Thriving in College and Beyond

Research-Based Strategies for Academic Success and Personal Development

Joseph B. Cuseo
Marymount
College

Viki Sox Fecas
University of South Carolina
—Columbia

Aaron Thompson
Eastern Kentucky
University

with Foreword by Mary Stuart Hunter

KENDALL/HUNT PUBLISHING COMPANY
4050 Westmark Drive Dubuque, Iowa 52002

Book Team

Chairman and Chief Executive Officer   Mark C. Falb
President and Chief Operating Officer   Chad M. Chandlee
Director of National Book Program   Paul B. Carty
Editorial Development Manager   Georgia Botsford
Developmental Editor   Tina Bower
Vice President, Operations   Timothy J. Beitzel
Assistant Vice President, Production Services   Christine E. O'Brien
Senior Production Editor   Charmayne McMurray
Permissions Editor   Elizabeth Roberts
Cover Designer   Jenifer Chapman

Cover photos courtesy of © JupiterImages Corporation

Contents

3 Educational Planning and Decision Making

Making Wise Choices about Your College Courses and Major 73

4 Strategic Learning

Applying Research on Human Learning and the Human Brain to Acquire Knowledge Effectively and Comprehend It Deeply 105

12 Health and Wellness
The Physical Dimension   387

13 Health and Wellness
Mental and Spiritual Dimensions   427

Epilogue: Thriving in College and Beyond
A Matter of Principles and Character   455

List of "Take Action Now!" Boxes

List of Snapshot Summaries

List of Take Action Now! Boxes

Foreword

By Mary Stuart Hunter

The very fact that you have this book in your hands and are reading these words is evidence that you are well on your way to becoming a successful student—congratulations. You join hundreds of thousands of other undergraduate students who each year take important steps toward ensuring their success through enrolling in a first-year seminar, by participating in a learning community, or engaging in other special programs on college and university campuses. College can be an exciting experience with challenges and opportunities that you've never faced before. It is a time for personal growth and development far beyond simply the learning of facts and figures. How you choose to spend your time in college will impact your life for years to come. You will discover new ideas about the world and your place in it both in the classroom and beyond as you accept the challenges before you and take responsibility for your own educational experience. And along the way, you will certainly learn more about yourself as an individual.

My own work with college students over the past 25 years tells me that students of all types, ages, and abilities can succeed. But I have also, unfortunately, seen far too many very bright and capable students fail. The fact that your college accepted you for admission is evidence enough that you have the capacity to succeed. But, making the transition from a high school learning culture to that of college is not automatic. Simply being a college student on a college or university campus doesn't mean that you will be as successful as you were in high school or in the world of your pre-college experience. What worked for you before may not work for you in this new environment. Understanding the difference in teaching and learning cultures is key to student success.

This book is one of the many resources available to you as a college student. The title itself, *Thriving in College and Beyond*, should tell you that college is just the beginning of a life full of learning. The pages of this book address the critical and multi-faceted opportunities in front of you as a college student. Throughout the book you will find information that will assist you as you navigate the complex and often mysterious collegiate experience. The authors have masterfully constructed a book that contains a wide variety of elements including exercises, checklists, cartoons, "take action now" suggestions, quotes, reflection guides, and thought questions all carefully chosen to engage and inform you while at the same time providing meaningful material to help you find success in college.

As individuals, the authors have a wealth of experience in assisting college students and they are sharing their best information, ideas, and strategies with you. Joe Cuseo is a well-respected first-year educator and professor of psychology who has many years experience helping new students successfully transition from high school to college. An award-winning faculty member at Marymount College, his passion for student success and creativity in teaching are hall-marks of his teaching and can be easily witnessed in the pages of this book. Viki Sox Fecas has helped countless students at the University of South Carolina transition to college and her campus through teaching sections of the first-year seminar and through her good work as a career counselor. Her positive attitude and enthusiasm for the collegiate experience has made her a sought-after and valuable resource for students at all levels. Aaron Thompson has many years of experience helping students attain educational success as well. With teaching and administrative experience at several public institutions, his contributions to this book are important and noteworthy. The partnership formed by these authors has resulted in a rich and practical book that will help countless students. You, too, can be one of these students.

So, read this book intentionally, apply what you read to yourself. Approach the exercises with vigor. Ask questions. Challenge the ideas. Discuss what you have read with your classmates and friends. Make the most of the generous resources in the book. But most of all, use what you learn in the book to help you be the very best student you can be. You'll be better for having done so. And then, you will be able to look back and appreciate all that this book has taught you!

Mary Stuart Hunter
Director
National Resource Center for The First-Year
Experience and Students in Transition
University of South Carolina

Preface

Welcome to Our Book

Activate Your Thinking

What do you think are the key characteristics or features of a textbook that:

a. enables you to *learn* from it?

b. makes it *interesting* to read?

●●● Plan and Purpose of This Book

The primary purpose of this book is to help you make a smooth transition to college, as well as equip you with strategies to promote your success in college and in life beyond college. Our book is designed to elevate personal performance and promote academic excellence among all students. No matter what your high school GPA, SAT or ACT scores were, college is a new ballgame played on a new playing field with different teammates and different rules. If you were not a strong student in high school, this book is designed to make you a strong student in college. If you were a strong student in high school, this book is designed to make you an equally strong or stronger student in college.

A major goal of this text is to help you put into practice one of the principles of effective learning that is discussed in Chapter 4: *Self-Monitoring*. Self-monitoring basically means "watching yourself" while you learn to be sure that you're learning in the most effective way. We think that this same principle of self-monitoring can be applied to college success in general. If you get in the habit of watching yourself as you "do" college and check to see if you are using the most effective strategies, then you can dramatically increase your chances of excelling in college. Rather than learning how to do college by random trial-and-error and hoping that you will eventually stumble on and discover what works best, we feel it's better to start with a game plan that rests on a solid base of research about what makes students successful in college and in life beyond college.

We believe that college can and should be done *strategically*. Consequently, you will find that specific success strategies make up the heart of this book. However, we also take time to point out the underlying rationale or theoretical principle that organizes these individual strategies and makes them effective, rather than presenting them to you as a laundry list of isolated tips. We feel it's important not only to know *what* you should do, but also *why* you should do it. If you understand the reason behind our suggested strategies, the more motivated you'll be to take action on them and put them into practice.

Furthermore, by organizing our strategies around general, powerful principles of human learning and development, you should be able to see how they may be applied across different academic or personal situations, as well as enable you to develop your own effective strategies that follow the same principle.

Thus, many of the individual strategies discussed in this book should not only facilitate your transition *into* college; they should also facilitate your transition *through* college and *from* college to post-college life.

> **·—· CLASSIC QUOTE ·—·**
>
> *The man who also knows why will be his boss. As to methods there may be a million and then some, but principles are few. The man who grasps principles can successfully select his own methods. The man who tries methods, ignoring principles, is sure to have trouble.*
>
> —Ralph Waldo Emerson, 19th-century author, poet, and philosopher

Since the strategies we recommend are research-based, you will find references cited in the body of the text that support their effectiveness. We have done this to assure you that there is evidence reinforcing our recommendations and that our suggestions are backed-up by solid research. We want you to know that the subject of college success is a well-established scholarly field—just like psychology, biology, history, or any other subject that is covered in the college curriculum. You will find a balanced blend of references in the text that include older, "classic" studies and more recent, "cutting edge" research. This demonstrates how the ideas presented are supported by research spanning from past to present, and points to the power of these ideas by showing how they have withstood the test of time.

••• Preview of Content

Here is a sneak preview of the key content contained in each chapter of this text.

Introduction

The introduction explains why your college experience has the potential to be the most enriching personal experience of your life, providing you with multiple, lifelong benefits. Probably more than any other time in the college experience, the first year is the stage when students undergo the greatest amount of learning and development. It is also the time when students experience the greatest academic and personal challenges, the most stress, the most academic difficulties, and the highest dropout rate.

The findings point to the importance of the first-year experience, the importance of this book, and the importance of courses designed to promote your college success. As we document in the introduction, beginning students who participate in first-year seminars or college-success courses are more likely to stay in college, complete their degree, and make the most of their college experience.

Chapter 1. Touching All the Bases

This chapter provides an overview and preview of the most powerful principles of college success. Its major goal is to equip you with a comprehensive set of personal success strategies, and to lay out the full range of student services and campus resources that are available to you, which you can use to support your success. You can utilize these strategies and capitalize on these support services to get off to a fast start in college, and you can continue to use them beyond the first year to sustain success throughout your entire college experience.

Chapter 2. The Value of Liberal Arts and General Education

This chapter is designed to show you how the college experience develops you as a *whole person*. The chapter's primary goal is to help you develop a deeper understanding of the meaning, purpose, and value of the liberal arts. This is the component of a college education that provides the essential foundation or backbone for your college education. It is designed to equip you with a wide range of skills that will promote your success in any academic majors, in any career, and in your personal life beyond college.

:SP: STUDENT PERSPECTIVES

"I could really relate to everything we talked about. It is a great class because you can use it in your other classes."
—First-year student comment made when evaluating a first-year seminar (college success course)

"Everything we learned we will apply in our lives."
—First-year student comment made when evaluating a first-year seminar (college success course)

"This is the only course I've ever taken that was about me."
—First-year student comment made when evaluating a first-year seminar (college success course)

Chapter 3. Educational Planning and Decision-Making

This chapter is designed to help you make wise choices about your college courses and your college major. Whether you are undecided, or think you've already decided on a college major, you need to be sure that you know *yourself* well and know all your options in order to reach the best possible decision. You should have a strategic plan in mind that will allow you to strike a healthy balance between exploration and commitment. The primary goal or purpose of this chapter is to help you strike this balance and develop an action plan for making educational decisions that will be most effective for reaching your long-term goals.

Pause for Reflection

What percentage of students entering college do you think have already made-up their mind about a major?

What percentage of these "decided" students do you think eventually change their mind and end up graduating with a different major?

(See Chapter 3 for the answers to these questions.)

Chapter 4. Strategic Learning

This chapter is intended to help you apply research on human learning and the human brain to acquire knowledge more efficiently and understand it more deeply. The chapter takes you through all key stages of the learning process—from the first stage of taking-in information through lectures and readings, to the second stage of studying and storing information in your brain, to the final stage of retrieving or recalling information that you've studied and stored. The ultimate goal of this chapter is to supply you with a full set of powerful strategies, supported by solid research on how humans learn and how the human brain works, which you can use to promote learning that is both *deep* (beyond surface memorization) and *durable* (long-lasting).

·—· **CLASSIC QUOTE** ·—·

What is the hardest task in the world? To think.

—Ralph Waldo Emerson, 19th-century American essayist and lecturer

Chapter 5. Improving Memory and Test Performance

The important final step or stage in the learning process is to recall what you have learned and to demonstrate or communicate that knowledge on your tests and exams. This chapter provides you with an organized set of memory-improvement strategies to strengthen your ability to recall information that you've studied and learned, plus a set of test-taking strategies to help you become more "test-wise" and less "test-anxious."

Chapter 6. Higher-Level Thinking

This chapter goes beyond learning and memory of factual knowledge to examine higher levels of critical and creative thinking. Since higher-level thinking is the primary teaching goal of college faculty, the primary goal of this chapter is to help you understand what higher-level thinking really is, and help you develop strategies and skills to think at this level. We break down the process of higher-level thinking into its different forms or types, lay out a set of self-assessment questions to help you become aware of whether you're thinking at a higher level, and suggest a series of practical strategies for demonstrating higher-level thinking on your exams and assignments.

The Thinker, by Auguste Rodin, 19th-century French sculptor

Your speech, Mr. Edwards, was, like, totally eloquent.

If students begin to develop their speaking skills during the first year of college, this scenario should not take place at college graduation.

Chapter 7. Three Key Academic Skills: Research, Writing, and Speaking

The goals of this chapter are to improve your ability to effectively communicate your ideas through writing and speaking, and to effectively acquire the ideas of others through research. Writing, speaking, and research are three key skills that can be "transferred" or applied to any academic field of study where they can be used to acquire and communicate knowledge. Not only are these portable skills that you can take with you and use across different subjects in the college curriculum, you can also use them to promote your success across different careers. This chapter is designed to help you start developing these key transferable skills during your very first term in college.

Pause for Reflection

Besides writing papers and reports, what do you think are other valuable uses or purposes of writing?

(See Chapter 7 for a discussion of the multiple uses, purposes, and advantages of writing.)

·—· **CLASSIC QUOTE** ·—·

I would like to be known as a person who is concerned about freedom and equality and justice and prosperity for all people.

—Rosa Parks, "mother of the civil rights movement" who took a stand for racial equality in 1955 by refusing to surrender her seat to a white passenger on a city bus

Chapter 8. Diversity

The primary purposes of this chapter are to clarify the meaning of "diversity" and show how experiencing diversity can promote learning, personal development, and professional success. The chapter includes ideas for overcoming cultural barriers that may interfere with the development of potentially rewarding relationships, and it supplies strategies to help you create opportunities to learn from others with prior experiences and cultural backgrounds that differ from your own.

Chapter 9. Finding a Path to Your Future Profession

The primary goal of this chapter is to alert you to strategies you can use in your first year of college to facilitate career exploration, preparation, and development. While it may seem odd or premature to find a chapter on career success in a book for beginning college students, effective career exploration, preparation, and development begins in the first term of college (Gore, 2005). Since career planning is really *life* planning, the earlier you start this process, the more likely you are to start moving toward creating a future life for yourself that will allow you to do what interests you and what you do well.

Chapter 10. Two Key Life-Management Skills: Managing Time and Money

Mastering the skills of managing time and money are critical for success in college and throughout life. Both of these key elements of life management require self-awareness of how each is "spent" since both time and money come in limited quantities and need to be budgeted for, or else we can quickly run out of both of them.

In college, you will encounter an academic calendar and schedule that differs greatly from high school. You will have more free time because you will be spending less time per week sitting in class, and you'll need to manage it effectively to attain success.

Similarly, the greater personal independence experienced in college often brings with it greater demands for economic self-sufficiency, critical thinking about consumerism, and effective management of personal finances. If you can gain greater control over how you spend your time and money, you can gain greater control over the quality of your life. The purpose of this chapter is to help you develop specific time- and money-management skills that will enable you to gain greater control of these two key aspects of your life.

Chapter 11. Interpersonal Relations

As a new college student, you are likely to find yourself surrounded with more social opportunities than you've ever had in your life. Among the key adjustments you will need to make in college is striking a healthy balance between too much and too little socializing, as well as finding and forming interpersonal relationships that will support (rather than sabotage) your educational success. More importantly, development of a good social support system is one of the major keys to achieving personal health and happiness. Studies show that people who have stronger social support networks are more likely to be healthier (Giles, et al., 2005) and happier (Myers, 1993).

In this chapter, you will be provided with strategies that are designed to improve the quality of your interpersonal relationships, which in turn, should improve your prospects for success, health, and happiness.

Chapter 12. Health and Wellness: The Physical Dimension

None of us can reach our full potential and function at our highest level without meeting our physical needs. Remaining healthy and attaining peak levels of performance depend on how well we attend to our *body*—what we put into it (healthy food), what we keep out of it (unhealthy substances), what we do with it (exercise), and how well we rejuvenate it (quality of sleep). This chapter will examine strategies for managing our nutrition, maintaining total fitness, sleeping well, and avoiding risky behaviors that can jeopardize our health.

Chapter 13. Health and Wellness: Mental and Spiritual Dimensions

In addition to the body, two other important elements of human experience that must be attended to are *mind*—how we manage our thoughts and emotions, and *spirit*—how we go about finding meaning or purpose in life, and how we come to grips with the connection between our self and the larger world around and beyond us. This chapter will provide strategies for continuing our thoughts, managing our emotions, and promoting our spiritual well being.

Epilogue: Success in College and Beyond— A Matter of Character

The concluding section of our text is designed to help you tie it all together and see the big picture. It attempts to provide you with a look back to get a panoramic overview of the most significant ideas contained in the book. We end the text with a recap of how the four bases of college success discussed in Chapter 1 contribute to and promote the development of personal

STUDENT PERSPECTIVE

"In high school, a lot of the work was done while in school, but in college all of your work is done on your time. You really have to organize yourself in order to get everything done."

—First-year student's response to a question about what was most surprising about college life (Bates, 1994).

STUDENT PERSPECTIVE

"Sometimes it seems harder to make friends because of the size of the school. But there are a variety of organizations and activities. Get involved and meet the people!"

—First-year college student (Rhoads, 2005)

STUDENT PERSPECTIVE

"I want to see how all the pieces of me come together to make me, physically and mentally."

—College sophomore

character, which can aid your success throughout college and life after college. Success stems from something larger than the application of a series of specific strategies. Success emerges when good strategies become good habits and develop into virtues that form a person's character. The Epilogue will explain how being successful depends on being a person of character who possesses the virtues of wisdom, initiative, motivation, integrity, and civic responsibility.

Personal Story

I've learned a lot from teaching the first-year seminar (college success course) and from co-writing this book. Before teaching the course, I didn't have a clear idea about what the liberal arts were and how my general education was so important for achieving personal and professional success. I also learned new strategies for managing my time, my money, and my health. The strategies and skills that I've learned from teaching a college-success course and co-writing this book have convinced me that this course and this book not only develop skills for success in college, but also develop skills for success in life beyond college.

—Joe Cuseo, co-author of this text

••• Sequencing of Chapter Topics

The chapters have been arranged in an order that allows you to ask and answer the following sequence of questions:

1. Why am I here?
2. Where do I want to go?
3. What do I do to get there?
4. How do I know when I've arrived?

Chapters 1 through 3 are intended to help you get immediately situated and oriented to your new campus environment, clarify your reasons for being in college, and decide where you want your college experience to take you. These chapters will provide you with a mental map for your trip through college and for navigating your total college environment, including the curriculum (college courses) and the co-curriculum (out-of-class learning and student development programs). Following your completion of these chapters, you should have a clearer sense of personal direction and purpose, and you should be able to see a clearer connection between where you are now and where you want to go.

Since motivation underlies and drives action, if the first three chapters work to help you clarify why you're in college and where college will take you, the more energized you'll be to learn about and take action on the strategies suggested in the chapters that follow (Chapters 4 through 8). These chapters focus on the nitty-gritty of *how* to actually "do" college and get the academic job done. These middle chapters focus on learning how to learn, how to improve your memory, how to think more deeply, how to acquire knowledge through research, and how to most effectively communicate your knowledge through writing and speaking.

The last four chapters of the text, Chapters 9 through 12, focus on the development of personal and professional skills you will need to achieve success in your career and other important life roles beyond college.

••• Process and Style of Presentation

How information is presented is as important as *what* information is presented. When writing this text, we intentionally attempted to deliver information in a manner that would strengthen your learning and your motivation to learn. We tried to do this by incorporating effective human learning and motivational principles throughout the text.

◆ At the start of each chapter, we begin with an **Activate Your Thinking** exercise that is designed to energize or "turn on" ideas or feelings you may already have about the upcoming material. This pre-reading exercise serves to "wind up" or "tune up" your brain so that it becomes ready to make connections between the ideas you'll encounter in the chapter and the ideas you already have in your head. It is an instructional strategy that implements one of the most powerful principles of human learning, namely: we learn most effectively by relating what we are trying to learn to what we already know or what is already stored in our brain.

◆ During each chapter, we periodically interrupt your reading with a **Pause for Reflection** that asks you to reflect on and think about the material you've read. These timely pauses should help you stay alert and remain mentally active during the reading process. They should also intercept the drop in attention that naturally tends to take place when the human brain spends an extended period of time receiving and processing information (such as reading). These periodic pauses for reflection should also deepen your understanding of the material because they encourage you to *write* something in response to what you've read, which stimulates greater reflection and deeper thinking than simply underlining or highlighting words while reading. As we mention in Chapter 1, effective learning takes place when there is both action and reflection

◆ At the end of each chapter, we include at least one **Exercise** that asks you to reflect back on knowledge you've acquired from the chapter and convert that knowledge in to action. Your instructor may ask you to complete these exercises or other exercises provided in the Instructor's Manual that accompanies this textbook. As shown in the Epilogue, we don't attain wisdom by just acquiring knowledge; we attain it by *acquiring* knowledge and then *applying* that knowledge by putting it into practice. Thus, the Activate Your Thinking exercises at the start of the chapter, the Pauses for Reflection within the chapter, and the Exercises at the conclusion of the chapter are strategically positioned to create an effective learning sequence that consists of a meaningful beginning, middle, and end. These different learning activities should work to keep you mentally active immediately before, during, and immediately after your reading of each chapter.

◆ Information is presented in a variety of formats that includes diagrams, pictures, cartoons, advice from current college students, words of wisdom from famous and successful people, and personal stories drawn from the authors' experiences as students, professors, and advisors. This variety of formats allows us to communicate with you through multiple modalities and sensory avenues, which should increase the number of ways that information reaches your brain and the number of places in your brain where that information gets stored.

Listed below is a more detailed description of the book's learning and motivational features.

Take Action Now Boxes

Throughout the book, you will find shaded boxes that contain short lists of *high-priority* tips for college success. These tips are introduced at times when you are most likely to need them.

For example, in the first chapter, a series of top tips on note-taking is included because you will be expected to take notes during your first week in college—probably on the very first day of class. At the midpoint of the book, in Chapter 5, you will find a series of test-taking strategies because you're likely to encounter your first major wave of college exams at midterm—the midpoint of the term. Toward the end of the book, in Chapter 10, you will find a set of stress-management strategies to prepare you for the second wave of stress that often rushes in around the time of major holidays and final exams. (Hopefully, you will experience manageable "ripples" of stress, not "tidal waves!").

We have attempted to introduce topics in a time-sensitive manner that is responsive to the natural rhythms of the academic term by introducing you to textbook topics at times when you are most likely to encounter them in your first-year experience. Humans are more likely to be receptive to, and motivated by, information that is delivered at a time when it is most relevant to what they are currently experiencing, dealing with, or worried about. Simply stated, you are more motivated to learn information that is delivered in a timely fashion—when it reaches you at a time when you can immediately apply it to your current interests and concerns.

Textbooks typically cover topics in separate chapters, one topic at a time. However, students do not experience college-related challenges or adjustments one at a time; instead, they often experience multiple challenges at the same time. For instance, during the first weeks of college you may be thinking about larger questions relating to whether college is really for you, whether the college you've chosen is the best fit for you, or whether going to college is really worth it. At the same time, you will be coping with the practical day-to-day tasks associated with the start of college life, such as taking notes during class lecture, doing the assigned readings, and trying to fit in socially.

To help you deal with this reality of multi-tasking, most of our chapters include inserted boxes that contain practical strategies for dealing with different issues, which you are likely to be experiencing along with the one being covered as the chapter's main topic. This feature of our text allows us to address the primary topic covered in the chapter (the major plot), while simultaneously addressing other topics (subplots) that relate to other issues you may be experiencing in college at that point in your first term.

Pause for Reflection

At this point in your first term, what is it about college experience that you're most enthusiastic about or excites you the most?

At this point, what concerns or worries you the most?

Snapshot Summary Boxes

Throughout the text, you will find boxes that contain summaries of key concepts and definitions. These boxed summaries are designed to pull together ideas related to the same concept and connect them in the same physical place, so that you will be more likely to connect them mentally in the same conceptual category.

"Remember" Cues

Periodically, you will encounter the word "remember" in orange, followed by content in bold-face type. This is a cue that the information appearing in boldface type is especially important to pay attention to and remember.

Classic Quotes

Dispersed throughout the text are quotes from famous and influential people. These quotes relate to and reinforce key ideas that are being discussed at different points in the chapter. We feel that you can learn a lot from the first-hand experiences and words of people who have actually achieved success. You will find quotes from accomplished individuals who have lived in many different time periods and who have succeeded in many different fields, such as politics, philosophy, religion, science, business, music, art, and athletics. The wide-ranging cultures, timeframes, and fields of study represented by the people who've issued these quotes serve to demonstrate how the ideas they convey are timeless and universal. The varied professional backgrounds of the successful people who are quoted also demonstrate how the book's strategies contribute to personal success in many careers or professions. It is our hope that these Classic Quotes will stimulate your personal motivation, and will inspire you to aspire to the same level of high achievement attained by these successful and influential people.

Personal Stories

In each chapter, you will find personal stories drawn from the authors' own experiences. We have learned a lot from our professional experiences working with students as teachers and advisors, and from being college students ourselves. We share our stories with the idea of personalizing our text, and with the hope that hearing about our college experience will enable you to improve the quality of your college experience. (Even if it's by learning not to make the same mistakes that we made!)

Student Perspectives

You will find comments and advice from students at different stages of the college experience and college graduates (alumni). As we point out in Chapter 1, research indicates that you can learn a lot from other students, especially from students who've been there and have experienced what you are about to experience. You can learn from both their success stories and stumbling blocks.

Pause for Reflection

Have you received any advice or tips about how to succeed in college from friends or family members? If yes, what did they suggest?

Chapter Outlines

Before each chapter, an outline of the chapter's content is presented. This feature is included because research shows that if learners are able to see how information is organized before they attempt to learn it, they are better able to comprehend and retain that information. In other words, if you see how different parts of the whole fit together to form the whole, much like seeing the whole picture of a completed jigsaw puzzle, you are better able to piece together the parts and solve the puzzle. Thus, we recommend that you take a moment to read through the chapter outline to get an overview and preview of its parts and how they are related, before you jump into the chapter and begin reading its content.

Concept Maps: Verbal-Visual Aids

Diagrams and concept maps are included throughout the text that relate to and reinforce the reading material. These visual images are designed to help you comprehend and retain the information presented in print. They serve to organize abstract (verbal) ideas and transform them into concrete (visual) form, which should improve your memory for these ideas by enabling you to record two different memory traces in your brain: verbal (words) and visual (images).

Cartoons: Emotional-Visual Aids

You will discover an ample supply of cartoons sprinkled throughout the text. These humorous illustrations have been included to provide you with a little entertainment, but more importantly, they are included to help you remember the concept illustrated by the cartoon, because that concept will be reinforced by a visual image (drawing) and an emotional reaction (humor). If the cartoon manages to trigger some laughter, your body will release adrenalin—a biochemical that improves memory storage. Furthermore, a little humor should also stimulate your brain to release endorphins—chemicals that serve to reduce your stress level and elevate your mood!

Case Studies

At the end of each chapter you will find a short case study. A case may be defined as a real-life event or a fictional scenario that closely matches a real-life event. It encourages you to think deeply and reach a decision or draw a conclusion about something that does not have a definite answer or easy solution. Some of the cases we've included in this book involve actual events that have taken place on college campuses and made national news, while others involve scenarios that closely match real-life college events. Each case is placed at the end of a chapter so that you can take the knowledge you've acquired from the chapter and apply it to a "real life."

Learning More through Independent Research

At the end of each chapter, you will find recommended Web-based resources that contain additional information relating to the chapter's topic. One of the major goals of a college education is to prepare you to become an independent, self-directed learner. Our hope is that the material presented in each chapter will stimulate your interest and motivation to learn more about the topic. If it does, you can use the power of electronic technology to further your learning by searching for additional information online about the ideas we've presented in print.

Pause for Reflection

What feature or features of this book do you think will:

a. *contribute most to your* learning?

b. *make the book most* interesting?

Ultimately, we hope the content of this book, and the process or style that we've used to deliver its content, will help you jumpstart, map out, and max out your college experience.

Furthermore, the skills discussed in this book, such as effective planning and decision-making, learning and remembering, thinking critically and creatively, speaking and writing persuasively, managing time and money, communicating and relating effectively with others, and maintaining health and wellness, are more than just "college" skills, they are "life" skills.

Remember: This book is more than just a textbook for first-term students. It is a *college-success* and *life-success* book, which contains ideas and strategies that should prove useful to you well beyond your first term in college.

We recommend that you not discard this book as soon as you finish your first term in college. Instead, save it, and continue using its ideas to promote your success throughout your college experience and beyond. Learning does not stop after college; it is a lifelong process. If you strive to apply the ideas included in this text and use them to continue learning throughout life, you should thrive in any profession or personal path you choose to follow.

Sincerely,

Joe Cuseo, *Viki Sox Fecas*, and *Aaron Thompson*

I'd like to take this opportunity to thank several people who have played an important role in my life and whose positive influence made this book possible:

Mildred and Blase Cuseo, my parents, for the sacrifices they made to support my education. James Vigilis, my uncle, for being a second father to me during my formative years. Jim Cooper, my best friend, for being a mentor to me in graduate school.

Mary and Tony Cuseo, my wife and son, for their courage and love.

I would also like to thank the following students for their contributions to this textbook: Joaquin Leon, for the many humorous cartoons he contributed throughout the text; Vicky Vermazen, for her excellent illustrations; and Lizzie Frazer and Britt Beard, for their poignant poems.

Joe Cuseo

If not for the love and support of my parents, Wyman and Fae Sox, and son, Matt Fecas, my involvement in this project would never have happened. Thanks also to Kendall/Hunt Publishing's Director of the National Book Program, Paul Carty, whose wisdom in assembling the writing team and assignment of a crackerjack editor, Tina Bower, made this idea a fun reality. I also tremendously value my colleagues for their encouragement and feedback through the writing and review process.

Viki Sox Fecas

I would like to thank my wife Holly and my children, Sonya, Sara, Michael, Maya, and Isaiah for being my continual inspiration and source of unconditional love. I would also like to thank my father and mother (Big "A" and Margaret) for instilling in me that education is the key to most all that is valuable in our society. In addition, I would like to acknowledge the support that Eastern Kentucky University gave me with my education and with their support to write this book. This support largely came through Rhonda who made sure that I could get the time to do the work. I would also like to thank my co-authors (Joe and Viki) and Kendall/Hunt (Paul and Tina) for the opportunity to be part of a great team. Lastly, I would like to thank my mentors and students who gave me the encouragement and motivation.

Aaron Thompson

We gratefully acknowledge the constructive criticism of the colleagues who provided reviews for individual chapters of this text, and who participated in the focus groups. They include:

Peg Adams
Northern Kentucky University

Linda Alvarez
University of Wisconsin—River Falls

Stephanie Adams
William Woods University

Scott Amundsen
Eastern Kentucky University

Anita Adkins
Northern Kentucky University

Suzanne Ash
Cerritos College

Treva Barham
Le Tourneau University

Andrea Berta
University of Texas—El Paso

Paula Bradberry
Arkansas State University

Cynthia Burnley
Eastern Tennessee State University

Norma Campbell
Fayetteville State University

Jay Chaskes
Rowan University

Regina Clark
Tennessee State University

Karen Clay
Miami-Dade College

Geoff Cohen
University of California—Riverside

Amy D'Olivo
Centanary College of New Jersey

Donna Dahlgren
Indiana University Southeast

Rachelle Darabi
Indiana Purdue University—Fort Wayne

Michael Denton
University of North Carolina—Charlotte

Louise Ericson
University of South Carolina Upstate

Betsy Eudey
California State University—Stanislaus

Carlisa Finney
Anne Arundel Community College

Janet Florez
Cuesta College

Stephanie Foote
University of South Carolina—Aiken

Paula Fuhst
Yavapai College

Stephanie Fujii
Estrella Mountain Community College

Jennifer Gay
Fort Lewis College

Latty Goodwin
Rochester Institute of Technology

Tracy Gottlieb
Seton Hall University

Virginia Granda
University of Texas—El Paso

Laurie Grimes
Lorain County Community College

Allen Grove
Alfred University

Robert Guell
Indiana State University

Laurie Hazard
Bryant College

Marge Jaasma
California State University—Stanislaus

Andrew Koch
Purdue University

Lora Lavery-Broda
St. Leo University

Deborah Lotsof
Mount Union College

Jane Owen
Waynesburg College

Denise Roade
Northern Illinois University

Chris Rubic
Grayslake North High School

Jane Snyder
Fontbonne University

Mary Taugher
University of Wisconsin—Milwaukee

Judy Termini
Gallaudet University

Kathie Wentworth
Tri-State University

Carol Williams
Arizona State University

Introduction

Welcome to College

Congratulations and welcome! We applaud your decision to continue your education. You've made it to college, also known as "higher education" (because it's "higher" than high school), and you are about to begin a new and exciting journey in your life. While your previous attendance in school was required, continuing your education in college is your choice, and you have made a choice that will surely better your life.

Your movement into higher education represents an important life transition. Similar to an immigrant moving to a new country, you will be moving into a new culture with different expectations, regulations, customs, and "language" (Chaskes, 1996) (See the Glossary and Dictionary of College Vocabulary at the end of this book for "translations" of special words and phrases that you are likely to encounter in the college culture.) Your transition to college means you will be moving into "higher education," where you will be moving up to higher levels of challenge, support, and development.

It is probably safe to say that, after college, you will never again be a member of any other organization or institution with as many resources and services available to you that have been intentionally designed to promote your learning, development, and success. Your college experience has the potential to be the most enriching and enjoyable stage of your life. If you capitalize on the numerous resources and opportunities that are available to you, and if you utilize effective learning strategies while in college, you are likely to create an experience that will bring you multiple, life-long benefits. (See Box 1.)

Your transition to college means you will be moving into "higher education," where you will be moving up to higher levels of challenge, support, and development.

BOX 1 *Snapshot* SUMMARY

Why College Is Worth It: The Economic and Personal Benefits of College

About 27 percent of Americans have earned a college (bachelor's) degree. When college graduates are compared with individuals from similar social and economic backgrounds who have not continued their education beyond high school indicates, the results indicate that college is well worth the investment. It has been found that college graduates experience multiple advantages, such as the following. (Explanations for these advantages are provided in Chapter 2.)

1. **Career Benefits**
   - Security and Stability—lower rates of unemployment
   - Versatility and Mobility—more flexibility to move out of a position and into other positions
   - Advancement—better opportunity to move up to higher professional positions
   - Interest—more likely to find their work stimulating and challenging
   - Autonomy—greater independence and opportunity to be their own boss
   - Satisfaction—enjoy their work more and feel that it allows them to use their special talents
   - Prestige—higher career status (job desirability)

(continued)

> **·—· CLASSIC QUOTE ·—·**
>
> *If you think education is expensive, try ignorance.*
>
> —Derek Bok, former President, Harvard University

2. Economic Advantages
   - Higher income—the gap in income between high school and college graduates is *increasing*. Individuals with a bachelor's degree now earn an average salary of about $50,000 per year—40 percent higher than high school graduates, whose average salary is less than $30,000 per year. The lifetime income of families headed by persons with a bachelor's degree is about 1.6 million more than families headed by persons with a high school diploma.
   - Make wiser consumer choices and decisions
   - Make more effective long-term investments

3. Advanced Intellectual Skills
   - Greater knowledge
   - More effective problem-solving skills
   - Better ability to deal with complex and ambiguous (uncertain) ideas
   - Greater openness to new ideas
   - More advanced levels of moral reasoning
   - A clearer sense of self-identity—more awareness and knowledge of personal talents, interests, values, and needs
   - More likely to continue learning throughout life

4. Better Physical Health
   - Better dietary habits
   - Exercise more regularly
   - Live longer and healthier lives

5. Social Advantages
   - Higher levels of social self-confidence
   - Understand and communicate more effectively with others
   - Greater popularity
   - More effective leadership skills
   - Greater marital satisfaction

6. Emotional Advantages
   - Lower levels of anxiety
   - Higher levels of self-esteem
   - Higher sense of self-efficacy—sense of control over their life
   - Higher levels of psychological well-being
   - Higher levels of personal happiness

7. More Effective Citizens
   - Greater interest in social and political issues
   - Greater knowledge of current affairs
   - Higher voting participation rates
   - Participate more frequently in civic affairs and community service

8. Better Quality of Life for their Children
   - Spend more time and energy on their children
   - Provide better health care for their children

(continued)

- More likely to involve their children in educational activities that stimulate their mental development
- Their children are more likely to graduate from college
- Their children are more likely to attain higher-status and higher-paying careers

References:
Astin, A. W. (1993). *What Matters in College?*
Bowen, H. R. (1977, 1997*). Investment in Learning: The Individual & Social Value of American Higher Education.*
Ottinger, C. (1990). *College graduates in the labor market: Today and the future.*
Feldman, K. A., & Newcomb, T. M. (1994). *The impact of college on students.*
Pascarella, E. T., & Terenzini, P. T. (1991). *How college affects students: Findings and Insights from Twenty Years of Research.*
Pascarella, E. T., & Terenzini, P. T. (2005). *How college affects students: A third decade of research* (volume 2). San Francisco: Jossey-Bass.
Postsecondary Education Opportunity (2000). *Private Benefit/Cost Ratios of a College Investment for Men and Women, 1967–1999.*
Tierney, W. G. (ed.) (1998). *The responsive university: Restructuring for high performance.* Baltimore: Johns Hopkins Press.
U.S. Census Bureau (2003). *Bureau of Labor Statistics.* Washington, D.C.: Author.

 Pause for Reflection

Why did you decide to go to college?

Why did you choose the particular college you're now attending?

••• Importance of the First Year of College

The *first* year of college is definitely the most critical stage of the college experience. It is the year during which students report the most change, the most learning, and the most development (MacGregor, 1991; Light, 2001). It is also the year during which students experience the most stress, the most academic difficulties, and the highest dropout rate (American College Testing, 2003; Cuseo, 1991). When graduating seniors look back on their college experience, many of them say that the first year was the time of greatest change and the time during which they made the most significant improvements in their approach to learning. Here is how one senior put it during a personal interview:

Interviewer: What have you learned about your approach to learning [in college]?

Student: I had to learn how to study. I went through high school with a 4.0 average. I didn't have to study. It was a breeze. I got to the university and there was no structure. No one checked my homework. No one took attendance to make sure I was in class. No one told me I had to do something. There were no quizzes on the readings. I did not work well with this lack of structure. It took my first year and a half to learn to deal with it. But I had to teach myself to manage my time. I had to teach myself how to study. I had to teach myself how to learn in a different environment (Chickering & Schlossberg, 1998, p. 47).

In many ways, the first-year experience in college is similar to ocean surfing or downhill skiing; it can be filled with many exciting thrills and also some potentially dangerous spills. The goal of skiing and surfing is to maximize the thrills, minimize the spills, and finish the run while still on your feet. The same is true for the first year of college; studies show that if you can complete your first-year experience in good standing, your chances for successfully completing the total college experience improves dramatically (American College Testing, 2003).

In a nutshell, college success depends on your taking advantage of what your college can do for you and what you can do for yourself. The research cited and the advice provided in this book point to one major conclusion: Success in college depends on *you*—i.e., you make it happen by what you *do*. The more motivated you are to get the most out of your college experience, the more successful you will be. In the graph below, you can see that there is a direct relationship between students' motivation and their college grades.

Percentage of Highly Motivated Students Attending a Particular College and the Average Grades Achieved by Students at that College (National Survey of Student Engagement, 2005)

After reviewing 40 years of research on how college affects students, two distinguished researchers concluded that:

> The impact of college is largely determined by individual effort and involvement in the academic, interpersonal, and extracurricular [co-curricular] offerings on a campus. Students are not passive recipients of institutional efforts to "educate" or "change" them, but rather bear major responsibility for any gains they derive from their postsecondary [college] experience (Pascarella & Terenzini, 2005, p. 602).

Compared to high school, your college experience will involve a much broader range of courses, far more resources to capitalize on, much more freedom of choice and many more decision-making opportunities. Your particular college experience will be different than that of any other college student because you will have the freedom to actively shape or create it in a way that is uniquely your own. So, don't let college happen *to* you; instead, make it happen *for* you—by taking charge of your experience and taking full advantage of all the resources that are at your command.

••• Importance of a First-Year Seminar (also known as a College Success or Student Success Course)

If you're reading this book, you are already beginning to take charge of your college experience because you're probably enrolled in a course that is designed to promote your college success. Research strongly indicates that new students who participate in courses such as the one you're in are more likely to stay in college, complete their degree, and achieve higher grades. These positive effects have been found for:

◆ all types of students (under-prepared and well-prepared, minority and majority, residential and commuter, male and female),

◆ students at all types of colleges (2-year and 4-year, public and private),

◆ students attending college of different sizes (small, mid-sized, and large), and

◆ students attending college in different locations (urban, suburban, and rural).

(References: Barefoot, 1993; Barefoot et al., 1998; Boudreau & Kromrey, 1994; Fidler & Godwin, 1994; Glass & Garrett, 1995; Grunder & Hellmich, 1996; Hunter & Linder, 2005; Shanley & Witten, 1990; Sidle & McReynolds, 1999; Starke, Harth, & Sirianni, 2001; Thomson, 1998; Tobolowski, 2005).

It is fair to say that there has been more carefully conducted research on first-year seminars or college-success courses, and more evidence supporting their effectiveness for increasing students' college success, than there is for any other course that has ever been offered in the history of higher education. You are fortunate to be enrolled in such a course. Give it your best effort and take full advantage of what it has to offer. If you do, you will be taking a major step toward thriving in college and beyond.

As you begin your college journey . . .

> **Remember:** On the higher education highway, don't be a passive passenger; instead, take charge of your college experience and be an active driver of your own vehicle. Ultimately, your effort and energy will provide the high-mileage fuel that carries you all the way to graduation, and your goal-setting and strategic planning will provide the steering wheel that guides you in the direction of future success.

Have a good trip!

STUDENT PERSPECTIVES

"Every first-semester freshman needs a class like this—whether they think so or not."
—First-year student comment made when evaluating a first-year seminar (college success course)

"I am now one of the peer counselors on campus, and without this class my first semester, I don't think I could have done as well, and by participating in this class again (as a teaching assistant), it reinforced this belief."
—First-year student comment made when evaluating a first-year seminar (college success course)

Joe Cuseo holds a Ph.D. in Educational Psychology and Assessment from the University of Iowa. Currently, he is a Professor of Psychology at Marymount College (California) where for 25 years he has directed the first-year seminar, a course required of all new students. He has been a member of the Advisory Board to the National Resource Center for The First-Year Experience and Students in Transition, and has received the Center's Outstanding First-Year Advocate award. He is also a 12-time recipient of the Faculty Member of the Year award on his home campus, an award based on student vote, for effective teaching and academic advising. He has authored numerous articles and chapters on the first-year experience, student success, and academic advising. He is currently completing a monograph on the first-year seminar, titled *The First-Year Seminar: Research-Based Guidelines for Course Design, Delivery, and Assessment.*

Viki Sox Fecas has a Ph.D. in Educational Administration from the University of South Carolina (USC). In her current role as Program Manager for Freshman and Pre-Freshman Programs, she coordinates the career component for all of the 150+ sections of the number one ranked University 101 Program in the country. She serves as a career resource for international scholars visiting the National Resource Center (NRC). She also is an Adjunct Professor in the Higher Education and Student Affairs graduate program at USC. She was recognized as the *Outstanding Freshman Advocate* in 1996.

She took University 101 as a freshman at USC, and has been teaching for the past 18 years. Since 1995, she has taught the sole section dedicated to transfer students. Her research interests center around the transition of college students, with a special interest in transfer students. She has written a career chapter for both the U101 *Transitions* book as well as *Your College Experience.* She regularly presents at both the National First-Year Experience and Students in Transition Conferences sponsored by the NRC.

Aaron Thompson, Ph.D., is the Associate Vice President for Academic Affairs and Professor of Sociology at Eastern Kentucky University. He has his Ph.D. in Sociology in areas of Organizational Behavior/Race and Gender relations. Dr. Thompson has risen through the faculty ranks at Eastern Kentucky University and was previously employed by the University of Missouri as Assistant Professor of Human Development and Family Studies. In addition to his administrative role as Associate Vice President for Academic Affairs, he served as Associate Vice President for Enrollment Management, Assistant Vice President for Academic Affairs, Executive Director of the Student Success Institute, Coordinator of Retention Services and Coordinator for Academic Success. Thompson has researched, taught and consulted in areas of assessment, ethics, research methodology and social statistics, multicultural families, cultural competence, leadership, race and ethnic relations, and organizational design. He is nationally recognized in the areas of educational attainment, race and gender diversity, poverty, divorce and fatherhood in the black family, overcoming obstacles, and achieving academic success. His latest books are *Focus on Success* and *Black Men and Divorce*. He has in excess of 50 research and peer reviewed publications and presentations and has given more than 150 workshops, seminars and invited lectures in the areas of diversity and cultural competence. He has been or is a consultant to educators, corporations, non-profit organizations, police departments and other governmental agencies. In addition, Thompson's research has been cited in popular publications such as *Cosmopolitan*, *Baltimore Sun*, *Orlando Sentinel* and others.

Touching All the Bases

An Overview and Preview of the Most Powerful Principles of College Success

Learning Goals

The major goal of this chapter is to supply you with a set of powerful strategies that you can immediately use to get off to a fast start in college and that you can continually use to achieve success throughout your remaining years of college.

Outline

Activate Your Thinking

1. How do you think college will be *different* than high school?
2. What do you think it will take to be *successful* in college? (In other words: What personal characteristics, qualities, or strategies do you feel are most important for college success?)
3. What do you imagine your first year here will be like?

••• The Most Powerful Research-Based Principles of College Success

Research on human learning and student development indicates that there are four powerful principles of college success:

1. active involvement,
2. utilizing resources,
3. social interaction/collaboration, and
4. self-reflection (Astin, 1993; Kuh, 2000; Light, 2001; Pascarella & Terenzini, 1991, 2005; Tinto, 1993).

These represent the four basic principles of college success, and they are introduced and examined carefully in this opening chapter for two important reasons:

1. so you can *immediately* put these strategies into practice to get off to a fast start in college and establish good habits, and
2. because these principles provide the essential *foundation* for all the success strategies that are recommended throughout this book. These four key principles of college success can be represented visually in the form of a diamond with four bases (Figure 1.1).

Figure 1.1 The Diamond of College Success

□ = Supporting Bases for College Success
▼ = Primary ("Home") Base for College Success

••• The Home Base of College Success: Active Involvement

Research indicates that active involvement is the most fundamental and most powerful principle of human learning and college success (Astin, 1993; Kuh, 2000). You could consider it to be the home base of college success, because it provides the basic foundation for all other college-success strategies. The bottom line is this: To maximize your success in college, you need to be an *active agent* in the learning process, not a passive sponge or spectator.

The basic principle of active involvement includes the following pair of key components or processes:

◆ the amount of personal *time* you devote to learning in college, and
◆ the degree of personal *effort* or *energy* (mental and physical) that you put into the learning process.

One way to ensure that you are actively involved in the learning process, and are expending high levels of energy or effort, is to act on what you are learning. In other words, you should perform some physical action on what you are attempting to learn. If you engage in any of the following physical actions with respect to what you are learning, you can be assured that you are investing a high level of involvement and energy in the learning process.

Writing—expressing what you are trying to learn in print

    ACTION: Write notes when reading, rather than passively underlining sentences.

Speaking—orally communicate what you are attempting to learn

    ACTION: Explain a course concept to a study-group partner, rather than just looking it over silently.

Organizing—grouping or classifying the concepts you are learning into logical categories that show how they are related.

    ACTION: Create an outline, diagram, or concept map (similar to Figure 1.1) that visually organizes concepts.

© Corbis.

Writing notes while reading is one way to become actively involved in the learning process.

The following section explains how you can apply both components of active involvement—spending time and expending energy—to some of the major learning tasks that you will encounter in college.

Time Spent in Class

Since the total amount of time you spend on learning is associated with how much you learn and how successful you are in college, this association naturally leads to a very straightforward recommendation: Attend all class sessions in all your courses. It may be tempting to skip or cut classes because college professors are less likely to monitor your attendance or call roll like your teachers in high school. Do not let this new freedom fool you into thinking that missing classes will not affect your grades. College research indicates that there is a direct relationship between class attendance and course grades—as one goes up or down, so does the other (Anderson & Gates, 2002; Grandpre, 2000). For instance, one study revealed that every 10 percent increase in the number of student absences in college classes resulted in a .2 drop in students' overall grade-point average (Kowalewski, Holstein, & Schneider, 1989). Figure 1.2 represents the results of another study conducted at the City Colleges of Chicago, which shows the relationship between students' class attendance during the first five weeks of the term and final course grades.

Time Spent on Coursework Outside the Classroom

In college, you will spend fewer hours per week sitting in class than you did in high school. However, in college, there are higher expectations for the amount of time that you should commit to academic work outside of class time. Studies clearly show that the greater amount of time college students spend on academic work outside of class results in greater learning and higher grades. For example, one study of over 25,000 college students found that the percentage of students receiving grades that were mostly "As" was almost three times higher for students who spent 40 or more hours per week on academic work than it was for students who spent 20 or

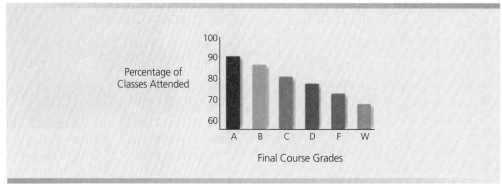

Figure 1.2 Relationship Between Class Attendance Rate and Final Course Grades

less. On the other hand, among students who spent 20 or fewer hours on academic work, the percentage of them receiving grades that were mostly "Cs" or below was almost twice as high as it was for students who spent 40 or more hours per week on academic activities (Pace, 1990a, 1990b).

Only 20 percent of first-year students expect to spend more than 25 hours per week studying, and although almost all (96%) first-year students agree that they can improve their academic ability through hard work and practice, almost one-third (30%) admitted that they did just enough work to get by (National Survey of Student Engagement, 2005).

Keep in mind that better grades in college equals better chances for career success after college. Research on college graduates indicates that the higher their grades were in college, the higher:

♦ the status (prestige) of their first job,

♦ their job mobility (ability to change jobs or move into different positions), and

♦ their total earnings (salary).

This relationship between college grades and career success exists for students at all types of colleges and universities, regardless of the reputation or prestige of the institution they are attending (Pascarella & Terenzini, 1991, 2005). In other words, how well you do academically in college matters more to your career success than where you go to college, or what particular college issues your diploma.

 Pause for Reflection

In high school, how many hours per week did you spend on schoolwork outside of class?

Active Listening and Note-Taking

You will find that professors frequently use the lecture method, whereby the instructor speaks continuously and the students' job is to listen and take notes. This method of instruction places great demands on students' ability to listen carefully and take notes that are accurate and complete.

> **Remember:** Research shows that, in all subject areas, the majority of test questions on college exams come from the professor's lectures and that students who take better class notes get better course grades (Brown, 1988; Kierwa, 2000).

The best way to apply the strategy of active involvement during a class lecture is to engage in the physical action of writing notes. Writing down what your instructor is saying in class essentially forces you to pay closer attention to what is being said and reinforces your retention of that information. By taking notes, you not only hear the information (auditory memory), you also see it—on paper (visual memory) and feel it—in the muscles of your hand as you write it (motor memory).

> **Remember:** Your role in the college classroom is not to be a passive spectator or sponge; instead, take on the role of an aggressive detective or investigative reporter who is on a "search and record" mission. Actively search for information by picking your instructor's brain and recording your "pickings" in your notebook.

See Box 1.1 for top strategies on classroom listening and note-taking that you should put into practice immediately. This is the first of a series of "Take Action Now!" boxes offered throughout the text that contain top-priority academic strategies. Compared to high school, achieving academic success in college will require working harder—investing more time and energy—and working smarter—using more effective learning strategies. However, academic success not only depends on the quantity of time you devote to your studies, it also depends on the quality of the time you spend; and the quality of your learning time increases when you use high-quality learning strategies, such as those suggested in this text.

Active Class Participation

You can become actively involved in the college classroom by coming to class prepared (e.g., having done the assigned reading), by asking relevant questions, and by contributing thoughtful comments during class discussions. Oral communication increases your level of active involvement because it requires you to exert both mental energy—thinking about what you are going to say—and physical energy—moving your lips to say it. Thus, thoughtful class participation increases the likelihood that you remain alert and attentive in class. It also sends a clear message to the instructor that you are a motivated student who takes the course seriously and really wants to learn. Since class participation accounts for a portion of your final grade in many courses, your attentiveness and involvement in class may have a direct, positive effect on your course grade.

If you do not feel confident or assertive enough to speak in class with many people present, consider contributing your questions and comments by e-mail to your instructor and/or classmates.

© Adobe.

Participating in class increases the likelihood that you will remain alert and attentive, and lets the instructor know you are motivated to learn.

Top Strategies: Listening and Note-Taking

One of the tasks that you will be expected to perform at the very start of your first term in college is to take notes in class. Studies show that professors' lecture notes are the number-one source of test questions (and test answers) on college exams. So, get off to a fast start by using the following strategies to improve the quality of your note-taking.

1. **Get to every class.** Whether or not your instructor takes roll, s/he may still be aware of whether you are in class, and you are still responsible for all material covered in class. Think of your class schedule as a full- time job that requires you to show up only about 13 hours a week. (If you happen to miss class, leave space in your notebook as a reminder to get those notes from a classmate.)

2. **Get to every class on time.** The first few minutes of a class session often contain very valuable information, such as reminders, reviews, and previews.

3. **Get organized.** Come to class with the right equipment—get a separate notebook for each class, get your name on it, date each class session, and store all class handouts in it.

4. **Get in the right position:**
   ⊙ The ideal place to sit—front and center of the room—where you can hear and see most effectively;
   ⊙ the ideal posture—sitting upright and leaning forward—because your body influences your mind; if your body is in an alert and ready position, your mind is likely to follow.
   ⊙ the ideal position socially—sit near people who will not distract your focus of attention or detract from the quality of your note-taking.

Remember: These attention-focusing strategies are particularly important during the first year of college because you are more likely to have large-sized classes. When class size increases, each individual tends to feel more anonymous, which may reduce feelings of personal responsibility and the need to stay focused and remain actively involved. So, in large-class settings, it is especially important to use effective strategies that eliminate distractions and attention drift.

5. **Get in the right frame of mind.** Get psyched up, and come into the classroom with the attitude that you are going to pick your instructor's brain and pick up answers to test questions.

6. **Get it down** (in writing) by actively looking, listening, and recording important points. Pay special attention to whatever information the instructor puts in writing—on the board, on an overhead, on a slide, or in a handout.

7. **Do not let go of your pen**—if you're in doubt, write it out—it's better to have it and not need it than to need it and not have it. Keep in mind that most professors do not write out all the important information on the board for you; instead, they expect you to listen carefully to what they are saying and write it down for yourself.

8. **Finish strong**—the *last few minutes* of class often contain very valuable information—such as reminders, reviews, and previews.

9. **Stick around.** As soon as class ends, don't bolt out—hang out—and quickly review your notes (by yourself or with a classmate); if you find any gaps, check them out with your instructor before s/he leaves the classroom. Also, this quick end-of-class review will help your brain retain the information it just received.

Note: More detailed information on listening and note-taking is provided in Chapter 4, *Strategic Learning*.

Pause for Reflection

When you enter a classroom, where do you usually sit? Why do you think you sit there? Is it a conscious choice or more like an automatic habit? Do you think that your usual seat places you in the best possible position for listening and learning in the class-room?

Finish class with a rush of attention, not a rush out the door!

Active Reading

Just as writing promotes active listening in class, writing also promotes active reading outside of class. Taking notes on important information that you highlighted in your first read, ensures active involvement because it requires more mental and physical energy than merely reading the material or passively highlighting sentences with a highlighter. (See Box 1.2 for top strategies on improving textbook reading that you should put into practice immediately.)

TAKE ACTION NOW! Box 1.2

Top Strategies: Improving Textbook-Reading Comprehension and Retention

You have already purchased textbooks for your courses, and you probably have already received reading assignments to complete. After lecture notes, information from reading assignments is the second most frequent source of test questions on college exams. In fact, your professors may deliver class lectures with the expectation that you have done the assigned reading; so, if you haven't done the reading, you may not be able to follow what your instructor is talking about in class. Also, college professors often expect you to relate or connect what they talk about in class to the reading they have assigned. Thus, it's important to start developing good reading habits right now. You can do so by using the following strategies to improve your reading comprehension and retention.

1. **Get the right equipment**
   - Pen or pencil to note important information that should be later reviewed and studied for exams.
   - Dictionary to find the meaning of unfamiliar words. This will not only help you understand what you are reading, it is also the most effective way to build your vocabulary, which will come in handy in all college courses and on all standardized tests, such as those required for entry to graduate schools and professional schools.
2. **Get in the right position**—sit upright and have light coming from behind you, over the opposite side of your writing hand. (This will reduce the distracting and fatiguing effects of glare and shadows.)
3. **Get a sneak preview** of the chapter by first reading its boldface headings and any chapter outline, summary, or end-of-chapter questions that may be provided. This will give you a mental map of the chapter's content before you begin reading, enabling you to see the big picture and helping you keep track of the chapter's most important concepts as you read through all the specific details.
4. **Use boldface headings and subheadings** as cues for important information. Turn these headings into questions, then read to find their answers. This will send you on an answer-finding mission , keeping you mentally active and helping you read with a purpose. This is also the ideal way to prepare for tests because you will be practicing exactly what you will be doing on tests—answering questions.
5. **Pay special attention to the first and last sentences** in sections of the text that lie beneath the chapter's major headings and subheadings. These sentences often contain an important introduction and conclusion to the material covered within that section of the text.
6. **Finish with a short review** of what you have highlighted or noted as important information (rather than trying to cover a few more pages). It is best to use the last few minutes of your reading time to lock in the most important information you have just read because most forgetting takes place immediately after you stop focusing and start doing something else (Underwood, 1983). So, read to find the most important information, but end your reading by re-reading your findings.

Note: More detailed information on reading comprehension and retention is provided in Chapter 4, *Strategic Learning*.

●●● Touching the First Base of College Success: Utilizing Campus Resources

Successful performance in college, like successful performance in any human endeavor, is influenced by both the individual and the environment. Your environment (college campus) is chock full of specialized resources that are available to you (in print, in person, and online), all of which can strongly support your quest for educational and personal success. Studies show that students who utilize these resources report higher levels of satisfaction with, and get more out of, the college experience (Pascaralla & Terenzini, 1991, 2005).

For example, two researchers who conducted a comprehensive review of over 2,500 research studies reached the following conclusion. "The impact of college is not simply the result of what a college does for or to a student. Rather, the impact is a result of the extent to which an individual student exploits the people, programs, facilities, opportunities, and experiences that the college makes available" (Pascarella & Terenzini, *How College Affects Students,* pp. 610–611).

Described in this section are some of the most valuable campus services that can support and promote your success.

> **Remember:** Involvement with campus services is not only valuable, but it's also free because the cost of these services has already been covered by your college tuition. By investing time and energy in these resources, you are not only increasing your prospects for personal success, you are also maximizing the return on your financial investment in college.

Learning Center

Also known as the Center for Academic Support or Academic Success, this is the place on campus where you can obtain individual assistance to support and strengthen your academic performance. The one-to-one and group tutoring provided by the Center can help you master difficult course concepts and assignments, and the people working there have been professionally trained to help you learn "how to learn." While your professors may have expert knowledge of the subject matter they teach, learning resource specialists are experts on the process of learning. These specialists can show students how to adjust or modify their learning strategies to meet the demands of the different courses and teaching styles they encounter in college.

Studies show that students who become actively involved with academic support services outside the classroom, such as the Learning Center or Academic Support Center, are more likely to attain higher college grades and complete their college degree. This is particularly true if they began their involvement with these support services during the first year of college (Cuseo, 2003). Also, students who seek and receive assistance from academic-support services show significant improvement in academic self-efficacy—that is, they develop a greater sense of personal control over their academic performance and develop higher self-expectations for future academic success (Smith, Walter, & Hoey, 1992).

Despite the multiple advantages of getting involved with academic support services outside the classroom, these services are typically under-utilized by college students, especially by those students who could gain the most from using them (Knapp & Karabenick, 1988; Walter & Smith, 1990). This could be due to the fact that some students feel that seeking academic help is an admission that they are not smart, or that they cannot succeed on their own. Do not be one of these students.

Remember: The purpose of the Learning Center (Academic Support Center) is not just to provide remedial repair work for academically under-prepared learners, to save floundering or failing students, or to fix struggling students' with academic problems. It is a place where all learners can benefit, including well-prepared and highly motivated students who want to be the best they can be and who are striving to achieve the highest possible levels of academic excellence.

Personal Story   At my college, it has been found that the grade-point average of students who use the Learning Center is higher than the college average, and honor students are more likely to use the Center than non-honors students.

–*Joe Cuseo, Professor of Psychology*

Writing Center

Many college campuses offer specialized support that is expressly designed to help students improve their writing skills. Typically referred to as the Writing Center, this is the place where you can receive assistance at any stage of the writing process, whether it be collecting and organizing your ideas in outline form, composing your first draft, or proofreading your final draft. Since writing is an academic skill that you'll use in almost all your courses, improvements in your writing will improve your overall academic performance. Thus, we strongly encourage you to capitalize on this campus resource.

Disability Services or Office for Students with Special Needs

If you have a physical or learning disability that is interfering with your performance in college, or think you may have such a disability, this would be the resource on your campus to consult for assistance and support. Programs and services typically provided by this office include:

- assessment for learning disabilities,
- verification of eligibility for disability support services,
- specialized counseling, advising, and tutoring,
- authorization of academic accommodations for students with disabilities.

College Library

Do not overlook the fact that librarians are educators who provide instruction outside the classroom. You can learn from them just as you do from faculty inside the classroom. Furthermore, the library is a place where you can acquire skills for locating, retrieving, and evaluating information that you may apply to any course you are taking or will ever take.

Academic Advisement

College students who have developed a clear sense of their educational and career goals are more likely to continue their college education and complete their college degree (Willingham, 1985; Wyckoff, 1999). However, most beginning college students need help with clarifying their educational goals, selecting an academic major, and exploring future careers. For instance, consider the following findings:

© JupiterImages Corporation.

Working with your academic advisor can help you develop clear educational and career goals.

- three of every four beginning college students are uncertain or tentative about their career choice (Frost, 1991);
- less than 10 percent of new students feel they know a great deal about their intended college major (Erickson & Strommer, 1991);
- over half of all students who enter college with a declared major change their mind at least once before they graduate (Noel, 1985); and
- only one of three college seniors end up majoring in the same field that they preferred during their first year of college (Cuseo, 2005).

These findings point to the conclusion that the majority of college students do not make final decisions about their major before starting their college experience; instead, they make these decisions during the college experience. It is only natural for you, a first-year student, to feel uncertain about your intended major because you have not yet experienced the variety of subjects and academic programs that make up the college curriculum. In fact, you will encounter fields of study in college that you probably never knew existed in high school.

Remember: Being undecided or unsure about your major and career is nothing to be embarrassed about because the process of long-range academic planning and effective decision-making is challenging and complex. So, connect early and often with an academic advisor to help you work through this challenging process and to help you find a major that best taps your educational interests, talents, and values.

Career Development Center

Research on college students indicates that they are more likely to stay in school and graduate when they have some sense of how their present academic experience relates to their future career goals (Levitz & Noel, 1989). Studies also show that the vast majority of new students are uncertain about what future careers they would like to pursue (Gordon & Steele, 2003). So, if you are uncertain about a career right now, welcome to the club. This uncertainty is entirely normal and understandable because you have not yet had the opportunity for hands-on work experience in the real world of careers. As Vincent Tinto, a nationally known scholar on student success, points out:

> Among any population of young adults who are just beginning in earnest their search for adult identity, it would be surprising indeed if one found that most were very clear about their long-term goals. The college years are an important growing period in which new social and intellectual experiences are sought as a means of coming to grips with the issue of adult careers. Students enter college with the hope that they will be able to formulate for themselves a meaningful answer to that important question (1993, p. 40).

The Career Center is the place to go for help in finding a meaningful answer to the important question of how to connect your current college experience with your future career goals. Although it may seem like beginning a career is light years away because you are just beginning college, the process of investigating, planning, and preparing for career success begins in the first year of college. You can start this important process by visiting the Career Center, which is a campus resource that has been explicitly created to help you:

- explore the rapidly changing world of careers,
- understand the often complex relationship between particular academic majors and related careers,
- identify what careers may be most compatible with your personal interests, abilities, or values,
- locate volunteer (service-learning) experiences and internships that will enable you to test your interest in different careers through direct, real-world experience, and
- develop your resume.

Your Career Center will typically provide such services as personal career counseling, workshops on career exploration and development, and "career fairs" where you are able to meet professionals working in different career fields. Although entering a career may appear to be a very long-term goal to you right now, successful career planning should begin in your first year. Thus, we strongly encourage you not to wait until your junior or senior year before taking advantage of this valuable campus resource.

Counseling Center

Students entering college today are reporting higher levels of stress than in years past (Astin, et al., 1997; Sax, et al., 2000). The first year in college can be particularly stressful because it represents a major life transition, which requires not only academic adjustments, but also involves significant changes in social relationships, emotional experiences, and personal identity. In fact, studies show that the vast majority of students who withdraw from college do not do so for strictly academic reasons. Most students who drop out do not flunk out; they leave because of other factors (Tinto, 1993).

These findings point to the importance of focusing not only on your academics, but also on non-academic aspects of your adjustment to college and your development as a whole person. In fact, studies of successful people indicate that social and emotional intelligence (EQ) are often more important for personal and professional success than intellectual ability (IQ) (Goleman, 1995).

Counseling services can provide you with a valuable source of support during your first year of college, not only for helping you cope with college stressors that may be interfering with your academic success, but also for helping you realize your full potential. Personal counseling can promote self-awareness and self-development in social and emotional areas of your life that are important for mental health, physical wellness, and personal growth.

 Remember: College counseling is not just for students who are experiencing emotional problems. It is for all students who want to enrich their overall quality of life.

 Pause for Reflection

Take a moment to visualize your campus environment. Can you "see" the locations of the following college services that are designed to support your academic success: Academic Advisement? College Library? Learning Center (Academic Support Center)? Career Center? Counseling Center?

Health Center

Making the transition from high school to college often involves taking more personal responsibility for your own health and wellness. In addition to making your own decisions about what to eat, when to sleep, and how to manage your own health, your stress level is likely to increase during times of change or transition in your life. Good health habits are one effective way to both cope with college stress and reach peak levels of performance. The Health Center on your campus is the key resource for information on how to manage your health and maintain wellness. It is also the place to go for help with physical illnesses, sexually transmitted infections or diseases, and eating disorders.

Experiential Learning Resources

The learning that takes place in college courses is primarily vicarious—that is, you learn from or through somebody else—by *listening* to the ideas professors present in class and by *reading* the print materials outside of class. While this academic learning is valuable, it should be complemented by experiential learning—that is, learning directly through first-hand experiences. This is supported by the work of two highly regarded scholars, who reviewed more than 2,500 studies on college students, and reached the following conclusion: "On the basis of the extensive body of evidence reviewed, one of the most inescapable conclusions we can make is that the impact of college is largely determined by the individual's quality of effort and level of involvement in both academic and nonacademic [experiential] activities" (Pascarella & Terenzini, 1991, 2005).

As a first-year college student, there are two major ways in which you can get involved in college life beyond academics and capitalize on experiential learning opportunities outside of the classroom:

1. through involvement in co-curricular experiences on campus, and
2. through volunteer experiences in the local community.

Here are some specific strategies for becoming actively involved in both of these important forms of experiential learning.

Co-Curricular Experiences on Campus

Colleges and universities no longer refer to involvement in campus life outside the classroom as "extra"-curricular activities, because these activities can be very powerful sources of experiential learning. Instead, they are referred to as "*co*"-curricular experiences, because the prefix "co" suggests that they are *equal* to curricular (course-related) experiences for promoting learning and development.

More specifically, research reveals that students who become actively involved in campus life are more likely to:

♦   enjoy their college experience,
♦   graduate from college, and
♦   develop leadership skills that are useful in the world of work after college (Astin, 1993).

For example, college graduates consistently report that their participation in co-curricular experiences involving leadership helped them to develop skills that were important for their work performance and career advancement. These reports have been confirmed by on-the-job evaluations of college alumni, which indicate that previous involvement in co-curricular activities on campus, particularly those involving student leadership, is the best predictor of successful managerial performance. In fact, these experiences are more strongly associated with the managerial success of college graduates than the prestige of the college they attended (Pascarella & Terenzini, 1991, 2005). Also, involvement in student leadership activities is associated with improved self-esteem (Astin, 1993).

Try to get involved in no more than two to three major campus organizations at any one time. Limiting the number of your out-of-class activities should enable you to keep up with your studies, and it is likely to be more impressive to future schools or employers because a long list of involvement with multiple activities may seem suspicious. As the director of a national bureau for college placement once said: "Just a [long] list of club memberships is meaningless; it's a fake front. Remember that quality, not quantity, is what counts" (Pope, 1990, p. 189). High-quality campus clubs and organizations to become involved with are those that relate to your academic major or career interests (for example, history or psychology club), and which place you in a position of providing leadership or help to others (for example: student government, college newspaper, college committees, peer counseling, or peer tutoring).

Volunteerism and Service Learning

When you volunteer to serve others, you are also serving yourself. Your self-esteem is boosted by knowing that you are doing something good. Volunteering also enables you to:

♦ acquire learning skills through hands-on experience (hence the term, "service *learning*"),

♦ strengthen your resumé, and

♦ explore areas of work that may relate to your future career interests.

One of the benefits of volunteering at a local elementary school is that it will give you the experience to determine if you want to major in education.

Service-learning experiences can function as exploratory internships that enable you to test the waters and gain real-life knowledge about careers relating to your area of volunteer work, while simultaneously providing you with career-related work experience. Volunteer experiences also allow you to network with professionals outside of college who may serve as excellent resources, references, and sources for letters of recommendation. Furthermore, if these professionals are impressed with your initial volunteer work, they may also hire you on a part-time basis while you are still in college, or on a full-time basis after you graduate.

Do not worry that putting some time into experiential learning outside the classroom will subtract time from your studies and lower your grades. Keep in mind that, in college, you will be spending much less time in the classroom than you did in high school. For instance, a full load of college courses (15 units) only requires that you be in class about 13 hours per week. This leaves enough out-of-class time for other activities. Just don't overdo it. In fact, there is evidence that college students who are involved in co-curricular, volunteer, and part-time work experiences outside the classroom that total *no more than 15 hours per week* actually earn higher grades than students who do not get involved in any out-of-class activities (Pascarella, 2001; Pascarella & Terenzini, 2005). This is probably because students who have commitments outside the classroom learn to manage their out-of-class time better, because their structured out-of-class schedule essentially forces them to use their time well. On the other hand, students who do not have to show up for anything other than their 13 hours of classes per week may have so much unstructured out-of-class time that they do not get into a regular routine for organizing it. Apparently, instead of effectively using their out-of-class time, they end up wasting or abusing it. If you work, we strongly recommend limiting it to 15 hours per week, because students who work more than 15 hours are more likely to eventually switch from full-time to part-time enrollment and are less likely to continue in college and complete their degree (Pascarella & Terenzini, 2005).

Learning More about Your Campus Resources through Your Own Research

Utilizing your resources is an important, research-based strategy for college success. An essential first step toward putting this strategy into practice is to become fully aware of all the key support services that are available at your college. You can find this information in three major forms:

1. **In print**—information published in written form. For in-print information on campus resources, consult your College Catalog (also known as the College Bulletin), and your *Student Handbook*. If you do not have a copy of the college catalog, you should be able to obtain one from the Office of Admissions or Center for Academic Advising. If you do not have a copy of the student handbook, you should be able to obtain one from the Office of Student Life or Student Affairs.

2. **Online**—information posted electronically on the Internet. For online information on campus resources, check your college's Web site. Your college may have its entire Catalog and Student Handbook available online.

3. **In person**—information communicated directly to you by a knowledgeable person For in-person information on campus resources, speak with a professional in different offices or centers on your campus, such as:

   a. Academic Support Services (Learning Resource Center)—ask about the type of support it provides for improving course learning and increasing academic success (e.g., study and test-taking strategies);

   b. College Library—ask about the type of support it provides for finding information and completing research assignments (e.g., term papers and group projects); and

   c. Student Development Services (Student Affairs)—ask about the type of support it provides on issues relating to social and emotional adjustment, involvement in campus life outside the classroom, and leadership development.

◆ *Pause for Reflection*

You have now reached the end of this unit on campus resources, so this is a good time to step back from your reading and reflect on what you have read thus far. Take a minute to look back at the major college resources that have been mentioned in this section, and identify two or three of them that you think you should use immediately. *Briefly explain* why *you have identified these resources as your top priorities at this time. (You might consider asking your course instructors what they think, and see what resources they would recommend for immediate use.)*

••• Touching the Second Base of College Success: Social Interaction and Collaboration

Learning is strengthened when it takes place in a social context that involves human interaction. As some scholars put it, human knowledge is socially constructed or built-up through interaction and dialogue with others. According to these scholars, our thinking is largely an internalization or internal incorporation of the conversations we have had with other people, and our personal knowledge is often a product of these interpersonal interactions (Bruffee, 1993). So, if we have frequent, high-quality dialogue with others, we increase the quality of our thinking and the quantity of our knowledge.

Modern advances in electronic technology (e-mail, instant messaging) now allow interpersonal interaction to occur at any time and any place—on or off campus. If you are a commuter student who does not live on campus, or if you are an adult student who is juggling family and work commitments along with your academic schedule, e-mail communication may be an especially effective and efficient mode of interaction for you.

Four particular forms of interpersonal interaction have been found to be strongly associated with improving students' performance in college and their motivation to complete college:

1. Student-faculty interaction,
2. Student interaction with academic advisors,
3. Student interaction with a mentor, and
4. Student-student (peer) interaction.

Student-Faculty Interaction

Many research studies demonstrate that students' college success is influenced heavily by the quality and quantity of their interaction with faculty members *outside the classroom*. More specifically, student-faculty contact outside of class is positively associated with the following student developments:

♦ improved academic performance,
♦ increased critical thinking skills,
♦ greater satisfaction with the college experience,
♦ increased likelihood of completing a college degree, and
♦ stronger desire to seek further education beyond college (Astin, 1993; Pascarella & Terenzini, 1991, 2005).

Because these positive results are so strong and widespread, we urge you to consciously seek interaction with college faculty outside of class time. Here are some of the most manageable ways to increase your out-of-class contact with college instructors during the first year of college.

1. Seek interaction with your course instructors *immediately after class*.

This may be an ideal time for you to interact with a faculty member because your interest, curiosity, or confusion may have been sparked by course material just covered in class. This is likely to be the time when you are most motivated to talk about a concept discussed in class, and it may also be the time when your instructor is most motivated to discuss it with you. Furthermore, interaction with your instructors immediately after class serves to increase their familiarity with you and their awareness of you as an individual, which in turn should increase your confidence and willingness to seek subsequent contact with them.

2. Seek interaction with your course instructors during their *office hours*.

One important piece of information on the syllabus you receive in college courses is your instructors' office hours. Make specific note of these office hours, and make an earnest attempt to capitalize on them. College professors spend most of their professional time outside the classroom preparing for class, grading papers, conducting research, and serving on college committees. However, some of their out-of-class time is reserved specifically for office hours, during which they are expected to be available for interaction with students.

National surveys reveal that 85 percent of first-year college students report having worked on academic matters with other students outside of class, but less than 20 percent have interacted with their instructors outside of class (Policy Center on the First Year of College, 2003). One way to be sure that you do not fall into this pattern is to schedule an office visit with your instructor during the early stages of the course. This is important for the purpose of discussing course assignments, term paper topics, and possible major or career choices. Try to make at least one visit to the office of all your instructors, preferably early in the term, because once midterm is reached, both instructors and students tend to become very busy, so quality time for student-faculty interaction is often harder to find.

Even if you meet with your instructors for only a few minutes, it will still serve as a valuable icebreaker that can help them to get to know you as a person, and help you to feel more comfortable about interacting with them again in the future.

3. Seek interaction with your instructors through e-mail.

Electronic communication is another effective way to interact with your instructors, particularly if their office hours conflict with your class schedule, work responsibilities, or family commitments. Also, if you are shy or hesitant about "invading" your instructors' office space, e-mail can provide a less threatening way for you to interact with your instructors, and may give you the initial self-confidence to eventually seek contact with them on a face-to-face basis.

STUDENT PERSPECTIVE

"I wish that I would have taken advantage of professors' open door policies when I had questions, because actually understanding what I was doing, instead of guessing, would have saved me a lot of stress and re-doing what I did wrong the first time."

–Advice to new students from a college sophomore (Walsh, 2005)

Student-Advisor Interaction

An academic advisor can be an effective referral agent who is well positioned to direct you to, and connect you with, campus support services that best serve your needs. An advisor can also help you understand college procedures and navigate the bureaucratic maze of college policies and politics.

> **Remember:** An academic advisor is not someone who you see just once per term—when you need to get a signature for class scheduling and course registration. An advisor is someone you should visit on a more regular basis than your course instructors. Your instructors will change from term to term, but your academic advisor may be the college professional with whom you have regular contact and a stable, ongoing relationship that can endure throughout your college experience.

Your academic advisor should be someone you feel comfortable talking to, who knows you by name, and who is familiar with your personal interests and abilities. Give your advisor the opportunity to get to know you personally, and seek that person's advice about courses, majors, and personal issues that may be interfering with your academic performance.

If your college does not assign you a personal advisor, but offers advising through an advisement center on a drop-by basis, this may result in your seeing a different advisor each time you visit the center. If you are not satisfied with this system of multiple advisors, find one advisor with whom you feel most comfortable and make him or her your personal advisor by scheduling your appointments in advance. This will enable you to consistently connect with the same advisor, with whom you can develop an ongoing relationship. On the other hand, if your college has assigned a personal advisor to you, and you find that you cannot develop a good relationship with this person, ask the Director of Advising or Academic Dean if you could

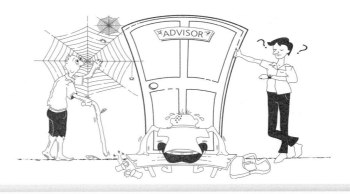

Make appointments to meet with an academic advisor at times other than during the "mad rush" of course registration and class scheduling.

be assigned someone else. If your college does not allow you to change from an advisor that you are unhappy with, then consider finding a *mentor* with whom you could develop a better relationship.

 Pause for Reflection

Do you have a personally assigned advisor?

If yes, do you know who this person is and where he or she can be found?

If no, do you know where you could go if you have questions about your class schedule or academic plans?

Interaction with a Mentor

A mentor may be described as an experienced guide who takes personal interest in you and the progress you are making toward your goals. (For example, in the movie "Star Wars," Yoda served as a mentor for Luke Skywalker.) Research in higher education is beginning to demonstrate that a mentor is someone who can make first-year students feel significant and who can encourage or enable them to stay on track until they complete their college degree (Campbell & Campbell, 1997). A mentor can assist you in trouble-shooting difficult or complicated issues that you may not be able to resolve on your own. A mentor is also someone with whom you can share good news, such as your success stories and personal accomplishments. Look for someone on campus with whom you can develop this type of trusting relationship. There are many people on campus who have the potential to be outstanding mentors, such as:

- ◆ Academic advisors
- ◆ Academic support professionals (e.g., professional tutors in the Learning Center)
- ◆ Your instructor for the first-year seminar or college-success course
- ◆ Faculty in your intended major
- ◆ Juniors, seniors, or graduate students in your intended field of study

- Working professionals in careers that interest you
- Career counselors
- Personal counselors
- Learning assistance professionals (for example, Learning Resource Center)
- Student Development professionals (for example, Director of Student Life or Residential Life)
- Residential Life advisors
- Work-study or volunteer-service supervisor
- Campus minister or chaplain
- Financial aid counselors or advisors

✒ Pause for Reflection

Four general categories or types of people in your college community who can contribute to your success are:

1. *Peers (to be discussed in the next section),*
2. *Faculty (instructors),*
3. *Administrators (e.g., office and program directors), and*
4. *Staff (e.g., student support professionals and administrative assistants).*

Think about your first interactions with faculty, staff, and administrators. Do you recall anyone who impressed you as being very approachable, personable, or helpful? If you did, make a note of that person's name for future reference, in case you would like to seek out the person again. If you have not met such a person yet, be sure not to forget him or her when you do.

Interaction with Peers (Student-Student Interaction)

Studies of college students repeatedly point to the importance of the peer group as a powerful source of social and intellectual support (Pascarella, 2005). One study of over 25,000 college students revealed that when students interact with each other while learning, they achieve higher levels of academic performance and are more likely to complete their college degree (Astin, 1993). Another study, which involved in-depth interviews with more than 1,600 college students, found one particular study habit that was shared by almost all students who struggled academically: They always studied alone (Light, 2001).

Peer interaction is especially important during the first term of college because this is a stage in the college experience when feeling socially accepted and "belonging" are high-priority needs for new students—many of whom have left the long-time security of their family and hometown friends. As a new college student, it might be best to view your early academic performance in terms of the classic need hierarchy theory of human motivation that was formulated by American psychologist Abraham Maslow (1954) (Figure 1.3). According to this theory, humans cannot reach their full potential and achieve peak performance until their more basic emotional and social needs have been met (for example, their needs for personal safety, social acceptance, and self-esteem). Making early connections with your peers can help you meet these basic human needs by providing you with a base of social support that can ease your integration into the college community, and enable you to move up to higher levels of

Figure 1.3 Abraham Maslow's Hierarchy of Needs Resembles a Pyramid

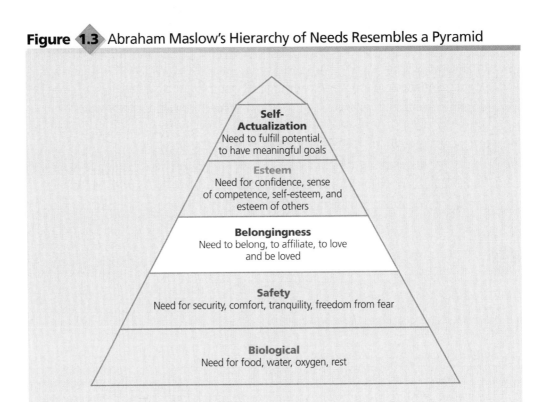

the need hierarchy (for example, striving for educational excellence and fulfilling your personal potential).

Studies repeatedly show that students who have become socially integrated or connected with other members of the college community are much more likely to complete their first-year of college and continue on to complete their college degree (Tinto, 1993). So, find ways to become involved with campus organizations or activities that connect you with other students. Also, try to get connected with experienced students who are at more advanced stages of college development. Sophomores, juniors, and seniors can often be a very valuable social resource for a new student, and they may be very willing to share their experiences with you because you have shown an interest in hearing what they have to say. In fact, you may be the very first person who has ever bothered to ask them what their experience has been like at your college. You can learn from their experiences by asking them about good courses they have taken, what instructors they would recommend, or what advisors they found to be most well informed and personable.

Remember: Your peers can be much more than competitors or sources of negative peer pressure; they can also be collaborators, a source of positive influence, and a resource for college success. Be on the lookout for first-year classmates who are motivated to learn and willing to learn with you, and keep an eye out for advanced students who are willing to assist you. Start building your own success-supporting social network by surrounding yourself with success-seeking and success-achieving students. They can be a stimulating source of positive "peer power" that can drive you to higher levels of academic performance and increase your motivational drive to complete college.

Collaboration with Peers

Simply defined, collaboration is the process of two or more people working interdependently toward the same goal, rather than working independently or competitively. Collaboration involves true teamwork, whereby individuals support each other's success and share equal responsibility for helping the team move toward its common goal. Research on students from kindergarten through college has shown that when students collaborate in teams, their academic performance and interpersonal skills improve significantly (Cuseo, 1996).

To maximize the power of collaboration, use the following guidelines to seek peers who will enhance the quality of your learning team.

Research shows that students who collaborate in teams improve their academic performance and their interpersonal skills.

1. Choose your teammates wisely; look for fellow students who are motivated and will contribute to your team's success, rather than those who are likely to be hitchhikers looking for a free ride. Observe your classmates with an eye toward identifying potentially good teammates.

2. Do not team-up only with peers who are similar to you, or have characteristics that are familiar to you. Instead, include teammates who are different than you in terms of age, gender, ethnic, racial, cultural or geographical backgrounds, learning styles, and personality characteristics. Such variety brings different life experiences, styles of thinking, and learning strategies to your team, which will serve not only to enrich its diversity but its quality as well. If you team-up only with friends or classmates whose interests and lifestyles are similar to your own, this familiarity and homogeneity can work against your team's performance because your common experiences can result in your learning group getting off track and on to topics that may have nothing to do with the learning task (for example, what you did last weekend or what you are planning to do next weekend).

Remember: Seek diversity—capitalize on the advantages of collaborating with peers from varied backgrounds and lifestyles. Simply stated, studies show that you learn more from people who are different than you than you do from people who are the same as you (Pascarella, 2001).

Another point to keep in mind about learning teams is that they are not simply study groups formed the night before an exam. Effective learning teams collaborate more regularly and work on a wider variety of academic tasks than late-night study sessions. Listed below is a series of important academic tasks and situations for which learning teams may be formed to improve your personal performance.

•—·· **CLASSIC QUOTE** ·—•

Surround yourself with only people who are going to lift you higher.

—Oprah Winfrey, actress and talk-show host

Note-Taking Teams

Immediately after class sessions end, take a couple of minutes to team-up with another student to compare and share notes. Listening and note-taking are demanding tasks, so what often happens is that one student will pick up an important point that others overlooked. Also, by teaming-up immediately after class, your team has the opportunity to consult with your instructor about any missing or confusing information before the instructor leaves the classroom.

During my first term in college, I was having difficulty taking complete notes in my biology course because the instructor spoke rapidly and with an unfamiliar accent. I noticed another student (Alex) sitting in the front row who was trying to take notes the best he could, but he was experiencing the same difficulty. Following one particularly fast and complex lecture, we both looked at each other and began to share our frustrations. We decided to "double-team" the instructor by pairing-up immediately after every class and comparing each other's notes to identify points that we missed or found confusing. First, we helped each other; then, if there were points that neither one of us could figure out, we went up together to consult with the instructor before he left the classroom. At the end of the course, Alex and I finished with the highest grades in class.

—*Joe Cuseo*

Reading Teams

After completing your reading assignments, you can team-up with classmates to compare your highlighting and margin notes. You can consult with each other to identify major points in the reading and reach decisions about what information is most important to study for upcoming exams.

Writing Teams

Teammates can provide each other with feedback that can be used to revise and improve the quality of their writing. You could connect with a writing team of peers at any or all of the following stages in the writing process:

♦ topic selection and refinement—to help generate a list of potential topics and related subtopics,

♦ pre-writing—to clarify your purpose and audience,

♦ first draft—to improve your general style and tone, and

♦ final draft—to proofread and correct mechanical errors before submitting your work.

Library Research Teams

Many first-year students are unfamiliar with the process of conducting library research, and some may experience library anxiety. Forming library research teams is an effective way for you to develop a social support group that can make trips to the library more enjoyable and transform the process of library research from something you do alone into something you do as a team.

Remember: It is ethical and acceptable for you to team-up with others to search for and share resources. This is not cheating or plagiarizing, as long as your final product is completed individually and what you turn into your instructor represents your own work.

Team-Instructor Conferences

Visiting course instructors during their office hours with other classmates is an effective way to get additional assistance in preparing for exams and completing assignments. This is a good team-learning strategy for the following reasons:

- You may feel more comfortable about visiting and soliciting help from instructors on their "turf" if you are accompanied by peers, rather than entering this unfamiliar territory on your own. As the old expression goes, "There's safety in numbers."

- When a team of students makes an office visit, the information shared by the instructor is heard by more than one person, so your teammates may pick up some useful information that you might miss, misinterpret, or forget.

- You save your instructors' time by enabling them to help multiple students simultaneously, rather than requiring them to engage in "repeat performances" for students who visit individually at different times.

- You send a message to instructors that you are serious about their course and are motivated to learn, because you have taken the time—in advance—to connect with your peers and prepare for the visit.

Test Results-Review and Assignment-Review Teams

After receiving results on your course examinations and assignments, you can collaborate with other classmates to review your results as a team. By comparing answers, you can better identify the sources of your mistakes. Also, observing the answers of teammates who received maximum credit on particular questions can provide you with a model for improving your future performance.

Teaming-up after tests and assignments given early in the term is especially effective, because it enables you to get a better idea of what the instructor expects from students throughout the remainder of the course. You can use it as early feedback to trouble-shoot problems, fine-tune your performance, and improve your grade—while there is still plenty of time left in the course to do so.

Copyright © by Ed Arno. Reprinted by permission.

Research shows that when peers work collaboratively to achieve a common goal, they learn more effectively and achieve "higher levels" of thinking.

Learning Communities

Your college may offer first-year students the opportunity to participate in a learning community program, in which the same group of students takes the same block of courses together during the same academic term. If this opportunity is available to you, try to take advantage of it because it's been found that students who participate in learning community programs are more likely to:

- become actively involved in classroom learning,
- form their own learning groups outside the classroom,
- report greater intellectual gains, and
- continue their college education (Tinto, 1997, 2000).

If learning community programs are not formally available to you on your campus, consider forming your own learning communities by identifying first-year students who are likely to be taking the same courses as you, and team-up with them to register for the same two to three courses. This will allow you to reap the benefits of a learning community, even though your college does not offer a formal learning-community program.

Pause for Reflection

Think about the students who are in your classes this term. Are there any students who might be good members to join-up with and form learning teams? Do you have any classmates who are in more than one class with you, and who you would consider collaborating with, so that you might work together on the courses you have in common?

TAKE ACTION NOW!   Box 1.3

Top Strategies: Making Connections with Key Members of Your College Community

Studies consistently show that students who become socially integrated or connected with other people in the college community are more likely to remain in college and complete their degree. Below is a list of ten tips for making important interpersonal connections in college. We encourage you to start making these connections right now so that you can begin constructing a base of social support that can strengthen your performance during your first term and serve as a solid foundation for your future success in college.

1. Connect with a favorite peer or student development professional that you may have met during orientation.
2. Connect with peers who live in your student residence or who commute to school from the same community in which you live. If your schedules are similar, consider carpooling together.
3. Join a college club, student organization, campus committee, intramural team, or volunteer-service group whose activities match your personal or career interests.
4. Connect with a peer leader who has been trained to assist new students (e.g., peer tutor, peer mentor, or peer counselor), or with a peer who has more college experience than you (e.g., sophomore, junior, or senior).
5. Look for and connect with a motivated classmate in each of your classes and try working together as a team to take notes, complete reading assignments, and study for exams. (Look especially to team-up with a peer who may be in more than one class with you.)
6. Connect with your favorite faculty in fields that you may be interested in majoring in by visiting them during office hours, conversing briefly with them after class, or communicating with them via e-mail.
7. Connect with an academic support professional in your college's learning resource center to receive personalized academic assistance or tutoring for any course in which you want to improve your performance.
8. Connect with an academic advisor to discuss and develop your future educational plans.
9. Connect with a college librarian to get early assistance and a head start on any major research project that you have been assigned.
10. Connect with a personal counselor at your college or a campus minister to discuss any difficult college-adjustment or personal-life issues that you may be experiencing.

••• Touching the Third Base of College Success: Self-Reflection

Success requires not only action, but also reflection—that is, reflecting on what you have *done*, what you are *doing*, and what you *will do*. In our current, fast-paced, fast food, fast Internet society, we need to make a conscious effort to take time to step back and reflect on our experiences. Such reflection or thoughtful review is the flip side of active involvement. Both processes are needed for learning to be complete. Active involvement is necessary for engaging your attention—which enables you to initially get information into your brain—and reflection is necessary for consolidation—keeping that information in your brain, by locking it into your long-term memory (Broadbent, 1970; Bligh, 2000). In fact, researchers have discovered that different brainwave patterns are associated with each of these two essential processes of human learning (Bradshaw, 1995) (Figure 1.4). This faster brain activity indicates that you are attending to the information and processing it in your brain. This slower brain activity indicates that you're taking the information that's reached your brain and are thinking deeply about it, which will consolidate or lock it into your memory. Thus, effective learning involves both active involvement and thoughtful reflection.

Figure 1.4

Faster Brain-Wave Pattern Associated with a Mental State of *Active Involvement*

Slower Brain-Wave Pattern Associated with a Mental State of *Reflective Thinking*

There are four specific forms of self-reflection that are particularly important for effective learning and college success:

1. Self-assessment,
2. Self-monitoring,
3. Reflecting on feedback, and
4. Reflecting on your future.

Self-Assessment

Simply defined, self-assessment is the process of evaluating your personal characteristics, traits, or habits, and their relative strengths or weaknesses. This process is essential for promoting self-awareness, which is a critical first step toward self-improvement, strategic planning, and decision-making. Listed below are key characteristics of the self that can strongly influence college success and, therefore, are important target areas for self-assessment.

♦ Personal Interests: What you like or enjoy doing.

♦ Personal Values: What is important to you; what you care about doing.

♦ Personal Abilities or Aptitudes: What you do well or have the potential to do well.

♦ Learning Habits: How you go about learning—the usual approaches, methods, or techniques you use when learning.

♦ Learning Styles: How you prefer to learn, that is, your preferred manner of:
   ◇ Receiving information (e.g., reading from books or listening to speakers),
   ◇ Perceiving information (e.g., through sight, sound, or touch), and

◇ Processing information—how you tend to deal mentally with information that you have received and perceived (e.g., thinking about it alone, or talking about it with others).

♦ Personality Traits: Your temperament, emotional characteristics, and social tendencies (e.g., whether you tend to be an introvert or extrovert).

♦ Academic Self-Concept: Your personal beliefs about what kind of student you think you are, and how you perceive yourself as a learner. In particular, two components of your academic self-concept play an important role in college success:

1. Academic Self-Efficacy—whether you think your academic success depends largely on you (e.g., your self-motivation and determination) and that you can change for the better (e.g., by increasing your effort and improving your habits); or, whether you believe that academic success depends largely on factors beyond your control (e.g., your upbringing or present life circumstances) and that you cannot change or improve your performance (e.g., due to low ability or insufficient intelligence).

2. Academic Self-Esteem—how you feel about yourself as a student (e.g., positive, negative, or neutral) and your level of self-confidence in academic situations (e.g., whether you expect success or fear failure).

Pause for Reflection

How would you rate your academic self-confidence at this point in your college experience? (Circle one)

VERY CONFIDENT   SOMEWHAT CONFIDENT   SOMEWHAT UNCONFIDENT   VERY UNCONFIDENT

Why did you make this choice?

Self-Monitoring

Research indicates that one key characteristic of successful college students is that they monitor their own performance. They maintain awareness of:

♦ How effectively they are learning—for example, they pay attention to whether they are really paying attention in class.

♦ Whether they are comprehending what they are attempting to learn—for example, if they are truly understanding the material they are studying or merely memorizing it (Weinstein, 1994; Weinstein & Meyer, 1991).

♦ What they are attempting to learn (for example, science or literature), and they self-regulate or adjust their learning strategies in a way that best meets the specific demands of the subject they are trying to learn (Pintrich, 1995). For instance, they read more slowly and stop to test their understanding more frequently when reading technical material in a science textbook than when reading a novel in a literature course. In contrast, unsuccessful students often do not maintain this high level of self-awareness during the learning process. This can result in their not being fully aware of what method they are using to learn, whether the method they are using is most effective for the type of material they are attempting to learn, or if they are actually understanding the material they are attempting to learn.

You can begin to establish good habits of self-monitoring right now by getting in the routine of periodically pausing to reflect on what you are doing in college. For instance, ask yourself these questions:

♦ Are you are really listening attentively to what your instructor is saying in class?

♦ Do you really comprehend what you are reading outside of class?

♦ Are you effectively utilizing campus resources that are designed to support your success?

♦ Are you interacting with campus professionals who can contribute to your current and future development?

♦ Are you interacting and collaborating with peers who can enhance your learning and social integration into the college community?

It is important to periodically stop and reflect on whether you are actually comprehending what you are reading.

♦ Are you effectively implementing the key success strategies identified in this book?

You can also engage in effective self-monitoring to reflect on what you should *not* be doing if you want to achieve academic excellence. In Box 1.4, the director of academic advising at a state university offers the list of behaviors to avoid if you want to excel in college.

BOX 1.4 *Snapshot* SUMMARY

How Not to Succeed in College: Self-Monitoring the Behaviors You Should Avoid

1. Either don't go to class at all or go very little. This way you won't be bothered with knowing anything about stuff that might be on exams.
2. After cutting class, be sure to ask the instructor, "Did I miss anything?"
3. Sit in the back of the classroom. This will immediately indicate a lack of interest in the class and a generally negative attitude toward school.
4. Forget to buy your textbooks.
5. Don't read your assignments before going to class. This way, you'll be nicely unprepared to answer questions, and you'll have no idea what the professor is lecturing about.
6. If you must take notes, let the reading and studying of them pile up until the night before an exam.
7. Ignore exam results. Throw them away. If you study them, you might do better next time.
8. Start term papers late. In fact, just throw them together.
9. Never visit with any of your professors during the term. That way you can avoid getting any valuable information that might help you.

Source: Bonnie Titley, *National On-Campus Report*, Aug. 12, 1994.

Reflecting on Feedback

Learning and decision-making are enhanced when you reflect on, and make use of information you receive from others on how to correct or improve your performance. In college, potential sources of valuable feedback include professors, academic advisors, academic support professionals, and student life professionals. While feedback from such experienced professionals is extremely valuable, do not overlook your peers as another potential source of useful academic and personal feedback.

Effective learning requires *self-monitoring*—periodically reflecting on whether you're truly understanding what you're learning, or simply "going through the motions."

Pause for Reflection

What positive feedback have you received from others about your personal characteristics or behavior?

Have you ever received feedback from others that you've used to improve yourself, your behavior, or your performance?

If yes, what type of feedback did you receive, and what changes did you make as a result of receiving this feedback?

Be alert and open to feedback that you receive from peers as well as professionals. Better yet, rather than just waiting and hoping that useful feedback floats your way, actively seek it out from people whose judgment you trust and value.

Reflecting on Your Future

Self-reflection not only involves reflecting on what you have done and what you are currently doing, it also involves self-projection—reflecting on what you will be doing in the more distant future. This process of futuristic thinking involves the twin tasks of goal-setting and long-range planning. To achieve success, you need to focus on the "big picture"—your long-term goals and dreams, which inspire motivation, and the "little details"—daily deadlines, due dates, and short-term commitments, that require perspiration. Try to view college as if you were using a dual-focus camera with two lenses: a narrow-angle lens to focus on the foreground that is immediately in front of you (e.g., completing your major assignment that is due next week) and a wide-angle lens to focus on the more distant background—one that enables you to keep in perspective how all your immediate academic chores and challenges are part of a larger picture (e.g., college graduation and a successful future). In other words, you need to periodically pick-up your head from the books in front of you and look farther ahead; then you need to shift back from this long-range vision to the here and now, lower your head again, put your nose to the grindstone, and refocus your sight on the day-to-day college tasks that immediately confront you.

By viewing college from both of these perspectives, you will not lose sight of how achieving your future goals connects with conquering your current challenges. Consider discussing your future plans on a regular basis with an academic advisor, career counselor, or mentor to help you stay focused and moving in the direction of your long-term goals, while simultaneously meeting your short-term objectives.

Remember: Keep both your future dreams and present realities in clear focus. Integrating these two perspectives will produce an image that can provide you with the inspiration to continue your college education and the determination to complete your day-to-day tasks.

◆ *Pause for Reflection*

Before exiting this chapter, we ask you to do one last thing to "lock into" your brain some of the chapter's major ideas. Take a look at the following "Checklist Summary of College-Success Principles and Strategies," and take a minute to see how these ideas compare with those you recorded at the start of this chapter—in response to the questions we asked you about how college would be different from high school and what it would take to be successful in college. What ideas from your list and our checklist tend to match? Were there any ideas on your list that were not on ours, or vice versa?

●●● A Checklist Summary of Key College-Success Principles and Strategies

1. **Active Involvement**

   Inside the Classroom:
   - ☑ Get to Class—treat it like a job—if you "cut," your pay (grade) will be cut.
   - ☑ Get Involved in Class—come prepared, listen actively, take notes, and participate.

   Outside the Classroom:
   - ☑ Read Actively—take notes while you read to increase attention and retention.
   - ☑ Spend a Significant Amount of Time on Academic Activities Outside of Class—make it a 40-hour work week (with occasional "overtime").

2. **Utilizing Campus Resources**

   Capitalize on Academic and Student Support Services:
   - ☑ Learning Center
   - ☑ Writing Center
   - ☑ Disability Services
   - ☑ College Library
   - ☑ Academic Advisement
   - ☑ Career Development
   - ☑ Personal Counseling
   - ☑ Health Center

Capitalize on Experiential Learning Opportunities:

☑ Participate in co-curricular experiences on campus.

☑ Participate in volunteer experiences and internships off campus.

3. **Social Interaction and Collaboration**

Interact with:

☑ Peers—by joining campus clubs and student organizations.

☑ Faculty—by connecting with them immediately after class, in their offices, or by e-mail.

☑ Academic Advisors—see them for more than just a signature to register; find an advisor you can relate to and with whom you can develop an ongoing relationship.

☑ Mentors—try to find experienced people on campus who can serve as trusted guides and role models.

Collaborate by:

☑ Forming Learning Teams—not only last-minute study groups, but teams that collaborate more regularly to work on such tasks as taking lecture notes, completing reading assignments, editing writing assignments, conducting library research, and reviewing results of exams and course assignments.

☑ Participating in Learning Communities—enroll in two or more classes with the same students during the same term.

4. **Self-Reflection**

☑ Self-Monitor Your Learning—maintain awareness of how you are learning, what you are learning, and if you are learning.

☑ Reflect on Feedback—seek information from others (professionals and peers) on the quality of your performance and what specifically you can do to improve it.

☑ Reflect on Your Future—take time from the daily grind to project yourself into the future, set long-term goals, and develop strategic plans for your major, your career, and your life.

●●● Learning More through Independent Research

Web-Based Resources for Further Information on College Success

For additional information relating to the ideas discussed in this chapter, we recommend the following Web sites:

http://steele.instrasun.tcnj.edu/travers6/college_success_formula.html

http://www2.ncsu.edu/for_student/success/text/fundamentals.html

http://www.lifehack.org/article/lifehack/from-a-freshman-five-tips-for-success-in-college

CHAPTER 1
Constructing a Master List of Campus Resources

Use each of the following information sources to gain more in-depth knowledge about the specific support services available on your campus.

1. Information published in your College Catalog and Student Handbook.

2. Online information posted on your college's Web site.

3. In-person information gathered by speaking with a professional in different offices or centers on your campus.

ASSIGNMENT

Using the above information sources, construct a master list of all support services that are available to you at your college. Your final product should be a list that includes:

1. The names of different support services your college offers,

2. The specific types of support each service provides,

3. A short statement next to each specific support service listed, indicating whether you think you would benefit from this particular type of support, and

4. The name of a person whom you could contact for support from this service.

NOTE:

◆ You can pair-up with a classmate to work collaboratively on this assignment. Working together with a peer on a research task can often reduce your anxiety, increase your energy, and generate synergy—which results in a final product that is superior to what could have been produced by either of you working alone (independently).

◆ Save your master list of support services for future use after this course is completed. You might not have an immediate need or use for some of these services during your first term of college, but they can become very valuable and useful to you at later stages of your college experience.

Support Services

LEARNING CENTER

Types of Support

Will I benefit? _____ Contact Person: _____

Will I benefit? _____ Contact Person: _____

Will I benefit? _____ Contact Person: _____

Will I benefit? _____ Contact Person: _____

Will I benefit? _____ Contact Person: _____

WRITING CENTER

Types of Support

Will I benefit? _____ Contact Person: _____

Will I benefit? _____ Contact Person: _____

Will I benefit? _____ Contact Person: _____

Will I benefit? _____ Contact Person: _____

Will I benefit? _____ Contact Person: _____

DISABILITY SERVICES

Types of Services

Will I benefit? _____ Contact Person: _____

Will I benefit? _____ Contact Person: _____

Will I benefit? _____ Contact Person: _____

Will I benefit? _____ Contact Person: _____

Will I benefit? _____ Contact Person: _____

COLLEGE LIBRARY

Types of Services

Will I benefit? _____ Contact Person: _____

Will I benefit? _____ Contact Person: _____

Will I benefit? _____ Contact Person: _____

Will I benefit? _____ Contact Person: _____

Will I benefit? _____ Contact Person: _____

ACADEMIC ADVISEMENT

Types of Services

Will I benefit? _____ Contact Person: _____

Will I benefit? _____ Contact Person: _____

Will I benefit? _____ Contact Person: _____

Will I benefit? _____ Contact Person: _____

Will I benefit? _____ Contact Person: _____

CAREER DEVELOPMENT CENTER

Types of Services

Will I benefit?	Contact Person:
Will I benefit?	Contact Person:
Will I benefit?	Contact Person:
Will I benefit?	Contact Person:
Will I benefit?	Contact Person:

COUNSELING CENTER

Types of Services

Will I benefit?	Contact Person:
Will I benefit?	Contact Person:
Will I benefit?	Contact Person:
Will I benefit?	Contact Person:
Will I benefit?	Contact Person:

HEALTH CENTER

Types of Services

Will I benefit?	Contact Person:
Will I benefit?	Contact Person:

Will I benefit? _____ Contact Person: _____

Will I benefit? _____ Contact Person: _____

Will I benefit? _____ Contact Person: _____

EXPERIENTIAL LEARNING RESOURCES

Types of Services

Will I benefit? _____ Contact Person: _____

Will I benefit? _____ Contact Person: _____

Will I benefit? _____ Contact Person: _____

Will I benefit? _____ Contact Person: _____

Will I benefit? _____ Contact Person: _____

OTHER

Types of Services

Will I benefit? _____ Contact Person: _____

Will I benefit? _____ Contact Person: _____

Will I benefit? _____ Contact Person: _____

Will I benefit? _____ Contact Person: _____

Will I benefit? _____ Contact Person: _____

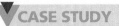

Alone and Disconnected: Feel Like Going Home

Josephine is a first-year student in her second week of college. She doesn't feel like she fits in with other students that she's met at the college thus far. She also feels separated from her family and former friends, and fears that her ties with them will be weakened or broken if she doesn't spend more time at home. In fact, Josephine is feeling so homesick right now that she is having thoughts about withdrawing from college altogether.

Reflection and Discussion Questions

1. What could you say to Josephine that might persuade her to stay in college?

2. Could your college have done more during her first two weeks on campus to make Josephine (and other students) feel more welcomed and less homesick?

3. What could Josephine do now to help herself feel less homesick and more at home at college?

The Value of Liberal Arts and General Education

How the College Experience Develops You as a Whole Person and Improves Your Total Quality of Life

Learning Goals

The primary goal of this chapter is to develop a deeper understanding of the meaning, purpose, and value of a *liberal arts* education. This is the part of your education that provides the essential foundation or backbone of the college experience because:

◆ it is the part that *all* students experience in common, no matter what their major may be, and

◆ it represents what *all* college students should *know* and be able to *do* by the time they graduate.

Outline

Activate Your Thinking

Which one of the following statements represents the most accurate meaning of the term *"liberal arts"* education?

a. Learning to be less conservative politically.

b. Learning to spend money more freely.

c. Learning to value the art of peace more than the martial arts.

d. Learning how to become a performing artist.

e. Learning skills for freedom.

••• The Meaning and Purpose of a Liberal Arts Education

If you are not certain about what the term "liberal arts" means, welcome to the club. Most first-year students do not have the foggiest idea about what a liberal arts education actually stands for (Hersh, 1997), and if they were to guess, they might say that it has something to do with liberal politics, as illustrated by the following story.

Personal Story I was once advising a first-year student (Laura) who intended to major in business, and I was helping her plan what courses she needed to complete her degree. I pointed out to her that one course she still needed to take was philosophy. Here is how our conversation went after I made that point.

Laura (in a somewhat irritated tone): "Why do I have to take philosophy? I'm a business major."

Dr. Joe: "Because philosophy is one important component of a liberal arts education."

Laura (in a very agitated tone): "I am not liberal and I don't want to be a liberal. I'm conservative and so are my parents. We all voted for Reagan in the last election!"

—*Joe Cuseo*

Many students (and their parents) do not know what the term *"liberal arts"* truly means.

In the multiple-choice question that we asked at the start of this chapter, Laura probably would have picked choice "a" as her answer. She would have been wrong because choice "e" actually is correct. Literally translated, the term "liberal arts" derives from the Latin words "liberales"—meaning to *liberate* or *free*, and "artes"—meaning *skills*. Thus, "skills for freedom" is the most accurate meaning of the term "liberal arts."

The roots of the term "liberal arts" date back to the origin of modern civilization—to the ancient Greeks and Romans—who argued that political power in a democratic society rests with the people because, in a democracy, the people elect their own leaders. Thus, in a democracy, people are freed from uncritical dependence on, or blind obedience to, a dictator or autocrat. However, to ensure that a democratic society is successful and political freedom is preserved, citizens in a democracy must be *well educated* so they can ask intelligent questions of their potential political leaders and make wise choices about whom they elect as their leaders and lawmakers (Bishop, 1986; Cheney, 1989).

The founding fathers of America also shared the ancient Greco-Roman emphasis on the importance of education as typified by Thomas Jefferson, third president of the United States and founder of the University of Virginia, who wrote in 1801:

> *I know of no safe depository of the ultimate powers of a society but the people themselves; and if we think them not enlightened enough to exercise control with a wholesome discretion [ability to make responsible decisions], the remedy is not to take power from them, but to inform their discretion by education" (Ford, 1903, p. 278).*

Although its original purpose was to preserve freedom in a democracy, a liberal arts education has taken on the added meaning of liberating or freeing people to be *self-directed* individuals whose choices, decisions, and behavior are determined or driven by their own thoughts and values, rather than by others around them (Gamson, 1984). Self-directed human beings have the mental power to resist excessive control by outside influences, such as:

◆ Politicians—who may try to manipulate or dominate.

◆ Parents—who may attempt to make decisions for their children after they reach an age of independence.

◆ Peers—who can exert excessive influence or pressure for conformity.

◆ Mass media—which may try to manipulate people into thinking how they should vote, act, look, and spend their money.

A liberal arts education encourages you to be "your own person" and to always ask: "Why?" It is the component of your college education that is designed to equip you with the mental tools needed to think independently, along with the inquiring mind needed to question authority and resist thought control by all authority figures, including your instructors! This is one reason why students in college, compared to high school, spend less time per week sitting in class under the direction of instructors and have more free time to work independently outside the classroom. This greater freedom also brings with it greater expectations about the amount of time college students are to commit to their studies outside the classroom, plus greater personal responsibility for planning and managing their own time. For some tips on exercising this freedom responsibly, see Box 2.1.

·—· CLASSIC QUOTE ·—·

❝*Knowledge will forever govern ignorance; and a people who mean to be their own governors must arm themselves with the power which knowledge gives.*❞

—James Madison, 4th president of the United States, and co-signer of the American Constitution and Bill of Rights

SP: STUDENT PERSPECTIVE

"I want knowledge so I don't get taken advantage of in life."

—*First-year student*

TAKE ACTION NOW! **Box 2.1**

Top Strategies for Exercising Personal Freedom Responsibly: Completing Tasks, Planning Time, and Preventing Procrastination

In high school, your educational time was frequently structured for you. In college, you will have more freedom and responsibility to structure your own time. For example, in college, you will typically spend only about 15 hours per week in class, and often you will not go directly from one class to the next; instead, you will often have gaps of "free time" between classes. To effectively manage your out-of-class time, consider implementing the following strategies.

1. **Plan Your *Term***
   ⊙ Review the *course syllabus (course outline)* for each course you are enrolled in this term, and highlight all major exams, tests, quizzes, assignments, papers, and the dates they are due.

SP: STUDENT PERSPECTIVE

"High school can be an assembly line-like time-table. Everything you do is pre-planned; you are given a schedule you must follow. You wish you would have some free time."

—*High school senior*

(continued)

Note: College professors are more likely to expect you to rely on your course syllabus to keep track of what you have to do and when you have to do it.

- ⊙ Obtain a *large calendar* for the academic term (available at your campus bookstore or learning center) and record all your exams, assignments, etc. for all your courses in the calendar boxes that represent their due dates. To fit this information within the calendar boxes, use creative abbreviations to represent different tasks—e.g., "E" for Exam, "TP" for Term Paper (not toilet paper). When you are done, you will have a centralized chart or map of deadline dates, and a potential "master plan" for the entire term.

2. **Plan Your *Week***

- ⊙ Make a map of your *weekly schedule* that includes times during the week when you are in class, when you typically eat and sleep, and if you are employed, when you work.

- ⊙ If you are a full-time college student, find *at least 25 total hours per week* when you can do *academic work outside the classroom*. (These 25 hours can be pieced together any way you like, including time between daytime classes and work commitments, evening time, and weekend time.) When adding these 25 hours to the time you spend in class each week, you will end-up with a 40-hour workweek, similar to any full-time job.

- ⊙ Make good use of your *"free time" between classes* by working on assignments and studying in advance for upcoming exams. 🖉 **Remember:** For the purpose of mastering course material and improving your course grade, out-of-class work includes such tasks as:
  - ○ completing reading assignments,
  - ○ reviewing class notes,
  - ○ integrating information in your class notes with related information that you have highlighted in your assigned reading, and
  - ○ breaking-up work for large, long-term assignments into smaller short-term tasks.

3. **Plan Your *Day***

- ⊙ Make a *daily "to do" list*. 🖉 **Remember:** If you *write it out*, you are less likely to block it out and forget about it. Studies of effective people show that they are "list makers," and they make lists not only for grocery items and wedding invitations, but also for things they want to accomplish each day (Covey, 1990).

- ⊙ Attack daily tasks in *priority order*. 🖉 **Remember:** "First things, first." So, *plan your work* by placing the most important and most urgent tasks at the top of your list, and *work your plan* by attacking tasks in the order that you have listed them.

4. **Carry *Portable* Work and Planning Materials with You at All Times**

- ⊙ Portable work is work that you can take with you and do in any place at any time, enabling you to take advantage of dead time during the day. For example, carry material with you that you can read while sitting and waiting for appointments or transportation during the day, which will resurrect this wasted time and transform it into productive time.

- ⊙ Carry a *small calendar or appointment book* with you at all times. This will enable you to record appointments that you may need to make on the run during the day, and it will also allow you to jot down creative ideas or memories of things you need to do—which can sometimes pop into your mind at the most unexpected times.

- ⊙ Wear a *watch* or carry a cell phone that can accurately and instantly tell you what *time* it is and what *date* it is. Obviously, you can't even begin to manage time if you don't know what time it is, and you can't plan a schedule if you don't know what date it is!

Note: For more on improving time management and preventing procrastination, see Chapter 10.

●●● The Liberal Arts Curriculum

The first liberal arts *curriculum* was intended to provide the type of education that would best preserve political democracy and personal freedom. It was driven by the belief that individuals who experienced these courses would be equipped with a *broad* base of knowledge—ensuring that they would be well informed in a variety of different subjects, and that they would develop a wide range of mental skills—enabling them to think *deeply* and *critically*. Based on this educational philosophy of the ancient Greeks and Romans, the first liberal arts curriculum was developed during the Middle Ages and consisted of two major divisions of knowledge:

A liberal arts education encourages students to ask questions.

1. The Verbal Arts, which included logic, language, and rhetoric (the art of persuasion), and
2. The Numerical Arts, which included mathematics, geometry, and astronomy (Ratcliff, 1997).

The liberal arts curriculum has survived the test of time, and today's colleges and universities continue to offer a liberal arts curriculum for the purpose of providing students with a broad base of knowledge in different subject areas. However, the liberal arts curriculum today is sometimes referred to as:

♦ The *general education* curriculum—"general" representing "broad" rather than narrow education;

♦ The *core* curriculum—"core" standing for what is central or essential for all students to know, regardless of their particular major; or

♦ *Breadth requirements*—required courses that are "wide-ranging," spanning across different subject areas.

Also, the major divisions of knowledge that comprise the liberal arts curriculum today have changed and include more divisions than those that made up the original curriculum devised by the Greeks and Romans. The contemporary liberal arts curriculum usually consists of the general divisions of knowledge and specific subject areas listed below. The *divisions* of the liberal arts curriculum, and the *courses* that make up each division, may vary somewhat from one college to another. Also, colleges vary in terms of whether they require students to take specific courses within each division of knowledge, or whether students are allowed to choose from a menu of courses within each of the divisions. However, what the liberal arts curriculum represents at every college and university are the areas of knowledge and the types of intellectual skills that all students should experience and master, no matter what their particular major happens to be.

◢ *Pause for Reflection*

What type of knowledge or skills do you think are needed to be successful in all majors and careers?

Major Divisions of Knowledge and Subject Areas in the Liberal Arts Curriculum

Humanities

Courses in this division of the liberal arts curriculum tend to focus on the human experience and human culture, asking important questions that arise in a human's life, such as: Why are we here? What is the meaning or purpose of our existence? How should we live? What is the good life? Is there life after death?

Primary Subject Areas:

◆ English Composition: improving written communication.

◆ Speech: public speaking (rhetoric).

◆ Literature: reading written works of artistic merit.

◆ Languages: learning foreign languages.

◆ Philosophy: understanding why logical thinking is essential for humans to live wisely, ethically, and achieve meaning or purpose in life.

◆ Theology: understanding how humans view their relationship with, and express their faith in, a transcendent or supreme being.

© Corbis.

Pottery is a visual art, one of the subject areas of Fine Arts, which focuses on the art of human expression.

Fine Arts

Courses in this division of the liberal arts curriculum focus largely on the art of *human expression*, asking such questions as: How do humans express and appreciate what is beautiful? How do humans express themselves aesthetically (through the senses) with imagination, creativity, style, and elegance?

Primary Subject Areas:

◆ Visual Arts: creative expression through painting, sculpture, and graphic design.

◆ Musical Arts: rhythmical and creative arrangement of sounds.

◆ Performing Arts: creative expression through drama and dance.

Mathematics

Courses in this division of the liberal arts curriculum are designed to promote skills in numerical calculation, quantitative reasoning, and problem solving.

Primary Subject Areas:

◆ Algebra: mathematical reasoning involving symbolic representation of numbers with letters that can vary in size or quantity.

◆ Statistics: mathematical methods for summarizing, estimating probabilities, and drawing conclusions from numerical data.

◆ Calculus: higher mathematical methods for calculating the rate at which the quantity of one entity changes in relation to another, and for calculating the areas enclosed by curves.

Natural Sciences

Courses in this division of the liberal arts curriculum are devoted to observation of the *physical world* and explanation of *natural phenomena*, asking such questions as: What causes physical events in the natural world? How can we predict and control physical events and improve the quality of interaction between humans and the natural environment that surrounds them?

Primary Subject Areas:

◆ Biology: understanding the structure and vital processes of all living things.

◆ Chemistry: understanding the composition of natural and man-made substances, and how they may be changed or developed.

◆ Physics: understanding the structural properties of the physical world and how they produce energy.

◆ Geology: understanding the composition of the earth, and the natural processes that take place to shape its development.

◆ Astronomy: understanding the make-up and motion of celestial bodies that comprise the universe.

© JupiterImages Corporation.

The natural sciences division of the liberal arts curriculum focuses on the observation of the physical world, and the explanation of natural phenomena.

Social and Behavioral Sciences

Courses in this division of the liberal arts curriculum focus on the observation of *human behavior*, individually and in groups, asking such questions as: What causes humans to behave the way they do? How can we predict, control, or improve human behavior and interpersonal interaction?

Primary Subject Areas:

◆ Psychology: understanding the human mind, its conscious and subconscious processes, and the underlying causes of human behavior.

◆ Sociology: understanding the structure, interaction, and collective behavior of organized social groups and societal institutions or systems (e.g., families, schools, and governmental services).

◆ Anthropology: understanding the cultural and physical origin, distribution, and classification of human beings.

◆ History: understanding past events, their causes, and their influence on current events.

◆ Political Science: understanding how societal authority is organized and how this authority is exerted to govern people, make collective decisions, and maintain social order.

◆ Economics: understanding how the monetary needs of humans are met by allocating limited resources, and how material wealth is produced and distributed.

◆ Geography: understanding how the place where humans live influences their cultural interactions and their interactions with the physical environment.

Physical Education and Wellness

Courses in this division of the liberal arts curriculum focus on the *human body* and how to best maintain health or develop physically, asking such questions as: How does the body function most effectively? What can we do to prevent illness, promote wellness, and improve the physical quality of our lives?

Primary Subject Areas:

◆ Physical Education: understanding the role of human exercise for promoting health and peak performance.

- Nutrition: understanding how nourishment is consumed by the body and is used to promote health and generate energy.
- Sexuality: understanding the biological, psychological, and social aspects of sexual relations.
- Drug Education: understanding how substances that alter the body and mind affect physical health, mental health, and human performance.

By the time you graduate from college with a bachelor's degree, roughly one-third of your total college credits will consist of required *liberal arts* courses, one-third will be required courses in your *major*, and one-third will be *electives*—courses in any subject that you choose or "elect" to take.

◢ *Pause for Reflection*

Look back at the subject areas within each of the six divisions of the liberal arts (general education) curriculum, and list those subjects in which you have never had a course. Then look back at your list and highlight any courses that strike you as particularly interesting or intriguing.

●●● **What Is the Value of a Liberal Arts Education?**

Most of the liberal arts courses required for general education are taken during your first and second year of college. Do not be disappointed if you see some general education courses that you have already taken in high school. College courses in these subject areas will not simply repeat what was covered in high school because, in college, you will examine these subjects at a higher level and in greater depth.

Also, if you have already decided on a specific major, do not assume that general education courses have nothing to do with your specialized field of study. Recall our story about Laura, the first-year student with a business major who questioned why she had to take a course in philosophy. Laura needed to take philosophy because she would encounter topics in her business major that relate either directly or indirectly to philosophy. For instance, in her business courses, she would likely encounter philosophical issues relating to (a) the logical assumptions and underlying values of capitalism, (b) business ethics—for example, hiring and firing practices, and (c) business justice—for example, how profits should be fairly or justly distributed to workers and shareholders. Philosophy would equip her with the fundamental logical and ethical thinking skills needed to understand these issues deeply and respond to them humanely. Similarly, other areas of the liberal arts would provide Laura, or any student in her major, with a foundation of knowledge and the fundamental thinking skills needed to succeed in the field of business. Some other courses in the liberal arts curriculum relevant to a business degree are:

- **History and Political Science**—understanding governmental policies toward business and regulations of industry;
- **Psychology and Sociology**—understanding what motivates individuals and groups, such as the work habits of employees and the purchasing habits of consumers;
- **Speech, English Composition, and Literature**—speaking confidently and persuasively at meetings, writing clear and concise memos, reading and interpreting business reports accurately and critically;
- **Mathematics**—analyzing statistical data from marketing surveys;

- **Natural Science**—determining effective and efficient ways to utilize energy and conserve natural resources;
- **Fine Arts**—devising creative and innovative advertisements;
- **Physical and Health Education**—selecting effective employee health-insurance plans and corporate-sponsored health services.

In addition to business, liberal arts subjects are relevant to successful performance in a wide variety of majors and careers, as is explained in the following section.

Gaining a Multi-Dimensional Perspective and Multiple Thinking Tools

Liberal arts courses provide a relevant foundation for success in any college major or professional career. The broad, balanced base of knowledge provided by a liberal arts education enables you to view issues or problems from *multiple* perspectives, angles, and vantage points.

Although you will specialize in one field (your college major), "real-life" issues and career challenges are not specialized into majors. For instance, such important issues as providing effective leadership, improving race relations, and promoting world peace, cannot be understood or solved by one single field of study. A narrow approach provides only a single-minded and often over-simplified explanation of, or solution to, complex issues. Similarly, the tasks that humans face in their personal lives and professional careers are also multi-dimensional, requiring perspectives and skills that go well beyond the boundaries of one particular field of study.

The multiple subject areas that you are exposed to in the liberal arts provide you with these multiple perspectives and equip you with a wider repertoire of thinking tools to work on the tasks we face in our personal and professional lives. Keep in mind that liberal arts courses do not just expose you to different subject areas; they also train your mind to think in different ways. This is why different academic subjects are often referred to as *disciplines*, because by learning them, you are developing the "mental discipline" that faculty in these fields have spent years of their lives developing. For instance, when you study history, algebra, biology, and art, you are disciplining your mind to think in new and different ways—you are learning to think chronologically (history), symbolically (algebra), scientifically (biology), and creatively (art). You will find that subjects in different divisions of the liberal arts will ask you to think in very different ways. For example, some subjects will require you to think:

© JupiterImages Corporation.

The different disciplines of a liberal arts education train your mind to think in different ways. An algebra class requires you to think symbolically.

- in the form of words, numbers, or images,
- in terms of specific parts or whole patterns,
- individually or globally,
- concretely or abstractly,
- systematically (in sequential steps) or intuitively (in sudden leaps),
- objectively or subjectively, and
- factually or imaginatively (Donald, 2002; Katz & Henry, 1993).

Different disciplines will also train your mind to develop the habit of asking powerful questions. Some will be important fact-seeking and fact-finding questions, such as: Who? What?

When? and Where? Others will be deeper questions designed to get beyond the facts and beneath the surface, such as: Why? Why not? How come? What if? The diversity of thinking and questioning styles you experience by taking a broad array of courses in the liberal arts provide you with a wide range of intellectual resources to draw from, along with a large repertoire of thinking tools. This rich supply of mental resources equip you with the intellectual curiosity, versatility, and agility needed to "think on your feet."

Furthermore, the liberal arts enhance your creativity. The different thinking styles you develop supply you with a myriad of strategies that you can modify and adapt to solve problems you may encounter in a range of contexts or situations. These diverse strategies can also be combined or rearranged in ways that result in unique or innovative solutions to problems. Thus, ideas you acquire in separate subject areas of the liberal arts can often feed off each other and "cross-fertilize," giving birth to new approaches for solving old problems.

Another advantage of liberal arts is that it can accelerate your learning curve, enabling you to learn new material more rapidly. Learning occurs when your brain makes a connection between the new concept you are trying to learn and something you already know. The greater the number and variety of learned connections that your brain has already made, the more pathways it has to build on and connect new ideas to, which leads to faster learning of new ideas.

Acquiring a Powerful Set of Fundamental Skills

Another key way in which the liberal arts provides a foundation for success in your major, your career, and your life is by equipping you with a *set of essential skills* that have two powerful qualities:

1. Transferability—skills that "travel" well, enabling you to apply them across a wide range of subjects, careers, and life situations, and
2. Durability—skills that are long-lasting and that can be continually used to learn new things throughout your entire lifetime.

To use an athletic analogy, what the liberal arts do for the mind is similar to what cross-training does for the body. In cross-training, you intentionally engage in a wide range of different exercises. As a result of this wide range of exercises, the body builds up a broad base of fundamental physical-performance skills, which include strength, endurance, flexibility, agility, and coordination. These physical skills are essential for successful athletic performance in all sports, whether it be basketball, baseball, tennis, or rowing.

Similar to cross-training, a liberal arts education builds-up the following set of basic academic and lifelong learning skills that can be applied to promote your success in any field of study or professional career.

 Pause for Reflection
Read each of the skills listed below and rate yourself according to the following scale:

4 = very strong
3 = strong
2 = needs some improvement
1 = needs much improvement

◆ **Communication Skills** for accurate *comprehension* and articulate *expression* of ideas.

There are five particular types of communication skills that provide an important foundation for future success in any specialized field of study or work:

1. **Reading Skills:** comprehending, interpreting, and evaluating writing in a variety of styles and subject areas.
2. **Written Communication Skills:** writing in a clear, creative, and persuasive manner.
3. **Oral Communication Skills:** speaking in a concise, confident, and eloquent fashion.
4. **Listening Skills:** comprehending spoken language with accuracy and empathy.
5. **Multi-Media Communication Skills:** comprehending and expressing ideas delivered through modes of communication other than language, which include visual representation (drawings, images) and technology-assisted communication (sound, film, and computer graphics).

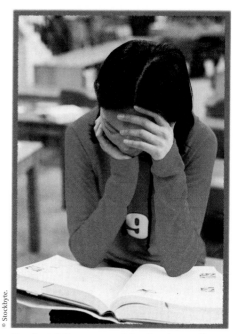
© Stockbyte.

Reading skills are one of the five types of communication skills needed to provide an important foundation for future success.

◆ **Computation Skills** for accurate calculation and comprehension of quantitative information, and to analyze, summarize, interpret, or evaluate statistical data.

◆ **Research Skills** for locating, accessing, retrieving, organizing, and evaluating information from a variety of sources, including library and technology-based systems.

◆ **Higher-Level Thinking Skills** that enable you to think at a deeper or higher level than merely memorizing facts.

In particular, the following four types of thinking skills are essential for success in any field:

1. **Analysis:** ability to break down or dissect information into its key parts and detect what is most important or relevant.
2. **Creativity:** ability to imagine alternative ideas, original viewpoints, and new or innovative strategies for addressing old problems.
3. **Evaluation:** ability to critically assess or judge the validity (truth), morality (ethics), or aesthetic (artistic) value of ideas, products, or practices.
4. **Synthesis:** ability to build up or connect separate ideas and integrate them into a meaningful whole, resulting in a more complete understanding of the "big picture."

Memory Tips A useful mnemonic device (memory-improvement strategy) for recalling these four powerful thinking skills is to take the first letter of each skill and form one word "ACES."

"Education is what's left over after you've forgotten all the facts" is an old saying that carries a lot of truth. Studies do show that students' memory of specific facts learned in college often fades with the passing of time (Pascarella & Terenzini, 1991, 2005). What is left over are the lifelong learning skills that students develop in college, such as thinking deeply, writing clearly, and speaking persuasively. Just as the physical skills of bicycle riding or roller skating can be remembered throughout an entire lifetime, so can mental skills and thinking habits. Memorized facts often fade with time, but learning skills remain with you, and can be repeatedly retrieved and recycled continually throughout life. They are the "gift that keeps on giving."

Lifelong learning skills are more essential for success in today's work world than ever before, because with the help of computer technology, new information is now being generated and communicated at a faster rate than at any other time in human history (Dryden & Vos, 1999). Existing knowledge and traditional methods quickly becomes obsolete due to the rapid communication of new information (Naisbitt, 1982). Thus, it is necessary for workers to update their skills continually in order to remain employed and advance in their careers (Niles & Harris-Bowlsbey, 2002). This results in an increased need for people to continue to acquire new knowledge *for* themselves and *by* themselves throughout their lifetime (Daly, 1992).

Today's rapidly changing information society places a high value on, and creates a great demand for, individuals who have learned *how to learn*—one of the key skills you will acquire from a liberal arts education. Remember that the wide range of different thinking styles and the broad base of knowledge developed by the liberal arts will accelerate your "learning curve," enabling you to continue to learn new things more rapidly and more effectively.

Furthermore, since so much new information is being produced at such a rapid rate, the research skills you develop as part of a liberal arts education will allow you to effectively locate, select, and organize the information you need to learn. The ability to research, evaluate, and integrate information are lifelong learning skills that can provide the lifeboat you need to stay afloat and navigate the tidal wave of information generated by current technology. Since one primary goal of a liberal arts education is to "liberate" or free you to become an independent, self-reliant learner, your college librarians will not just simply supply you with this information; instead, they will educate you on *how* to find it on your own. Thus, you acquire a lifelong learning skill that can be used to locate any information you need whenever you need it, at any time or stage of your life.

"WHEN DID THEY START USING A SEARCH ENGINE?"

A liberal arts education develops *lifelong learning skills* that you can use to continue learning new things more effectively throughout life.

Pause for Reflection

Reflect on the four key skill areas developed by a liberal arts education (communication, computation, research, and critical thinking), and choose one that is most important or most relevant to you. Write a one-paragraph explanation about why you chose this skill.

••• Achieving Career Success

Studies show that college students, as well as their parents, are extremely concerned about majors and careers, but they often overlook or underestimate the relationship between liberal arts education and career performance (Hersh, 1994). They often believe that the "liberal arts" are something idealistic or impractical, which cannot be put to use in the "real world" and will not help you get a "real job" (Hersh, 1997). Actually, this is far from the truth. Just as the core skills developed by a liberal arts education prepare you for success in your major, they are also important for success in your eventual career.

Skills

The skills developed by a liberal arts education are strikingly similar to the types of skills that employers desire and seek in new employees. In many national surveys and in-depth interviews, employers and executives in both industry and government consistently report that they seek employees with skills that fall into the following three categories.

Writing skills are one of the communication skills employers look for when hiring.

1. **Communication Skills,** which include listening, speaking, writing, and reading (National Association of Colleges & Employers, 2003).

   "There is such a heavy emphasis on effective communication in the workplace that college students who master these skills can set themselves apart from the pack when searching for employment." Marilyn Mackes, Executive Director of the National Association of Colleges and Employers (Mackes, 2003, p. 1).

2. **Thinking Skills,** which include problem solving and critical thinking (Van Horn, 1995).

   "We look for people who can think critically and analytically. If you can do those things, we can teach you our business." Paul Dominski, Store Recruiter for the Robinson-May Department Stores Company (Indiana University, 2004, p. 1).

3. **Lifelong Learning Skills,** which include learning how to learn and how to continue learning (The Conference Board of Canada, 2000).

   "Employers are virtually unanimous that the most important knowledge and skills the new employee can bring to the job are problem solving, communication, and 'learning to learn' skills. The workers of the future need to know how to think and how to continue to learn." David Kearns, former Chief Executive Officer for the Xerox Corporation (Kearns, 1989, p. 8).

This trio of skills shows up in studies that ask employers for skills they are currently seeking in employees and skills they will be seeking from employees in the future. These same skills are also consistently cited by employers in different regions of the United States and in different countries around the world, including Canada (The Conference Board of Canada, 2000), England (QHE, 1993, 1994), Australia (Business/Higher Education Round Table, 1991, 1992), and Germany (Laur-Enrst, 1990).

If you compare the key work skills sought by employers with the key academic skills developed by a liberal arts education, you will find that there is a remarkable resemblance between the two. This similarity is not surprising when you think about the typical duties or responsibilities of working professionals. They need to have good communication skills because they listen, speak, and explain things to co-workers and customers. They read and critically interpret reports, and they write letters, memos, and reports. They need to have well-developed thinking skills to analyze problems, construct well-organized plans, come up with creative solutions to problems, and evaluate whether their plans and strategies are effective.

In his classic book, *The Idea of a University*, John Henry Newman (1852) eloquently explains how a liberal arts education prepares students for any career or any major:

> *It is the education which gives a man [woman] a clear conscious view of his own opinions and judgments, a truth in developing them, an eloquence in expressing them, and a force in urging them. It teaches him to see things as they are, to go right to the point, to detect what is sophisticated, and to discard what is irrelevant. It prepares him to fill any post with credit, and to master any subject with facility (1852, pp. 177–178).*

 Remember: The liberal arts component of your college education is not only providing you with academic skills needed to succeed in your chosen major; it is simultaneously providing you with practical skills to succeed in your future career. Do not underestimate the importance of these fundamental skills: Work hard at developing them, and take pride in their development.

The academic skills developed by a liberal arts education are also *practical* skills that contribute to successful performance in *any career*.

Do not lose sight of the fact that these essential skills are durable and transferable, so they can be transported and applied to different types of careers throughout your entire working life. This is one way in which a liberal arts education "liberates"—freeing you from narrow job training or career overspecialization that only equip you with a small set of technical skills to perform a specific task.

Lastly, keep in mind that the transferability and durability of liberal arts skills serve not only to increase your chances of being hired immediately after college graduation (career entry); these skills also increase your freedom of career choice—the ability to move into different types of careers, and your career mobility—the ability to move out of a career or back into a career after taking time off from it.

During your college experience, you might hear students state that they need to get their general education (liberal arts) courses out of the way so they can get into courses that relate to their major and career. Based on what you've read thus far in this chapter, what may be inaccurate or untrue about this statement?

••• Developing the Whole Person

Figure 2.1 Key Elements of Holistic (Whole-Person) Development

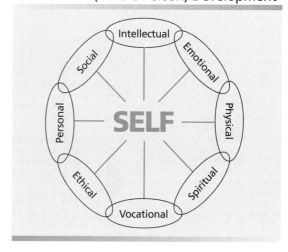

While the development of intellectual skills are important for success in your major and career, there are other aspects of yourself that need attention and development in order to achieve success in both college and life. Your "self" is comprised of multiple elements or dimensions, and each one of them can affect your success and happiness. As you can see in Figure 2.1, there are a number of key elements of the self that join together to form the "whole person," and their development is an essential goal of a liberal arts education (Kuh, Shedd, & Whitt, 1987). These elements include the following eight aspects of self-development:

1. intellectual
2. social
3. emotional
4. physical
5. spiritual
6. ethical
7. vocational
8. personal

We are not just intellectual beings or working beings; we are also social, emotional, physical, ethical, and spiritual beings. Furthermore, notice in the figure that all of these elements are joined or linked, and they are interrelated because they work interdependently (Love & Love, 1995). For instance, our intellectual performance can be influenced by our emotional state (e.g., whether we are bored or excited); our emotional state can be influenced by our social relationships (e.g., whether we feel lonely or loved); and our social relationships can be influenced by our physical condition (e.g., whether we have a positive or negative physical self-image). Thus, if we can strengthen one element of the self, other elements can often be strengthened simultaneously. In fact, research shows that when college students gain more knowledge, they also attain higher levels of self-esteem, greater social popularity, and greater popularity with the opposite sex (Pascarella & Terenzini, 1991, 2005).

Research also suggests that our quality of life depends on our attention to and integration of all the important elements of the self. It has been found that people who are healthy (physically and mentally) and successful are typically individuals who have effectively attended to and blended all key dimensions of the self, enabling them to lead well-balanced and well-rounded lives (Covey, 1990; Goleman, 1995; Heath, 1977).

Since wholeness seems so essential for wellness, success, and happiness, we ask you to carefully read the following descriptions and specific skills associated with each of the eight elements of holistic development. Keep in mind that even though these elements are discussed separately, in real life they are interrelated and influence each other.

•—• **CLASSIC QUOTE** •—•

The research portrays the college student as changing in an integrated way, with change in any one area appearing to be part of a mutually reinforcing network or pattern of change in other areas.

—Pascarella & Terenzini, *How College Affects Students*

STUDENT PERSPECTIVE

"Being successful is being balanced in every aspect of your life."

—First-year college student

"I thought I was going to college to get a good job. Now they tell me I'm going to develop critical thinking, social intelligence, emotional intelligence, ethical perspective, personal wellness, and spiritual awareness! I don't think I'll even have enough time to sleep!!"

A liberal arts education is designed to develop your whole person.
(And still leave you enough time to sleep.)

Pause for Reflection

As you are reading the specific skills listed beneath each of the following eight elements of holistic development, place a checkmark in the space next to any skill that is especially important to you. You may check more than one skill within each area.

Skills and Abilities Associated with Each Element of Holistic Development

Intellectual Development: Acquiring knowledge, learning how to learn, and how to think deeply.

Key Skills and Specific Abilities:

- Becoming aware of your different intellectual abilities, interests, or learning styles.
- Attaining and maintaining attention and concentration.
- Using effective strategies for improving long-term learning and memory.
- Moving beyond memorization to think at a higher level.
- Using effective research skills to obtain information from a variety of sources and systems.
- Viewing issues from multiple angles or viewpoints (psychological, social, political, economic, etc.) in order to attain a balanced, comprehensive perspective.
- Critically evaluating ideas in terms of their truth and value.
- Thinking creatively or imaginatively.
- Responding rationally and constructively to differing viewpoints or opposing arguments.
- Resisting persuasion tactics that appeal to emotions, to responding to them logically or rationally.

Emotional Development: Strengthening skills for understanding, controlling, and expressing emotions.

Key Skills and Specific Abilities:

- Dealing with emotions in an honest, non-defensive manner.
- Maintaining a healthy balance between emotional control and emotional expression.
- Responding with empathy and sensitivity to emotions experienced by others.
- Dealing effectively with depression.
- Dealing effectively with anger.
- Using effective stress-management strategies to control anxiety or tension.
- Responding positively to life changes and challenges.
- Dealing effectively with fear of failure, criticism, or poor performance.
- Accepting feedback in a constructive, non-defensive manner.
- Being optimistic and enthusiastic.

Social Development: Enhancing the quality and depth of interpersonal relationships.

Key Skills and Specific Abilities:

- Using effective interpersonal communication skills.
- Relating effectively to others in one-to-one, small-group, and large-group situations.
- Overcoming shyness or loneliness and initiating new relationships.
- Forming meaningful friendships.
- Effectively handling interpersonal conflict in an assertive manner, rather than in a passive or aggressive manner.
- Providing advice and feedback to others in a constructive and considerate manner.
- Using effective collaboration and teamwork skills to work productively with others.
- Relating effectively to others from different cultural backgrounds and with different personal lifestyles.
- Developing effective leadership skills.

Ethical Development: Acquiring a clear value system for guiding life choices and decisions, and developing consistency between moral convictions (beliefs) and moral commitments (actions).

Key Skills and Specific Abilities:

- Being self-aware of personal values and ethical assumptions.
- Making important personal choices and life decisions based on a meaningful value system (for example, decisions about majors, careers, and relationships).
- Having the courage to think and act with personal integrity or honesty, including honesty with respect to schoolwork, both inside and outside the classroom (academic integrity).
- Using electronic technology in an ethical and responsible manner.
- Fulfilling personal commitments and responsibilities to others.
- Knowing how to exercise individual freedom without infringing on the rights of others.
- Developing a concern and commitment for human rights and social justice.
- Becoming a responsible citizen.

Physical Development: Applying knowledge about how the human body functions to prevent disease, maintain wellness, and promote peak performance.

Key Skills and Specific Abilities:

- Being aware of your physical condition and state of health.
- Applying knowledge about exercise and fitness training to promote physical and mental health.
- Understanding the role of rest and sleep patterns for promoting health and increasing energy.
- Applying knowledge on nutrition and diet to enhance your health and physical performance.
- Maintaining healthy balance between work, relaxation, and recreation.
- Having a healthy and positive body image.
- Being aware of and avoiding eating disorders.
- Being aware of the effects of drugs on the body and how they affect physical and mental performance.
- Being knowledgeable about the biology and psychology of human sexuality and sexually transmitted diseases.
- Being knowledgeable about the physical and physiological differences between the sexes and their implications for male-female relationships and gender orientation.

Spiritual Development: Searching for the meaning or purpose of life and death, and exploring eternal relationships that transcend human life and the physical world.

Key Skills and Specific Abilities:

- Developing a personal philosophy or world view about the meaning and purpose of human existence.
- Appreciating what cannot be completely understood.
- Appreciating the mysteries associated with the origin of the universe.
- Exploring the connection between yourself and humanity.
- Exploring the connection between yourself and the physical world that surrounds you.
- Being open to examining questions relating to death and life after death.
- Being open to examining questions about the possible existence of a supreme being or higher power.
- Being aware of different approaches to spirituality and their underlying beliefs or assumptions.
- Understanding the difference and relationship between faith and reason.
- Being knowledgeable and tolerant of religious beliefs and practices.

Vocational Development: Exploring career options, making career choices wisely, and developing skills needed for lifelong career success.

Key Skills and Specific Abilities:

- Being knowledgeable about the relationship between college majors and careers.
- Using effective strategies for exploring and identifying potential careers.
- Selecting career options that are consistent with your personal values, interests, and aptitudes.
- Acquiring work experience in fields that relate to your career interests.

- Developing an effective resumé and portfolio.
- Adopting effective strategies for selecting individuals to serve as personal references and improving the quality of your letters of recommendation.
- Developing effective job-search strategies.
- Acquiring effective strategies for writing letters of inquiry and letters of application to potential employers.
- Developing effective networking skills for making personal contacts with potential employers.
- Learning strategies for effective job-interview preparation and performance.

Personal Development: Developing positive self-beliefs, personal attitudes, and personal habits.

Key Skills and Specific Abilities:

- Developing a sense of personal identity and a coherent self-concept. (Who am I?)
- Finding a sense of future direction and purpose. (Who am I becoming?)
- Developing self-respect and positive self-esteem.
- Acquiring self-confidence.
- Developing self-efficacy—a strong belief that success is yours for the taking.
- Setting realistic goals and establishing personal priorities.
- Becoming self-motivated and self-disciplined.
- Developing the patience and perseverance to persist on tasks despite personal setbacks or frustration.
- Managing personal affairs effectively and efficiently.
- Becoming independent, self-reliant, and self-sufficient.

Pause for Reflection

Look back and count the number of checkmarks you placed in each of the eight general areas of self-development. Did you find that you placed roughly the same number of checks in all eight areas, or did you place a large number of checks in certain areas and very few checks in others?

Based on your answers to these questions, would you say that your interests in self-development are balanced across different elements of the self, or are they slanted toward strong interest in certain elements of self-development with little interest in others?

••• The Co-Curriculum

For the college experience to have maximum positive impact on all key areas of self-development, you need to take advantage of the "total" college environment. This includes not only courses in the curriculum, but also the learning experiences available to you outside the classroom (the co-curriculum) because research consistently shows that they are equally important to your overall development as the course curriculum (Kuh, 1995; Kuh et al., 1994). The co-curriculum includes all educationally-related discussions you have with your peers and professors outside the classroom, as well as the wide variety of support services and programs that are offered on college campuses. Listed below are some of the college services and programs that comprise the co-curriculum, preceded by the primary element of the self that they are designed to develop:

- **Intellectual development:** Academic Advising, Learning Center, Library, Tutoring Services, Information Technology Services, Campus Speakers, Publications, Concerts, Plays, and Galleries
- **Emotional development:** Counseling Services, Peer Counseling, and Peer Mentoring Programs
- **Social development:** Student Activities, Student Organizations, Campus Clubs, Residential-Life Programs, Commuter Programs
- **Physical development:** Student Health Services, Athletics, Intramural Sports
- **Spiritual development:** College Chaplain, Campus Ministry, Peer Ministry
- **Ethical development:** Judicial Review Board, Academic Integrity Committee, Student Government
- **Vocational development:** Career Development Services, Internships, Service Learning, Work-Study Programs, Major Fairs, Career Fairs
- **Personal development:** Counseling Services, Financial Aid Services, Campus Workshops, Peer Counseling, Peer Mentoring Programs

This list is just a sample of the total number of programs and services that may be available at your school. As you can see from this lengthy list, colleges and universities have been organized to promote your development in multiple ways, and a liberal arts education is the component of your college experience that has been intentionally designed to provide you with this multi-faceted, well-rounded form of development.

 Remember: To develop a "whole person," a liberal arts education relies on both the curriculum *and* co-curriculum, and requires student use of the *total* college environment.

Leadership skills cannot be developed solely by listening to lectures and reading books about leadership; they need to be accompanied by leadership *experiences*, such as those developed by "leading a [discussion] group in class, holding office in student government, or by being captain of a sports team" (Association of American Colleges & Universities, 2002, p. 30). Recall that using campus resources is one of the key bases for college success, so take full advantage of your whole college to develop yourself as a whole person.

Developing all aspects of yourself will not only help you become a more complete human being and improve the quality of your personal life, it will also help you prepare for a career and succeed in your professional life. You may recall that earlier in this chapter we identified three clusters of skills that employers consistently look for in college graduates: communication skills, thinking skills, and lifelong learning skills. While these three sets of intellectually oriented skills rank high in importance to employers, they do not account for the complete list of skills that employers seek in college graduates. There are other characteristics that employers value, which relate to different elements of the self, such as:

Interpersonal (Social) Skills, including leadership, ability to collaborate, negotiate, work in teams, and relate to others with diverse characteristics and backgrounds—such as people of different age, race, gender, and cultural backgrounds (National Association of Colleges & Employers, 2003).

Personal Attitudes and Behaviors, including motivation, initiative, effort, self-management, independence, personal responsibility, enthusiasm, flexibility, good work habits, and self-esteem (National Association of Colleges & Employers, 2000).

Personal Ethics, namely: honesty, integrity, and ethical standards of conduct (National Association of Colleges & Employers, 2003).

Pause for Reflection

Look at the above three skills and jot down something you could do in college to develop or demonstrate each of them.

1. Interpersonal (Social) Skills:

2. Personal Attitudes and Behaviors:

3. Personal Ethics:

Do you recognize that the qualities sought by employers correspond closely to different elements of holistic development promoted by a liberal arts education? Note also that some of the skills correspond closely to the liberal arts goal of developing the "liberating" skills needed for independence, such as personal initiative, self-management, and personal responsibility. You can start developing these skills right now by taking the initiative to assume personal responsibility for managing your independent work in college. See Box 2.2 on the following page, for some quick tips on how to do so.

••• Broadening Your Perspective of the Whole World

Thus far, the focus of this chapter has been on you, and how the liberal arts benefit you as an individual. However, another major goal of a liberal arts education is to help you step outside yourself and expand your perspective of the world around you. The components of this larger perspective are organized and illustrated in the following concept map (Figure 2.2).

In Figure 2.2, the center circle represents you as an individual. Fanning out to the right is a series of arches, labeled as the **social-spatial perspective.** This broadening perspective includes increasingly larger social groups and more distant places, ranging from the narrowest perspective (self) to the widest perspective (universe). A liberal arts education frees you from the narrow tunnel vision of an egocentric viewpoint and provides you with a panoramic perspective of the world, enabling you to move outside yourself and see yourself in relation to other people and other places.

 STUDENT PERSPECTIVE

"College was not something I regarded as the next step after high school. It was not something I deemed important in order to be really rich later on in life. It was something I considered fundamental to learning about myself and the world around me."

—First-year student (Watts, 2005)

Top Strategies: Working Independently Outside the Classroom

Unlike high school, homework in college often does not involve turning things in to your instructor on a daily or weekly basis. Instead, the academic work you do outside the classroom may not be collected and graded, but is done for your own benefit to prepare yourself for upcoming exams and major assignments (e.g., term papers or research reports). Rather than formally assigning work to you as homework, your professors expect that you will do this work on your own and without supervision. Listed below are strategies for working independently and in advance of college examinations and assignments, which should serve to increase your performance on them.

INDEPENDENT WORK IN ADVANCE OF EXAMS

⊙ **Complete reading assignments** in advance of lectures that will relate to the same topic as the reading. This will make lectures easier to understand and will prepare you to ask intelligent questions and make relevant comments in class.

⊙ **Review your class notes** between class periods so you can construct a mental bridge from one class to the next and make each upcoming lecture easier to follow. When reviewing your notes before the next class, rewrite any class notes that may be sloppily written, and if you find notes relating to the same point that are all over the place, reorganize them by getting notes relating to the same point in the same place. Lastly, if you find any information gaps or confusing points in your notes, seek-out the course instructor or a trusted classmate to clear them up before the next class takes place.

⊙ **Review information** that you have highlighted in your reading assignments in order to improve your memory of the information, and if there are certain points that are confusing to you, discuss them with your course instructor or fellow classmate.

⊙ **Integrate key ideas** in your class notes with information that you have highlighted in your assigned reading that relate to the same major point or general category. For example, get related information from your lecture notes and your readings in the same place.

⊙ **Use a part-to-whole study method,** whereby you study key material from your class notes and readings in small parts during short, separate study sessions that take place well in advance of the exam; then make your last study session prior to the exam a longer review session, during which you re-study all the small parts together (the "whole").

Memory Tips   The belief that studying in advance is a total waste of time because you will forget it all anyway is a myth. As you will see in Chapter 4, information studied in advance of an exam remains in your brain and is still there when you later review it. Even if you cannot recall the previously studied information when you first start reviewing it, you will re-learn it much faster than you did the first time, thus proving that some memory of it was retained.

INDEPENDENT WORK IN ADVANCE OF TERM PAPERS OR RESEARCH REPORTS

Work on these large, long-term assignments by breaking them into the following smaller, short-term tasks:

⊙ Search for and select a topic.

⊙ Locate sources of information on the topic.

⊙ Organize the information obtained from these sources into categories.

⊙ Develop an outline of the report's major points and the order or sequence in which you plan to discuss them.

⊙ Construct a first draft of the paper (and, if necessary, a second draft).

⊙ Write a final draft of the paper.

⊙ Proofread the final draft of your paper for minor mechanical mistakes, such as spelling and grammatical errors, before submitting it to your instructor.

In Figure 2.2, to the left of the individual, you see a different series of arches that are labeled the **chronological perspective**, which represents the perspective of time—past (historical), present (contemporary), and future (futuristic). A liberal arts education not only widens your perspective, it also lengthens it—by stretching your vision beyond the present, enabling you to see yourself in relation to those who have lived before us and those who will live after us.

Figure 2.2 The Broadening Perspectives of a Liberal Arts Education

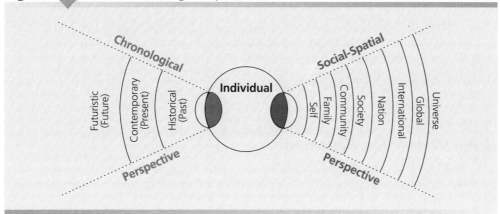

This chronological perspective gives you hindsight to see where the world has been, insight into where it is now, and foresight to see where it may be going.

The social-spatial perspective can be seen as providing you with a telescope for viewing aspects of the world that are far away, while a chronological perspective provides you with a mental "time machine" that you can use to flash back to the past and fast-forward to the future. We will now provide a brief description of the specific elements that make up each of these two major perspectives developed by a liberal arts education.

Elements of the Chronological Perspective

The **historical element** of the chronological perspective is an important one to understand because it represents the root causes of our current human condition and world situation. We are products of both social and natural history. Don't forget that our earth is estimated to be more than 4.5 billion years old, and our human ancestors date back more than 250,000 years (Knoll, 2003). Our current lives represent a very small frame in a very long reel of time, and every modern convenience we now enjoy reflects the cumulative knowledge and collective efforts of humans that span across thousands of years of history. By studying the past and understanding how it has influenced our present circumstances, we can learn to reproduce its achievements and avoid its mistakes.

The **contemporary element** of a chronological perspective focuses on understanding the current world situation and the current events that comprise today's news. For example, we are now living in a world of such rapid technological change that it is being referred to as the technology revolution (Glassman, 2000). So, it is important to understand how modern technology is affecting the world we currently live in, and how it will affect the world of tomorrow. One major goal of a liberal arts education is to increase your understanding of contemporary society (Miller, 1988) and its effectiveness for doing so is supported by research on college graduates, which consistently shows that they have greater knowledge of current affairs, popular culture, and contemporary news media than people who have not experienced a college education (Pascarella & Terenzini, 1991, 2005).

The **futuristic element** of the chronological perspective focuses on looking forward and envisioning what the world will be like years from now. It is concerned with such questions as: Will the world be in better shape and a better place for humans who will live after us, including our children and grandchildren? How can humans avoid short-term or shortsighted think-

·—· **CLASSIC QUOTE** ·—·

Those who cannot remember the past are damned to repeat it.

—George Santayana, Spanish-born American philosopher

ing and adopt a long-range vision that will enable them to anticipate, prepare for, and adapt to the future?

Thus, a complete chronological perspective enables us to see our lives, and the world we live in, as an ongoing process that began well before we arrived on the current scene and that will likely continue long after we have departed. "We all inherit the past. We all confront the challenges of the present. We all participate in the making of the future" (Boyer & Kaplan, 1977, p. 16).

Pause for Reflection

How might you use the information you've just read to interpret or explain the meaning of the following statement: "We can't know where we're going until we know where we've been?"

Elements of the Social-Spatial Perspective

As you can see in Figure 2.2, the first element of the social-spatial perspective is the **self**. Among the many goals of a liberal arts education, the one that has the longest history and most frequent emphasis is "Know thyself" (Cross, 1982). To do so, you need to step outside yourself and view yourself objectively. This enables you to remove personal blinders and increase your self-awareness, which is the first step toward self-development and personal success. As an old saying goes, "It is difficult to see the picture when you are inside the frame."

Moving beyond the self, an individual is part of a larger social unit—the **family**. The people with whom you were raised have almost certainly influenced the person you are today and how you got to be that way. You also influence your family. For example, your decision to go to college may make your parents and grandparents proud, and may influence the decision of other members of your family to attend college. Furthermore, if you have children, graduating from college is likely to positively influence their future welfare. As mentioned in the introduction to this book, the children of college graduates experience improved intellectual development, physical health, and economic security (Bowen, 1977, 1997; Pascarella & Terenzini, 1991, 2005).

Moving beyond your family, you are also a member of a larger social unit—your **community**. This social circle includes your friends and neighbors at home, at school, and at work. These local communities are where you can begin to take action to improve the world around you. If you want to make the world a better place, this is the place to start—get involved in your home or college community.

Moving beyond your local community, you are also a member of a larger **society** that includes people from different regions of the country, cultural backgrounds, and social classes. As we will discuss more thoroughly in Chapter 8, there is more diversity in our society today than at any other time in history. Being willing and able to understand, relate to, and learn from people with diverse backgrounds has become a critical skill for success in today's world (Smith, 1997; National Association of Colleges & Employers, 2003).

Not only are you a member of a society, you are a citizen of a **nation**. As such, you are expected to participate in its political system—as a voter—and in its judicial system—as a juror. It is noteworthy that American citizens between the ages of 18 and 24 consistently have the lowest voter-turnout rate of any age group that is eligible to vote (Cummings, 2002). If you are a student in this age group, we strongly encourage you to involve yourself in the voting process because it is the foundation of a democratic nation and is the original purpose of a liberal arts education—to educate citizens broadly so they could vote wisely.

Although you are expected to vote as a citizen of a nation, American citizens between the ages of 18 and 24 have the lowest voter turnout.

Moving beyond our nation of citizenship, we are members of an **international world** that includes citizens of other countries. Today, there is more interaction among citizens of different countries and more "international interdependence" among nations than at any other time in world history. Boundaries between countries are breaking down as a result of more international trading, more multinational corporations, more international travel, and more international communication—due to rapid advances in electronic technology (Dryden, & Vos, 1999; Smith, 1994). Employers of college graduates are beginning to place higher value on prospective employees who have international knowledge and foreign language skills (Fixman, 1990; Office of Research, 1994). Today's world truly is a small world, and your success in it will be enhanced if you gain an international perspective. You can do this by interacting with international students who may be attending your college, by taking foreign language and cross-cultural courses, or by participating in a study-abroad program. By learning from and about different nations, you become much more than a citizen of your own country, you become cosmopolitan—a citizen of the world.

Even broader than the international perspective is the **global perspective**. This perspective goes beyond relations between people of different nations to include relationships among all life forms that inhabit planet earth, and the relationship between these life forms and their environment. Don't forget that humans share the earth and its natural resources (minerals, air, water) with millions of other animal species and several hundred thousand forms of vegetative life (Knoll, 2003). As members of this global village, we need to balance our human needs and our industrial-technological progress with the preservation of other life forms and the earth's natural resources. Striking this balance may be the only way to ensure long-term survival of our species and our planet.

Beyond the global perspective is the broadest of all perspectives—the **universe**. We should not lose sight of the fact that the earth is just one planet among other planets sharing the solar system and that our planet is just one celestial body sharing a galaxy with millions of other types of celestial bodies, which include stars, moons, meteorites, and asteroids. Also, we need to remember that our planet is not the center of the universe, and all these other heavenly bodies do not revolve around us! As one physics professor put it: "In astronomy, you must get used to viewing the earth as just one planet in the larger context of the universe" (Donald, 2002, p. 49).

Astronauts who have traveled beyond the earth's force of gravity and explored the universe from the perspective of outer space have often described this perspective as being a spiritual experience. Even mental exploration of the universe by contemplating its massive and mysterious nature, how it may have begun, where it may be going, and whether it will ever end, are issues that some educators have referred to as spiritual questions (Zohar & Marshall, 2000). Whether you view the universe through the physical telescope of astronomy or the spiritual scope of introspection (or both), it qualifies as the broadest of all social-spatial perspectives developed by a liberal arts education.

·—· **CLASSIC QUOTE** ·—·

A liberal [arts] education frees a person from the prison-house of class, race, time, place, background, family, and nation.

—Robert Hutchins, former president, University of Chicago

·—· **CLASSIC QUOTE** ·—·

Without exception, the observed changes [during college] involve greater breadth, expansion, and appreciation for the new and different. These changes are eminently consistent with values of a liberal [arts] education, and the evidence for their presence is compelling.

—Ernest Pascarella and Pat Terenzini, *How College Affects Students*

The Synoptic Perspective: Integrating Diverse Perspectives to Form a Unified Whole

By broadening your perspective on time, place, and people, a liberal arts education liberates you from the here and now, enabling you to view things "long ago and far away." In addition to this liberating purpose of a liberal arts education, it also has an *integrating* purpose. You are enabled to see how, as an individual, you are a single strand that is embedded within a progressively wider web of social-spatial interconnections with your family, community, society, nation, world, and universe—all of which are united along a chronological spectrum of time—past, present, and future. Seeing how these different perspectives of time, place, and person are interrelated to form a unified whole is sometimes referred to as a synoptic perspective (Cronon, 1998; Heath, 1977).

The term synoptic refers to a comprehensive, integrated perspective. The word derives from a combination of two different roots: "syn"—meaning 'together' (as in the word 'synthesize'), and "optic"—meaning 'to see.' Thus, a *synoptic* perspective literally means to "see things together" or to "see the whole."

> **Memory Tips**
>
> Breaking down technical terms into smaller parts that contain the roots of their meaning is an effective strategy for making sense of what you're trying to learn and for locking it into your long-term memory.

So, in addition to the wholeness that comes from integrating different elements of the self to develop the whole person, there is another type of wholeness that a liberal arts education attempts to develop—how you, as an individual, are integrated or connected with other people, places, and times to form the whole world.

When we view ourselves as connected with others from different places and different times, we become aware of the common humanity we all share, and this increased sense of integration with mankind serves to decrease our feelings of isolation or alienation (Bellah, et al., 1985). In his book, *The Perfect Education*, Kenneth Eble skillfully describes this benefit of a liberal arts education:

> *It can provide that overarching life of a people, a community, a world that was going on before the individual came onto the scene and that will continue on after [s]he departs. By such means we come to see the world not alone. Our joys are more intense for being shared. Our sorrows are less destructive for our knowing universal sorrow. Our fears of death fade before the commonness of the occurrence (Eble, 1966, pp. 214–215).*

· — · CLASSIC QUOTE · — ·

A truly great intellect is one which takes a connected view of old and new, past and present, far and near, and which has an insight into the influence of all these on one another, without which there is no whole, and no center.

—John Henry Newman, English Cardinal and educator, *The Idea of a University*, 1852

Thus, by stepping outside ourselves to view the similarities we share with other people and other times, we then return to view ourselves from a new perspective and in a new light. Stepping outside ourselves and seeing how we differ from other people and other times provides us with reference points for comparison and contrast that sharpens our self-awareness and insight. We see what is distinctive about ourselves, and how we may be uniquely advantaged or disadvantaged. For instance, by seeing what limited opportunities there are for people to attend college in many countries today, and what limited opportunities there were for certain groups of people in our own country some time ago, we become instantly aware that the opportunity all Americans have today to attend college and advance themselves—regardless of their race, gender, age, or prior academic record—is truly a distinctive advantage that should neither be overlooked nor taken for granted.

By looking outside yourself and taking the perspective of other people and other times, you acquire a sort of reflective mirror that also allows you to see yourself and your present situation more clearly by comparison and contrast. This dual vision provided by a liberal arts education supplies you with a double-purpose tool that you can use to simultaneously better yourself and the world in which you live. For example, by broadening your perspectives and widening your range of knowledge, you gain greater social self-confidence. You are able to relate to a wider range of people with different interests, and you can contribute to conversations on a wider variety of topics. You become a more interested and interesting person who is less likely to be left out of a conversation or to have the topic of conversation go over your head. Furthermore, broadening your perspectives and discovering new knowledge is simply a very stimulating mental experience, which can prevent you from becoming bored (and boring).

Pause for Reflection

What information or ideas in this chapter might be used to support the following statement: "Knowledge is power."

••• Summary and Conclusion

Before leaving this chapter, there are three key ideas we hope you will take with you.

1. Being a generalist is as important for career success as being a specialist.

Studies show that college students, as well as their parents, are extremely concerned about what majors and careers to specialize in. However, they often overlook or underestimate the value of general education provided by the liberal arts (Hersh, 1994, 1997). As a result, liberal arts courses are sometimes seen as unnecessary requirements that students need to get out of the way before they can get into what is really important—their specialized major. This negative view probably stems from lack of knowledge about what the liberal arts stand for and what they are designed to do, as well as misinterpreting general education to mean something that is non-specific and without any particular value or practical purpose. However, as we have demonstrated repeatedly in this chapter, a liberal arts education develops very practical, durable, and transferable skills that provide the foundation for success in all majors and all careers.

Your general education classes provide you with skills that are stable and portable.

In fact, research indicates that as an individual's career progresses, specific skills learned in a major tend to decline in importance and are replaced by more general skills (Pascarella & Terenzini, 2005). Specific, technical skills may be important for moving you into a career, but general, professional skills are more important for moving you up the career ladder. They are the skills that prevent you from being stuck at a dead-end position and help you avoid the tendency to rise to a position that you cannot perform successfully because the position requires broader professional skills and responsibilities than those needed for success at a lower level. The importance of general professional skills will become even more important for people entering the workforce during the twenty-first century because the demand for upper-level positions that involve management and leadership will exceed the supply of people in the workforce who are prepared to fill these positions (Herman, 2000).

While many people see the career advantages of specializing in a particular field, they often fail to see its potential disadvantage—overspecialization. There is an old saying that goes something like this: "A specialist is someone who knows more and more about less and less until he knows a whole lot about very little (and isn't interested in learning anything outside his specialty because then he wouldn't be a specialist)." There is some truth to this old adage because when you are very narrowly trained, you are restricted by knowledge limited to one specific type of job or specialized position.

Furthermore, if changes in society create less demand for the specialized career you trained for, then your risk of unemployment is higher. You may end up preparing for a very specific career that will no longer be in demand (or may no longer exist) after graduation.

Personal Story My father is a good example of someone whose education was too narrow and whose career was too specialized. He spent approximately two years of his life learning to be a horologist—a specialist in watch and clock repair. He found regular employment until the 1980s, when advances in technology at that time made it possible for companies to produce and sell high-performance watches at a much cheaper price than ever before. As a result, instead of having their watches repaired when they began to malfunction, people simply threw them away and bought new ones. This reduced society's need for watch repairmen, such as my father, who soon lost his position with the watch company he was working for and was eventually forced into early retirement.

—*Joe Cuseo*

Our society is undergoing rapid technological change and dramatic growth in knowledge. Existing jobs can become obsolete and unnecessary, while at the same time, entirely new positions get created that never existed before (Brown, 2003). Naturally, nobody is specifically trained or prepared to fill these new positions because no one knew they would come into existence. The growing number of such unanticipated positions is now creating a greater demand for generalists who have a broad base of knowledge, flexible lifelong-learning skills, plus the mental versatility needed to take on changing job responsibilities and different professional roles (Niles & Harris-Bowlsbey, 2002; Herman, 2000).

The best way to prepare for such a changing future is by equipping yourself with durable, transferable learning skills—those timeless skills that always have been and always will be useful, and that can be employed anywhere in any way. While certain technological skills may be "hot" right now, the specific technological skills needed for current technological tasks, such as word-processing programs and Web-page designs, will likely change considerably in the future. However, the general education (liberal arts) skills of clear writing and visual creativity are likely to withstand the test of time and continue to remain in demand.

Remember: Do not look at general education as something to get out of the way so that you can get into your major and career. Instead, look at it as something to get into and be ready to take away from general education those general, transferable skills that will remain *stable*—which you can continue to use during changing times, and which are *portable*—that you can take with you and use successfully to adapt to different work situations and career roles.

"I hear this school likes to emphasize the value of a Classical Education."

Recent, rapid changes in information technology are increasing society's demand for the type of *timeless* and *flexible* mental skills developed by a liberal arts education.

2. Building your skills, broadening your perspectives, and keeping track of your development is as important as earning credits, completing courses, and checking off degree requirements.

While completing assignments, getting good grades, and getting a degree are all important accomplishments, it is equally important to step back, reflect, and keep track of what you are actually learning. More important than memorizing facts, figures, and formulas are the new skills you are acquiring or refining, the new perspectives or vantage points from which you are viewing things, and the different dimensions or elements of the "self" that you are developing. Save the lists of specific skills, perspectives, and areas of self-development that have been identified in this chapter, and use them as checklists to keep track of how many of them you are acquiring.

It is important to make a conscious attempt to increase your awareness and memory of your developing skills and perspectives because their improvement can often be subtle and subconscious. Development of these important skills and perspectives sometimes gets embedded within or buried below all the factual material you are consciously trying to learn. Skills and perspectives are mental habits, and like other habits that are repeatedly practiced, their growth can be so gradual, we often do not notice how much has actually occurred.

3. Attending college is not just about earning a better living; it's also about learning to live a better life.

Research shows that the primary reasons why students go to college are to "prepare for a career" and "get a better job" (Sax, et al., 2004). We acknowledge that these are important reasons and that your career is an important element of your life. However, as previously noted, a person's vocation or occupation represents just one element of the self. It also represents just one of many different roles or responsibilities that you are likely to have in life, such as being a son or daughter, a friend, a spouse, a parent, a co-worker, and a citizen.

Remember: Living a successful and rewarding life depends on your ability to fulfill multiple roles effectively. The broad-based knowledge, wide-ranging perspectives, and transferable skills developed by a liberal arts education will help prepare you for these multiple life roles.

Personal Story   One life role that a liberal arts education helped prepare me for was the role of parent. Courses that I took in psychology and sociology proved to be very useful in helping me understand how children develop and how a parent can best support them at different stages of their development. Surprisingly, however, there was one course I took in college that I never expected would ever help me as a parent. That course was *statistics*, which I took to fulfill a general education requirement in mathematics. It was not a particularly enjoyable course; in fact, some of my classmates sarcastically referred to it as "sadistics" because they felt it was a somewhat painful or torturous experience. However, what I learned in that course really become valuable to me many years later as a parent when my 14-year-old son (Tony) developed a life-threatening disease, known as leukemia—a cancer that attacks blood cells. Tony's form of leukemia was a particularly serious one because it had only a 35% average cure rate; in other words, 65% of those who develop the disease do not recover and eventually die from it. This statistic was based on patients that received the traditional treatment of chemotherapy, which was the type of treatment that my son began receiving when his cancer was first detected.

Another option for treating Tony's cancer was a bone-marrow transplant, which involves using radiation to destroy all of his own bone marrow (that was making the abnormal blood cells) and replace it with bone-marrow donated to him by another person. My wife and I got opinions from doctors at two major cancer centers—one from a center that specialized in chemotherapy, and one from a center that specialized in bone-marrow transplants. The chemotherapy doctors felt strongly that drug treatment would have the best chance of curing Tony, and the bone-marrow transplant doctors felt strongly that his chances of survival would be much better if he had a transplant. So, my wife and I had to decide between two opposing recommendations, each made by a respected group of doctors.

To help us reach a decision, I asked both teams of doctors for research studies that had been done on the effectiveness of chemotherapy and bone-marrow transplants for treating my son's particular type of cancer. I read all of these studies and carefully analyzed their statistical findings. I remembered from my statistics course that when an "average" is calculated for a general group of people (for example, average cure rate for people with leukemia), it tends to "lump together" individuals from different subgroups of people (for example, males and females; children and teenagers). Sometimes, when separate statistics are calculated for different subgroups, the results may be different than the average statistic for the whole group. So, when I read the research reports, I looked to find any subgroup statistics that may have been calculated. I found that there were two subgroups of patients with my son's particular type of cancer that had a higher rate of cure with chemotherapy than the general (whole-group) average of 35%. One subgroup included people with a low number of abnormal cells when the cancer was first detected and chemotherapy first began, and the other subgroup consisted of people whose cancer cells dropped rapidly after their first week of chemotherapy. My son belonged to both of these subgroups, which meant that his chance for cure with chemotherapy was higher than the overall 35% average. Furthermore, I found that the statistics showing higher success rate for bone-marrow transplants were based only on patients whose bodies accepted the donor's bone marrow, and did not include those who died because their body "rejected" the donor's bone marrow. So, the success rates for bone-marrow patients were not actually as high as they appeared to be, because the overall average did not include the subgroup of patients who died because of transplant rejection. Based on these statistics, my wife and I decided not to have the transplant and to continue with chemotherapy.

Our son has now been cancer-free for over five years, so we think we made the right decision. However, I never imagined that a statistics course, which I took many years ago to fulfill a general education requirement, would help me fulfill my role as a parent and help me make a life-or-death medical decision about my own son.

—Joe Cuseo

 Remember:
A liberal arts education not only prepares you for a career, it prepares you for *life*.

●●● Learning More through Independent Research

Web-Based Resources for Further Information on the Liberal Arts

For additional information relating to the ideas discussed in this chapter, we recommend the following Web sites:

http://www.aacu-edu.org/issues/liberaleducation/index.cfm
http://www.educationindex.com/liberal/

CHAPTER 2

Planning Your Liberal Arts Education

The liberal arts are such an important component of your college experience that it should be intentionally planned. By so doing, you can become actively involved in shaping or creating your liberal arts education in a way that will have maximum impact on your personal development and career success.

STEPS:

1. **Become aware of the general education requirements at your college.** You can find this information by consulting your college catalog. Since college catalogs can sometimes be difficult to navigate, you might consider teaming-up with a classmate to make this task a little easier. You and your teammate will be pursuing a common goal of finding information that applies to both of you because general education requirements apply to all students. Another personal resource on campus that you can consult for help with interpreting the college catalog and accurately identifying general education requirements is an academic advisor.

2. Use the index in your college catalog to **find the general education or liberal arts requirements**, and go to the pages on which these requirements appear. You are likely to find that general education requirements are organized into general divisions of knowledge that make up the liberal arts curriculum, such as Humanities, Fine Arts, Natural Sciences, etc. Within each of these liberal arts divisions, you will see specific courses listed that fulfill the general education requirement for that particular division. In some cases, you will have no choice about what courses you must take to fulfill the general education requirement, but in most cases, you will have the freedom to choose from a group of courses. You can exercise this freedom of choice to plan and build a liberal arts experience that will have the most positive impact on your development. (Remember that courses you are taking this term may be fulfilling certain general-education requirements, so be sure to include them in your plan.)

3. **Highlight the specific courses** in the catalog that you plan to take to fulfill your general education requirements in each area of the liberal arts, and use the form at the end of this chapter to list these courses. Before making your final selections, be sure to read the descriptions of these courses that are provided in your college catalog. It is recommended that you use the following criteria or guidelines when selecting general education courses:

   ◆ Select courses that will expose you to **new areas of knowledge**, particularly those that capture your curiosity and interest. (Your answer to the "pause for reflection" on page 44 of this chapter may help you identify these courses.) Exploring new fields of knowledge that attract your interest will stimulate your motivation to learn and may lead to discovery of fields in which you eventually want to major or minor.

   ◆ Select courses that will enable you to attain all of the **broadening perspectives** developed by a liberal arts education, which are described on pages 57–61. Use the perspectives provided on the form at the end of this chapter (p. 70) as a checklist to ensure that your overall perspective is comprehensive and that there are no blind spots in your liberal arts education. Remember that general education courses you are taking this term may already be developing some of these broadening perspectives. So, any general education courses that you listed in your "pause for reflection" on page 62 could be included on the checklist.

   ◆ Select courses that will enable you to **develop elements of the whole person** (pp. 51–55). A list of these elements is provided on the planning form (p. 72). Use this as a checklist to ensure that you are not overlooking any important area of self-development. Remember that development of your whole self also includes co-curricular learning experiences (for example, leadership and volunteer experiences) that take place outside the classroom. So, be sure to consider including these experiences as part of your plan to develop yourself as a whole person. Your *Student Handbook* probably represents the best resource for information about co-curricular experiences offered by your college. The best person to contact for this information on your campus would be the Director of Student Development, Student Life, or Student Activities at your college.

◆ Try to take courses that encourage you to **make connections** between different disciplines or fields of knowledge, and between academic learning in the classroom and service to the community. Courses that encourage these types of connections are described briefly below.

Interdisciplinary courses are courses that are designed to help you connect or integrate two or more different academic disciplines. For example, psychobiology is an interdisciplinary course that examines connections between the mind (psychology) and the body (biology). Research indicates that students who participate in interdisciplinary courses report greater gains in learning and greater satisfaction with the learning experience (Astin, 1993; Terenzini & Pascarella, 2004).

Service-learning courses are courses designed to help you integrate or connect classroom learning with volunteer service in the community. For example, a sociology course may include assignments that involve volunteer service in the local community, which students then reflect on and relate to course material through writing or class discussions. Research indicates that students who participate in such service-learning courses have been found to experience strong gains in multiple areas of self-development, including critical thinking skills and leadership skills (Astin, et al., 2000; Strage, 2000).

Enrolling in service-learning and interdisciplinary courses will help you develop the synoptic perspective described in this chapter (p. 62), and will enable you to see how different pieces and parts of your learning experience connect together to form a more meaningful whole.

Liberal Arts Education-Planning Form

Division of the Liberal Arts Curriculum: _____

General education courses you are planning to take to fulfill requirements in this division:
(Record the course number and course title)

_____   _____   _____

_____   _____   _____

Division of the Liberal Arts Curriculum: _____

General education courses you are planning to take to fulfill requirements in this division:

_____   _____   _____

_____   _____   _____

Division of the Liberal Arts Curriculum: _____

General education courses you are planning to take to fulfill requirements in this division:

_____   _____   _____

_____   _____   _____

Division of the Liberal Arts Curriculum: _____

General education courses you are planning to take to fulfill requirements in this division:

_____   _____   _____

_____   _____   _____

Division of the Liberal Arts Curriculum: _____

General education courses you are planning to take to fulfill requirements in this division:

_____   _____   _____

_____   _____   _____

Division of the Liberal Arts Curriculum: _____

General education courses you are planning to take to fulfill requirements in this division:

_____   _____   _____

_____   _____   _____

Planning Checklist for Developing the Broadening Perspectives of a Liberal Arts Education

(See pages 57–61 for descriptions of these perspectives.)

BROADENING CHRONOLOGICAL PERSPECTIVES   Course developing this perspective:

_____ Historical (Past)   _____

_____ Contemporary (Current)   _____

_____ Futuristic (Future)   _____

BROADENING SOCIAL-SPATIAL PERSPECTIVES   Course developing this perspective:

_____ Self   _____

_____ Family   _____

_____ Community   _____

_____ Society   _____

_____ Nation   _____

_____ International   _____

_____ Global   _____

_____ Universe   _____

Planning Checklist for Developing Key Elements of the Whole Person

(See pages 51–55 for further descriptions of these elements.)

ELEMENTS OF THE WHOLE PERSON	Course or co-curricular experience developing this element:
_____ Intellectual (Cognitive)	_____
_____ Emotional	_____
_____ Social	_____
_____ Ethical	_____
_____ Physical	_____
_____ Spiritual	_____
_____ Vocational	_____
_____ Personal	_____

▼ CASE STUDY

Dazed and Confused: General Education versus Career Specialization

Joe Tech was really looking forward to college because he thought he would have freedom to select the courses he wanted and the opportunity to get into the major of his choice (computer science). However, he is shocked and disappointed with his first-term schedule of classes because it consists mostly of required general education courses that do not seem to relate in any way to his major, and some of these courses are about subjects that he already took in high school (English, history, and biology). He's beginning to think he would be better off transferring out of college and going to a technical school where he could get right into computer science, and immediately begin to acquire the knowledge and skills he'll need to prepare him for his intended career.

Reflection and Discussion Questions

1. If this student decides to leave college for a technical school, what would be the possible short-term and long-term consequences of his decision?

2. Can you relate to this student, or know of other students who feel the same way as he does?

3. Do you see any way this student might strike a balance between pursuing his career interest and his college degree, so that he could work toward achieving both goals at the same time?

Educational Planning and Decision Making

Making Wise Choices about Your College Courses and Major

Learning Goals

The primary goals of this chapter are to help you achieve a balance between academic exploration and commitment to a specific academic field, and develop a plan for making educational decisions that is best for attaining your personal and professional goals.

Outline

Activate Your Thinking

Regarding your college major, are you decided or undecided? If you selected "undecided," please list any subjects that you would consider to be possibilities for a major:

If you selected "decided," note your choice here _____, and indicate how *sure* you are about that choice by circling one of the following options.

a. absolutely sure
b. fairly sure
c. not too sure
d. likely to change

••• To Be or Not to Be Decided about a College Major: What the Research Shows

Whether you have or have not decided on a major, here are some research findings related to student decisions about college majors that may be worth keeping in mind:

◆ Less than 10 percent of new college students feel they know a great deal about the field that they are intending to major in.

◆ As students proceed through the first year of college, they grow more uncertain about the major they chose when they began college.

◆ Over two-thirds of new students change their mind about their major during the first year of college.

◆ Only one in three college seniors eventually major in the same field that they chose during their first year of college (Cuseo, 2005).

These findings point to the conclusion that the vast majority of students entering college are truly undecided about a college major. They do not make a final decision about their major before starting college; instead, they reach a final decision during their college experience. Even if you think you're absolutely sure about a major, you will still need to explore specialized fields within your major to identify one that is most compatible with your personal interests, abilities, and values.

Thus, whether or not you have decided on a college major, you still need an action plan that will allow you to continue exploring and testing your options while you make steady progress toward a final decision. In other words, you need an action plan that allows you to strike a balance between exploration and commitment.

As a beginning college student, it is only natural to feel at least somewhat uncertain about your intended major because you have not yet experienced the variety of subjects or fields of study that make up the college curriculum. Being uncertain about a major is nothing to be embarrassed about. The term "undecided" or "undeclared" doesn't mean that you have somehow failed or are lost.

As a new student, you may be undecided for a variety of good reasons. For instance, you may be undecided simply because you have interests in a variety of subjects. This is actually a healthy form of indecision because it shows that you have a broad range of interests and a high level of motivation to learn about different subjects. You may also be undecided simply because you are a careful, reflective thinker whose decision-making style is to gather more information before making any long-term commitments. In one study of students who were undecided about a major when they started college, 43 percent had several ideas in mind but were not yet ready to commit to one of them (Gordon & Steele, 2003). These students were not "totally clueless"; instead, they had some ideas but still wanted to explore them and keep their options open, which is a very effective way to go about making decisions.

While it is true that decisions sometimes can be put off too long, resulting in procrastination, it is also true that they can be made too quickly, resulting in premature decisions that are reached without taking enough time to carefully think through all options. Judging from the large number of students who end up changing their minds about a college major, it is probably safe to say that more students make the mistake of reaching a decision about a major too quickly, rather than procrastinating about it indefinitely. This may be due to the fact that students hear the same question over and over again, even before they step a foot on a college campus: "What are you going to major in when you go to college?" You probably also saw this question on your college applications, and you are likely to hear it again during your first term in college. This is a prime time in your college experience for meeting new people, and when you meet them, almost immediately after they ask the typical opening question: "What's your name?", get ready for the typical follow-up question: "What's your major?" Also, if members of your family are helping you pay for the rising cost of a college education, they may frequently ask this same question—hoping you will have a definite answer to it—because paying for college becomes a little easier for them if they know you have a definite idea about what you're going to do while you're there (your major) and what you'll do with it after you leave (your career).

Despite any pressure you may be receiving from others to make an early decision, we encourage you not to officially commit to a particular major until you gain more self-knowledge and more knowledge of your options. Even if you think you're sure about your choice of major, before you make a commitment to it, take a course or two in the major to test it out.

 Pause for Reflection

If you have chosen a major or are considering a particular major, what has led you to choose or consider this option?

Studies show that students learn more when the material covered in their courses tends to match their personal interests and abilities (Cook, 1991; Dunn et al., 1995). Furthermore, research indicates that students are more likely to continue in college and graduate when they choose majors that reflect their personal interests (Leuwerke, et al., 2004).

In fact, it may be unrealistic for you, a first-term student, to make a final decision about a college major before you've had at least some experience with the courses that comprise the liberal arts curriculum. One key purpose of a liberal arts education is to help new students develop the critical thinking skills needed to make wise choices and well-informed decisions, such as choice of your college major. The liberal arts curriculum is also designed to introduce you to a variety of academic subjects, and as you progress through this curriculum, you may discover subjects that really captivate you and capture your interest. Some of these subjects may represent fields of study that you never experienced before, and all of them represent possible choices for a college major.

In addition to finding new fields of possible interest, as you gain experience with the college curriculum, you are likely to gain more self-knowledge about your academic strengths and weaknesses. This is important knowledge to take into consideration when choosing a major, because you want to select a field that builds on your academic abilities and talents.

Remember: Make sure that your *first* choice is your *best* choice—the one that is most compatible or consistent with your personal abilities and interests.

When Should You Reach a Firm Decision about a College Major?

National surveys indicate that colleges and universities vary in terms of when they expect students to make a decision about their college major. Some institutions require or strongly en-

"I've decided to change my major."

courage first-year students to declare a major, some discourage or forbid it, and others leave it entirely up to the student (Policy Center on The First Year of College Year, 2003). If you have been pressured or forced to make an early decision, try to remain flexible and open to the possibility of changing your original choice. Changing decisions about a major is not necessarily a bad thing; it may represent your discovery of other academic fields that are more interesting to you or that are more compatible with your personal skills and abilities. Exercise your right to change your mind and don't lock yourself in a situation where you feel trapped or believe there is no turning back.

Naturally, there is a downside to changing majors—if you make the change late in your college experience. This can result in added time to graduation (and added tuition costs) because you may need to complete additional courses required for your newly chosen major.

Remember: As a general rule of thumb, you should reach a fairly firm decision about your major during your second (sophomore) year in college. However, in order to reach a good decision within this time frame, the process of exploring and planning should begin now—during your first term in college.

••• The Importance of Long-Range Educational Planning

Compared to high school, college will allow you more choices about what courses to enroll in and the choice of what field to specialize in. Your advisor's job, as the job title implies, is to "advise." Advisors are not academic dictators who tell you what to do; ultimately, you are in charge of making your own academic choices and decisions. Through advanced planning, you can actively take charge of your academic future, *making* it happen *for* you, rather than passively *letting* it happen *to* you. By looking ahead and developing a tentative plan for your courses beyond the first term of college, you're able to view your college experience as a full-length movie and get a sneak preview of the total picture. In contrast, scheduling your classes one term at a time just prior to each registration period (when everyone else is making a mad rush to get their advisor's signature for the following term's classes) forces you to view your academic experience as a series of separate snapshots that do not come together to form a big picture.

Furthermore, long-range educational planning enables you to take a proactive approach to your future. Being proactive means you are taking early, preventative action that anticipates your future before it sneaks up on you and forces you to react to it without enough time to plan and develop your best strategy. As the old saying goes, "If you fail to plan, you plan to fail."

Lastly, by doing some advanced educational planning, you reduce your anxiety about the future because you gain some control over it. To begin this process of advanced planning and gaining control of your educational future, you are strongly encouraged to complete the exercises at the end of this chapter. Remember that any long-range plan you develop is not set in stone—it can change—depending on changes in your academic interests and future plans. The purpose of long-range planning is not to lock you into a particular plan; instead, its purpose is to free you from shortsightedness, which if uncorrected, can lead to procrastination or denial.

Don't take the denial and avoidance approach to planning your educational future.

◆ Pause for Reflection

Choosing a major is a life-changing decision because it will determine what you do for the rest of your life.

Would you agree or disagree with the above statement? Why?

●●● Myths about the Relationship between Majors and Careers

Good decisions are informed decisions that are based on accurate information, rather than misconceptions or myths. Since there is a relationship between majors and careers, to be able to plan effectively for a college major, you first need to have an accurate understanding of this relationship. Described below are some common myths about the relationship between majors and careers that can lead to uninformed or unrealistic choices of a college major.

Myth 1: When You Choose Your Major, You're Choosing Your Career

While some majors lead directly to a particular career, most do not. Those majors that do lead directly to specific careers are often called pre-professional majors, which include such fields as accounting, engineering, and nursing. However, the vast majority of college majors do not channel you directly down one particular career path. Instead, they leave you with a variety of career options. The career path of most college graduates is not like walking a straight line directly from your major to your career. For instance, all physics majors do not become physicists, all philosophy majors do not become philosophers, all history majors do not become historians, and all English majors do not become Englishmen (or Englishwomen). The trip from your college experience to your eventual career(s) is more like climbing a tree. As illustrated in Figure 3.1, you begin with the tree's trunk (the foundation of liberal arts), which grows into separate limbs (choices for college majors), which in turn, lead to different branches (different career paths or options).

Figure 3.1 The Relationship between General Education (Liberal Arts), College Majors, and Careers

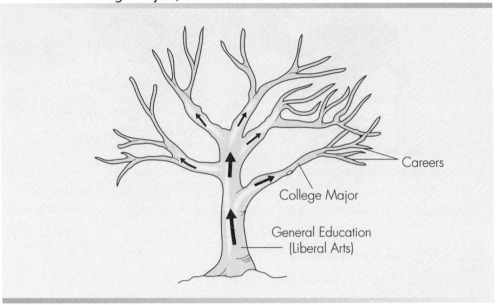

Careers

College Major

General Education
(Liberal Arts)

Note that the career branches grow from the same major limb, so typically a particular major will lead to a "family" of related careers. For example, an English major will often lead to careers that involve use of the written language (e.g., editing, journalism, publishing), while a major in art will often lead to careers that involve use of visual media (e.g., illustration, graphic design, art therapy). The Web site, MyMajors.com, provides useful information on what groups or families of jobs tend to be related to different majors.

Furthermore, different majors can lead to the same career. For instance, many different majors can lead a student to law school and to an eventual career as a lawyer, because there really is no law or pre-law major. Similarly, there really is no pre-med major. Students interested in going to medical school after college typically major in some field in the natural sciences (e.g., biology or chemistry); however, it is possible for students to go to medical school with majors in other fields, particularly if they take and do well in certain science courses that are emphasized in medical school (e.g., general biology, general chemistry, organic and inorganic chemistry).

Your major does not equal your career (major ≠ career), nor does it automatically turn into your career (major → career), but this is why some students may procrastinate about choosing a major; they think they are making a lifelong decision. They are afraid that if they make the "wrong" one, then they will be stuck doing something they hate for the rest of their lives. The key point we are making here is that the relationship between most majors and careers is not a direct, one-to-one relationship.

 Remember: Do not assume that choosing your college major means that you're choosing what you will do for a living for the remainder of your working life.

Research on college graduates indicates that they change careers numerous times, and the further they continue along their career path, the more likely they are to work in a field that is unrelated to their college major (Millard, 2004). While this may seem hard to believe, remember that the liberal arts curriculum is a significant part of your college education and exposes you to different subjects, promotes your development of key skills (e.g., writing, speaking, organizing), and serves to qualify you for a number of different careers—regardless of what your particular major happens to be.

 Remember: Deciding on a major and deciding on a career are typically different decisions that are made at different times.

The order in which decisions about majors and careers are covered in this book reflects the order that they are made in life. First, you make a decision about your major, and later, you make a decision about your career. Although it is important to think about the relationship between your choice of major and your choice of career(s), these are different choices that are made at different times. Both choices do relate to your future goals, but they involve different timeframes: Choosing your major is a short-range goal, whereas choosing your career is a long-range goal.

Myth 2: If You Want to Continue Your Education after College, You Must Continue in the Same Field as Your College Major

After college graduation, you have two main options or alternative paths available to you:

1. You can enter a career immediately, or
2. You can continue your education in graduate school or professional school. (See Figure 3.2 for a visual map of the signposts or stages in the college experience and the basic paths available to you after college graduation.)

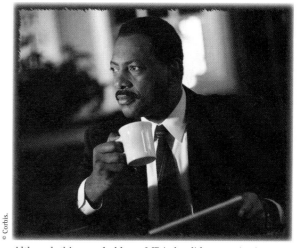

Although this man holds an MBA, he did not major in business as an undergraduate.

Once you complete your bachelor's degree, it is possible to continue your education in a field that is different than your college major. This is particularly true for students majoring in fields that do not lead directly to a particular career after graduation (Pascarella & Terenzini, 2005). For example, if you major in English, you can still go to graduate school in a subject other than English, or go to law school, or get a master's degree in business administration. In fact, it is common to find that the majority of graduate students in master's of business administration (MBA) programs were not business majors in college (Dupuy & Vance, 1996).

 Pause for Reflection

Reflecting back on the timeline above:

1. *Do you see yourself completing your bachelor's degree in four years?*

2. *What do you think will help you the most to stay on track and finish your degree in four years?*

3. *Do you see any possible interfering factors or potential obstacles that might prolong the time you need to complete your degree?*

Figure 3.2 Timeline to the Future: A Snapshot of the College Experience and Beyond

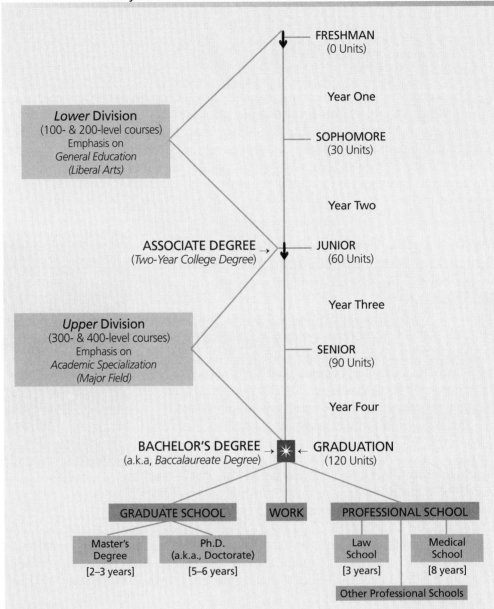

Notes:

1. The total number of *general education* units and the total number of units needed to *graduate* with a bachelor's degree may vary somewhat from school to school. Also, the total number of units required for a *major* will vary somewhat from major to major and from school to school.

2. It often takes college students longer than four years to graduate due to a variety of reasons, such as working part-time and taking fewer courses per term, needing to repeat courses that were failed or dropped, or making a late change to a different major and needing to fulfill additional requirements for the new major.

3. *Graduate* and *professional* schools are options for continuing to higher levels of education after completion of an undergraduate (college) education.

4. Compared to graduate school, *professional* school involves advanced education in more "applied" professions (e.g., pharmacy or public administration).

Myth 3: To Work in a Business or Corporation, You Need to Major in Business or a Technical Field

The former director of a national college-placement bureau puts it this way: "Employers are far more interested in the prospect's ability to think and to think clearly, to write and speak well, and how he works with others than in his major or the name of the school he went to. Several college investigating teams found that these were the qualities on which all kinds of employers, government and private, base their decisions" (Pope, 1990, p. 213). So, do not restrict your range of choices for a major by believing in the myth that you must major in business to work for a business after graduation. Research shows that in the long run, the career mobility and career advancement of non-business majors in the business world are equal to those attained by business majors (Pascarella & Terenzini, 1991, 2005).

Myth 4: If You Major in a Liberal Arts Field, the Only Career Available to You Is Teaching

Liberal arts majors enter and advance in careers other than teaching. There are many college graduates with majors in liberal arts fields who have proceeded to, and succeeded in, careers other than teaching. Among these graduates are such notable people as:

- ◆ Jill Barad (English major), CEO, Mattel Toys
- ◆ Steve Case (political science major), CEO, America Online
- ◆ Brian Lamb (speech major), CEO, C-Span
- ◆ Willie Brown (liberal studies major), Mayor, San Francisco

(Source: Indiana University, 2004).

In fact, studies show that students in liberal arts majors are just as likely to advance to the highest levels of corporate leadership as majors in pre-professional fields, such as business and engineering (Pascarella & Terenzini, 2005). If you are considering a major in a liberal arts field, you should not be dismayed or discouraged by those who may question your choice by asking: "What are you going to do with a degree in *that* major?"

(A good career-information Web site for liberal arts majors can be found at: www.eace.org/networks/liberalarts.html)

Myth 5: Specialized Skills Are More Important for Career Success than General Skills

You may find that liberal arts courses are sometimes viewed by students as unnecessary requirements, which they have to get out of the way before they can get into what is really important—their major or academic specialization. However, as we documented extensively in Chapter 2, a liberal arts education develops very practical, durable, and transferable skills that provide a strong foundation for success in any major or any career.

Also, don't forget that the general skills and qualities developed by the liberal arts serve to increase career mobility (your ability to move into different career paths) and career advancement (your ability to move up the career ladder). While specific, technical skills may be important for getting into a career, the general, professional skills are more important for moving up the career ladder. The courses you take as part of your liberal arts education will prepare you for your advanced career positions, not just your first one (Boyer, 1987; Miller, 2003). Furthermore, general professional skills will grow even more important for college graduates who enter the workforce in the twenty-first century because the demand for upper-level positions that

STUDENT PERSPECTIVE

"They asked me during my interview why I was right for the job and I told them because I can read well, write well and I can think. They really liked that because those were the skills they were looking for."

—English major hired by a public relations firm (Source: Los Angeles Times, *April 4, 2004)*

involve management and leadership will exceed the supply of workers available to fill these positions (Herman, 2000).

Pause for Reflection

How do you think your general education courses will strengthen your performance in your chosen major?

●●● Making Decisions about a College Major

Reaching an effective decision about a college major involves three steps:

1. Gaining awareness of yourself—your personal abilities, interests, and values;
2. Becoming aware of your options—the academic fields that are available to you as choices for a college major; and
3. Developing awareness of what options best match your personal abilities, interests, and values.

Strategies relating to each of these steps in the decision-making process for selecting a college major are discussed below.

Step 1: Gaining Self-Awareness

This is a critical first step in making decisions about a college major, or any other important decision. You must know yourself before you can know what choice is best for you. While this may seem obvious, self-awareness and self-discovery are often overlooked aspects of the decision-making process. Being true to yourself is the first and foremost step when choosing a major or making any other important choice.

As we mentioned in Chapter 2, "know thyself" is the most frequently cited purpose of a liberal arts education. The wide range of courses that you will experience in the liberal arts curriculum will help you become more deeply aware of different dimensions of yourself. However, you can begin to deepen your self-awareness right now by engaging in some introspection. No one is in a better position to know who you are, and what you want, than *you*. One of the most effective ways to access information about yourself is through effective self-questioning—asking yourself key questions that trigger deep thinking about who you are and what matters most to you. Effective self-questioning launches you on a quest that leads to valuable personal insights and self-discoveries. When your goal is self-awareness for the purpose of choosing a college major that best fits you, good questions are those that increase self-awareness of your:

◆ interests—what you like doing,
◆ abilities—what you're good at doing, and
◆ values—what you feel good about doing.

Select one question from each of the following three categories that you can relate best to, or which brings to mind the most ideas about yourself. Record your ideas in the space provided at the end of each category. When thinking about your answers to these questions, consider all areas of your life—home, school, jobs, volunteer experiences, athletics, hobbies, etc.

Personal Interests

1. What do you really enjoy doing and tend to do as often as you possibly can?
2. What do you look forward to or get excited about?
3. What tends to grab your attention and hold it for long periods of time?
4. What sorts of things are you naturally curious about or do you tend to seek more information about?
5. What are your favorite hobbies or pastimes?
6. When you're with your friends, what do you like to talk about or do together?
7. What has been your most stimulating or enjoyable learning experience?
8. If you've had previous work or volunteer experience, what jobs or tasks did you most enjoy doing?
9. What do you like to read about?
10. When you open a newspaper, what do you tend to read first?
11. When time seems to "fly by," what are you usually doing?
12. If you daydream about your future, does it tend to be about anything in particular?

Pause for Reflection

Choose one of the above questions relating to your personal interests, and record your response to it in the space below.

Personal Abilities

1. What comes easily or naturally to you?
2. What would you say is your greatest gift or talent?
3. What do you really excel at when you apply yourself and put forth your best effort?
4. What are your most advanced or well-developed skills?
5. What would you say has been the greatest accomplishment or achievement in your life thus far?
6. What about yourself are you most proud of, or take most pride in doing?
7. Do you notice people coming to you for advice or assistance with anything? (If yes, what do they usually come to you for advice or help with?)
8. What would your best friend(s) say is your most positive quality?
9. What have you had the most success doing?
10. What has been your most successful learning experience?
11. In what types of courses do you tend to earn the highest grades?
12. If you have received any special awards or other forms of recognition, what have they been for?

Pause for Reflection

Choose one of the above questions relating to your personal abilities, and record your response to it in the space below.

Personal Values

1. What do you really care about?
2. What would be one thing that you really stand for or believe in?
3. What would you say are your highest priorities in life?
4. What makes you feel good about yourself when you're doing it?
5. If there was one thing in the world you could change, or could make a difference in, what would it be?
6. When you have extra spending money, what do you usually spend it on?
7. When you have free time, what do you usually find yourself doing?
8. What does living a "good life" mean to you?
9. How would you define success?
10. Do you have any heroes or anyone you admire, look up to, or feel has set an example worth following? (If you do, why do you admire this person?)
11. Would you rather be thought of as:
    a. smart,
    b. wealthy,
    c. creative, or
    d. caring?

    (Rank from 1 to 4, with 1 being the highest)
12. What would you say is your strongest conviction or commitment?

Pause for Reflection

Choose one of the above questions relating to your personal values, and record your response to it in the space below.

Multiple Intelligences: A Tool for Identifying Your Personal Abilities and Talents

Intelligence was once considered to be a single, general intellectual trait that could be detected and measured by an IQ (Intelligence Quotient) test. Now the singular word "intelligence" has been replaced by the plural word "intelligence*s*" because humans can display intelligence or mental ability in many forms other than just their intellectual performance on an IQ test.

Listed in Box 3.1 are different forms of intelligence that have been identified by Howard Gardner (1983; 1993), based on his studies of gifted and talented individuals, experts in different lines of work, and a variety of other sources. As you read through these different types of intelligence, think about which types seem to best reflect your personal talents or abilities. (You can possess more than one type.) Keep your type(s) of intelligence in mind when you are deciding on a college major. Ideally, you want to select a major that most closely taps into and builds on your strongest skills or talents. Choosing a major that is compatible with your strongest abilities may enable you to master the concepts and skills required by your major more easily, rapidly, and deeply, as well as strengthen your academic self-esteem.

BOX 3.1 *Snapshot* **SUMMARY**   **Multiple Forms of Intelligence**

1. *Linguistic* Intelligence: ability to communicate through words or language. For example: verbal skills in the areas of speaking, writing, listening, or reading.

2. *Logical-Mathematical* Intelligence: ability to reason logically and succeed in tasks that involve mathematical problem-solving. For example, skill for making logical arguments and following logical reasoning or the ability to think effectively with numbers and make quantitative calculations.

3. *Spatial* Intelligence: ability to visualize relationships among objects arranged in different spatial positions and the ability to perceive or create visual images. For example, forming mental images of three-dimensional objects; detecting detail in objects or drawings; artistic talent for drawing, painting, sculpting, or graphic design; or skills related to sense of direction and navigation.

4. *Musical* Intelligence: ability to appreciate or create rhythmical and melodic sounds. For example, playing, writing, or arranging music.

5. *Interpersonal (Social)* Intelligence: ability to relate to others, to accurately identify others' needs, feelings, or emotional states of mind; or ability to effectively express emotions and feelings to others. For example: skills involving interpersonal communication and emotional expression; ability to accurately "read" the feelings of others, or to meet the emotional needs of others.

6. *Intrapersonal (Self)* Intelligence: ability to self-reflect, become aware of, and understand one's own thoughts, feelings, and behavior. For example: capacity for personal reflection, emotional self-awareness, and self-insight into personal strengths and weaknesses.

7. *Bodily-Kinesthetic (Psychomotor)* Intelligence: ability to use one's own body skillfully and to acquire knowledge through bodily sensations or movements. For example: skilled at tasks involving physical coordination; ability to work well with hands; mechanical skills; talent for building models and assembling things; or skills relating to technology.

8. *Naturalist* Intelligence: ability to carefully observe and appreciate features of the natural environment. For example: keen awareness of nature or natural surroundings; ability to understand causes or results of events occurring in the natural world.

Source: Howard Gardner (1993). *Frames of Mind: The theory of multiple intelligences* (2nd ed.)

Learning Styles: A Tool for Identifying Your Personal Interests and Learning Preferences

In contrast to multiple intelligences, learning styles refers to differences in learning preferences, or different ways in which individuals prefer to perceive information (receive or take it in) and process information (deal with it after taking it in). For instance, different individuals may prefer to take-in information by reading about it, listening to it, seeing an image or diagram of it, or physically touching and manipulating it. Individuals may also vary in terms of whether they like to receive information in a form that is very structured and orderly, or in an unstructured form that allows them the freedom to explore, play with, and restructure it in their own way. After information has been received, individuals may also differ in terms of how they prefer to process or deal with it. For instance, some might like to think about it on their own, while others may prefer to talk about it with someone else, make an outline of it, or draw a picture of it.

> *Personal Story* In my family, whenever there's something that needs to be assembled or set-up (e.g., a ping-pong table or new electronic equipment), I've noticed that my wife, my son, and myself have different learning styles in terms of how we go about doing it. I like to read the manual's instructions carefully and completely before I even attempt to touch anything. My son prefers to look at the pictures or diagrams in the manual and uses them as models to find parts; then he begins to assemble those parts. My wife seems to prefer not to look at the manual at all! Instead, she prefers to figure things out as she goes along by grabbing different parts from the box and trying to assemble parts that look like they should fit together—like piecing together pieces of a jigsaw puzzle.
>
> *—Joe Cuseo*

There are specially designed tests that you can take to assess your particular learning style and how it compares with others. If you're interested in taking a learning styles test, the Learning Center or Career Center are the two most likely sites on campus where you can take one. Perhaps the most frequently used learning styles test is the *Myers-Briggs Type Indicator (MBTI)* (Myers, 1976; Myers & McCaulley, 1985), which is based on the personality theory of psychologist Carl Jung. It consists of four dimensions, each of which has a pair of opposite traits or preferences, along which people vary on a scale or continuum (lower to higher). The four dimensions and opposite traits are illustrated in Figure 3.3.

Pause for Reflection

As you read the following scales, place a mark along the line where you think you fall with respect to these traits. For example, place a mark in the middle of the line if you think you are midway between these opposite traits, or place a mark at the far left or far right if you think you lean very strongly toward the trait listed on either end.

Figure 3.3 Traits and Learning Styles Measured by the Myers-Briggs Type Indicator (MBTI)

Extraversion Prefer to focus on "outer" world of persons, actions, or objects	*Introversion* Prefer to focus on "inner" world of thoughts and ideas
Sensing Prefer interacting with the world directly through concrete, sensory experiences	*Intuition* Prefer dealing with symbolic meanings and imagining possibilities
Thinking Prefer to rely on logic and rational thinking when making decisions	*Feeling* Prefer to rely on human needs and feelings when making decisions
Judging Prefer to plan for and control events	*Perceiving* Prefer flexibility and spontaneity

Figure 3.4 Students With Each MBTI Learning Style Have a Preferred Style of Writing

In one study, it was found that college students who score differently on the MBTI have different learning styles when it comes to the style of writing and type of writing assignments they prefer (Jensen & Ti Tiberio, as cited in Bean, 2001). See Figure 3.4 for the details on the findings.

These research findings clearly indicate that students have different learning styles, which in turn influence the type of writing assignments they feel most comfortable doing. This may be important to keep in mind when choosing your major because different academic fields emphasize different styles of writing. Some fields place heavy emphasis on writing that is structured and tightly focused (e.g., science and business), while other fields encourage writing with personal style, flair, or creativity (e.g., English and art). How your writing style meshes with the style emphasized by different academic fields may be one key factor to consider when making decisions about your college major.

Another popular learning styles test that may be available on your campus is the *Learning Styles Inventory (LSI)* (Dunn, Dunn, & Price, 1990), which was originally developed by David Kolb, a professor of philosophy (Kolb, 1976; 1985). It is based on how individuals differ with respect to the following two key elements of the learning process:

How Information Is *Perceived* (Taken in)

Concrete Experience
Learning through direct involvement
or personal experience

Reflective Observation
Learning by watching or observing

How Information Is *Processed* (Dealt with after it has been taken in)

Abstract Conceptualization
Learning by thinking about things
and drawing logical conclusions

Active Experimentation
Learning by taking chances
and trying things

When these two dimensions are crisscrossed to form intersecting lines, four sectors (areas) are created, each of which represents a different learning style, as illustrated in Pause for Reflection. As you look at the four styles in Figure 3.5, circle the style that you think reflects your most preferred way of learning.

Figure 3.5 Learning Styles Measured by the *Learning Styles Inventory (LSI)*

Concrete Experience

Accommodators
Prefer to learn through trial-and-error, hands-on experience; act on gut feelings; get things done; and rely on or accommodate the ideas of others.

Divergers
Prefer to observe, rather than act; generate many creative or imaginative ideas; view things from different perspectives; and pursue broad cultural interests.

Active Experimentation

Reflective Observation

Convergers
Prefer to use logical thinking to focus on solutions to practical problems and to deal with technical tasks rather than interpersonal issues.

Assimilators
Prefer to collect and evaluate lots of information, then systematically organize it into theories or conceptual models; prefer to deal with abstract ideas rather than people.

Abstract Conceptualization

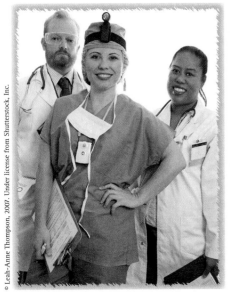

© Leah-Anne Thompson, 2007. Under license from Shutterstock, Inc.

People working in the medical field are most often found to be convergent thinkers.

Research indicates that students majoring in different fields tend to display differences in these four learning styles (Svinicki & Dixon, 1987). For instance, "assimilators" are more frequently found majoring in mathematics and natural sciences (e.g., chemistry and physics), probably because these subjects stress reflection and abstract thinking. In contrast, academic fields where "accommodators" tend to be more commonly found are business, accounting, and law, perhaps because these fields involve taking practical action and making concrete decisions. "Divergers" are more often attracted to majors in the fine arts (e.g., music, art, drama), humanities (e.g., history, literature) or social sciences (psychology, political science), possibly because these fields emphasize different viewpoints and multiple perspectives. In contrast, "convergers" are more likely found in fields like engineering, medicine, and nursing, probably because these fields focus on finding specific solutions to practical and technical problems (Kolb, 1976). This same clustering of fields took place when faculty were asked to classify different academic fields in terms of what learning styles they emphasized (Biglan, 1973; Carnegie Commission on Higher Education, cited in Svinicki & Dixon, 1987).

The Engineering and Humanities majors settle their differences in the Fine Arts quad!

Personal Story The first time I noticed that students in different academic fields may have different learning styles occurred when I was teaching a psychology course that was required for students majoring in nursing and social work. I noticed that some students in class seemed to lose interest (and patience) when we got involved in lengthy class discussions about controversial issues or theories, while others seemed to love it. On the other hand, whenever I lectured or delivered information for an extended period of time, some students seemed to lose interest (and attention), while others seemed to get "into it" and took great notes. After one class period that involved quite a bit of class discussion, I began thinking about who the students were that seemed most involved in the discussion and who seemed to drift off or lose interest. I suddenly realized that the students who did most of the talking and seemed most enthused during the class discussion were the students majoring in social work. On the other hand, most of the students who appeared disinterested or a bit frustrated were the nursing majors.

When I began to think about why this happened, it dawned on me that the nursing students were accustomed to gathering factual information and learning very practical skills in their major courses, and that was the learning style they were expecting to use in my psychology course. The nursing majors felt more comfortable with structured class sessions in which they received lots of factual, practical information from the professor. On the other hand, the social work majors were more comfortable with unstructured class discussions because courses in their major often emphasized debating about social issues and hearing different viewpoints or perspectives.

I left class that day with the following question on my mind: Did nursing majors and social work majors select their major because the style of learning it emphasized tended to "match" their preferred learning style?

–Joe Cuseo

The point we're making here is that students do have different learning styles, and academic fields do emphasize different styles of learning. Thus, if you are thinking about majoring in a particular field, it is important to consider how your learning style matches up with the style of learning emphasized by that field. If the match seems to be close or compatible, then the "marriage" between you and that major could be one that leads to a satisfying or enjoyable learning experience.

We recommend taking a trip to the Learning Center or Career Center on your campus, where you can take a test designed to assess your learning style. Even if the test doesn't help you choose a particular major, it will at least help you become more aware of your particular learning style. This alone could contribute to your academic success because studies show that just becoming more self-aware of your learning style can improve your academic performance in college courses (Claxton & Murrell, 1988).

Pause for Reflection

In addition to taking formal tests to assess your learning style, you can gain some awareness of your learning styles or preferences through some simple introspection or self-examination. Please take a moment to complete the following sentences that are designed to stimulate some awareness of your learning style:

I learn best if . . . .

I learn most from . . . .

I enjoy learning when . . . .

The most important factor to consider when reaching decisions about a major is whether it is compatible with four key characteristics of your "self": your *learning style*, your personal *abilities*, your personal *interests*, and your personal *values* (Figure 3.6). These are the four pillars that provide the foundation for effective decisions about a college major.

Figure 3.6 Personal Characteristics that Provide an Effective Foundation for Choice of a College Major

Step 2: Gaining Awareness of Your Options (the academic subjects available to you as choices for a college major)

The second critical step in any effective decision-making process is to gain awareness of the options available to you as possible majors. Here again, your trip through the liberal arts will help you take this step. These courses help you examine yourself and gain greater self-awareness. Your trip through the liberal arts curriculum may result in discovery of new personal interests and new possibilities for majors, some of which may be in fields that you didn't even know existed.

Also, your exposure to a wide range of subjects in the liberal arts curriculum will provide you with a general context for making an intelligent selection of your specific major. This will enable you to understand how your particular major fits into the bigger picture.

Lastly, experiencing these different fields of study may lead you to discover a second field of interest, which you could pursue as a *minor* to complement your major. (See p. 96 in this chapter for more details about college minors.)

Before moving on to Step 3 in the decision-making process, be sure you have taken the first two steps: Knowing yourself (step 1) and knowing your options (step 2) should take place before making a firm decision and final commitment.

Step 3: Gaining Awareness of Options That Best Match Your Personal Abilities, Interests, and Values

This is the final step in our three-step process for making decisions about a college major. When linked together, these three steps form the following chain of explorations and discoveries:

1. Exploring and discovering your personal abilities, interests, and values;

2. Exploring and discovering your range of options for a college major;

3. Exploring and discovering what college major best matches your personal abilities, interests, and values.

In the following section, we identify some key strategies for completing the last step in this process.

Strategies for Discovering a Personally Compatible Major

If you are currently undecided about a major, this is perfectly fine because you are at the earliest stage of your college experience. Although you are postponing your decision about a major, this does not mean you are postponing the process of exploring and planning for your major. You shouldn't put all thoughts about your major on the back burner and drift until the time comes when a choice must be made. Now is the time to start the process of exploring and developing a game plan that will lead you to a good decision about your major.

Similarly, if you have already chosen a major, this doesn't mean that you'll never have to give any more thought to the decision you've made, and that you can just shift into cruise control and go along for a thought-free ride in the major you've chosen. Instead, you should continue the exploration process while you carefully test drive your first choice, making sure it's the choice that best fits your abilities, interests, and values. In other words, you should adopt a strategy that enables you to either verify or modify your first decision.

·—· **CLASSIC QUOTE** ·—·

When you have to make a choice and don't make it, that is in itself a choice.

—William James, American philosopher and psychologist

·—· **CLASSIC QUOTE** ·—·

When you get to a fork in the road, take it.

—Yogi Berra, Hall of Fame Baseball Player

To explore and identify majors that may be compatible with your personal strengths and interests, consider using the following specific strategies.

◆ Think about what subjects you've been successful at in high school and during your first year of college.

As the old saying goes, "Nothing succeeds like success itself." If you have done well, and continue to do well in a certain field of study, this may indicate that your mental skills and learning style correspond well with the academic skills required by that particular field. This could spell future success and satisfaction in that field if you decide to pursue it as your college major.

You can enter information about your learning experiences with high school courses at a Web site (e.g., MyMajors.com), which will analyze this information and provide you with several majors that may be a good match for you, based on your academic experiences in high school.

◆ Use your elective courses to test your interests and abilities in subjects that you are considering as a major.

As its name implies, elective courses are those that you elect or choose to take. In college, electives come in two forms: free electives and restricted electives.

Free electives are courses that you may elect to enroll in, if you choose to, which count toward your college degree but are not required for either general education or your major.

Restricted electives are courses that you must take, but you choose them from a restricted list of possible courses that have been specified by your college as fulfilling a requirement in general education or your major. For example, your school may have a general education requirement in the area of Social or Behavioral Sciences that requires you to take two courses in this area, but you are allowed to choose them from a menu of different subjects, such as anthropology, economics, political science, psychology, or sociology. If you are considering one of these subjects as a possible major, you can take an introductory course in this subject and test your interest in it, while simultaneously fulfilling a general education requirement needed for graduation. In addition to using your restricted electives in this way, you can use your free electives to select courses in fields that you are considering as possible majors. By using some of your free and restricted electives in this manner, you can test your interest and ability in these fields, and if you find one that is a good match, you may have found yourself a major.

Naturally, you don't have to use all your electives in this fashion. Depending on your major, you may have as many as 40 units (credits) of elective courses in college. This leaves you with a great deal of freedom to shape your college experience in a way that best meets your personal needs and interests. For suggestions on how to make the best use of your free electives, see Box 3.2.

◆ Be sure you know the specific courses that are required for the major you're considering.

In college, it is expected that students know the specific requirements for the major they have chosen, and these requirements can vary considerably from one major to another. Be sure to review your college catalog carefully to determine what specific courses are required for the major you are considering. If you have trouble tracking the requirements in your college catalog, don't become frustrated. These catalogs are often written in a very technical manner that can sometimes be difficult to follow or interpret. If you need help identifying or understanding the requirements for a major that you're considering, don't be embarrassed about seeking assistance from a professional in your school's Academic Advisement Center.

Top-Ten Suggestions for Making the Most of Your College Electives

Your elective courses in college will give you some degree of academic freedom and personal control of your college coursework. You can exercise this freedom of choice by strategically selecting your electives in a way that will enable you to get the most out of your college experience and degree.

As you read these 10 suggestions, select two that represent your top-two strategies for using your electives. In the space at the end of this box, write a short explanation about why you chose each of these strategies.

Use Your Electives to:

1. Complete a minor or build an area of concentration that will complement and strengthen your major, or that will allow you to pursue another field of interest in addition to your major.

2. Help you make a career choice.

   Just as you can use electives to help you choose a college major, you can use them to help you choose a career. For instance, you could enroll in

   ⊙ career planning or career development courses,

   ⊙ courses that involve internships or service learning experiences, or an independent study course that allows you to study a career that you are considering.

3. Strengthen your skills in areas that may appeal to future employers.

   For example, courses in leadership development, foreign language, or argumentation and debate are educational experiences that may be attractive to future employers and may improve your employment prospects.

4. Help you develop practical life skills that you can use now or in the near future.

   For instance, you might take courses in managing personal finances, marriage and family, or child development to help you manage your money and your future family.

5. Seek personal balance and develop yourself as a whole person.

   You can use your electives strategically to cover all the key dimensions of self-development. For instance, you could take courses that promote your *emotional* development (e.g., stress management), *social* development (e.g., inter-personal relationships), *mental* development (e.g., critical thinking), *physical* development (e.g., nutrition, self-defense), and *spiritual* development (e.g., world religions; death and dying).

 Remember: Choose college courses that will not only contribute to your major and career, but also to your quality of life.

---

6. Make connections across different subjects and academic disciplines.

   Courses that are specifically designed to connect or integrate two or more academic disciplines are typically referred to as interdisciplinary courses. For example, psychobiology is an interdisciplinary course that combines or integrates the fields of psychology (focusing on the mind) and biology (focusing on the body), thus enabling you to see how the mind influences the body and vice versa. Making connections across different subjects and seeing how they can be combined to provide a more complete understanding of a subject or issue can be a stimulating experience. Furthermore, the presence of interdisciplinary courses on your college transcript may also be attractive to future employers.

7. Help you develop broader perspectives on life and the world in which we live.

   As suggested in Chapter 2, you can take courses that progressively widen your perspective. For example, you could strategically select courses that provide you with a *societal* perspective (e.g., sociology), a *national* perspective (e.g., political science), an *international* perspective (e.g., cultural geography), or a *global* perspective (e.g., ecology). These broadening perspectives serve to widen your scope of knowledge and deepen your understanding of the world.

8. Appreciate different cultural viewpoints and improve your ability to communicate with people from diverse cultural backgrounds.

   For instance, you can take courses relating to diversity across nations (e.g., international or cross-cultural awareness), or ethnic and racial diversity within America (e.g., multicultural awareness). For more detailed information on how these courses can contribute to your personal and professional success, see Chapter 8.

(continued)

9. Stretch beyond your familiar or customary learning style to experience different ways of learning and to develop new skills.

Courses are likely to be available to you in college that were never previously available to you, and which focus on skills that you've never had a chance to test-out or develop.

10. Learn something you were always curious about, or something you simply wanted to know more about.

For instance, if you've always been curious about how members of the other sex think and feel, you could take a course on the psychology of men or the psychology of women; or, if you've always been fascinated by movies and how they are made, you might elect to take a course in film-making or cinematography.

Pause for Reflection

What were the top-two strategies you selected from the above list? Why?

After you have accurately identified the requirements for the major you're considering, ask yourself the following two questions:

1. Do the course titles and descriptions appeal to my interests and values?
2. Do I have the abilities or skills needed to do well in these courses?

Also, be aware that college majors often require courses in fields outside of the major. For instance, psychology majors are often required to take at least one course in biology, and business majors are often required to take calculus. If you are interested in majoring in any particular subject area, be sure you are fully aware of such outside requirements and are comfortable with them. You don't want to be surprised by unexpected requirements after you have already committed to a major, particularly if these unanticipated requirements do not match-up well with your personal abilities, interests, or learning styles.

◆ Look over an introductory textbook in the field that you're considering as a major.

Find an introductory book in a major that you are considering, review its table of contents, and ask yourself if the topics are compatible with your academic interests and talents. Read a few pages of the text to get some sense of the writing style used in the field and how comfortable you are with it. You should easily find introductory textbooks for all courses in your college bookstore, the college library, or by asking a faculty member in the field.

◆ Talk with students majoring in the field that you're considering as a major and ask them about their experiences.

Try to speak with several students in the field so that you get a balanced perspective that goes beyond the opinion of just one individual. A good way to find students in the major you're considering is by visiting Major Clubs (e.g., psychology club, history club, etc.) on campus. Also, you could check the catalog for required courses in the major you're considering, and then check the schedule of classes to see when and where these classes meet. This would enable you to find and speak with students who are taking these classes (e.g., by conversing with them before or after the class period). The following questions may be good ones to ask students in a major that you're considering:

◇ What first attracted you to this major?

◇ What do you think are the advantages and disadvantages of majoring in this field?

◇ Knowing what you know now, would you choose the same major again?

Also, ask these students about the quality of teaching and advising in the department. Studies show that different departments within the same college or university can vary greatly in terms of the quality of teaching, as well as their educational philosophy and attitude toward students (Pascarella & Terenzini, 1991).

◆ Sit in on some classes in the field you're considering as a major.

If the class you want to visit is a large class, you probably could just slip into the back row and listen. However, if the class is small, you should ask the instructor's permission. When visiting a class, focus on the content or ideas being covered in class, rather than the instructor's personality or teaching style. (Keep in mind that you're trying to decide if you will major in the subject, not in the teacher.)

◆ Discuss the major you are considering with an academic advisor.

It is probably best to speak with an academic advisor who advises students in a variety of majors, rather than someone who advises only students in one particular academic department or major field. You want to discuss the major with an advisor who is more likely to be neutral and will give you unbiased feedback about the pros and cons of majoring in that field.

Speaking with students majoring in the discipline you are considering is a good way to get a balanced perspective.

◆ Speak with some faculty members in the department that you're considering as a major. Consider asking them the following questions:

◇ What academic skills or qualities are needed for a student to be successful in your field?

◇ What are the greatest challenges faced by students majoring in your field?

◇ What do students seem to like most and least about majoring in your field?

◇ What can students do with a major in your field after college graduation?

◇ What types of graduate programs or professional schools would a student in your major be well prepared to enter?

◆ Visit your Career Center to see if information is available on what college graduates majoring in the field you're considering have gone on to do with that major after graduation. This will give you some idea about the type of careers the major can lead to, or what type of graduate and professional school programs that students may enter after completing a major in the field you're considering.

◆ Surf the Web site of a professional organization associated with the field that you're considering as a major. For example, if you are thinking about becoming an anthropology major, check out the Web site of the American Anthropological Association. If you're considering history as a major, take a look at the Web site of the American Historical Association. The Web site of a professional organization often contains useful information for students who are considering that field as a major. For example, the Web site of the American Philosophical Association contains information about non-academic careers for philosophy majors, and the American Sociological Association's Web site identifies a variety of careers that sociology majors are qualified to pursue after college graduation.

To locate the professional Web site of the field that you might want to explore as a college major, ask a faculty member in that field or complete a search on the Web by simply entering the name of the field, followed by the word "association."

◆ Be sure you know what academic standards must be met for you to be accepted for entry into the major that you're considering. Because of their popularity, certain college majors are impacted or oversubscribed, that is to say, there are more students interested in majoring in these fields than there are openings for them. For instance, pre-professional majors that lead directly to a particular career path can frequently become oversubscribed (e.g., accounting, education, engineering, pre-med, nursing, or physical therapy). On some campuses, these majors are called restricted majors, meaning that departments control their enrollment by limiting the number of students they let into the major. For example, departments may restrict entry to their major by admitting only students who have achieved an overall grade-point average of at least a 3.0 or higher in certain introductory courses required by the majors or by ranking all students who apply by their GPA and counting down until they have filled their maximum number of available spaces (Strommer, 1993).

Students who would like to major in one of these restricted fields, but have not yet been accepted or admitted to it, are sometimes called "shadow majors." In effect, shadow majors are students who have been admitted to their college or university, but have not yet been admitted to their intended major. These students may eventually be admitted to their preferred major, or they may be shut out if they fail to meet the specific standards of the department.

So, be sure you know whether the major you are considering is oversubscribed and has special standards that must be met before you can be admitted. As you complete courses and receive grades, check to see if you are meeting these standards. If you are, then continue your pursuit of that major. If you find yourself failing to meet these standards, increase the amount of time and effort you devote to your studies, and seek assistance from your campus Learning Center. If you are working at your maximum level of effort and are regularly using the learning assistance services available on your campus, but are still not meeting the academic standards of your intended major, then consider consulting with an academic advisor to help you identify an alternative field that may be closely related to the restricted major that you were hoping to enter.

Pause for Reflection

What major(s) at your school are oversubscribed, i.e., have more students wanting to major in the field than there are openings in the field?

◆ Consider the possibility of a college minor in a field that may complement your major.

A college minor usually requires about one-half the number of credits (units) that are required for a college major. Most schools allow you the option of completing a minor along with your major. Check your college catalog to determine which minors are available at your school and what courses are required to complete any minor that appeals to you.

If you have strong interests in two different fields, a minor will allow you to major in one of these fields while minoring in the other. Thus, you can pursue two fields that interest you without having to sacrifice one for the other. Furthermore, a minor can be completed along with most college majors without delaying your time to graduation. (In contrast, a "double major" will typically lengthen your time to graduation because you must complete the separate requirements of two different majors.) Other ways in which you can pursue another field of study along with your major without delaying your time to graduation are through completion of a *cognate* area—which requires fewer courses to complete than a minor (e.g., 4 to 5 courses)—or a *concentration* area—which may require only two to three courses.

Taking a cluster of courses in another field outside your major can be an effective way to strengthen your resume and increase your employment prospects because you demonstrate versatility and gain experience in areas that may be missing or underemphasized by your major. For example, students majoring in the fine arts (music, theatre) or humanities (English, history) may take courses in the fields of mathematics (e.g., statistics), technology (e.g., computer science) and business (e.g., economics), which are not emphasized by their major. In fact, some colleges and universities offer business classes that are open only to liberal arts majors. Employment and career opportunities for non-business majors are enhanced if they have some course work in business (e.g., economics, business administration) (The Board of Trustees, 2005).

Similarly, students majoring in such fields as business or computer science could take a cluster of courses in fine arts or humanities to develop skills and perspectives that are not strongly emphasized in their own major. For instance, they could take foreign language or cross-cultural courses to enhance their career prospects in today's global economy.

●●● **Summary and Conclusion**

This chapter has focused on the *curriculum*, which refers to the total set of courses that your college offers. By the time you graduate, the total set of courses that appear on your college transcript will represent your curriculum. You will have much more choice and control of your curriculum in college than you did in high school. You will choose what field to specialize in (your major), and you will decide what particular electives to take within your major and within the academic areas required for general education.

One of the primary advantages of taking the wide range of courses that make up the liberal arts curriculum is that they enable you to become more aware of different aspects of yourself, while at the same time, you become more aware of the variety of academic disciplines and subject areas that are available to you as possible majors. Your trip through the liberal arts curriculum will likely result in your discovery of new personal interests and new choices for majors, some of which may be in fields that you didn't even know existed.

Also, your exposure to a wide range of subjects provides you with the general context that is needed to make an intelligent selection of your specific major and to understand how your particular major fits into the bigger picture. In other words, you need to take a trip through the forest before you can select the right tree. So, look at your trip through the liberal arts curriculum as an exploratory journey in which you are searching to make three key discoveries:

1.   Discovering the full range of choices for majors that are available to you,
2.   Discovering where your special interests, values, needs, and abilities lie, and
3.   Discovering what specialized major best matches your special interests, values, talents, and abilities.

Even if you have already decided on a major, you will still need to explore specialized fields within your major to find one that is most compatible with your personal interests, abilities, and values. For instance, if you have decided to major in communications, you will still need to select what particular field or communication media to specialize in, such as visual media, print media, or sound media. Similarly, if you are interested in pursuing a career in law, you will eventually need to decide what branch of law you wish to practice.

So, if you have decided on a major field of study, the liberal arts component of your college experience will help you explore specializations within that field by exposing you to a wide variety of subject areas and by testing your skills and interests in these areas. Furthermore, your exposure to different fields of study in the liberal arts curriculum may result in your discovery of a second field that interests you, which you may decide to pursue as a *minor* to accompany your major.

Lastly, keep in mind that approximately one of every three or four courses you'll take in college will be a free elective—your choice of any of the many courses that are listed in your college catalog. This freedom of choice will allow you the opportunity to shape and create an academic experience that is uniquely your own. Seize this opportunity, and exercise your freedom responsibly and reflectively. Do not make choices thoughtlessly, randomly, or solely on the basis of scheduling convenience (e.g., choosing courses to create a schedule with no early morning or late afternoon classes). Instead, make strategic choices of courses that will contribute most to your educational, personal, and professional development. Intentionally select courses with one or more of the following purposes in mind:

Choosing courses that best enable you to achieve your long-term educational and personal goals should take precedence over creating a class schedule that leaves your Fridays free for three-day weekends.

◆ to choose a major or confirm whether your first choice is a good one;
◆ to acquire a minor or build a concentration that will complement your major;
◆ to broaden your perspectives on the world around you;
◆ to become a more balanced or complete human being;
◆ to handle the practical life tasks that face you now and in the future; and
◆ to strengthen your career development and employment prospects after graduation.

With "higher" education comes a "higher" degree of freedom of choice and a greater opportunity to determine your own academic course of action. *Enjoy* it and *employ* it—use your freedom strategically to make the most of your college experience and college degree.

••• Learning More through Independent Research

Web-Based Resources for Further Information on Educational Planning

For additional information relating to the ideas discussed in this chapter, we recommend the following Web sites:

College majors: www.Mymajors.com

Careers for liberal arts majors: www.eace.org/networks/liberalarts.html

Assignment 1. Planning for a College Major

At the end of Chapter 2, you made a tentative plan for the liberal arts (general education) component of your college experience. We now ask you to consider developing a plan for your college major.

STEPS:

1. Go to your college catalog and use its index to locate pages containing information relating to the major you have chosen or are considering. Even if you are "totally undecided," select a field that you might consider as a possibility. To help you identify possible majors, you can use your catalog, or go online and complete the short interview at the following Web site: http://www.Mymajors.com.

   The point of this assignment is not to force you to commit to a major right now, but to familiarize you with the process of developing a plan, so that you can apply it when you do make a firm decision about the major you intend to pursue.

2. Once you've selected a major for this assignment, use your college catalog to identify what courses are required for the major you selected. Use the form below to list the course number and course title of all courses that are required by the major you've selected.

   You will find certain courses required by the major that you must take; these are often called *"core" requirements* for the major. For instance, at most colleges, all business majors must take the course microeconomics. In other cases, you will find that there are courses required for a certain area within your major, but you are allowed to choose them from a list of possible courses (e.g., "choose any three courses from among the following six courses"). Such courses are often called *"restricted electives"* in the major. When you find restricted electives in the major you've selected, read the course descriptions and choose those courses from the list that appeal most to you. Just list the course titles and numbers of these courses on the planning form. You don't need to write down all the possible choices that are listed in the catalog.

   College catalogs can sometimes be tricky to navigate or interpret, so if you run into any difficulty, don't panic. Seek help from an academic advisor, or check with the department secretary in the field you selected as a major to see if the department has created any summary sheets of requirements for a major in that field. Your college may also have a "degree audit" program that allows you to track your degree requirements electronically. If your college has such a program, take advantage of it.

Major Selected _____

Major Core Course Requirements:
Specific courses in your major that you must take

Course #	Course Title	Course #	Course Title

Restricted Electives in the Major:
Courses required for your major that you choose to take from a specified list.

Course #	Course Title	Course #	Course Title

PERSONAL REFLECTIONS ON THIS ASSIGNMENT

After competing this assignment, take a moment to think back on it and answer the following questions.

1. Looking over the courses required for the major you've selected, would you still be interested in majoring in this field?

2. Were there courses required by this major that you were surprised to see, or that you did not expect would be required?

3. Are there any unanswered questions that remain in your mind about this major?

Assignment 2. Developing a Comprehensive, Long-Range Graduation Plan

A comprehensive, long-range graduation plan includes all three key types of courses you need to complete a college degree:

1. Liberal arts requirements,
2. College major requirements, and
3. Free electives.

By combining your plan for required liberal arts courses (assignment at the end of Chapter 2) and your plan for a college major (Assignment 1 of this chapter), you could then add in your free electives to create a comprehensive graduation plan.

Use the form on the following page to develop this complete graduation plan. Use the slots to pencil in the liberal arts courses you're planning to take to fulfill your general education requirements, your major requirements, and your free electives. (Use a pencil so that you can easily make any changes to this plan as you develop or implement it.)

SUGGESTIONS:

1. If you haven't decided on a major, a good strategy might be to concentrate on taking liberal arts courses to fulfill your general-education requirements during your first year of college. This will open more slots in your course schedule during your sophomore year. By that time, you may have a better idea of what you want to major in, and you can fill these open slots with courses required by your major. This may be a particularly effective strategy if you choose to major in a field that has many requirements, because it may be necessary for you to complete several of those requirements before the end of your sophomore year.

2. For ideas on choosing your free electives, see pp. 93–94 in this chapter.

3. Keep in mind that the course number indicates the year in the college experience that the course is usually taken. Courses numbered in the 100s (or below) are typically taken in the first year of college, 200-numbered courses in the sophomore year, 300-numbered courses in the junior year, and 400-numbered courses in the senior year. Also, be sure to check if the course you are planning to take has any pre-requisites—which are courses that need to be completed before you can enroll in the course you're planning to take. (For example, if you're planning to take a course in literature, it is likely that you cannot enroll in it until you have completed at least one pre-requisite course in writing or English composition.)

4. To complete a college degree in four years, you should complete about 30 credits each academic year. Summer term is considered part of an academic year, and we encourage you to use that term to help keep you on a four-year timeline.

5. Check with your course instructor or an academic advisor to see if your college has developed a "projected plan of scheduled courses" for the next few years, which indicates when courses listed in the catalog are scheduled to be offered (e.g., fall, spring, summer). If such a long-range plan of scheduled courses is available, take advantage of it because it will enable you to develop a personal educational plan that includes not only what courses you will take, but also *when* you will take them. This can be a very important advantage because some courses you may need for graduation will not be offered every term. For example, if you're planning to take a course that you need to graduate during your final term in college, and that course is not offered during your final term, you may have to wait until it is offered again. While you wait for the term when that course is offered again, you end-up delaying your graduation and taking a longer time to complete your college degree. So, we strongly encourage you to inquire about and acquire any long-range plan of scheduled courses that may be available at your college or university, and use it to develop your personal, long-range graduation plan.

6. Don't forget to include out-of-class learning experiences as part of your educational plan, such as volunteer service, internships, and study abroad. (For information on these learning experiences, see Chapter 9.)

This long-range graduation plan is not something set in stone. Like clay, its shape can be molded and changed into a different form as you gain more experience with the college curriculum. Nevertheless, your development of this initial plan will remain useful because it provides you with a blueprint to work from. Once you have created slots specifically for your general education requirements, your major courses, and your electives, then you have all the key categories of courses covered and changes to your plan can often be made easily by simple substitution of different courses into the slots you've already created for the three categories of courses.

Remember: The purpose of this long-range planning assignment is not to "lock" you into a "rigid" plan, but to help you create a rough "map" that will enable you to visualize your future years in college. Vision can provide you with a sense of direction that leads to a plan of action, which, in turn, enables you to see a connection between where you are now and where you want to be. Furthermore, this process of visualizing can be energizing, because when you're able to see what's ahead of you, you can see the finish line and what it will take to get you there.

PERSONAL REFLECTIONS ON DEVELOPING A LONG-RANGE GRADUATION PLAN

After completing this assignment, take a moment to think back on it and answer the following questions.

1. Do you think this was a useful assignment? Why? (Or, why not?)

2. Do you see any way in which this assignment could be improved or strengthened?

Whose Choice Is It Anyway?

Ursula, a first-year student, was in tears when she showed up at the Career Center. She had just returned from a weekend visit home, where she informed her parents that she was planning to major in art or theatre. When Ursula's father heard about her plans, he exploded and insisted that she major in something "practical," like business or accounting, so she could earn a living after she graduates. Ursula replied that she had no interest in these majors, nor did she feel she had the skills needed to complete the level of math required by them, which included calculus. Her father shot back that he had no intention of "paying four years of college tuition for her to end up as an unemployed artist or actress!" He went on to say that if she wanted to major in art or theatre, she'd "have to figure out a way to pay for college herself."

Reflection and Discussion Questions

1. What options (if any) do you think Ursula has right now?

2. If Ursula were your friend, what would you recommend she do?

3. Do you see any way(s) in which Ursula might pursue a major that she's interested in, while at the same time, ease her father's worries that she will end up jobless after college graduation?

Strategic Learning

Applying Research on Human Learning and the Human Brain to Acquire Knowledge Effectively and Comprehend It Deeply

Learning Goals

The goal of this chapter is to supply you with a well-designed set of learning strategies that are supported by solid research on how humans learn and how the human brain works.

Outline

Activate Your Thinking

Do you think there is a difference between learning and memorizing?

If yes, what do you think the difference is?

You are likely to experience greater academic challenges in college than you did in high school. Studies show that the percentage of students earning "As" and "Bs" drops from about 50 percent in high school to about 33 percent in college (Astin, 1993; Sax et al., 2004). Learning strategies that enabled you to earn "As" and "Bs" in the past may not earn you those grades now. Thus, to maintain or exceed your level of academic performance in high school, you will need to elevate your performance to a higher level in college. Attaining this higher level of academic performance will probably not involve just working "harder"; it will involve working "smarter" and learning to use effective strategies that are supported by research on how humans learn and how the human brain works.

●●● Brain-Based Learning Principles

Learning becomes more effective and efficient when it is "brain-based" or "brain-compatible" (Hart, 1983) and capitalizes on the brain's natural learning tendencies (Caine & Caine, 1994). Despite the fact that there are differences among us in terms of our intellectual talents and learning styles, we are all members of the human species and we all possess a human brain. Just as all humans have bodily organs that perform specific functions, such as our heart and liver, we also have a brain that functions as the "learning organ" of the body (Zull, 1998). By understanding how the human brain learns, we can capitalize on this knowledge to identify general principles or common themes of learning that work effectively for all humans. You can then convert these general principles into specific strategies that may be used to learn effectively in all subject areas to promote your success across the curriculum (Weinstein, 1982).

The Brain Is Biologically Wired to Seek Meaning

Perhaps the most distinctive and most powerful feature of the human brain is that it is biologically wired to seek meaning (Caine & Caine, 1994). The human brain naturally looks for meaning by trying to connect what it is trying to learn and understand to what it already knows. For instance, when the brain perceives the external world, it looks for meaningful patterns and connections rather than isolated bits and pieces of information (Nummela & Rosengren, 1986). In Figure 4.1, notice how your brain naturally ties together and fills in the missing information to perceive a meaningful whole pattern.

Figure 4.1 Triangle Illusion

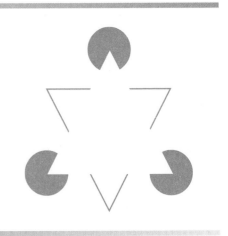

You perceive a white triangle in the middle of this figure. However, if you use three fingers to cover up the three corners of the white triangle that fall outside the other (background) triangle, the white triangle suddenly disappears. What your brain does is take these corners as starting points and fills in the rest of the information on its own to create a complete or whole pattern that has meaning to you. (Notice also how you perceive the background triangle as a complete triangle, even though parts of its left and right sides are missing.)

The brain's natural tendency to seek whole patterns with meaning applies to words as well as images. The following passage once appeared (anonymously) on the Internet. See if you can read it and grasp its meaning.

"Aoccdrnig to rscheearch at Cmabridge Uinverstisy, it deosn't mattaer in what order the ltteers in a word are, the only iprmoetnt thing is that the frist and lsat ltteer be at the rghit pclae. The rset can be a total mses and you can still raed it wouthit a porbelm. This is bcusae the human mind deos not raed ervey lteter by istlef, but the word as a wlohe. Amzanig huh?"

Notice how your brain found the meaning of the misspelled words by naturally transforming them into correctly spelled words that it already knew or understood. We tend to see whole patterns because the knowledge we have in our brain is stored in the form of a connected network of brain cells (Coward, 1990). Thus, whenever we learn something, we do so by connecting what we're trying to understand to what we previously know and what we have already stored in our brain.

When we learn by making meaningful connections, this is referred to as *deep learning* (Entwistle & Ramsden, 1983). To "deeply" learn the challenging concepts you'll encounter in college will require active mental involvement and personal reflection on the information you receive. You will need to move beyond shallow memorization to deeper levels of comprehension. When you learn deeply, you don't just take in information; you take the additional step of actively reflecting on it. This also involves a shift away from the old view that learning occurs by passively absorbing information like a sponge, whereby you receive it from the teacher or text and study it in exactly the same, pre-packaged form you received it. Instead, you want to adopt a different approach to learning that involves actively transforming information you receive into a form that is meaningful to you (Entwistle & Marton, 1984; Feldman & Paulsen, 1994).

Pause for Reflection

When you try to acquire knowledge or learn new information, do you tend to memorize it in the form in which it's presented to you, or do you usually try to transform it into your own words?

Personal Story When my son was about 3 years old, we were riding in the car together and listening to a song by the Beatles titled, "Sergeant Pepper's Lonely Heart Club Band." You may be familiar with this tune, but in case you're not, there is a part in it where the following lyrics are sung over and over: "Sergeant Pepper's Lonely, Sergeant Pepper's Lonely, Sergeant Pepper's Lonely . . . ."

When this part of the song was being played, I noticed that my 3-year-old son was singing along. I thought that it was pretty amazing for a boy his age to be able to understand and repeat those lyrics. However, when that part of the song came on again, I noticed that he wasn't singing "Sergeant Pepper's Lonely, Sergeant Pepper's Lonely . . ." etc. Instead, he was singing: "Sausage Pepperoni, Sausage Pepperoni . . ." (which were his two favorite pizza toppings).

So, I guess my son's brain was doing what it tends to do naturally. It took unfamiliar information (song lyrics) that didn't make any sense to him and transformed it into a form that was very meaningful to him!

—Joe Cuseo

New Knowledge Is Built on Knowledge Already Possessed

Acquiring knowledge isn't a matter of pouring information into the brain, as if it were an empty jar; it's a matter of building new knowledge onto knowledge you already possess (Piaget, 1978; Vygotsky, 1978), or attaching it to information that is already stored in the brain.

When people understand a concept, a physical or biological connection is made between brain cells, whereby the new information gets connected into a network of connections that have already been made in the brain (Alnon, 1992). Thus, deep learning is learning that actually changes the brain. The following figure (Figure 4.2) shows a microscopic section of the human brain that specializes in the learning of language. Notice that the number of brain cells (black spots) in a newborn baby and a 6-year-old child are about the same. However, the 6-year-old's brain almost looks like a forest because there are many more connections between brain cells; these connections represent all the language (e.g., vocabulary words) the child has learned in six years of life.

Figure 4.2

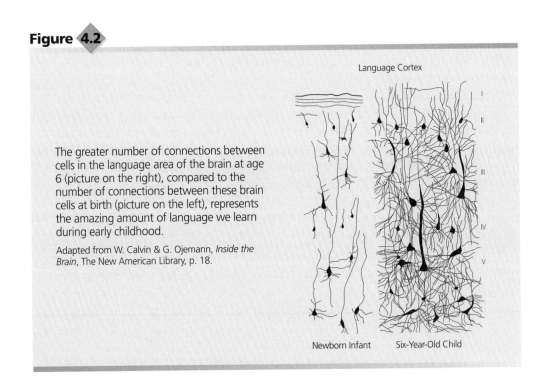

Language Cortex

The greater number of connections between cells in the language area of the brain at age 6 (picture on the right), compared to the number of connections between these brain cells at birth (picture on the left), represents the amazing amount of language we learn during early childhood.

Adapted from W. Calvin & G. Ojemann, *Inside the Brain*, The New American Library, p. 18.

Newborn Infant   Six-Year-Old Child

Shallow, Surface-Oriented versus Deep, Meaning-Oriented Approaches to Learning

It has been found that students have different methods of processing or handling information they are trying to learn (Schmeck, 1981; Entwistle & Marton, 1984). Some students take a shallow, surface-oriented approach to learning in which they spend most of their study time repeating and memorizing information in the exact form that it's presented to them. Other students use a deep, meaning-oriented style of learning in which they deal with new information by elaborating on it—changing it from the form they received it into a form of their own—by restating it in their own words and relating it to their own experiences. They spend most of their study time thinking about and trying to understand what they're learning, rather than repeating and memorizing it.

Figure 4.3 Memorizing Factual Information

SURFACE /Shallow LEARNING

DEEP LEARNING

(Going beneath the surface to a deeper level of learning involves comprehension rather than memorization)

Studies show that academically successful students dive below the surface of shallow memorization to a deeper level of learning that involves seeking meaning and understanding.

Studies of these two methods of learning reveal that the shallow, surface-oriented approach tends to result in poorer memory for studied material (Watkins, 1983) and lower college grades than the deep, meaning-oriented approach (Ramsden, 2003). For example, in a study of engineering students, those students who used a surface approach to learning earned lower grades, even though they had high class-attendance rates and spent a great amount of time studying outside of class. Despite the fact that these students attended class regularly and put in sufficient study time, their method of study was not as effective as those students who took a deeper, meaning-oriented approach to learning (Kember, Jamieson, Pomfret, & Wong, 1995).

Although there may be times in college when you simply have to remember information that is presented to you, the primary goal of your studying should be to seek deep learning and comprehension, rather than settling for shallow memorization and repetition. Seeking meaning not only results in learning that is deeper, but also results in memory that is more *durable*—it's more likely to "stick" or remain in your brain for a longer period of time (Craik & Lockhart, 1972; Craik & Tulving, 1975).

 Remember: Deep, long-lasting learning requires an active search for meaning via personal reflection, rather than passive memorizing via mindless repetition.

Finding meaning in what you're learning means you truly understand it, which enables you to connect it with the knowledge you already possess and apply it to new situations you'll encounter in the future (Ramsden, 2003).

Since our brains naturally seek meaning, when you learn by searching for meaning, it also makes the process of learning more stimulating and more motivating than learning by memorizing and repeating, which can quickly become very monotonous, mindless, and boring. In fact, interviews with students show that those who use a deep approach to learning are more likely to report a higher level of personal satisfaction and interest in what they're learning than students who use a surface approach (Biggs, 1987; Marton, et al., 1997; Marton & Saljo, 1984).

Pause for Reflection

Look back at your response to the question asked at the very start of this chapter about whether there is a difference between learning and memorization. Based on the information you've read thus far in this chapter, would you modify or change your answer in any way?

••• Stages in the Learning and Memory Process

Although deep learning is the ultimate goal or final stage you want to achieve, to get there requires successful completion of a series of stages in the process of learning and memory. Learning deeply, and remembering what you've learned, is a process that involves three key stages:

1. getting information into your brain (*perception*),
2. keeping it there (*storage*), and
3. finding it when you need it (*retrieval*).

You can consider these stages of human learning and memory to be similar to the way information is processed by a computer: (a) information first gets typed onto the screen, (b) the information is kept or stored by saving it in a memory file, and (c) the information is found by calling up or retrieving that file when it's needed.

We'll now take a more detailed look at each of these three key stages in the learning-memory process and relate them to learning in college.

Stage 1. Perception: Receiving Information from the Senses and Sending It to the Brain

If you are not actively paying attention while looking at a sign, the message can reach your eyes but not register in your brain.

This is the first step in the learning process because we must first attend to and receive information in order to get it into our brain—where it is then registered or perceived. All information from the outside world gets to the brain through our senses (e.g., sight and sound), but it will only reach and get registered in our brain if we pay attention to it.

Contrary to popular belief, not all information that reaches our senses is received and registered in our brain (Rose, 1993). Although information may reach our eyes and ears, if we are not paying close enough attention to it, it will not register in our brain and we will not perceive it. Have you ever had the experience of driving right past an exit that you were supposed to take? Your eyes were fully open and the exit sign was in your field of vision when you passed it, but because you weren't paying close enough attention to it, it didn't register in your brain and you never perceived it.

Only information that we pay attention to gets registered by our conscious brain because the lower, subconscious part of our brain works as an attention filter by selectively letting in or keeping sensory information from reaching the upper parts of the brain—where it is consciously perceived (Figure 4.4).

Figure The Brain's Human Attention System

Information reaching our senses must pass through lower, subconscious parts of the brain that act as an attention filter or gatekeeper, determining whether sensory information will be sent to upper parts of the brain where it is consciously received (perceived).

Pause for Reflection

People often forget the name of someone immediately after being introduced. What do you think causes this memory failure?

In fact, one of the major causes of forgetting is our failure to pay enough attention to what we want to remember; as a result, this information never registers in our brain in the first place. For example, forgetting where we put our keys or where we parked our car are classic examples of inattention or "absentmindedness." We forget these sorts of things because our brain never received the information in the first place. Our mind was not consciously present.

As these examples illustrate, attention is a critical prerequisite for learning and memory to take place.

 Remember:
If there is no attention, there can be no retention.

In college, there are two key sensory channels or routes through which you will receive information:

1. Hearing—listening to lectures, and
2. Seeing—reading information from textbooks.

For learning to occur through either of these routes, the critical first step is to attend to and make note of the information you receive. Simply stated, you cannot learn and retain information that you've never attended to and acquired in the first place.

Personal Story

My son Michael is notorious for wanting to do everything that we ask his younger sister to do, and very little of what we ask him to do. A classic example is when we send him to any room to retrieve any object. My wife and I now measure how long it will take him to bring the wanted item back to us. (However, if we're in a hurry, we usually get it ourselves.) This is how it usually goes. "Michael, please go into the master bathroom and get the nail clippers." Michael, who will be seven at the time of this publication, walks slowly toward the bathroom. In a few minutes, he'll walk back into the room where we are, carrying some object he has started to construct (perhaps he'll grow up to be an engineer). When we ask him for the clippers, he'll say: "Oh, I forgot." In reality, he was not paying attention to our request, and it never registered in his brain. However, if we asked Maya (our daughter) to retrieve the item, Michael bowls her over to retrieve it. He listens well when Maya's name is called. The plan in our household now is to ask Maya for everything and let her actually get it when Michael is not around.

—*Aaron Thompson, Professor of Sociology*

Stage 2. Storage: Keeping Information in the Brain

If information passes through our attention filter and is consciously perceived by our brain, it enters into one of the following memory systems:

◆ short-term memory—where it lasts for only a few seconds; or

◆ working memory—where you can consciously hold it in your mind and "work on it" for an extended period of time.

Have you ever walked into a room to do or get something, but once you got there, you had no idea why you were there? This experience illustrates the difference between short-term and working memory. What happened is that you had an idea in your short-term memory about something you were going to do or get in that room, but you then began thinking about something else after you had this thought, and by the time you got to the room, the thought had faded from your working memory. If you had kept that thought in your working memory, you would have been able to hold onto it and would have remembered why you went into the room after you got there.

To get information to stay in the brain for more than a short period of time, it has to be transferred from working memory, which is a temporary memory system, and moved into a different memory system known as *long-term memory*. Similar to a computer, we can get information onto the screen (short-term memory) and work on it (working memory), but if we want our computer to save the information we've worked on, we have to store it in the computer's long-term memory system.

The part of the brain that enables you to transfer memories from short-term to longer-term memory is known as the hippocampus (Squire, 1992) (Figure 4.5). If the hippocampus is permanently damaged, an individual cannot store long-term memories. Or, if the hippocampus is temporarily slowed down by alcohol or marijuana, it can interfere with memory storage (for example, memory "blackouts" experienced by someone for events that occurred during a night of excessive drinking).

The process of storing information in long-term memory is referred to as *coding*, and the information that's stored is referred to as a *memory trace*—a physical or biological trace of the memory in the brain. (Note: The term memory "trace" is consistent with the word "learning"—which derives from the root word meaning "footprint" or "track.") Relating this to college learning, when you're studying, you are trying to register a memory trace by transferring

Brain image © David Huntley, 2007. Under license from Shutterstock, Inc.

The hippocampus is the part of the brain that enables us to transfer information from short-term memory to association areas in the upper part of the brain where it is stored in long-term memory.

Long-Term Memory Storage

Hippocampus (Short-Term Memory)

information from working memory to encode it in long-term storage so that you can recall it at test time. How well the information you have studied will stick in your brain depends on how effectively or deeply you learned it—the deeper the learning, the stronger its memory trace.

Memory Tips

The following strategies will help you to learn more deeply and better retain information that you're studying:

- connect or relate the information to something you already know;

- organize it into some classification system;

- take it in through multiple sensory modalities—e.g., see it, hear it, draw it, and feel it; and

- practice it at different times. (These strategies are discussed more fully later in the chapter.)

Pause for Reflection

It's common to hear students say, "I knew it when I studied it, but I forgot it on the test."

What do you think causes this common occurrence?

How might students study differently to prevent this from happening?

Stage 3. Retrieval: Finding Information That's Been Stored in the Brain and Bringing It Back to Consciousness

Getting information into the brain and getting it to stay there are the first two critical stages in the learning-memory process. The final stage is finding the stored memory and bringing it back to mind. To use the computer analogy, when your computer retrieves a file, it searches through the stored files, finds the particular file you need, and then brings it back to the screen in front of you. Relating this to college learning, the retrieval stage of memory corresponds to test taking. You first attend to and receive information from lectures and readings; you later study that information; and, finally, you attempt to retrieve that information at test time.

Evidence supporting the importance of the retrieval stage of memory comes from what researchers call the "tip of the tongue" phenomenon (Brown & McNeill, 1966). You've probably said to yourself: "Oh, I've got it (the memory) on the tip of my tongue." For example, you're taking an exam, you studied the material well, and you know the information that's being asked for in the test question, but you just can't quite get it to come back to you. However, after the test is over, it suddenly comes back to you when it's too late to use it! This demonstrates the memory trace was in your brain the entire time; you just weren't able to access and retrieve it.

Thus, retrieval represents the third and final stage of the memory process. All of the key stages in the processes of learning memory that we have discussed so far are summarized visually in Figure 4.6.

Figure 4.6 Key Stages in the Learning and Memory Process

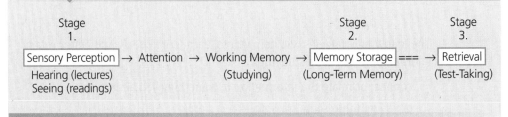

Pause for Reflection

For each of the three stages that make up the learning and memory process, how would you rate yourself in terms of your ability or past performance?

1. *Attention to information presented in class and in reading assignments (strong, average, or weak?)*

2. *Studying—preparing for exams and getting information to "store" in your brain (strong, average, or weak?)*

3. *Test-taking—retrieving information that you've studied at test time and getting it down on paper (strong, average, or weak?)*

This information about the key stages in the learning-memory process can be applied to generate a series of practical strategies that you can use to improve your performance on each of the following academic tasks:

◆ listening to lectures and note-taking,
◆ textbook reading, and
◆ studying.

●●● Lecture Listening and Note-Taking Strategies

Information from class lectures represents one of the major sources of information that your brain must first take in for successful learning to eventually take place. Described are strategies for effective lecture listening and note-taking.

The Importance of Taking Notes

Studies show that information found in professors' lectures is the number-one source of test questions (and answers) on college exams (Brown, 1988; Kuhn, 1988). When lecture information appears on a test and has not been recorded in students' notes, it has only a 5 percent chance of being recalled (Kiewra, et al., 2000). This means that you should view each lecture like it is a test-review session during which your instructor is giving out test answers.

The importance of effective listening and note-taking for college success is highlighted by a study conducted with an entire freshman class of over 400 students who were given a listening test at the start of their first term in college. At the end of their first year, 49% of those students who scored low on the listening test were on academic probation at the end of their freshman year, compared to only 4.4% of students who scored high on the listening test. On the other hand, 68.5% of students who scored high on the listening test were eligible for the Honors program at the end of their first year, compared to only 4.17% of those students who had low listening-test scores (Conaway, 1982).

Contrary to popular belief that writing interferes with listening, students themselves report that taking notes actually increases their attention and concentration in class (Hartley & Marshall, 1974; Hartley, 1998). Studies also show that when students write down information that is presented to them rather than just listening to it, they are more likely to remember the most important aspects of that information when they are later given a memory test. Students who write notes during lectures have been found to achieve higher course grades than students who just listen to lectures (Kiewra, 1985), and students with a more complete set of notes tend to demonstrate higher levels of academic achievement (Kiewra & Fletcher, 1984). For instance, one study discovered that successful students (GPAs of 2.53 or higher) record more information in their notes and retain a larger percentage of the most important information than students with GPAs less than 2.53 (Einstein, Morris, & Smith, 1985). These findings are not surprising when you consider that *hearing* lecture information, *writing* it, and *seeing* it while writing, provide three different memory traces in the brain that can combine to improve your memory for that information. Furthermore, students with a good set of notes have a written record of that information, which can be re-read, reflected on, and studied later.

Students who take notes during lectures have been found to achieve higher class grades than those who just listen.

© JupiterImages Corporation.

Remember: Come to class with the attitude that your instructors are throwing out answers to test questions as they speak; your purpose for being there is to pick-out and pick-up these answers. Take on the role of an active, investigative reporter who has an inquiring mind and an intense interest in acquiring important information.

Focus Your Attention

Attention is the critical first step to successful learning and memory. However, our attention span is limited, so it's impossible to attend to and make note of every piece of information that an instructor delivers in class. Thus, you need to use *selective attention* to attend to and select the most relevant or important information to record in your notes. Listed below are some key strategies for doing so.

◆ Pay special attention to any **information your instructors put in writing**—on the board, on an overhead, on a slide, or in a handout. If your instructor has taken the time and energy to write it out, that's usually a good clue that it is important information and you're likely to see it again—on an exam.

◆ Pay close attention to **information presented during the first few minutes and last few minutes of class.** Instructors are more likely to provide valuable reminders, reviews, and previews at the very start and very end of class.

◆ **Use your instructor's verbal and nonverbal cues** to detect important information. What the instructor writes out is not the only information that is important. It has been found that students record almost 90 percent of information that is written on the board, but they only record about 50 percent of important ideas that instructors state but don't write on the board (Locke, 1977). So, don't fall into the reflex-like routine of just writing something in your notes when you see your instructor writing something on the board. You also have to listen actively to record important ideas in your notes that you hear your instructor saying. In Box 4.1 are some specific strategies for detecting important information being delivered orally by your instructors during lectures.

TAKE ACTION NOW! | Box 4.1

How to Detect When Instructors Are Delivering Important Information During Class Lectures

1. **Verbal cues:**
   ⊙ Using phrases that signal important information, such as: "The key point here is . . ." "What's most significant about this is . . ."
   ⊙ Repeating information or rephrasing it in a different way (such as saying: "In other words, . . .").
   ⊙ Following stated information with a question to check students' understanding (e.g., "Is that clear?" "Do you follow that?" "Does that make sense?" "Are you with me?").

2. **Vocal (tone of voice) cues:**
   ⊙ Information that is delivered louder or at a higher pitch than usual, which may indicate excitement or emphasis.
   ⊙ Information delivered at a slower rate or with more pauses than usual, which may be your instructor's way of giving you more time to write down these especially important ideas.

3. **Nonverbal cues:**
   ⊙ Information delivered by the instructor with more than usual:
      a. facial expressiveness—e.g., raised or furrowed eyebrows;
      b. body movement—e.g., more gesturing and animation;
      c. eye contact—e.g., looking at the faces of students to see if they are following or understanding what is being said.
   ⊙ Information delivered with the instructor's body oriented directly toward the class—i.e., delivering information with both shoulders directly (squarely) facing the class.
   ⊙ Moving closer to the students—e.g., instructor moving away from the podium or blackboard to move closer to the class.

Taking Notes

Adopt a seating location that will maximize your focus of attention and minimize possible sources of distraction. Studies show that students who sit in the front and center of the classroom tend to attain higher exam scores (Rennels & Chaudhair, 1988). One study discovered a direct relationship between test scores and seating distance from the front of class: Students in the front scored 80 percent; those seated in the middle scored 71.6 percent; and those seated in the back rows of class scored 68.1 percent on course exams (Giles, 1982). Such results are found even when students are assigned seats by their instructor, so they are not simply due to the fact that more motivated students tend to sit in the front and center of the room. Instead, the higher academic performance of students sitting front and center is likely to have something to do with a learning advantage provided by these seating positions. Front-and-center seating probably improves academic performance by allowing students better vision of the blackboard, better hearing of what is being said by the instructor, and greater eye contact with the instructor—which may increase their sense of personal responsibility to listen and take notes on what their instructor is saying.

© JupiterImages Corporation.

Studies show that students who sit in the front and center of a classroom tend to earn higher test scores.

When you enter the classroom, step up to the front of class and sit down. In large-sized classes, it is particularly important that you sit in front and "get up close and personal" with your instructors. This will not only improve your attention and note-taking; it should also improve your instructor's ability to remember who you are and how well you performed in class, which will work to your benefit if you ever need a letter of recommendation from that instructor.

Be aware of how your social seating position affects your behavior in the classroom. Intentionally sit near classmates who will not distract you or interfere with the quality of your note-taking. Attention comes in degrees or amounts; you can give all of it or part of it to whatever task you're performing. When you are in class trying to grasp complex information, this task demands your undivided attention.

> **Remember:** When you enter a classroom, you have a choice about where you are going to sit. Choose wisely by selecting a location that will maximize your focus of attention and the quality of your note-taking.

The evolution of student attention from the back to the front of class.

Adopt a seating posture that screams attention. Sitting upright and leaning forward is more likely to maximize your attention because these signals from your body will reach and influence your mind. If your body is in an alert and ready position, your mind tends to pick up these bodily cues and follow your body's lead by becoming more alert and ready to learn. Just as baseball players assume their "ready position" in the field before a pitch is delivered so that they are in a better postural position to catch batted balls, learners who assume a ready position in the classroom put themselves in a better position to mentally "catch" spoken ideas. Studies show that when humans are ready and expecting to capture an idea, greater amounts of the brain chemical C-kinase is released at the connection points between different brain cells, which increases the likelihood that a branched learning connection is formed between them (Howard, 2000).

Also, be aware that we may sometimes give others and ourselves the impression that we're actively listening because it is the polite thing to do; however, we may just be listening passively, partially, or not at all. For instance, when we're being introduced to someone for the first time, we may appear to be politely listening and paying attention to the person's name; however, we may not be listening carefully at all because we're thinking about what to say next or worrying about the type of impression we're making. When we run into that same person again five minutes later, we're embarrassed to learn that we've forgotten the person's name—which indicates that we weren't really listening and paying attention when we first heard it.

So, one aspect of effective listening in the classroom is to pay attention to whether you're really paying attention. Often the best way to do so is to check your own body language. Listed in Box 4.2 are some key nonverbal signals that often provide a good indication of whether or not you're listening actively and attending closely to what your instructor is saying in class.

Making a conscious effort to focus your attention in the classroom is particularly important during the first year of college because class sizes for introductory courses are often larger than other college courses or courses you had in high school. When class size gets larger, individuals tend to feel more anonymous, which may reduce their feelings of personal responsibility and their sense of active involvement. In large-class settings, it becomes especially important to fight off both distractions and the tendency to slip into "attention drift."

Lastly, there is another major advantage of maintaining your focus of attention in class: You send a clear message to your instructor that you're a motivated, conscientious, and courteous

---

TAKE ACTION NOW!   Box 4.2

Nonverbal Signals Indicating That You're Paying Close Attention During Lectures

1. Your body is oriented directly toward the instructor, so that your shoulders line up squarely with the instructor's shoulders (as opposed to one shoulder facing the instructor and your other shoulder facing away—which is known as giving someone "the cold shoulder").

2. Your body is upright or tilting slightly forward (rather than leaning back—which may mean you are "kicking back" and "zoning out").

3. You make occasional eye contact with the instructor—rather than making no eye contact at all (e.g., looking out the window) or continually staring/gazing at the instructor like you're in a mesmerized trance. Studies show that when a person makes periodic eye contact and then looks away for a moment to the left or right (referred to as "lateral eye movements" or "LEMS"), this indicates that the person is really listening to and thinking about what is being said (Glenberg, Schroeder, & Robertson, 1998).

4. Your head nods periodically and slowly—not continuously and rapidly—which usually means that you want the speaker to hurry up and finish so you don't have to listen anymore.

student. This can influence your instructor's perception and evaluation of your academic performance, either consciously or subconsciously. If you're on the border between two grades at the end of the term, you may get the benefit of the doubt. In contrast, inattentive or discourteous behavior in the classroom is likely to have the opposite effect on your instructors' perception and evaluation of you, which may lower your grade.

One survey revealed that college professors found the following student behaviors in the classroom to be especially irritating, so be sure to avoid them (Box 4.3).

 BOX 4.3 Snapshot SUMMARY

Pet Peeves of College Professors

Surveys show that professors really hate it when students:

1. Carry on personal conversations with others during a lecture.
2. Miss class and ask, "Did I miss anything important?"
3. Place their head on the desk or fall asleep during class.
4. Are excessively tardy.
5. Fail to bring required materials to class.
6. Are excessively absent.
7. Miss a lecture and then expect the professor to provide them with a personal encore.

Source: Larry Ludewig, college professor, cited in Vogt (1994).

Question Frequently Asked by Students After Missing a Class

Responses from Tom Wayman, Professor of Creative Writing, University of Calgary.

Nothing. When we realized you weren't here we sat with our hands folded on our desks in silence, for the full two hours.

Everything. I gave an exam worth 40 percent of the grade for this term and assigned some reading due today on which I'm about to hand out a quiz worth 50 percent.

Nothing. None of the content of this course has value or meaning. Take as many days off as you like: Any activities we undertake as a class I assure you will not matter either to you or me and are without purpose.

Everything. A few minutes after we began last time, a shaft of light descended and an angel or other heavenly being appeared and revealed to us what each woman or man must do to attain divine wisdom in this life and the hereafter. This is the last time the class will meet before we disperse to bring this good news to all people on earth . . .

And you weren't there.

"The student question that drove Professor Jenkins over the edge!"

Take organized notes. Keep taking notes in the same paragraph if the instructor is continuing on the same point or idea; for each new concept the instructor introduces, skip a few lines and shift to a new paragraph. Be alert to phrases that your instructor may state to indicate a shift to a new or different idea (e.g., "Let's turn to . . ."), and use these phrases as cues for taking notes in paragraph form. This will strengthen the organization of your notes, which, in turn, will improve your comprehension and retention of them. Also, leaving extra space between paragraphs will give you some room to add information that you may have missed and to add your own thoughts or to paraphrase lecture notes into your own words.

Take your own notes in class. Do not rely on someone else to take notes for you. Taking your own notes in your own words will ensure that they have meaning to you. You can rely on classmates for the purpose of comparing notes for completeness and accuracy, or to get notes if you are forced to miss class. However, do not routinely rely on others to take notes for you. Studies show that students who record and review their own notes earn higher scores on memory tests for that information than students who review the notes of others (Fisher & Harris, 1973). These findings point to the importance of taking and studying your own notes because they have personal meaning to you.

If you do not immediately understand what your instructor is saying, don't stop taking notes. Keep taking notes, even if you are temporarily confused, because this will at least leave you with a record of the information that you can reflect on later, when you will have more time to think about it and grasp it. If you still don't understand it after taking more time to reflect on it, then you can check with your textbook, your instructor, or a classmate.

Remember: Your primary goal during lectures is to get important information into your brain long enough to note it mentally and then physically—by recording it in your notes. Fully comprehending and deeply understanding that information may have to come later, when you have time to reflect on the ideas you've written.

Before individual class sessions, check your syllabus to see where you are in the course and determine how the upcoming class fits into the total course picture. This strategy will strengthen your learning by allowing you to see how the parts relate to the whole.

If possible, get to class ahead of time, so you can look over your notes from the previous class session and your notes from any reading assignment relating to the day's lecture topic. Research indicates that when students review information relating to a lecture topic before hearing the lecture, it improves their ability to take more accurate and complete notes during the lecture (Ladas, 1980). This research supports the strategy of reading textbook information relating to the lecture topic *before* hearing the lecture, because this will help you better understand the lecture and take better notes. A brief review of previously learned information serves to activate your previous knowledge, getting it into your working memory so you'll be in a better position to build a mental bridge from one class to the next. This will help you relate new information to what you've already experienced, which is essential for deep learning.

What do you tend to do immediately after a class session ends?

Why?

As soon as class ends, quickly check your notes for missing information or incomplete thoughts. You can do this by yourself, or better yet, with a motivated classmate. If you both have gaps, check them out with your instructor before s/he leaves the classroom. Even though it may be weeks before you will be tested on this material, the quicker you address missed points and misunderstood ideas, the better, because you'll be able to avoid the last-minute, mad rush of students seeking help from the instructor just before test time. You want to reserve the critical time period just before exams to review a whole set of complete and accurate notes—rather than rushing around, trying to find missing information and trying to understand concepts that were presented weeks ago.

As soon as possible after the end of a class session, reflect on your notes and make them meaningful to you.

In college, your professors will often be lecturing on information that you may have little prior knowledge about, so it is unrealistic to expect that you will understand everything that's being said the first time you hear it. Instead, you'll need to take time to reflect on and review your notes to make sense of them. During this review and reflection process, we recommend that you take notes on your notes by:

◆ translating technical information into your own words to make them more meaningful to you, and

◆ reorganizing your notes to get ideas relating to the same points in the same place or category.

Studies show that when students are instructed to organize lecture information into meaningful categories, they show greater recall on a delayed memory test for that information than students who were simply told to review their notes (Howe, 1970). We recommend that you do this review and reorganization of your notes as soon as possible after class because the information may still be fresh in your mind and will become more easily locked into memory storage before forgetting takes place.

Remember: Look at note-taking as a two-stage process; stage one is aggressively taking notes in class (active involvement), and stage two occurs at a later point in time—when you think about those notes more deeply (personal reflection).

Honestly rate yourself in terms of how frequently you use the following note-taking strategies, using the following scale: 4 = always, 3 = sometimes, 2 = rarely, 1 = never.

1. *I take notes aggressively in class.* 4 3 2 1

2. *I sit near the front of the room in my classes.* 4 3 2 1

3. *I sit upright and lean forward while in class.* 4 3 2 1

4. *I take notes on what my instructors say, not just what they write on the board.* 4 3 2 1

5. *I pay special attention to information presented at the very start and very end of class.* 4 3 2 1

6. *I take notes in paragraph form.* 4 3 2 1

7. *I review my notes immediately after class to check if they are complete and accurate.* 4 3 2 1

••• Strategies for Improving Textbook-Reading Comprehension and Retention

Following lecture notes, information from reading assignments is the second most frequent source of test questions on college exams (Brown, 1988). You will encounter test questions based on information found in your assigned readings that your professors may not have explicitly talked about in class. College professors often expect you to relate or connect what they are lecturing about in class with the reading they have assigned. Furthermore, professors often deliver class lectures with the assumption that you have done the assigned reading, so if you haven't done it, you may have great difficulty following what your instructor is saying in class. Unfortunately, studies show that only about 25 percent of students in class complete the course reading that their professor has assigned them to read before coming to class on any particular day (Hobson, 2004).

The bottom line is this: Do the assigned reading and do it according to the schedule that your instructors have assigned. This will help you comprehend lectures and improve the quality of your participation in class. Better yet, when you complete your reading assignments, use reading strategies that capitalize on the most effective principles of human learning and memory, such as those listed below.

© Stockbyte.

Although keeping up with class reading is important, you should also utilize effective learning strategies to get the most from the material you read.

Before Beginning to Read

Before beginning to read, first see how the assigned reading fits into the overall organizational structure of the book and the course. You can do this efficiently by just taking a look at the book's table of contents to see where the chapter you're about to read is placed in the sequence of chapters in the book, particularly the chapters that immediately precede and follow it. This will give you a sense of how the particular part you're focusing on relates to the whole. Research shows that if learners have advance knowledge of how information is organized, and if they "see the whole" (how all the information is connected) before examining its parts, their ability to understand and remember that information is improved (Ausubel, 1978; Kintsch, 1994).

Before you begin to read a chapter, preview it by reading its boldface headings and any chapter outline, objectives, summary, or end-of-chapter questions that may be provided. Sometimes when you dive into details too quickly, you lose sight of how the details relate to the big picture. As we've previously discussed, the brain's natural tendency is to perceive and comprehend whole patterns rather than isolated bits of information. Start by seeing how the different parts of the text are integrated into the whole. In so doing, you're essentially seeing the total picture of a completed jigsaw puzzle. By seeing how its separate pieces will fit together, you can more effectively comprehend the content of the chapter.

So, get in the habit of previewing what is in a chapter to get an overall sense of its organization before jumping right into the content.

After previewing the chapter, take a moment to think about what ideas or knowledge you may already have that relates to the chapter's topic. By taking a minute to think about what you may already know about the topic you're about to read, you can activate the areas of your brain where that knowledge is stored, thereby preparing it to make meaningful connections with the information you are about to read.

While Reading

Read selectively by noting or highlighting the most important information for later review. Here are three key strategies that will help you decide what to note or highlight in your reading as important information.

1. Use boldface or dark-print headings and subheadings as cues for identifying important information.

    These headings serve to organize the chapter's content, and you can use them as "traffic signs" to direct you to the chapter's most important concepts. These headings are the key clues to finding the important information in the chapter.

    Better yet, turn the headings into questions, and then read the information beneath them to find their answers. This will send you on an answer-finding mission that can keep you mentally active and allow you to read with a purpose—to find answers to the questions you've created out of the headings.

 Memory Tips To help you remember to use this strategy, we recommend that you place a question mark after each heading while you're previewing or surveying the chapter.

Creating and answering questions while you are reading is also motivating because you feel rewarded when you find answers to the questions you've created (Walter, Knudsbig, & Smith, 2003). Furthermore, answering questions while you are reading is an ideal way to prepare for tests because you're practicing exactly what you'll be doing on tests, which will be to answer questions. Also, you can conveniently use the heading questions as "flash cards" to review for exams by trying to remember the key information you've highlighted under each heading.

2. Pay special attention to the first and last sentences in each paragraph.

These sentences often contain an important introduction and conclusion to the ideas covered in that passage of the text. In fact, when reading sequential or cumulative material that requires you to understand what was previously covered in order to understand what's covered next, it is a good idea to quickly reread the first and last sentences of each paragraph you've just finished reading before moving on to read the next paragraph.

3. Re-read the chapter after you've heard your instructor lecture on the chapter's topic.

You can use your lecture notes as a guide to help you focus on what particular information in the chapter your instructor feels is most important. If you adopt this strategy, you will be able to read before lectures to help you better understand the lecture and take better class notes, and you can use your reading after lectures to help you better identify and understand the most important information contained in your textbook.

 Remember: Your goal when reading is not merely to "cover" the assigned pages, but to "uncover" the most important information and ideas contained in those pages.

Adjust your reading speed to the type of subject matter that you're reading. Academic reading is more technical and mentally challenging than popular reading, such as reading magazines or newspapers, so do not attempt to read college texts all at the same speed. Furthermore, certain academic subjects place greater demands on your working memory than others, so you cannot expect to read all types of academic material at the same rate. For instance, material in the natural and social sciences is likely to have more technical terminology and will need to be read at a slower rate than a novel or short story. For more technical subjects, you may not understand the material when you first read it, so you may need to re-read what you have just read to get a better understanding of it.

Remain aware of your reading rate. If you find yourself reading different subjects at the same speed, you may need to better regulate and accommodate your reading speed to the type of material you are reading.

Find the meaning of unfamiliar words that you encounter while reading. Knowing the meaning of specific terms is important in any college course, but it is absolutely critical in courses whose subject matter builds on knowledge of previously covered information, such as math and science. If you do not learn the meaning of key terms as you read them, you cannot build upon this knowledge to understand information that is covered later.

Have a dictionary available, and if the textbook has a glossary, make regular use of it. In fact, you may want to make a photocopy of the textbook's glossary (typically located at the end of the text) because this will save you the hassle of having to repeatedly hold your place in the chapter with one hand while using the other to find the meaning of unfamiliar terms at the back of the textbook. The more effort it takes to look up words you don't know, the less likely you are to do it, so make your access to a glossary and dictionary as convenient as possible.

Take written notes on what you're reading. Just as you take notes in response to your instructor's spoken words in class, take notes in response to the author's written words in your text. For example, write short answers to the boldface heading questions in a reading notebook or in the text itself, using its side, top, and bottom margins. Writing requires more active thinking than highlighting because you are generating words on your own, which are words that have personal meaning to you (rather than passively highlighting words written by someone else). Try not to get into the habit of using your textbook as a coloring book, where you get so into the

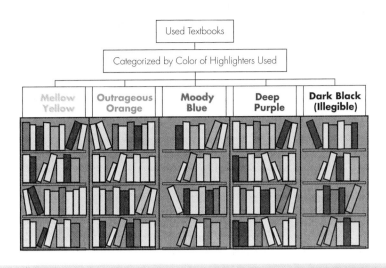

Highlighting textbooks in spectacular colors is a very popular reading strategy among college students, but it's a less effective strategy for producing deep learning than taking written notes on what you read.

artwork of highlighting in metallic, kaleidoscopic colors that the artistic process becomes more important than the process of thinking actively and deeply about what you are reading.

Remember that you can write in your textbook because you own it. Even if you intend to sell it at the end of the term, you can still write in it by using a pencil and you can even highlight it in pencil—by simply bracketing or underlining key sentences. If you eventually decide to sell your book back, then you can erase the pencil markings and probably end up with a book that will have higher resale value than one covered with hallucinogenic-like highlighting. In fact, pencils are more versatile reading tools than highlighters because they can be used more easily to do a variety of things, such as recording written notes, drawing figures or symbols, and making changes to your notes by erasing and rewriting.

Pause for Reflection

When reading a textbook, which of the following items do you usually have on hand?

Highlighter: Yes No

Pen or pencil: Yes No

Notebook: Yes No

Class notes: Yes No

Dictionary: Yes No

Make use of the visual aids that are provided in your textbooks. Don't fall into the trap of thinking that visual aids can or should be skipped because they merely supplement the written words of the text. Visual aids, such as charts, graphs, diagrams, and concept maps are powerful learning and memory tools for a couple of reasons:

1. They enable you to visualize information as a picture or image, and
2. They can organize many separate pieces of information into one meaningful whole.

Furthermore, viewing them gives you a periodic break from continually reading written words, allowing you to experience a different form of mental stimulation, which should increase your attention to what you're reading, as well as your motivation to read.

After Reading

Finish your reading session with a short review of the information that you've noted or highlighted. Forgetting information that your brain has just processed tends to occur most rapidly immediately after you stop focusing on it (Underwood, 1983). Taking a few minutes at the end of your reading time to review the most important information that you've noted or highlighted serves to lock in your memory of it before you turn your attention to something else and forget what you have just read.

Collaborate with peers to improve the effectiveness of your reading. The same benefits of participating in small-group discussions and study groups can be experienced when you form reading groups. After you complete your reading assignments, you can team-up with classmates to compare your highlighting and margin notes. You can consult with each other to identify major points in the reading, and help each other identify what information is most important to study for upcoming exams.

If you find that a certain concept explained in your text is difficult to understand, take a look at how another textbook explains that concept. Not all textbooks are created equally; some do a better job of explaining certain concepts than others. Another text may be able to explain a hard-to-understand concept much better than the textbook you purchased for the course. So, keep this option open by checking to see if your library has other texts in the same subject as your course, or check your campus bookstore for other textbooks in the same subject area as the course you're taking.

Pause for Reflection

Honestly rate yourself in terms of how frequently you use the following reading strategies according to the following scale:

4 = always, 3 = sometimes, 2 = rarely, 1 = never.

1. *I read the chapter outlines and summaries before I start reading a chapter.*	*4 3 2 1*
2. *I preview a chapter's boldface headings and subheadings before I begin to read the chapter.*	*4 3 2 1*
3. *I adjust my reading speed to the type of subject I am reading.*	*4 3 2 1*
4. *I look up the meaning of unfamiliar words and unknown terms that I come across before I read any further.*	*4 3 2 1*
5. *I take written notes on information I read.*	*4 3 2 1*
6. *I use the visual aids included in my textbooks.*	*4 3 2 1*
7. *I finish my reading sessions with a review of the important information that I noted or highlighted.*	*4 3 2 1*

●●● Study Strategies

Effective note-taking and reading ensures that you receive and gain access to the information that will show up on exams. The next step is to get that information stored in your brain so that you can later retrieve it at test time. Described below is a series of strategies for effectively storing information in your brain while studying.

Minimize Distractions

Maximize your attention while studying by blocking out all distracting sources of outside stimulation. As mentioned earlier, attention comes in a fixed quantity or amount; you can give all of it or part of it to whatever task you're working on. When you're involved with the task of studying complex material, this requires your complete and undivided attention. You don't want to divide your attention among multiple tasks by trying to study and process other information at the same time, such as listening to music, watching television, or exchanging instant messages with a friend.

Research on such multi-tasking consistently shows that trying to do more than one task at the same time interferes with the performance of the primary task you're working on—especially if that primary task involves complex thinking (Crawford & Strapp, 1994). In fact, when people multi-task, studies show that they don't pay equal and maximum attention to different tasks at the same time; instead, what they do is alternate or shift their attention back and forth from one task to another (Howard, 2000). The result is that they lose attention to one of the tasks for a while before returning to it.

When studying complex material, you need to give your complete and undivided attention to this task. Listening to music is a distraction that will shift your focus away from the information you are trying to learn.

Probably the most common example of the dangers of trying to focus on more than one task at the same time is driving a car while talking on a cell phone. Studies have repeatedly shown that a person's driving attention and performance are reduced when they try to drive and use a cell phone simultaneously (Redelmeier & Tibshirani, 1997).

Studies show that doing challenging academic work while multi-tasking divides up attention and drives down comprehension and retention.

Sights and sounds unrelated to what we're trying to learn tend to compete for and interfere with our attention during the learning process. When people say that they learn just as well or better while they listen to music or watch TV, this doesn't turn out to be true when they are actually tested (Crawford & Strapp, 1994). Even all the hype about how listening to classical music while studying can accelerate learning is not supported by research (Wagner & Tilney, 1983). The bottom line is that when you are learning challenging concepts or performing mental tasks that you cannot do automatically, competing external stimulation interferes with the quiet, internal reflection time needed to form deep, long-lasting connections between brain cells (Jensen, 1998).

Find Meaning in Terms

Each academic field has its own specialized vocabulary that can almost sound like a foreign language to someone who has no experience in the subject area. Before you start to brutally beat these terms into your brain through sheer repetition, try to find some meaning in them, or in some part of them. You can make a meaningless term more meaningful to you by looking up its word root in the dictionary or by identifying its prefix or suffix that may give away the term's meaning. For instance, if you were studying the autonomic nervous system in biology, which is the part of the nervous system that operates without our conscious or voluntary control (e.g., our heart beating and lungs breathing), its meaning is given away by its prefix "auto"—which means self-controlling, as in the word "automatic."

If the term's root, prefix, or suffix does not give away its meaning, then see if you can make it more meaningful to you in some other way. For instance, suppose you looked up the root of the term "artery," and nothing about the origins of this term reveals its meaning or purpose. You could then create your own meaning for this term by taking its first letter ("a"), and have it stand for "away"—to help you remember that arteries carry blood *away* from the heart. Thus, you've taken a meaningless biological term and made it more personally meaningful (and memorable).

Compare and Contrast

When you're studying something new, get in the habit of asking yourself the following questions:

Is this similar or comparable to something I've already learned?

How does this differ from, or contrast with, what I already know?

Research indicates that this simple strategy is one of the most powerful ways to promote learning of academic information (Marzano, Pickering, & Pollock, 2001). The power of the compare-and-contrast strategy probably stems from the fact that asking yourself, "How is this similar to and different than something that I already know?" makes learning more personally meaningful by encouraging you to relate what you're trying to learn to what you already know.

Integrate Information

Pull together information from your class notes and your assigned reading that relate to the same major concept or category; for example, get them in the same place by recording them on the same index card under the same category heading. The category heading can function like the hub of a wheel, around which individual pieces of information are attached like spokes. This will improve your learning and memory by strengthening its organization, plus it will enable you to study all course material relating to the same topic at the same time.

In contrast, when information relating to different concepts is separated in physical space, it helps you to separate them mentally, and prevents all that information from running together in your mind and confusing you.

Divide and Conquer

Effective learning depends not only on your study method, it also depends on when you learn—your timing. Although cramming just prior to exams is better than not studying at all, it is far less effective than studying that is spread out across time. Rather than cramming all your studying into one long session, use the *distributed practice* method, which spreads out study time into several shorter sessions. Research consistently shows that short, periodic practice sessions are more effective than a single marathon session. For instance, in one study of students who were learning Spanish, half of them studied many Spanish words in a single day, while another group studied the same number of words for the same amount of time, but their study time was broken up into a number of

Spreading out your studying into shorter sessions improves your memory by reducing loss of attention due to fatigue.

shorter sessions held at different times. Eight years later, the students were tested for their memory of these Spanish words. Those students who learned the words in the one-day cram session recalled an average of 6 percent of the words, while students who studied the words in several shorter sessions remembered 25 percent of the words—more than four times the amount remembered by the cramming group (Bahrick & Phelps, 1987).

Spreading out your studying into shorter sessions serves to improve your memory because it:

- reduces loss of attention due to fatigue or boredom, and
- reduces mental interference by giving the brain some "cool down" time to process and lock-in information that it has received without being interrupted by the need to take in additional information (Murname & Shiffrin, 1991).

If this downtime is interfered with by the need to process additional information, the brain gets overloaded and its memory for new information becomes impaired. This is exactly what cramming does—it interferes with the brain's need for downtime by overloading it with lots of information in a limited period of time. In contrast, distributed study does just the opposite—it spreads out learning into shorter sessions with downtime in-between sessions, which allows the brain to store information that has been previously studied. To illustrate this point, consider how difficult it would be to recall the names of ten new people you meet in one evening, compared with recalling the names of ten people you meet on ten separate evenings.

Another major advantage of distributed study is that it is less stressful and more motivating than cramming. You should feel more motivated to study because you know that you're not going to have to do it for a long stretch of time and lose any sleep over it. Furthermore, you should feel more relaxed because if you discover something that you don't understand, you know that you still have time to get help with it before you'll be tested and graded on it.

Distributing study time throughout the term is particularly crucial in college courses because tests are often given less frequently than in high school. In some college courses, you may take only two to three tests per term, and those tests will cover large amounts of material. So, resist the temptation to procrastinate and cram all information into your brain on the day (or night) before the exam; and don't buy into the belief that "I work better under pressure" (which often really means, "I *only* work under pressure because I procrastinate and have no other choice").

Use a "Part-to-Whole" Method of Studying

Divide your studying into small parts or units, and then learn these parts in several short, separate study sessions in advance of exams.

The part-to-whole method of studying is consistent with and flows naturally from the distributed practice method of studying that we just discussed. With the part-to-whole method, your last study session prior to the exam is one in which you re-study what you previously studied in short sessions altogether at one time. Thus, your last study session is a review session, not a session during which you're trying to learn information for the first time.

Do not underestimate the power of studying small pieces of course material in short, separate study sessions in advance of exams. The part-to-whole study method is often resisted because of the following common (and dangerous) belief: Studying done in advance of an exam is a total "waste of time" because you'll "forget it all by the time you take the test." This is a flat-out fallacy because memory for information that you study in advance of an exam is still in your brain when you later review the day or night before the exam. Even if you cannot recall the previously studied information when you first start reviewing it, you will re-learn it much faster than you did the first time you studied it, thus proving that some memory of it was still retained in your brain (Kintsch, 1994).

The time you save when you review and re-learn something a second time is referred to by memory researchers as "re-learning savings time" (Gordon, 1989) in other words, it is the amount of time saved when re-learning and remembering something a second time compared to the time it took to learn and remember it the first time. For example, suppose a student took French in high school and knew the French words for chair, table, floor, and ceiling, but two years later, this person can no longer recall the French translations of these words. So, it appears as if these French words learned in high school were completely forgotten. However, if you were to calculate the time this person would need to re-learn these French words and compare it to the amount of time it took to first learn them two years ago, much less time would be needed to re-learn these words the second time. The amount of time saved when re-learning the words the second time indicates that those French words learned in high school have not been totally forgotten; instead, traces of their memory are still in the student's brain, which enables them to be relearned much faster the next time around.

So, the old expression, "If you don't use it, you'll lose it," is not quite accurate when it comes to material that has been studied during the course of a term. Traces of these previous memories are not totally lost or erased from your brain; they are just weakened or lightened (Alnon, 1992). Often, all it takes is a mental "tune up" to get them up and working again. Thus, distributing studying into smaller parts in advance of a test is not a waste of time because it allows for re-learning savings time—plus reduced memory interference, reduced stress, and improved sleep that occur with distributed study compared to last-minute, late-night cramming.

Consuming large doses of caffeine or other stimulants to stay awake for all-night cram sessions is likely to maximize anxiety and minimize memory.

Begin with a Review

For sequential or cumulative subjects that build on understanding of previously covered information to learn new information (e.g., math), begin each study session with a quick review of what you learned in your previous study session.

Research shows that students of all ability levels learn course material more effectively when it's studied in small units, and when progression to the next unit takes place only after the previous unit has been mastered or understood (Pascarella & Terenzini, 1991, 2005). This strategy ensures that students build on their previous knowledge to understand what's coming next, and it enables *over-learning* to take place—that is, reviewing information that has already been learned further reinforces and strengthens its memory. This is particularly important in cumulative subjects that require memory for problem-solving procedures or steps, such as math and science. Continued practice of these procedures serves to make them become more automatic so you're able to retrieve them quicker (e.g., on a timed test) and use them without devoting all your mental energy to them (Newell & Rosenbloom, 1981). This frees up your working memory to focus on higher-level thinking and creative problem-solving (Schneider & Chein, 2003).

Change Things Up

Periodically change the type of academic tasks you're performing while studying. Change in work routine and in the type of mental task performed serves to increase your level of alertness and concentration by reducing "habituation"—attention loss that tends to occur after repeated exposure to the same learning task (McGuiness & Pribram, 1980). So, look to vary the type of task or work you're doing while studying. For instance, shift periodically across tasks that involve reading, writing, studying (e.g., rehearsing or reciting) and practicing skills (e.g., solving problems).

Study different subjects in different places. Different study locations provide different environmental contexts for learning, which tends to reduce the amount of interference that would normally build up if all the information was studied in the same place (Anderson & Bower, 1974). Memory research shows when lists of information are learned in different environments, memory interference is reduced. In one study, students who learned a group of 40 words in two separate study sessions held in the same room recalled an average of 15.9 words on a later memory test. In contrast, students who studied the words for the same amount of time, but whose study sessions took place in two distinctively different rooms, recalled an average of 24.4 words (Smith, Glenberg, & Bjork, 1978).

Thus, it may not only be a good idea to spread out your studying at different times, it may also be a good idea to spread out your studying in different places. In fact, ancient Greek and Roman speakers used this method of changing places to remember long speeches by walking through different rooms, mentally associating different parts of their speech with different rooms (Higbee, 1998).

The brain's attention system has a particular area that is specialized for attention to location (Ackerman, 1992), so changes in the place or space where learning occurs can stimulate greater attention (Schacter, 1992), in part because the change and novelty of the new environment provides greater sensory stimulation to the brain (La Berge, 1995). Even the act of standing up and moving to a new location can have positive effects on mental performance and brain functioning (Jensen, 1998) because it increases circulation of oxygen-carrying blood to the brain and stimulates areas of the brain that play a key role in learning (Middleton & Strick, 1994).

This research suggests that changes in the nature of the learning task and the learning environment provide changes of pace that infuse some variety into the learning process, which can improve your attention to and concentration on what you're studying. Although it may be useful to have a set schedule of study times during the week to get you into a regular, habit-forming work routine, this doesn't mean that learning occurs best by habitually performing the same learning tasks while sitting in the same seat at the same place. Instead, you should make periodic changes in the learning tasks you're performing and the environments in which you perform them to maximize attention and minimize interference (Druckman & Bjork, 1991).

 Remember: Studying will be more effective if:

- there is separation of your study material into smaller parts and separation of your study time into shorter sessions; and
- there is variation in the type of study tasks you perform and in the study places where you perform them.

Use All of Your Senses

When studying course material, try to use as many different sensory channels as possible because research clearly indicates that information stored through more than one sensory modality is better remembered (Bjork, 1994; Schacter, 1992). When a memory is stored in the brain, different sensory aspects of it are stored in different areas. For example, the visual, auditory, and motor sensations associated with what you're learning are all stored in different parts of the brain. Thus, when you use all of these sensory channels while learning, multiple "memory traces" of what you're studying are recorded in your brain, which leads to stronger memory (Education Commission of the States, 1996). Listed below are some of the major channels through which learning occurs and memories are stored, accompanied by specific strategies for using each of these channels while studying.

1. Visual Learning

   The human brain consists of two halves or hemispheres: the left hemisphere and the right hemisphere (Figure 4.7). Each of these hemispheres specializes in a different type of learning. In most people, the left hemisphere specializes in verbal learning, dealing primarily with words. In contrast, the right hemisphere specializes in visual-spatial learning, dealing primarily with images. Thus, if you use both words and images to learn the information you're studying, two memory traces are recorded in different halves of your brain: One memory trace is recorded in the left hemisphere—where words are encoded—and one in the right hemisphere—where images are encoded. This process of laying down a double memory trace (verbal and visual) is referred to as *dual coding* (Paivio, 1990). When this happens, memory for what you're learning is substantially strengthened, primarily because two memory traces are better than one.

   To capitalize on the advantage of dual coding, make use of any visual aids that are available to you. Use the visual aids provided in your textbook and by your instructor, and create your own by drawing pictures, symbols, or concept maps—such as flow charts or branching tree diagrams. Drawing is not just an artistic exercise; it can be used as a learning tool as well—you can draw to learn. By taking words and ideas and representing them in visual form, the resulting drawing enables you to dual code the information you're studying, doubling the number of memory traces recorded in your brain.

Figure 4.7

The human brain consists of two halves, known as the left hemisphere and the right hemisphere.

© JupiterImages Corporation.

Pause for Reflection

People remember faces better than they do names. Why do you think this is?

2. Motor Learning (also known as Muscle Memory)

In addition to hearing and seeing, movement is another sensory channel that provides the brain with kinesthetic stimulation—the sensations we get from our body's muscles as a result of physical movement. Memory traces for movement are commonly stored in the cerebellum—an area in the lower back of the brain. Brain research indicates that this part of the brain plays a major role in all types of learning (Middleton & Strick, 1994). Thus, associating movement with what you're learning can improve your ability to retain it because you record an additional "muscle memory trace" of it to another area of your brain.

Personal Story I was talking about memory in class one day and mentioned that if I forget how to spell a word, when I start to write it out, I often remember its correct spelling. One of my students then raised her hand and said the same thing happens to her when she forgets a phone number—it comes back to her when she starts dialing it. Both cases of memories coming back when movement began (writing and dialing) are classic cases of how a muscle memory trace can trigger recall of verbal or factual information that is associated with movement.

—Joe Cuseo

STUDENT PERSPECTIVE

"I have to *hear* it, *see* it, *write* it, and *talk* about it."

—First-year student, responding to the question: "How do you learn best?"

You can use movement to help you learn and retain academic information by using your body to act out what you're studying or to symbolize it with your hands (Kagan & Kagan, 1998). For example, if you're trying to remember five points about something (e.g., five key consequences of the Civil War), when you're studying these points, count them out on your fingers as you try to recall each of them. Also, remember that talking itself involves muscle movement of your lips and tongue. Thus, by speaking aloud when you're studying, either to a friend or to yourself, your memory of what you're studying should be improved by adding kinesthetic stimulation to your brain (along with the auditory or sound stimulation your brain receives from hearing what you're saying).

TAKE ACTION NOW! **Box 4.4**

Adjusting Your Academic Work to Your Biological Rhythms

⊙ When planning your daily work schedule, be aware of your natural "biological rhythms"—your *peak periods* and *down times*. Studies show that humans vary in terms of when they naturally prefer to fall asleep and wake up; some are "early birds" who prefer to go to sleep early and wake up early, and others are "night owls" who prefer to stay up late at night and get up late in the morning (Natale & Ciogna, 1996). (Teenagers more often fall into the category of "night owls.") As a result of these differences in sleeping patterns, individuals will vary with respect to the times of day when they experience their highest and lowest levels of physical energy. Naturally, "early birds" are more likely to be "morning" people whose peak energy period occurs before noon; and "night owls" are likely to be more productive in the late afternoon and evening. Also, most people experience a "post-lunch" dip in energy in the early afternoon (Monk, 2005).

⊙ Be aware of your most productive hours of the day and schedule your highest priority work and most challenging tasks at times when you tend to work at peak effectiveness. For example, schedule your out-of-class work so that you're tackling academic tasks that require intense thinking (e.g., technical writing or complex problem-solving) at times of the day when you tend to be most productive, and schedule lighter work (e.g., light reading or routine tasks) at times when your energy level tends to be lower. Also, keep your natural peak and down times in mind when you schedule your courses. Attempt to arrange your class schedule in such a way that you experience your most challenging courses at times of the day when your body and mind are most ready to accept that challenge.

Emotional Learning and Memory

Just as information reaches the brain through the senses and is stored in the brain as a memory trace, the same is true of emotions. There are numerous connections between brain cells in the emotional and memory centers of the human brain (Zull, 1998). For instance, when we're experiencing emotional excitement and energy about what we are learning, adrenaline is released and is carried through the blood stream to our brain. Once adrenaline reaches the brain, it increases blood flow and glucose production, which can stimulate learning and strengthen memory (LeDoux, 1998; Rosenfield, 1988). In fact, if an experience is very emotionally intense, the amount of adrenaline that is released can immediately and permanently store the memory in the brain for the remainder of a person's life. For instance, most people can remember exactly what they were doing at the time they experienced such emotionally intense events as the September 11th terrorist attack on the United States, or their first kiss, or when their favorite team won a world championship.

What does this emotion-memory link have to do with helping you remember academic information that you're studying? Research on human emotions suggests that emotional intensity, excitement, and enthusiasm do make a real difference for learning and memory. If you get "psyched up" about what you're learning, you have a much better chance of learning and remembering it. Even telling yourself that you want to learn and that you intend to remember what you're learning can increase your memory of it (Minninger, 1984; Howard, 2000).

Form Study Groups

Group learning is a natural, "brain compatible" form of learning. The human brain is biologically wired for interpersonal communication because social interaction and collaboration are critical to survival of the human species (Jensen, 1998). In fact, brain-imaging studies reveal that more activity occurs in thinking parts of the brain when people learn through social interaction than when they are learning alone or in isolation (Carter, 1998).

Research has shown that college students learn as much, or more, from peers than they do from instructors and textbooks (Astin, 1993; Pascarella, 2005). When seniors at Harvard University were interviewed, nearly every one of them who had been part of a study group considered this experience to be crucial to their academic progress and success (Light, 1990, 1992).

To fully capitalize and maximize the power of study groups, each member should study individually *before* studying in a group. Research on study groups indicates that they are effective only if each member has done required course work in advance of the group meeting—for example, if each group member has done the required readings and other course assignments (Light, 2001). All members should come prepared with specific information or answers to share with teammates as well as specific questions or points of confusion about which they hope to receive help from the team. This ensures that all group members are individually accountable or personally responsible for their own learning and for contributing to the learning of their teammates.

Forming a study group is an excellent learning strategy.

CLASSIC QUOTE

Education is not the filling of a pail, but the lighting of a fire.

—William Butler Yeats, Irish poet and playwright

SP STUDENT PERSPECTIVE

"I learn best through teaching. When I learn something and teach it to someone else, I find that it really sticks with me a lot better."

—College sophomore's response to the question: "How do you learn best?"

Personal Story

When I was in my senior year of college, I had to take a theory course by independent study because the course would not be offered again until after I planned to graduate. There was another senior who found himself in the same situation. Thus, the theory instructor allowed both of us to take this course together and agreed to meet with us every two weeks. My fellow student and I studied independently for the first two weeks. I prepared for the bi-weekly meeting by reading thoroughly, yet I had little understanding of what I had read. After our first meeting, I left with a strong desire to drop the course; however, I stayed with it. Over the next two weeks, I spent many sleepless nights trying to prepare for our next meeting and had feelings of angst about not being the brightest theory student in my class of two. During the next meeting with the instructor, I found out that the other student was also having difficulty. Not only did I notice this, but the instructor also noticed. After that meeting, the instructor gave us study questions and asked us to read separately and then get together to discuss the questions. During the next two weeks, my classmate and I met several times for some stimulating discussions on theory. By being able to communicate with each other about the issues we were studying, we both ended up gaining greater understanding. Our instructor was delighted to see that he was able to suggest a learning strategy that worked for both of us.

—Aaron Thompson

Pause for Reflection

Honestly rate yourself in terms of how frequently you use the following study strategies, according to the following scale:

4 = always, 3 = sometimes, 2 = rarely, 1 = never.

1. I block out all distracting sources of outside stimulation when I study. 4 3 2 1

2. I look for meaning in technical terms by looking at their prefix or suffix, or by looking up their word root in the dictionary. 4 3 2 1

3. I compare and contrast what I'm currently studying to what I've already learned. 4 3 2 1

4. I organize the information I'm studying into categories or classes. 4 3 2 1

5. I integrate or pull together information from my class notes and readings that relate to the same concept or general category. 4 3 2 1

6. I distribute or "spread out" my study time into several short sessions in advance of the exam and use my last study session before the test to review the information I previously studied. 4 3 2 1

7. I participate in study groups with my classmates. 4 3 2 1

••• Self-Reflection and Self-Monitoring

Rather than mindlessly going through the motions of learning, *deep* learning requires self-reflection. Effective learners reflect and check on themselves to see if they're really understanding what they're attempting to learn, monitoring their comprehension as they go along by asking themselves questions such as, "Am I following this?" "Do I really understand it?"

How do you know if you really know it? Probably the best answer to this question is: you know if you really know it and truly comprehend it when you find meaning in it—that is, when you can relate to it personally or can understand it in terms that make sense to you

(Ramsden, 2003). When you comprehend a concept, you've learned it at a deeper level than mere memorization; and when you comprehend it, you're more likely to remember it because learning that is deep is also more durable—it stays in long-term memory for a greater length of time (Kintsch, 1970).

Discussed below are some specific strategies for checking whether you're truly understanding what you are attempting to learn. These can be used as indicators or checkpoints for determining whether you've moved beyond memorization to deeper understanding of what you're studying.

Comprehension Self-Monitoring Strategies

◆ Can you paraphrase what you're learning? Can you restate or translate it into your own words? When you can paraphrase what you're learning, you're able to describe it by completing the sentence that begins with the phrase, "In other words, ..." This is a good indication that you've moved beyond memorization to comprehension because you have transformed what you're learning into words that are meaningful to you. Even better than saying it in your own words is writing it in your own words, because this will reinforce your memory of it and give you a record of it for later review.

◆ Can you explain what you're learning to someone else who is unfamiliar with it? If you can explain to a friend what you've learned, this is a good sign that you've moved beyond memorization to comprehension because you are able to translate it into less technical language that someone hearing it for the first time can understand. Studies show that students gain deeper levels of understanding for what they're learning when they are asked to explain it to someone else (Chi, et al., 1994). Often, we don't realize how well we know or don't know something until we have to explain it to someone else who's never heard of it before (just ask any teacher). If you cannot find anyone to explain it to, then explain it aloud as if you were talking to an "imaginary friend."

◆ Can you think of an example of what you've learned? If you can provide an example or instance that is your own—not one that has already been given by your teacher or text—this is a good sign that you truly comprehend it because you're taking a general and abstract concept or principle and applying it to a specific and concrete experience. In fact, research indicates that when humans recall technical terms they have learned, they don't retrieve the definition first; instead, they retrieve an example or concrete instance of the term and use that example or instance to reconstruct the term's meaning (Norman, 1982; Tulving, 1985). This illustrates how important concrete examples are to understanding and retaining abstract concepts. (Have you ever noticed that when students are having trouble understanding something abstract or theoretical, they often ask their instructor: "Can you give me an example?")

◆ Can you represent or describe what you've learned in terms of an analogy or metaphor, which compares it to something else that has similar meaning or works in a similar way? Analogies and metaphors are basically ways of learning something new by understanding it in terms of something else that is similar and that we already understand. For instance, in this chapter we used the computer as a metaphor for the human brain to better understand learning and memory as a three-stage process. If you can use an analogy or metaphor to represent what you're learning, this is a good sign that you understand it at a deep level because you've built a mental bridge to connect what you're trying to understand to something that you already understand.

◆ Can you apply what you're learning to solve a particular problem that you've never encountered before? Perhaps the strongest sign of deep learning and comprehension is the ability to transfer something you've learned in one situation and apply it in a different context. Learning specialists sometimes refer to this mental process as "de-contextualization"—taking what has been learned in one context or situation and applying it to another (Bransford, Brown, & Cocking, 1999).

For instance, you know that you've really understood a mathematical concept when you can use that concept to solve math problems that are different than those which were used by your instructor or textbook to help you learn it in the first place. This is why it's unlikely that your math instructors will include on exams the exact same problems they solved in class or were solved in your textbook. They're not trying to trick you at test time; they're just trying to test your comprehension to determine if you've deeply learned the concept or principle, rather than simply memorized it. Similarly, if you took a course in human relations and learned the principles of conflict management, and you were later able to use those principles to settle a dispute between yourself and your roommate, this suggests you have deeply learned and understood those principles.

In fact, one of the key differences between deep learning and surface memorization is that when you've learned something deeply, you're able to continually put that learning to use in future situations that you have never encountered before (Anderson & Krathwohl, 2001). When you have simply memorized something, its future use is restricted to exactly the same situation in which you originally learned it.

Knowledge Awareness Strategies

Remain aware of the type of knowledge that you're trying to acquire and adjust your study strategy accordingly. Knowledge comes in different forms and involves different learning and memory systems. The key types of knowledge you will acquire in college usually fall into one of the following major categories.

Declarative (Semantic) Knowledge: knowing what is accurate or true and that you can "declare" or state it in words (e.g., factual information). Acquiring this type of knowledge requires studying that involves effective use of recitation or memory-improvement strategies, such as meaningful association, acrostics, or rhythm and rhyme.

Procedural (Skill) Knowledge: knowing how to do something, which usually involves procedures or skills that have multiple steps (e.g., solving math problems, conducting science experiments). Acquiring this type of knowledge requires repeated practice or rehearsal, such as practicing delivery of a speech or lines in a play. However, this repeated practice should be reflective practice, not mindless repetition. Although repetition is needed to develop certain skills, they are often developed more deeply and more rapidly if you reflect on and remain aware of the learning and thinking *process* that you are using while practicing.

Studies show that students who consciously attend to their own thought processes when solving math and science problems become more effective problem solvers than those who just go through the motions (Resnick, 1986). For instance, expert problem-solvers ask themselves such questions as, "How did I go about solving this problem correctly?" "What were the key steps I took to arrive at the correct solution?" These are important questions to ask yourself while practicing any problem-solving skill, because you want to understand and recall the thought process behind the skill so you can use that successful thought process again in the future (e.g., on upcoming exams).

Episodic Knowledge: knowing where something is located—its place in space. The term episodic derives from "epi" meaning "on" or "at" and "odic" meaning "path." So, literally, it refs to knowing the specific place or space where something is located in relation to other things along the same path. For example, if you are taking a course in anatomy and you are trying to learn the location of each one of the internal organs of the body or each major part of the human brain, you are trying to acquire episodic knowledge. Acquiring this type of knowledge requires study strategies that make effective use of visual learning techniques, such as diagrams, concept maps, and visual imagery.

◆━ *Pause for Reflection*

Do you change or adjust your studying strategy, depending on the type of test you're going to take, or do you tend to study the same way for all tests?

••• Summary and Conclusion

We covered a lot of territory in this chapter, moving through all stages of the learning and memory process—from the very first stage of perceiving and receiving information through lectures and readings, to studying and storing information in the brain, and finally, to the stage of retrieving and recalling information.

The major principles and strategies associated with academic success at all stages in the learning and memory process are consistent with, and strongly reinforce, the four major bases of college success that we discussed in the first chapter of this text, namely: active involvement, self-reflection, social interaction/collaboration, and utilizing campus resources. These four bases can be used to summarize the most important learning and memory strategies that were discussed in this chapter.

Active Involvement

This principle of college success suggests that college students need to be active agents in the learning process (rather than passive sponges or spectators), and that academic success depends on the amount or degree of personal time, effort, and energy invested in learning. The importance of this principle emerged at the very start of this chapter when it was noted that deep learning involves active building of knowledge, whereby you shape and mold information to be learned into a form that has personal meaning for you. This importance of active involvement was also evident throughout all three key stages of the learning and memory process that were discussed in the chapter. First, active attention is needed for information to be perceived and received by your conscious brain. Second, information is saved in the brain through the investment of mental, physical, and emotional energy. Third, information is actively retrieved from the brain and brought back to consciousness when taking exams.

Remember: We learn most effectively when we actively involve all our senses, and when we learn with passion and enthusiasm. In other words, learning becomes deeper and lasts longer when you put your "whole self" into it—your mind, your body, and your heart.

Self-Reflection

Deep learning not only requires action, it also requires reflection. Both mental processes are needed for learning to be complete. Active involvement is necessary for engaging our attention—which enables us to initially get information into our brain—and quiet reflection is necessary for consolidation—keeping that information in our brain, by locking it into our long-term memory. Rather than immediately jumping in and pounding in what we're trying to learn through mindless repetition, take a pause for a worthy cause—reflect and connect it with something that's already in our brain.

Reflection also involves awareness of ourselves as learners. We need to periodically pause and reflect on what is going on in our mind during different learning tasks. For instance, you should occasionally step back and think about whether you are actively listening to what your instructor is saying in class, and whether you are deeply understanding what you're studying outside of class. Also, you should occasionally step back and reflect on whether you are using learning strategies that are effective for the type of material you're studying and the type of test you'll be taking.

Said in another way, you want to be a self-regulated learner (Pintrich, 1995) who is self-aware and is in control of your own effort and attention, and who can regulate or adjust:

- *how* you learn to what you are learning—adjusting your study strategies to the type of subject you're studying and the type of test you're taking,
- *when* you are learning—adjusting your study time and timing, and
- *where* you are learning—adjusting your study situation or environment.

Social Interaction/Collaboration

As we noted in Chapter 1, one of the four key bases of college success is interpersonal interaction and collaboration. Learning is strengthened when it takes place in a social context that involves human interaction.

Your two primary sources for social interaction relating to your classes are your faculty instructors and your classmates. As we documented in Chapter 1, student interaction with faculty is positively associated with improved academic performance and increased likelihood of completing a college degree (Astin, 1993; Tinto, 1993), so take advantage of opportunities to discuss course material with your instructors immediately after class and during their office hours. The educational benefit of interacting and collaborating with your peers is well supported by research (Johnson, Johnson, & Smith, 1991). As we noted earlier in this chapter, you can collaborate with your classmates at any stage of the learning and memory process. You can form:

- note-taking teams immediately after class by taking a few minutes to team up with a classmate to compare your notes for accuracy and completeness;
- reading teams, teaming up with classmates to compare your highlighting and margin notes;
- study teams to prepare for upcoming exams, and
- test-results review teams by collaborating with other classmates to review your results together, compare answers, and identify the sources of your mistakes.

Utilizing Campus Resources

The professionals who work in the Learning Resource or Academic Success Center on your campus have been professionally trained to help you learn "how to learn." These professionals are experts on the process of learning and can help you adjust or regulate your learning strategies to meet the demands of different courses and teaching styles. This Center provides learning support in multiple formats, including instructional videos, self-assessment instruments for assessing your personal learning habits, strategies or styles, and peer tutors—who can be especially effective teachers because they are developmentally closer to you in terms of their stage of intellectual development and level of communication (Vygotsky, 1978; Whitman, 1988).

Take full advantage of the multiple forms of support that your Learning Resource or Academic Success Center can offer you. Utilizing its services should strengthen your learning and elevate your grades.

Before you exit this chapter, we would like to remind you that the learning and memory strategies discussed here are more than just "study" skills or "academic" success skills; they are *life success* skills or *lifelong learning* skills that you can and will use throughout the remainder of your personal and professional life. For example, the skills of focusing attention and active listening are not only useful in the classroom, but in social relationships outside of class and throughout life; and note taking itself is a skill that you will continue to use throughout your career (e.g., during professional meetings and committee work).

Furthermore, these lifelong learning skills are probably more important today than at any other time in history because we are now living in an era characterized by rapid technological change and dramatic growth of knowledge. This information and communication explosion is creating a greater need for people to learn continuously throughout life and a higher demand for working professionals who are skilled learners—who have learned how to learn (Niles & Harris-Bowlsbey, 2002; Herman, 2000).

 Remember: Putting into practice the learning strategies discussed in this chapter will not only prepare you for taking college tests, it will also prepare you for lifelong learning.

●●● Learning More through Independent Research

Web-Based Resources for Further Information on Strategic Learning

For additional information relating to the ideas discussed in this chapter, we recommend the following Web sites:

www.Dartmouth.edu/~acskills/success/index.html

www.utexas.edu/student/utlc/lrnres/handouts.html

www.muskingum.edu/~cal/database/general/

www2.gsu.edu/~wwwrld/Resources/helpfultips.htm

CHAPTER 4
Self-Assessment of Learning Strategies and Habits

Look back at the ratings you gave yourself for effective note-taking strategies (p. 122), reading strategies (p. 126) and studying strategies (p.136). Add up your total score for each of these three sets of learning strategies (maximum score for each set would be 28):

Note Taking _____

Reading _____

Studying _____

Total Learning Strategy Score = _____

SELF-ASSESSMENT QUESTIONS

1. In what learning strategy area did you score lowest?

2. Do you think that the strategy area in which you scored lowest has anything to do with your lowest course grade at this point in the term?

3. Of the seven specific strategies listed within the area that you scored lowest, which ones could you immediately put into practice to improve your lowest course grade?

4. What is the likelihood that you will put the above strategies into practice this term?

Too Fast, Too Frustrating: A Note-Taking Nightmare

Joanna Scribe is a first-year student who is majoring in journalism, and she's currently enrolled in an introductory course that is required for her major (Introduction to Mass Media). Her instructor for this course lectures at a very rapid rate and uses vocabulary words that go right over her head. Since she cannot get all the instructor's words down on paper and can't understand half the words she does manage to write down, she has become frustrated and has now stopped taking notes altogether. She wants to do well in this course because it's the first course in her major, but she's afraid she will fail it because her class notes are so pitiful.

Reflection and Discussion Questions

1. Can you relate to this case personally, or know any students who are in the same boat as Joanna?

2. What would you recommend that Joanna do at this point?

3. Why did you make the above recommendation?

Improving Memory and Test Performance

Strategies for Remembering What You Have Learned and Demonstrating What You Know

Learning Goals

In this chapter, we will focus on the final stage of the memory process, which involves finding and retrieving information that has been stored in the brain. The primary goals of this chapter are to strengthen your ability to remember information that you've studied and to effectively demonstrate your knowledge of that information on college exams.

Outline

Memory and Learning
Memory-Improvement Strategies
    Mnemonic Devices
    Meaningful Association
    Organization: Classifying or Categorizing What You're Trying to Remember
    Visualization
    Rhythm and Rhyme
    Acrostics
    Link System
    Loci System
Test-Taking Strategies
    Before the Test
    On the Day of the Test
    During the Test
    After the Test: Troubleshooting Test-Taking Errors and Sources of Lost Points on Exams
Summary and Conclusion
Learning More through Independent Research
Exercises:
    Self-Assessment of Learning Strategies
    Midterm Self-Evaluation
Case Study: Bad Feedback: Shocking Midterm Grades

Activate Your Thinking

Are learning and remembering the same?

How are they similar?

How are they different?

⦿⦿⦿ Memory and Learning

If you are not sure about the answers to the "Activate Your Thinking" questions, welcome to the club. There is still debate among scholars about the similarities and differences between learning and memory. Certainly, these are not totally different mental processes. When we learn something, it's stored in our brain as a memory, so learning and memory are definitely related; we can only remember things that we've learned. However, if we've learned something and stored it in our brain, we cannot always recall it; thus, learning and remembering are not identical. As we mentioned in the previous chapter, deep learning and long-term memory is a multi-step process that involves three distinct stages:

1. Getting information into your brain (perception),
2. Keeping it there (storage), and
3. Finding it later when you need it (retrieval).

Although college courses will often emphasize comprehension and higher-level thinking skills, there will be numerous occasions when you'll be asked just to recall information. Memory, like any other learning skill, can be improved by using effective strategies or techniques. Contrary to popular belief, most people with good memories do not possess any extraordinary ability, such as photographic memory. The vast majority of people with outstanding memory have successfully developed a set of effective memory strategies and practiced them diligently.

If you can learn to use memory-improvement methods effectively, you will not only reduce the risk of forgetting information that you've studied, but you'll also reduce the amount of study time spent on trying to memorize information through sheer repetition; this will open up more time for comprehension and "higher" forms of thinking. Furthermore, using memory-improvement methods, such as those we are about to discuss, are simply more stimulating and motivating than memorizing by repetition.

⦿⦿⦿ Memory-Improvement Strategies

Mnemonic Devices

Mnemonic devices, also known as mnemonics (pronounced "neh-mon-iks"), are specific memory-improvement methods designed to prevent forgetting. The mnemonic devices we are about to discuss should not be viewed as tricks or gimmicks but as legitimate strategies that are based on one or more of the following research-based, memory-improvement principles:

◆ meaning
◆ organization
◆ visualization
◆ rhythm and rhyme

What all mnemonic devices have in common is that they help us remember by providing us with a partial *cue* to bring the memory back to mind. When humans try to retrieve memories that have been stored, studies show they usually do not remember all parts or pieces of the information in one shot; instead, they "build back" their memory around one or two points that they do remember (Loftus, 1979). For instance, when college students are asked to recall stories, pictures, or geometrical designs that they have been shown days or weeks before, they tend to organize their recall around one or two major details—for example, they'll remember one character or episode in a story and will then try to fill in the missing details. This process

Figure 5.1 A "Map" of the Functions Performed by the Outer Surface of the Human Brain

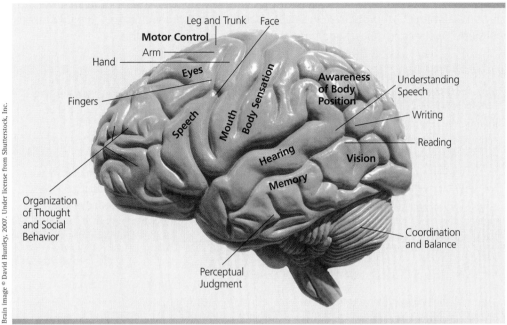

Brain image © David Huntley, 2007. Under license from Shutterstock, Inc.

of building up and building back a memory piece-by-piece is called *reconstruction*. Retrieval works this way because different elements of a memory are stored in different parts of the brain (Pribram, 1991). For example, you may store the place where you saw the information in the part of our brain specialized for visual memory, the words you heard your instructor speak about it in an area of the brain specialized for auditory memory, and the printed words you read about it in an area of the brain involved with reading. See Figure 5.1, a map of the surface of the human brain, to get an idea of how different parts of the brain are specialized for different mental activities. When we retrieve a memory, we often retrieve different parts of the memory that are stored in different areas of the brain, and we use the process of reconstruction to try to rebuild the whole memory.

The effectiveness of mnemonics for reconstructing memory has been demonstrated in many research studies. For instance, one study showed that college students using mnemonics remembered 72 percent of words they studied, compared to an average of 28 percent for students who tried to memorize these words through mere repetition (Bower, 1973). Listed below are seven mnemonic devices that you could use to recall hard-to-remember information in any field of study (Buzan, 1991; Higbee, 1998; Lorayne & Lucas, 1974). These mnemonics can be adapted to remember information in different subject areas, whether it is a single piece of information, multiple ideas, or a sequence of steps in a procedure. Some of them may work more effectively on certain types of information than others, but the variety should give you a menu to choose from, allowing you to select different ones for different learning tasks or situations. (For additional mnemonics designed for remembering information in particular academic subjects, see: www.eudesign.com. To find mnemonics specifically for medical and health-related fields, see: www.medicalmnemonics.com.)

Meaningful Association

Relating what you're trying to remember to something that you already know can be a powerful memory aid because learning is all about making connections in the brain. So, the first and most effective way to improve memory would be to find *meaning* in what you're learning. Before starting to repeatedly pound what you're learning into your head like a hammer and nail, first look for a hook to hang it on by relating it to something already stored in your brain. It may take a little while to discover the right hook, but once you've found it, the information will store in your brain quickly and remain there for a long period of time.

Personal Story   Some time ago, I had to give up running because of damage to my right hip, so I decided to start riding a stationary bike instead. My wife found an inexpensive, used stationary bike at a garage sale. It was an old and somewhat rusty bike that made a noise when I rode it that sounded like "ee-zoh" over and over again as the wheel spun. One evening I was riding it and I noticed that, after about 10 minutes, I was hearing the words "zero," "rosy," and "Rio" off and on in my head. Now that I think about it, what my brain was doing was taking a meaningless sound ("ee-zoh"), which apparently it was becoming bored with hearing over and over again as the wheels spun, and transformed that sound into actual words that provided it with variety and meaning. Perhaps this was a classic case of how the human brain naturally seeks meaning and variety, and naturally resists mindless repetition.

—Joe Cuseo

There are many everyday examples of how effective meaningful associations can be for improving memory. Here are some of the most well-known uses of meaningful association to improve recall of information.

◆ Remembering to turn the clock one hour ahead in the spring and one hour back in the fall by associating it with: "Spring forward, fall back."

◆ Remembering how to spell the word "principal" (as opposed to principle) by associating it with the idea that a principal should be a "pal."

◆ Remembering Italy's geographic location at the bottom of Europe because it's shaped like a boot.

◆ Remembering dates—for example, remembering that the Magna Carta (a key historical document that led to constitutional laws designed to protect personal freedoms and rights) was written in the year 1215—by associating it with a "free lunch" given at lunchtime (12:15 p.m.).

Here is a meaningful association we recommend for remembering one of the most frequently misspelled words in the English language: Remember to spell "separate" correctly (instead of the frequently misspelled "seperate,") by remembering that "par" means to divide, as in the words "*par*ts," "*par*tition," and "se*par*ate."

◢ *Pause for Reflection*

Can you think of information you're learning in a course this term that you could form a meaningful association to remember?

What is the information you're attempting to learn?

What is the meaningful association you could use to help you remember it?

Organization: Classifying or Categorizing What You're Trying to Remember

Bits or pieces of information are more easily learned and better remembered if they are organized into a classification system. Studies show that if students study a list of words that fall into different categories (e.g., 12 grocery items that fall into categories like fruit or meat), their recall is much better than when they study 12 unrelated words that cannot be grouped into categories (Mandler, 1967).

The memory advantage for categorized information is even greater if the words that belong to the same category are grouped or clustered together in blocked form (Bower et al., 1969). For instance, it's easier to remember "10-10-987" than it is to remember "1-0-1-0-9-8-7."

So, look for categories and sub-categories to organize information you're studying. For example, create a mental filing system by using index cards, with each card containing a separate category of information. Research suggests that we can hold up to about six items in our working memory, so try to create categories of no more than six items (Cowan, 2001). If you end up with a category that contains seven or more items then use a "divide and conquer" strategy by subdividing it into two smaller groups of six or fewer items.

The power of organization on learning and memory is so strong that some studies have shown that when college students are instructed simply to "organize" information, they tend to remember that information just as well as students who are specifically instructed to "study" or "memorize" the same information (Mandler, 1967; Kintsch, 1982). Although it may take you a little extra time to organize the information at first, you save study time in the long run because you're actually learning the information at the same time that you're organizing it. Furthermore, once the information has been organized, it is much less time-consuming to review at a later date because you've got all the parts together in a file system. In fact, if you organized the information on index cards, with each index card representing a separate category of information, you could put a rubber band around the cards and carry them with you to review at any time or any place. This not only makes studying more convenient, it also tends to reduce your level of test anxiety because you've got it altogether in a neat package, which is a lot more comforting than having it all over the place.

Personal Story Whenever I meet a new class of students at the start of the term, the first thing I try to do is learn their names as quickly as possible. I have found that I can learn student names more rapidly if I do not study the names individually, but group them into certain categories. I first divide the names by gender, putting all the male and female students into separate groups. Then I subdivide the male and female names into two subgroups: American student names and international student names. Thus, I end up with four groups: (1) American male students, (2) American female students, (3) international male students, and (4) international female students. I have found that I can learn and remember student names faster when I group them into these categories than by trying to learn them one name at a time.

—Joe Cuseo

Visualization

This mnemonic involves:

◆ visualizing a mental *image* or *picture* of what you want to remember, or

◆ imagining what you want to remember in a familiar *place* or *location*.

Visual imagery strengthens memory because it allows you to "see" what you're learning. This improves memory by making abstract ideas more concrete and tangible. Also, visualizing an idea puts it in a concrete place or physical location that gives it a spatial dimension. Have you ever had the experience of first remembering the place on a page where a certain piece of information was located (e.g., upper-right-hand corner) which then triggered your memory of the information you were trying to recall? This example points to the important role that space and place can play in improving our memory.

Studies also show that visual images takes less rehearsal and are more easily recalled than words and sentences (Buzan, 1991; Roediger & McDermott, 2000). In fact, images can be recalled instantly because all of the parts can be "seen" at once (Nadel & Welmer, 1980). The power of visual memory may be due to the fact that it is the oldest form of human memory. Before humans were able to speak, write, and remember words, our early ancestors relied on site and visual memories of objects and places. The ability to visualize may have been critical for enabling early humans to survive, such as using their visual memory to recall places where food and shelter were located (Milner & Goodale, 1998). Thus, the human brain may be biologically wired for effective visual memory, so capitalize on it to reduce forgetting.

You can use *visual imagery* as a mnemonic device by imagining visual scenes depicting the information you want to remember. This is illustrated by the common strategy for remembering that the mathematical symbol ">" means "greater than" by imagining it as a mouth taking a bite out of something smaller. Studies show that when students are asked to associate two words (e.g., "cow" and "ball"), they display better memory for the associated words if they visually imagine the two words interacting in some way (e.g., the cow chasing the ball). In learning foreign languages, it has been found that visual imagery improves learning word translations. For example, one student effectively learned and remembered the Spanish word caballo (pronounced "cab-eye-oh"), which means "horse," by associating it with a visual image of a horse with a huge eye (Atkinson, 1975). Visual images that are vivid, emotional, humorous, outrageous, or action-packed are often the most effective ones for improving memory (Bower, 1972; Carney & Levin, 2001).

Another way to capitalize on the memory-improving power of visualization and organization is to create *concept maps*, which organize all the pieces of information you're trying to remember into a visual map. Figure 5.2 represents a concept map that could be used to remember the parts and functions of the human nervous system.

Drawing concept maps help improve your memory by enabling you to become actively involved with the material you're trying to remember and by providing you with a visual picture of that information.

Pause for Reflection

Think of a course you're taking this term in which you're learning related pieces of information that could be joined together to form a concept map. Below, make a rough sketch of this map that includes the information you need to remember.

Figure 5.2 Concept Map for the Human Nervous System

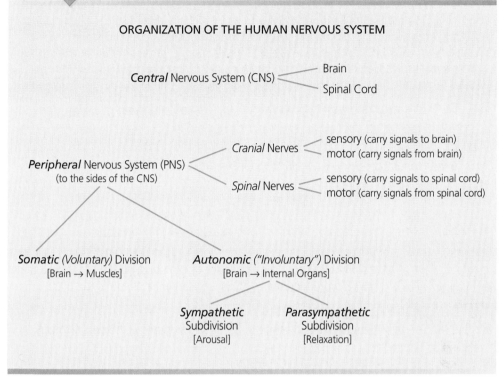

ORGANIZATION OF THE HUMAN NERVOUS SYSTEM

Central Nervous System (CNS)
— Brain
— Spinal Cord

Peripheral Nervous System (PNS)
(to the sides of the CNS)

Cranial Nerves
— sensory (carry signals to brain)
— motor (carry signals from brain)

Spinal Nerves
— sensory (carry signals to spinal cord)
— motor (carry signals from spinal cord)

Somatic (Voluntary) Division
[Brain → Muscles]

Autonomic ("Involuntary") Division
[Brain → Internal Organs]

Sympathetic
Subdivision
[Arousal]

Parasympathetic
Subdivision
[Relaxation]

Rhythm and Rhyme

This mnemonic device involves creating a short poem, song, or jingle that ties together the pieces of information you're trying to remember. Studies show that if information is arranged in a rhythmical-rhyming pattern, it is better remembered (Higbee, 1998). You may have had the experience of hearing a song or melody that you hadn't heard in years, but as soon as you hear the melody, the song lyrics immediately come back to mind. There are many well-known examples of using rhythm and rhyme to improve memory, such as the following:

◆ Remembering the letters of the alphabet by singing the alphabet song—"A, B, C, D, E, F, G, . . . H, I, J, K, L, M, N, O, P," etc.

◆ Remembering the correct number of days in each month—"Thirty days hath September, April, June, and November," etc.

◆ Remembering spelling rules—for example, "i" before "e" except after "c" or when sounded like "a" as in "neighbor" and "weigh."

◆ Remembering directions—for example, when using a screwdriver: "left-loose, right-tight" or, the more rhythmic: "lefty-loosey, righty-tighty."

◆ Remembering dates—for example, "In fourteen hundred and ninety-two, Columbus sailed the ocean blue."

There are many other examples that could be added to this list, which suggests that rhythm and rhyme can be applied to almost any information you're trying to remember. So, be on the lookout for how you could use this powerful mnemonic to remember course information by converting that information into a short poem or jingle.

The following mnemonic devices are effective for remembering multiple pieces of information in their correct order or sequence.

Acrostics

The term acrostic stems from the same root as the words "order" or "line," and refers to a mnemonic device that involves lining up the first letter of each item you're trying to remember in an order that creates a word (acronym), phrase, or sentence. Some of the most famous acrostics are:

◆ "HOMES"—to remember the names of the Great Lakes: Huron, Ontario, Michigan, Erie, and Superior;

◆ "Roy G Biv"—to remember the colors of the visual spectrum: Red, Orange, Yellow, Green, Blue, Indigo, and Violet;

◆ "Every Good Boy Does Fine"—to remember the notes on the musical scale's treble clef: E-G-B-D-F;

◆ FOIL—to remember how to multiply algebraic expressions—First Outer, Inner Last.

You can create an acrostic for anything that you're studying that has multiple parts or pieces. For instance, in Chapter 4 (Strategic Learning), you read about five different indicators or signs that you could use to see if you really comprehend or understand something at a deeper level than memorization. We could take the first letter of each indicator of comprehension to form the sentence, "I RATE"—to remember: I = Illustration (give an example of it), R = Representation (represent it in a different form, such as an analogy or metaphor), A = Application (apply it to solve a problem), T = Translation (paraphrase it in your own words), and E = Explanation (explain it to a friend).

An acrostic can be an invaluable memory aid when you are trying to remember any information that can be arranged in a list or sequence. A good strategy would be to list the first letters of individual items you're attempting to remember and rearrange their order until you come up with a sequence that spells out an acrostic, just as you would rearrange the letters in a "word jumble" that you see in newspapers. Be creative; it may take a while, but once you've found one, it's likely to be an effective way to store information in long-term memory that can help you prepare for exams. In fact, when you take exams, as soon as you receive the test, immediately write down your acrostics so you don't forget them once you begin to turn all your attention to taking the test. Then, you can just refer to the acrostics when you need them during the exam. Once you've got an acrostic down on paper, it can serve as a powerful memory trigger for the information associated with it.

◆ Pause for Reflection

Take a few moments and try to create an acrostic (word, phrase, or sentence) to serve as a mnemonic device for remembering the four key memory-improvement strategies that we've discussed thus far, namely: (1) meaningful association, (2) organization, (3) visualization, and (4) rhythm and rhyme.

(For one possibility, go to the bottom of the last page in this chapter.)

Link System

This mnemonic device uses meaningful associations to create a *story* containing the pieces of information that need to be remembered in a set order or sequence. It consists of two basic steps:

1. Make a list of the items you want to remember, arranging them in the order that you want to recall them.
2. Make an association between each successive pair of items on the list—that is, between the first and second items, then the second and third items, then the third and fourth items.

In other words, you associate two items at a time—linking each pair of items together until you form a complete association chain, which links all the items into one logically sequenced story.

For instance, suppose your biology course requires you to remember the following taxonomy of living organisms: (1) Kingdom, (2) Phylum, (3) Class, (4) Order, (5) Family, (6) Genus, and (7) Species. You might use the link system to weave all seven of these classifications into a meaningful story sequence, such as the following: "A mad ruler wanted to take over the world and create his own intelligent <u>kingdom</u>, so he decided to take his people and file 'em (<u>phylum</u>) into different <u>classes</u> of intelligence. He then delivered an <u>order</u> requiring that only members of the brightest groups be allowed to marry and have a <u>family</u> because they would be more likely to have genius (<u>genus</u>) children, which would improve the intelligence of the human <u>species</u>.

By linking all seven items into a short story such as this, seven unrelated bits of information are organized into one meaningful chunk. Thus, the link or chain system capitalizes on the power of the brain-based learning principles of organization and meaningfulness to improve memory.

You can also use the link system to help you remember parts of a speech you're planning to deliver, or the parts to a long essay answer you're preparing. You can do this by picking out a key phrase or catchword to represent the major point of each section of your speech or essay, and then devise a link between each of these catchwords, connecting them in the order in which you want to recall them. Thus, successive catchwords serve as memory cues to help you recall the specific piece of information associated with each of them, as well as their correct order or sequence.

Loci System

The word loci means place or location. This mnemonic device involves thinking of a natural sequence of places or locations along a path that you regularly travel and visually associating the items of information you're trying to remember at each of these sites. More specifically, this method consists of the following three steps:

1. Take a familiar location you pass through quite often and note the natural sequence of various sites (loci) you see along the way. For example, the location could be your home and the typical sequence of sites might be: the flower in your front yard, the concrete front steps, the oak front door, a narrow hallway, the numbered door leading to your room or apartment, etc.

2. Associate each of the items you want to remember with one of the sites along your route—in the order that you want to recall them. Associate the first item to be remembered with the first site on the route, the second item to be remembered with the second site, etc.

3. When you want to recall all the items in their proper sequence, just take an imaginary walk along your route, using each site as a cue to recall the item you associated with it.

The loci system mnemonic device uses a familiar location to trigger memory.

This memory strategy was discovered and used by famous Greek and Roman orators who delivered their speeches as they walked through their mansions, using each successive room as a visual cue to remember each successive part of their long speeches (Lofus, 1980). One current carry-over from this old tradition is the expression, "in the first place," which we tend to say when we're about to make a number of different points.

If you were to use the loci system to remember the Ten Commandments, you would visually associate one of the commandments with each successive site along your familiar route. To briefly illustrate: First, you could visualize a statue of a pagan god sitting in your front yard (for commandment #1: Thou shalt have no other gods before me). Second, you might imagine a salesman standing on your front steps cursing because your mother has just rejected his attempt to sell her a new encyclopedia (for commandment #2: Thou shalt not take the name of the Lord in vain), etc.

The loci system can be used to remember anything that comes in a series or sequence, such as:

◆ lists of information (e.g., Bill of Rights) or amendments to the Constitution,

◆ parts of a speech (letting each site stand for each section of your speech), or

◆ major sections of your answer to an essay question.

It is recommended that you visualize the images you want to remember as if you were seeing them with your own eyes, rather than watching yourself walking through the rooms as if you were a spectator. Also, as you go from place to place, try to feel the actual sensations you get from moving, because this will add a kinesthetic memory trace to your visual memory trace. Studies show that when people not only visualize a movement, but also imagine making the movement, it enhances their performance (Garfield, 1984). This technique is referred to as visual-motor behavior rehearsal (VMBR), and athletes have used it successfully to improve their recall of motor (muscle) memories (Suinn, 1985).

Some of the mnemonic devices we've just described may appear to be very involved or elaborate. However, the best strategy for using them effectively is to keep the process simple. Use Box 5.1 as a guide to developing mnemonic devices that are likely to be more effective than trying to memorize the information through continual repetition.

Pause for Reflection

Have you ever created a mnemonic of your own for information that you were studying and trying to remember?

If yes, what was it?

If no, why do you think that you've never created one?

••• Test-Taking Strategies

The last stage in the learning-and-memory process involves remembering what you've learned and demonstrating that knowledge on tests or exams. The first stage of the process involves attention to and reception of key information from lectures and readings; the second stage involves studying that information and storing it in your brain; and the third stage involves remembering that information by either recognizing or recalling it on exams. Described below is a series of test-taking strategies for improving your ability to remember information at test time, which in turn, should improve your test performances and course grades.

Before the Test

Be well prepared for the exam.

Studies show that college students who are well prepared for exams not only achieve higher test scores; they also experience lower test anxiety (Zohar, 1998). For instance, not cramming before the exam will reduce the usual anxiety associated with the frantic rush to obtain and retain information in a very short period of time.

There is evidence that college students who display greater amounts of procrastination also experience higher levels of test anxiety (Rothblum, Solomon, & Murakami, 1986). High levels of pre-test tension associated with rushing and late-night cramming are likely to carry over to the test itself, resulting in higher levels of test-taking tension. Furthermore, loss of sleep caused by previous-night cramming is likely to decrease your amount of dream (REM) sleep, which in turn, will likely increase the level of anxiety you experience the following day—i.e., test day. Also, research on test anxiety indicates that the most effective strategy for reducing high levels of test anxiety is the use of effective learning strategies prior to the exam (Benjamin, McKeachie, Lin, & Holinger, 1981; Jones & Petruzzi, 1995; Zeidner, 1995).

Adjust your study strategies to the type of test you will be taking.

Your memory for information you have studied will depend not only on how you studied, but also on how your memory will be tested (Stein, 1978). It may be that you can remember what you've studied and demonstrate knowledge of it in one way (e.g., multiple-choice test), but not if you are tested in a different format (e.g., essay test). So, in addition to adjusting your study strategies to the type of knowledge you're acquiring, you also need to adjust your study strategies so that they match the type of test you'll be taking.

College test questions tend to fall into either one of two general categories, and there are study strategies that work most effectively for each type.

1. Recognition Test Questions

This category of test questions asks you to select or choose the correct answer from answers that are provided to you. Falling into this category are multiple-choice, true-false, and matching questions. These test questions do not require you to retrieve and produce the correct answer entirely on your own. Instead, you're asked to recognize the correct answer by identifying it or picking it out—similar to identifying the "correct" criminal from a line-up of potential suspects.

2. Recall Test Questions

In contrast to recognition test questions, recall test questions require you to go into your memory bank, retrieve the information you've stored in your brain, and reproduce it on your own at test time. As the root term for recall implies, you have to "call back" to mind what you are trying to remember. Falling into the category of recall test questions are essay and short-answer questions that ask you to write your own response.

Recall test questions ask you, "What is it?" In contrast, recognition test questions ask you, "Is it this one?" As you probably already know, we can usually remember information on recognition tests more easily than we can on recall tests (Gordon, 1989) because recognition just involves identifying the correct answer; it does not demand that we retrieve and provide the answer on our own. For instance, we can remember faces more easily than names because

"IT'S NUMBER THREE, MR. HUGO, OUR SEVENTH GRADE TEACHER—THE ONE WHOSE EXAMS CONTAINED QUESTIONS NOT COVERED IN THE ASSIGNED READING."

Multiple-choice questions require recognition memory similar to that used to identify the correct criminal from a line-up of possible suspects.

seeing someone's face is similar to being given a recognition test—the only thing we have to do is say, "Yes, I recognize you (your face is familiar)." However, when we try to remember the name that goes with the face, it's similar to taking a recall test—now we have to come up with the name on our own, which is a more difficult memory task than simply recognizing a face that's presented to us. You have probably heard people say, "I've got a great memory for faces, but I'm terrible with names." However, you never hear them say, "I've got a great memory for names, but I'm terrible with faces!" It's also common to hear people say, "You're face is familiar, but I can't recall your name." But, you never hear them say, "Your name is familiar, but I can't recall your face!"

What does all this have to do with how you prepare for tests in college? Since recognition test questions ask you to recognize or identify the correct answer from among answers that are provided for you, a study strategy that involves looking over your notes and becoming familiar with key information may be an effective way to prepare for tests containing these questions. This study strategy works because reading over, becoming familiar with, and understanding the information written in your class notes and textbook matches the type of mental activity that you'll be asked to perform on the exam—reading over and identifying correct answers.

In contrast to recognition, recall test questions that require you to retrieve information and generate correct answers on your own (e.g., writing essays), require more elaborate study strategies. Recall test questions require *you* to generate or produce the correct answer, such as short-answer questions (e.g., "Explain what happens during photosynthesis") and longer essay questions (e.g., "Trace the causes and consequences of the industrial revolution").

Your recall memory may be tested in three basic ways:

1. **Paired-Associate Recall:** memory for one single piece of information that is "paired" or "associated" with another piece of information. For example, a test question that asks you to recall the Spanish word for "head," or the capital of Alaska.

2. **Free Recall:** memory for two or more pieces of information, which you are free to recall in any order or sequence that you like. For example, a test question that asks you to, "Name the countries of South America" or, "List and describe the major causes of World War I."

"When I looked at the first essay question, my whole life flashed before my eyes, then my whole mind went totally blank!"

Students can go "completely blank" on essay tests because they face a blank sheet that requires them to provide information on their own—as opposed to multiple-choice tests, which ask students to recognize or pick-out a correct answer from information that is provided for them.

3. Serial Recall: memory for two or more pieces of information in a specific series (order or sequence). For example, a test question that asks you to recall the names of all the vertebrae in the spinal column—in their correct order, from top to bottom.

What these three forms of recall memory have in common is that they require you to retrieve information on your own—a task that places greater demands on your memory than recognition. So, your study strategy for tests that require recall memory should be to practice retrieving the information on your own without looking at it, rather than just reading over information while it is in front of you. Research shows that practicing retrieval while studying information results in better recall memory for that information than just looking it over or re-reading it (Bjork, 1994). Simply reviewing information when studying for a recall test is similar to a football team reading the playbook or reviewing game films prior to a game, rather than actually practicing the plays. Or, imagine if actors were to prepare for their roles in a play by just looking over their lines—without practicing dress rehearsals during which they actually retrieve and say their lines without looking at the script. Obviously, these practice strategies do not match the actual performance situation, so the performance results will be much weaker. Similarly, studying for essay tests by looking over your class notes and highlighted reading will not prepare you to retrieve and recall information on your own, because it does not simulate what you'll actually be doing on the test itself.

Two of the most effective strategies for practicing memory retrieval while studying for recall tests are:

1. Recitation

Recitation involves saying to yourself the information you need to recall—*without looking at it*. Research studies indicate that memory for information is significantly strengthened when students study by trying to generate that information on their own, rather than reviewing or re-reading it (Graf, 1982). In particular, recitation strengthens recall memory in three key ways:

- Reciting essentially forces you to actively retrieve the information on your own, instead of just looking at that information while it's right in front of you. When preparing for recall tests that involve essay questions, it is more effective to write out what you are reciting so your practice will more closely match what you'll be expected to do on the test.
- Reciting gives you clear feedback on whether or not you can actually recall the information you're studying. If you cannot retrieve and recite the information to yourself without looking at it, then you know for sure you will not be able to recall it at test time, so you need to study it further. One way to ensure that you give yourself this feedback is to put the question on one side of an index card and the answer on the other side. If you find yourself turning over the index card to look at the answer before saying it, this is a good sign that you're not able to recall the information and it needs additional study.
- Reciting encourages you to use your own words, which gives you feedback on whether you are able to paraphrase it, which is one good indicator of whether you really understand what you're studying. Also, this is a good sign that you will be able to recall the information because if it is more deeply comprehended, it's more likely to be remembered.

Reciting while studying can be done silently, by speaking aloud, or by writing what you are saying. We recommend speaking aloud and writing out what you're reciting because these strategies involve physical action, which will keep you more actively involved or engaged with what you're studying. Speaking and writing also increases the number of sensory channels you use while learning, which, in turn, will increase the number of memory traces stored in your brain. For example, speaking aloud provides auditory stimulation and writing allows for motor and visual stimulation where you can feel and see what you have written.

2. Creation of Retrieval Cues

Suppose you're trying to remember a person's name that you know, but you just cannot seem to recall it. If a friend gives you a clue (e.g., the first letter of the person's name or a name that rhymes with it), this will suddenly trigger your memory of the person's entire name. What your friend did was provide you with a "retrieval cue." A retrieval cue can be considered to be a type of memory clue or reminder (like a string tied around your finger), which brings back to your mind what you've temporarily forgotten. The retrieval cue represents a piece of information that is connected to a whole chunk of information you're trying to recall; it helps you build back or reconstruct the total memory, because human memories are stored as parts in an interconnected network (Pribram, 1991) (Figure 5.3).

Figure 5.3

Human memories are stored in the brain as parts of an interconnected system or network. A retrieval cue represents one piece or part of a memory network that can activate and trigger your memory for other information stored in the same network.

© Jurgen Ziewe, 2007. Under license from Shutterstock, Inc.

If you're able to recall one key piece or segment of an interconnected network, it has the potential to trigger total recall by spreading and activating other pieces of information contained within the same organizational network (Collins & Loftus, 1975).

Relating this to studying for recall tests, studies show that students who are unable to remember information they studied will recall it if they are given a retrieval cue. For instance, suppose students have studied a list of items that includes some animals, but are unable to recall these animals on a later memory test. If these students are given a retrieval cue, such as "animals" at the time of the recall test (e.g., if the term "animals" is listed on the answer sheet), what often happens is that the student will then be able to recall some or all of the animals that they had temporarily forgotten (Kintsch, 1968). These research findings suggest that category names can serve as powerful retrieval cues. By taking information that you'll need to recall on an essay test and organizing it into categories, you can then use their category names as retrieval cues at the time of the test.

Pause for Reflection

Think of a course you're taking this term that contains information that could be easily grouped into categories.

What is the course?

What are the categories that could be used to organize information contained in that course?

Also, if you are studying for a recall test, you can intentionally create retrieval cues in the form of catchwords or catchphrases as a net to "catch" related ideas that you want to recall. You can then use that catchword or phrase to trigger your memory of the related information at the time of the exam. For example, an acronym can serve as a catchword, with each letter serving as a retrieval cue for a set of related ideas. Suppose you are studying for a test in abnormal psychology that will include essay questions that ask you to write about different types of mental illness. You might create an acronym like "SCOT" that could serve as a retrieval cue to help you remember to discuss *symptoms* (S), *causes* (C), *outcomes* (O), and *therapies* (T) for each type of mental illness you'll be writing about on the test.

Try to match your study environment as closely as possible to the test environment.

Athletic teams hold their last practice sessions on the field where they will actually play so that their practice environment and performance (game) situation match as closely as possible. Theatrical performers also practice their dress rehearsals on the same set where they will actually perform. Similarly, you want to make your last study (practice) session as similar to the test environment as possible in order to maximize transfer of what you've learned in your study situation to the test situation. For example, if you know how many essay questions you'll need to answer and the total amount of time you'll have to answer them, it would be ideal to practice writing the same number of essays under the same time deadline that you will encounter in the actual test situation.

Studies show that when students take a test in the same environment that they studied in, they tend to remember more of that information at test time than do students who study in one place and take the test in a different place (Smith, Glenberg, & Bjork, 1978). While it is unlikely that you'll be able to do all your studying in the same room that you will take your test in, it may be possible to do your final review in your classroom or in an empty classroom with similar features. This could strengthen your memory for the information you studied because the features of the room in which you studied the information may become associated with the information you studied, and seeing these features again at test time may help trigger memory of the information you studied (Tulving, 1983).

© JupiterImages Corporation.

Studying or doing a final review in the classroom where you will take a test could make recall easier during the exam.

Other studies demonstrate that if students are exposed to a distinctive or unique aroma while they are studying (e.g., the smell of chocolate) and are exposed to that same smell again during a later memory test, they display better memory for the information they studied than do students who didn't study and take the test with the same aroma present (Schab, 1990). Perhaps one practical application of this finding is to wear a distinctively smelling cologne or perfume while studying, and use it again on the day of the test. This might improve your memory for the information you studied by matching the scent of your study environment with the scent of your test environment. Although this strategy may seem silly, keep in mind that the area of the human brain where smell is perceived has connections with the brain's memory pathways (Jensen, 1998). This may account for why people commonly report that certain smells can trigger memories of past experiences (e.g., the smell of a summer breeze triggering memories of summer games played during childhood). Thus, don't underestimate the sense of smell's potential for promoting memory.

On the Day of the Test

Come to the test room fully equipped with all the test-taking tools you'll need (e.g., #2 pencil, pen, blue book, Scantron, calculator, etc.).

Also, bring back-up equipment in case you experience equipment failure (e.g., an extra pen in case your first one runs out of ink, or extra pencils in case your original one breaks); this will ensure that you don't lose test time and elevate your text anxiety while searching for replacements.

Sit in the same seat that you normally occupy in class.

As previously mentioned, there is some research indicating that memory is improved when information is recalled in the same place or environment where it was originally perceived and studied (Sprenger, 1999). Taking the test in the same seat that you normally occupy during lectures, which is the place where you originally heard much of the information that appears on the test, may also improve your test performance.

Try to get to the test a few minutes early.

Getting to the test ahead of time will give you time to review any mnemonic devices or memory-improvement shortcuts that you may have created, as well as hard-to-remember terms, formulas, equations, etc. This strategy will help get them on your mind and into your

Using Nutritional Strategies to Strengthen Your Academic Performance

Is there a "brain food" that can strengthen our mental performance? Can we "eat to learn?" Some animal studies suggest that memory may be improved by consumption of foods containing lecithin, which is a substance that helps the brain produce acetylcholine—a brain chemical that plays an important role in memory formation (Ulus & Wurtman, 1977). Fish contains a high amount of lecithin, which may have something to do with why some people refer to fish as "brain food."

·—· **CLASSIC QUOTE** ·—·

To keep the body in good health is a duty, otherwise we shall not be able to keep our mind strong and clear.

—Hindu Prince Gautama Siddharta, a.k.a., Buddha; founder of Buddhism, 563–483 BC

·—· **CLASSIC QUOTE** ·—·

No man can be wise on an empty stomach.

—George Elliot, 19th-century English novelist

Despite the results of some animal studies, there is not enough research yet available to conclude that there is any one miraculous food item humans can consume that will dramatically increase their ability to comprehend and retain knowledge. However, there is evidence that the following nutritional strategies may be used to improve mental performance on days when our knowledge is tested.

1. **Eat breakfast on the day of the exam.**

    Numerous studies show that students who eat a nutritious breakfast on the day they are tested typically attain higher test scores than students who do not (Martin & Benton, 1999; Smith, Clark, & Gallagher, 1999).

    Breakfast on the day of an exam should include grains, such as whole-wheat toast, whole-grain cereal, oatmeal, or bran, because those foods contain complex carbohydrates that will deliver a steady stream of energy to the body throughout the day; this should help sustain your test-taking endurance or stamina. Also, these complex carbohydrates should help your brain generate a steady stream of serotonin, which may reduce your level of nervousness or tension on test days.

2. **Make the meal you eat before an exam a light meal.**

    You don't want to take tests while feeling hungry, but the meal you consume nearest test time should not be a large one. Humans tend to get sleepy after consuming a large meal because it elevates our blood sugar to such a high level that large amounts of insulin are released into the bloodstream in order to reduce our high blood-sugar level. This draws blood sugar away from the brain, which results in a feeling of mental fatigue.

3. **If you feel you need an energy boost immediately before an exam, eat a piece of fruit rather than a candy bar.**

    Candy bars are processed sweets that can offer a short burst of energy provided by the sugar. Unfortunately, however, this short-term rise in blood sugar and quick jolt of energy is accompanied by an increase in nervous tension and is followed by a sudden, sharp decrease in energy and increase in sluggishness (Haas, 1994).

    The key is to find a food that can produce a state of elevated energy without elevating tension (Thayer, 1996) and maintains that state of energy at an even level. The best nutritional option we have for accomplishing this sustained level of energy is the natural sugar contained in a piece of fruit, not processed sugar that's artificially slipped into a candy bar.

4. **Avoid consuming caffeine before an exam.**

    Even though caffeine is a stimulant that increases alertness, it's also a legal drug that can increase your level of tension and make you jittery, which is not what you want to be feeling during a test, particularly if you tend to experience test anxiety. Also, caffeine is a diuretic, which means it will increase your urge to urinate. Naturally, this is an urge that you could do without during an exam when you're confined to a classroom for an extended period of time, sitting on your butt (and bladder).

short-term memory, so that you can retrieve them as soon as you receive the exam. Arriving early will also allow you to take a few minutes to get into a relaxed pre-test state by thinking positive thoughts, taking slow, deep breaths, or stretching and relaxing your muscles. Try to avoid discussing the test with other students just before the test begins because their last-minute questions, confusion, and anxiety may "rub off" on you. (Anxiety can be contagious.)

During the Test

As soon as you receive the test, write down any mnemonic devices or memory-improvement shortcuts that you may have created, as well as hard-to-remember terms, formulas, equations, etc.

This strategy ensures that you don't forget key information after you begin the test and get involved in the process of reading and answering questions, which can create memory interference for information you studied prior to the exam.

Answer the easier test questions first.

As soon as you receive the test, before launching into the first question, take a moment to check out the layout of the test. Note the questions that are worth the most points and the questions that you know well. Studies show that when easier questions are answered at the start of a test, students tend to perform better on more difficult questions that come later (Savitz, 1985) and achieve higher overall test scores (Roos et al., 1996). A good test-taking strategy is to place a checkmark by any difficult questions that you encounter and come back to them later. This strategy is recommended for several reasons:

- It will prevent you from devoting so much time trying to answer difficult questions that you end up running out of time before getting to questions you know well and would earn you full credit.

- After you've answered and obtained full credit for all the questions you know well, you will feel more confident and relaxed because you already have a good number of points "under your belt." This should reduce your anxiety level when you return to the more difficult items. Research shows that our ability to solve difficult problems and think creatively is improved when our anxiety levels are not high (Teigen, 1994).

- It allows you to put the difficult questions out of your mind for a while before coming back to them. Sometimes, answers or solutions suddenly pop into your mind after you get away from them and come back to them later (Csikszentmihalyi, 1996).

- By skipping difficult questions and proceeding to the more manageable ones, you may find information in the easier questions that relate to the more difficult ones and may help you answer them. You could then take this information and go back to solve some of the difficult questions that you previously skipped.

If you experience "memory block" for information that you know you've studied and have stored in your brain, try using the following strategies:

- Mentally put yourself back in the environment or situation in which you studied the information. Recreate the steps in which you learned the information that you've temporarily forgotten by mentally picturing the place where you first heard or saw it and where you studied it, including its sights, sounds, smells, time of day, etc. This memory-improvement strategy is referred to as "guided retrieval," and research supports its effectiveness (Glenberg et al., 1983). In fact, people use it all the time to help them remember a lost item by retracing their steps and trying to recall where they saw it last. Also, detectives use guided retrieval to help witnesses recall details of a crime that they are having difficulty remembering (Czaja, et al., 1994).

- Think of any idea or piece of information that may be related to the information you cannot retrieve. This related piece of information may trigger your memory for the forgotten information because related pieces of information are usually stored as memory traces within the same network of brain cells. Studies show when students experience

STUDENT PERSPECTIVE

"Avoid flipping through notes (cramming) immediately before a test. Instead, do some breathing exercises and think about something other than the test."

—Advice to first-year students from a college sophomore (Walsh, 2005)

temporary forgetting, they're more likely to suddenly recall that information if they first recall partial information that relates to it in some way (Reed, 1996).

◆ Take your mind off the question and turn to another question. Just taking your mind off it for a while may allow your subconscious to work on it and trigger your memory. Also, you may find information appearing in later *test questions* that may serve as a retrieval cue for stimulating your recall of the information you've forgotten.

During tests, when I experience memory block, I usually _____.

I am most likely to experience memory block in the following subject areas:

To manage test anxiety, consider the following practices and strategies.

1. Focus your attention on the here and now—concentrate fully on the process of answering the test question that you're currently working on, and avoid thinking or worrying about what the future outcome may be—i.e., your eventual test grade.

2. Focus your vision on the test in front of you, not the students around you. Do not spend valuable test time looking at what others are doing and wondering whether they are doing better than you are. If you came to the test well prepared and are still finding the test to be difficult, it's very likely that other students are finding it difficult too. (And if you happen to notice that other students are finishing before you do, don't assume they "breezed through" the test or that they're smarter than you. Their faster finish may simply reflect the fact that they didn't know many of the answers and decided to give up and get out, rather than prolong the agony.)

3. Do not focus an excessive amount of attention to the amount of time remaining to complete the exam. Repeatedly checking the clock during the test can distract your thought process and increase your stress level, so only check the time periodically. Also, do your time checking after you've completed test questions, rather than during your answers and interrupting your train of thought. (You might also consider taking off your wristwatch or taking out your cell phone and laying it on your desk during the test, so you can check the time more easily during the exam.)

4. Control your thoughts—focus on thinking positively and showing what you know, rather than worrying about what answers you don't know and how many points you have lost. Our thoughts can influence our emotions (Ellis, 1995), and positive emotions, such as those associated with optimism and a sense of accomplishment, can improve mental performance by enhancing the brain's ability to process, store, and retrieve information (Rosenfield, 1988).

5. Keep the test in perspective. The exam does not represent a test of your general intelligence or your overall academic ability, and the score you receive is not a reflection on you as a person (e.g., your character or self-worth). In fact, a low test-grade may not

reflect lack of effort or ability on your part, but instead may reflect the complexity of the course material or the complexity of the test itself. College exams are going to be more difficult than high school tests, and it's less likely that college students will get 90 to 100 percent of the total points on any given exam. Remember that you can achieve good grades on college exams without having to achieve near-perfect test scores.

BOX 5.3 Snapshot SUMMARY

Test Anxiety

- Understand what test anxiety is and what it's not. Do not confuse anxiety with stress. Stress is something that cannot be completely eliminated when you are involved in situations where your performance is being evaluated. Instead of trying to block out stress altogether, your goal should be to control it, contain it, and maintain it at a level that maximizes the quality of your performance. Actually, it is beneficial to experience a moderate amount of stress during tests and other performance situations because moderate stress tends to improve your levels of alertness, concentration, and memory (Sapolsky, 2004). Stress is a physical reaction that prepares your body for action by arousing and energizing it, and this arousal and energy can be used productively to strengthen your performance. In fact, if you were totally stress-free during an exam, this may indicate that you are too laid back and could care less about how well you're doing. Thus, your goal should not be to eliminate or ignore the stress you experience during exams; instead, your goal should be to remain aware of it and keep it at a moderate level, capitalizing on its capacity to help you get "psyched up" and "pumped up," but preventing it from reaching such a high level that you become "psyched out" or "stressed out."

- Identify the symptoms of test anxiety. If your stress level gets too high during exams, you may begin to experience test anxiety—a negative emotional state that can weaken your mental performance by producing mental interference (Tobias, 1985), such as interfering with your attention (Jacobs and Nadel, 1985), memory (O'Keefe & Nadel, 1985), and the ability to think at a higher level (Caine & Caine, 1991). If you experience the following symptoms during tests, your stress level may be at a level high enough to be accurately called test anxiety.

  1. You feel physical symptoms of anxiety during the test, such as: pounding heartbeat, rapid pulse, muscle tension, sweating, or an upset stomach.

  2. You having difficulty concentrating or focusing your attention while answering test questions.

  3. Negative thoughts and feelings run through your head (e.g., fear of failure or self-putdowns such as: "I always mess up on exams").

  4. You rush through the test just to get it over with (and alleviate the anxiety you may be experiencing).

  5. Even though you studied and know the material, you go blank during the exam and forget what you studied. However, you're able to remember the information after you turn in your test and leave the test situation.

- One final note on the topic of text anxiety: If you continue to experience test anxiety after implementing the strategies we have just suggested, seek assistance from a student support professional in your Learning (Academic Support) Center or Personal Counseling Office.

How would you rate your general level of test anxiety during most exams?

High _____

Moderate _____

Low _____

Do you tend to experience different levels of anxiety depending on the type of test you're taking?

On what type(s) of tests do you tend to experience the most anxiety?

Consider the following test-taking strategies for multiple-choice questions.

◆ Read all of the choices that are listed and use a process-of-elimination strategy, whereby you eliminate choices that are clearly wrong and continue doing so until you narrow them down to one answer that seems to be the best choice.

Keep in mind that the correct answer is often the one that is *most probably* true; it does not have to be absolutely true—just "more true" than the other choices listed.

A *process-of-elimination* approach is an effective test-taking strategy to use when answering difficult multiple-choice questions.

◆ Use *test wise* strategies when you do not know the correct answer.

Your decision to choose a particular answer on a multiple-choice question should first be based on your knowledge of the material, rather than an attempt to outsmart the test by figuring out the correct answer based on how the question is worded. However, if you have used all your knowledge and the process-of-elimination strategy still leaves you with two or more answers that appear to be correct, then you should rely on being "test-wise," which is the ability to use the characteristics of the test question itself (such as its wording or format) to increase the probability of choosing the correct answer (Millman,

Bishop, & Ebel, 1965). Listed below are three key, test-wise strategies for making wise choices on a multiple-choice question whose answer you do not know or cannot remember.

1. Pick an answer that contains qualifying words, such as: "usually," "probably," "likely," "sometimes," "perhaps," or "may." Truth often does not come in absolute statements, so options that contain broad generalizations or definitive words are more likely to be false. For example, answers containing words such as: "always," "never," "only," "must," and "completely" are more likely to be false than true.

2. Pick the longest answer. True statements often require more words to make them true.

3. Pick a middle answer rather than the first or last answer. For example, on a question with four choices, select answer "b" or "c" rather than "a" or "d." Studies show that instructors have a greater tendency to place correct answers as middle choices, rather than as the first or last choice (Linn & Gronlund, 1995), perhaps because they think the correct answer will be too obvious or "stand out" if it's listed as the very first or very last choice.

◆ When reviewing your test and checking answers to multiple-choice (or true-false) questions, be especially careful to check for any questions that you may have skipped and intended to go back to later.

In some cases when students skip a question, they forget to skip the number of that question on the answer form, so it throws off the order of their remaining answers by one space or line. On a computer-scored test, this can result in answers being marked wrong because they are off by one space or line on the answer form.

When checking your answers on multiple-choice or true-false tests, do not be afraid to change an answer after you have re-read it and given it more thought.

Since 1928, there have been over 30 studies on the topic of changing answers on multiple-choice and true-false tests (Kuhn, 1988). These studies consistently show that most changed test answers go from an incorrect to a correct answer, and the majority of students who changed answers improved their test scores (Benjamin, Cavell, & Shallenberger, 1984; Shatz & Best, 1987). For example, in one study of more than 1,500 students' midterm exams in an introductory psychology course, it was found that when students changed their answers, 51 percent of the time they went from wrong to right and only 25 percent of the time they went from right to wrong (Kruger et al., 2005). This is probably because students may catch a mistake they made when they read the question the first time, or they discover some information later in the test that causes them to reconsider their first answer. However, you should not go overboard on your answer-changing. If you find yourself changing a large number of your original answers, this may indicate that you were not well prepared for the exam and are just doing a lot of guessing and second-guessing.

 Pause for Reflection

On exams, do you ever change your original answers?

If you do change answers, what is the usual reason why you make a change?

Consider the following test-taking strategies for essay questions.

♦ Make a brief outline or list of bullet points representing the main ideas to be included in your answers before you begin to write them. This strategy is effective for several reasons:

◊ An outline will help you remember the major points you intend to make and the order in which you intend to make them. This should help prevent forgetting of any major points once you begin writing and focusing your attention on your sentences and word selection.

◊ An outline will improve your answer's organization, which is one key aspect of your essays that your instructor will likely take into consideration when grading them. (You can make your answers' organization even clearer by underlining your major sections or numbering your major points.)

◊ Having some advanced idea about what you're going to write about should reduce your test anxiety. The outline will take care of the answer's organization in advance, so you don't have to pay attention to both organizing and explaining your answer at the same time while writing it out.

◊ By making an outline for your answers to each essay question before beginning to write any of them, if you happen to run out of test time, your instructor will be able to see your outline for any questions that you didn't have time to complete. Your outline should earn you points, even if you didn't have the opportunity to convert it into sentence form, because it demonstrates your knowledge of the major ideas relating to that unfinished question. (In contrast, if you begin the test by writing out your answers to essay questions one at a time, you run the risk of running out of time before getting to questions you knew well and having nothing on your test to show that you knew them.)

♦ Get directly to the point on each essay question.

Avoid elaborate introductions to your answers that take-up your test time (as well as your instructor's grading time) and don't earn you any points. For example, don't start your answers by writing something like, "This is a very interesting question that we had a great discussion on in class . . . ." Your time on essay tests is often limited, so you cannot afford to spend valuable test time on flowery introductions. One strategy for getting right to the point of the question is to immediately include part of the question in the first sentence of your answer. For example, if the question asks, "Discuss how capital punishment may or may not reduce the nation's murder rate," your first sentence might be, "Capital punishment may not reduce the murder rate for the following reasons . . ."

♦ Answer all essay questions as precisely and completely as possible.

Do not assume that your instructor already knows what you're talking about, or will be bored by details. Instead, take the approach that you are writing to someone who knows little or nothing about the subject—as if you are a teacher and the reader is a student.

 Remember: As a general rule, it is better to *over*-explain than to under-explain your answers to essay questions.

♦ Whenever possible, cite specific evidence—facts, stats, quotes, and figures—rather than general statements and personal opinions.

Assume the role of a criminal lawyer who is making a case by presenting concrete evidence ("exhibit A," "exhibit B," etc.). Also, keep in mind that the time allotted for

Exhibit 1

Identical twins
adoption
Parents/family tree

6/6

2. There are several different studies that scientists conduct, but one study that they conduct to find out how genetics can influence human behavior is in <u>identical twins</u>. Since they are identical, they will most likely end up very similar in behavior because of their identical genetic makeup. Although environment has some impact, genetics are still a huge factor, and will more likely than not, behave similarly. Another type of study is with <u>Parents and their family trees</u>. Looking at a subjects family tree will alleviate why a certain person is bi-polar or depressed. It is most likely a cause of a gene in the family tree, even if it was last seen decades ago. Lastly, another study is w/ <u>adopted children</u>. If adopted children act a certain way, that is unique to that child, and researchers find the parents/family tree, they will most likely see similar behavior in the parents/siblings as well.

No freewill
No afterlife

6/6

2. The monistic view of the mind-brain relationship is so strongly opposed and criticised because there is belief or assumption that <u>freewill</u> is taken away from people. For example, if a person commits a heinous crime, it can be argued "monistically" that the chemicals in the brain were the reason, and that a person cannot think for themselves to act otherwise. This view limits responsibility.
Another reason that this view is opposed is because it has been said that <u>there is no afterlife</u>. If the mind and brain are one in the same, and there is NO difference, then once the brain is dead, and is no longer functioning, so is the mind, thus, it cannot continue to live beyond what we know today as life. And this goes against many religions, which is why this reason, in particular, is heavily opposed.

Written answers to two short essay questions given by a college sophomore, which demonstrate effective use of bulleted lists or short outlines to ensure recall of most important points.

---

essay tests may not allow you to write down all the evidence you know. Be selective and choose to write down your most powerful or persuasive pieces of evidence first.

◆ Leave extra space between your answers to each essay question. This strategy will enable you to easily add information to your original answer that you may happen to recall at a later point in the test.

◆ When reviewing and checking your answers on essay test questions, proofread what you have written and correct any spelling or grammatical errors that you find. Elimination of such errors is likely to improve your test score. Even if your instructor does not explicitly state that grammar and spelling will be counted in determining your grade, these mechanical mistakes may still subconsciously influence your professor's overall evaluation of your written work.

◆ Neatness counts. Research indicates that neatly written essays tend to be scored higher than sloppy ones, even if the answers are essentially the same (Klein & Hart, 1968). This is understandable when you consider that grading essay answers is a time-consuming task that forces your weary-eyed instructor to plod through multiple styles of handwriting—whose readability may range from crystal clear to cryptic code. So, make a point of writing as clearly as possible; and if you happen to finish the test with time to spare, "clean up" your writing by re-writing any sloppily written words or sentences.

◆ Before turning in your test, carefully review and double-check your answers.

This is the critical last step in the process of effective test taking. Sometimes the rush and anxiety of taking a test can cause test-takers to overlook details, misread instructions, unintentionally skip questions, or make absentminded mistakes. When taking essay tests, there may also be a natural tendency to grow tired of writing toward the end of the test and fall into the mindset that you just want to finish it up, turn it in, and get the whole thing over with. Try to avoid this tendency, as well as any ego-trip tendency to be among the fastest students in class to turn in their test. Instead, take some time after you're done to systematically review your answers and be sure that you didn't make any mindless mistakes. If you take into account the amount of time and effort you put into preparing for the exam, it certainly makes good sense to take just a few more minutes to be sure that you get the "maximum mileage" out of the time and effort you spent on test preparation.

Pause for Reflection

Honestly rate yourself in terms of how frequently you use the following test-taking strategies, according to the following scale:

4 = always, 3 = sometimes, 2 = rarely, 1 = never.

1. I take tests in the same seat that I usually sit in to take class notes.	4 3 2 1
2. I answer the easier test questions first.	4 3 2 1
3. I use a "process-of-elimination" approach on multiple-choice tests by eliminating choices until I find one that is correct or most accurate.	4 3 2 1
4. On essay test questions, I outline or map-out my ideas before I begin to write the answer.	4 3 2 1
5. I look for information included on the test that may help me answer difficult questions, or may help me remember information I've forgotten.	4 3 2 1
6. I leave extra space between my answers to essay questions in case I want to come back to them to add more information later.	4 3 2 1
7. I carefully review my work, double-checking for errors and skipped questions before turning in my tests.	4 3 2 1

After the Test: Troubleshooting Test-Taking Errors and Sources of Lost Points on Exams

Your test results represent a potential source of valuable feedback that you can use to improve your future test performances and your final course grade. Examine your tests carefully when you get them back, being sure to note any written comments that your instructor may have made. See where you went right—so you can do it again, and see where you went wrong—so you can avoid making the same mistake again.

Consider reviewing your test with other classmates. In particular, review your test with a classmate who did exceptionally well because it can provide you with a model that you can learn from and get a better idea about the type of work your instructor expects on exams. Also, con-

Seeking feedback from your peers is a good test-review strategy to identify correct answers after exams, but it's a violation of academic integrity to use it *during* exams.

sider making an appointment with your course instructor to seek feedback on how you might improve your performance on the next test.

When seeking feedback from others, seek quality feedback, which has the following features:

◆ Quality feedback is specific—it precisely identifies what you should do to improve your performance and how you should go about doing it. For example, after a test, seek feedback from your instructors that provides you with more than just information about what your grade is, or why you lost points; instead, seek specific information about what you could do to improve your performance next time.

◆ Quality feedback is prompt—it comes soon after completing a task, because this is the time when you are most motivated to receive it and most likely to retain it. For example, as soon as possible after completing tests or assignments, review your performance with classmates or your professor.

◆ Quality feedback comes early in the learning process—when you still have plenty of time to use it to improve your performance. For example, seek feedback from instructors early in the term, so you have more time to use that feedback to improve your course performance and course grade.

Receiving feedback from your instructor can be an excellent way to improve future performance.

Whatever you do, try not to let a bad test grade get you mad or sad, particularly if it occurs during the first half of the term. Look at mistakes in terms of what they can do *for* you, rather than *to* you. A poor test performance can be turned into a valuable learning experience by using test results as feedback or as "error detectors" for locating the specific source of your mistakes.

 Remember: Your past mistakes shouldn't be ignored or neglected; instead, they should be inspected, detected, and corrected so you don't replay them on future tests.

On those test questions where you lost points, try to pinpoint what stage in the learning process the breakdown occurred by asking yourself the following key questions about the source of lost points on exams:

1. **Did you *have* the information you needed to answer the question correctly?**

   If you didn't have the information, what was the source of the missing information? Was it information presented in class that didn't get into your notes? If so, take a look at the strategies for improving listening and note-taking habits (pp. 115–122). If the missing information was from your assigned reading, check whether you're using effective reading strategies (pp. 122–126).

2. **Did you have the information, but did not study it because you didn't think it was important?**

   If this occurred, then you might want to review the study strategies for finding and focusing on the most important information in class lectures and reading assignments (pp. 127–131).

3. **Did you know the information, but not well enough?**

   This may mean one of three things:

   a. You didn't store the information adequately in your brain, so your memory trace for it wasn't strong enough for you to recall it at the time you took the test. This suggests that more study or practice time needs to be spent on recitation or rehearsal (pp. 158–159).

   b. There may have been too much interference built-up across all the information you studied, because you crammed too much of it in just before the test. The solution here would be to distribute your study time more evenly in advance of the next exam, and take advantage of the effective "part-to-whole" study method (pp. 130–131).

   c. You put in enough study time and you spread out your study time well enough, but you didn't study effectively or strategically. For example, you may have studied for essay questions by just reading over your class and reading notes, rather than writing them out and rehearsing them. The solution to this type of error would be to adjust or align your study strategy to better match the type of test you are taking (pp. 156–160).

4. **Did you study the material but didn't really understand it or comprehend it deeply?**

   If so, you may need to self-monitor your comprehension more carefully while studying to monitor whether you truly understand the material (pp. 136–138).

5. **Did you know the information but were not able to retrieve it during the exam?**

   If you had the information on the "tip of your tongue" during the exam, this indicates that the memory of it was stored in your brain, but the problem was that you couldn't get at it when you needed it. This error may be corrected by making more use of retrieval cues and mnemonic devices (pp. 146–154).

6. **Did you know the answer but just made a careless test-taking mistake?**

   If so, the solution may be simply to take more time to review your test after finishing it, double-checking it for absentminded mistakes before turning it in (pp. 170–172, 174).

BOX 5.4 *Snapshot SUMMARY*

How to Compute Your Grade-Point Average (GPA)

Most colleges and universities use a grading scale that ranges from 0 to 4.0 to represent a student's grade-point average (GPA) or quality-point average (QPA). Some schools use letter grades only, while other institutions use letter grades with pluses and minuses.

Grading System Using Letters Only

Grade	=	Point Value
A	=	4
B	=	3
C	=	2
D	=	1
F	=	0

GRADE POINTS Earned Per Course = Course Grade Multiplied by the Number of Course Credits

GRADE POINT AVERAGE (GPA) = $\dfrac{\text{Total Number of Grade Points for All Courses}}{\text{Divided by Total Number of Course Units}}$

SAMPLE/EXAMPLE GPA

Course	Units	×	Grade	=	Grade Points
Roots of Rock 'n' Roll	3	×	C (2)	=	6
Daydreaming Analysis	3	×	A (4)	=	12
Surfing Strategies	1	×	A (4)	=	4
Wilderness Survival	4	×	B (3)	=	12
Sitcom Analysis	2	×	D (1)	=	2
Love and Romance	3	×	A (4)	=	12
	16				48

GPA = $\dfrac{48}{16}$ = 3.0

Grading System Using Letters with Pluses and Minuses

Grade	=	Point Value
A	=	4.0
A–	=	3.7
B+	=	3.3
B	=	3.0
B–	=	2.7
C+	=	2.3
C	=	2.0
C–	=	1.7
D+	=	1.3
D	=	1.0
D–	=	.7
F	=	0

GRADE POINTS Earned Per Course = Course Grade *Multiplied* by the Number of Course Credits

GRADE POINT AVERAGE (GPA) = $\dfrac{\text{Total Number of Grade Points for All Courses}}{\textit{Divided} \text{ by Total Number of Course Units}}$

(continued)

SAMPLE/EXAMPLE

Course	Units	×	Grade	=	Grade Points
Roots of Rock 'n' Roll	3	×	C (2.0)	=	6.0
Daydreaming Analysis	3	×	A (4.0)	=	12.0
Surfing Strategies	1	×	B (3.0)	=	3.0
Wilderness Survival	4	×	B+ (3.3)	=	13.2
Sitcom Analysis	2	×	C– (1.7)	=	3.4
Love and Romance	3	×	A– (3.7)	=	11.1
	16				48.7

$$GPA = \frac{48.7}{16} = 3.04$$

Semester or *Quarter* GPA = GPA for one academic term (semester or quarter)*
Cumulative GPA = GPA for *all* semesters or quarters combined

Academic *Sanctions* or *Penalties***
Academic Probation = GPA less than 2.0 in first term
Academic Dismissal = Cumulative GPA continuing to remain below 2.0 beyond first term

Awards for Academic Excellence**
Dean's List = Achieving an outstanding semester GPA (e.g., *3.5* or higher)
Summa Cum Laude = Graduating with Highest Honors (e.g., achieving a cumulative GPA of *3.8*)
Magna Cum Laude = Graduating with High Honors (e.g., achieving a cumulative GPA of *3.5*)
Cum Laude = Graduating with Honors (e.g., achieving a cumulative GPA of *3.3*)

* An academic term at most colleges and universities is either a *semester* (15 weeks) or *quarter* (10 weeks)

** The criteria or standards for academic sanctions/penalties and academic awards can vary from college to college. See your *College Catalog* (*Bulletin*) or *Student Handbook* for details.

Pause for Reflection

When this term began, what grade-point average (GPA) were you hoping to attain?

Based on your grades thus far this term, what GPA do you think you'll end-up with at the end of the term?

••• Summary and Conclusion

We started this chapter by noting that learning and memory are interrelated mental processes, both of which are critical for academic success. It may be said that learning relates more to the *input* (storage) of information into our brain, and memory relates more to the *output* (retrieval) of that stored information when we need it. However, strategies that are effective for improving information storage (learning) and information retrieval (remembering what we've learned) involve similar principles. Both learning and memory can be improved by implementing three key principles:

1. meaningful association—relating what you want to learn and remember to something you already know,
2. organization—grouping or classifying it into categories (also, chunking information into a rhythmic and rhyming pattern, such as a short poem or jingle, can strengthen your ability to remember it), and
3. visualization—creating a visual image of it in your mind.

Furthermore, the way in which your memory is tested may influence your ability to remember what you've learned. You are able to remember information more easily when you're asked to recognize or identify it, such as identifying the correct answer on a multiple-choice test. In contrast, it is more difficult to remember information when you have to recall it entirely on your own, such as recalling information on an essay test or short-answer test. When you are asked to recall information, you are being asked to retrieve it on your own—without any cues or clues provided for you. To handle this more demanding memory task, you need to create your own retrieval cues. In fact, all the effective memory-improvement strategies or mnemonic devices discussed in this chapter have one thing in common: they provide you with a retrieval cue that effectively triggers recall.

We conclude this chapter with a reminder of three key ingredients of successful test performance:

1. Be aware of how your knowledge will be tested and employ memory-improvement strategies that will best enable you to remember and demonstrate what you know.
2. Be "test wise"—maintain awareness of how the characteristics and formats of the test itself, such as the way test questions are worded, can provide clues to correct answers.
3. Manage test anxiety—maintain awareness of the amount of stress you're experiencing during exams and keep it at a moderate level to produce optimal performance.

●●● Learning More through Independent Research

Web-Based Resources for Further Information on Improving Memory and Test Performance

For additional information relating to ideas discussed in this chapter, we recommend the following Web sites:

For improving memory:
www.utexas.edu/student/utlc/class/mkg-grd/memory.html
http://memory.uva.nl/memimprovement/eng/

For improving test-taking:
http://web.mit.edu/arc/learning/modules/test/testtypes.html
http://cws.unc.edu/content/view/71/0/1/2/

CHAPTER 5

Exercise #1. Self-Assessment of Learning Strategies

Look back at the ratings you gave yourself for effective test-taking strategies (p. 170). Add up your total score for this set of strategies (maximum score for the set would be 28):

Test-Taking Strategy Score: _____

SELF-ASSESSMENT QUESTIONS

1. In what strategy area did you score lowest?

2. Do you think that the strategy area in which you scored lowest is related to your lowest course grade at this point in the term?

3. Of the seven specific strategies listed within the area that you scored lowest, do you see any that you could immediately put into practice to improve your lowest course grade?

Exercise #2. Midterm Self-Evaluation

Since you are at about the midpoint of this textbook, you may be at about the midpoint of your first term in college. It is at this time of the term when you are likely to experience the midterm crunch—a wave of midterm exams and due dates for certain papers and projects. This may be a good time for you to step back and assess your academic progress thus far.

Use the form below to list the courses you're taking this term and the grades you are currently receiving in each of these courses. If you do not know what your grade is, take a few minutes to check your syllabus for your instructor's grading policy, and check your scores on completed tests and assignments. This should give you at least a rough idea of where you stand in your courses. If you're having difficulty determining your grade in any course, even after checking your course syllabus and returned tests or assignments, then ask your instructor how you could estimate your current grade.

Course No.	Course Title	Instructor	Grade
1.			
2.			
3.			
4.			
5.			

1. Were these the grades you were *hoping* to get? Are you pleased or disappointed?

2. Were these the grades you *expected* to get? (Or, were they better or worse than expected?)

3. If these grades turn out to be your final course grades for the term, what would your overall Grade Point Average (GPA) be? (See pp. 168–169 for information on "How to Compute Your GPA.")

4. Do you see any patterns in your performance that suggest specific things you are doing well or things that you need to improve?

5. If you had to pinpoint one action step you could immediately take to improve your lowest course grades, what would it be?

▼ CASE STUDY

Bad Feedback: Shocking Midterm Grades

Joe Frosh has really enjoyed his first weeks on campus. He has met lots of interesting people and feels that he really fits in socially. He also likes the fact that his college schedule does not require that he be in class for five to six hours per day, like it did in high school. This is the good news. The bad news is that, unlike high school where his grades were all "A's" and "B's", his first midterm grades in college are three "C's", one "D," and one "F." He was totally stunned and a bit depressed by his midterm grades because he thought he was doing well. Since he never received grades this low in high school, he's beginning to think that he is not college material and may flunk out.

Reflection and Discussion Questions

1. What factors may have caused or contributed to Joe's bad start?

2. What are Joe's options at this point?

3. What do you recommend Joe do now to get his grades up and avoid being placed on academic probation?

4. What might Joe do in the future to prevent this midterm setback from happening again?

Higher-Level Thinking

Moving Beyond Basic Knowledge and Comprehension to Higher Levels of Critical and Creative Thinking

Learning Goals

The primary goal of this chapter is to increase your awareness and understanding of the thinking process, and help you develop the type of higher-level thinking skills needed to excel in college.

Outline

Activate Your Thinking

Please start this chapter by completing the following sentence:

To me, *critical thinking* means . . .

_____

_____

(At a later point in this chapter, we will discuss critical thinking and flash back to your response to this incomplete sentence.)

●●● What Is Thinking?

"Thinking" refers to the mental process of consciously experiencing thoughts, ideas, and images. Psychologists often refer to thinking as "cognition" or as "cognitive" activity (from "cogito," meaning "to think" or "to know"), and distinguish it from emotions (e.g., anger or anxiety) or drives (e.g., hunger or sex). Brain research confirms that thought and consciousness occur in the upper part of the brain, nearer its outer surface, whereas emotions and drives originate from deep within the middle area of the brain (LeDoux, 1996) (Figure 6.1).

Figure 6.1 Where Thoughts, Emotions, and Drives are Experienced in the Brain

The ability to think at higher levels is a key characteristic that distinguishes human beings from other living creatures. When the human brain is compared to the brains of other animals, it is clear that the area that is most responsible for higher thinking—the frontal lobe—is much larger in humans than other animals. This gives humans a distinctive biological advantage in intelligence and enables us to think at higher levels than any other living species (Figure 6.2).

Some scholars argue that it is the presence of thinking that defines a "living" or an "alive" human being. In contrast, prolonged absence of any electrical activity (flat line) in the upper parts of the human brain that are responsible for conscious awareness and thinking is referred to as "cerebral brain death" (Figure 6.3).

Figure 6.2

The part of the brain responsible for higher thinking (frontal lobe) is much larger in humans than other animals, including the highly intelligent chimpanzee.

Frontal Lobe

Figure 6.3

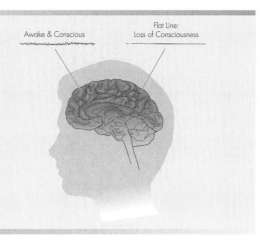

Awake & Conscious

Flat Line:
Loss of Consciousness

"Flat Line": prolonged absence of activity in the uppermost part of the brain, which is responsible for conscious awareness and thought, may indicate that a human being is no longer alive, even though lower parts of the brain may still be functioning.

●●● What is Higher-Level Thinking?

Thinking includes all those mental processes that are involved in learning, acquiring knowledge, and comprehending ideas. However, when we use the term "higher-level" thinking, we are referring to thinking that is "higher" than that used for basic learning, and which involves a more advanced level of thought. For instance, reviewing textbook information that you've highlighted and taken notes on does involve thinking, and it will help you learn and remember that information. However, *higher-level* thinking occurs when you reflect on that information and perform a more advanced mental act, such as evaluating its usefulness or integrating it with your class notes to create a larger, more comprehensive product. When you see contestants perform on TV quiz shows (e.g., "Jeopardy" or "Who Wants to Be a Millionaire?"), they are responding with factual knowledge to questions asking for information about who, what, when, and where. If these contestants were to be tested for higher-level thinking, they would be answering more challenging questions, such as: "Why?" "How?" or "What if?"

As its name implies, higher-level thinking involves setting the bar higher and "jacking up" your thinking to levels that go beyond merely remembering, reproducing, or regurgitating factual information. In college, simply remembering information may get you a grade of "C," comprehending the information at a deeper level may get you a "B," and going beyond comprehension to demonstrate higher-level thinking should get you an "A."

> **Remember:** Your college professors want you to do more than just *retain* information; they want you to *attain* higher levels of thinking. So, don't stop thinking as soon as you understand something; instead, take it a step higher and analyze it, evaluate it, build on it, or connect it with other concepts you've learned.

Also, your future employers will expect you to apply higher-level thinking skills to meet challenges and solve problems that arise in the workplace (Business/Higher Education Round Table, 1991, 1992; Secretary's Commission on Achieving Necessary Skills, 1992; Education Commission of the States, 1995).

This is not to say that basic knowledge and comprehension are unimportant. Factual knowledge and basic comprehension in different subject areas provide the necessary foundation for the steps that enable you to climb up to reach higher levels of thinking (Figure 6.4).

STUDENT PERSPECTIVE

"To me, thinking at a higher level means deep thought. It is when you have to put your time and effort into whatever you are thinking or writing."

—First-year college student

STUDENT PERSPECTIVES

"To me, thinking at a higher level means to think and analyze something beyond the obvious and find the deeper meaning."

—First-year college student

"To me, thinking at a higher level means going beyond understanding something on a superficial and general level; it requires a deep and profound thought process."

—First-year college student

Figure 6.4 The Relationship between Knowledge, Comprehension, and Higher-Level Thinking

For example, we cannot do higher-level thinking in math until we've acquired factual knowledge (e.g., memorizing our multiplication tables) and basic comprehension (understanding what the concept of multiplication really means). However, higher-level thinking doesn't stop there. It builds on this basic knowledge to reach higher levels of thought, which enables us to solve more complex mathematical problems.

••• Defining and Classifying the Major Forms of Higher-Level Thinking

As we mentioned in Chapter 2, self-awareness or to "know thyself" is a major goal of a liberal arts education. One important aspect of yourself that you should know well is *how you think*. Consequently, our first major objective in this chapter is to dissect the process of higher-level thinking in order to help you gain a deeper understanding of what this thought process consists of, and to help you gain greater self-awareness about whether you're actually using it.

Thinking often takes the form of a private monologue in which we speak silently to ourselves, or sometimes speak out loud to ourselves. The language or vocabulary words we hear and learn to speak with also become part of our "thinking vocabulary," and can strongly influence what or how we think (Carroll, 1964). So, by understanding the "language" of higher-level thinking, such as the words we'll use to define and describe the different forms of higher thinking that we provide in this chapter, you will be taking an important first step toward training your mind to think at higher levels. This will help you demonstrate higher-level thinking in your college courses, which in turn, should help you earn higher grades.

College professors in different academic disciplines will define and emphasize higher-level thinking in different ways (Gardiner, 2005). We think that the various forms of higher-level thinking emphasized in college are most effectively described and classified in terms of seven types of mental skills, each of which will be explained in upcoming sections of this chapter. Our hope is that this classification system may be used as a guide to promote your awareness and use of higher-level thinking skills when you read, write, speak, listen, and study. Here is an overview of the seven major types of thinking skills that will be discussed in this chapter:

1. **Analysis (Analytical Thinking):** *breaking down* information and identifying its key parts or underlying elements.
2. **Synthesis:** *building up* ideas by integrating separate pieces of information to form a larger whole or more comprehensive product.
3. **Multidimensional Thinking:** taking *multiple perspectives* and considering *multiple theories*.

4. **Balanced Thinking:** carefully considering reasons *for and against* a particular position or viewpoint.

5. **Inferential Reasoning:** Using *deductive* and *inductive* reasoning to formulate arguments and reach conclusions.

6. **Critical Thinking:** making well-informed *evaluations* or *judgments* of arguments and conclusions.

7. **Creative Thinking:** producing *new* and *different* ideas, works, methods, or strategies.

We will first describe and illustrate each of these forms of higher-level thinking and then discuss specific strategies for using these skills to improve your academic performance in college.

Analysis (Analytical Thinking)

When you analyze something, you break it down or take apart the whole to identify its key parts or elements. For example, an analysis of a novel would involve identifying such elements as its main protagonist(s), key passages, or its underlying themes. Analysis of a textbook chapter would go beyond simply reading to "cover" the assigned content; it would involve attempting to "uncover" the author's main ideas. We are using analytical thinking in this chapter right now as we attempt to break down the whole process of higher-level thinking into its key elements or forms. Analysis may also involve identification of underlying reasons or causes, which is referred to as *causal analysis.* For instance, a causal analysis of the September 11th attack on the United States would involve identifying the factors that caused or motivated the attack, or the reasons why the attack took place.

STUDENT PERSPECTIVE

"In Physics, you have to be analytical and break it [the problem] down into its parts, and not look at the question all at once."

—Physics student (quoted in Donald, 2002, p. 1)

Pause for Reflection

A TV commercial for a particular brand of liquor (which shall remain nameless) shows a young man getting out of his car in front of a house where there's a party. The driver gets out of his car, takes out a knife, slashes his tires, and goes inside to join the party. Using the higher-level thinking skill of analysis, identify the underlying messages that you think this commercial is sending to viewers.

Synthesis

Synthesis is a form of higher-level thinking that is just the opposite of analysis. When you analyze something, you break it down; when you synthesize, you build it up by integrating separate pieces of information to form a larger whole or more complete product. For example, you would be using synthesis if you took related ideas discussed in separate sections or units of a course and connected them together to form a single, unified product—such as a speech, paper, or concept map. You would also be engaging in synthesis if you were to connect ideas presented in different courses; for instance, integrating ethical concepts you learned in a philosophy course with marketing concepts you learned in a business course to produce a set of ethical guidelines for business marketing and advertising practices.

As you may be able to tell from these examples, synthesis involves more than a summary of information on a topic. Instead, it involves finding and forming meaningful connections among separate pieces of information and weaving them together to form a bigger picture. When you are synthesizing you are thinking *conceptually* by converting isolated facts and separated bits of information and integrating them into a *concept*—a larger system or network of related ideas. For instance, when you connect separate facts you know about the sun, the earth, and how the earth rotates and tilts toward the sun at different times of the year, they can be synthesized to form the larger concept of "season" (Anderson & Krathwohl, 2001).

Although synthesis and analysis are opposite thought processes, they work well together. When you analyze, you disassemble wholes into their key parts. When you synthesize, you reassemble these parts to build a new whole. For instance, when writing this book, we analyzed published material in many different fields (e.g., psychology, education, philosophy) and identified parts of these fields that were most important for beginning college students to know. We then synthesized or reassembled these parts to create a new whole—the textbook that you're now reading.

Multidimensional Thinking

A multidimensional thinker is someone who draws conclusions and makes decisions by:

◆ taking multiple perspectives and
◆ considering multiple theories.

We will discuss both of these characteristics of multidimensional thinking in the following sections of this chapter.

Taking Multiple Perspectives

This feature of multidimensional thinking involves viewing ourselves, and the world around us, from different angles or vantage points. In particular, multidimensional thinkers consider issues from four key perspectives:

1. Person
2. Place
3. Time
4. Culture

Multidimensional thinkers consider how these four perspectives influence, and are influenced by, the issue they are discussing or debating. For example, they would ask the following types of questions:

1. How would this issue affect my personal health? (The perspective of Person)
2. What impact would this issue have on people living in different countries? (The perspective of Place)
3. How would future generations of people be affected by this issue? (The perspective of Time)
4. How would this issue be interpreted or experienced by groups of people who share different social customs and traditions? (The perspective of Culture)

For instance, global warming is a current issue that refers to the earth's atmosphere gradually thickening and trapping more heat due to a collection of greenhouse gases, which are produced primarily by the burning of fossil fuels. It is theorized that the increase of man-made pollution is causing temperatures to rise (and sometimes fall) around the world and is contributing to natural disasters, such as droughts, wildfires, and dust storms (National Resources Defense Council, 2005; Joint Science Academies Statement, 2005).

A comprehensive understanding and solution to this problem involves taking each of the four major perspectives we just cited, as depicted in Figure 6.5.

Figure 6.5

PERSPECTIVE	IMPLICATION
Person	Global warming involves us on an individual level because our personal efforts at energy conservation in our homes and our willingness to purchase energy-efficient products can play a major role in solving this problem.
Place	Global warming is an international issue that extends beyond the boundaries of one's own country to all countries in the world, and its solution will require worldwide collaboration.
Time	If the current trend toward higher global temperatures caused by global warming continues, it could seriously threaten the lives of future generations of people who inhabit our planet.
Culture	The problem of global warming has been caused by industries in technologically advanced cultures, yet the problem of rising global temperatures is likely to have its most negative impact on less technologically advanced cultures that lack the resources to respond to it (Joint Science Academies Statement, 2005). To prevent this from happening, technologically advanced cultures will need to use their advanced technology to devise alternative methods for generating energy that does not continue to release heat-trapping gases into the atmosphere.

Each one of these four key perspectives has different dimensions or elements embedded within it. The four major perspectives, along with the key dimensions that comprise each of them, are listed and described in the box below. (Note how these perspectives are consistent with those developed by a liberal arts education, which we discussed in Chapter 2.)

BOX 6.1 *Snapshot* SUMMARY

Key Perspectives Associated with Multidimensional Thinking

Perspective 1: PERSON

Individual or Self

Key Components:

- Cognitive—personal knowledge, thoughts, and self-concept.
- Emotional—personal feelings, emotional adjustment, and mental health.
- Social—personal relationships and interpersonal interactions.
- Physical—personal health and bodily wellness.
- Vocational (Occupational)—personal means of making a living and earning an income.
- Ethical—personal values and moral convictions.
- Spiritual—personal beliefs about the meaning or purpose of life and the hereafter.

(continued)

Perspective 2: PLACE

Broader perspectives representing wider circles of social and spatial distance beyond the individual

Key Components:

- Family—perspective of parents, children, and relatives.
- Community—perspective of local communities and neighborhoods.
- Society—perspective of societal institutions (e.g., schools, churches, hospitals) and different groups within society (e.g., groups that differ in age, gender, race, or social class).
- Nation—perspective of one's country or place of citizenship.
- International—perspective of different nations or countries.
- Global—perspective on the planet Earth (e.g., all its life forms and natural resources).
- Universe—perspective on the relationship between earth and its place in a galaxy that includes all other planets and heavenly bodies.

Perspective 3: TIME

The chronological perspective

Key Components:

- Historical—perspective of the past.
- Contemporary— perspective of the present.
- Futuristic—perspective on the future.

Perspective 4: CULTURE

The distinctive way or style of living of a group of people who share the same social system, heritage, and traditions

Key Components:

- Linguistic (Language)—how its members communicate through written or spoken words, and through nonverbal communication (body language).
- Political—how the group organizes societal authority and uses it to govern themselves, make collective decisions, and maintain social order.
- Economic—how the material wants and needs of the group are met through the allocation of limited resources, and how wealth is distributed among its members.
- Geographic—how the group's physical location influences the nature of their social interactions and affects the way they adapt to and use their environment.
- Aesthetic—how the group appreciates and expresses artistic beauty and creativity through the fine arts (e.g., visual art, music, theater, literature, and dance).
- Scientific—how the group views, understands, and investigates natural phenomena through systematic research (e.g., scientific tests and experiments).
- Ecological—how the group views the interrelationship between the biological world (human beings and other living creatures) and the natural world (surrounding physical environment).
- Anthropological—how the group's culture originated, evolved, and developed over time.
- Sociological—how the group's society is structured or organized into social subgroups and social institutions.
- Psychological—how its individual members tend to think, feel, and interact; and how their attitudes, opinions, or beliefs have been acquired.
- Philosophical—the group's ideas or views on wisdom, goodness, truth, and the meaning or purpose of life.
- Theological—its members' conception of or beliefs about a transcendent, supreme being, and how they express shared faith in a supreme being.

Most real-life issues, problems, and challenges do not exist in isolation, but as parts of interconnected systems. Using global warming again as an example, this is an issue that is intertwined with ecology—the interrelationship between humans and their natural environment; science—research and development of alternative sources of energy; economics—cost to industry to change their existing sources of energy; national politics—laws may need to be created to encourage or enforce changes in industry's use of energy sources; and international relations—collaboration among all countries that are currently contributing to the problem and could contribute to its future solution.

Reaching conclusions and making decisions that are both accurate and effective requires use of what some scholars call "systems thinking"—taking into account how our decisions affect and are affected by other parts of a larger, interrelated system (Senge, 1990). Systems thinking highlights the importance of viewing issues from multiple perspectives, such as those contained in the lists we have just provided. It is unlikely that you will need to consider all the perspectives on these lists for each issue you study or discuss. Issues you examine in college will probably have implications for some of these perspectives and not for others. It is best to use the four lists of perspectives as checklists; they can be easily scanned to check for perspectives that relate to the issue you're examining and to identify whether an important perspective has been overlooked in your thinking, or in the thinking of others.

Pause for Reflection

Think of a problem in today's world other than global warming. Look back at the key perspectives of multidimensional thinking in Box 6.1, and briefly explain how one dimension within each of these perspectives may be involved in causing it or providing a potential solution to it.

Considering Multiple Theories

In addition to taking multiple perspectives, multidimensional thinking also involves considering multiple theories. A *theory* may be defined as a body of related concepts and general principles that help us organize, understand, and apply knowledge that has been acquired in a particular field of study. For example, in Chapter 4 we used information-processing theory to organize a large amount of research in the field of learning and memory, so that we could deliver it to you in a form that was connected and coherent, rather than random and piecemeal. Information-processing theory helps us understand the concepts of learning and memory by explaining it in terms of a three-stage process (input, storage, and retrieval) similar to that used by a computer. We also used this theory to generate a series of practical strategies that could be applied to improve academic performance.

One major misconception about a theory is that it's impractical. When people hear the word "theoretical," they often interpret it as being the opposite of practical, and they mistakenly conclude that a theory has no practical use, value, or benefit. However, theories do have practical benefits; they help us organize and make sense of research so that we can apply its results to improve the quality of our lives (for example, information-processing theory can improve the quality of our learning and memory).

Another common misconception about a theory is that it's nothing more than an opinion or guess. However, scholars in an academic field will not label something a theory until its ideas have been supported by at least some evidence. Don't confuse theory—which is supported by some evidence, with a *hypothesis*—which is an informed guess that *might* be true, but still needs to be tested to confirm whether it *is* true.

Although theories are supported by evidence and have practical value, no single theory can account for the whole truth or tell the whole story. This is why more than one theory exists in virtually every field of study. Different theories explain different portions of the total truth or knowledge that exists in any given field. For instance, information-processing theory alone cannot explain all aspects of human learning and memory. This theory is based on a computer model, and since computers do not experience emotions or feelings, it does not adequately account for the influence of motivation on human learning—for example, how humans often learn information more quickly and retain it longer if they're excited about it or interested in it. So, we also need to consider another theory (motivational theory) to account for how human interest and motivation affects learning and memory.

Although no single theory can account for the whole truth, the good news is that elements of different theories may be combined to explain a larger portion of the total truth. Also, elements of different theories may be combined to give us a more complete and versatile set of tools to use for practical purposes. For example, in Chapters 4 and 5, we were able to generate a wide variety of strategies for improving learning and memory by combining elements of the following theories:

- information-processing theory—e.g., strategies for creating memory cues to retrieve stored information,
- brain-based learning theory—e.g., strategies for using the left and right halves of the brain to record dual (verbal and visual) memory traces, and
- constructivist learning theory (which takes the position that we learn by constructing or building new knowledge on what we already know)—e.g., strategies for using analogies and metaphors that relate what we're trying to learn to what we already know.

If you find yourself thinking or asking the question, "Why do we need all these theories anyway?" keep in mind that scholars in different fields are attempting to understand, explain, and improve the human experience and the world around us. These are not simple, one-dimensional subjects; they are complex, multi-dimensional subjects that involve many factors and perspectives. Thus, multiple theories are needed to understand these multiple factors and perspectives, and to help us develop a more comprehensive set of strategies for improving the human and world condition.

Dialectical (Dialogic) Thinking

Don't be surprised if you find that scholars in the same field disagree about what particular theory accounts for the largest portion of "truth" in their field. Don't be frustrated by such disagreement; it's just part of the normal process of intellectual dialogue that gradually brings us closer and closer to a more complete understanding of the issues and questions found in any field of study. This thought process is referred to as *dialectical* or *dialogic thinking* (Paul & Elder, 2002) (from the root word meaning "conversation"). When you think dialectically, you consider opposing viewpoints—a *thesis* and an *antithesis*; then you engage in an exchange of arguments for and against each viewpoint. During this dialogue, the thesis and antithesis are cross-examined and tested for their strengths and weaknesses. This process of cross-examination gradually leads to a *synthesis*—an integrated and intermediate viewpoint, which is closer to the truth than either the thesis or antithesis.

"NOW I'M CONFUSED."

The mental confusion or contradiction caused by considering opposing viewpoints simultaneously helps reduce oversimplified, "dualistic" (black-or-white) thinking.

Dialectical thinking stimulates and sharpens our thinking skills by forcing the mind to consider the strengths of opposing viewpoints simultaneously, creating a mental experience called cognitive *dissonance*—a state of mental contradiction or disequilibrium (Kurfiss, 1988; Meyers, 1986). When you consider the strengths of opposing positions at the same time, it reduces *dualistic* thinking—an oversimplified form of thinking in which "truth" is seen as something that is always clear-cut and black-or-white, with one answer or position being right and all the others wrong (Perry, 1970, 1999). Thus, your first step in the process of seeking truth is not to immediately jump in and look to take an either-or (for-or-against) stance on a debatable issue. Instead, your first step should be to look at the pros and cons of each position, acknowledge the strengths and weaknesses of each, and identify what additional information may still be needed to reach a conclusion.

Studies consistently show that the majority of first-year college students think in a dualistic (black-white) manner, believing their professors' role is to give them the correct answers and their role is to learn (or memorize) these answers (Baxter-Magolda, 1992; Belenky, et al., 1986; King & Kitchener, 1994). However, in college (and in reality), truth often does not come in the form of absolute answers that are either true or false and conveniently packaged in boxes that are marked "right" or "wrong." This is not to say that there are only opinions and "everybody has a right to their own opinion," or that "everything is relative," or "anything goes." What we are saying is that although there may not be one absolutely correct answer, there are still some answers that are better than others because they are more accurate, and some viewpoints are better than others because they're more *informed*—that is to say, they are based on more accurate information or stronger evidence. Answers are usually not black or white but come in different shades of gray, ranging from lighter to darker, with some answers being closer to the truth than others because they are better supported by evidence.

So, when you encounter multiple theories in college, try not to look at them in dualistic (right-or-wrong) terms. Instead, take an *eclectic* approach, which means that you are open to different theories and are ready to borrow elements from each of them in order to create a more comprehensive understanding of complex issues, and are open to acquiring a more complete set of tools for solving practical problems.

Balanced Thinking

Balanced thinking involves seeking out and giving careful consideration to evidence for and against a particular position. The process of supporting a position with evidence is technically referred to as *adduction*; when you "adduce," you offer reasons *for* a particular position. The process of arguing against a position by presenting contradictory evidence is called *refutation*; when you "refute," you supply evidence against a particular position.

Balanced thinking involves both adduction and refutation. The goal of a balanced thinker is not to stack-up evidence for one position or the other, but to be an impartial investigator who looks at both supporting and contradictory evidence, and attempts to reach a conclusion that is neither biased nor one-sided. If that conclusion favors one position over another, the opposing position's stronger arguments are acknowledged and its weaker ones are refuted (Fairbairn & Winch, 1995).

Balanced thinking requires more than just adding up the number of arguments for and against a position; it also considers the degree of importance of each argument. For instance, suppose you find the following three arguments for a particular position: (1) it would be profitable (economic advantage), (2) it would beautify the environment (aesthetic advantage), and (3) it would help us understand how our environment works (scientific advantage). The only sound argument against this position is that it will increase the risk of cancer for people living in the nearby environment (health disadvantage). Although there are three times as many arguments for this position than against it, its one opposing argument outweighs the combined weight of all three of its supporting arguments, because the preservation or protection of human life is much more important than economic gain, artistic beauty, or scientific advancement. Because preserving human life is such an important or heavily weighed value, this case represents a rather clear-cut example of why arguments for and against a position need to be weighed, not merely added up or tallied like a debit-credit sheet. However, in other cases, the weights that should be assigned to different arguments may be more subtle and subject to disagreement; for example, whether or not to build needed housing for a growing community in a location that may cause the extinction of a rare species of butterfly. In such debatable cases, the weight given to opposing arguments will depend on the value system of the individual who is judging and weighing them.

Remember: A key characteristic of balanced thinking is being aware of the value you place on different arguments, and acknowledging how you weighed them when you reach a conclusion (e.g., in a written report or class presentation).

In some cases, after reviewing both supporting and contradictory evidence for a particular position, balanced thinking may lead you to conclude that you cannot reach a firm conclusion for or against it. For instance, as a balanced thinker, you may occasionally reach conclusions such as, "Right now, I see equally strong arguments for and against this position" or, "I need more information or evidence before I can make a final judgment or reach a firm conclusion." This is not being wishy-washy; it is a perfectly legitimate conclusion to draw, as long as it is an informed conclusion that is supported with sound reasons or evidence. In fact, it is better to hold an undecided, but informed viewpoint that's based on balanced thinking than to hold a definite, but uninformed opinion that's based on emotion—such as those often displayed by people on radio and TV talk shows.

Personal Story For years I really didn't know what I believed. I always seemed to stand in the no man's land between opposing arguments, yearning to be won over by one side or the other, but finding instead degrees of merit in both. But in time, I came to accept, even embrace, what I called "my confusion," and to recognize it as a friend and ally, no apologies needed. I preferred to listen rather than to speak; to inquire, not crusade.

—*"In Praise of the 'Wobblies'" by Ted Gup (2005), journalist who has written for* Time, National Geographic, *and* The New York Times

Remember: When you combine balanced thinking with multidimensional thinking, you become a comprehensive thinker who views ideas and issues from both sides and all angles.

Pause for Reflection

Consider the following positions:

1. *Course requirements should be eliminated; college students should be allowed to choose the classes they will take for their degree.*
2. *Course grades should be eliminated; college students should take classes on a pass-fail basis.*

Choose one of these positions and use balanced thinking to make two arguments: one for and one against this position.

Inferential Reasoning

Inferential reasoning is a thought process for making arguments and drawing conclusions; it starts with a premise (a statement or an observation) and uses it to *infer* or "step to" a conclusion. For example, the following sentence starters demonstrate the inferential reasoning process:

"Because this is true, it follows that . . . "
"Based on this evidence, I can conclude that . . ."

If you were to represent inferential reasoning in the form of a flow chart, it would look something like this:

Premise	→	Inference	→	Conclusion
(because/since)		(thus/therefore)		(it can be concluded that . . .)

In college, you will frequently be required to reach conclusions and support those conclusions with evidence. For example, if you are asked to formulate an *argument*, you are being asked to use inferential reasoning to reach a conclusion and support your conclusion with logical reasons or evidence. In a sense, you're being asked to take on the role of a lawyer who is trying to build a strong case by supporting it with solid logic and concrete evidence (exhibit A, exhibit B, etc.).

Inferential reasoning takes place through either of two routes:

1. Deductive reasoning (deduction) or
2. Inductive reasoning (induction).

Since these are the primary ways that humans make arguments and reach conclusions, we will take a close look at both of these forms of inferential reasoning.

·—· **CLASSIC QUOTE** ·—·

The trouble with English is that there are no answers. There are only evaluations and critical judgments backed up with evidence and strong argument. It requires the ability to make a case through reasoned, logical argument, and the ability to marshal evidence.

—English professor
(quoted in Donald, 2002, p. 1)

Deductive Reasoning (deduction)

When we reason *deductively*, we start with a general statement (the premise); we then infer (step to) a conclusion about a specific instance or particular case by arguing for what follows logically from the general premise. A clear-cut example of deductive reasoning is the *syllogism*—a formal argument that involves a major premise, a minor premise, and a conclusion, such as the following:

All college students like pizza. (Major premise)
Greg is a college student. (Minor premise)
Therefore, Greg likes pizza. (Conclusion)

Notice that this argument starts with a general statement (about college students and pizza), then proceeds to a conclusion about a more specific instance or example (Greg).

When you deduce a conclusion, your logic flows from top to bottom—in other words, it trickles down from a general premise and steps down to infer a conclusion about something more specific. Deduction derives from the same root as the word "deduct," which means to "take away" or "reduce"; thus, deductive reasoning takes from something larger (general premise) to reach a conclusion about something smaller (a specific instance or example).

Inductive Reasoning (induction)

When we reason *inductively*, we start with an observation of a specific instance or case (the premise); we then infer a conclusion that consists of a general statement by arguing that the conclusion follows logically from the specific instance. Here is an example of inductive reasoning that will allow us to compare and contrast it with deductive reasoning:

I questioned fifty college students and found that each of them likes pizza.
(Observation of specific instances)
Therefore, all college students like pizza. (Conclusion)

Notice that this argument starts with a specific observation (individual college students and pizza), and proceeds to a conclusion about something more general (all college students and pizza). Thus, inductive reasoning moves in a direction that's opposite to deductive reasoning. When you induce a conclusion, your logic flows from bottom to top—in other words, it bubbles up to a more general conclusion by taking an inferential step up from individual instances or specific examples. Induction derives from the same root word as "induct," meaning to "take into." Just as an individual can be inducted or taken into a larger group (e.g., an honor society or the hall of fame), inductive reasoning involves taking an individual instance to reach a larger (more general) conclusion.

Both deductive and inductive reasoning are important forms of higher-level thinking because they represent the primary mental processes humans use to reach conclusions about themselves and the world around them. These are also the two key thought processes that you will use to make arguments and reach conclusions about ideas presented in your college courses. For example, in an art history class, you may be asked to provide specific examples of artwork that represent the same general artistic style; this mental process requires deductive reasoning. Or, you may be shown specific works of art and asked to identify what general style or form of art that each of these instances represent; this mental process requires inductive reasoning.

Critical Thinking

Critical thinking is a higher-level thought process that involves making a judgment or evaluation. This evaluation can be either positive or negative; for example, a movie critic can give a good ("thumbs up") or bad ("thumbs down") review of a film.

Pause for Reflection

Flash back to the first page of this chapter and take a look at your response to the incomplete sentence. How does it match up with the definition of critical thinking we've just provided?

If you wrote that critical thinking means "being critical" or negatively criticizing something or somebody, don't feel bad. Many students think that critical thinking has this negative meaning or connotation.

Critical thinking can also be used to critique many things in addition to evaluating films, art or music; it's also used to judge the quality of ideas, beliefs, choices, and decisions, whether they are our own or belong to others. Often, we use critical thinking to make judgments about something's:

◆ validity (Is it accurate or true?)

◆ morality (Is it fair or just?)

◆ beauty (Is it artistic or aesthetic?)

◆ practicality (Is it useful?)

◆ priority (Is it the best or most important?)

Critical thinking may be considered to be one of the highest forms of thinking because we use it to evaluate the quality of other forms of higher-level thinking. For instance, we use critical thinking to judge the quality of our analysis and synthesis, or to evaluate whether our thinking is multidimensional and balanced. In particular, critical thinking is most frequently used to evaluate the inferential reasoning process involved in making arguments and reaching conclusions (King & Kitchener, 1994; Paul & Elder, 2004). Since this is probably the most common function or purpose of critical thinking, we will provide a detailed description of how critical thinking is used to evaluate the two key forms of inferential reasoning: deductive and inductive reasoning.

Using Critical Thinking to Evaluate Deductive Reasoning

When critical thinking is used to evaluate arguments that involve deductive reasoning, two key elements of the argument require careful judgment:

1. Is the premise true? (In other words: Does the argument begin with and build on a statement that is accurate?)

2. Is the conclusion logically consistent with the premise? (In other words: Does the conclusion logically follow or flow from the premise?)

For example, let's apply critical thinking to evaluate the deductive reasoning used in the following argument.

> Mind-altering drugs are harmful to you. (Major premise)
> Alcohol is a mind-altering drug. (Minor premise)
> Therefore, alcohol is harmful to you. (Conclusion)

In this argument, there are two premises that may not be true:

1. The major premise states, "Mind-altering drugs are harmful to you." This is not necessarily true, because taking mind-altering drugs may not be harmful to someone who is

STUDENT PERSPECTIVE

"Critical thinking is an evaluative thought process that requires deep thinking."

—First-year student's response to the question, "What does critical thinking mean to you?"

experiencing extreme physical pain (e.g., morphine given to a patient who has just recovered from a major operation), or for someone experiencing extreme emotional pain (e.g., giving an anti-depressant drug to someone who's extremely depressed and suicidal, due to a chemical imbalance in the brain).

2. The minor premise that alcohol is a mind-altering drug is not true in all cases. It is a mind-altering drug if taken in sufficiently large doses; however, if taken in small doses, alcohol may be classified as a beverage (e.g., drinking a glass of wine with dinner). So, a critical thinker would judge the quality of this argument to be weak because its conclusion is built on weak premises.

Now, let's apply critical thinking to evaluate a second key element of deductive reasoning: whether an argument's conclusion is logically consistent with its premises. Consider the following argument:

> Alcohol is a dangerous drug because it increases the rate of violent and sexual crimes committed in our society. (Premise)
> During the prohibition, drinking alcohol was illegal and people still continued to make alcohol illegally and abuse it. (Premise)
> This proves that alcohol is a dangerous drug that should be banned. (Conclusion)

In this argument, both of the premises are true. Studies do show that drinking alcohol does increase the rate of violent and sexual crimes (e.g., date rape). The second premise is also true: During prohibition, people did continue to make alcohol and get drunk. However, the conclusion that alcohol should be banned does not follow logically from the second premise. If alcohol was banned during the prohibition and people still used and abused it, why would there be any reason to conclude that banning it now would provide a solution to the problem? (In fact, it could be argued that it would make the problem worse because prohibition led to the birth and growth of organized crime groups whose booming illegal business was the selling of illegal or "bootleg" alcohol.) Thus, critical thinking would lead us to question this argument because its conclusion does not logically follow from one of its premises. (In the field of logic, this type of thinking error is referred to as a *non-sequitir*, which literally means: "It does not follow.")

Using Critical Thinking to Evaluate Inductive Reasoning

When critical thinking is used to evaluate arguments that involve inductive reasoning, two different aspects of the argument require careful judgment:

1. Is the size of the sample large enough to make a generalized statement?
2. Is the sample representative—does it accurately reflect the characteristics of the larger group that's referred to in its conclusion?

For example, let's apply critical thinking to evaluate the quality of inductive reasoning used in the following argument.

> My father drank alcohol and became an alcoholic. (Specific instance)
> My uncle drank alcohol and became an alcoholic. (Specific instance)
> Therefore, people should not drink alcohol. (General conclusion)

In this argument, the conclusion is based on just two instances or cases. Critical thinking would lead us to judge this argument as weak, because the number of cases or size of the sample on which it is based is too small to reach a conclusion about people in general. In the field of logic, this reasoning error is sometimes referred to as a *hasty generalization*.

Another criticism of the above argument is that its conclusion refers to people in general; however, the particular instances that have been observed (the two brothers), which form the basis of its conclusion, may not accurately represent or reflect people in general. Said in another way, the argument may be using apples to draw a conclusion about oranges. The two brothers have something in common (their genes), so it is very possible that they may share the same genetic tendency toward alcoholism because they share similar genes. Other people who are unrelated to these brothers are likely to have an entirely different set of genes; thus, it is questionable whether the two brothers can be used as a representative sample to reach the general conclusion that, "People (in general) should not drink alcohol." In the field of logic, this type of "comparing apples to oranges" reasoning error is referred to as a *false* or *weak analogy*.

BOX 6.2

Logical Fallacies and Errors of Reasoning

As you read the following list of logical errors, make a brief note in the margin of any example of these errors that you have personally observed or experienced.

■ **Dogmatism:** Stubbornly clinging to a personally held viewpoint that is not supported by evidence and remaining totally closed-minded (non-receptive) to other viewpoints.

For example, believing that capitalism is the only economic system that can work in a successful democracy, and not acknowledging the existence of other countries with capitalistic economies, which are successful democracies.

■ **Selective Perception:** The tendency to focus on and perceive instances that confirm one's position or conclusion, while overlooking those that contradict it.

For example, two groups of people that have opposing moral viewpoints on an issue, yet each of them interprets the Bible in a way that supports their own viewpoint. Or, someone believing in astrology who only notices and talks about people whose personalities fit their astrological sign, but fails to notice those who don't.

■ **Double Standard:** Having two sets of standards for judgment—a higher standard for judging others and a lower standard for judging oneself.

This is the classic, "Do as I say, not as I do" hypocrisy. For example, people who critically evaluate and challenge the opinions of others, but not their own.

■ **Denial:** Ignoring factual evidence that contradicts one's personal opinions or beliefs.

For example, saying to someone who presents evidence that contradicts our own opinion: "Anybody can find evidence to support anything they want to believe."

■ **Wishful Thinking:** Thinking that something is true, not because logic or evidence indicates that it's true, but because the person *wants* it to be true.

For example, a teenage girl who does not want to become pregnant and believes that she will not become pregnant, even though she and her boyfriend always have sex without using any contraceptive.

■ **Hasty Generalization:** Reaching a general conclusion based on a very limited number of observations or experiences.

For example, concluding that people belonging to a group are "all that way" or "most of them are that way" on the basis of only one or two personal experiences.

·— **CLASSIC QUOTE** ·—·

It's better not to know so much than to know so many things that ain't so.

—Josh Billings, pen name of Henry Shaw, nineteenth-century American humorist

·— **CLASSIC QUOTE** ·—·

Belief can be produced in practically unlimited quantity and intensity, without observation or reasoning, and even in defiance of both by the simple desire to believe.

—George Bernard Shaw, Irish playwright and Nobel Prize winner for literature, 1925

(continued)

- **Jumping to a Conclusion:** Making a huge leap of logic to reach a conclusion that is based on only one reason or factor, and ignores other possible reasons or contributing factors.

  For example, after being rejected for a date or a job, the rejected person concludes that, "I must be a real loser." (While this may be a possible explanation for the rejection, there are many other reasons or factors that could have been responsible for it.)

- **Glittering Generality:** Making a positive general statement without supplying specific details or evidence to back it up.

  For example, writing a letter of recommendation for someone and claiming that the person is a "wonderful human being" with a "great personality," but not providing any specific reasons or evidence indicating why this person is so "wonderful" or has such a "great" personality.

- **Straw Man Argument:** Distorting an opponent's argument position and then attacking it.

  For example, a politician attacks an opposing candidate for supporting censorship and restricting civil liberties, when the opponent merely supported a ban on violent pornography.

- **Ad Hominem Argument:** Aiming an argument at the person who is being debated, rather than at the issue being debated. (Literally translated, the term "ad hominem" means "to the man.")

  For example, an older person telling a younger person, "You're too young and inexperienced to know what you're talking about." Or, a younger person telling an older person, "You're too old and behind the times to understand this issue."

- **Red Herring:** Bringing up an irrelevant issue that disguises or distracts attention from the real issue being discussed or debated. ("Red herring" derives from an old practice of dragging a herring—a strong-smelling fish—across a trail to distract the scent of pursuing dogs.)

  For example, someone responds to criticism of former president Nixon's involvement in the Watergate scandal by arguing that, "He was a good president who accomplished many good things while he was in office." (Nixon's effectiveness as a president is an irrelevant issue or a "red herring"; the real issue being discussed is Nixon's behavior in the Watergate scandal.)

- **Smoke Screen:** Intentionally disguising or covering up one's true reasons or motives with reasons that are designed to confuse or mislead others.

  For example, a politician opposes gun control legislation by arguing that it is a violation of our constitutional right to bear arms; however, his true reason for opposing it is that he's receiving financial support from gun manufacturing companies.

- **Slippery Slope:** Basically a fear tactic, whereby the person argues that not accepting his or her position will result in a "domino effect"; that is, it will result in a negative event, which will lead to another negative event, which in turn, will lead to yet another negative event, etc. (like a series of falling dominoes).

  For example, "If you experiment with marijuana it will automatically lead to harder drugs, you will lose your motivation, drop out of college, end up in rehab, and ruin your life."

- **Rhetorical Deception:** Using deceptive language to conclude that something is true, without actually providing any reasons or evidence that it is true.

  For example, confidently making such statements as: "*Clearly* this is . . ." or, "It is *obvious* that . . . " or, "Any *reasonable* person can see . . ." without ever explaining why it is so "clear," "obvious," or "reasonable."

- **Begging the Question** (*Circular Reasoning*): Arguing in circles whereby the conclusion is nothing more than a rewording or restatement of the premise.

  For example, concluding that, "Cursing is immoral because it's a sinful thing to do."

- **Appealing to Authority or Prestige:** If someone in authority or who has prestige says it's true or should be done, then it is true and we should do it.

  For example, "Buy product X because this famous and prestigious actor or athlete uses it." Or, "My supervisor told me to do it, so I must do it, whether it's right or wrong, otherwise I wouldn't be following orders."

(continued)

- **Appealing to Tradition or the Familiar:** Concluding that what currently *is* or what has traditionally been is what *should* be or *ought to* be.

  For example, "This is the way it's always been done, so this is the way we should do it."

- **Appealing to Popularity or the Majority** *(Jumping on the Bandwagon)*: Concluding that if a belief is very popular or is held by the majority, then it is true.

  For example, "So many people believe in psychics, it has to be true; they can't all be wrong."

- **Appealing to Emotion** (rather than reason): Reaching conclusions on the intensity of feelings experienced rather than the quality of reasons considered.

  For example, "If I feel strongly about something, it must be true." The expressions, "always trust your feelings" and "just listen to your heart" may not always lead to the most accurate conclusions and the best decisions, because emotions can overpower rational thinking. For instance, when people become involved in a romantic relationship (an emotionally intense experience), their quality of thinking can become seriously impaired, as reflected in expressions such as:

  □ "*madly* in love"—losing ability to think rationally;

  □ "love is *blind*"—failing to see obvious flaws in the partner

  □ "*insanely* jealous"—having irrational thoughts about the partner "cheating."

Sources: Bassham, et al., (2005); Ruggiero (2004); Wade & Tavris (1990).

Creative Thinking

To think creatively is to develop something new or different, whether it may be a product, an idea, a method, or a strategy. In contrast to critical thinking, which leads you to ask the question, "*Why?*" (For example, Why are we doing it this way?), creative thinking leads you to ask the question, "*Why not?*" (For example, "Why not try doing it this different way?"). When you think critically, you look "inside the box" and evaluate the quality of its particular content; when you think creatively, you look "outside the box" to imagine other possible packages containing different types of content. Your past schooling may have trained you to answer questions that other people ask. However, when you think at a higher level, you're the one asking the questions; and when you think creatively, you're asking new or original questions.

Creative ideas have changed the course of human history and are responsible for many modern conveniences, medical advances, and cultural arts we enjoy today. In a world that is rapidly changing due to advances in technology and faster production of new information, the ability to think creatively is a skill that may be more valuable today than at any other time in history (Pink, 2005). Surveys of employers indicate that they place high value on creativity (BCA, 2006) and personal qualities related to creativity, such as "thinking on your feet," "finding the right problems to solve," and "identifying new solutions" (Education Commission of the States, 1995).

Although creative and critical thinking represent different forms of higher-level thinking, they go hand-in-hand. We use creative thinking to ask new questions and generate new ideas, and we use critical thinking to evaluate the ideas we create (Paul & Elder, 2004). A creative idea must not only be different or original; it must also be effective (Sternberg, 2001; Runco, 2004). If critical thinking reveals that the quality of what we've created is poor, we then shift back to creative thinking to generate something that's new and improved. Or, we may start by using critical thinking to evaluate an old idea or approach and come to the judgment that it's not very good. This unfavorable evaluation naturally leads to and turns on the creative thinking process, which tries to come up with a new idea or different approach that is better than the old one.

·—· **CLASSIC QUOTE** ·—·

The principle mark of genius is not perfection but originality, the opening of new frontiers.

–Arthur Koestler, Hungarian novelist and philosopher

·—· **CLASSIC QUOTE** ·—·

Creativity is allowing oneself to make mistakes; art is knowing which ones to keep.

–Scott Adams, creator of the Dilbert comic strip and author of *The Dilbert Principle*

Creative and critical thinking often involve complementary mental processes, known as *divergent* and *convergent* thinking (Guilford, 1967). When you think creatively, you are using divergent thinking—that is, your thinking "diverges" (spreads out) in different directions, with the goal of generating many different possibilities. In contrast, when you think critically, you are using convergent thinking—that is, your thinking "converges" (narrows in) on each particular idea that you've created and evaluates it. In other words, creative thinking involves generating ideas that *could* be used; critical thinking involves determining which of these ideas *should* be used.

The problem-solving process of *brainstorming* is a classic example of how creative and critical thinking work together. See Box 6.3 for the key steps or stages involved in the process of brainstorming.

BOX 6.3 *Snapshot* SUMMARY

The Process of Brainstorming

Steps:

1. Produce and list as many ideas as you possibly can, generating them rapidly without stopping to evaluate the quality of the ideas. Studies show that worrying about whether an idea is correct often blocks creativity (Basadur, Runco, & Vega, 2000). So, let your imagination run wild; don't worry about whether the idea you generate is impractical, unrealistic, or outrageous.

2. Use the ideas on your list as a springboard to think about and generate additional ideas. In other words, use your listed ideas to trigger new ideas and build on them to produce other ideas.

3. After you run out of ideas, review and evaluate the list of ideas you've generated and eliminate those that you think are least effective.

4. From the remaining list of ideas, choose the best idea or best combination of ideas.

Note that the first two steps in the brainstorming process involve divergent thinking, which goes off in different directions to generate multiple ideas. These first two steps represent the creative thinking stage of the brainstorming process. In contrast, the last two steps in the process involve *convergent* thinking that narrows-in, evaluates, and selects the best idea(s) generated. These final steps represent the *critical* thinking stage of the brainstorming process.

Personal Story

Several years ago, I was working with a friend to come up with ideas for a grant proposal that he was going to write. We started out by sitting at his kitchen table, sipping coffee, and then we both got up and began to pace back and forth, walking all around the room while throwing out different ideas and bouncing ideas off each other. Whenever a new idea was thrown out, one of us would jot it down (whoever was pacing closer to the kitchen table at the moment).

After we ran out of ideas, we shifted gears, slowed down, and sat down at the table to carefully review each of the ideas we just generated during our "binge-thinking" episode. After some debate, we finally settled on an idea that we judged to be the best one of all the ideas we produced, and he made it his grant proposal.

Although I was not fully aware of it at the time, the stimulating thought process we were using was called brainstorming, which first involved creative thinking—our fast-paced walking and idea-production stage, followed by critical thinking—our slower-paced sitting and idea-evaluation stage.

—Joe Cuseo

As the brainstorming process suggests, creativity does not just happen suddenly or effortlessly, like the so-called "stroke of genius"; instead, it takes conscious mental effort (Torrance, 1963; Paul & Elder, 2004). Although it may involve some sudden or intuitive leaps, it also involves carefully reflecting on those leaps and critically evaluating whether any of them actually landed on a good idea.

Furthermore, to think creatively doesn't mean that you have to be an artistic genius. Creative thinking is not restricted to the arts; it can occur in all subject areas, even in fields that seek precision and definite answers. For example, in math, creative thinking may involve using new approaches or strategies for arriving at a correct solution to a problem. In science, creative thinking takes place whenever a scientist uses imaginative thinking to create a hypothesis or logical hunch ("What might happen if . . .?"), then conducts an experiment and collects evidence to see if the hypothesis turns out to be true.

Anytime you combine two old ideas to generate a different idea or a new product, you are engaging in creative thinking. In fact, creative thinking can be viewed as just an extension or higher form of synthesis, whereby parts of separate ideas are combined or integrated, resulting in a final product that turns out to be significantly different from what existed before (Anderson & Krathwohl, 2001). Even in the arts, products that are created are not totally original or unique. Instead, creative art typically involves a combination or rearrangement of previously existing elements to generate a new "whole"—a different total product. For instance, Bob Dylan combined elements of acoustic folk music and amplified rock music to help create a new musical form or genre, which became known as folk rock (Shelton, 2003).

••• Strategies for Developing and Applying Higher-Level Thinking Skills to Improve Academic Performance

This section of the chapter is devoted exclusively to practical strategies for developing and applying higher-level thinking skills to improve your performance on academic tasks you face in college, such as: note-taking, reading, discussions, studying, and writing papers or reports. We offer these strategies for the dual purpose of elevating your thinking skills and raising your course grades.

Self-Questioning Strategies

As we mentioned in Chapter 4, effective learners are effective self-monitors—they watch themselves while learning and monitor whether they are really understanding what they're attempting to learn (Weinstein & Underwood, 1985). Similarly, effective thinkers engage in a slightly different form of self-monitoring known as *meta-cognition*—they think about how they are thinking (Flavell, 1985).

One simple but powerful way to think about your thinking is through self-questioning. Since thinking often involves talking silently to yourself, if you remain consciously aware of the types of questions you ask yourself, you can become more aware of the types of thinking you are using and more able to control the quality of your thinking. In fact, one standard for judging the quality of any question you ask yourself is its ability to stimulate your thinking and elevate it to a higher level. It could be said that a good question is one that provides rocket fuel for the mind—it launches your thinking upward to higher levels in a quest to answer it.

Asking yourself a good question can stimulate your higher-level thinking about almost any experience, whether it takes place inside or outside the classroom.

Pause for Reflection

In the above cartoon, what do you think are the advantages and disadvantages associated with the common practice of bars selling alcoholic drinks at reduced prices?

What do you think are the assumptions or implications of calling this practice "happy hour?"

Since questions have the power to activate and elevate our thinking, you can capitalize on their power by intentionally asking yourself good questions. The higher the level of thinking called for by the questions you regularly ask yourself, the higher the level of thinking you will display in class discussions, on exams, and in the papers you write. Listed in Box 6.4 is a set of questions that have been intentionally designed to promote the major forms of high-level thinking that have been discussed in this chapter. These questions are constructed in a way that will allow you to easily "fill in the blank" with any type of idea or issue that you may be discussing in almost any college course and academic discipline. Considerable research evidence indicates that students can use questions such as these as effective triggers for stimulating their use of higher-level thinking skills in a variety of academic subjects (King, 1990, 1995).

We recommend that you save a copy of these higher-level thinking questions so that you can use them regularly to monitor and strengthen your own thinking skills on academic tasks, such as studying or writing papers, and to stimulate the thinking of others during class discussions or study-group sessions.

Questions for Stimulating Different Forms of Higher-Level Thinking

Analysis (Analytical Thinking): to break down information into its essential elements or parts.

Trigger Questions

⊙ What are the main ideas contained in _____?

⊙ What are the important aspects of _____?

⊙ What are the key issues raised by _____?

⊙ What are the major purposes of _____?

⊙ What assumptions or biases lie hidden within _____?

⊙ What were the reasons behind _____?

Synthesis: to combine and integrate separate bits or pieces of information to form a larger product or pattern.

Trigger Questions

⊙ How can this idea be joined or integrated with _____ to create a more complete or comprehensive understanding of _____?

⊙ How could these different _____ be grouped together into a more general class or category?

⊙ How could these separate _____ be reorganized or rearranged to produce a more comprehensive understanding of the "big picture?"

Taking Multiple Perspectives: thinking that involves viewing ourselves, and the surrounding world, from different angles or vantage points.

Trigger Questions

⊙ How would _____ affect different dimensions of myself (e.g., emotional, physical, etc.)?

⊙ What broader impact would _____ have on the social and physical world around me?

⊙ How might people living in different times (e.g., past and future) view _____?

⊙ How would people from different cultural backgrounds interpret or react to _____?

⊙ Have I taken into consideration all the major factors that could influence _____ or be influenced by _____?

Balanced Thinking: carefully considering reasons for and against a particular position or viewpoint.

Trigger Questions

⊙ What are the strengths/advantages and weaknesses/disadvantages of _____?

⊙ What evidence supports and contradicts _____?

⊙ What are the arguments for and the counterarguments against _____?

⊙ Have I considered both sides of _____?

Adduction: arguing for a particular idea or position by supplying supporting evidence.

Trigger Questions

⊙ What proof is there for _____?

⊙ What are logical arguments for _____?

⊙ What research evidence supports _____?

Refutation: arguing against a particular idea or position by supplying contradictory evidence.

Trigger Questions

⊙ What proof is there against _____?

⊙ What logical arguments indicate that _____ is false?

⊙ What research evidence contradicts _____?

(continued)

Deductive Reasoning: inferring conclusions about specific instances or particular cases that follow logically from a general statement.

Trigger Questions

⊙ What specific conclusion can be drawn from the general statement that _____?

⊙ What particular actions or practices would be consistent with the general statement that _____?

⊙ If the general statement _____ is true, it logically follows that _____.

Inductive Reasoning (Induction): inferring conclusions that involve a general statement, which follows logically from observation of specific instances or examples.

Trigger Questions

⊙ What are the broader implications of _____?

⊙ What are the common themes or patterns in _____?

⊙ What general concept or principle can be drawn from _____?

Critical Thinking: making well-informed evaluations or judgments.

Trigger Questions for Evaluating Validity:

⊙ Is _____ true or accurate?

⊙ Is there sufficient evidence to support the conclusion that _____?

⊙ Is the reasoning behind _____ strong or weak?

Trigger Questions for Evaluating Morality:

⊙ Is _____ fair?

⊙ Is _____ just?

⊙ Is _____ ethical?

⊙ Is this action consistent with the professed or stated values of _____?

Trigger Questions for Evaluating Beauty (Aesthetics):

⊙ What is the artistic merit of _____?

⊙ Does _____ have any aesthetic value?

⊙ Does _____ contribute to the beauty of _____?

Trigger Questions about Practicality (Usefulness):

⊙ Will this _____ work?

⊙ Can this _____ be put to good use?

⊙ How would _____ provide help or benefit for _____?

Trigger Questions about Priority (Order of Importance or Quality):

⊙ Which one of these _____ would be most effective?

⊙ Is this _____ the best option or choice available?

⊙ How should these _____ be ranked from first to last (best to worst) in terms of their quality?

Creative Thinking: producing new or different ideas, products, methods, or strategies.

Trigger Questions

⊙ What could be invented to _____?

⊙ What might happen if _____?

⊙ What might be a different way to _____?

⊙ How would this change if _____?

⊙ What would be an original idea for _____?

Look back at the forms of thinking described in Box 6.4. Take one question listed under each of these forms of thinking and fill in the blank with a concept or issue you're learning about in a course you're taking this term.

Personal Story   When I teach classes or give workshops, I often challenge students or participants to debate me on either politics or religion. I ask them to choose a political party affiliation, a religion or a branch of religion for their debate topic, and a social issue that they have a stance on that can be backed up politically or religiously. The ground rules are as follows: I will let them choose the topic for debate, they can only use facts to pose their argument and/or rebuttal, and they can only respond in an analytical, balanced manner without letting emotions drive their answers. This exercise demonstrates that the topics we feel strongly about are often the topics we don't look at critically. People often say they are Democrat, Republican, Independent, etc., and argue that they are sure this is where they stand, and who they are. However, very few people actually spend time critically thinking about whether that description really fits. Have they read the core document (i.e., party platform) that outlines the party stance? Have they determined whether those core documents hold up to higher-level thinking processes? What kind of examination has this belief been through (thought, debate, discussions, etc.)? Do *your* beliefs hold up to careful examination?

—*Aaron Thompson*

Listening Strategies

When listening to lectures and professional presentations, pay attention not only to the content of the message, but also to the thinking process that lies behind it.

You can use the list of higher-level thinking questions in Box 6.4 to help you detect the type of thinking your instructors are using and to keep your thinking at higher levels during lectures.

Asking yourself higher-level thinking questions during lectures should prevent you from asking questions like this one.

Reading Strategies

When completing reading assignments and listening to class lectures, try to get in the habit of *cross referencing* or connecting ideas you come across that relate to ideas you've previously encountered.

When you discover information that relates to something you've learned about elsewhere, make a note of it in the margin of your text or your class notebook. This practice will help you develop and demonstrate synthesis on course exams and writing assignments.

Creating Cognitive Dissonance

To increase your ability to engage in balanced thinking, intentionally hold opposing ideas in your mind at the same time to put yourself in a mental state of cognitive dissonance.

Studies show that this type of cognitive contradiction or friction serves to decrease dualistic thinking and increase balanced thinking (Kurfiss, 1988; Meyers, 1986). Listed below are some specific strategies for creating cognitive dissonance.

◆ Find arguments for a position, then reverse your thinking and switch sides to argue for the opposing viewpoint.

◆ When doing research on a controversial issue, proceed as if you are going to defend and refute both sides of the issue. For instance, seek out readings that take opposing viewpoints and compare or contrast them. This will enable you to develop and demonstrate balanced thinking in your assignments and discussions.

◆ During group discussions with classmates, seek out different viewpoints or positions. For example, ask questions such as: "Who doesn't agree with what's being said?" or, "Would someone else like to express an opposing viewpoint?"

Studies show that the positive impact of interacting with peers on developing higher-level thinking skills is greatest when peers challenge each other's beliefs, which promotes personal reflection and re-evaluation (Pascarella & Terenzini, 2005). Seeking out different ideas doesn't mean that you are indecisive, looking to conform to someone else's viewpoint, or that you want to be a "yes man" who always agrees with others. Nor does it mean that you don't want to be a "no man" who always disagrees with others or ignores their viewpoints. Instead, you want to be an "open person" who seeks out and listens to different viewpoints in order to gain access to additional ideas that may make your viewpoint more balanced and complete.

By seeking out and discussing opposing viewpoints during group discussions, your group benefits by what social psychologists call the "group depolarization" effect—the tendency for each group member's position to become less extreme (depolarized) as a result of being exposed to an alternative viewpoint (Taylor, Peplau, & Sears, 2006). This strategy is not only valuable for improving the balance and quality of your group discussions in college, but it will also improve the group discussions you're likely to become involved in beyond college (e.g., committee work and jury duty).

◆ During group discussion, periodically play the role of *devil's advocate*—the person who points out the shortcomings or weaknesses in the position that everyone else seems to be taking. This will promote your group's awareness of the limitations or disadvantages of its viewpoint, and will help them avoid what social psychologists call "group think"—the tendency for a tight-knit group of like-minded people whose thinking is so much alike that they become blind to its weaknesses (Janis, 1982). Even if you are persuaded by your group's position, always be on the lookout to find and acknowledge its possible limitations or weaknesses.

Remember: The goal of group work is not to encourage rigid conformity or blind loyalty among its members, nor is it to discourage disagreement or dissent. As a responsible group member, one of your key roles is to encourage other members to express their individual viewpoints, even if they differ from the majority. If you are the person who holds a view that differs from other members, your role is to help your group seek *consensus*—which means one of three things:

1. you change your mind and agree with other members of your group,
2. group members change their minds and agree with you, or
3. you and other members of your group agree to disagree and move on with your work.

Pause for Reflection
Complete the following sentence with the first idea that comes to your mind:

To come up with creative ideas, you should _____

Creative Thinking Strategies

◆ Carry a small notepad or packet of post-its with you at all times because creative ideas can come to mind at the most unexpected times. The process of having a creative idea suddenly pop into your mind is referred to as *incubation*—because, just like an egg, an idea can suddenly hatch and emerge from your subconscious after you've sat on it for a while. However, just as creative ideas can suddenly slip into your mind, they can just as quickly slip out of your mind when you start thinking about something else. So, be sure to have the right equipment on hand to record and save your creative ideas before you lose them.

◆ When working on a problem that you cannot seem to solve, stop working on it for a while, and come back to it later. Creative solutions to a problem can sometimes appear after you stop thinking about it, take your mind off it, and return to it at a later point in time. Sometimes, when you're working intensely on a problem or challenging task, your attention may become mentally set or rigidly fixed on one aspect of it (Maier, 1970). Taking your conscious mind off it for a while may relax you and allow the problem to incubate in your subconscious, which may produce a sudden insight. Also, when you come back to the task later, your focus of attention is likely to shift to a different feature or aspect of it. This new focus point may enable you to view the problem from a different angle or vantage point, which can sometimes lead to a breakthrough idea that was blocked by your previous perspective (Anderson, 2000).

◆ When you're stuck on a problem, try rearranging its parts or pieces. The rearrangement can transform the problem into a different pattern and provides you with a new perspective. This new perspective may, in turn, allow you to suddenly see a solution that you previously missed, just like changing the order of letters in a word jumble may suddenly enable you to see the hidden, scrambled word. Similarly, you may increase your creative insights by changing the wording of any problem you're working on, or by recording ideas on index cards (or post-it notes) and laying them out in different orders and arrangements.

There are several strategies for coping with a difficult problem, such as coming back to it later, rearranging its parts, or working at the problem backwards.

◆ If you are having trouble solving problems that involve a sequence of steps (e.g., math problems), try changing the sequence by reversing their order and working backwards, or starting in the middle. The new sequence may change your approach to the problem by forcing you to come at it from a different direction, which could provide you with an alternative path to its solution.

◆ Represent what you're thinking about in different sensory modalities. For instance, take verbal information and represent it in visual form, such as a diagram, flow chart, or idea map. This will increase the number of brain areas that become stimulated and engaged in the creative thinking process.

◆ Use multiple sources by drawing on ideas from different people and different fields of study. Trading ideas with different people and bouncing ideas off them is a good way to generate energy, synergy, and serendipity (accidental discoveries). Studies show that creative people have a wide range of knowledge and interests, and they tend to combine ideas from different sources (Riquelme, 2002). For instance, creative people in specialized fields often build on a large store of knowledge that goes beyond the boundaries of their particular area of specialization and seek connections across different subject areas (Baer, 1993; Kaufman & Baer, 2002). As we mentioned in Chapter 2, the broad base of knowledge and wide range of thinking skills you acquire from the liberal arts will enhance your creativity. The general knowledge acquired from different subject areas that comprise the liberal arts can be combined and connected to form bridges to new ideas.

◆ Be flexible. Think about ideas and objects in unusual or unconventional ways. The power of flexible and unconventional thinking was well illustrated in the nonfiction movie, "Apollo 13," when an astronaut saved his life by creatively using duct tape as an air filter. Johannes Gutenberg discovered the idea of a printing press when he was watching a machine being used to crush grapes at a wine harvest. He thought that the same type of machine could be used to press letters onto paper (Dorfman, Shames, & Kihlstrom, 1996).

◆ Be experimental. Play with different ideas. Try out new ideas to see if they will work, and whether they will work better than the status quo. Studies show that creative people tend to take risks by experimenting with different ideas and techniques (Sternberg, 2001). Don't take the attitude that "it won't work" or "if it ain't broke, don't fix it." Instead, adopt an experimental attitude that asks: "How do we know it won't work until we try it?" And if it's already working, how might it work even better—more effectively, efficiently, or aesthetically. In other words, strive for continuous quality improvement by continually thinking about ways to create new and improved versions of what already exists. Actively resist settling for the security of familiarity. Doing things the way they've always been done doesn't mean you're doing them the best way they could be done. It may mean that it's just the most habitual (and mindless) way to do them. When we cling rigidly or stubbornly to what is conventional or traditional, we may be clinging to the comfort and security of what is most familiar and predictable while resisting the challenge of creativity and change.

- Be mobile. Get up and move around. By just standing up, studies show that our brain gets approximately 10 percent more oxygen than it does when we're sitting down (King, 1996). Since oxygen provides fuel for the brain, our ability to think creatively may be enhanced when we think on our feet and move around, rather than thinking while sitting down for extended periods of time.

- Be persistent. Studies show that creativity takes time, dedication, and hard work (Ericsson & Charness, 1994). Creative thoughts do not often emerge in one sudden stroke of genius, but evolve after continuous reflection and persistent effort.

Pause for Reflection

Post-It® Notes are very popular, perhaps because they stick on almost anything and can be stuck in any place; then they can be removed (without a mess) and re-stuck in a different place. Think creatively for a minute and come up with as many possible ways that students could use Post-Its to handle different tasks they face in college.

••• Summary and Conclusion

In this chapter, we analyzed the process of higher-level thinking and examined its individual forms separately in order to highlight their differences. However, in reality, these different forms of thinking typically work together in pairs, with one skill complementing the other. The various forms of higher-level thinking that have been discussed in this chapter may be concisely summarized in terms of the following complementary pairs of mental processes:

- **Analysis and Synthesis:** we use *analysis* to break down ideas into their parts or elements, and we use *synthesis* to build-up larger ideas (concepts) by connecting or integrating separate pieces of information.

- **Multidimensional and Balanced Thinking:** we look at issues from all angles (different perspectives and theories) to attain *multidimensional* thinking, and from both sides (pros and cons) to attain *balanced* thinking.

- **Dialectical and Dualistic Thinking:** we look at opposing arguments at the same time (dialectical thinking) to prevent us from thinking in overly simplistic, black-or-white terms (dualistic thinking).

- **Deductive and Inductive Reasoning:** we use *deductive* reasoning to move logically from general principles to reach conclusions about specific instances, and we use *inductive* reasoning to move logically from specific instances to reach conclusions that involve general statements or principles.

- **Divergent and Convergent Thinking:** we use *divergent* thinking to spread out our thinking in different directions to consider multiple ideas, and we use *convergent* thinking to narrow in and focus our thinking on a single idea.

- **Critical and Creative Thinking:** we use *critical* thinking to evaluate existing ideas, and we use *creative* thinking to generate new ideas.

Benefits of Higher-Level Thinking

Higher-level thinking is the most important teaching goal of college faculty.

Simply stated, college professors are more concerned about teaching you *how* to think than teaching you *what* to think (e.g., what facts to remember, or what position to take). In a national survey of 40,000 college professors teaching freshman-level through senior-level courses in a wide variety of fields, 97 percent of them reported that the most important goal of a college education is to develop students' ability to think critically (Milton, 1982). Similarly, college professors who teach introductory courses to freshmen and sophomores indicate that the primary educational purpose of their courses is to develop students' critical thinking skills (Stark et al., 1990).

Since thinking skills are valued by professors who are teaching students at all stages in the college experience and all subjects in the curriculum, if you work on developing these skills, it should be time well spent and should improve your academic performance significantly.

Higher-level thinking and research skills are increasingly important in today's information age, in which increasing amounts of information are being produced at increasingly faster rates.

As futurologist John Naisbitt (1982) predicted in *Megatrends*, "Running out of [information] is not a problem, but drowning in it is" (p. 24). The tidal wave of factual information currently being produced cannot be simply remembered or memorized, and even if it could, most of it would soon become outdated and replaced by the next wave. Thus, acquiring factual knowledge is less important than developing:

◆ information-literacy skills—which will allow you to efficiently search for and find information that is most relevant to your needs, and

◆ critical thinking skills—which will enable you to evaluate and select only the best information from the overwhelming amount that's at your fingertips (Cross, 1993).

The majority of new workers in the information age will no longer work with their hands but with their heads (Miller, 2003), and employers will value college graduates who have inquiring minds and possess higher-level thinking skills (Harvey, et al. 1997).

Higher-level thinking skills are vital for citizens in a democracy.

Authoritarian political systems, such as dictatorships and fascist regimes, suppress critical thought and demand submissive obedience to authority. In contrast, citizens living in a democracy are expected to control their political destiny by choosing (electing) their political leaders; thus, judging and choosing wisely is a crucial civic responsibility in a democratic nation. Citizens living and voting in a democracy must use higher-level reasoning skills, such as balanced and critical thinking, to make wise choices.

Research indicates that political campaigns in America are making more frequent use of manipulative media advertisements. These ads rely on short sound bites, one-sided arguments, and powerful visual images, which are intentionally designed to appeal to emotions and encourage simplistic thinking (Goleman, 1992). The need for Americana citizens to develop and deploy higher-level thinking skills may be more important today than at any other time in the nation's history, because these are the mental skills that empower voters to detect and resist the growing use of political propaganda.

· —· CLASSIC QUOTE ·—·

In a nation whose citizens are to be led by persuasion and not by force, the art of reasoning becomes of the first importance.

—Thomas Jefferson

Higher-level thinking is an important safeguard against prejudice, discrimination, and hostility.

Racial, ethnic, and national prejudices often stem from narrow, self-centered, or group-centered thinking (Paul & Elder, 2002). Prejudice often results from oversimplified, dualistic thinking that can lead individuals to categorize other people into either in-groups ("us") or out-groups ("them"). This type of dualistic thinking can lead, in turn, to ethnocentrism—the tendency to view one's own racial or ethnic group as the superior "in-group," while other groups are seen as inferior "out-groups." Development of higher-level thinking skills, such as taking multiple perspectives and using balanced thinking, counteracts the type of dualistic, ethnocentric thinking that can lead to prejudice, discrimination, and hatred.

●●● Learning More through Independent Research

Web-Based Resources for Further Information on Higher-Level Thinking

For additional information on concepts covered in this chapter, see the following Web sites.

Critical Thinking: www.criticalthinking.org
Creative Thinking: www.amcreativityassoc.org

Exercise 1: Plan to Demonstrate Higher-Level Thinking in Your Courses

Take a look at the syllabus for each course you're enrolled in this term. Find a major assignment or exam that will strongly influence your grade in each course. List four of these assignments or exams in the space below. If you are taking fewer than four courses, you can choose more than one assignment or exam from the same course.

Course   Major Assignment/Test

1. _____

2. _____

3. _____

4. _____

Using the matrix below, place a check mark in the boxes representing forms of higher-level thinking that you feel you can demonstrate on each of these major assignments or tests. (See the higher-level thinking definitions on pages 182–183 and the higher-level thinking questions on pages 201–202 to help you determine what form(s) of higher-level thinking you could use on each assignment or test.)

MAJOR COURSE ASSIGNMENT/TEST

	1.	2.	3.	4.
Analysis				
Synthesis				
Multiple Perspectives				
Multiple Theories				
Balanced Thinking				
Critical Thinking				
Creative Thinking				

HIGHER-LEVEL THINKING SKILL

Choose one box you checked in each column, and use the spaces provided below to explain how you would demonstrate that particular form of higher-level thinking on that particular assignment or test. For instance, if you checked a box indicating that you will use multiple perspectives in assignment #1, note the particular course concept or topic you will apply these multiple perspectives to, and what particular perspectives you will apply.

Exam/Assignment #1: _____

Form of Higher-Level Thinking: _____

How This Form of Thinking Will Be Demonstrated:

Exam/Assignment #2: _____

Form of Higher-Level Thinking: _____

How This Form of Thinking Will Be Demonstrated:

Exam/Assignment #3: _____

Form of Higher-Level Thinking: _____

How This Form of Thinking Will Be Demonstrated:

Exam/Assignment #4: _____

Form of Higher-Level Thinking: _____

How This Form of Thinking Will Be Demonstrated:

NOTES:

◆ Save the matrix on page 211 and use it as a visual reminder to ensure that you are using at least one form of higher-level thinking in your course assignments and exams.

◆ Use the matrix in study groups and group projects by having each member of your team take a different thinking role (e.g., analysis, synthesis, or balanced thinking). After each group member works individually, he or she could then share their thinking with the rest of the team. This would enable your team to pool the individual efforts of all its members to create a final product that demonstrates a variety of higher-level thinking skills.

Exercise 2: Self-Assessment of Higher-Level Thinking Characteristics

Listed below are four general characteristics of higher-level thinkers along with a set of specific traits relating to each characteristic. When you read the specific traits listed beneath each of the general characteristics, place a checkmark in the space next to any specific trait that you think is true of you.

CHARACTERISTICS OF A HIGHER-LEVEL THINKER

1. **Tolerant and Accepting**

    ___ Keeps emotions under control when someone criticizes his or her viewpoint.

    ___ Does not tune-out ideas that conflict with one's own.

    ___ Feels comfortable with disagreement.

    ___ Is receptive to hearing different points of view.

2. **Inquisitive and Open-Minded**

___ Eager to continue learning new things from different people and different experiences.

___ Has an "inquiring mind" that's curious, inquisitive, and ready to explore new ideas.

___ Finds differences of opinion or opposing viewpoints interesting and stimulating.

___ Attempts to understand why people hold very different viewpoints and tries to find common ground between them.

3. **Reflective and Tentative**

___ Suspends judgment until all the evidence is in, rather than making snap judgments before knowing the whole story.

___ Acknowledges the complexity, ambiguity, or uncertainty of some issues and may say things like, "I need to give this more thought" or "I need more evidence before I can draw a conclusion."

___ Takes time to think things through before drawing conclusions, making choices, and reaching decisions.

___ Periodically reexamines personal viewpoints to see if they should be maintained or changed as a result of new experiences and evidence.

4. **Honest and Courageous**

___ Gives fair consideration to ideas that other people may instantly disapprove of, or find distasteful.

___ Willing to express personal viewpoints that may not conform with the majority.

___ Willing to change old opinions or beliefs when they are contradicted by new evidence.

___ Willing to acknowledge the limitations or weaknesses of one's own attitudes and beliefs.

Look back at the list and count the number of checkmarks you placed underneath each of the four general areas.

1. Tolerant and Accepting   _____

2. Inquisitive and Open-Minded   _____

3. Reflective and Tentative   _____

4. Honest and Courageous   _____

Under which characteristic did you have the most checkmarks?

Under which did you have the fewest checkmarks?

How would you interpret the meaning of this difference?

Why do you think this difference occurred?

Trick or Treat: Confusing or Challenging Test?

Students in a philosophy course just got their first exam back, and Professor Plato is going over the test with students in his class. Some students are really angry because they feel that Professor Plato deliberately made up a test that was designed to confuse them by creating "trick questions." In his defense, Professor Plato states that he did not construct a confusing test with trick questions, but a college-level test that was designed to "challenge students to think!"

Reflection and Discussion Questions

1. Why do you think the students may have felt that the professor was trying to "trick" or "confuse" them on the exam?

2. What do you think the professor meant when he said that his test questions were designed to "challenge students to think?"

3. What might these students do to reduce the likelihood that they'll feel tricked on future tests?

4. What might the professor do to reduce the likelihood that students will feel tricked on future tests?

Three Key Academic Skills

Research, Writing, and Speaking

Learning Goals

The goals of this chapter are to help you develop effective skills for:

◆ acquiring ideas of others through research, and

◆ communicating your own ideas through writing and speaking.

These are key general-education or liberal arts skills that can be applied to any academic field or discipline to help you acquire and communicate knowledge.

Outline

Activate Your Thinking

What would you say is the difference between learning factual knowledge and learning a transferable skill?

_____

_____

_____

●●● The Importance of Research and Communication Skills

We are now living in an era referred to as the "information age" and the "communication age" because more information is being generated and communicated in today's world than at any other time in history (Breivik, 1998; Thornburg, 1994). Since information is being generated at such a rapid rate, developing "information literacy" skills—the ability to search for, locate, and evaluate information for relevance and accuracy—is critical for managing and making sense of the overload of information that's currently available to us. In addition, communication skills—such as speaking and writing—are becoming increasingly critical for career success (National Association of Colleges & Employers, 2003; The Conference Board of Canada, 2000). Such strong emphasis is being placed on effective communication in today's work world that college graduates with well-developed communication skills will have a clear advantage in today's job market (Mackes, 2003). Said in another way, *linguistic intelligence*—the ability to communicate with others through words or language—is an ability that will contribute immensely to your career entry and career advancement.

If you improve your research, writing, and speaking skills, you will likely improve your overall academic performance in college and your occupational performance after college. In this chapter, we will discuss specific strategies for improving your skills in each of these key areas.

●●● Research Strategies

In addition to completing writing assignments and making class presentations relating to material covered in course readings and class lectures, you are likely to be assigned research projects that involve writing in response to information that you locate, read, and evaluate. If you recall from Chapter 2, a key goal of a liberal arts education is to help you become a self-reliant, lifelong learner. One key characteristic of a self-reliant, lifelong learner is *information literacy*—the ability to find, evaluate, and use information. If you are information literate, you know where and how to find the information you need whenever you need it (National Forum on Information Literacy, 2005).

In this section, we discuss six major strategies for searching, locating and evaluating information, and how you can use that information to write college research papers that demonstrate higher-level thinking.

Identify Your Research Topic or Question

If your instructor does not assign a specific topic or research question for your paper, this is a golden opportunity for you to select a topic that has the most interest or value to you. Just be sure that your topic is relevant to the assignment and that its scope is neither:

◆ too *narrow*—that is, there is too little information available (or accessible) on the topic, or
◆ too *broad*—that is, there is too much information on the topic to reasonably cover within the maximum number of pages allowed for your paper.

If you have any doubts about your topic's relevance or scope, before you go any further, seek feedback from your instructor or from a professional in your college library.

 Remember: Librarians are information-research experts who are also out-of-class instructors, so capitalize on their expertise.

Locate Potential Sources of Information

You have two major resources you can use to search for and locate information:

1. Print resources—e.g., card catalogs, published indexes, and guidebooks; and

2. Online resources—e.g., online card catalogs, Internet search engines, and electronic databases.

Since different information-search tools are likely to generate different results, it's best not to rely exclusively on one research tool alone. For regularly updated summaries of different electronic search engines, how they work, and the type of results they produce, check the following Web sites:

The two main sources of information are print resources and online resources.

> searchenginewatch.com
> researchbuzz.com.

For a summary of key computer-based research terms, see Box 7.1.

Naturally, when you locate a source, your first step is to determine its relevance to your paper's topic. One strategy for efficiently determining the relevance of a source is to ask if it will help you answer one or more of the following questions about your topic: Who? What? When? Where? Why? How?

However, the most important question to ask yourself about potential sources is whether they are acceptable to the instructor who assigned your research paper. Before you even begin the information-search process, be sure you know what sources your instructor requires or prefers.

Evaluate the Quality of the Sources

When writing a research paper, the primary purpose of your sources is to provide *documentation*—to serve as references that support or reinforce your conclusions. Since sources of information can vary widely in terms of their quality, you will need to think critically and make sound judgments about what are "good" sources to select and use for documentation. The Internet has made this selection process more challenging because most of its posted information is "self-published" (Academic Integrity at Princeton, 2003). This means that the posted information was not subjected to the same quality control measures as information published in journals and books—which go to press only after they are reviewed for acceptance by a neutral panel of experts and are carefully edited by a professional editor. If you have any doubt about the quality or authenticity of a reference that you've located, play it safe and double-check with your instructor or a professional librarian.

Listed below are some criteria to help you critically evaluate the quality of the sources you locate.

◆ **Credibility:** Is the source written by an authority or expert in the field, such as someone with an advanced educational degree and/or professional experience related to the topic? For example, if your topic relates to an international issue, a highly credible source would be an author who has an advanced degree in international relations, or professional experience in international affairs.

◆ **Scholarly:** Is the source a scholarly publication that has been reviewed by a panel or board of impartial experts in the field before being published? If you see that the source

BOX 7.1 *Snapshot* SUMMARY

Key Computer-Based Research Terms

As you read the following list, make a note after each item indicating

- whether you've heard of it before, and
- whether you've used it before.

Database: a collection of data (information) that is organized for the purpose of easy access and retrieval.

A database may include:

a. *reference citations*—e.g., author, date, and publication source,

b. *abstracts*—summary of the contents of a scholarly article,

c. *full-length documents*, or

d. a combination of (a), (b), and (c).

Subscription Database: a database that can be accessed only through a subscription.

For instance, most of the electronic databases available in libraries are paid for through subscriptions. Subscription databases usually contain information sources that are more scholarly and closely monitored for quality than do databases that are free and accessible to anyone who accesses the Web.

Catalog: a library database that contains information about what information sources the library owns, and where they are located. Most catalogs are now in electronic form; however, a library may have some or all parts of its catalog available on cards (i.e., a *card catalog*).

Key Word: a word used to search multiple databases by matching the search word to items found in the databases.

Key words are very specific, so if the exact word is not found in the database, any information related to the topic being researched that does not exactly match the key word will be missed. For example, if the key word is "college," it will not pick up relevant sources that may have "higher education" instead of "college" in their titles.

Wildcard: a symbol, such as an asterisk (*), question mark (?), or exclamation point (!) that may be used to substitute different letters into a search word or phrase, so that an electronic search will be performed on all words represented by the symbol.

For example, the asterisk in the key word, *econom**, may be used to search for all information sources containing the words "economy," "economical," or "economist."

Descriptor (a.k.a., **Subject Heading**): a key word or phrase in the index of a database (or Catalog) that describes the subjects or content areas found within it, which can help researchers find relevant sources when they do a search.

For example, "emotional disorders" may be a descriptor for a psychology database to help researchers find information related to anxiety and depression. (Some descriptors or subject headings suggest different words or phrases to use in a search.)

Search Thesaurus: a list of words or phrases that have similar meaning provided by some databases that also identify which version of these words or phrases are used as key words, descriptors, or subject headings in the database.

This feature enables researchers to choose the correct search term before they begin the search process.

Source: Adapted from "Glossary of Library and Web Terms" by Diana Hacker, 2006 (http:www.dianahacker.com).

For a complete glossary of Internet terms, see: "Matisse's Glossary of Internet Terms" at http://www.matisse.net/files/glossary.html.

has been "peer reviewed" or "peer refereed," it means that it has been reviewed, evaluated, and approved for publication by other experts in the field. This is a good indication that the source represents a scholarly publication. For example, professional journals are peer reviewed (e.g., *New England Journal of Medicine*) but not popular magazines (e.g., *Newsweek*) or popular Web sites (e.g., Wikipedia.org).

"But Professor Jenkins, I researched my topic thoroughly on Wikipedia."

All sources are not created equally; some are more scholarly than others.

◆ Currency: Is it a recent or current source of information? In certain fields of study, such as the natural and social sciences, recent references may be strongly preferred because new data is generated rapidly in these fields and information can become quickly outdated. In other fields, such as history and philosophy, older references may be viewed as "classics," and citing them is perfectly acceptable. If you're not sure if current references are strongly preferred, check with your instructor before you begin the search process.

◆ Objectivity: Is the author likely to be impartial or unbiased toward the subject? Consider how the professional position or personal background of the authors may influence their ideas or their interpretation of evidence. Scholarly authors should attempt to write with objectivity, minimize emotional or political involvement with the topic, and not be in a position to gain personally from favoring a certain conclusion about the topic. For instance, you are more likely to suspect that biased information may appear on Web sites whose address ends with ".com"—indicating that it's a *com*mercial site whose primary purpose is to sell products and make profits, rather than to educate the public and engage in the objective pursuit of truth. Or, suppose your topic relates to a controversial medical issue and you find an article written by a medical doctor who is likely to benefit economically from taking one side on the issue. It would be reasonable to expect that this author may have a conflict of interest and will be biased toward reaching a conclusion that favors the side of the issue that will provide personal benefits. Since the objectivity of this article may be questionable, you may not want to use it as a source in your paper. If you feel that it is a well-written article containing good arguments, you can cite it in your paper, but demonstrate critical thinking by noting that its conclusions may have been biased by the author's background or position.

If authors or researchers are not neutral, it increases the risk that they will find what they *want* to find. In scientific research, this risk is referred to as experimenter bias, and it stems from the natural tendency for people to see what they expect to see, or what they hope to see (Rosenthal, 1966, 1974).

Personal Story

Soon after my wife and I got married, we moved to a new city and tried to find a place to live. We got up early, skipped breakfast, and drove to the town where we were planning to live. We were determined to find an apartment to rent before lunch, but we found ourselves still driving around town looking for a place in the middle of the afternoon. By this time, both of us were extremely hungry because we hadn't eaten anything since the night before, so we decided to stop looking for a place to live and start looking for a place to eat.

Unfortunately, we had about as much luck finding a place to eat as we did finding a place to live. It was approaching 4 p.m. and we were now beginning to hear each other's stomach growling like lions. Then, suddenly, my wife elbowed me (hard) while I was driving and said: "Joe, look—fried chicken!" She pointed to a flashing sign in the distance that I couldn't read clearly, but I figured she had better long-range vision than me. I put the pedal closer to the metal and sped up to get there as fast as was legally possible. As we continued down the road, I still couldn't see any sign that clearly read "fried chicken," but finally I did see a flashing sign and thought to myself, "Yee-hah, food!" However, as I drove closer and closer to the flashing sign, it became clearer and clearer to me that it didn't spell FRIED CHICKEN at all. Instead, it was a sign flashing the words: FREE CHECKING! FREE CHECKING!

We had a great laugh, but my hungry wife wasn't joking when she first saw the flashing sign in the distance; she really did think it was flashing the words, "fried chicken." That experience proved to me beyond a doubt that human beings do tend to see what they *expect* to see, or what they *hope* to see!

—Joe Cuseo

Pause for Reflection

Have you ever had the experience of seeing what you hoped or expected to see, rather than seeing things accurately (objectively)? Or, have you ever observed this happen to someone else?

What was the situation?

Why do you think that you (or the person you observed) did not view the situation accurately or objectively?

Evaluate the Number and Variety of References

Your research will be judged not only in terms of the quality of your individual references, but also in terms of the overall set or collection of references you use as research for your paper. Your total set of references is likely to be judged in terms of the following criteria:

◆ Quantity of references: Are there enough references? As a general rule, it is better to use as many references as possible because this should result in a paper with more perspectives and one that is more comprehensive or complete. Also, this will prevent you from relying only on one or two sources and reduce your risk of being accused of plagiarism. Lastly, use of multiple sources gives you more opportunity to demonstrate the higher-level thinking skill of synthesis, because you will have the opportunity to integrate ideas drawn from many different sources to create a final product that is uniquely your own. However, be sure to include only sources in your reference section that you actually used and cited in the body of your paper.

◆ Variety of references: Have you used different *types* of sources? For some research papers, not only the number but the *variety* of sources you use may be important to your instructor. You can intentionally vary your sources by drawing on different types of references, such as:

   ◇ books,

   ◇ scholarly journals—written by professionals and research scholars in the field,

   ◇ magazine or newspaper articles—written by journalists,

   ◇ course readings or class notes, and

   ◇ personal interviews or personal experiences.

Sources can also vary in terms of whether they are *primary sources*—first-hand information or original documents (e.g., research experiments or novels), or *secondary sources*—publications that rely on or respond to primary sources (e.g., a textbook, or an article that critically reviews a novel or movie). Using a balanced blend of older, classic sources and newer, cutting-edge references may also be desirable because it will enable you to demonstrate how certain ideas have changed or evolved over time, or how certain ideas have withstood the test of time and continue to remain important.

As a general rule, it is better to include a wider variety of sources than it is to rely on just one or two types of references. However, the best rule is to know exactly what types of references your instructor requires or prefers, and if you are unsure, find out before beginning the search process.

Use Your Sources of Information as Stepping-Stones to Higher-Level Thinking

Your paper should represent something more than summarized information obtained from your sources. Simply collecting and compiling the ideas of others will result in a final product that reads more like a high school book report than a college research paper. Remember that your sources just provide the raw material for your paper; you shape that raw material into a finished product by using higher-level thinking skills to analyze, synthesize, and evaluate it. Since it's your name that appears on the front cover of the paper, *you* should be in it—for example, it should contain *your* critical judgments and original ideas.

Remember: Research involves both generating some of your own ideas and placing those ideas in a larger context that includes the ideas of others. You want to show that you've done your research by citing the ideas of others, but you also want to connect, evaluate, and expand on those ideas to create your own. Do not just report or describe information you've drawn from your sources; instead, react to them, draw conclusions from them, and use them as evidence to support your reactions and conclusions.

Cite Your Sources

Properly citing and referencing your sources is a form of academic integrity or intellectual honesty that gives credit where credit is due. It credits others whose work you have borrowed, and it credits you for the research you have done. Furthermore, when you carefully cite and reference the information you have borrowed from others, what you do not cite stands out more clearly as your own thoughts and original ideas.

When should sources be cited?

You should cite a source for anything you *include in your paper that does not represent your own work or thoughts*. This includes other people's words, ideas, statistics, research findings, and visual work (e.g., diagrams, pictures, or drawings). **There is only one exception to this rule: You do not need to cite sources for factual information that is *common knowledge*—information that most people already know.** For example, common knowledge includes well-known facts (e.g., the earth is the third planet from the sun) and familiar dates (e.g., the Declaration of Independence was signed in 1776). If you are not sure if a piece of information represents common knowledge, one rule of thumb is to check an encyclopedia. If you find it there, then you probably don't need to cite its source in your paper. However, there may be exceptions to this rule (Academic Integrity at Princeton, 2003). If you're in doubt about whether or not to cite a reference, the best rule to follow is to consult with your instructor or a librarian.

The Internet has allowed us to gain easy access to an extraordinary amount of information and has made research much easier—that's the good news. The bad news is that it has also made proper citation more challenging. Determining the true "owner" or original author of posted information or where it was first produced isn't as clear-cut as it is for published books and articles. If you have any doubt, print it out and check it out—with your instructor or a professional librarian. If you don't have the time or opportunity to consult with either one of them, then play it safe and cite the source in your paper. If you cannot find the name of an author, at least cite the Web site, the date of the posted information (if available), and the date you accessed or downloaded it.

> **Remember:** As a general rule, whenever you're unsure about the need to cite a source, it's better to cite it and risk being corrected for over-citing than it is to run the risk of being accused of plagiarism—a serious violation of academic integrity that can have grave consequences (e.g., probation, suspension, or expulsion).

Where and how should sources be cited?

There are two places where you should cite your sources:

1. The body of your paper and
2. The reference section at the end of your paper (also known as a "bibliography" or "works cited" section).

How you should cite your sources depends on the referencing style of the particular academic field or discipline in which you are writing your paper, so be sure that you know the citation style your instructor prefers. It is very likely that you will be expected to use either one of two referencing styles during your first year of college:

1. *MLA* style—standing for the *Modern Language Association*, which is the citation style commonly used in humanities and fine arts (e.g., English and theatre arts); or

2. *APA* style—standing for the *American Psychological Association*, which is the citation style most commonly used in the social and natural sciences (e.g., sociology and anthropology).

It's also possible that you may be asked to use other styles in advanced courses in specialized fields, such as *The Chicago Manual of Style* for papers in history, or the Council of Biology Editors (CBE) style for papers in the biological sciences. Thus, be sure you are aware of the referencing style that is expected or preferred by your instructor before you begin to write your paper.

When you use someone else's *exact words* in the body of your paper, place parentheses around those words and cite the specific page number of your source. If you do not use someone else's exact words, summarize that person's ideas by paraphrasing them and immediately cite the author's name and the year of the publication. To ensure that you are paraphrasing and not plagiarizing your source, write your summary without looking directly at the source itself. After you've completed your summary, check the source to see if you accurately captured the author's main ideas without copying the author's actual words (Purdue University Online Writing Lab, 1995–2004). If you paraphrase several ideas from the same source within the same paragraph, you do not need to cite the author after every single sentence. Instead, cite the source only once—at the end of the paragraph.

BOX 7.2 Snapshot SUMMARY

What Is Plagiarism?

Definition

Deliberate or unintentional use of someone else's work without acknowledging it, thus giving the reader the impression that it's your own work.

Common Forms of Plagiarism

1. Submitting an entire paper written by someone else.
2. Copying an entire section of someone else's work and inserting it into your own work.
3. Cutting paragraphs from separate sources and pasting them into the body of your own paper.
4. Paraphrasing (re-wording) someone else's words or ideas without citing that person as a source. (For specific examples of paraphrasing versus plagiarism, go to: www.princeton.edu/pr/pub/integrity/pages/plagiarism.html)
5. Not placing quotation marks around someone else's exact words that appear in the body of your paper.
6. Failing to cite the source of factual information included in your paper if it is not common knowledge.

Note: If the source for information included in your paper is listed in your reference section or list of works cited at the *end* of your paper, but is not cited in the *body* of your paper, this still qualifies as plagiarism.

Sources: Academic Integrity at Princeton (2003); The Pennsylvania State University (2005); Purdue University Online Writing Lab (1995–2004).

●●● Writing

Writing is a transferable skill that you can use across the curriculum, including general education courses and your academic major. Different academic disciplines will emphasize different styles of writing, which will help you to learn how to communicate for different purposes and audiences (Griffin, 1982; Spear, 1988; Smith, 1983–84). Some fields will place heavy emphasis on writing that is structured and tightly focused (e.g., science and business), while other fields may encourage writing with personal style, flair, or creativity (e.g., English and literature).

The power of writing is highlighted in interviews with graduating seniors who were asked the following question: "Think of all the courses you have taken at college. Which course, or courses, had the most profound impact on you, on the way you think, about learning, about life, about the world?" When seniors answered this question, they tended to cite courses in which they had done a significant amount of writing (Light, 2001).

Your ability to write clearly, concisely, creatively, and persuasively is a skill that will not only enable you to succeed academically; it will also help you to succeed professionally. In one study, college alumni were asked about the importance of different skills to their current work responsibilities more than ten years after they graduated, and over 90 percent of the alumni ranked "need to write effectively" as a skill they considered to be of "great importance" to their current work (Worth, cited in Light, 2001). Other surveys have revealed that working professionals spend anywhere from 4 to 16 hours of their work week on writing activities alone, such as writing reports, memos, and letters (Anderson, 1985). In fact, the first contact and first impression you will make on future employers is likely to be your letter of application or cover letter that you write when applying for positions. Constructing a well-written letter of application may be your first step toward converting your college experience and college degree into a future career.

> **Remember:** Writing skills will contribute to your academic success across all subjects throughout all your years in college, and they will promote your professional success in any career you may pursue after college.

Types of Writing

The types of written products that you can produce other than the traditional formal essay, research report, or term paper, include a host of shorter and more informal types of writing. Writing scholars have classified different forms of writing into two major classes or categories:

Transactional writing and *expressive* or informal writing (Britton, et al., 1976; Connolly, 1989; Tchudi, 1986). These two major types of writing are defined and illustrated below.

1. Transactional Writing: public writing that is primarily intended for others to read, and which is commonly used for the purposes of communicating, informing, reporting,

explaining, persuading, or entertaining. This type of writing includes written products such as:

◆ Letters, such as writing a letter to a newspaper editor, an elected official, student body president, or college administrator, to offer persuasive suggestions for improving the college experience on your campus.

◆ Manuals or "How to" Guides, such as writing a college-success guide for beginning college students.

◆ Editorials or Feature Articles, such as writing editorials or articles for your college newspaper.

◆ Critical Reviews, such as writing reviews of books, films, plays, musical performances, or TV programs.

◆ Creative Literature, such as writing poems, fictional stories, science fiction, and scripts for plays, movies, or videos.

2. Expressive or Informal Writing: personal writing that is intended for the writer and is used for the purpose promoting self-awareness and personal growth. This category would include written products such as:

◆ Diaries
For example, keeping a diary of autobiographical entries that includes key past experiences and future plans.

◆ Journals
A journal may be defined as an ongoing series of written reactions to, or reflections on personal experiences that take place over an extended period of time. For example, in Chapter 9, we recommend keeping a "career-exploration journal." In it, you would record your reflections on the results of career tests and self-assessments. Also, included in this journal could be any self-insights or self-discoveries about your career interests, values, and abilities that may result from your coursework in different subjects or your experiences outside the classroom (e.g., co-curricular activities, volunteer service, and part-time employment). You can also use journals as a personal incentive to stimulate and motivate your use of effective learning strategies, such as keeping weekly journals in which you note how you have applied effective learning strategies that have been discussed in this book. (Note: You're more likely to actually use learning strategies if you know you are going to keep track of them.)

Writing in a journal is a type of expressive or informal writing.

In a journal, since your written entries are made over an extended period of time, you are left with a historical record of your thoughts and feelings. This record can be checked to detect patterns of consistency or change, which may give you a window of self-insight through which you can see how you are developing academically and personally.

◆ Lists or Memos to Self
For example, you can get in the habit of listing specific advantages and disadvantages associated with difficult personal choices, along with their relative weights (strong or weak), in order to help you make important decisions in an informed and balanced way.

♦ Checklists

A checklist may be defined as an inventory or itemized list of all key elements or steps involved in a task, which allows you to check (and double-check) whether you have missed or overlooked any of them. For example, we wrote a checklist of steps for college success in Chapter 1 (pp. 29–30). Similarly, you can write a checklist for any college task to be sure that you do it completely, carefully, and effectively, such as creating a checklist of criteria or factors that your instructor will use to grade your performance on a major assignment.

♦ Logs

A log may be defined as a written record of personal habits or behaviors that include specific information about when and where they took place. For instance, you could keep a log of how you spend your time or your money.

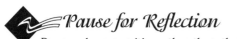 *Pause for Reflection*

Do you do any writing other than that which is assigned to you in your classes?

If yes, what are the other types of writing you do and what purposes do they serve?

Writing-to-Learn Strategies

As we mentioned in Chapter 1, humans learn most effectively from experience when they become actively involved in the experience and when they reflect on the experience after it has taken place. Writing can be used as a strategy to help us learn from any experience by increasing our level of involvement with it and our ability to carefully reflect on it. The phrase "writing-to-learn" has been coined by scholars to capture the idea that writing is not only a communication skill that is learned in English composition classes, but is also a skill that can promote learning in any academic subject or from any life experience. Thus, writing to learn and learning to write are complementary goals, and you can use writing not only as a channel for communicating your knowledge or ideas to others, but also as a tool to promote your own learning (Applebee, 1981; Elbow, 1973; Murray, 1984).

Writing-to-learn activities differ from traditional writing assignments, such as essays or term papers, in three major ways:

1. They are shorter—requiring less amount of student time to complete.
2. They are written primarily for the benefit of the writer—as an aid to thinking and learning (Tchudi, 1986).
3. They are not done for teachers as required assignments, but are done by students for their own benefit—to promote learning and understanding.

See Box 7.3 to see how writing-to-learn activities can be used for a wide variety of academic purposes and tasks encountered in college.

Writing-to-Learn Activities: Academic Tasks and Purposes

As you read the following writing activities and purposes, make a short note in the margin indicating whether you do this type of writing; if you don't do it, indicate whether you think it would be worth doing.

Writing to Listen

You can actively take notes in class, during study-group sessions, or office visits with your instructors, in order to increase your focus of attention and concentration on what is being said. *Hearing*, *writing*, and *seeing* information after it's been written provides three different memory traces in the brain that can combine to improve your comprehension and retention of that information.

For instance, you could write a "one-minute paper" immediately after each class session, which only takes a minute or less to complete, yet enables you to assess whether you've actively listened to and grasped the most important message delivered in class that day (e.g., "What was the most significant concept I learned in class today?" or, "What was the most confusing thing that I experienced in today's class that I should ask my instructor to clarify?")

Writing to Read

Just as writing promotes active listening, writing also promotes active reading. Taking notes on *what* you're reading *while* you're reading ensures active involvement because it requires more mental and physical energy than merely reading and highlighting sentences.

Writing to Remember

Writing lists or memos to yourself, such as ideas generated at a group meeting or creating lists of definitions of vocabulary words you need to remember, is an old-fashioned but sure-fired way not to forget them. When you've recorded an idea in print, you have created a permanent record of it that will enable you to remember it forever. The act of writing itself creates a "muscle memory" associated with movement that can trigger recall of the information you've written.

STUDENT PERSPECTIVE

"Write notes to yourself while reading your assignments. This helps you understand what you are reading and helps you make 'connections' to additional discussions or readings."

—Advice to new students from a college sophomore (Walsh, 2005)

Personal Story Whenever I have trouble remembering the spelling of a word, I take a pen or pencil and start to write the word out. I'm surprised at how many times the correct spelling comes back to my mind once I begin to write the word. However, the more I think about it, it's not surprising that my ability to remember the spelling immediately returns when I start writing it. This memory "flashback" is probably due to the fact that when I start using the muscles in my hand to write the word, it activates the "muscle memories" in my brain from the times in the past when I've written that word correctly.

—Joe Cuseo

Writing to Organize

Constructing summaries and outlines, or writing ideas on different index cards that relate to different categories or concepts are effective ways of organizing information. This type of organizational writing requires synthesis of different ideas and restatement of ideas in your own words, both of which are effective learning strategies.

Writing to Study

Writing study guides or practice answers to potential test questions represents an effective study strategy that can be done when learning alone or when preparing for study groups. This is particularly effective preparation for essay tests because it enables you to study in a way that closely matches what you will be expected to do on the test.

Writing to Understand

Paraphrasing or restating what you're trying to learn by writing it in your own words is an effective way to get feedback about whether you've truly understood it rather than just memorized it, because you have transformed it into words that are meaningful to you.

(continued)

·—· **CLASSIC QUOTE** ·—·

I write to understand as much as to be understood.

—Elie Wiesel, world-famous American novelist, Nobel Prize winner, and Holocaust survivor

Writing to Discuss

Prior to participating in class or group discussions, you can gather your thoughts in writing before expressing them orally. This will ensure that you've carefully reflected on your ideas, which, in turn, should improve the quality of ideas you contribute to class or group discussions. This strategy should also make you a less anxious and more confident speaker because you reduced the pressure of trying to think about what you're going to say at the same time that you're trying to say it. Your written notes give you a script to build on—and to fall back on—in case you experience speech anxiety while expressing your ideas.

Final Note: Any of the above writing-to-learn strategies can be done collaboratively as well as individually. The benefits of using writing-to-learn activities can be magnified by pairing-up with another student and doing them as a duet, or by teaming-up with two or three other students and doing them as a trio or quartet.

 Pause for Reflection

Have you ever teamed up with a classmate to complete a writing assignment?

If yes, did you think it was effective?

If no, why do you think you have never done so?

Writing and Higher-Level Thinking

Writing can be used as a tool to strengthen your ability to think at higher levels. Since writing requires physical action, it implements the effective learning principle of active involvement; it essentially forces you to focus attention on your own thoughts and activate your thinking. Writing not only helps to jump start your thinking, it also elevates its quality by slowing down your thought process, allowing it to proceed in a more careful, systematic fashion that makes you more consciously aware of specific details. Furthermore, the act of writing results in a visible product that you can review and use as feedback to improve the quality of your thoughts (Applebee, 1984; Langer & Applebee, 1987). In other words, writing allows you to "think out loud on paper" (Bean, 2003, p 102).

Writing can also stimulate your discovery of new ideas because these may emerge *during* the act or process of writing (Ambron, 1991). As the poet William Stafford puts it, "A writer is not so much someone who has something to say as he is someone who has found a process that will bring about new things he would not have thought of if he had not started to say [write] them" (quoted in Connolly, 1989, p. 3). Viewed from this perspective, writing is not just the end result or final product of your thinking; it is also a means or process of stimulating your thinking.

In particular, we strongly encourage you to write for the purpose of discovering or creating new ideas. You can use *free-writing* to capture your free-floating thoughts by getting them down rapidly on paper, without worrying about spelling and grammar. You can use this writing strategy as a warm-up exercise to help you generate ideas for a research topic, to keep track of original ideas you may happen to discover while brainstorming, or to record creative ideas that suddenly pop into your mind at unexpected times (before you forget them).

We also strongly encourage you to write for the purpose of capturing your thought process during problem-solving tasks in math and science. Try to get in the habit of writing down the thoughts that are going through your mind at each major step in the problem-solving process. This type of reflective writing enables you to think about your thinking (meta-cognition), which is a practice that is strongly associated with effective higher-level thinking. It will increase awareness of your own thinking process and will leave you with a written record of your train of thought. Also, you can review this written record later to help you retrieve the path of thought that led you to solve the problem successfully, so that you can reuse the same path to solve similar problems in the future.

Try to get into the habit of periodically stepping back to reflect on your thinking process. Ask yourself what type of thinking you are doing (such as analysis, synthesis, evaluation) and record your personal reflections in writing. You could even keep a "thinking log" or "thinking journal" to increase self-awareness of the thinking strategies you develop across time, or how your thinking strategies may vary across different courses and academic fields.

Writing to Communicate

You may have many great thoughts in your head, but unless you can get those thoughts out of your head and effectively communicate them, your instructors will never know that you have them, and you will never receive full credit for them in your college courses. Writing is a major route or avenue through which you can communicate your ideas, and it is one that your instructors will use to judge the quality of your thinking. Thus, if you improve your writing skills, you will improve your ability to communicate and demonstrate your higher-level thinking skills.

Studies show that a very small percentage of high school students' class time and homework time is spent on writing assignments that are as lengthy and demanding as those given in col-

"JUNIOR'S WRITING HAS IMPROVED. HIS LETTERS FROM COLLEGE, PLEADING FOR MORE MONEY, ARE FORCEFULLY AND FLAWLESSLY WRITTEN."

College writing assignments are often intended to develop your persuasive reasoning skills.

lege. For example, high school writing is more likely to involve summaries or descriptive reports that do not require the type of higher-level reasoning used for persuasive writing—which is the type of writing most frequently assigned in college (Applebee, 1981; Applebee, et al., 1990).

We acknowledge that people have different writing styles, and that there may not be one best method or formula for effective writing. However, there are some common themes or general approaches to effective writing that can help weak writers become stronger, and help good writers become better. One general approach to effective writing is to divide the writing process into separate stages and concentrate on one stage at a time. When writing is done in smaller steps with a timeline for completing each of these steps, you are less likely to feel overwhelmed by trying to do all things at once. Studies show that when writers divide their writing into small, manageable tasks, they are less likely to experience anxiety, procrastination, and "writer's block"—the inability to start or to continue writing (Boice, 1994).

In this section, we provide a plan for writing papers that involves dividing the total task into ten stages. This division of time and labor should make your writing more manageable, less stressful, and more successful. Writing is a multi-stage process, and its multiple stages cannot be completed in one night. Just as breaking up studying into separate sessions that take place in advance of an exam serves to improve your test performance, breaking up the writing process into separate stages and completing them in advance of the due date serves to improve the quality of your written product.

Dividing large writing assignments into smaller, manageable steps can reduce late-night frustration and the risk of permanent computer damage.

Stage 1. Know the Purpose or Objective of the Assignment

Having a clear understanding of the purpose or goal of the writing assignment is a critical first step to completing it successfully. Knowing what you're going to do not only helps you to stay on track and moving in the right direction, it also helps you get on the track and get going in the first place. Studies show that one major cause of writer's block is uncertainty about the goal or purpose of the writing task (Rennie & Brewer, 1987).

Therefore, before you attempt to do anything else, be sure you are addressing the question that is being asked by your instructor. You can do so by asking yourself these three questions about the assignment:

1. What is this assignment asking you to accomplish?
2. What type of thinking is your instructor asking you to demonstrate in this assignment?
3. What criteria or standards will your instructor use to judge and grade your performance on this assignment?

In college, it is unlikely that the purpose of your writing assignment will be to simply report information, as it would be when writing a summary or book report. Instead, you will be expected to react or respond to the information you report by using one or more of the forms of higher-level thinking that we've described in Chapter 6. To help determine what particular form(s) of thinking you are expected to demonstrate in a writing assignment, make special note of any action verbs that are included in the description of the assignment. These verbs can provide valuable clues to the type of thinking that your instructor wants you to demonstrate. Listed in Box 7.4 are some thinking verbs that you are likely to see in the description of college writing assignments, accompanied by the type of mental action typically called for by each of these verbs.

BOX 7.4 *Snapshot* **SUMMARY** **Thinking Verbs and Corresponding Mental Actions Commonly Found in College Writing Assignments**

As you read the following list, make a short note after each mental action, indicating whether or not you've been asked to use such thinking on any assignments you completed prior to college.

Compare—find key ideas, noting their similarities and differences.

Contrast—find key ideas, noting the differences between them, particularly sharp differences or distinctions.

Describe—identify key parts and give details about these parts (e.g., who, what, where, and when).

Discuss—analyze into parts and evaluate the parts (e.g., strengths and weaknesses).

Document—support your ideas or conclusions with sources (references).

Explain—provide reasons that answer the questions Why? or How?

Illustrate—provide concrete examples or specific instances.

Interpret—draw your own conclusion about something, and support your conclusion with evidence.

Justify—back-up your arguments and viewpoints with evidence.

Prioritize—arrange in order from highest to lowest in terms of importance or value.

Stage 2. Brainstorming Ideas

Use the mental process of brainstorming to generate possible ideas or points you will include in your paper. (Brainstorming is described in Chapter 6, p. 198.) At this stage, the only thing you are concerned about is getting the ideas you have in your head, out of your head, and on to paper. Writing scholars refer to this process as "focused freewriting"—writing nonstop for a certain period of time just to generate ideas, without worrying about writing complete or correct sentences (Bean, 2001). Remember that the act of writing itself can stimulate ideas, so if you're not sure what ideas you have, start writing because it will likely focus your thoughts

I'm in the middle of an intense brainstorm; ideas are pouring out of my mind at lightning speed! Write 'em down fast!!

and trigger ideas, which, in turn, can lead to additional ideas. One way to overcome writer's block is to start writing something (Zinsser, 1990). It could be anything, as long as it jump-starts the process. Once you run out of ideas, take a break, come back later, and try again. Chances are that you will generate more ideas after you've stopped thinking about the task for a while, which can allow additional ideas to incubate subconsciously. Sometimes, even changing your working environment or format may stimulate new ideas, such as shifting from writing ideas in pen or pencil to typing them on your computer. Also, generating ideas with a friend or testing your ideas with a classmate can make the brainstorming stage more stimulating and productive.

Stage 3. Organize Your Ideas

There are two key ways in which ideas need to be organized in a paper.

1. Separate pieces of information relating to the same idea need to be organized conceptually into the same categories.

   Strategy: Review the ideas that you've brainstormed and group together those ideas that relate to the same general category.

   For instance, if your topic is terrorism, and you find three ideas on your list that refer to different causes of terrorism, group those ideas together under the category of "causes." Similarly, if you find ideas on your list that relate to possible solutions to the problem of terrorism, then group those ideas under the category of "solutions."

   Index cards can be very useful tools for organizing your ideas into separate categories. You can conveniently write the category heading on the top of the card and record any ideas relating to the same category on the same card.

2. General categories of ideas need to be organized sequentially into an order that flows smoothly or logically from start to finish.

   Strategy: Arrange your general categories of ideas into an orderly sequence that creates a beginning, a middle, and an end.

   Index cards come in handy when trying to find the best progression of your major ideas because the cards can be arranged and rearranged easily until you discover an order that produces the smoothest, most logical sequence. You can use that sequence of index cards to create an outline for your paper, which lists your major categories of ideas and the order in which they will appear in your paper.

   Strategy: Another effective way to organize and sequence your ideas is by creating a *concept map* or *idea map*, which represents your main categories of ideas in a visual-spatial format that's similar to a road map. Below is a concept map (Figure 7.1) that we used to organize and sequence the main ideas relating to higher-level thinking that we wrote about in Chapter 6. We call this type of concept map a "clock map" because its main ideas are organized and sequenced like the hour hands of a clock, beginning at the top and then moving sequentially in a clockwise direction.

◆ *Pause for Reflection*

When you attempt to organize your ideas, are you more likely to use a map (diagram) format *or an* outline format—*in which you list major ideas as headings (A, B, C, etc.) and related minor ideas as subheadings (1, 2, 3, etc.)?*

Figure 7.1 Concept Map Used to Organize and Sequence Major Ideas Relating to Higher-Level Thinking

Why do you think you tend to favor one method over the other?

Which method for organizing ideas appears more natural or comfortable to you?

Stage 4. Writing a First Draft

The stages of writing we've discussed thus far are referred to as "prewriting" because they focus on generating and organizing your own ideas rather than expressing or communicating them to someone else (Murray, 1993). When you write a first draft, you begin the formal writing process by beginning to convert your major ideas into sentences—without worrying about the mechanics of writing (e.g., punctuation, grammar, or spelling).

Remember: Do not expect to write a perfect draft of your paper on the first try. Even professional writers report that it takes them more than one draft (often three or four) before they produce their final draft. Although the final product of award-winning writers may look great, what precedes it is a messy process that includes lots of revisions in-between the first try and the final product (Bean, 2001).

In your first draft, your goal is to "talk through" your key ideas on paper. After you have completed your first draft, it's a good idea to step away from it for a while. When you return to it later, after you've given your mind some time to cool off and incubate, you may think of new ideas and better ways to express the ideas you previously had. In your later drafts, you can convert your informal writing into more formal and polished prose.

Stage 5. Write a Second Draft Focusing on Your Paper's Organization

After getting your main ideas in sentence form (first draft), you can turn your attention to organizing your sentences into paragraphs, and organizing your paragraphs into a logical sequence. Here are some strategies for accomplishing each of these steps:

◆ When writing, keep separate ideas in separate paragraphs. Do not scatter information pertaining to the same idea across different paragraphs, or pack information relating to different ideas within the same paragraph. A paragraph should represent a chain of sentences that are linked to the same thought or idea; when you shift to a different idea, shift to a different paragraph.

◆ Whenever possible, start new paragraphs with a topic sentence that relates or connects the first sentence of the new paragraph with the last sentence of the previous paragraph. This will allow you to make smooth transitions from one paragraph to another.

◆ Use your first paragraph to provide a meaningful introduction, overview, or preview of the major points you will make in the body of the paper. Pay particular attention to your opening paragraph because it creates the all-important first impression of your paper and sets the stage for what will follow. Your introduction should include a *thesis statement*—a one-sentence summary of your key point or main argument—which the body of your paper will support with evidence. Your thesis statement is the most important sentence in your introduction; consider it to be the compass or map for your "trip" (paper) that guides your thinking, and keeps you and your audience on track toward the same destination (your conclusion). You may also consider writing your thesis statement in the form of a question, and use the body of your paper as a quest or journey to reach an answer to that question.

◆ Use your final paragraph to deliver a summary of the "big picture" that ties together and drives home your paper's major points. This will leave your paper with three distinctive parts:

1. The introduction—an opening paragraph that includes a thesis statement;

2. The body—a series of paragraphs following the introduction, each of which contains one of your major points or ideas, and

3. The conclusion—a final paragraph that summarizes your major points and relates them to the thesis statement included in your introduction.

◆ Make sure that your conclusion and introduction are aligned or interrelated. The most important sentence in your conclusion should be a restatement of your original thesis statement in a way that answers the question you presented in your introduction. In fact, when writing your conclusion you may come up with a sentence that turns out to be a better thesis statement than the one you originally wrote in your opening paragraph. In fact, it is a good idea to review and perhaps slightly revise your introductory thesis statement after completing the body of your paper because, in the process of writing, you are likely to discover new thoughts and better ideas. If this happens, you can modify your opening thesis statement so that it more closely matches your concluding statement (Bean, 2001). However, if you find yourself making radical changes to your thesis statement, this may indicate that you radically changed directions while writing the body of your paper and you didn't accomplish what you said you were going to do in your introduction.

Connecting your thesis statement with a concluding statement provides a pair of book ends that effectively anchors your paper at its two most pivotal points—the beginning and the end. This enables you to capitalize on your paper's two most powerful points of impression—the first and the last.

Stage 6: Reading and Editing

After completing a second draft of your paper, take your mind off it for a while, and come back to it in a different role—as *reader* and *editor*. Up to now, your role has been that of a writer; at this stage, you shift roles from writer to reader and you read your own work as if someone else had written it, critically evaluate its ideas, organization, and writing style. As a reader of your own writing, if you find that your choice of words and sentences are effectively communicating the message you intended to send, then there is no need to change them. However, if the words you've chosen and the sentences you've constructed are not really capturing or reflecting what you meant to say, then *revision* is necessary. At this stage, make sure your paper is double-spaced, so you have ample room for editing and revising.

When reading your paper, critically evaluate each of the following features:

◆ Higher-Level Thinking

Does your paper demonstrate any of the forms of higher-level thinking we discussed in Chapter 6 (e.g., analysis and synthesis, critical and creative thinking)? Are its major points and final conclusion well supported by evidence—such as:

◇ direct quotes from authoritative sources,

◇ specific examples,

◇ statistical data,

◇ scientific research findings, or

◇ first-hand experiences?

◆ Overall Organization

Take a *panoramic* or aerial view of your paper to see if you can clearly identify its three major parts: the beginning (introduction), middle (body), and end (conclusion). Do these form a connected whole? If the sections don't seem to be well connected, try rearranging their order. If the paper's key sections seem difficult to identify or distinguish, try highlighting them with headings that are underlined, capitalized, or boldfaced; this may make it clearer to the reader where different sections begin and end. Also, check to see if there is *continuity* across major sections of your paper: Does your train of thought stay on track from start to finish? If you find yourself getting away from the main topic at certain points in your paper, eliminate that information or rewrite it in a way that re-routes your thoughts back onto its main track (your thesis statement).

◆ Sentence Structure

Do the sentences make sense and flow smoothly? Are they easy to read and follow? Check for:

◇ Sentences that are too long—rambling sentences that go on and on without any punctuation or pauses that allow readers to catch their breath. You can correct rambling sentences by

    a. punctuating them with a comma—signaling a short pause,

    b. punctuating them with a semi-colon—signaling a longer pause than a comma (but not as long as a period), or

    c. dividing them into two shorter sentences (separated by a period).

◇ Sentences that are too short—choppy sentences that "chop up" what you've written into such short statements that they interfere with the natural flow or rhythm of reading. Correct choppy sentences by joining them to form a larger sentence.

One strategy for helping you to determine if your written sentences flow smoothly is to read them aloud. Note the places where you naturally tend to pause and stretches where you tend to keep going. Your natural pauses may serve as cues for places where your sentences need punctuation, and your natural runs may indicate sentences that are flowing smoothly and should be left alone. Reading your writing out loud can also help you find run-on sentences and awkward phrases.

◆ Word Selection

Are certain words or phrases used so frequently that they become *repetitious*? If so, try to vary your vocabulary by substituting words that have the same or similar meaning. This substitution process can be made easier by using a thesaurus, which may be conveniently available on your computer's word processing program.

> **Remember:** Your writing style should not obscure or obstruct the thoughts you intend to send from your mind to the reader's mind; instead, it should function as a smooth-running vehicle that "drives home" your thoughts efficiently and powerfully.

Stage 7. Seek Feedback from Other Readers

You are always the first reader of your paper, but you don't have to be the only reader before you submit to your instructor and receive a grade. Sometimes, no matter how honest or objective we try to be about our own work, we may still be blind to its weaknesses. All of us may have a natural tendency to see what we hope or want to see in our work, rather than what's really there—especially after we've put a great deal of time, effort, and energy into the process of creating it. So, get a second opinion on your paper by asking a trusted friend or a tutor in the Writing or Learning Center to read it. You can seek feedback at any stage of the writing process—whether it be for help with understanding the assignment, brainstorming ideas, writing your first draft, or writing your final draft. Seeking feedback from the Writing or Learning Center is something that should not only be done by students experiencing writing problems or writer's block. Feedback should be sought by all students who want to push the quality of their writing to a higher level. Studies show that when students with different levels of writing ability receive feedback from others prior to submitting a paper, it improves their quality of writing as well as the grade they receive on the paper (Dudenhyer, 1976; Thompson, 1981).

Since writing and speaking both involve communicating with words, the same benefits that students experience from participating in small-group discussions and study groups can be experienced when they participate in writing groups (Bruffee, 1993). Your peers can provide you with a unique source of feedback because they represent a live audience of readers who speak the same language as you do. Because writing is something we usually do alone and without any social support, we do not receive the immediate response or reaction to our words like we do when we're speaking to others. However, writing groups can provide this social support and interpersonal feedback, making the writing process more comfortable and more motivating for the writer by making it more similar to the speaking process (Elbow, 1973). In fact, research reveals that when individual students interact with their peers during the writing process, they tend to show higher levels of involvement and commitment to writing (Hillocks, 1986). Research also demonstrates that interaction with peers in writing groups improves the quality of student writing. For instance, in one semester-long study of 250 students' writing in 13 different classes, it was discovered that students who worked in writing groups made better revisions in their papers and demonstrated greater gains in essay-writing performance by the end of the term than did students who worked alone (Nystrand, 1986).

Furthermore, writing groups not only help the writer who receives feedback from other students, it also benefits students who read and provide the feedback because this helps them to read and edit their own writing more effectively (Gere, 1987). So, consider forming writing

STUDENT PERSPECTIVE

"There are countless ways in which an individual can avoid academic dishonesty. An excellent idea is going to a tutor or professor to have the paper read [before turning it in]."

—*First-year student reflection on a plagiarism violation*

STUDENT PERSPECTIVE

"Students can avoid plagiarism by getting help from someone who knows how to cite correctly. I know now that I have my citations double-checked."

—*First-year student reflection on a plagiarism violation*

groups, just as you would form study groups. Schedule regular meetings to help each other stay on schedule to meet writing deadlines. Even if you consider yourself to be a good writer, your writing can get even better if you seek and receive feedback from others before submitting your final product. Consider pairing up with a partner to exchange and assess each other's papers, using a checklist of criteria that your instructor will use to evaluate and grade your papers. Once you have checked each paper, assist each other in the revision process if they do not meet the standards of your instructor.

Lastly, keep in mind that in the real world of work, professionals regularly seek help from co-workers when they write reports, memos, and proposals. Even professional writers share their drafts with other writers to obtain feedback at different stages in the writing process (Leahy, 1990).

> **Remember:** You can form writing teams with peers at any stage in the writing process, whether it may be brainstorming possible ideas to include in your paper, reviewing your first draft, or proofreading your final draft.

Stage 8. Writing the Final Draft

The final draft of your paper is the version that includes all revisions you've made during your reading and editing stage, plus any feedback you may have received from other readers. Your final draft is only complete after you are satisfied with the quality of your paper's *content* (ideas), *structure* (organization), and *form* (writing style). Realistically, a high-quality final draft requires completion of at least two previous drafts. Writing multiple drafts of a paper does not mean that you are a slow or ineffective writer; to the contrary, it is a sign of a good writer whose final product has been carefully reviewed, revised, and improved.

·—· **CLASSIC QUOTE** ·—·

I'm not a writer; I'm a rewriter.

—James Thurber, award-winning American journalist and author

Pause for Reflection

Reflect back on your high school experience, and try to recall your writing assignments:

a. *What was the longest paper you wrote in high school?*

b. *What type of thinking were you usually asked to do on your writing assignments? (For example: Memorize? Summarize? Analyze? Criticize? Compare and contrast?)*

Stage 9. Proofread Your Paper Carefully for Any Mechanical Mistakes Before Officially Submitting It

Proofreading entails a microscopic form of editing in which you focus on detecting errors relating to such details as referencing, grammar, punctuation, and spelling. It represents an important final step in the editorial process because small, technical errors may be easily overlooked during earlier stages of the writing process when you were focusing on the content, form, and style of your paper. Proofreading focuses your attention on another key element of your paper: its mechanics.

Although it may be tempting to turn your paper in and get it out of your hair as soon as you finish the final draft, before you unload your paper, take time to re-load and re-read it one last time at a fine-grained level. Your instructors are unlikely to forgive many (or any) mechanical errors, particularly when word-processing programs make correction of them so much easier than in the not-so-good-old days of typewriters (when erasing words required the use of white-out, and when "cut and paste" literally meant cut with scissors and paste with glue)!

It is recommended that you proofread your paper after printing it out, rather than attempting to proofread it on screen. It has been our experience that writing errors are harder to detect on screen, perhaps because you're peering through an artificially narrow window. Also, remember that your computer's spell-check may not correct all misspelled words that appear on the screen. Your spell-checker checks spelling on a word-by-word basis, without considering whether the word's meaning is accurate in the context (sentence) that you're using it. For instance, our spell-checker did not correct the three "correctly" spelled words that are actually misspelled in the following sentence: "She <u>war</u> her high-<u>heal</u> sneakers to the <u>bawl</u>."

When you proofread your paper, we also recommend that you read it out loud because actually hearing the words you've written provides sensory input that can alert you to mechanical mistakes that may go unnoticed during silent reading. Also, just as in other stages of the writing process, it is a good idea to proofread your paper once, then put it aside, take your mind and eyes off it for a while, and come back to proofread it one last time before letting it go.

Remember: Careful proofreading represents the key, final step in the process of writing a high-quality paper. Earlier stages of the writing process are more mentally demanding and time-consuming than proofreading, so it would be a shame to overlook this simple last step and lose points for mistakes that can be easily detected and corrected.

Stage 10. Carefully Review Your Paper after It's Returned to You

When you receive your paper back after it's been graded, try not to get emotional or react defensively if the grade you receive is lower than you expected. Sometimes, no matter how hard you try to anticipate and demonstrate everything your instructor expects from you on the first major assignment, there are just some things that can only be learned and corrected after you've received feedback from your instructor on your first performance.

So, review your paper closely when you get it back and pay special attention to any written comments provided by your instructor. View these comments as constructive feedback that can improve your performance on future assignments. Also, make special note of your most common and costly mistakes that resulted in the largest loss of points. If you are unclear about what went wrong or what needs correction or improvement, make an appointment to see your instructor. If your instructor is willing to meet with you during office hours and review your paper with you, take full advantage of this opportunity. Receiving personalized feedback from the very person who has evaluated your work, and who will be evaluating your future work, may be the most powerful way to improve your future performance and final grade. In addition to obtaining this powerful form of feedback, there is another advantage of making an appointment with your instructor to review your performance: It sends a clear message to the instructor that you are a serious student who wants to learn from mistakes and achieve excellence.

••• Speaking

In addition to writing, the second major channel you will use to convey and demonstrate your knowledge and higher-level thinking is *oral communication*. In addition to elevating your academic performance, developing your speaking skills can also strengthen your interpersonal skills and improve the quality of your relationships by boosting your social self-confidence, helping you overcome shyness, and enabling you to converse more effectively with others in one-to-one, small-group, and large-group situations. This improved social self-confidence should, in turn, contribute to the development of your leadership skills by enabling you to work more productively in teams, communicate more effectively with people of different cultural backgrounds, and provide better advice or feedback to others.

Furthermore, developing your ability to speak in a clear, concise, and confident manner will also contribute to your career development. The oral communication skills you demonstrate during your job interviews may play a major role in determining whether you are initially hired, and your ability to speak effectively during meetings and professional presentations may contribute significantly to your prospects for promotion. National surveys and interviews with employers reveal that oral communication skills are one of the top-ranking characteristics they seek in prospective employees (AC Neilsen Research Services, 2000; National Association of Colleges & Employees, 2003; The Conference Board of Canada, 2000).

Speaking is more than just a communication skill; just as writing can be used as a tool to improve learning and thinking, so too can speaking. Speaking helps to keep you actively involved in the learning and thinking process because it requires physical action (moving your tongue and lips). It also enables you to "hear" your thoughts, which puts you in a better position to evaluate whether or not they make sense. The former director of Harvard University's Center for Teaching and Learning explains the relationship between speaking and thinking in the following fashion: "Until a student hears herself expounding [explaining] or questioning, she may not know what she thinks, which is why speaking empowers future thinking and speaking. As soon as she hears that she has asserted [stated] something, even in the form of a question, she puts herself in the position of being able to criticize her own thought" (Gullette, 1989, p. 34). So, just as writing provides you with a visual product that can be seen and used as feedback to improve the quality of your thoughts, speaking provides an *audible* product that can be heard and used as feedback to improve the quality of your thinking.

Speaking Strategies to Promote Higher-Level Thinking Skills

Think aloud while you attempt to solve problems. When you're solving problems in math or science, think about the mental steps you're taking and state them aloud. This will enable you to become more aware of the process of thinking you're using to solve the problem. Research indicates that the quality of students' higher-level thinking is enhanced when they are asked to think out loud while they solve problems (Ahlum-Heather & DiVesta, 1986). This is probably due to the fact that thinking aloud causes you to:

◆ consciously attend to your thought process, and

◆ convert your silent (internal) thoughts into audible (external) sounds that you can hear, respond to, and use as feedback to improve your thinking (Resnick, 1986).

Pair up with another student. Pose higher-level thinking questions to each other, such as the ones listed in Chapter 6 (pp. 201–202). One member's role is to pose the question; the other uses higher-level thinking to answer it. Periodically switch roles, so both of you take turns playing the role of questioner and respondent.

Research indicates that students who work in pairs and use this type of question-and-answer interchange are more likely to display higher levels of thinking on course examinations (King, 1995).

Form discussion groups or learning teams of three or more students to create opportunities for yourself to practice higher-level thinking skills by speaking in small groups about course material.

Research consistently shows that when college students engage in group discussions about class material with their peers they are more likely to develop critical thinking skills than by just listening to lectures and recording notes (Kulik & Kulik, 1979).

Enroll in small seminar classes where you are less anonymous. These classes provide you with opportunities to become actively involved by expressing your thoughts orally and receiving feedback on the quality of your thinking.

Sit in the front of class. You may feel more comfortable responding to your instructor's thought-provoking questions and asking questions of your instructor if you're not sitting behind a large number of classmates who turn around to look at you every time you speak.

Public Speaking: Oral Presentations and Speeches

National surveys indicate that beginning college students rate their public speaking skills lower than virtually all other academic abilities, including their writing skills, mathematical ability, computer skills, creativity, and leadership ability (Sax et al., 2004). Studies also show that many college students experience "communication apprehension" in the classroom—that is, they are fearful about speaking in class (Richmond & McCloskey, 1997). Other national surveys show that fear of public speaking is extremely common among people of all ages, including adolescents and adults (Motley, 1997). So, if you are at least somewhat nervous about public speaking, that's not unusual or "abnormal"; in fact, you should feel like you're a member of a worldwide club that includes lots of other "normal" people just like you.

In this section, we provide strategies that you could use immediately to improve your ability to express your thoughts in oral presentations and speeches. Since speaking and writing both involve communicating thoughts in the form of words, you will find that many of the strategies suggested here for improving oral reports overlap with those suggested for improving written reports. To avoid repetition, we will not describe these overlapping strategies in great detail; instead, we refer you to the pages in the writing section where they are discussed more thoroughly. The good news about this overlap is that you should be able to "double dip" and transfer the effective strategies you've learned for writing papers to improve your oral presentations, and vice versa.

STUDENT PERSPECTIVE

"I was really nervous during the entire thing, but I felt so relieved and proud afterwards."

—*First-year student commenting on her first public speech.*

Francie reprinted by permission of Sherrie Shepherd.

Surveys reveal that fear of public speaking is very common and ranks high on the list of most intense human fears.

Identifying Your Purpose

Be sure you know the purpose or objective of your oral presentation. Knowing what your presentation is supposed to accomplish represents the key first step toward making an effective presentation. You cannot begin to plan what you're going to do until you know why you're doing it. If you have any doubt, seek clarification from your instructor before proceeding.

Oral presentations usually fall into one of the following two categories, depending on their purpose or objective:

1. *Informative (expository)* presentations that are intended to inform the audience by providing accurate information or explanation, and

2. *Persuasive* presentations that are intended to persuade the audience to agree with a certain conclusion or position by providing supporting evidence.

In college, most of your oral presentations will likely be the persuasive type, which means that you will search for information, draw conclusions about your research, and document your conclusions with evidence. Similar to writing research papers, oral presentations will usually require that you think at a higher level, cite sources, and demonstrate academic integrity.

Identifying Your Topic

If you are given a choice about what topic to speak about, seize this opportunity to pursue a subject that captures your interest and enthusiasm. If you do, your interest and enthusiasm is likely to show through in your delivery, which should increase your self-confidence, your audience's attention, and your overall grade for the presentation.

◆ Use brainstorming to generate ideas about your topic.
(See p. 198 for the key steps involved in brainstorming.)

◆ Organize your major ideas categorically and sequentially.
(For more information, see stage three of the writing process, pp. 230–232.)

◆ Develop an introduction to your presentation that provides an overview or preview of what will follow.
Like a written report, your introduction should include a thesis statement in which you state (orally) what you propose to accomplish in your presentation.

◆ Develop a conclusion that includes a statement which drives home your presentation's most important point or most memorable idea.
Your conclusion should tie everything together and include a statement that refers back to, and reinforces your original thesis statement, thereby connecting your ending with your beginning.

· — · CLASSIC QUOTE · — ·

Enthusiasm is everything.

—Pelé, Brazilian soccer player; arguably the most famous player in the sport's history

STUDENT PERSPECTIVE

"I think that better organization and an increased sense of formality would have improved the quality of my work."

—*First-year student commenting on her first speech*

"If somebody asked me what my like favorite class is,
you know, I'd hafta go, 'Speech'."

Rehearsing what you plan to say, before you say it, can increase the clarity
of your oral presentations by decreasing your use of unnecessary fillers
("like," "you know," "I'm all," etc.)

Delivering Your Presentation

Rehearse and Revise

Just as you would write several drafts of a paper before turning it in, rehearse and revise your oral presentation several times before delivering it. Rehearsal will improve your memory and increase the clarity of your presentation by reducing long pauses, the need to stop and re-start, and your use of distracting "fillers" (e.g., "uh," "umm," "like," "you know").

Rehearsal also helps reduce speech anxiety. Studies show that fear of public speaking is often really a fear of failure—fear of being negatively evaluated by the audience. So, if your oral presentation is well prepared and well rehearsed, your fear of receiving a negative evaluation should decrease, which, in turn, should decrease your level of speech anxiety.

Listed below are some speech-rehearsal strategies that you may use to improve your preparation and delivery of oral presentations.

 STUDENT PERSPECTIVE

"The only time I get nervous is when I am not very familiar with my topic or if I'm winging my assignment and I'm not prepared."

—First-year student commenting on her previous oral presentations

◆ During rehearsal, use index cards to trigger your memory of your major points and arrange the order of the cards in a sequence that will keep your presentation on track from start to finish. If you write your major points on separate index cards, they can serve as memory cues to trigger your recall of specific details that are hard to remember without a cue or clue. Index cards are also compact and easy to handle, so you can bring them with you and use them during your presentation.

◆ If possible, rehearse your speech in the same place where you will be delivering it (e.g., in the same classroom or a similar classroom). When you rehearse and deliver your presentation in the same place, seeing the same visual features of the room may serve as memory cues that help trigger your memory of information that you rehearsed in the very same place. Furthermore, the room's familiarity should make you feel less anxious during the actual delivery of your presentation.

During rehearsal, pay special attention to the following parts of your presentation:

◇ Your introduction should be rehearsed carefully because it sets the stage and creates a powerful first impression.

◇ Statements that signal your transition from one major category of ideas to another (e.g., statements that move you from one index card to another) because they serve to highlight your presentation's organization, showing how its separate parts are connected.

◇ Your conclusion should be carefully rehearsed because this is your chance to finish strong and create a powerful last impression.

◆ Rehearse the total time it takes to complete your presentation to see if it falls within the time range set by your instructor, making sure that it's neither too short nor too long.

◆ Practice making periodic eye contact with an imaginary audience by periodically lifting your head from your notes or index cards to look at different chairs in the room. During your presentation, you can occasionally look at your notes or index cards and use them as cues to help you recall the key points you intend to make, but they should not be used as a script that's read verbatim (word for word). An oral presentation is a form of public *speaking*, not a public *reading* of a paper that has been written out entirely in advance. On the other hand, an oral presentation is not an impromptu speech that's given off the top of your head without prior preparation. Instead, your oral presentation should be *extemporaneous*—something in-between a formal reading and an impromptu speech, which involves advanced preparation and use of some notes but is not something written out entirely in advance and read (or memorized) word for word (Luotto, et al., 2001). Extemporaneous speaking also allows the opportunity to ad lib, which can be useful when you stumble while speaking or forget a main part of the speech. It can help keep you from getting flustered, and even prevent the audience from noticing that any mistake was made.

Incorporate some creativity into the delivery of your presentation.

For example, develop some original visual aids to illustrate or reinforce your points, or include some higher-level thinking questions to stimulate your audience's attention and involvement.

Get feedback on your presentation before officially delivering it.

Ask a friend or group of friends to listen to your presentation and ask for their input. Not only can peers give you valuable feedback, they can also provide a "live audience" that makes your rehearsal more realistic by making it more closely match your actual performance. The closer the match between your practice and performance situations, the more comfortable you should feel during the actual delivery of your presentation. In fact, research indicates that fear of speaking in front of a class is reduced if students first have the opportunity to share their ideas with a small group of peers (Neer, 1987).

Another way to obtain feedback prior to your actual presentation is to have a friend videotape your delivery of it. This allows you to view your presentation as if you were a member of the audience. Viewing yourself on tape is almost like having an "out-of-body experience" because it enables you to step outside of your body and view yourself as others view you. This can provide you with a unique form of feedback that can dramatically increase awareness of your own behavior while you are communicating, particularly your nonverbal communication (body language).

Earlier in the chapter, we noted that one of the key advantages of writing is that it provides you with a visible product of your own thoughts that can be reviewed and used to improve the quality of your thinking. Similarly, videotapes provide a visible product of your spoken thoughts, which can be reviewed and used as feedback to improve the quality of your thinking as well as the quality of your public speaking.

One final warning about being videotaped: Don't freak out when you first see yourself on tape. It's a normal reaction for people to be a bit shocked when they first see and hear themselves on tape. However, this initial shock will soon wear off and then you will feel more comfortable viewing yourself and reviewing your performance.

◆ Pause for Reflection

Have you ever received feedback on the quality of your speaking skills from a teacher, a peer, or by observing yourself on videotape?

If you have, what did you learn from this feedback?

If you haven't, would you be willing to seek out feedback on your speaking skills?

To reduce your level of speech anxiety or fear of public speaking, consider implementing the following strategies:

Before delivering your speech:

◆ When practicing your speech, try to match your practice situation to the actual performance situation. For instance, speak out loud at the same volume that you'll use when you actually deliver your speech. Also, if possible, try to practice your speech at least once in the classroom where you will be delivering it.

◆ Carefully observe presentations made by other students and note the things that relaxed, effective speakers do during their speeches for hints about what you could do to be equally relaxed and successful when you deliver your speech.

◆ Practice and learn your introduction especially well. This will enable you to get off to a smooth start and give you an early sense of confidence, which should reduce your anxiety for the remainder of your presentation.

◆ Prepare your body and brain for the speech by getting adequate sleep the night before your presentation and eating well on the day of the presentation. Also, avoid consuming caffeine or any other stimulating substance prior to speaking because this may serve to elevate your level of tension during your speech.

◆ Come prepared with all the equipment you can use to support your presentation (e.g., notes, index cards to jog your memory, and visual aids to illustrate your points). Also, come with backup equipment in case you encounter any unexpected technological problems (e.g., bring overhead transparencies in case you experience technical problems with PowerPoint). Knowing that you're fully equipped should reduce your worries about something going wrong, and if something does go wrong, you'll have a plan to deal with it immediately and you'll avoid the anxiety-producing hassle of trying to figure out what to do at the spur of the moment.

◆ Try to get to the site of your speech early, so you have time to settle in and settle down before delivering your presentation. In the minutes just prior to delivering your speech, relax yourself by taking deep breaths and visualizing a successful performance.

BLOOM COUNTY   by Berke Breathed

© 1980. Berkeley Breathed. Distributed by *The Washington Post*. Reprinted with permission.

Stress-management techniques—such as deep breathing—
are often effective strategies for reducing speech anxiety.

◆ Since thoughts can influence our emotions and positive thoughts trigger positive emotions (Ellis, 2000), come to your speech with a positive mindset. For example:

1. Keep in mind that it's natural to experience at least some anxiety in any performance situation, especially in a public speaking situation. This is not necessarily a bad thing, because if your anxiety is kept at a moderate level, it will actually increase your enthusiasm, energy, concentration, and memory (Rosenfield, 1988; Sapolsky, 2004).

2. Don't expect to deliver "the perfect speech" like a TV reporter who is delivering (actually reading) the nightly news. A few verbal mistakes or lapses of memory are common during speeches, just as they are during normal conversations. You can still receive an excellent grade on an oral presentation without delivering a flawless speech.

3. Remember that if you happen to forget a point or two, the audience will not know that you forgot those points, only you will. Similarly, most of the anxiety you may feel internally during your speech will not be externally visible or noticeable to your audience.

4. Think of your speech as something similar to a normal conversation; the only difference is that you're speaking to more than one person and that it's a conversation you've had the opportunity to prepare in advance. Since you've been speaking every day since you were a toddler, speaking to more than one person is just a slight extension of what you've done your entire life. To help get into this mindset, look at one person at a time while you're delivering different parts of your speech. (However, periodically change your focus to a person in different sections of the room to ensure that you're making eye contact with different members of the audience.)

5. Keep in mind that the audience to whom you are speaking is not made up of expert speakers. Most of them do not have any more public speaking experience than you do, nor are they experienced critics. These are your peers who are fully aware that getting up in front of a class is a stressful thing to do for most students; thus, they are likely to be very accepting of any mistakes you happen to make.

During delivery of your speech:

◆ Feel free to move around, rather than standing still or remaining motionless. When you're experiencing even moderate stress, your body releases more adrenaline—an energy-generating hormone. So it may be natural for your body to want to move during your speech in order to expend this extra energy. Physical movement during your speech will help you burn up that extra energy and burn off any extra anxiety that you may be experiencing. Furthermore, research shows that some movement and gesticulation by the speaker helps hold the attention of the audience more effectively than standing rigidly in one place (Andersen, 1985). (You can even move in a way that reinforces your transition from one key point to another during your speech by moving to a different position or place in the front of the room as you move conceptually from one point to the next). Although some movement during a speech is good, fidgeting is not (e.g., playing with things in your pockets or clicking your pen). Such nervous fidgeting can distract the audience from your spoken message and detract from the quality of your speech.

◆ Focus your attention on the *message* you're delivering (the content of your speech), *not the messenger* (yourself as a speaker). By remaining conscious of the ideas you're communicating to your listeners, you'll become less self-conscious about the impression you're making on them and their evaluation of you.

◆ Final Note: If you continue to experience high levels of speech anxiety after implementing the strategies we've suggested, seek the advice and help from a professional in your Learning Center or Academic Support Center.

Pause for Reflection

Rate your level of speech anxiety in the following situations.

1. *Large Groups (e.g., asking a question in a class of 30 or more students):*

   highly anxious   somewhat nervous   fairly relaxed   very relaxed

2. *Small Groups (e.g., speaking in a discussion group of 3–5 students):*

   highly anxious   somewhat nervous   fairly relaxed   very relaxed

3. *Pairs (e.g., talking over an assignment with a classmate):*

   highly anxious   somewhat nervous   fairly relaxed   very relaxed

---

••• Summary and Conclusion

We began this chapter by asking you what the difference was between learning factual knowledge and learning a transferable skill. As you may have known before beginning this chapter, or discovered while reading it, a transferable skill has more flexibility than factual knowledge because it can be applied or transferred to different situations or contexts. The three key skills discussed in this chapter—research, writing, and speaking—are all powerful, transferable skills that can be applied across different academic subjects that you encounter in college and across different careers you may encounter after college.

Research, writing, and speaking may be viewed as interrelated and complementary success tools. Research tools are needed to acquire high-quality ideas from others, and writing and speaking tools are needed to actively stimulate your own thinking about the ideas you acquire and as vehicles for communicating your ideas to others. Said in another way, *research* skills enable you to locate, evaluate, and integrate information, while *writing* and *speaking* skills enable you to comprehend, communicate, and demonstrate your mastery of that information to others.

These three key skills have always been relevant to the educational and professional success of college students and college alumni, but they are even more critical to the success of students and alumni in today's information and communication age.

We strongly encourage you to work hard at developing the transferable skills that were discussed in this chapter and take full advantage of the campus resources that have been intentionally designed to help you develop them, such as your College Library and Academic Support Center. The time and energy you invest in developing your research, writing, and speaking skills will pay huge dividends toward your success in college and beyond.

••• Learning More through Independent Research

Web-Based Resources for Further Information on Research, Writing, and Speaking

For additional information relating to ideas discussed in this chapter, we recommend the following Web sites:

Research Skills: http://www.bedfordstmartins.com/researchroom

Writing Skills: www.quintcareers.com

Speaking Skills: www.public-speaking.org

Exercise 1. Internet Research

Go to **www.itools.com/search**. This Web site allows you to conveniently access multiple search engines, Web directories, and newsgroups. Type in the name of a subject or topic you'd like to research in each of the following "search for" windows provided at this site: (a) Search Engines, (b) Web Directories, and (c) Newsgroup Search. (Be sure to type the same subject or topic in each of these three "search for" windows.)

1.   What were the major differences in the type of information that was generated by these three searches?

2.   Was the information provided by any one of these searches more useful than the others?

3.   Would you return to this Web site again to conduct future research?

Exercise 2. Chapter Synthesis

Suppose you were given a class assignment to deliver an oral presentation or construct a written report that synthesizes or summarizes the key concepts presented in this chapter. Construct an outline or concept map that you could use to organize your ideas for this assignment (see p. 233 for an example).

Crime and Punishment: Plagiarism and Its Consequences

In an article that appeared in an Ohio newspaper, titled "Plagiarism persists in classrooms," an English professor was quoted as saying: "Technology has made it easier to plagiarize because students can download papers and exchange information and papers through their computers. But technology has also made it easier to catch students who plagiarize." This professor's college now subscribes to a Web site that matches the content of students' papers with content from books and online sources. Many professors now require students to submit their papers through this Web site. If students are caught plagiarizing, for a first offense, they typically receive an "F" for the assignment or the course. A second offense can result in dismissal or expulsion from college, which has already happened to a few students (Source: Mariettatimes.com, March 22, 2006).

Reflection and Discussion Questions

1. Why do you think students plagiarize? What do you suspect are its primary motives, reasons, or causes?

2. What do you think is a fair or just penalty for those found guilty of plagiarism? For a first violation? A second violation?

3. How do you think plagiarism could be most effectively reduced or prevented from happening in the first place?

4. What could students do to minimize or eliminate plagiarism?

5. What could professors do to minimize or eliminate plagiarism?

Diversity

Appreciating the Value of Human Differences for Enhancing Learning and Personal Development

Learning Goals

The primary goal of this chapter is to show how experiencing diversity in college can promote your learning, personal development, and career success.

Outline

Activate Your Thinking

Complete the following "sentence starter":

When I hear the word "diversity," the first thoughts that come to my mind are . . .

••• The Spectrum of Diversity

As you may have already detected by the title of this chapter, diversity simply means "variety" or "difference." Thus, human diversity refers to the variety or differences that exist among people that comprise humanity (the human species). When we use the word "diversity" in this chapter, we will be referring primarily to *different groups* of humans. The relationship between humanity and diversity is represented visually in Figure 8.1.

**Figure ** Humanity and Diversity*

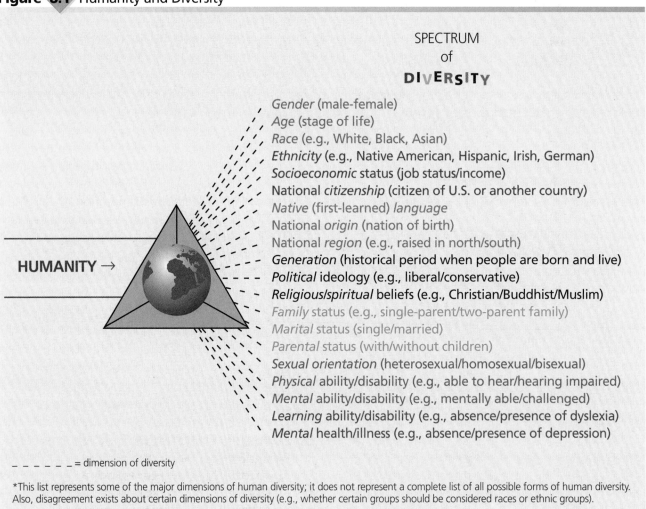

SPECTRUM
of
DIVERSITY

HUMANITY →

Gender (male-female)
Age (stage of life)
Race (e.g., White, Black, Asian)
Ethnicity (e.g., Native American, Hispanic, Irish, German)
Socioeconomic status (job status/income)
National *citizenship* (citizen of U.S. or another country)
Native (first-learned) *language*
National *origin* (nation of birth)
National *region* (e.g., raised in north/south)
Generation (historical period when people are born and live)
Political ideology (e.g., liberal/conservative)
Religious/spiritual beliefs (e.g., Christian/Buddhist/Muslim)
Family status (e.g., single-parent/two-parent family)
Marital status (single/married)
Parental status (with/without children)
Sexual orientation (heterosexual/homosexual/bisexual)
Physical ability/disability (e.g., able to hear/hearing impaired)
Mental ability/disability (e.g., mentally able/challenged)
Learning ability/disability (e.g., absence/presence of dyslexia)
Mental health/illness (e.g., absence/presence of depression)

_ _ _ _ _ _ _ = dimension of diversity

*This list represents some of the major dimensions of human diversity; it does not represent a complete list of all possible forms of human diversity. Also, disagreement exists about certain dimensions of diversity (e.g., whether certain groups should be considered races or ethnic groups).

The relationship between humanity and human diversity is similar to the relationship between sunlight and the spectrum colors. Just as sunlight passing through a prism reflects all the different groups of colors that make up the visual spectrum, humanity occupying planet earth reflects all the different groups of people that make up the spectrum of human diversity. As you can see in Figure 8.1, groups of people can differ from one another in a wide variety of ways, including their physical features, values, beliefs, abilities, geographical locations, social backgrounds, and other personal dimensions.

Diversity has been viewed by some people to be a "political" issue. However, we view diversity as an *educational* issue—a learning experience that can have a powerful impact on an individual's college and career success. Since there have been different interpretations (and misinterpretations) about what diversity actually is, we would like to begin by clarifying some key terms that are essential to an accurate understanding of the meaning and value of diversity.

What Is Culture?

"Culture" can be broadly defined as a distinctive pattern of beliefs and values that develop among a group of people who share the same social heritage and traditions. Culture is the whole way in which a group of people has learned to live (Peoples & Bailey, 1998), which includes style of speaking (language), fashion, food, art, and music, as well as values and beliefs. Different cultures exist across different nations—often referred to as *cross-cultural* differences; and different cultures can exist within the same nation—commonly called *multicultural* differences. Thus, cultural diversity may take the forms of *international* diversity and *national* (*domestic*) diversity. Although the terms "culture" and "society" are used as if they have the same meaning, they refer to different things. *Society* refers to a group of people who are organized under the same social system. For example, all members of American society are organized under the same system of government, justice, and education. On the other hand, culture is what members of certain groups of people in a society actually share with each other in terms of traditions and lifestyle (Nicholas, 1991). So, within the same society, multiple cultures can exist; hence, we use the term "multicultural society."

Culture is a distinctive pattern of beliefs and values that develop among a group of people who share the same social heritage and traditions.

What Is an Ethnic Group?

An *ethnic group* (or *ethnicity*) refers to a group of people who share the same culture. Thus, culture refers to *what* an ethnic group shares in common, and ethnic group refers to the particular group of people *who* share a common culture. Major ethnic groups in the United States include Native Americans (American Indians), African Americans, Hispanic Americans (Latinos), Asian Americans, and European Americans. Ethnic subgroups also exist within each of these major ethnic groups. For example, Hispanic Americans include people who have cultural roots in Mexico, Puerto Rico, Central America, South America, etc.; Asian Americans include cultural descendents from Japan, China, Korea, Vietnam, etc.; and European Americans include descendents from Scandinavia, England, Ireland, Germany, Italy, etc. In the United States, European Americans are the *majority* ethnic group, meaning that the majority of the American population belongs to this ethnic group. Native Americans, African Americans, Hispanic Americans, and Asian Americans are considered to be ethnic *minority* groups.

Pause for Reflection

What ethnic group(s) do you belong to, or identify with? What common cultural values do you think are shared by your ethnic group(s)?

The different cultures associated with different ethnic groups may be viewed simply as variations in the way groups of people express the same theme: being human. You may have heard the question: "We're all human, aren't we?" The answer to this important question is, "yes and no." Yes, we are all the same, but not in the same way.

One way to understand this apparent paradox is to visualize humanity as a quilt in which all humans are joined together by the common thread of humanity—we are all human beings; yet, the different patches that makes up the quilt represent diversity—the distinctive or unique cultures that comprise our common humanity. This quilt metaphor acknowledges the identity and beauty of all cultures. It differs from the old American "melting pot" metaphor—which viewed differences as something that should be melted down or eliminated, and the "salad bowl" metaphor—which suggests that America is a hodgepodge or mishmash of different cultures thrown together without any common connection. In contrast, the quilt metaphor suggests that the cultures of different ethnic groups can and should be recognized. Yet these differences may be woven together to create a unified whole—as in the Latin expression: "E pluribus Unum" ("Out of many, one"). This expression has become a motto of the United States, and you will find it printed on all its coins.

 Personal Story When I was 12 years old and living in New York, I returned from school one Friday afternoon, and my mother asked me if anything interesting happened at school that day. I mentioned to her that the teacher went around the room, asking students what we had for dinner the night before. At that moment, my mother began to become a bit agitated and nervously asked me: "What did you tell the teacher?" I said: "I told her and the rest of the class that I had pasta last night because my family has a tradition of eating pasta on Thursdays and Sundays." My mother then exploded and yelled back at me: "Why couldn't you tell her that we had steak or roast beef!" For a moment, I was stunned and couldn't figure out what I had done wrong or why I should have lied about eating pasta. Then it suddenly dawned on me: My mother was extremely embarrassed about being an Italian American. She wanted me to hide our family's ethnic background and make it sound like we were very "American." After this became clear to me, a few moments later, it also became clear to me why her maiden name was changed from the very Italian-sounding "DeVigilio" to the more American-sounding "Vigilis."

I never forgot this incident because it was such an emotionally intense experience. For the first time in my life, I became aware that my mother was ashamed of being a member of the same group to which every other member of my family belonged, including me. After her outburst, I felt a combined rush of astonishment and embarrassment. However, these feelings didn't last long because, in the long run, my mother's reaction actually had the opposite effect on me. Instead of making me feel inferior or ashamed about being Italian-American, my mother's reaction that day caused me to become more aware of, and take more pride in, my Italian heritage.

I later learned why my mother felt the way she did. She grew up in America's "melting pot" generation—a time when different American ethnic groups were expected to melt down and melt away their ethnicity. They were not to celebrate diversity; they were to eliminate it.

—*Joe Cuseo*

·—· **CLASSIC QUOTE** ·—·

We have become not a melting pot but a beautiful mosaic.

—Jimmy Carter, thirty-ninth president of the United States and winner of the Nobel Peace Prize

What Is a Racial Group?

A *racial group (race)* refers to an ethnic group that also shares some distinctive physical traits, such as skin color or facial characteristics; however, there continues to be disagreement among scholars about what groups of people actually constitute a human "race," or whether totally distinctive races truly exist (Wheelright, 2005). Unlike an ethnic group, whose shared culture has been passed on through social experiences, a racial group's shared physical characteristics are those that they are born with and which have been passed on genetically. The United States Census Bureau (2000) identifies three races: White, Black, and Asian. Nevertheless, Anderson & Fienberg (2000) caution that racial categories are social-political constructs (concepts) and are not scientifically based.

Remember: There are no specific genes that differentiate one race from another. In other words, there is no way you could do a blood test or any type of "internal" genetic test to determine a person's race. Humans have simply decided to categorize people into "races" on the basis of certain external differences in physical appearance, particularly the color of their outer layer of skin.

The differences in skin color that exist among humans is likely due to biological adaptations that evolved among groups of humans. These differences helped them survive in different environmental regions where they were living and breeding. For instance, darker skin tones were more likely to develop among humans who inhabited and reproduced in hotter regions nearer the equator (e.g., Africans), where darker skin may have enabled them to adapt and survive in that environment. Their darker skin provided their bodies with better protection from the potentially damaging effects of the sun (Bridgeman, 2003) and better ability to use the sun's source of vitamin D (Jablonski & Chaplin, 2002). In contrast, lighter skin tones were more likely to develop among humans inhabiting colder climates more distant from the equator (e.g., Scandinavians) to allow their bodies to absorb greater amounts of sunlight because it was less plentiful and direct.

While humans may display racial diversity, the biological reality is that all members of the human species are remarkably similar. There is much less genetic variability among us than members of other animal species; in fact, approximately 98 percent of our genes are exactly the same (Bridgeman, 2003; Molnar, 1991). This accounts for all the similarities that exist among humans, regardless of what differences in color appear at the surface of our skin. For example, all humans have similar external features that give us a "human" appearance and clearly distinguish us from other animal species; we have internal organs that are similar in structure and function; and we have similar facial expressions for expressing our emotions (Figure 8.2).

Other human characteristics that anthropologists have found to be shared across all groups of people in every corner of the world include storytelling, poetry, adornment of the body, dance, music, decoration of artifacts, families, socialization of children by elders, a sense of right and wrong, supernatural beliefs, explanations of diseases and death, and mourning of the dead (Pinker, 1994).

It is important to realize that human *variety* and human *similarity* exist side-by-side. For instance, humans all over the world communicate verbally via language; in fact, newborn babies in all cultures babble by using the same wide range of sounds. However, these babies will eventually speak only in the sounds of the language(s) they are exposed to in their particular culture and other sounds they used while babbling will eventually drop out (Oller, 1981). Thus, language is a characteristic that all humans share as part of their common humanity, but the variety of languages spoken by people around the world is a reflection and expression of their diverse cultural experiences.

It is also important to keep in mind that *individual* differences *within* the same group of people are *greater* than the average differences between different groups of people. For example, although we live in a world that is very conscious of differences between races, the fact is that physical differences (e.g., height and weight) and behavioral differences (e.g., personality char-

Figure 8.2

Humans all over the world display the same facial expressions when experiencing certain emotions.
See if you can detect the emotions being expressed in the following faces.
(To find the answers, turn your book upside down.)

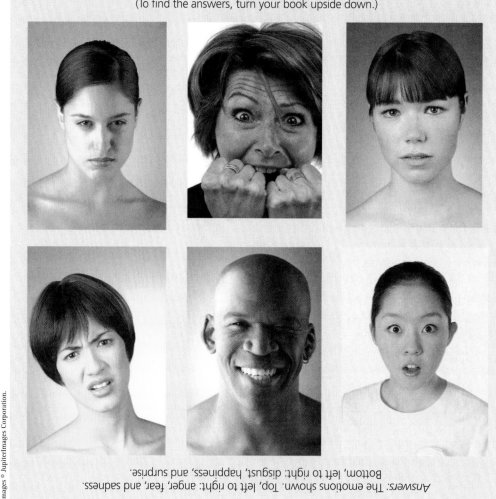

Bottom, left to right: disgust, happiness, and surprise.
Answers: The emotions shown. Top, left to right: anger, fear, and sadness.

All images © JupiterImages Corporation.

acteristics) among individuals within the same racial group are actually greater than the average differences between different racial groups (Caplan & Caplan, 1994).

As you proceed through this chapter, keep in mind the following distinctions among humanity, diversity, and individuality:

◆ Humanity—we are all members of the *same group* (the human species).
◆ Diversity—we are all members of *different groups* (e.g., our gender and ethnic groups).
◆ Individuality—each of us is a *unique person* who is different from any person in any group to which we may belong.

••• Diversity and the College Experience

The ethnic and racial diversity of students is increasing in American colleges and universities. In 1960, Whites comprised almost 95 percent of the total college population; in 2005, the percentage decreased to 69 percent. At the same time, the percentage of Asian, Hispanic, Black, and Native American students attending college increased (Chronicle of Higher Education, 2003). Approximately 35 percent of today's 18- to 24-year-olds are non-white, making it the most diverse generation in American history (The Echo Boomers, 2004).

American colleges are also becoming more diverse in terms of gender and age. In 2000, the percentage of females enrolled in college was almost 66 percent, compared to 25 percent in 1955 (Postsecondary Education Opportunity, 2001). The percentage of students enrolled in college today that are 24 years of age or older has grown to 44 percent (Chronicle of Higher Education, 2003).

You are also likely to find students on your campus from different nations. From 1990 to 2000, the number of international students attending American colleges and universities increased by over 140,000 (Institute of International Education, 2001).

© Stockbyte.

The ethnic and racial diversity of students in American colleges is increasing.

Colleges and universities often intentionally recruit students with different cultural experiences and geographical backgrounds in order to create a campus environment that enriches the variety and quality of your learning experience. Thus, your campus may be the ideal environment for experiencing diversity. The college experience can provide you with the time, the place, the variety of people, and the quality of educational resources (courses, programs) needed to learn the most about and from diversity.

As a first-year student, this may be the first time in your life that you are a member of a community that includes so many people from such a variety of backgrounds. In fact, students report more experience with diversity during their first year of college than at any other time in the college experience (Kuh, 2002). So, this year may be the prime time for you to capitalize on the diversity around you and take full advantage of its many educational and personal benefits.

Pause for Reflection

1. What diverse groups do you see represented on your campus?

2. Are there groups on your campus that you did not expect to see, or to see in such large numbers?

3. Are there groups on your campus that you expected to see, but do not see, or see in smaller numbers than you expected?

••• Advantages of Experiencing Diversity

Diversity Increases the Power of a Liberal Arts Education

As we discussed in Chapter 2, an effective liberal arts education should liberate or free you from the "tunnel vision" of an egocentric (self-centered) viewpoint and enable you to move outside yourself and see yourself in relation to the world around you. There is simply no way you can gain this global perspective without understanding human diversity. If we could reduce the world's population to a village of precisely 100 people, with all existing human ratios remaining the same, the demographics would look something like this:

> The village would have 60 Asians, 14 Africans, 12 Europeans, 8 Latin Americans, 5 from the United States and Canada, and 1 from the South Pacific.
>
> 51 would be male, 49 would be female
>
> 82 would be non-white; 18 white
>
> 67 would be non-Christian; 33 would be Christian
>
> 80 would live in substandard housing
>
> 67 would be unable to read
>
> 50 would be malnourished and 1 dying of starvation
>
> 33 would be without access to a safe water supply
>
> 39 would lack access to improved sanitation
>
> 24 would not have any electricity (and of the 76 that do have electricity, most would only use it for light at night)
>
> 7 would have access to the Internet
>
> 1 would have a college education
>
> 1 would have HIV
>
> 2 would be near birth; 1 near death
>
> 5 would control 32 percent of the entire world's wealth; all 5 would be citizens of the United States
>
> 33 would be receiving—and attempting to live on—only 3 percent of the income of "the village"

(Source: *State of the Village Report* by Donella H. Meadows, originally published in 1990 as "Who lives in the Global Village?" and updated in Family Care Foundation, 2005.)

Another perspective that should be developed as part of your liberal arts education is a *national* perspective, which involves understanding and appreciating your own nation. To appreciate the United States as a nation is to appreciate human diversity. Today, the United States is more ethnically and racially diverse than at any other time in its national history, and it will continue to grow more diverse throughout the twenty-first century (Torres, 2003). In 1995, about 75 percent of America's population was White; by 2050, it will shrink to about 50 percent (U.S. Census Bureau, 2004).

Because of this increasing diversity, "multicultural competence"—the ability to understand cultural differences and to interact effectively with people from different cultural backgrounds—has become an important liberal arts skill that is essential for success in today's world (Pope et al., 2005).

Just as the different subjects you take in the liberal arts curriculum opens your mind to multiple perspectives, so does experience with people from different backgrounds. Exposure to the different perspectives of people with different cultural experiences serves to expand your consciousness; it stretches your perspective and liberates you from viewing the world through the narrow perspective of a single culture—your own.

One cultural viewpoint cannot provide a complete understanding of any issue because it represents a one-sided viewpoint that is likely to be partial to its particular vantage point (Elder & Paul, 2002). Obtaining a wide range of cultural perspectives allows you to detect the partiality and weaknesses of partial viewpoints, but also allows you to combine their particular strengths to form a multi-sided perspective that is more comprehensive and balanced.

If you recall from Chapter 2, one of the major divisions of the liberal arts curriculum is the humanities. Courses in this division of knowledge focus on understanding humanity—the common elements of the human experience that are shared by all human beings.

> **Remember:** By learning about diversity (our differences), we simultaneously learn more about what we have in common—our shared humanity.

Experiencing diversity not only enhances your appreciation of the unique features of different cultures, it also provides you with a larger perspective on the universal aspects of the human experience that are common to all people, no matter what their particular cultural background happens to be.

Pause for Reflection

List three human experiences that you think are universal, i.e., that are experienced by all human beings in all cultures.

1.

2.

3.

Diversity Promotes Self-Awareness

Learning from people with diverse backgrounds and experiences also serves to sharpen your self-awareness and self-understanding by allowing you to compare and contrast your life experiences with people whose life experiences differ sharply from your own. This *comparative perspective* can give you an important reference point, putting you in a better position to see more clearly how your unique cultural experiences have influenced the development of your personal beliefs, values, and lifestyle. When students around the country were interviewed about their diversity experiences in college, many of them reported that these experiences enabled them to learn more about themselves. Some said that their interactions with students from different races and ethnic groups produced "unexpected" or "jarring" self-insights (Light, 2001).

Diversity Strengthens Development of Learning and Thinking Skills

Just as the quality of your physical health and performance are improved by consuming a varied and balanced diet of foods from different food groups, the quality of your mental performance is improved by helping yourself to a balanced diet of ideas obtained from different groups of people. Experiencing their rich variety of cultural perspectives nourishes your mind with good "food for thought." Research consistently shows that we learn more from people who are different from us than we do from people who are similar to us (Pascarella, 2001; Pascarella & Terenzini, 2005). This result is probably best explained by the fact that when we encounter what is unfamiliar or uncertain, we are forced to stretch beyond our mental comfort zone to actively compare and contrast it to what we already know in order to understand it (Acredolo & O'Connor, 1991; Nagda, Gurin, & Johnson, 2005).

Keep in mind that learning is strengthened when it takes place in a social context that involves human interaction. As some scholars put it, human knowledge is "socially constructed"—it is built up through interaction and dialogue with others (Bruffee, 1993). According to these scholars, our thinking is largely an "internal" (mental) representation of conversations we have had with other people (Vygotsky, 1978). So, the nature and quality of our conversations with others affects the nature and quality of our own thinking. If we have multiple conversations with humans from very different backgrounds, then the nature of our thinking becomes more diverse and complex. In contrast, when we restrict the diversity of people who we interact with, we artificially restrict the range and complexity of our thought—by limiting the variety of lenses or angles we can use to view issues and solve problems.

Research on first-year college students shows that students who experience the highest level of exposure to different dimensions of diversity (e.g., interactions and friendships with peers of different races, or participating in multicultural courses and events on campus) report the greatest gains in:

◆ thinking complexity—the ability to think about all parts and all sides of an issue (Gurin, 1999),
◆ reflective thinking—the ability to think deeply (Kitchener et al., 2000), and
◆ critical thinking—the ability to think logically (Pascarella et al., 2001).

Lastly, experiencing diversity can enhance your ability to think *creatively*. Just as experiences with academic disciplines (subjects) can equip you with different thinking styles and strategies that may be combined to generate new ideas, so do experiences with different dimensions of diversity. Although a major advantage of culture is that it helps bind people together, it can also blind people from other perspectives. Since culture shapes the way we think, it can cause groups of people to view the world solely through their own cultural frame of reference (Colombo, Cullen, & Lisle, 1995). Diversity experiences supply us with different thinking styles

Figure 8.3 Optical Illusion

that can help us think outside the boundaries of our own cultural framework. These experiences also help us to be aware of our perceptual "blind spots" and to avoid the dangers of *group think*—the tendency for tight, like-minded groups of people to think so much alike that they overlook the flaws in their own thinking—which can lead to poor choices and faulty decisions (Janis, 1982).

Optical illusions are a good illustration of how our cultural perspectives can blind us or cause us to misperceive things. For instance, compare the length of the two lines in Figure 8.3.

If you perceive the line on the right to be longer than the line on the left, welcome to the club. Virtually all Americans and people from Western cultures perceive the line on the right to be longer. Actually, both lines are equal in length. (If you don't believe it, take out a ruler and check it out.) However, people from non-Western cultures who live in environments with circular architecture rather than buildings with lines and corners, do not make this perceptual error (Segall, Campbell & Herskovits, 1966).

The key point underlying this optical illusion is that our cultural experiences shape and sometimes distort our perceptions or interpretations of reality. We think we are seeing things objectively or "as they really are," but we are often seeing things subjectively from our limited cultural vantage point. Being open to people from different backgrounds who perceive the world from different cultural vantage points opens up our range of perception and helps us overcome our cultural blind spots. As a result, we can see and think about the world around us with greater clarity and balance.

The people who live in these circular huts would not be fooled by the optical illusion in Figure 8.3.

Diversity Enhances Career Preparation and Success

Learning from diversity also has a very practical benefit: It better prepares you for the world of work. Whatever career you may choose to enter, you will likely find yourself working with employers, employees, co-workers, customers, and clients from diverse cultural backgrounds. America's workforce is now more diverse than at any other time in its history, and work today takes place in a global economy that involves greater economic interdependence among nations (e.g., international businesses), more international trading (imports/exports), more multinational corporations, more world travel, and more effective worldwide communication—due to advances in the World Wide Web (Dryden, & Vos, 1999; Smith, 1994). Consequently, employers of college graduates have begun to place higher value on job candidates with international knowledge and foreign language skills (Fixman, 1990; Office of Research, 1994).

Successful career performance in today's diverse workforce requires sensitivity to human differences and the ability to relate to people from different cultural backgrounds who work in the United States and across different nations (National Association of Colleges & Employers, 2003; Smith, 1997). One national survey of business leaders and policymakers revealed that they want college graduates to have more than just "awareness" or "tolerance" of diversity; they want graduates to have actual *experience* with diversity (Education Commission of the State, 1995). Today's world truly has become a "small world," and your success in it will be enhanced if you gain a multicultural and cross-cultural perspective.

Diversity Stimulates Social Development

Experiencing diversity also promotes your social development. When you interact with people from a variety of groups, you widen your social circle by expanding the pool of people with whom you can associate and develop relationships. As the old American proverb goes, "Variety is the spice of life." Or, as the French might say: "Viva la difference!" (Long live difference!)

Just as the quality of your dining experiences are enriched by the range and variety of ethnic foods you can choose from to stimulate your taste palate, so too can the quality of your learning experiences be enriched by the range and variety of ethnic groups with which you can choose to interact. In fact, research indicates that students who have more diversity experiences in college report higher levels of satisfaction with their college experience (Astin, 1993).

••• Blocks to Experiencing Diversity

Although there are multiple benefits associated with diversity, there are also some human tendencies that can interfere with or block us from experiencing diversity and reaping its benefits. Three of these potential stumbling blocks are *stereotyping*, *prejudice*, and *discrimination*.

Stereotyping

The word stereotype is a combination of two root words: "stereo" (to look at in a fixed way) and "type" (typical). It is the tendency to *view* individuals of the same type (group) in the same (fixed) way. In effect, stereotyping ignores or disregards a person's individuality; instead, all individuals who share a similar group characteristic (e.g., race or gender) are viewed as having similar personal characteristics—as in the expression: "You know what they are like; they're all the same." If virtually all members of a stereotyped group are *judged or evaluated* in the same way, this results in *prejudice*.

◢═*Pause for Reflection*

1. Have you ever been stereotyped, based on your appearance or group membership? If so, how did it make you feel and how did you react?

2. Have you ever unintentionally perceived or treated someone in terms of a stereotype rather than as an individual? What assumptions did you make about that person? Was that person aware of, or affected by, your stereotyping?

Prejudice

The word "prejudice" literally means to "pre-judge." It represents a judgment, attitude, or belief about another person or group of people, which is formed before the facts are known. Stereotyping and prejudice often occur together because individuals who are placed in a stereotyped group are commonly pre-judged in a biased (slanted) way. When this bias is negative, it is referred to as *stigmatizing*—associating inferior or unfavorable traits with people who belong to the same group. Although, technically, prejudice may be either positive or negative, the term is most often used to refer to negative pre-judgment or stigmatizing, which is the way it will be used in this chapter.

Someone with a prejudice toward a group typically avoids contact with individuals from the stigmatized group. Thus, the prejudice continues because there is little or no chance for the prejudiced person to have positive experiences with a member of the group that could contradict or disprove the prejudice. Thus, a vicious cycle is established in which the prejudiced person avoids contact with the stigmatized group, and this lack of contact keeps the prejudice going by not allowing any opportunities for it to be contradicted.

A prejudice can also remain intact because facts that contradict it are often ignored through the psychological process of *selective perception*—the tendency for the prejudiced person to see what he or she *expects* to see (Hugenberg & Bodenhausen, 2003). This results in the prejudiced person choosing to pay attention to information that is consistent with the prejudice and "seeing" that information, while ignoring or overlooking information that contradicts the prejudice. Have you ever noticed that fans rooting for their favorite sports team tend to focus on and "see" the calls or decisions of referees that go against their own team, but do not seem to notice or react to calls that go against the other team? This is a classic, everyday example of selective perception. It could be said that selective perception changes the process of "seeing is believing" into "believing is seeing." Even if a contradictory piece of information happens to slip through the prejudiced person's attention filter, it is likely to be dismissed as an "exception to the rule," or as an exception that "proves" the general rule (Aronson, et al., 2005).

Selective perception can also be accompanied by *selective memory*—the tendency to remember only information that is consistent with the prejudice, while forgetting information that is inconsistent or contradictory (Judd et al., 1991). It is possible for the psychological processes of selective perception and selective memory to operate *unconsciously*, so the prejudiced person may not be fully aware that they are using them or that they are resulting in prejudice (Baron, Byrne, & Brauscombe, 2006).

Whether prejudice is conscious or unconscious, the bottom line is that it can cause a person to minimize or cut off interaction with a whole group of people. As a result, the prejudiced person fails to experience and profit from the particular dimension of diversity (e.g., ethnic, racial, or national) that members of the stigmatized group have to offer. Worse yet, the person's prejudice can lead to acts of *discrimination* against members of the stigmatized group.

Discrimination

Literally translated, the term discrimination means division or separation. While prejudice is an attitude or belief, discrimination is an *action* taken toward another individual, which results in that person receiving different treatment. So, it could be said that discrimination is prejudice put into action.

"Hate crimes" represent an extreme form of discrimination. These are crimes motivated solely by prejudice against members of a stigmatized group—for example, damaging their personal property or physically assaulting them (e.g., "gay bashing"). Hate crimes are acts of discrimination that are committed consciously and maliciously. However, just like prejudice, some forms of discrimination can be very subtle and may take place without people being fully aware that they are discriminating. For example, there is some evidence that white, male college professors tend to treat female students and students from ethnic or racial minority groups differently than they do males and non-minority students. In particular, females and minority students tend to:

◆ receive less eye contact from the instructors,

◆ be called on less frequently in class,

◆ be given less time to respond to questions asked by instructors in class, and

◆ have less contact with instructors outside the classroom (Hall & Sandler, 1982, 1984; Sedlacek, 1987; Wright, 1987).

In the vast majority of these cases, the discriminatory treatment that these students received was subtle and not done consciously or deliberately by the instructors (Green, 1989). Nevertheless, these unintended actions are still discriminatory, and they may send a message to these students that their ideas are not worth hearing, or that they are not as capable as other students (Sadker & Sadker, 1994).

Have you noticed classroom teaching behaviors or strategies used by instructors that clearly treated all students equally and promoted appreciation of student diversity?

What did these instructors do?

Personal Story

Being African American and living in southeastern Kentucky, the heart of Appalachia, did not provide for the grandest of living styles. Even though my father worked twelve hours a day in the coal mines, he earned only enough pay to supply staples for the table. Our family also worked as tenant farmers to have enough vegetables for my mother to can for the winter and to provide a roof over our heads.

My mother was a direct descendent of slaves and moved with her parents from the deep south at the age of seventeen. My father lived in an all-black coal mining camp, into which my mother and her family moved in 1938. My dad would say to me, "Son, you will have opportunities that I never had. Many people, white and black alike, will tell you that you are no good and that education can never help you. Don't listen to them because soon they will not be able to keep you from getting an education like they did me. Just remember, when you do get that education, you'll never have to go in those coal mines and have them break your back. You can choose what you want to do, and then you can be a free man."

My father lived through a time when freedom was something he dreamed his children might enjoy someday, because before the civil rights movement succeeded in changing the laws, African Americans were considerably limited in educational opportunities, job opportunities, and much else in what was definitely a racist society. My father remained illiterate because he was not allowed to attend public schools in eastern Kentucky.

In the early 1960s my brother, my sister, and I were integrated into the white public schools. Physical violence and constant verbal harassment caused many other blacks to forgo their education and opt for jobs in the coal mines at an early age. But my father remained constant in his advice to me: "It doesn't matter if they call you n_____; but don't you ever let them beat you by walking out on your education."

Being poor, black, and Appalachian did not offer me great odds for success, but constant reminders from my parents that I was a good and valuable person helped me to see beyond my deterrents to the true importance of education. My parents, who could never provide me with monetary wealth, truly made me proud of them by giving me the gift of insight and an aspiration for achievement.

—Aaron Thompson

••• Causes of Prejudice and Discrimination

There is no single or definitive answer to the question of what causes people to be prejudiced and to discriminate against other groups of people. However, research indicates that the following factors can play an influential role.

The Influence of Familiarity and Stranger Anxiety

Research has repeatedly demonstrated that when humans encounter things that are unfamiliar or strange, they tend to experience feelings of discomfort or anxiety. In contrast, what is familiar tends to be more accepted and better liked (Zajonc, 2001).

When we encounter people who are not familiar to us, experiencing at least some feeling of discomfort is a natural human tendency that probably occurs automatically. In fact, these feelings may be "wired into" our bodies because it was once important to the survival and evolution of our species (Figure 8.4). When we encountered strangers in our primitive past, it was to our advantage to react with feelings of anxiety and a rush of adrenaline, known as the "fight or flight" response, because those strangers may have been potential predators who were about to threaten or attack us. This evolutionary response may also explain why "stranger anxiety" is a very normal part of human development during infancy. Between about 8 and 18 months of life, virtually all infants when seeing a stranger will react with anxiety (increased heart rate, breathing, crying) (Papalia & Olds, 1990).

Familiarity and stranger anxiety may contribute to prejudice by causing members of the same group to favor members of its own group and to be "on guard" to defend them from members of other groups who are less familiar or strange (Aronson, et al., 2005). Members of minority groups are less familiar to the majority group because they are fewer in number. Also, members of minority groups are less likely to have regular contact with members of the majority group because they are less likely to live in the same area (e.g., the same neighborhood), due to residential segregation of racial and ethnic groups, which is still common today (Massey,

Figure 8.4 "Fight-or-Flight" Reaction

When primitive humans encountered members of strange or unfamiliar groups, an automatic "fight or flight" survival response kicked in, providing a rush of anxiety and adrenaline to prepare them to fight or run away from these potential predators.

Lungs expand

Blood vessels near skin contract

Adrenal glands secrete adrenaline

Large blood vessels dilate to speed blood flow

Heart rate and blood pressure rise

Liver releases glucose for energy to muscles

Sweat glands activated (moist palms)

Muscle tension increases

2003; Tienda & Cortes, cited in Nagda, Gurin, & Johnson, 2005). Thus, members of the majority group may view minority group members as "unfamiliar," and this lack of familiarity may automatically trigger negative feelings of uncertainty and anxiety. These negative feelings may then become associated with the minority group, which can lead to negative prejudices toward that group.

Pause for Reflection

Prejudice can be subtle and only begin to surface when the social or emotional distance between members of different groups grows closer. Rate your level of comfort (high, medium, low) with the following situations.

Someone from another racial group:

1. *going to your school*	*high*	*medium*	*low*
2. *working in your place of employment*	*high*	*medium*	*low*
3. *living on your street as a neighbor*	*high*	*medium*	*low*
4. *living with you as a roommate*	*high*	*medium*	*low*
5. *socializing with you as a personal friend*	*high*	*medium*	*low*
6. *being your most intimate friend or romantic partner*	*high*	*medium*	*low*
7. *being your partner in marriage*	*high*	*medium*	*low*

For any item you rated "low," why do you think it received that rating?

The Tendency to Categorize People

Humans have a tendency to put groups of people into mental categories in order to organize their complex social world and make it simpler to understand (Jones, 1990). While this is a normal human tendency, it can lead to stereotyping members of other groups, which blinds us to their individuality. It also can contribute to prejudice because we tend to create categories of *in*-groups ("us") and *out*-groups ("them"). One negative consequence of this tendency is that it can lead to *ethnocentrism*—the tendency to view one's own culture or ethnic group as the central or "normal" in-group and other cultures as less important or "abnormal" out-groups. This tendency can, in turn, lead to prejudice and discrimination toward people with cultural backgrounds that differ from our own.

Our cultural experiences can affect our judgments and conclusions about what is perceived as socially acceptable or "normal." For instance, in American culture, it may be socially acceptable for males to tell others of their achievements or accomplishments; however, in English and German cultures, such behavior is likely to be perceived as immodest or immature (Hall & Hall, 1986). Failure to appreciate cultural differences can lead to ethnocentric thinking, which fails to consider that groups of people may have attitudes and behaviors that are different but equally acceptable or "normal" when viewed from the perspective of their respective cultures. Ethnocentric thinking is a form of simplistic, dualistic (black-white) thinking that can lead to the conclusion that the way things are done by the in-group ("us") must be "right," and the behavior of out-groups ("them") must be "wrong."

Group Perception

Research studies show that humans are more likely to see members of groups that they do not belong to as more similar to each other in attitudes and behavior than members of their own group (Baron, Byrne, & Brauscombe, 2006). For instance, individuals perceive people older than themselves as being more alike in their attitudes and beliefs than members of their own age group (Linville, Fischer, & Salovey, 1989).

One explanation for this tendency to see members of other groups as being more alike than members of our own group is that we have more experience with members of our own group, so we have more opportunities to observe and interact with a wide variety of individuals within our group. In contrast, we have less experience with members of other groups, so the variety of individuals we have had contact with is narrower, perhaps leading us to conclude that the individual differences among them are narrower, i.e., they are more alike in attitudes and behavior than members of our own group. This effect can be so strong that we often fail to detect differences in the faces of individuals who are members of groups that we're unfamiliar with, i.e., "They all seem to look alike" (Levin, 2000). A dramatic example of this tendency is the case of Lenell Geter, an African-American engineer, who spent over a year of a life sentence in prison for a crime he didn't commit. Four of five non-black witnesses misidentified him for another black man who actually committed the crime and was later apprehended.

Majority Group Members' Attitudes

Research shows that if negative behavior occurs at the same rate among members of both majority and minority groups (e.g., the rate of criminal behavior in both groups is 10 percent), members of the majority group are more likely to develop negative attitudes (prejudice) toward the minority group than their own group (Baron, Byrne, & Brauscombe, 2006). For example, it has been found that whites in the United States tend to overestimate the crime rates of African-American men (Hamilton & Sherman, 1989).

One possible explanation why the negative behaviors of minority group members are more likely to produce negative views of their group is the tendency for majority group members to better remember instances of negative behavior associated with members of the minority group. Since minorities are more likely to be seen as different or distinctive, their behavior is more likely to stand out in the minds of majority group members, which makes it more likely that these negative behaviors will be remembered (McArthur & Friedman, 1980). Since these negative behaviors are more likely to be retained in the minds of the majority group, they are more likely to negatively influence their view of the minority group, thus increasing the possibility of prejudice.

Although prejudice on the part of the majority group toward minority groups has led to the most extreme form of discrimination and domination (Baron, Byrne, & Brauscombe, 2006), any group can become a target for prejudice. (See pages 268–269 for a snapshot summary of the many different groups of people that have been the target for prejudicial theories and beliefs.) Members of a minority group can also be prejudiced toward the majority group, as illustrated by the student perspective in the margin.

Group Membership and Self-Esteem

Self-esteem—how you feel about yourself—can be influenced by group membership. If people think that the group they belong to is superior, it enables them to feel better about themselves (Tajfel, 1982). In other words, "My group is superior, and since I belong to it, I am superior." This type of thinking is even more likely to occur when an individual's self-esteem has been threatened or damaged as a result of some personal frustration or failure. When this happens,

STUDENT PERSPECTIVE

"My friend said that he 'hates white people because they try to dominate people of color.' I, on the other hand, feel differently. One should not blame all white people for the mistakes and prejudiced acts that white people have made. Unfortunately, my friend has yet to learn this."

Student of color, quoted in Nagna, Gurin, & Sohnson, 2005, p. 102.

the person whose self-esteem has been threatened or damaged can boost it by stigmatizing or putting down members of another group (Rudman & Fairchild, 2004), or by blaming them and making them the "scapegoat" (Gemmil, 1989). For example, they might say, "If it weren't for 'them,' we wouldn't have this problem." Probably the most extreme example of "scape-goating" in human history took place in Nazi Germany, where Jews were blamed for the country's economic problems and became targets of the Holocaust. Studies have shown that when times are tough (e.g., when unemployment is high) and people are frustrated, prejudice and discrimination tend to increase (Aronson, et al., 2005).

Although the causes of prejudice are still not completely understood, we can help guard ourselves against prejudice by remaining aware of the five tendencies discussed in this section, namely:

1. The tendency to favor familiarity and fear strangers;
2. The tendency to mentally categorize people into "in" and "out" groups;
3. The tendency to perceive members of other groups as more alike than members of our own group;
4. The tendency for the attitudes of majority group members to be more influenced by negative behaviors committed by members of minority groups than members of their own (majority) group; and
5. The tendency to build our self-esteem through group membership.

BOX 8.1 *Snapshot* SUMMARY

Stereotypes and Prejudiced Belief Systems about Group Inferiority

As you read this list, make a note next to each item indicating: (a) whether you've heard of this form of stereotype or prejudice, and (b) whether you've observed or experienced it.

Ethnocentrism: considering one's own culture or ethnic group to be "central" or "normal," and viewing cultures that are different as "deficient" or "inferior."

For example, claiming that another culture is "weird" or "abnormal" for eating certain animals that we consider unethical to eat, even though we eat certain animals that they consider unethical to eat.

Racism: prejudice or discrimination based on skin color.

For example, Cecil Rhodes (Englishman and empire builder of British South Africa), once claimed: "We [the British] are the finest race in the world and the more of the world we inhabit the better it is for the human race."

Apartheid: a strict system of racial separation and discrimination against non-white people, which was once national policy in South Africa.

Classism: prejudice or discrimination based on social class, particularly toward people of low socioeconomic status.

For example, focusing only on the contributions made by politicians and wealthy industrialists to America, while ignoring the contributions of poor immigrants, farmers, slaves, and pioneer women.

Nationalism: excessive interest and belief in the strengths of one's own nation without acknowledgment of its mistakes or weaknesses, and without concern for the needs of other nations or the common interests of all nations.

For example, "blind patriotism" that blinds people to the shortcomings of their own nation, and views any questioning or criticism of their nation as being disloyal or "unpatriotic." (As in the slogan, "America: right or wrong!")

Regionalism: prejudice or discrimination based on the geographical region of a nation in which an individual has been born and raised.

For example, a northerner thinking that all southerners are racists.

(continued)

Xenophobia: extreme fear or hatred of foreigners, outsiders, or strangers.

For example, someone believing that all immigrants should be kept out of the country because they will increase the crime rate.

Anti-Semitism: prejudice or discrimination toward Jews.

For example, the mass murdering of Jews in Nazi Germany.

Religious Bigotry (Religious Intolerance): not respecting the fundamental human right of other people to hold religious beliefs that are different than one's own.

For example, stating that all people who hold another religious belief are immoral; or, forcing one's own religious practices (or lack thereof) on others against their will.

Terrorism: intentional acts of violence against civilians that are motivated by political or religious prejudice.

For example, the September 11th attacks on the United States.

Ageism: prejudice or discrimination based on age, particularly toward the elderly.

For example, believing that all "old" people are bad drivers with bad memories.

Ableism: prejudice or discrimination toward people who are disabled or handicapped.

For example, avoiding interaction with handicapped people because of anxiety about not knowing what to say or how to act around them.

Sexism: prejudice or discrimination based on sex or gender.

For example, believing that no one should vote for a woman president because she would be too "emotional."

Heterosexism: belief that heterosexuality is the only acceptable sexual orientation.

For example, using the phrase, "You're so gay" as an insult or put down; or believing that gays should not have the same legal rights and opportunities as heterosexuals.

Homophobia: extreme fear and/or hatred of homosexuals.

For example, people who create or contribute to anti-gay Web sites.

STUDENT PERSPECTIVE

"Most religions dictate that theirs is the only way, and without believing in it, you cannot enter the mighty kingdom of heaven. Who are we to judge? It makes more sense for God to be the only one mighty enough to make that decision. If other people could understand and see from this perspective, then many religious arguments could be avoided."

—First-year student

●●● Strategies for Making the Most of Diversity

We can learn the most from diversity by taking each of the following three steps:

1. Self-reflection,
2. Personal action, and
3. Interpersonal interaction.

Each of these steps represents a progressively higher level of involvement with diversity, so the higher you go, the more you will learn.

Self-Reflection: Gaining Self-Awareness and Developing Diversity Tolerance

The first step to learning from diversity is to develop self-awareness about our attitudes toward diversity, particularly awareness of any stereotypes and prejudices we may have that are biasing our perceptions of, or behaviors toward, different groups of people. At the bare minimum, we want to behave in a way that demonstrates tolerance or acceptance of diversity.

By writing a constitution that failed to grant female citizens the right to vote, America's founding fathers forgot their mothers (along with all other women) and provided a very vivid example of sexism.

As previously mentioned, research indicates that prejudice and discrimination can occur unconsciously or unintentionally (Baron, Byrne, & Branscombe, 2006). Listed below are some specific strategies for increasing your conscious awareness of attitudes and feelings about diversity.

Keep a journal or diary of your personal reflections on diversity.

Studies show that students learn most effectively from diversity experiences when they take time to reflect on these experiences, particularly when they record these reflections in writing (Lopez, et al., 1998; Nagda, et al., 2003). If you decide to reflect on your diversity experiences, it might be useful to keep the following questions in mind:

- What type of feelings or emotions did you experience?
- When and where did you experience these feelings? (What was the situation or context?)
- Why do you think you felt that way?

Becoming aware of our subtle and sometimes subconscious prejudices is the first step toward eliminating them. Reducing prejudice not only benefits those who are the targets of prejudice, it also benefits those who reduce their own prejudice. Research indicates that people who are less prejudiced report more satisfaction with their lives (Feagin & McKinney, 2003)—perhaps because they are more open to social experiences and less distrustful or fearful of the people around them (Baron, Byrne, & Branscombe, 2006).

Pause for Reflection

Have you ever been prejudiced against a certain group of people?

If you have, what was the group, and why do you think you held that prejudice?

Consciously avoid preoccupation with physical appearances.

Go deeper and get beneath the superficial surface of appearances to view people in terms of *who* they really are and how they really act, not in terms of how they look. Remember the old proverb: "It's what's inside that counts." Judge others by the quality of their personal character, not by your familiarity with their physical characteristics.

Personal Story
When I was a new college student at a large university in the south, I encountered a student who talked loudly, had her ears pierced all around the lobes, and used words my mom never allowed me to use. At first, I was turned off by these differences, but I was also absolutely intrigued by her. It appeared that other students were too, because she seemed to be "together" and very cool. I'm ashamed to admit it, but it took me the whole year to realize that my way was not necessarily the right way (it was just more familiar), and her way was not really wrong or deficient (it was just different).

—*Viki Sox Fecas, Program Manager for Freshman and Pre-Freshman Programs and co-author of this text*

Make a conscious attempt to perceive people as individuals—not as group members, and form your impressions of them on a case-by-case basis—not by using a "general rule."

This may seem like an obvious and easy thing to do, but remember, research shows that there is a natural tendency for humans to consider members of another group as being more alike (or all alike) than members of our own group (Taylor, 2006). Thus, we may have to deliberately fight off this grouping or "lumping together" tendency and consciously focus on each person's individuality.

Personal Action: Learning about Diversity by Acquiring Knowledge of Different Cultures

While self-awareness is an important first step toward learning from diversity, we also need to step outside ourselves and make an active attempt to learn about other social groups and cultures. Our perception of reality is a blending of fact (objectivity) and our interpretation (subjectivity)—which is shaped and molded by our particular cultural perspective (Paul, 1995). Viewing issues from different cultural perspectives allows you to perceive "reality" and see "truth" from different vantage points, which advantages your thinking by making it more comprehensive and less ethnocentric.

Thus, to think in a balanced and unbiased fashion, we need to acquire knowledge about the diverse groups that make up our social environment and how their experiences may be different from our own. In order to acquire this knowledge, we must first acknowledge that diversity exists. It means not being blind to, or in denial about human differences, and it is more than simply saying, "We're all human, so let's get over our differences and move on." This comment ignores the fact that different groups of people have had very different life experiences and continue to face different challenges. More importantly, it denies their group identity, which is an important element of their self-concept and self-esteem.

Remember: Don't let cultural differences get in the way of potentially rewarding relationships. The more opportunities you create to learn from others who are different from yourself, the more opportunities you will create to learn about yourself.

Someone who merely tolerates diversity (level 1) might say things like, "Let's just get along," "live and let live," or "to each his own." Learning about diversity (level 2) involves taking a step beyond diversity tolerance to the higher level of diversity *appreciation*—becoming interested in the cultures and experiences of different groups of people and wanting to learn more about them. Listed below are some strategies for taking this second step.

To increase your understanding and empathy for the experiences of members of another group, imagine yourself as a member of a different group, and attempt to visualize what the experience might be like.

Better yet, see if you can place yourself in the position or situation of someone from that group. For instance, ride in a wheelchair to experience what it is like for someone who is physically disabled, or wear blinders to experience what it's like to be visually impaired.

Incorporate diversity into your work on course assignments.

If you have a choice about what topic to do research on in a particular course, consider choosing a topic relating to diversity; or, consider discussing the diversity implications of whatever topic you may be writing or speaking about (e.g., use multicultural or cross-cultural examples as evidence to illustrate your points).

Take courses that cover material relating to diversity.

You can actively plan to do this by reviewing your college catalog for course descriptions and identify courses that are designed to promote understanding or appreciation of multicultural diversity within the United States or cross-cultural diversity across different nations.

Strongly consider taking a foreign language course.

This will not only benefit you educationally, but it should also benefit you professionally because employers of college graduates are placing increasing value on employees who have foreign language skills (Fixman, 1990; Office of Research, 1994).

Participate in co-curricular activities on campus that relate to diversity.

You can actively plan to do this by reviewing your student handbook for co-curricular programs, student activities, or student clubs that promote diversity awareness and appreciation. Planning in advance to attend some of these programs may be easy to do, because they often coincide with annually scheduled "national" weeks or months, such as Black History Month, Women's History Month, Latin Heritage Month, and Asian American Month.

Studies indicate that taking diversity courses and participating in co-curricular programs helps to reduce unconscious prejudice (Blair, 2002) and strengthens mental development (Pascarella & Terenzini, 2005). Furthermore, what you learn in these courses and programs can provide you with the preparation and confidence to move on to the next step—direct interaction with people from diverse backgrounds.

Interpersonal Interaction: Learning through Interaction and Collaboration with Members of Diverse Groups

Through formal courses and programs, you can learn about diversity. However, you can also learn through diversity experience—direct, first-hand interaction with people from diverse groups and backgrounds. Studies show that learning is maximized when students step beyond just learning about diversity through reading and attending lectures to actually experiencing diversity by interacting with others from diverse groups (Nagda et al., 2003). Such interpersonal experiences move you from the level of multicultural or cross-cultural awareness to a higher level that involves intercultural interaction. This represents a significant increase in your level of involvement with diversity. It is almost like the difference between learning about a foreign country by taking a class or reading about it and actually traveling to the country, interacting with its natives, and immersing yourself in its culture.

This third step involves actively seeking out interaction with members of diverse groups of people who can contribute to your learning and who can learn from you. It requires being open to interaction, dialog, and cultivation of personal relationships with individuals from diverse groups. If you have taken the previous step and learned about different cultures, you may now be more confident about interacting with people from different cultural backgrounds. However, your comfort level with this level of involvement may depend on how much experience you have had with diversity prior to college.

Cultivating relationships with others from diverse groups increases your awareness and comfort level when interacting with those from different cultural backgrounds.

 Pause for Reflection

How would you rank the amount or variety of diversity you have experienced in the following settings?

1. *The neighborhood in which you grew up*

2. *The places where you have worked or been employed*

3. *The high school you attended*

4. *The college or university you now attend*

Which setting had the most and least diversity? What do you think accounts for this difference?

If there is diversity on your campus that you have had little previous exposure to, seeking out and initiating interaction with members of unfamiliar groups may not come easily or naturally for you. On the other hand, if you have had little or no prior experience with diverse groups, you also have the most to gain from experiencing the diversity that is now available on your campus. Research on human learning consistently shows that new experiences that differ from an individual's prior experiences are those that tend to produce the greatest learning and the greatest gains in mental development (Piaget, 1985; Acredolo & O'Connor, 1991).

Even if you had experience living in diverse environments prior to college, you may not have experienced the particular types or dimensions of diversity that exist on your campus, or you may have not yet developed the most effective ways for interacting with and learning from members of diverse groups. Whatever your prior experience with diversity may be, look at the diversity on your campus as a new educational opportunity. Consider it to be a campus resource, and capitalize on this social resource to promote your educational and personal success.

Listed below is a series of strategies for increasing the quantity and quality of your interaction with members from diverse groups on campus.

Intentionally create opportunities for interaction and conversation with students from diverse groups.

Fight off the natural tendency to associate only with people who are similar to you. One way to do this is by placing yourself in situations where you are close enough for conversation to take place with individuals from diverse groups. Research indicates that meaningful interpersonal interactions and friendships are more likely to develop among people who are within close distance to one another (Latané, et al., 1993). So, make an intentional attempt to create this condition. For example, in class, sit near a student from another country; or, at lunch, sit near a student from a different ethnic or racial group.

Keep in mind that the definition of discrimination is giving unequal treatment to different groups of people. If we interact solely with members of our own group and separate ourselves from members of a group who are different than us, we are treating these two groups unequally. This qualifies as discrimination, even if we are not doing it maliciously or consciously.

Make an earnest attempt to learn the names and interests of students from diverse groups.

This will enable you to establish early, personal rapport that can serve as a foundation for further interaction and deeper conversation. Pay particular attention to interests that you may have in common, because shared interests can provide a source of interesting conversation, and perhaps, lead to the development of a long-term friendship.

"I have a love of words, too."

Finding interests you have in common with others is an effective way to start conversations and potential friendships.

Consider spending some time at the multicultural center on your campus, or join a campus club or organization that is devoted to diversity awareness (e.g., international student club).

This will enable you to make contact with members of groups other than your own, and clearly sends a message to them that you are interested in doing so, because you have taken the initiative to visit them on "their turf."

Participate in a multicultural or cross-cultural retreat sponsored by your college.

A retreat setting can provide a comfortable environment for getting to know people at a personal level, without the everyday interference and distractions that take place on campus.

Become involved in volunteer or community service activities that may allow you to work in diverse communities or neighborhoods.

Research suggests that college students who participate in volunteer experiences report significant gains in learning and leadership development (Astin, et al., 2000).

Attempt to locate and participate in an internship in a company or organization that will allow you the opportunity to work with people from diverse backgrounds and cultures.

This will not only provide you with a good learning experience, it will also improve your preparation and qualifications for career entry after college. Surveys of employers indicate that they value college graduates who have actual "hands on" experience with diversity (Education Commission of the States, 1995).

If possible, participate in a study abroad program that allows you to live in another country and interact directly with its natives.

In preparation for this international experience, take a course in the language, culture, or history of the nation to which you will be traveling.

Take advantage of the Internet to "chat" with students from diverse groups on your campus, or with students in different countries.

Electronic communication can be a more convenient and more comfortable way to initially interact with members of diverse groups with whom you have had little prior experience. After you've communicated successfully online, you may then feel more comfortable about communicating in person.

Deliberately seek out the views and opinions of students from diverse backgrounds.

For example, ask students from different backgrounds if there was any point made or position taken in class that they would strongly question or challenge. Seeking out divergent (diverse) viewpoints has been found to be one of the best ways to develop critical thinking skills (Kurfiss, 1988).

Join or form discussion groups with students from diverse backgrounds.

You can experience diverse perspectives by joining groups of students who may be different from you in terms of such characteristics as gender, age, race, or ethnic group. When ideas are generated freely in groups comprised of people from diverse backgrounds, a powerful "cross-stimulation" effect occurs, whereby one group member's idea often triggers different ideas from other group members (Brown et al., 1998).

You might begin by forming discussion groups of students who are different with respect to one characteristic but similar with respect to another. For instance, join a group of students of your gender but who differ with respect to race, ethnicity, or age. This strategy can give your diverse group some common ground to build on, as well as increase their awareness that humans who are members of different groups can, at the same time, be members of the same group—and share similar experiences, needs, or concerns.

> **Remember:** Including diversity in your discussion group not only increases social variety, it also increases the quality of the group's thinking. Diverse discussion groups allow each member to access the different perspectives and thinking styles of people with different background experiences.

For instance, older students may have more life experience for younger students to draw upon and learn from, while younger students may bring a fresh, idealistic perspective to group discussions with older students. Also, males and females tend to contribute different thinking styles to group discussions. Studies show that males are more likely to be "separate knowers" who have a greater tendency to "detach" themselves from the concept or issue being discussed so they can analyze it, whereas females are more likely to be "connected knowers" who have a stronger tendency to relate personally to concepts and connect them to their own experiences. For example, when confronting a poem, males are more likely to ask themselves, "What techniques can I use to analyze it?" In contrast, females are more likely to ask themselves, "What is the poet trying to say to me?" (Belenky, et al., 1986, p. 101). It has also been found that females generally adopt a more collaborative style during group discussions and are more likely to collect ideas of others in a group-learning situation, whereas males are more likely to adopt a competitive approach and debate the ideas of others (Magolda, 1992).

Pause for Reflection

How would you define teamwork?

What do you think are the key factors that make study groups or group projects successful?

Form collaborative learning teams.

A learning team is much more than a discussion group; it moves beyond discussion to collaboration—whereby teammates rely on each other as part of a united effort to reach a shared goal.

Studies show that interpersonal contact between members of different ethnic and racial groups, which takes place while they work collaboratively to achieve a common goal, tends to reduce racial prejudice and promote interracial friendships (Allport, 1954; Amir, 1976). This may be due to the fact that when these individuals from diverse groups work collaboratively on the same team, they become members of the same group. Thus, they all become members of the "in group," with no one being an "outsider."

The greatest gains in reducing prejudice and improving relationships among members of different ethnic and racial groups take place when collaboration occurs under the six conditions described in Box 8.2. Research also indicates that these are the same conditions that are most likely to produce the largest gains in learning among team members (Slavin, 1995; Johnson, et al., 1998).

At the conclusion of collaborative teamwork and group discussions, take some time to pause and reflect on the social interaction that took place.

Ask yourself questions that cause you to think back on the ideas that emerged from diverse members of the group and think about what impact these ideas had on you. For instance, after group discussions you could ask yourself the following questions:

◆ What major differences did you detect among group members during your discussion?
◆ What major similarities in viewpoints or background experiences did all group members share?
◆ Did the discussion cause you to reconsider or change any ideas you previously held?

Take a leadership role with respect to promoting diversity.

There are a variety of ways in which you can demonstrate diversity leadership, such as those listed below.

◆ During group discussions, take on the role of a moderator, who ensures that the ideas of people from minority groups are included, heard, and respected.

For example, encourage and reinforce the contributions of students who may be reluctant to speak up because of their minority status. Putting members with diverse cultures on the same team may serve to reduce prejudice, but only if each member's

Tips for Teamwork: Creating Successful Collaborative Learning Groups

1. **Teammates should have a common goal.**

   To help your team identify and work toward a common goal, plan to produce a final product that can serve as visible evidence of the group's effort and accomplishment (e.g., a completed sheet of answers to questions, a list or chart of specific ideas, or an outline). This will help keep the team focused and moving in a common direction.

2. **Teammates should have equal opportunity and individual responsibility for contributing to the team's final product.**

   For example, each member of the team should have equal opportunity to participate during group discussions and should be responsible for contributing something specific to the team's final product—such as a different perspective (e.g., national, global, or ethical) or a different form of thinking (e.g., application, synthesis, evaluation).

3. **Teammates should work interdependently—that is, they should depend on or rely upon each other to achieve their common goal.**

   Similar to a sports team, each member of the learning team has a specific position and role to play. For instance, each member of the team could assume a different role, such as:

   - manager—who assures that the team stays focused on their goal and doesn't get off track,
   - moderator—who assures that all members have equal opportunity to contribute,
   - summarizer—who identifies what the team has accomplished and what remains to be done, or
   - recorder—who keeps a written record of the team's ideas.

4. **Before beginning their work, teammates should take some time to interact informally with each other to develop a sense of team identity and group solidarity.**

   For example, take some "warm up" time for teammates to get to know each other's names and interests before tackling the learning task. Teammates need to feel comfortable with each other in order for them to feel comfortable about sharing personal thoughts and feelings, particularly if the team is comprised of individuals from diverse backgrounds.

5. **Teamwork should take place in a friendly, informal setting.**

   The surrounding atmosphere can influence the nature and quality of interaction among members of the group. People are more likely to work openly and collaboratively with others when they are in a social environment that is warm and friendly. For example, a living room or a lounge area would provide a more informal and friendlier atmosphere than a classroom or library.

6. **Learning teams should occasionally change membership so that each member gets an opportunity to work with different individuals from other ethnic or racial groups.**

   If someone with a prejudice toward a certain ethnic or racial group has the experience of working on multiple teams, which include different individuals from the same racial or ethnic group, the prejudiced person is less likely to conclude that any positive experience was due to having interacted with someone who was an "exception to the rule."

When contact between people from diverse groups takes place under the above conditions, it can have the most powerful effects on diversity appreciation and team learning. Working in teams under these conditions is a win-win situation: Prejudice is decreased, and at the same time, learning is increased.

References: Amir (1969); Allport (1979); Aronson, Wilson, & Akert (2005); Cook (1984); Sherif et al. (1961); and Wilder (1984).

cultural identity and perspective is sought and acknowledged, not ignored or abolished (Baron, Byrne, & Brauscombe, 2006).

◆ Serve as a community builder by identifying similarities or recurring themes you see across the ideas and experiences of students from varied backgrounds.

   For example, all humans live in communities, develop relationships, have emotional needs, and undergo life experiences that affect their self-esteem and personal identity. So, be on the lookout for patterns of unity that underlie diversity.

   Diversity without unity allows for no sense of community and can lead to feelings of group separation and divisiveness, because we fail to detect the deeper similarities that

·—· **CLASSIC QUOTE** ·—·

The nation's future depends upon leaders trained through wide exposure to that robust exchange of ideas which discovers truth out of a multitude of tongues.

—William J. Brennan, former Supreme Court Justice

lie beneath our more obvious differences. We need to dig more deeply to find the common ground from which our differences grow. By raising your fellow students' consciousness of the common or universal themes that bind different groups of people together, you can help ensure that highlighting diversity will not heighten divisiveness.

Remember: Diversity represents variations on the common theme of humanity. Although people have different cultural backgrounds, they are still cultivated from the same soil—they are all grounded in the common experience of being human.

◆ Take a stand against prejudice or discrimination by constructively expressing your disagreement with those who make stereotypical statements or prejudicial remarks. You may avoid risk by saying nothing, but your silence may be perceived by others to mean that you agree with the person who made the remark. A number of studies have shown that when a person in a group observes others making prejudiced comments, that person's prejudice can increase, perhaps due to the pressure of group conformity (Stangor, Sechrist, & Jost, 2001). On the other hand, if a prejudiced person sees that his views are out of line with others, particularly others who are liked or respected, the person's prejudice can be reduced (Baron, Byrne, & Brauscombe, 2006). So, by taking a leadership role and not remaining silent when people make prejudiced remarks, you may not only help reduce that one person's prejudice, you may also reduce the prejudice of others who heard the remark.

◆ Take the initiative in forming friendships with members of diverse groups. These friendships not only enrich your social life, they can also help reduce prejudice among members of your own group. Research indicates that when people see a member of their own group develop a positive relationship with someone from a group that they are prejudiced against, their prejudice tends to decline (Paolini, et al., 2004).

Remember: When you take a leadership role in modeling appreciation of diversity and combating prejudice in others, you are taking a stand for social injustice and for the ethical principle of *equity*—equal opportunity and impartial treatment of all people.

Furthermore, you are demonstrating responsible citizenship by doing something good for your community and, ultimately, your country. Let us not forget that the United States is a nation that was originally built and developed by members of diverse immigrant groups, many of whom left their native countries to escape different forms of prejudice and discrimination, and to experience the freedom of equal opportunity in America (Levine, 1996).

As a democracy, the United States is a nation that is built on the foundation of individual rights and freedom of opportunity, which are guaranteed by its constitution. When the personal rights and freedom of fellow citizens are threatened by prejudice and discrimination, the political stability and survival of any democratic nation is threatened.

Diversity and democracy go hand-in-hand; by appreciating the former, you preserve the latter.

Turn back to the diversity spectrum on page 252 of this chapter and look over the list of groups that make up the spectrum. Do you notice any groups that are missing from the list that should be added, either because they have distinctive cultures or because they have been targets of prejudice and discrimination?

·—· **CLASSIC QUOTE** ·—·

A progressive society counts individual variations as precious since it finds in them the means of its own growth. A democratic society must, in consistency with its ideal, allow intellectual freedom and the play of diverse gifts and interests.

—John Dewey, U.S. educator, philosopher, and psychologist

••• Summary and Conclusion

The growing diversity in America and on American college campuses represents a social resource that we can intentionally capitalize on to promote our personal development. By seeking out and learning from diversity, rather than separating ourselves from it, we gain a more complete understanding of our nation and our world; we sharpen our self-awareness and self-insight; we learn to think with greater complexity and creativity; we acquire cultural knowledge and intercultural communication skills that are relevant to career success; and we enrich our social lives by increasing the variety of human beings with whom we interact, network, and develop relationships.

Last, but certainly not least, diversity is an opportunity to develop your personal character and leadership. By serving as a moderator, mediator, and community builder, you assume the role of a leader who helps to build bridges of unity across islands of diversity.

> **Remember:** By being open to diversity and opposed to prejudice and discrimination, you also demonstrate character. You become a role model whose actions visibly demonstrate to others that diversity has both educational and ethical value—it's not only the *smart* thing to do; it's also the *right* thing to do.

••• Learning More through Independent Research

Web-Based Resources for Further Information on Diversity

Learn more about current issues relating to prejudice and discrimination by exploring the information provided at the following two Web sites.

Tolerance.org

This is the site of an educational and public service organization for people interested in fighting bigotry in America and creating communities that value diversity. It tracks hate groups, hate crimes, hate Web sites, and hate music, and it supplies research-based strategies for promoting social justice on campus and in the community. You can subscribe to a free newsletter that provides updates on the latest social, educational, and legal news relating to bigotry and diversity.

If you visit this site, try taking one of the *Hidden Bias Tests* that have been developed by psychologists at Harvard, the University of Virginia, and the University of Washington.

Amnesty.org

This is the Web site of Amnesty International (AI), which is a worldwide organization of people who are committed to preserving human rights. While Tolerance.org is a national organization, AI is an international movement that includes almost 2 million members from over 150 countries in every region of the world. Many of these people have very different political and religious beliefs, but they share the common concern and goal: to prevent violation of human rights. Its Web site includes strategies for protecting and promoting human rights, and information on how you can join this organization or its local volunteer groups.

If you visit this site, consider reading AI's *Universal Declaration of Human Rights*, which has been translated into more than 300 different languages for worldwide use.

CHAPTER 8

Diversity Self-Awareness

Further your diversity self-awareness by completing the following four exercises.

1. **Diversity Spectrum**

   We are members of different groups at the same time, and our membership in these groups can influence our personal development and self-identity. In the figure below, the shaded center circle represents yourself, and the six non-shaded circles represent six different groups that you belong to, which you feel have influenced your personal development.

   Fill in these circles with the names of those groups to which you belong that have had the most influence on your personal development. You can use the diversity spectrum that appears on the first page of this chapter to help you identify different groups. Do not feel you have to come up with six groups to fill all six circles. What is most important is to identify those groups that you think have had significant influence on your personal development or identity.

   After you identify these groups, take a moment to reflect on the following questions:

   a. Which one of your group memberships has had the greatest influence on your personal identity and why?

   b. Have you ever felt limited or disadvantaged by being a member of any group(s)?

   c. Have you ever felt that you experienced advantages or privileges because of your membership in any group(s)?

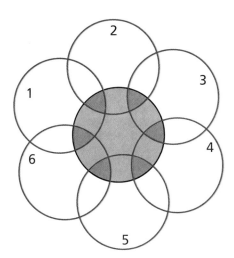

2. When Have You Felt Different?

   Describe an experience in your life when you felt that you were different from, or didn't fit in with, the majority of people around you.

   Why did you feel that way? How do you think members of the majority felt about you?

3. Questions about Other Groups or Cultures

   Write down, in question form, anything that you have wondered about people from a particular group or culture that is different than your own.

   Would you feel comfortable approaching and posing these questions to someone from this group or culture? Why or why not?

4. Personal Experience

   Have you ever been the personal target of prejudice or discrimination?

   What happened? Who was involved? How did you feel?

▼ CASE STUDY

Hate Crime: Racially Motivated Murder

Jasper County, Texas, has a population of approximately 31,000 people, 80 percent of whom are White, 18 percent Black, and 2 percent are of other races. The county's poverty rate is considerably higher than the national average, and its average household income is significantly lower. In 1998, the mayor, president of the Chamber of Commerce, and two councilmen were Black. From the outside, Jasper appeared to be a town with racial harmony, and its Black and White leaders were quick to state there was racial harmony in Jasper.

However, on June 7, 1998, James Byrd, Jr., a 49-year-old African-American male, was walking home along a road one evening and was offered a ride by three White males. Rather than taking Mr. Byrd home, Lawrence Brewer (31), John King (23), and Shawn Berry (23), three individuals linked to white-supremacist groups, took Mr. Byrd to an isolated area and began beating him. They then dropped his pants to his ankles, painted his face black, chained Mr. Byrd to their truck and dragged him for approximately 3 miles. The truck was driven in a zigzag fashion in order to inflict maximum pain on the victim. Mr. Byrd was decapitated after his body collided with a culvert in a ditch alongside the road. His skin, arms, genitalia, and other body parts were strewn along the road, while his torso was found dumped in front of a Black cemetery. Medical examiners testified that Mr. Byrd was alive for much of the dragging incident.

While in prison awaiting trial, Lawrence Brewer wrote letters to King and other inmates. In one letter, Brewer wrote: "Well, I did it and am no longer a virgin. It was a rush and I'm still licking my lips for more." Once the trials were completed, Brewer and King were sentenced to death. Both Brewer and King, whose bodies were covered with racist tattoos, had been on parole prior to the incident, and they had previously been cellmates. King had spent an extensive amount of time in prison where he began to associate with White males in an environment where each race was pitted against the other.

As a result of the murder, Mr. Byrd's family created the James Byrd Foundation for Racial Healing in 1998. On January 20, 1999, a wrought iron fence that separated Black and White graves for more than 150 years in Jasper Cemetery was removed in a special unity service. Members of the racist Ku Klux Klan have since visited the gravesite of James Byrd, Jr. several times, leaving stickers and other markers that have angered the Jasper community and Mr. Byrd's family.

Sources: *San Antonio Express News*, September 17, 1999, *Louisiana Weekly*, February 3, 2003, *Houston Chronicle*, June 14, 1998, Two Towns of Jasper, PBS.

Reflection and Discussion Questions

1. What social factors (if any) do you think led to the incident?

2. Could the incident have been prevented? If yes, how? If no, why not?

3. What do you think will be the long-term effects of this incident on the town?

4. How likely do you think it is that an incident such as this could occur in your hometown or near your college campus?

5. How would you react if it did happen?

Finding a Path to Your Future Profession

Career Exploration, Preparation, and Development

Learning Goals

The primary goal of this chapter is to supply you with specific strategies that you can use now and throughout your remaining years of college to promote your career exploration, preparation, and development.

Outline

Activate Your Thinking

Before you start digging into the meat of this chapter, take a moment to answer the following question: Have you decided on a career?

a. If yes, why did you pick this career? (Was your decision influenced by anybody or anything?)

b. If no, are there any careers you're considering as possibilities?

••• Why Career Planning Should Begin in the First Year of College

We know what you might be thinking: "Have I decided on a career? Give me a break; I've barely begun college!" This is probably the way most college seniors felt when they were first-year students. However, if you ask these seniors how they feel now, they would probably say something like: "I can't believe I'm about to graduate. How did time fly by so fast?" For these seniors and other students who will be graduating in this century, they are likely to continue working until age 75 (Herman, 2000). Also, consider the fact that once you begin full-time work, you will spend the majority of your waking hours at work. The fact is, the only other single activity that you will spend more time doing in your lifetime is sleeping. When you consider that such a sizable amount of our lifetime is spent working, plus the fact that work can influence our sense of self-esteem and personal identity, it is never too early to start thinking about your career choices.

 Remember: When you are doing *career* planning, you're also doing *life* planning; you are planning how to spend your future life doing what you want to do.

It is true that college graduation and career entry are years away, but the process of investigating, planning, and preparing for career success should begin during your first year of college. If you are undecided about a career, or have not even begun to think about what you'll be doing after college, don't be discouraged. In fact, you can join the club, because research indicates that the majority of college students are in the same boat. Three of every four beginning students are uncertain or have doubt about their career choice (Frost, 1991; Cuseo, 2005).

Even if you may have already decided on a career that you've been dreaming about since you were a preschooler, you will still need to make decisions about what specific type of specialization within that career you will pursue. For example, if you are interested in pursuing a career in law, you will eventually need to decide what branch of law you wish to practice (for example, criminal law, corporate law, or family law). You will also need to decide about what employment sector or type of industry you'd like to work in, such as: for profit, non-profit, education, or government. Each of these sectors will provide you with different options relating to the same career. For example, a student who is interested in an advertising career may work for an advertising agency (for profit) to encourage the purchase of a certain product, or may work in the non-profit sector to create a campaign for increasing public awareness of safety issues (e.g., persuade the public not to drink and drive). This student could also decide to create an effective advertisement designed to increase reading (education sector), or attempt to persuade people to enter public service positions (government). As these examples illustrate, there are still many options to consider and decisions to be made, even if you have decided on a particular career path.

Thus, no matter how certain or uncertain you are about your career path at this point in time, you will need to begin exploring different career options and start taking your first steps toward formulating a career development plan.

●●● Career Exploration and Development Strategies

Reaching an effective decision about a career involves four steps:

Step 1. Awareness of yourself—such as your personal abilities, interests, and values.

Step 2. Awareness of your options—the variety of choices (career fields) available to you.

Step 3. Awareness of what particular options (careers) best fit you—that is, deciding on what are the best matches for your personal abilities, interests, and values.

Step 4. Awareness of how to prepare for and gain entry into the career of your choice.

Step 1. Self-Awareness

The more you know about yourself, the better your choices and decisions will be. Self-awareness is a particularly important step to take when making career decisions because the career you choose to pursue says a lot about who you are and what you want from life. Your personal identity and life goals should not be based on or built around your career choice; instead, it should be the other way around: **Your personal identity and life goals should be considered first and should provide the foundation on which you build your career choice.**

One way to gain greater self-awareness of your career interests, abilities, and values is by taking psychological tests or assessments. These assessments allow you to see how your interest in certain career fields compares with other students who have taken the same assessment, and how your interests compare with people working in different career fields who have experienced career satisfaction and success. These *comparative perspectives* can give you important reference points for assessing whether your level of interest in different careers is high, average, or low, relative to other students and working professionals. By seeing how your results compare with others, you may become aware of your distinctive or unique interests. Your Career Development Center is the place on campus where you can find these career-interest tests, as well as other instruments that may allow you to assess your career-related abilities and values.

In addition to career assessments, the learning styles instruments described in Chapter 3 may sharpen self-awareness of your personal interests and preferences, and may provide useful information for making career choices. Also, the self-assessment questions about your personal interests, abilities, and values that were included in Chapter 3 (pp. 83–84) to help you select a college major may also be used to help you select a career path.

Lastly, when making choices about a career, you may also have to consider one other important aspect of yourself: your personal needs. A personal "need" may be best understood as something stronger than an interest. When you satisfy a personal need, you are doing something that makes your life more satisfying or fulfilling. Psychologists have identified a number of important human needs that vary in strength or intensity from one individual to another. Listed in Box 9.1 are personal needs that we feel are the most relevant or important ones to consider when making decisions about careers.

Pierce Howard, author of *The Owner's Manual for the Brain*, puts it this way: "It is stressful to attempt to be someone different from who we are, to try to be solitary when our nature is to be gregarious. Being true to our nature is, in some ways, the ultimate goal. Attempting to be something different is an obstacle to that goal. Don't expect a recluse to be motivated to sell, a creative thinker to be motivated to be a good proofreader day in and day out, or a sow's ear to be happy in the role of a silk purse" (2000, pp. 386–387).

Personal Needs to Consider When Making Career Choices

As you read the needs listed in the box below, make a note after each one, indicating how strong the need is for you (high, moderate, or low).

When exploring career options, keep in mind how different careers may or may not satisfy your level of need for autonomy, affiliation, competence, and sensory stimulation, each of which is described below.

1. **Autonomy:** Need to work independently, without close supervision or control.

   Individuals high in this need may experience greater satisfaction working in careers that allow them to be their own boss, make their own decisions, and control their own work schedule. Individuals low in this need may be more satisfied working in careers that are more structured and involve a supervisor who provides direction, assistance, and frequent feedback.

2. **Affiliation:** Need for social interaction, a sense of belongingness, and the opportunity to collaborate with others.

   Individuals high in this need may be more satisfied working in careers that involve frequent interpersonal interaction and teamwork with colleagues or co-workers. Individuals low in this need may be more satisfied working alone, or in competition with others, rather than careers that emphasize interpersonal interaction or collaboration.

3. **Achievement:** Need to experience challenge and achieve a sense of personal accomplishment.

   Individuals high in this need may be more satisfied working in careers that push them to solve problems, generate creative ideas, and continually learn new information or master new skills. Individuals low in this need may be more satisfied with careers that do not continually test their abilities, and do not repeatedly challenge them to stretch their skills by taking on new tasks or different responsibilities.

4. **Sensory Stimulation:** Need to experience variety, change, and risk.

   Individuals high in this need may be more satisfied working in careers that involve frequent changes of pace and place (e.g., frequent travel), unpredictable events (e.g., work tasks that vary considerably from day to day), and moderate stress (e.g., working under pressure of competition or deadlines). Individuals with a low need for sensory stimulation may feel more comfortable working in careers that involve regular routines, predictable situations, and minimal levels of risk or stress.

 STUDENT PERSPECTIVE

"To me, an important characteristic of a career is being able to meet new, smart, interesting people."

—*First-year student*

STUDENT PERSPECTIVE

"I want to be able to enjoy my job and be challenged by it at the same time. I hope that my job will not be monotonous and that I will have the opportunity to learn new things often."

—*First-year student*

 STUDENT PERSPECTIVE

"For me, a good career is very unpredictable and interest-fulfilling. I would love to do something that allows me to be spontaneous."

—*First-year student*

Personal Story

　　While enrolled in my third year of college with half of my degree completed, I had an eye-opening experience. I wish this experience had happened in my first year, but better late than never (although earlier is best)! Although I had chosen a career during my first year of college, the decision-making process was not a good critical thinking, systematic one. I chose a major based on what sounded best, and would pay me the most money. Although these are not necessarily bad variables, the lack of a good process to determine these variables was bad. In my junior year of college I asked one of my professors why he decided to get his Ph.D. and become a professor. He simply answered, "I wanted autonomy." This was an epiphany for me! He explained that when he looked at his life he determined that he needed a career that offered independence, so he began looking at career options that would offer that. After that explanation, autonomy became my favorite word, and this story became a guiding force in my life. After going through a critical self-awareness process, I determined that autonomy was exactly what I desired, and a professor is what I became.

　　　　　　　　　　　—*Aaron Thompson, Professor of Sociology, and co-author of this text*

Figure 9.1 Personal Characteristics Providing the Foundation for Effective Career Choice

Taken altogether, there are four key aspects of yourself that should be considered when exploring careers: your personal *abilities*, *interests*, *values*, and *needs*. As illustrated in Figure 9.1, these are the four pillars that provide a solid foundation for effective career choices and decisions. You want to choose a career that you're good at, interested in, passionate about, and that fulfills your personal needs.

Lastly, since a career decision is a long-range decision that will involve your life beyond college, self-awareness should not only involve personal reflection about who you are now, it also involves *self-projection*—reflecting on how you see yourself in the more distant future. When you engage in the process of self-projection, you begin to see a connection between where you are now and where you want to be.

Pause for Reflection

Project yourself ten years into the future and visualize your ideal career and life.

Try to answer the following questions about your ideal future-life scenario:

1. *What are you spending most of your time doing during your typical workday?*
2. *Where and with whom are you working?*
3. *How many hours are you working per week?*
4. *Where are you living?*
5. *Are you married? Do you have children?*
6. *How does your work influence your home life?*

© JupiterImages Corporation.

Your career choice should make you look forward to going to work each day.

Ideally, your choice of a career would be one that leads to a future career scenario in which your typical workday goes something like this: You wake up in the morning and hop out of bed enthusiastically—eagerly looking forward to what you'll be doing at work that day. When you're at work, time flies by, and before you know it, the day's over. When you return to bed that night and look back on your day, you feel good about what you did and how well you did it. For this ideal scenario to have any chance of really happening or even coming close to happening, you have to select a career path that is true to yourself—that closely matches your abilities (what you do well), your interests (what you like to do), your values (what you feel good about doing), and your needs (what brings you satisfaction and fulfillment in life).

Step 2. Awareness of Your Options

In order to make effective decisions about your career path, you need to have accurate knowledge about the nature of different careers and the realities of the work world. The Career Development Center is the first place to go for this information, as well as for help with career exploration and planning. In addition to helping you explore your personal career interests and abilities, the Career Development Center is also your key campus resource for learning about the nature of different careers and for strategies on how to locate career-related work experiences.

"HUNTER OR GATHERER? THOSE ARE MY ONLY OPTIONS?"

There are many more career choices in today's work world than there were for our early ancestors.

The federal government lists more than 30,000 different career fields, many of which you may have never heard of, but which may represent good career options for you. You can learn about careers through nine major routes or avenues:

1. Reading about careers,
2. Becoming involved in co-curricular programs on campus relating to career development,
3. Taking career development courses,
4. Interviewing people in different career fields,
5. Observing people at work in different careers,
6. Internships,
7. Co-op programs,
8. Volunteer service, and
9. Part-time work.

Strategies for using each of these routes to acquire accurate information about careers are discussed below.

1. Reading about Careers

Your Career Development Center and your College Library are key campus resources where you can find a wealth of reading material on careers, either in print or online. Here are some of the most useful sources of written information on careers:

- *Dictionary of Occupational Titles (DOT)*
  (http://www.occupationalinfo.org)

  This is the largest printed resource on careers; it contains concise definitions of over 17,000 jobs. It also includes such information as:
  - ◇ specific work tasks that people in the career typically perform on a regular basis;
  - ◇ type of knowledge, skills, and abilities that are required for different careers;
  - ◇ the interests, values, and needs of individuals who find working in their careers to be personally rewarding; and
  - ◇ background experiences of people working in different careers that qualified them for their positions.

- *Occupational Outlook Handbook (OOH)*
  (http://www.bls.gov/oco)

  This is one of the most widely available and frequently used resources on careers. It contains descriptions of approximately 250 positions, including information on the nature of work, work conditions, places of employment, training/education required for career entry and advancement, salaries, careers in related fields, and sources of additional information about particular careers (e.g., professional organizations and governmental agencies). A distinctive feature of this resource is that it contains information about the future employment outlook for different careers.

There are many resources for finding information on careers, many of which can be accessed on the Internet.

- *Encyclopedia of Careers and Vocational Guidance* (Chicago: Ferguson Press)

  As the name suggests, this is an encyclopedia of information on qualifications, salaries, and advancement opportunities for a wide variety of careers.

- *Occupational Information Network (O*NET) Online* (http://online.onetcenter.org)

  This is America's most comprehensive source of online information about careers. It contains an up-to-date set of descriptions for almost 1,000 different careers, plus lots of other information similar to that found in the *Dictionary of Occupational Titles (DOT)*.

In addition to these general sources of information, the Career Development Center or College Library should have books and other published materials relating to specific careers or occupations (e.g., careers for English majors). You can also learn a lot about careers by simply reading advertisements for position openings. You can find them in your local newspaper or at online sites, such as careerbuilder.com and monstertrak.com. When reading job descriptions, note the particular tasks, duties, or responsibilities that they involve, and ask yourself if these positions fit your profile of abilities, interests, needs, and values.

2. Becoming Involved in Co-Curricular Programs on Career Planning and Development

Periodically during the academic year, co-curricular programs devoted to career exploration and career preparation are likely to be offered on your campus. For example, your Career Development Center may sponsor career exploration or career planning workshops, which you can attend free of charge. Also, your Career Development Center may organize a "career fair" in which professionals working in different career fields are given booths on campus where you can visit with them and ask them questions about their careers. (See the end-of-chapter assignment for questions that you could ask.)

We strongly encourage your involvement in co-curricular programs that relate to career exploration and development. They have already been covered by the cost of your tuition, so get your money's worth and take advantage of them. Research suggests that such programs have positive effects on college students' career planning and decision-making (Brown & Krane, 2000; Hildenbrand & Gore, 2005).

3. Taking Career Development Courses

Many colleges offer career development courses for elective credit. These courses typically include self-assessment of your career interests, information about different careers, and strategies for career preparation. The things that students do in these courses are what they should do anyway (on their own), so why not do them as part of a career development course and receive academic credit for doing them? Studies show that students who participate in career development courses experience significant benefits in terms of their career choice and career development (Pascarella & Terenzini, 2005).

It might also be possible for you to take an *independent study* course that will allow you to investigate issues in the career area you are considering. An independent study is a project that you work out with a faculty member, which usually involves writing a paper or detailed report. It allows you to receive academic credit for an in-depth study of a topic of your choice, without having to enroll with other students in a traditional course that has regularly scheduled classroom meetings. You could use this independent-study option to choose a project that relates to a career you may be interested in pursuing. (To see if this option is available at your campus, check the college catalogue or consult with an academic advisor.) Also, if you have a free choice of a topic to write about in a writing course or to speak about in a speech course, consider researching your career interest and use this as a topic for your paper or presentation.

4. Information Interviews

One of the best and most overlooked ways to get accurate information about careers is to interview professionals who are actually working in careers that you are considering. Career development specialists refer to this strategy as "information interviewing." Although you might think that working professionals would have little interest in taking time out of their day to speak with a student, most of them do not mind being interviewed about their careers; in fact, they often enjoy it (Crosby, 2002).

Information interviews provide you inside information about what careers are really like, because you're getting that information directly "from the horse's mouth." Participating in information interviews can also help you gain experience and confidence with interview situations, which may help you prepare for future job interviews. Furthermore, if you make a good impression during the information interview, the person you interviewed may suggest that you contact him or her again after graduation in case there are any position openings. If there are, you might be the person being interviewed and possibly being hired.

Because information interviews can be a source of valuable information about careers (and provide possible contacts for future employment), we strongly recommend that you complete the information interview assignment that is included at the end of this chapter.

5. Observing People at Work in Different Careers

In addition to learning about careers from reading and interviews, you can experience careers more directly by placing yourself in workplace situations or environments that enable you to observe workers actually performing their jobs. Two college-sponsored programs that may allow you to observe working professionals are the following:

♦ Job Shadowing Programs: These programs allow you to follow around ("shadow") and observe a professional during a "typical" workday.

♦ Externship Programs: An externship is basically an extended form of job shadowing, which lasts for a longer period of time (e.g., 2–3 days).

Visit your Career Development Center to find out about what job shadowing or externship programs may be available at your college. If none are available in a career field that interests you, then consider finding one on your own, using strategies similar to those we recommend for information interviews in the end-of-chapter assignment (p. 310). The only difference would be that, instead of asking the person for an interview, you would be asking if you could observe that person at work. In fact, you might ask the same people who were willing to give you an information interview if they would also be willing to let you observe them at work. Just remember that one or two days of observation will give you some first-hand information, but not a thorough understanding of that field.

Pause for Reflection

If you were to observe or interview a working professional in a career that interests you, what position would that person hold?

6. Internships

In contrast to job shadowing or externships, whereby you observe someone at work, an internship program involves you with the work itself; that is to say, you actually *participate* and *perform* work duties related to the career. The word "internship" implies that you are involved "internally" with the work process, and actually doing the work—as opposed to an "externship" where you are "external" to the work process, observing someone else doing the work.

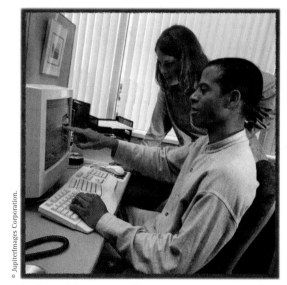

An internship is an excellent way to get experience in a career before you graduate.

Another distinguishing feature of internships is that you can receive academic credit, and, sometimes, financial compensation for the work you do. An internship usually totals 120 to 150 work hours, which may be completed at the same time you're enrolled in a full schedule of classes; or, internship hours could be completed during the summer.

A key advantage of an internship is that it enables college students to avoid the classic "catch-22" situation they often run into when interviewing for their first career position after graduation. The interview scenario often goes something like this: Employer asks the college graduate, "What work experience have you had in this field?" The recent graduate replies, "I haven't had any work experience because I've been a full-time college student." This situation can be avoided if students have an internship *during* their college experience. We strongly encourage you to participate in an internship while in college; this will enable you to beat the "no experience" rap after graduation and will distinguish yourself from many other college graduates. In fact, research reveals that students who have internships while in college are more likely to experience positive gains in development of career-related skills and find employment immediately after college graduation (Pascarella & Terenzini, 2005).

Although internships are typically available to students during their junior or senior year, there may also be internships available to first- and second-year students on your campus. If your school offers internships only for juniors or seniors, or does not offer internships that relate to your particular career interests, you can pursue an internship on your own. There are published guides that describe a wide variety of career-related internships, along with information on how to apply for them (e.g., *Peterson's Internships* and the *Vault Guide to Top Internships*). You could also search for internships on the Web (e.g., www.internships.com and www.vaultreports.com). Another good resource for possible information on internships is the local Chamber of Commerce in the town or city where your college is located, or the local Chamber of Commerce in your hometown.

"Got Experience?"—The "killer question" that college graduates can't answer after college unless they've had some career-related work experience during college (e.g., internships or volunteer service).

7. Cooperative Education (Co-op) Programs

A co-op is similar to an internship, but involves work experience that lasts longer than one academic term and often requires students to stop their course work temporarily in order to participate in the program. There are, however, some co-op programs that allow students to continue to take classes while working part time at their co-op position; these are sometimes referred to as "parallel co-ops." Students are paid for participating in co-op programs, but do not receive academic credit—just a notation on their college transcript (Smith, 2005).

Typically, co-ops are only available to juniors or seniors, but you can begin now to explore co-op programs by looking through your college catalog and visiting your Career Development

Center to see if your school offers co-op programs in career areas that may interest you. If you find any, plan to get involved with one, because it can provide you with an authentic source of career information and work experience.

The value of co-ops and internships is strongly supported by research, which indicates that students who have these experiences during college:

♦ are more likely to report that their college education was relevant to their career,

♦ receive higher evaluations from employers who recruit students on campus,

♦ have less difficulty finding an initial position after graduation,

♦ are more satisfied with their first career position after college,

♦ obtain more prestigious positions after graduation, and

♦ report greater job satisfaction (Gardner, 1991; Knouse, Tanner, & Harris, 1999; Pascarella & Terenzini, 1991, 2005).

In one statewide survey, which asked employers to rank a variety of factors in terms of their importance for hiring new college graduates, internships and cooperative education programs received the highest ranking from employers (Education Commission of the States, 1995). Furthermore, employers often report that when full-time positions become available in their organization or company, they are more likely to turn first to their own interns and co-op students (NACE, 2003).

8. Volunteer Service

In addition to helping your community, volunteer service can help *you*. It can serve to promote your career exploration and preparation by allowing you to experience different work environments and to gain work experience in fields related to your areas of service. For example, volunteer service to different age groups (e.g., children, adolescents, or the elderly) and service in different environments (e.g., hospital, school, or laboratory) can provide you with first-hand work experience, while simultaneously giving you a chance to test out your interest in possibly pursuing future careers relating to these areas of service. Volunteer experiences also enable you to network with professionals outside of college who may serve as excellent references and resources for letters of recommendation. Furthermore, if these professionals are impressed with your volunteer work, they may become interested in hiring you on a part-time basis while you're still in college, or on a full-time basis after you graduate from college.

Personal Story

I am an academic advisor and was once advising two first-year students, Kim and Christopher. Kim was thinking about becoming a physical therapist, and Chris was thinking about becoming an elementary school teacher. I suggested to Kim that she visit the hospital nearby our college to see if she could do volunteer work in the physical therapy unit. The hospital did need volunteers, so she volunteered in the physical therapy unit, and she absolutely loved it. That volunteer experience confirmed for her that physical therapy is what she wanted to pursue as a career. She completed a degree in physical therapy and is now a professional physical therapist.

I suggested to Chris, the student who was thinking of becoming an elementary school teacher, that he visit some of the local schools to see if they could use a volunteer teacher's aide. One of the schools did need his services, and Chris volunteered as a teacher's aide for about 10 weeks. At the halfway point during his volunteer experience, he came into my office to tell me that the kids were just about driving him crazy and that he no longer had any interest in becoming a teacher! He ended up majoring in communications.

Kim and Chris were the first two students whom I ever advised to get involved in volunteer work for the purpose of testing their career interests. Their volunteer experiences proved so valuable for helping both of them—in different ways—to make their career decision that I now encourage all students I advise to get volunteer experience in the field they're considering as a career.

—Joe Cuseo

It might also be possible to do volunteer work on campus by serving as an informal teaching assistant or research assistant to a faculty member. Such experiences are particularly valuable for students intending to go to graduate school. If you have a good relationship with any faculty members on campus who are working in an academic field that interests you, consider asking them if they would like some assistance, either with their teaching or research responsibilities. It is possible that your volunteer work for a college professor may enable you to make a presentation with your professor at a professional conference, or may even result in your name being included as a co-author on an article published by the professor you assisted.

Pause for Reflection

Have you done volunteer work prior to college? If you have, did you learn anything from your volunteer experiences that might help you decide what types of work best match your interests or talents?

9. Part-Time Work

Jobs that you hold during the academic year or during the summer should not be overlooked as sources of career information and as resume-building experiences. Part-time work can provide you with opportunities to learn or develop skills that may be relevant to your future career (e.g., organizational skills, communication skills, and ability to work effectively with co-workers from diverse backgrounds or cultures).

Also, work in a part-time position may eventually turn into a full-time career. The following personal story illustrates how this can happen.

Personal Story One student of mine, an English major, worked part time for an organization that provides special assistance to mentally handicapped children. After he completed his English degree, he was offered a full-time position in this organization, which he accepted. While working at his full-time position with handicapped children, he decided to go to graduate school on a part-time basis and eventually completed a Master's Degree in Special Education, which qualified him for a promotion to a more advanced position in the organization, which he also accepted.

—Joe Cuseo

It might also be possible for you to obtain part-time work experience on campus through your school's *work-study program*. A work-study job allows you to work on campus in a variety of possible work settings, such as the Business Office, college library, Office of Public Relations, or Computer Services. On-campus work can provide you with valuable career-exploration and resume-building experiences, and the professionals for whom you work can serve as excellent references for letters of recommendation to future employers. To see if you are eligible for your school's work-study program, visit the Financial Aid Office on your campus.

Learning about careers through first-hand experience in actual work settings (e.g., shadowing, internships, volunteer services, and part-time work) is critical to successful career exploration and development. These first-hand experiences represent the ultimate "career-reality test." They allow you direct access to information about what careers are truly like—as opposed to how they are portrayed on television or in the movies, which often paint an inaccurate or unrealistic picture of careers, making them appear more exciting or glamorous than they actually are. We strongly recommend using the strategies suggested in this section to get direct, first-hand experiences in real work environments, so you can make realistic career choices, rather than unrealistic choices that are based on second-hand information that reaches you indirectly—after passing through the sanitized and fantasized filter of popular media.

In summary, first-hand experiences in actual work settings equip you with five powerful career advantages. Such experiences enable you to:

1. Learn about what work is really like in a particular field,
2. Test your interest and skills for certain types of work,
3. Strengthen your resume by adding experiential learning to your classroom learning,
4. Acquire references for letters of recommendation, and
5. Make personal contacts that allow you to network with employers who may refer or hire you for a position after graduation.

So, get actively involved in first-hand work experiences. Use your campus resources (e.g., Offices of Career Development Center and your Financial Aid Office), read items posted on campus kiosks and hallway bulletin boards, use your local resources (e.g., Chamber of Commerce), and use your personal contacts (family and friends) to locate and participate in work experiences that are related to your career interests. When you land an internship, work hard at it, learn as much as you can from it, and build relationships with as many people as possible because these are the people who can provide you with future contacts, references, and referrals.

If you start gaining work experience early in college through volunteerism and part-time work, and participate later in an internship or cooperative education program as junior or senior, you will be able to graduate from college with an impressive amount of work experience under your belt (and on your resume).

Pause for Reflection

1. *Have you had first-hand work experiences?*

2. *Did you learn anything from these previous work experiences that may influence your future career plans?*

3. *If you could get first-hand work experience in any career right now, what career would it be?*

Step 3. Awareness of What Career Options Represent the Best Fit for You

When considering your career options, do not be misinformed and mislead by popular myths about careers. The following myths can lead students to make poor career choices or decisions.

Myth #1. Once you have decided on a career, you have decided on what you'll be doing for the rest of your life.

This is simply and totally false. The term "career" derives from the same root word as "racecourse," and like a racecourse, a career involves movement that typically takes different turns and twists. Like any race on any course, it's not how fast you start, but where you finish that matters most. This ability to move and change direction is what distinguishes a professional career from a dead-end job. According to the United States Bureau of Labor, Americans average four different careers in a lifetime; it also predicts that today's college graduates will change jobs 12 to 15 times, and these jobs will span across 3 to 5 different career fields (United States Bureau of Labor Statistics, 2005). You might find these statistics hard to believe because one of the reasons you are going to college is to prepare for a particular career. However, don't forget that the liberal arts component of your college education provides you with general, transferable skills that can be applied to many different jobs and careers.

> **Remember:** It is highly unlikely that your first career choice after college is what you will be doing for the remainder of your working life. Instead, your first career choice is likely to be a temporary choice, not a permanent choice that determines how you will make a living until the day you retire (or die).

Myth #2. You need to pick a career that's in demand, which will get you a job with a good starting salary right after graduation.

· — · CLASSIC QUOTE · — ·

Money is a good servant but a bad master.

—French proverb

Looking only at careers that are "hot" now and have high starting salaries can distract students from also looking at themselves, causing them to overlook the most important question of whether or not these careers are truly compatible with their personal abilities, interests, needs, and values.

Starting salaries and available job openings are factors that are external to us that can be easily "seen" and "counted," so they may get more attention and be given more weight in the decision-making process than things that are harder to see or put a number on, such as our inner qualities and whether they are really compatible with the choices we're considering. In the case of career decision-making, this tendency can result in college students choosing careers based exclusively on external factors (salaries and openings) without giving equal consideration to internal factors such as personal abilities, interests, and values. This, in turn, can lead some college graduates to choose and enter careers that eventually leave them bored, frustrated, or dissatisfied.

· — · CLASSIC QUOTE · — ·

There is perhaps nothing worse than reaching the top of the ladder and discovering that you're on the wrong wall.

—Joseph Campbell, American professor and writer

Also, keep in mind that careers which may be in high demand now may not be in such high demand by the time you graduate, nor may they remain in high demand for many years after you graduate. On the other hand, there will always be at least some demand for employees in almost all careers, because there will always be natural attrition (loss) of workers due to retirement or death.

The number of job offers you receive immediately after graduation and the number of dollars you earn as your first (starting) salary are very short-term and short-sighted standards for judging whether you've made a good career choice. Keep in mind the distinction between career *entry* and career *advancement*. Some college graduates may not bolt out of the starting gate and begin their career path with a well-paying first position, but they will steadily work their way up and get promoted to more advanced positions. Beware of advice from others who may tell you that you need to pick a career that's in demand. All this means is that you may be able to enter the field immediately and easily after graduation; it does not necessarily mean you will advance in that field just as quickly and easily. In other words, what is good in the short run (career entry) may not necessarily be good in the long run (career advancement).

Criteria to Consider When Evaluating Career Options

Effective decision-making requires identification of important factors that should be taken into consideration when evaluating your options, plus determining how much weight each of these factors should carry. As we have emphasized throughout this chapter, the factor that should carry the greatest weight or amount of influence in career decision-making is how compatible your choice is with your personal abilities, interests, needs, and values.

Suppose you have discovered more than one career option that is compatible with these four key dimensions of yourself. What other aspects of a career should be considered to help you reach a decision or make a selection? Many people would probably say salary, but as the length of the following list suggests, there are other important aspects or characteristics of careers that should be factored into the decision-making process.

1. Work Conditions

These would include such considerations as:

♦ the nature of the work environment (e.g., physical and social environment);

♦ geographical location of the work (e.g., urban, suburban, rural);

♦ work schedule (e.g., number of hours per week, flexibility of hours); and

♦ work-related travel (opportunities to travel, frequency of travel, locations traveled to).

2. Career Entry

Can you enter into the career without much difficulty, or does the supply of people pursuing the career far exceed the demand (e.g., professional acting), thus making entry into that career very competitive and difficult? If your first and ideal career choice is very difficult to enter, this doesn't mean you should automatically give up on it, but you should have a career to fall back on—in case you can't (or until you can) break into your ideal career.

3. Career Advancement (Promotion)

An ideal first job educates and prepares you to advance to an even better one. Does the career provide opportunities to be promoted to more advanced positions?

4. Career Mobility

Is it easy to move out of the career and into a different career path? This may be an important factor to consider because careers may rise or fall in demand, and because your career interests or values may change as you gain more work and life experience.

© JupiterImages Corporation.

When evaluating career options, be sure to take into account things like the amount of travel required.

5. Financial Benefits

This includes salary—including both starting salary and expected salary increases with greater work experience or advancement to higher positions; it also includes fringe benefits—such as: health insurance, paid vacation time, paid sick-leave time, paid maternity- or paternity-leave time, paid tuition for seeking advanced education, and retirement benefits.

6. Impact of Career on Personal Life

How would the career affect your family life, your physical and mental health, or your self-concept and self-esteem? Remember that you should not build your life around a career; you should build your career around your life. Your work life and personal life have to be considered simultaneously when making career choices, because the nature of your work can affect the nature (and quality) of your personal life.

Remember: A good career decision should involve consideration of how the career may affect all key dimensions of your "self" (social, emotional, physical, etc.) at all key stages of your life cycle—young adulthood, middle age, and late adulthood.

 Pause for Reflection

Think about a career you are considering, and answer the following questions:

1. *Why are you considering it? (What led or caused you to become interested in this choice?)*

2. *Would you say that your interest in this career is motivated primarily by intrinsic factors—that is to say, factors "inside" of you, such as your personal abilities, interests, needs, and values? Or, would you say that your interest in the career is influenced more heavily by extrinsic factors—that is to say, factors "outside" of you, such as starting salary, pleasing parents, meeting family expectations, or meeting an expected role for your gender (male role or female role)?*

3. *If money was not an issue and you could earn a comfortable living in any career, would you choose the same career?*

Don't let gender stereotypes limit your choice of a major or career.

Since the cost of college can be very high, family members paying this hefty cost (or helping you pay it) may sometimes get nervous about making such a steep financial commitment if you choose a career path that they are not familiar with, do not agree with, or do not understand (Helkowski & Shehan, 2004). If you happen to choose such a path, they may strongly oppose it, or may pressure you to change your mind. It may be tempting to reduce their anxiety, or your guilt about causing their anxiety, and conform to their wishes. However, **the decision you make about what career path to follow should really be *your* choice because it's really a decision about *your life*.** Although you should be grateful to those who have provided you with the financial support to attend college and should be open to their input, the final decision is yours to make.

Step 4. Awareness of How to Prepare for and Gain Entry into the Career of Your Choice

Whether you're keeping your career options wide open, or if you think you've already decided on a particular career, you can start preparing for success in any career field right now. In this section, we will discuss specific strategies that you can begin using immediately to prepare for successful career entry and development.

Self-Monitoring: Watching and Tracking Your Personal Skills and Positive Qualities

Many students think that a college credential or diploma itself is the passport to a good job and career success (Ellin, 1993; Sullivan, 1993). However, for most employers of college graduates, what matters most is not the credential but the specific skills and personal qualities an applicant possesses and can bring to the position (Educational Commission of the States, 1995). You can start building these personal skills and qualities by *self-monitoring*—watching or observing yourself, and keeping track of the skills you are using and developing during your college experience.

Although completing assignments, getting good grades, and getting a degree are all important end products, it is equally important to reflect on and keep track of the particular skills you've used, learned, or developed in the process of completing these products. More important than memorizing facts, figures, and formulas are the new skills you are acquiring or refining, the new perspectives or vantage points from which you are viewing things, and the different dimensions or elements of the "self" that you are developing. In Chapter 2, we provided a list of specific liberal arts skills, perspectives, and areas of self-development associated with a liberal arts education (pp. 52–55). We suggest that you save that list and use it periodically as a checklist to keep aware of, and to keep track of, the skills and perspectives you are developing in college. It is important to make a conscious and deliberate attempt to do so, because the development of skills and perspectives can occur subtly and subconsciously, often getting embedded within or buried below all the factual material you are consciously trying to learn. Skills and perspectives are mental habits, and like other habits that are repeatedly practiced, their development can be so gradual that you may not even notice how much growth is actually taking place (like watching grass grow).

Don't overlook the fact that *learning* skills are also *earning* skills. The skills you are acquiring in college may appear to be just *academic*-performance skills, but they are also *career*-performance skills. For instance, in the process of completing such academic tasks as taking tests and writing papers, you are often using a variety of career-relevant skills, such as: analyzing, organizing, communicating, and problem-solving.

·—· **CLASSIC QUOTE** ·—·

Whoever wants to reach a distant goal must take many small steps.

—Helmut Schmidt, former Chancellor of West Germany

Career development specialists recommend that you track your skills and "sell" them to employers and enhance your career prospects (Lock, 2000). Be sure to make a conscious effort to track the specific skills and perspectives you are developing in college, so you will be able to showcase and sell them to future employers.

One specific strategy you can use to track your developing skills is to keep a *career-development journal* of your completed academic tasks and assignments, accompanied by the specific skills you used to complete them. Also, be sure to record skills in your journal that you are developing in non-academic situations, such as those skills used while performing part-time jobs, personal hobbies, co-curricular activities, or volunteer services. Keep in mind that a skill is any positive or productive action that you can apply in different situations, which usually include most work situations. Since skills are actions, it is best to record them as action verbs in any career-development journal you may be keeping.

Personal Story

One day after class I had a conversation with one of my students (Max) about his personal interests. He said he was considering a career in the music industry and was now working part time as a disc jockey at a night club. I asked him what it took to be a good disc jockey, and in less than five minutes of conversation, we discovered that there were many more skills involved in doing his job than either of us had realized. He was responsible for organizing 3–4 hours of music each night he worked; he had to "read" the reactions of his audience (customers) and adapt or adjust his selections to their musical tastes; he had to arrange his selections in a sequence that periodically varied the tempo (speed) of the music he played throughout the night; and he had to continually research and update his music collection to track the latest trends in hits and popular artists. Max also said that he had to overcome his fear of public speaking in order to deliver announcements that were a required part of his job.

Although we were just having a short, friendly conversation after class about his part-time job, Max wound up reflecting on and identifying multiple skills that were involved in doing it. We both agreed that it would be a good idea to get these skills down in writing, so he could use them as selling points for future jobs in the music industry, or in any industry.

—Joe Cuseo

In addition to reflecting on your developing skills, also reflect on and keep track of your positive traits or personal qualities. While it is best to record skills as verbs because they represent actions, it may be best to record positive traits or qualities as adjectives because they are descriptions.

The key to discovering career-relevant skills and qualities is to get in the habit of stepping back from your academic work and out-of-class experiences to reflect on the skills and qualities you're developing, and then get them down in writing before they slip your mind. You are likely to find that many of the performance skills and personal qualities that you develop in college will be the very same ones that your future employers will seek from you in the workforce. Box 9.2 contains lists of some important career-success skills and personal qualities that you are likely to develop during your college experience.

BOX 9.2 *Snapshot* SUMMARY

Personal Skills Relevant to Successful Career Performance

The following behaviors represent a sample of useful *skills* that are relevant to success in a wide variety of careers (Bolles, 1998). As you read these skills, underline or highlight any of them that you have performed, either inside or outside of school.

advising	assembling	calculating	coaching	coordinating
creating	delegating	designing	evaluating	explaining
measuring	motivating	negotiating	operating	planning
researching	supervising	initiating	mediating	producing
proving	resolving	sorting	summarizing	synthesizing
translating				

The following represent a sample of *personal traits* or *qualities* that are relevant to success in multiple careers. As you read these traits, underline or highlight any of them that you feel you possess.

energetic	enthusiastic	ethical	outgoing	imaginative
industrious	loyal	precise	observant	open-minded
patient	persuasive	positive	productive	reasonable
reflective	sincere	tactful	thorough	flexible
broad-minded	cheerful	congenial	conscientious	considerate
courteous	curious	dependable	determined	prepared
punctual	persistent	productive		

Remember: Keeping track of your developing skills and your positive qualities is as important to your career success as completing courses, and compiling credits.

Self-Marketing: Packaging and Presenting Your Personal Strengths and Achievements

As we mentioned in the introduction to this book, there are many more advantages and benefits associated with the college experience than "getting a better job" and "making more money." However, national surveys of new college students indicate that these are the primary reasons why they're attending college (Sax, et al., 2004). We acknowledge that this is an important goal for beginning students, so we devote this section to a discussion of strategies for packaging and presenting the skills you've developed in college to future employers. To do this most effectively, it might be useful to view *yourself* (a future college graduate), as an eventual "product" and *employers* as future "customers" who could potentially purchase you and your skills. As a first-year student, it could be said that you are in the early stages of the product-development process. You want to begin the process of developing yourself into a high-quality product, so that by the time you graduate, your "finished product" will be one that employers will be interested in purchasing.

All the career-development strategies we've discussed thus far may be viewed as strategies for developing yourself into a quality product that will be attractive to future employers (or future schools) after graduation. However, using these strategies effectively to develop yourself into a high-quality product may still not close the deal. You also have to effectively *market* yourself so that employers or schools will notice your product, be attracted to it, and be persuaded to purchase it. An effective marketing plan will allow you to give employers a clear idea of what you have to offer and will reduce the likelihood that you will accept the first job you are offered (if it does not match your capabilities).

The major routes or channels through which you can effectively "advertise" or market your personal skills, qualities, and achievements to future employers are your:

1. College transcript
2. Co-curricular experiences
3. Personal portfolio
4. Personal resume
5. Letters of application (cover letters)
6. Letters of recommendations (letters of reference)
7. Networking skills
8. Personal interviews.

These are the primary tools you will use to showcase yourself to employers and that employers will use to evaluate you. We'll now discuss how you can strategically plan, prepare, and sharpen each one of these tools in a way that maximizes its power and persuasiveness.

1. Your College Transcript

A college transcript is a listing of all the courses you enrolled in, along with the grades you received in those courses. There are two key pieces of information included on your college transcript that can influence decisions to hire you, or influence decisions to admit you to graduate or professional school: (1) the grades you earned in your courses, and (2) the types of courses you completed.

Simply stated, the better your grades are in college, the better are your employment prospects after college. Research on college graduates indicates that the higher their grades are, the higher:

♦ the prestige of their first job,
♦ their total earnings, and
♦ their job mobility.

This relationship between college grades and career success exists for students at all types of colleges and universities, regardless of the reputation or prestige of the institution they are attending (Pascarella & Terenzini, 1991; 2005). In other words, research indicates that *how well* students do academically in college has a greater influence on their career success than does the name of the school that appears on their diploma.

The particular types of courses that are listed on your college transcript can also influence employment and acceptance decisions. Listed below are the types of courses that should be good selling points if they appear on your college transcript.

♦ Honors Courses

If you achieve excellent grades during your first year of college, you may apply or be recommended for the honors program at your school, which qualifies you to take courses that are more academically challenging. If you qualify for the honors program, we recommend that you accept the challenge. Even though "A" grades may be more difficult to achieve in honors courses, the presence of these courses on your college transcript clearly shows that you were admitted to the honors program and that you were willing to accept this academic challenge.

◆ Leadership Courses

Many employers hire college graduates with the hope or expectation that they will advance and eventually assume important leadership positions in their company or organization. Although a leadership course is not likely to be required for general education, or for your major, it is an elective course worth taking. It can enrich the quality of your college experience and the quality of your college transcript.

◆ Interdisciplinary Courses

An interdisciplinary course is one that interrelates or integrates two or more disciplines (academic fields). As we mentioned in Chapter 2, most career challenges cannot be fully addressed or understood by any one single field of study. For instance, careers that involve the challenge of effective management and leadership rely on principles drawn from multiple fields of study, including psychology (e.g., understanding human motivation), sociology (e.g., promoting harmonious group relationships), business (e.g., managing employees effectively), and philosophy (e.g., incorporating social ethics).

We recommend that you strongly consider taking at least one interdisciplinary course while in college. Even if interdisciplinary courses are not required for general education or your major, taking them will enable you to see connections across different subjects, which can be a very stimulating learning experience in its own right. Also, their appearance on your college transcript would clearly distinguish your transcript from those of most other college graduates. Furthermore, interdisciplinary courses may enhance your employment prospects because studies indicate that executives value new employees who have interdisciplinary experiences and who take an interdisciplinary approach to solving work-related problems. For instance, national surveys have shown that, "Business leaders point to the need for entry-level employees who have the practical ability to reach across artificial disciplinary boundaries to bring all relevant information to bear on concrete problems" (Daly, 1992).

◆ International or Cross-Cultural Courses

International or cross-cultural courses are those that cross national and cultural boundaries. The importance of such courses is highlighted by the fact that today's world is characterized by more international travel, more interaction among citizens from different countries, and more economic interdependence among nations than at any other time in world history (Office of Research, 1994). Boundaries between countries are also breaking down as a result of more international trading (importing-exporting goods), more multinational corporations, and more international communication—resulting from rapid advances in electronic technology (Dryden & Vos, 1999; Smith, 1994). As a result, employers have begun to place higher value on employees who have international knowledge and foreign language skills (Fixman, 1990; Office of Research, 1994). Taking courses that have an international focus, or which focus on cross-cultural comparisons, can help you develop the type of global perspective that strengthens the quality of your liberal arts education and the attractiveness of your college transcript to potential employers. In addition to gaining a global perspective from courses that emphasize international knowledge and foreign language skills, you might also consider participating in a study-abroad program in a country outside of the United States, which may be available to you during the regular academic year or during the summer.

Are you aware of what study-abroad opportunities are available at your college or university?

Are you seriously considering a study-abroad experience? If not, why not?

◆ Diversity (Multicultural) Courses

America's workforce is more ethnically and racially diverse today than at any other time in history, and it will grow even more so in the years ahead (United States Bureau of Labor Statistics, 2005). Successful career performance in today's diverse workforce requires sensitivity to human differences and the ability to relate to people from different cultural backgrounds (National Association of Colleges & Employers, 2003; Smith, 1997). Your participation in college courses relating to diversity awareness and appreciation, and your involvement in courses emphasizing effective multicultural interaction and communication, represent valuable additions to your college transcript that will strengthen your career preparation.

◆ Senior Seminars or Senior Capstone Courses

These courses are designed to put a "cap" or final touch on your college experience, helping you tie it all together and make a smooth transition from college to life after college. They may include such topics as resume building, portfolio preparation, job-interview strategies, job-location strategies, development of a college-to-career plan, and strategies for applying to and preparing for graduate or professional school after college. Some capstone courses may also involve a senior thesis or research project in your major field, which can provide a powerful finishing touch to your major and may be particularly valuable for helping you gain acceptance to graduate or professional school.

2. Your Co-Curricular Experiences

Participation in student clubs, campus organizations, and other types of co-curricular activities can be a very valuable source of experiential learning that can complement classroom-based learning and contribute to your career preparation and development. When college graduates are asked to look back at their college experience and identify what aspects of it helped prepare them for their career, they frequently report that their co-curricular experiences helped them develop skills that enhanced their work performance and career advancement (Marchese, 1990; Kuh, 1993). These personal reports have been confirmed by employers' on-the-job evaluations of college graduates, which indicate that the best predictor of success in careers involving management or leadership was previous involvement in co-curricular experiences during college, particularly those involving student leadership (Howard, 1986; Pascarella & Terenzini, 1991, 2005). It has also been found that student involvement in leadership experiences during college is associated with increased self-esteem (Astin, 1993).

Participation in campus organizations can be a valuable source of experience that contributes to your career preparation and development.

© PeterG, 2007. Under license from Shutterstock, Inc.

Because there is such a solid body of research supporting the value of co-curricular experiences, we strongly recommend your involvement in campus clubs and organizations. We especially recommend involvement with co-curricular activities that:

♦ allow you to develop leadership and helping skills (e.g., leadership retreats, student government, college committees, peer counseling, or peer tutoring),

♦ enable you to interact with others from diverse ethnic and racial groups (e.g., multicultural club, international club), and

♦ provide you with out-of-class experiences that relate to your academic major or career interests (e.g., student clubs relating to your college major or intended career field).

Keep in mind that co-curricular experiences are also resume-building experiences that provide evidence of involvement in your educational community and commitment to your school. So, be sure to showcase these experiences to prospective employers. Furthermore, the campus professionals with whom you may interact while participating in co-curricular activities (e.g., the Director of Student Activities or Dean of Students) can serve as valuable references for letters of recommendation to future employers, or graduate and professional schools.

Lastly, some colleges allow you to officially document your co-curricular achievements on a special transcript, often referred to as a *student development transcript* or *co-curricular transcript*. If your college offers such a transcript, we recommend that you take full advantage of it. When the idea of such a transcript was first introduced, national surveys were conducted to assess its potential usefulness. These surveys revealed that college admissions officials and employers of college students both thought the transcript would be very useful in helping them select applicants (Bryan et al., 1981). If your college does not offer such a transcript, be sure to describe your co-curricular experiences on your resume and your letters of application. Do not just cite or list the names of these activities. Provide details about the duties you performed and the specific skills that were required of you and acquired by you.

3. Personal Portfolio

You may have heard the word "portfolio," and associated it with a collection of artwork that professional artists put together to showcase or advertise their artistic talents. However, a portfolio can be a collection of any materials or products that illustrates an individual's skills and talents, or demonstrates an individual's educational and personal development. For example, a portfolio could include such items as written papers, exam performances, research projects, senior thesis, audiotapes or videotapes of oral presentations, artwork, DVDs of theatrical performances, or CDs of musical performances.

You can start the process of portfolio development right now by saving your best work and performances. Store them in a traditional portfolio folder, or save them on a computer disc and create an electronic portfolio. Another option would be to create a Web site and upload them there. Eventually, you should be able to build up a well-stocked portfolio that documents your skills and demonstrates your development for possible presentation to future employers or future schools. (For useful information and assistance on how to develop an elec-

The ritual of burning completed coursework in high school is not recommended in college. (Instead, save your best work, and include it in a personal portfolio.)

tronic portfolio, starting early in your first year and continuing through your senior year, go to www.kzoo.edu/pfolio.)

Pause for Reflection

If you were to predict what your best "work products" in college will be—those most likely to appear in your personal portfolio—what do you think they'd be?

---

4. Personal Resume

Unlike a portfolio, which contains actual products or samples of your work, a resume may be described as a listed summary of your most important accomplishments, skills, and credentials. If you have just graduated from high school, you may not have accumulated enough experiences to construct a fully developed resume. However, you can start now to build a "skeletal resume," which contains major categories or headings (the skeleton), under which you'll eventually include your specific experiences and accomplishments. See Box 9.3 for a sample skeleton resume. As you acquire experiences, you can then flesh-out the resume's skeleton by gradually filling in its general categories with specific skills, accomplishments, and credentials.

This process can be an excellent strength-recognition exercise that elevates your self-esteem. It essentially forces you to focus on your accomplishments by providing a visual record of them. Furthermore, developing a framework for organizing your accomplishments will also provide an outline for your personal goal setting—by serving as a visible reminder of the things you plan to do or accomplish. As you fill in and build up your resume, you can literally see how much you have achieved, which, in turn, can boost your confidence and motivation to continue achieving. Every time you look at your growing resume, you are reminded of your past accomplishments, which, in turn, can energize and motivate you to reach your future goals.

5. Letters of Application (a.k.a., Cover Letters)

A letter of application refers to the letter you write when applying for an employment position or acceptance to a school. When writing this letter, we recommend that you demonstrate your awareness or knowledge of:

◆ *you*—e.g., your personal interests, abilities, and values (use specific, concrete examples);
◆ the *organization* or *institution* to which you are applying—show them that you know something specific about its purpose, philosophy, programs, and the position you are applying for; and
◆ the *"match"* or *"fit"* between you and the organization (e.g., between the skills you possess and the skills that the position requires).

Focusing on these three major points should make your letter complete, and will allow the letter to flow in a natural sequence that moves from a focus on *you*, to a focus on *them*, to a focus on the *relationship* between you and them. Here are some suggestions for developing each of these three points in your letter of application.

◆ **Organize information about yourself into a past-present-future sequence of personal development.**
For instance, point out:

Constructing a Resume

Use this "skeletal resume" as an outline or template for beginning construction of your own resume and for setting your future goals. (If you have already developed a resume, use this template to identify and add categories that may be missing from your current one.)

Name (First, Middle, Last)
e-mail address

Current Address:	Permanent Address:
P.O. Box or Street Address	P.O. Box or Street Address
City, ST	City, ST
Phone #	Phone #

EDUCATION: Name of College or University, City, State
Degree Name (e.g., Bachelor of Science)
College Major (e.g., Accounting)
Graduation Date, GPA

RELATED WORK   Position Title, City, State   Start and stop dates
EXPERIENCES: (begin list with most recent date)

List skills used or developed

VOLUNTEER (COMMUNITY SERVICE) EXPERIENCES:

NOTABLE COURSEWORK
(e.g., leadership, international, or interdisciplinary courses)

CO-CURRICULAR EXPERIENCES
(e.g., student government, peer leadership)

List skills used or developed

PERSONAL SKILLS and POSITIVE QUALITIES:
List as bullets, and list as many as you think relate (directly or indirectly) to the position.

HONORS/AWARDS: In addition to those received in college, you may include those received in high school.

PERSONAL INTERESTS: Include items that showcase any special hobbies or talents that are not directly related to school or work. (Employers may use this information to see how well you may fit in with the work culture or relate to current employees.)

- where you have been—your past history or background experiences that qualify you to apply (academic, co-curricular, and work experiences)
- where you are now (why, at the present point in time, you've elected to apply to them)
- where you intend to go (what you hope to do or accomplish for them once you get there).

This past-present-future strategy should result in a smooth chronological flow of information about you. Also, by focusing on where you've been and where you're going, you demonstrate the ability to self-reflect on your past and self-project to your future.

When describing yourself, try to identify specific examples or concrete illustrations of your positive qualities and areas in which you have grown or improved in recent years. While it is important to highlight all your major strengths, this doesn't necessarily mean you must cover up any area in which you feel you still need to improve or develop. No human being is perfect; in fact, one indication of someone with a healthy self-concept is that person's ability to recognize and acknowledge both personal strengths and personal weaknesses—areas in need of further development. Including a touch of honest self-assessment in your letter of application demonstrates both sincerity and integrity. (And it may reduce the risk that your letter will be perceived or interpreted as a "snow job" that piles on mounds and pounds of self-flattery, under which even the tiniest ounce of self-honesty or personal humility is totally buried and concealed.)

◆ **Do some advanced research about the particular organization to which you're applying.**

In your letter of application, mention some specific aspects or characteristics of the organization that you've read or learned about; for example, one of its programs that impressed you or attracted your interest to them. This sends the message that you have taken the time and initiative to learn something about their organization, which is a very positive message for them to receive about you.

Pause for Reflection

Have you met a faculty member or other professional on campus who is getting to know you well enough to write a personal letter of recommendation for you?

If yes, who is this person, and what position does he or she hold on campus?

◆ **Make it clear why you feel there is a good fit or match between you and the organization to which you've applied.**

Point out how your specific qualities, skills, interests, or values are in line with the organization's needs or goals. By doing some research on the particular institution or organization that you're applying to, and including this information in your letter of application, you will immediately distinguish your application from the swarms of standard form letters that companies receive from applicants who mail-out multiple copies of the exact same letter to multiple companies.

6. Letters of Recommendation (a.k.a., Letters of Reference)

Your letters of recommendation can be one of your most powerful selling points. However, to maximize the power of your recommendations, you need to give careful thought to:

◆ *who* you want to serve as your references,
◆ *how* to approach them, and
◆ *what* to provide them.

Specific strategies for improving the quality of your letters of recommendation are suggested in Box 9.4.

7. Networking Strategies

Would it surprise you to learn that 80 percent of jobs are never advertised? This means that the jobs you see listed in a classified section of the newspaper and posted in a career development office or employment center represent only 20 percent of available openings at any given time. Almost one-half of all job hunters find employment through people they know or have

The Art and Science of Requesting Letters of Recommendation: Effective Strategies and Common Courtesies

⊙ **Select recommendations from people who know you well.**

Think about people with whom you've had an ongoing relationship, who know your name, and who know your strengths; for example, an instructor who you've had for more than one class, an academic advisor whom you see frequently, or an employer for whom you've worked for an extended period of time.

⊙ **Seek a balanced blend of letters from people who have observed you perform in different settings or situations.**

The following are key settings in which you may have performed well and key people who may have observed you perform well in these settings:

a. *the classroom*—for example, a professor for an academic reference

b. *on campus*—for example, a student life professional for a co-curricular reference

c. *off campus*—for example, a professional for whom you've performed volunteer service, part-time work, or an internship.

⊙ **Pick the right time and place to make your request.**

Be sure to make your request well in advance of the letter's deadline date (e.g., at least two weeks). First, ask the person if s/he is willing to write the letter, then come back with forms and envelopes. Do not approach the person with these materials in hand because this may send the message that you have assumed or presumed the person will automatically say "yes." This is not the most socially sensitive message to send someone whom you're about to ask for a favor.

Lastly, pick a place where the person can give full attention to your request. For instance, make a personal visit to the person's office, rather than making the request in a busy hallway or in front of a classroom full of students.

⊙ **Waive your right to see the letter.**

If the organization or institution to which you are applying has a reference-letter form that asks whether or not you want to *waive* (give-up) your right to see the letter, waive your right—as long as you feel reasonably certain that you will be receiving a good letter of recommendation.

By waiving your right to see your letter of recommendation, you show confidence that the letter to be written about you will be positive, and you assure the person who receives and reads the letter that you didn't inspect or screen it to see if it was a good one before sending it off.

⊙ **Provide your references with a fact sheet about yourself**, which includes your specific experiences and achievements—both inside and outside the classroom.

This will help make your references' job a little easier by giving them points to focus on. More importantly, it will help you because your letter becomes more powerful when it contains concrete examples or specific illustrations of your positive qualities and accomplishments (rather than sweeping generalizations or glittering generalities that could be said about anybody).

On your fact sheet, be sure to include any exceptionally high grades you may have received in particular courses, as well as volunteer services, leadership experiences, special awards or forms of recognition, and special interests or talents that relate to your academic major and career choice. Your fact sheet is the place and time for you to "toot your own horn," so don't be afraid of coming across as a braggart or egotist. You're not being conceited; you're just documenting your strengths.

⊙ **Provide your references with a stamped, addressed envelope.**

This is a simple courtesy that makes their job a little easier and demonstrates your social sensitivity.

⊙ **Follow up with a thank-you note** to your references about the time your letter of recommendation should be sent.

This is simply the right thing to do because it shows your appreciation, and it is the smart thing to do because if the letter hasn't been written yet, the thank-you note serves to gently remind your reference to write the letter.

⊙ **Let your references know the outcome of your efforts** (e.g., your successful admission into graduate school or acceptance of a job offer). This is a courteous thing to do, and your references are likely to remember your courtesy, which could strengthen the quality of any future letters they may write for you.

met, such as friends, family members, and casual acquaintances. When it comes to locating positions, *who* you know can be as important as *what* you know or how good your resume looks. Consequently, it's important to continually expand the circle of people who know your career interests and abilities, because they can be a powerful source of information about employment opportunities.

You can start expanding your circle of contacts by visiting the Career Development Center on your campus to find out what employers come to campus to interview graduating seniors. See if it is possible to obtain the names of representatives from those companies who have come to your college. Some of this information may also be available on your Career Center's online job listings. Also, ask if it is possible to receive the names of college alumni who may be working in fields related to your career interests. Some career centers have an online database that allow you to network with alumni who are working in careers that relate to your interests. Once you have selected a major, you may begin networking with seniors who will be graduating in your major by joining a club or organization that involves students majoring in the same field as you (e.g., philosophy club, business club). Lastly, be sure to share copies of your resume with friends and family members, just in case they may come in contact with employers who are looking for somebody with your career interests and qualifications.

8. Personal Interviews

A personal interview is your opportunity to make a positive "in-person" impression. You can make a positive first impression during any interview by showing that you've done your homework and have come prepared. In particular, you should come to the interview prepared with knowledge about yourself and your audience.

You can demonstrate knowledge about yourself by bringing a mental list of your strongest selling points to the interview and being ready to speak about them when the opportunity arises. You can demonstrate knowledge of your audience by doing some homework on the organization you are applying to, the people who are likely to be interviewing you, and the questions they are likely to ask. Try to acquire as much information as possible about the organization and its key employees that may be available to you online and in print.

To prepare for interviews, visit your Career Development Center and inquire about questions that are commonly asked during personal interviews. You might also try to speak with seniors who have interviewed with recruiters and ask them if certain questions tended to be frequently asked. Once you begin to participate in actual interviews, try to recall and make note of the questions you were asked. Although you may be able to anticipate some of the general questions that are asked in almost any interview, it's likely there will be unique questions asked of you that relate specifically to your personal qualifications and experiences. If these questions are asked in one of your interviews, there is a good chance they may be asked again in a future interview. So, try to get in the habit of mentally reviewing your interview as soon as you complete it, and attempt to recall the major questions you were asked while they're still fresh in your mind. This will also make it much easier to explain why you are a good candidate in a thank-you letter you may send the person who interviewed you. Consider developing an index-card catalog of questions that you've been asked during interviews—with the question on one side and your prepared response on the reverse side. The better organized and prepared you are for personal interviews, the quality of your answers will increase and the level of your anxiety will decrease.

When you know yourself (what about yourself you're going to say), and when you know your audience (who they're likely to be and what they're likely to ask), you should then be ready to answer what probably is the most important interview question of all: "What can *you* do for *us*?"

••• Summary and Conclusion

When it comes to converting a college degree into successful career entry, studies show that students who make this conversion most successfully have two characteristics in common: a *positive attitude* and *personal initiative* (Pope, 1990). They do *not* take a passive approach that assumes a good position will just fall into their lap, nor do they feel that they are owed a good career simply because they have a college degree. Instead, they become actively involved in the job-hunting process and use multiple job-search strategies (Brown & Krane, 2000).

In national surveys, employers rank attitude of the job applicant as the number-one factor in making hiring decisions, rating it higher in importance than such other factors as reputation of the applicant's school, previous work experience, and recommendations of former employers (Education Commission of the States, 1995; Institute for Research on Higher Education, 1995). Graduation from college with a diploma is not a guarantee that you'll be hired immediately after graduation, nor is it an automatic passport to a high-paying job. Your college degree will open career doors, but it's your attitude, initiative, and effort that will enable you to step through those doors and into a successful career.

This scenario can be avoided when students take a *proactive* approach to *career planning* before their senior year, and take an *active* approach to *job-hunting* during their senior year.

One study tracked a large number of college students after graduation to determine how successful they were in finding jobs. The results of this study indicated that those students who were most successful in getting outstanding career positions after graduation had two characteristics in common:

1. They engaged in career preparation and career development activities while in college, and
2. They took personal initiative during the job-hunting process.

These successful graduates were later interviewed and asked what advice they would give new college students. The advice they gave is nicely summarized in the following statement issued by a nationally known college advisor:

> *A big reason for their success, which shines through their answers and the advice they give, is initiative. They tell students to get involved in campus activities, but for substance, not for show; to take some career-related courses; to get internships and to have summer work experiences; and finally, to use initiative in investigating career possibilities and in looking for an actual job. Eighty-six percent of them said their own personal initiative was crucial to their being hired for their first job (Pope, 1990, p. 57).*

The advice of these successful graduates reinforces the key points made in this chapter and in the opening chapter of this book: Your career success *after* college depends on what you do *during* college. Touching all the bases that lead to *college* success will also lead to *career* success, namely:

1. **Get actively involved in the college experience**—get good grades in your classes and get work-related experiences outside of the classroom.

2. **Use your campus resources**—capitalize on all the career preparation and development opportunities that your Career Development Center has to offer.

3. **Interact and collaborate with others**—network with students in your major, college alumni, and career professionals.

4. **Take time for personal reflection**—deepen awareness of who you are, so you follow a career path that's true to you; and maintain awareness of your developing skills and personal qualities, so that you can successfully sell yourself to future employers.

Remember: When you make the most of your college experience, you get the most out of your college degree, and you maximize the value of both for your future career.

••• Learning More through Independent Research

Web-Based Resources for Further Information on Careers

For additional information relating to the ideas discussed in this chapter, we recommend the following Web sites:

For career descriptions and future employment outlook:
www.bls.gov/oco

For internships:
www.internships.com and www.vaultreports.com

CHAPTER 9

Conducting an Information Interview

One of the best and most overlooked ways to get accurate information about a career is to interview professionals who are actually working in that career, which is known as "information interviewing." An information interview has multiple advantages for your career exploration and development, which include:

◆ getting inside information about what a career is really like,

◆ networking with professionals in the field, and

◆ enabling you to gain experience and confidence with interview situations that may help you prepare for future job interviews.

STEPS

1. **Select a career that you may be interested in pursuing.**

   Even if you are currently keeping your career options wide open, pick a career that might be a possibility. You can use the resources cited on page 291 in this chapter to help you identify a career that may be most appealing to you.

2. **Find someone who is working in the career you selected and set up an information interview with that person.**

   To help locate possible interview candidates, consider members of your family, friends of your family members, and family members of your friends. Any of these people may be working in the career you selected and may be good interview candidates, or they may know other people who could be good candidates. The Career Development Center and the Alumni Association on your campus may also be able to provide you with graduates of your college, or professionals working in the local community near your college, who are willing to talk about their careers with students. Lastly, you might consider using the Yellow Pages or the Internet to find names and addresses of possible candidates. Send them a short letter or e-mail, asking about the possibility of scheduling a short interview. Mention that you would be willing to conduct the interview in person or by phone, whichever would be more convenient for them.

   If you do not hear back within a reasonable period of time (e.g., within a couple of weeks), send a follow-up message; if you do not receive a response to the follow-up message, then consider contacting someone else.

3. **Conduct an information interview with the professional who has agreed to speak with you.**

   Use the suggested strategies and potential questions in the following box.

Suggested Strategies for Conducting Information Interviews

◆ **Thank the person for taking the time to speak with you.**

This should be the first thing you do after meeting the person, before you officially begin the interview.

◆ **Take notes during the interview.**

This not only benefits you—by helping you remember what was said; it also sends a positive message to the person you're interviewing—by showing the person that his or her ideas are important and worth writing down.

◆ **Prepare your interview questions in advance.** Here are some questions that you might consider asking:

1. How did you decide on your career?
2. What qualifications or prior experiences did you have that enabled you to enter your career?
3. How does someone find out about openings in your field?
4. What specific steps did you take to find your current position?
5. What advice would you give to beginning college students about things they could start doing now to help them prepare to enter your career?
6. During a typical day's work, what do you spend most of your time doing?
7. What do you like most about your career?
8. What are the most difficult or frustrating aspects of your career?
9. What personal skills or qualities do you see as being critical for success in your career?
10. How does someone advance in your career?
11. Are there any moral issues or ethical challenges that tend to arise in your career?
12. Are members of diverse racial and ethnic groups likely to be found in your career field?

    This is an especially important question to ask if you are a member of an ethnic or racial minority group.
13. What impact does your career have on your home life or personal life outside of work?
14. If you had to do it all over again, would you choose the same career?
15. Would you recommend that I speak with anyone else to obtain additional information or a different perspective on this career field? (If the answer is "yes," you may follow-up by asking: "May I mention that you referred me?") This question is recommended because it's always a good idea to obtain more than one person's perspective before making an important choice or decision, especially one that can have a major influence on your life—such as a career choice.

If the interview goes well, consider asking if it might be possible to observe or "shadow" your interviewee during a day at work.

PERSONAL REFLECTION QUESTIONS

After completing your interview, take a moment to reflect on it and answer the following questions:

1. What information did you receive that impressed you about this career (if any)?

2. What information did you receive that distressed or depressed you about this career (if any)?

3. What was the most useful thing you learned from conducting this interview?

4. Knowing what you know now, would you still be interested in pursuing this career? (If "yes," why?) (If "no," why not?)

Career Choice: Conflict and Confusion

Josh is a first-year student whose family has made a great financial sacrifice to send him to college. He deeply appreciates the tremendous sacrifice his family has made for him and wants to pay them back as soon as possible. Consequently, he has been looking into careers that offer the highest starting salaries to college students immediately after graduation. Unfortunately, none of these careers seem to match Josh's natural abilities and personal interests, so he's confused and starting to get stressed out. He knows he'll have to make a decision soon because the careers with high starting salaries involve majors that have a large number of course requirements, and if he expects to graduate from college in four years, he'll have to start taking some of these courses during his first year.

Reflection and Discussion Questions

1. If you were Josh, what would you do?

2. Do you see any way that Josh might balance his desire to pay back his parents as soon as possible with his desire to pursue a career that's compatible with his interests and talents?

3. What other questions or factors do you think Josh should consider before making his decision?

Life-Management Skills

Managing Time and Money

Learning Goals

The primary goal of this chapter is to strengthen your skills and strategies for managing time and money.

Outline

Activate Your Thinking

When you read each of the following words, what are the first words that come to your mind?

Time: _____

Money: _____

The Importance of Time and Money Management

For many students, beginning college means the beginning of more independent living and the development of life-management skills. Two of those skills involve managing time and money. Each of them can serve as valuable resources to support your progress and success; however, they can also be sources of stress or distress that can block your progress. If you look back at your responses to "time" and "money" on the previous page, chances are that the first thoughts that came to your mind about these words were either very positive or very negative. Thus, we need to be consciously aware of these two key areas of our life and manage them effectively so that they work for us, not against us, and enable us to progress toward our life goals.

Strengthening your skills in each of these areas of life management will enhance your academic performance in college, as well as enrich your personal life and career performance beyond college.

Managing Time

Time management is a skill that grows in importance when your time is less structured or controlled by others, and you have more decision-making power about how your time will be spent. New students encounter an academic calendar and schedule in college that differs greatly from high school. It presents them with more free time to manage because less time is controlled or managed by others; for example, there is less mandatory "seat time" in college and less supervision by school authorities or parents.

Managing personal time is also an important issue for college students because they are expected to do more academic work on their own outside of class. Approximately four out of every five full-time college students are trying to complete this academic work while working part-time (U.S. Department of Education, 2002). Some students have family responsibilities outside of college as well. Thus, it is no surprise that research shows that the ability to manage time effectively plays a crucial role in college success (Erickson, Peters, & Strommer, 2006).

Simply stated, college students who have more difficulty managing their time have more difficulty managing college. In one study, sophomores who had an outstanding first year in college (both academically and socially) were compared with another group of sophomores who struggled during their freshman year. Interviews conducted with these students revealed one key difference between the two groups: The sophomores who experienced a successful first year repeatedly brought up the topic of "time" during the interviews. The successful students said they had to think carefully about how they spent their time and that they needed to budget time because it was a scarce resource. In contrast, the sophomores who experienced difficulty in their first year of college hardly talked about the topic of time at all during their interviews, even when they were specifically asked about it (Light, 2001).

Studies of working adults also indicate that managing time plays a pivotal role in their professional and personal success. Setting priorities and balancing multiple responsibilities (work, family, school) that compete for our limited time and energy can be a juggling act and is often a major source of stress for people of all ages (Harriott & Ferrari, 1996).

STUDENT PERSPECTIVES

"The major difference [between high school and college] is time. You have so much free time on your hands that you don't know what to do for most of the time."

—First-year college student, Erickson & Strommer (1991)

"In high school we were given a homework assignment every day. Now we have a large task assigned to be done at a certain time. No one tells [us] when to start or what to do each day."

—First-year student, Rhoads (2005)

STUDENT PERSPECTIVE

"I cannot stress enough that you need to intelligently budget your time."

—Words written by a first-year student in a letter of advice to students who are about to begin college

Personal Story I started the process of earning my doctorate a little later in life than some of my cohorts. I was a married father living with a preschool daughter. Since my wife left for work early in the morning, it was always my duty to get up and get my daughter's day going in the right direction. In addition, I had to do the same for me—which in most cases was tougher than what I had to do for Sara, my daughter. Three days of my week was spent on campus in class or in the library. We did not have quick access to research on computers then as you do now. The other two days of the work week and the weekend was spent on household chores, family time, and studying. In my mind, for me to be successful and finish my Ph.D. in a reasonable amount of time and have a decent family life, I had to adopt a schedule to help me manage my time. Needless to say, I had a very strict schedule to follow each day of the week. I got up, drank coffee, read the paper, took a shower, got my daughter ready for school and fed her breakfast. I then took her to school. Once I returned home, I would put a load of laundry in the washer, study, write, research, and spend time concentrating on what I needed to do to be successful from 8:30–12:00 every day. For lunch I had a pastrami and cheese sandwich and a soft drink while rewarding myself by watching *Perry Mason* reruns until 1:00. I then continued to study until it was time to pick up my daughter from school. Sometimes, I would start dinner. Each night I spent time with my wife and daughter and prepared for the next day. As you can see, I lived a life that had a preset schedule. By following this schedule, I was able to successfully complete my doctorate in a reasonable amount of time while giving my family the time they needed. By the way, I still watch *Perry Mason* reruns.

—*Aaron Thompson*

For these reasons, time management should be viewed not only as a college-success strategy, but also as a life-management strategy and life-success skill. Studies show that people who manage their time well report they are more in control of their lives and feel happier (Myers, 1993). In short, when you gain greater control of your time, you experience greater satisfaction with your life.

Strategies for Improving Time Management

Develop Self-Awareness about How You Spend Time

Have you ever asked yourself: "Where did all the time go?" or said to yourself: "I just can't seem to find the time!" One way to find out where your time went is by taking a time inventory (Webber, 1991) or doing a time analysis, which involves tracking your time by recording what you do and when you do it. By writing or mapping out how you spend time, you become more fully aware of how much time you actually have and where it actually goes, including patches of wasted time when you get little or nothing accomplished. You don't have to do this time analysis for more than a week or two; this should be long enough to give you a good sense of where your time is going and enough information to help you develop some strategies or habits for using time more effectively.

Pause for Reflection

What is your greatest "time waster?"

Is there anything you can do right now to stop or eliminate it?

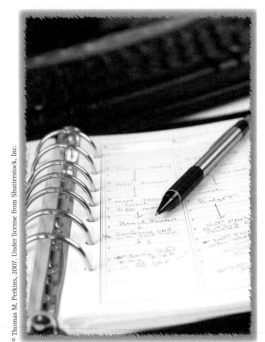

Using an assignment book is an effective way to keep track of your assignments and exams.

Itemize: Identify what specific tasks you need to accomplish and when you need to accomplish them.

Most of us have developed the habit of making lists for items we need to buy at the grocery store or lists of people we want to invite to a party. We make these lists to be certain that we don't forget anything or anybody. We can use exactly the same list-making strategy for tasks that we want to accomplish to ensure that we don't forget to do them, or forget to do them on time.

One practical strategy for itemizing your work tasks is by keeping an assignment booklet in which you list all your major assignments and exams for the term, along with their due dates. By pulling together all your work tasks from different courses in one place, you're less likely to overlook them or forget to do them.

Another itemizing option is to obtain a large calendar and record your commitments for the academic term and the dates they are due in the calendar's date boxes. Place the calendar in a location where it is in full view so you can't help but see it every day (e.g., on your bedroom or refrigerator door). If you regularly look at the things you should do, you're less likely to "overlook" and forget about them (or subconsciously push them out of your mind). Also, be sure that things you enjoy and look forward to are listed on the calendar and seen every day, because they can serve as strong incentives that motivate you to meet your work commitments.

Pause for Reflection

Do you have a calendar for the current academic term that you carry with you?

Do you carry a work list with you during the day?

If you carry either or both of the above items, why do you do so?

If you carry neither a calendar nor a work list, why do you think you don't?

Personal Story

As most of us who had moms in our household when we were kids, my mom was the person who ensured I got up for school on time. Once I got to school the bell would ring to let me know to move on to the next class. When I returned home I had to do my homework and chores. My daily and weekly schedule was dictated by someone else. When I came to college, I quickly realized that I needed to design a way to be organized, focused, and productive without the assistance of others. Where was mom when I really needed her? Since I came from a modest background, I had to work my way through college. Juggling schedules became an art for me. I knew the things that I could not miss (work and school) and the things I could miss (student organizations and girls). (Ok, not girls.) Thus, flexibility in my life existed only in terms of optional activities. After college, I spent 10 years in business, a world where I was measured on certain outcomes. It was during this time that I discovered a scheduling book. When I moved into academia as a professor I had other mechanisms to make sure I did what I needed to do when I needed to do it. This was largely based on when my classes were offered. Other time was dedicated to working out and spending time with my family. Now as an administrator, I have an assistant who keeps my schedule. She tells me where I am going, how long I should be there, and what I need to accomplish while I am there. Unless you take your parents with you or have an assistant, it is important to determine activities that are required and also allow time in your schedule for fun. Use a planner!

—Aaron Thompson

Prioritize: Rank your tasks in order of their importance.

Once your major commitments have been itemized by listing all the things that you need to do, they then need to be prioritized by deciding what order to do them in—i.e., what must be done first, what should be done next, and what could be done later. Prioritizing basically involves ranking your tasks in terms of their importance, with the highest ranked tasks appearing on the top of your list to ensure that they are tackled first. You want to be sure you invest your work time on work tasks that matter most.

How do you determine what tasks are most important and should be ranked highest? Two key criteria or standards of judgment can be used to help determine what tasks should be your highest priority:

1. Urgency—tasks that are closest to their deadline or due date should receive high priority (for example, finishing an assignment that's due tomorrow should receive higher priority than starting an assignment that's due next month);
2. Gravity—those that carry the heaviest "weight" should receive high priority (for example, if an assignment worth 100 points and another worth 10 points are due at the same time, working on the 100-point task should receive higher priority).

One strategy for making the task of prioritizing more manageable is to divide your tasks into "A," "B," and "C" lists (Lakein, 1973). The "A" list would include essential things—what you "must do," the "B" list would include important things—what you "should do," and the "C" list would include trivial things—what you "could do" or "might do" (e.g., if there's time left over after you've completed the tasks on lists "A" and "B").

Dividing our tasks in this fashion can help us decide how to divide our labor in a way that ensures we put "first things first." What we don't want to do is waste time doing less important things, and deceive ourselves into thinking that we're keeping busy and getting things done, when actually, we're doing things that just take our time (and mind) away from the more important things that should be done.

At first glance, itemizing and prioritizing may appear to be somewhat mechanical or clerical tasks. However, if we look at these mental tasks carefully, they require some of the key higher-level thinking skills we discussed in Chapter 6, such as:

a. analysis—breaking down commitments into specific tasks and breaking down time into its component elements or segments;
b. evaluation—critically evaluating our time-spending choices in terms of their importance or value; and
c. synthesis—organizing and integrating tasks into classes or categories based on priority.

Thus, developing self-awareness about how we spend time is a challenging exercise in self-reflection and higher-level thinking.

Develop a Time-Management Plan

Humans are creatures of habit. Regular routines help us organize and gain control of our life by doing things by design rather than leaving them to chance or accident, and planning our time increases the likelihood that we can make things happen for us rather than allowing them to happen to us—randomly or haphazardly. Thus, one valuable routine we can get into to help us organize our life and gain greater control of our life (and perhaps our destiny) is by planning how we're going to manage or spend our time.

Don't buy into the myth that you "don't have time to plan ahead" and that planning slows you down from getting started and getting things done. Time-management experts estimate that the amount of time you spend on planning your work time actually saves your total work time by a ratio of 3 to 1. In other words, for every one unit of time you spend planning, you save three units of time working; thus, 5 minutes of planning time will typically save you 15 minutes of total work time, and 10 minutes of planning time will save you 30 minutes of work time. This work-time savings probably results from the fact that planning ensures that before beginning our work, we know exactly what needs to be done and in what order to do it. This serves to reduce the number of mistakes we make due to "false starts"—starting our work but then having to re-start because we started off in the wrong direction, causing us to backtrack and reorganize our work after discovering its parts didn't fall naturally into an effective sequence or pattern. As the old proverb goes, "A stitch in time saves nine." Planning represents a "stitch" in time that saves "nine" stitches (units) of eventual work time.

••• Elements of a Comprehensive Time-Management Plan

Once we've accepted the notion that planning our time actually saves us time in the long run, the next thing to do is to design a time-management plan. Listed below are elements of an effective, total time-management plan.

A good plan should include:

a. a long-range plan for the entire academic term that identifies deadlines for reports and papers due toward the end of the term;
b. a mid-range plan for the upcoming month and week; and
c. a short-range plan for the following day.

The above timeframes may be integrated into a total time-management plan for the term by taking the following steps:

1. Identify the deadline dates of all assignments, i.e., the time when each of them must be completed (long-range plan),
2. Work backward from these final deadlines to identify dates when you plan to begin taking action on these assignments (short-range plan), and
3. Identify intermediate dates when you plan to finish particular parts or pieces of the total assignment (mid-range plan).

This three-stage plan should help you make steady progress throughout the term on assignments that are due later in the term, while reducing your tendency to procrastinate and your risk of running out of time at the end of the term.

A good time-management plan should include a balance of work and recreation.

A good plan should include reserve time to take care of the unexpected.

We should always hope for the best, but our plan should be built to anticipate and accommodate the worst. That is, our plan should include a buffer zone or safety net that builds in some extra time that can be used in case of any unforeseen or unexpected developments. Just as we should plan to save extra money in our bank in case emergency expenses crop up, we should also plan to save extra time in our schedule for the unexpected (e.g., unexpected tasks or tasks taking longer to complete than expected).

A good plan should include a balance of work and recreation.

Do not only plan work time; also plan time to relax, refuel, and recharge. Your overall plan shouldn't turn you into an obsessive-compulsive workaholic. Instead, your plan should contain a balanced blend of work and play, including activities that promote your mental and physical health—such as relaxation, recreation, and reflection.

Remember: A good time-management plan should help you stress less, learn more, and earn better grades, while leaving you more time for other important aspects of your life. Your plan should not only enable you to get your work done on time; it should also enable you to attain and maintain balance in your life.

What activities do you engage in:

a. *for fun?*

b. *to relieve stress?*

Your plan should have some flexibility.

Your time-management plan should be flexible enough to allow you to occasionally bend it without breaking it. Some people are immediately turned off by the idea of developing a schedule and planning their time because they feel it over-structures their lives and limits their freedom. It's natural for us to prize our personal freedom and resist any attempts to restrict it in any way. However, when you create a personal time-management plan, remember: It is *your* plan—you own it and you run it; it shouldn't run or own you. A good plan actually preserves your freedom by helping you get done what must be done, reserving free time for you to do what you want and like to do.

A good time-management plan should not force you to become a slave to a rigid work schedule. Just as work commitments and family responsibilities can crop up unexpectedly, so too can fun opportunities and other pleasant experiences. Your plan should allow you the freedom to modify your schedule so that you can take advantage of these enjoyable opportunities and experiences. The only restriction is that you should plan to make up the work time you lost. In other words, you can borrow or trade work time for play time, but don't steal it—you should plan to pay back the work time you borrowed by planning to make up that work at another time in your schedule.

· — · CLASSIC QUOTE · — ·

Some people regard discipline as a chore. For me, it is a kind of order that sets me free to fly.

—Julie Andrews, Academy-award winning English actress who starred in the Broadway musicals, "Mary Poppins" and "The Sound of Music"

Converting Your Time-Management Plan into an Action Plan

Step one is planning the work; step two is working the plan. A good action plan is one that guides your work on a day-to-day basis, provides a preview of what you intend to accomplish, and allows you to review what you actually accomplished. You can implement such an action plan simply by drawing up a daily list, bringing that list with you as the day begins, and checking off items on the list after getting them done. At the end of the day, review your list, and identify what was completed and what still needs to be done. The uncompleted tasks should become high priorities for the next day.

If you find yourself left with many unchecked items on your daily to-do list at the end of the day, it's possible that you may be spreading yourself too thin by trying to do too many things in a single day. You may need to be more realistic about the number of things you can reasonably expect to accomplish on a daily basis by shortening your daily list. However, not getting many of your intended tasks done may also mean that you need to tweak your work schedule by adding work time or subtracting activities that are taking time and attention away from your work (e.g., taking cell-phone calls during your planned work times).

Pause for Reflection

1. *Do you write down things you need to get done?*

_____ *never*

_____ *seldom*

_____ *often*

_____ *almost always*

If you selected "never" or "seldom," why do think this is?

2. By the end of a typical day, do you find that you accomplish most of the important tasks you hoped to accomplish?

_____ *never*

_____ *seldom*

_____ *often*

_____ *almost always*

Why?

Dealing with Procrastination

Procrastination Defined

The word "procrastinate" derives from two roots: "pro" meaning "forward" and "crastinus" meaning "tomorrow." Thus, it could be said that procrastinators do not abide by the proverb, "Why put off to tomorrow what can be done today?" Instead, the procrastinator's philosophy is: "Why do today what can be put off to tomorrow?" This philosophy results in a perpetual pattern of postponing what needs to be done until the last possible moment, then rushing anxiously to get it done by sacrificing quality, getting it only partially done, or not getting it done at all.

Research shows that three out of four college students label themselves as "procrastinators" (Potts, 1987). Over 80 percent of them procrastinate at least occasionally (Ellis & Knaus, 1977), and almost half do so consistently (Onwuegbuzie, 2000). Furthermore, these percentages seem to be on the rise (Kachgal, Hansen, & Nutter, 2001). Procrastination is such a serious issue for college students that some colleges and universities have opened "procrastination centers," which provide help exclusively for students experiencing problems with procrastination (Burka & Yuen, 1983).

Next time, I'll start sooner!

A procrastinator's idea of planning ahead and working in advance often boils down to this scenario.

However, procrastination is by no means limited to college students. It is a widespread problem that afflicts people of all ages and occupations (Harriott & Ferrari, 1996), which is why you see lots of books on the subject of time management in the self-help section of any bookstore, and why you see lots of people at the post office mailing their tax returns at the last possible moment ("Haven't filed yet," 2003).

Myths That Promote Procrastination

Before there can be any hope of putting a stop to procrastination, people need to let go of two very popular myths or misconceptions about time and performance.

Myth 1: "People work better under pressure" (e.g., on the day or night before something is due).

It is true that people can work more rapidly and with more nervous energy when they're under pressure, but that does not mean they're working more *effectively* and are producing work of higher *quality*. Because they're playing "beat the clock," their focus is no longer on how *well* they can do the job, but how *fast* they can do it and whether they'll be able to get it done before running out of time. This is a classic case of "haste makes waste" and a formula that is destined to result in an inferior work product or work outcome.

Don't confuse rapidity with quality; it typically takes time to do a high-quality job, particularly if that job requires higher-level thinking skills such as critical thinking, creative thinking, or problem solving. Academic work in college often requires these forms of deeper learning and complex thinking, which cannot be rushed because they require time for reflection. As we mentioned in Chapter 6, creative ideas take time to formulate, incubate, and eventually "hatch," which is not likely to happen under time pressure (Amabile, Hadley, & Kramer, 2002). Working under pressure on tasks that require higher-level thinking is like trying to complete a long, challenging test under a short time limit. What happens is we have less time to think, to attend to fine details, to double-check our work, and to fine-tune our final product.

Although you may work quicker under pressure, you are probably not working better.

Remember: Procrastinators often confuse desperation with motivation. Their belief that they "work better under pressure" is often just a rationalization to justify or deny the truth, which is that they will work *only* under pressure—i.e., they will work only when they are forced to work because they're under the gun to finally get the job done.

Myth 2: "Studying in advance is a waste of time because you will forget it all by test time."

This misconception is commonly used to justify procrastinating with respect to preparing for upcoming exams. As we demonstrate in Chapter 4, distributed (spread-out) studying is more effective than massed (crammed) studying for producing deeper learning and stronger memory. Furthermore, last-minute studying the night before exams often results in lost sleep time due to the need to pull "late- or all-nighters." This practice reduces memory for information that has been studied and increases test anxiety because of lost dream (REM) sleep—which is needed for memory formation and stress management (Hobson, 1988; Voelker, 2004).

Lastly, working under time pressure adds to performance pressure and performance anxiety by leaving you no margin of error to correct mistakes, no opportunity to get help along the way, and no chance to work around random catastrophes that may arise at the last minute (e.g., a head cold or a family emergency).

Pause for Reflection

Do you tend to put off work for so long that getting it done turns into an emergency or panic situation?

If your answer is "yes," why do you think this happens? If your answer is "no," what is it that you do to prevent this from happening?

Psychological Causes of Procrastination

Sometimes, procrastination has deeper psychological roots. People may procrastinate for reasons not directly related to poor time-management skills, but because of emotional issues involving self-esteem or self-image. For instance, studies show that a psychological strategy that some procrastinators use to protect their self-esteem is *self-handicapping*. People use this strategy (consciously or unconsciously) to give themselves a handicap or disadvantage so that if their performance turns out to be less than spectacular, they can say it was caused by the fact that they were performing under a handicap (Smith, Snyder, & Handelsman, 1982). For example, if their academic performance does not turn out to be great, they can conclude that they could have attained a higher grade if they just had more time, and that they had the ability or potential to achieve an "A"; they just didn't put in enough time to demonstrate their true ability. Or better yet, if they happened to get a good grade despite procrastinating, they could conclude they got it without putting in much time, which really proves how brilliant they are! Either way, the procrastinator's self-image is totally protected from any possible damage because conditions are arranged to guarantee that any performance that's less than outstanding can be attributed to external factors (lack of time), and any outstanding performance can be attributed to something within the person (extraordinary ability).

In addition to self-handicapping, research also shows that there are other psychological factors that can contribute to procrastination, such as the following:

a. fear of failure—feeling that it's better to postpone the job or not do it at all, rather than fail at it (Burka & Yuen, 1983; Soloman & Rothblum, 1984);

b. perfectionism—having unrealistically high personal standards or expectations, which lead to the belief that it's better to postpone work or not do it at all than to risk doing it less than perfectly (Flett et al., 1992; Kachgal, Hansen, & Nutter, 2001);

c. fear of success—fear that doing well will show that the procrastinator has the ability to achieve success and will be expected to do "repeat performances" in the future (Ellis & Kraun, 1977; Beck, Koons, & Milgram, 2000); and

d. indecisiveness—difficulty making decisions, including decisions about what to do or how to begin doing it (Anderson, 2003; Steel, 2003).

If these or any other issues are involved, it may mean that procrastination is merely a reflection of underlying psychological causes. These psychological causes must be dealt with first before procrastination can be overcome, and because they have deeper roots, it may take some time and professional assistance to uproot them. A good place to get such assistance is the Personal Counseling Office. The personal counselors on college campuses are professional psychologists who have been trained to deal with the psychological issues that can contribute to procrastination. Furthermore, these counseling psychologists are easily accessible to students because they provide their services on campus, and their services are free because their cost is covered by student tuition.

Self-Help Strategies for Beating the Procrastination Habit

Once inaccurate beliefs and emotional issues underlying procrastination have been dealt with, the next step is to overcome the actual habit of procrastinating. Listed below are our top strategies for minimizing or eliminating the procrastination habit.

Make the work meaningful.

Visualize your goals each time you feel procrastination rearing its ugly head. Take a moment to think about why the work is meaningful or important to achieve your goals and realize your dreams. Even if the nature of the work does not relate directly to your future aspirations, take a moment to think about how getting it done is a necessary stepping stone that will get you one step closer to your ultimate goal.

Make the start of work as inviting or appealing as possible.

Getting started can be a key stumbling block for many procrastinators. Procrastination often involves overcoming "start-up stress" that leads to work postponement and work avoidance (Burka & Yuen, 1983). If you have trouble starting your work, one strategy for jump-starting yourself is to arrange your tasks in a way that allows you to begin working on those tasks you find most interesting or are most likely to experience success. Once the work is begun, procrastinators may discover that the work wasn't as difficult, boring, or painful as they feared it would be; and as soon as they begin to make some progress, their apprehension starts to decline. As with any experience that's dreaded and avoided, the anticipation of the experience turns out to be worse than the actual experience itself. Once you are on a roll, you can ride the momentum you've created to attack your less appealing or more daunting tasks.

For many procrastinators, getting *started* is often their biggest obstacle.

Make the work manageable.

Work becomes less overwhelming and less stressful when it's handled in smaller chunks or pieces. You can conquer procrastination for large tasks by using a "divide and conquer" strategy: Divide the large task into smaller, more manageable units, then attack and defeat them one at a time.

Don't underestimate the power of short work sessions. They can be much more effective than longer sessions because it's easier to maintain maximum concentration and energy for shorter periods of time. If you're working on a large project or preparing for a major exam, dividing your work into short sessions gives you the opportunity to punch away at it in quick jabs and poke more and more holes in it. This will enable you to see the continual progress you're making and will gradually take away the pressure of having to go for the big "K.O." right before the bell.

Organization matters.

Research indicates that disorganization is a factor that contributes to procrastination (Steel, 2003). How well we manage and organize work materials can help us manage our time and reduce our tendency to procrastinate. Having the right materials in the right place at the right time can make our work easier to get to and easier for us to get going. When we've made a decision to get the job done, we don't want to waste time looking for the tools we need to begin doing it. For procrastinators, this time delay may give them just enough time to change their mind and not bother to start at all.

One simple but effective way to organize your college work materials is by developing your own file system. You can begin creating an effective file system by storing materials from different courses in different colored folders or notebooks. This will allow you to gather all materials relating to the same course in the same place, while keeping materials belonging to different classes in separate places. Such a system will help you get organized, help you beat procrastination by making it easier for you to start working, and help reduce stress caused by disorganization.

Location matters.

Where you work is as important as when and how you work. Distraction is a factor that has been found to contribute to procrastination (Steel, 2003). Thus, it may be possible for you to choose a work environment whose location and arrangement can combat procrastination by maximizing your concentration and minimizing distractions—which force you to stop and restart (or not restart at all).

Distractions tend to come in two major forms: social—e.g., people around who are not working, and media—e.g., cell phones, e-mailing, text messaging, CDs, and TV. Research indicates that the number of hours per week that college students spend watching television is *negatively* associated with academic success, including lower college GPA, less likelihood of graduating college with honors, and lower levels of personal development (Astin, 1993). So, pick a workplace and arrange your workspace to minimize media distractions.

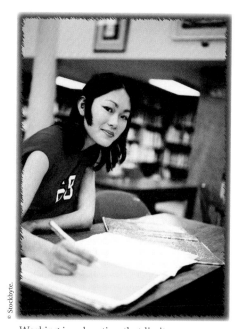

© Stockbyte.

Working in a location that limits your distractions will make it more difficult to procrastinate.

 Remember: Remove anything and everything from your work place that is not relevant to your work.

Pause for Reflection

List your two most common sources of distraction while working, and next to each distracter, identify a strategy that you might use to reduce or eliminate it.

Source of Distraction   *Strategy for Reducing This Source of Distraction*

_____   _____

_____   _____

Lastly, remember that you can arrange your work environment in a way that not only disables distractions but also enables concentration. You can "enable" your concentration by working in an environment that allows you easy access to work-support materials (e.g., class notes, textbooks, dictionary) and easy access to social support—such as working with a group of motivated students who help you stay focused and get your work done.

Adjust your sequence of work tasks to intercept procrastination at times when it's most likely to take place.

While procrastination frequently involves difficulty in starting work, it can also involve difficulty continuing and completing work (Lay & Silverman, 1996). As previously mentioned, if you have trouble starting work, it might be best to do your most stimulating tasks first. However, if you have difficulty maintaining or sustaining your work until it's finished, you might try scheduling work tasks that you find easier and more interesting *at the middle or end* of your planned work time. If tasks of greater interest and ease are scheduled at a time in the work sequence when you typically lose interest or energy, you may be able to maintain that interest and energy long enough to continue working until all your tasks are completed. Also, by doing your enjoyable tasks later, they can provide an incentive for completing your less enjoyable tasks first.

Momentum matters.

It often takes less effort to finish a task that's close to completion than it is to restart a task, because you can ride the momentum that you've already created. Furthermore, finishing a task can give you a sense of closure—the feeling of personal accomplishment and self-satisfaction that comes from knowing you've "closed the deal." Seeing a checkmark next to a completed task and realizing that it's one less task to do can increase your energy and drive to accomplish all the other tasks on your list.

••• Managing Money

Just as time management is a key life-management skill, so is money management. In fact, managing time and managing money have a lot in common. You may be familiar with the expressions, "Time is money," "A day late and a dollar short," and "I lost track of my time (or money)." Also, when people commit a crime, they pay their "debt" to society by doing time (jail or doing community service) and/or paying a fine. Both time management and money management require self-awareness of how they're "spent"; both can be saved or wasted, and since both come in limited quantities, they need to be budgeted for and saved or else we'll "run out" of them. Lastly, and perhaps most importantly, how we spend our time and money can tell us a lot about what really matters to us or what we truly value.

For new college students, greater personal independence often brings with it greater demands for economic self-sufficiency, critical thinking about consumerism, and effective management of personal finances. The importance of money management for college students is growing for two major reasons. One is the rising cost of a college education, which is leading more students to work while in college and to work more hours per week (Levine & Cureton, 1998). The rising cost of a college education is also requiring students to make more complex decisions about what options (or combination of options) they will use to finance their college education. Unfortunately, research indicates that many students today are not choosing financial strategies that contribute most effectively to their educational success in college and their long-term financial success after college (King, 2005).

A second reason why money management is growing in importance for college students is the availability and convenience of credit cards. For students today, credit cards are easy to get, easy to use, and easy to abuse. College students can do everything right, such as getting solid grades, getting involved on campus, and getting work experience while in college, but a poor credit history due to irresponsible use of credit cards in college can reduce students' chances of obtaining credit after college and their chances of being hired immediately after graduation. Research also indicates that accumulating high levels of debt while in college is also associated with higher levels of stress (Kiecolt, et al., 1986), lower academic performance (Susswein, 1995), and greater risk of withdrawing from college (Ring, 1997).

On the positive side of the ledger, studies show that when students learn to use effective money-management strategies, they can decrease unnecessary spending, prevent accumulation of significant debt, and reduce personal stress (Health & Soll, 1996; Walker, 1996).

Strategies for Managing Money Effectively

Develop Financial Self-Awareness

Effectively managing any personal habit begins with the critical first step of self-awareness. Developing the habit of effective money management begins with awareness of *cash flow*—the amount of money we have flowing in and flowing out. As illustrated in Figure 10.1, cash flow can be tracked by:

◆ watching how much money you have coming in (income) versus going out (expenses or expenditures) and

◆ watching how much money you have accumulated but not spent (savings) versus how much money you've borrowed but not paid back (debt).

Income for college students typically comes from one or more of the following sources:

a. scholarships or grants—which don't have to be paid back,

b. loans—which must be repaid,

c. salary earned from part-time or full-time work,

Figure 10.1 Two Key Avenues of Cash Flow

Income ⟷ Expenses

Savings ⟷ Debt

d.   personal savings, and

e.   gifts or other forms of monetary support from parents and other family members.

Sources of *expenses* (expenditures) may be classified into the following three categories:

1.   Basic needs or essential necessities—expenses that tend to be fixed because you cannot do without them (e.g., expenses for food, housing, tuition, textbooks, phone, transportation to and from school, and health-related costs).

2.   Incidentals or extras—expenses that tend to be flexible because spending money on them is optional or discretionary, i.e., you choose to spend at your own discretion or judgment. These expenses typically include:

     a.   money spent on entertainment, enjoyment, or pleasure (e.g., CDs, movies, concerts, club hopping, spring-break vacations) and

     b.   money spent primarily for reasons of promoting personal status or self-image (e.g., brand-name products, fashionable clothes, jewelry, or a "hot" new car).

3.   *Emergency* expenses—unpredicted, unforeseen, or unexpected costs (e.g., money paid for doctor visits and medicine because of illnesses or accidents).

Pause for Reflection

What do you estimate to be your 2 to 3 most expensive incidentals (optional purchases)?

Do you think you should reduce these expenses or eliminate them altogether?

Personal Story

When I was four years old living in the mountains of Kentucky, it was safe for a young lad to walk the railroad tracks and roads alone. My mother knew this and would send me to the general store to buy a variety of small items we needed for our household. Since we had very little money, she was aware of the fact that we had to be cautious and only spend money on the staples we needed to survive. I could only purchase items from the general store that I could carry back home by myself and the ones my mother strictly ordered me to purchase. Most of these items cost less than a dollar and in many cases you could buy multiple items for that dollar in the early 1960s. At the store I would hand my mother's handwritten list to the owners. They would pick the items for me, and we would exchange the items for my money. On the checkout counter there were jars with different kinds of candy or gum. You could buy two pieces for $.01. As a hard-working good son who was fulfilling the wishes of my parents, I didn't think there would be any harm in rewarding myself with two pieces of candy after doing a good deed. After all, I could devour the evidence of my disobedience on my slow walk home. Upon my return, my mother being the protector of the vault and the sergeant-of-arms in our household, would count each item I brought home to make sure I had been charged correctly. She always found that I had either been overcharged by one cent or that I had spent one cent. In those days, parents believed in behavior modification. After she gave me the direction that I so richly did not deserve, she would say: "Boy, you better learn how to count your money if you're ever going to be successful in life." I learned the value of $1 and the discomfort of overspending at a very young age.

—*Aaron Thompson*

Develop a Money-Management Plan

Once you're aware of the amount of money you have coming in—and from what sources, as well as how much money you're spending—and for what reasons, the next step is to develop a plan for managing this cash flow. The bottom line is to ensure that money you have coming in is equal to or greater than the money going out. If the amount of money you're spending exceeds the amount you have coming in, you're "in the red" or have negative cash flow.

STUDENT PERSPECTIVE

"I keep track of my money on Excel."

—First-year student

Strategic Selection and Use of Financial Tools for Tracking Cash Flow

Several financial tools or instruments are available to us that can be used to track your cash flow and manage your money. These cash-flow instruments include:

◆ checking accounts,
◆ credit cards,
◆ charge cards, and
◆ debit cards.

Checking Account

Long before credit cards were created, a checking account was the instrument most people used to keep track of their money. Checking accounts are still used by many people in addition to (or instead of) credit cards.

A checking account may be obtained from a bank or credit union, and its typical costs include a deposit ($20–25) to open the account, a monthly service fee (e.g., $10), and small fees for checks. Some banks charge customers a service fee based on the number of checks written, which is a good option if you don't plan to write many checks each month. If you maintain a high enough balance of money deposited in your account, the bank may not charge any extra fees, and if you're able to maintain an even higher balance, the bank may also pay you interest—known as an "interest-bearing checking account."

Along with your checking account, banks usually provide you with an ATM (Automatic Teller Machine) card that you can use to get cash. Look for a checking account that does not charge you fees for ATM transactions, but provides this as a free service along with your account. Also, look for a checking account that doesn't charge you if your balance drops below a certain minimum figure.

Personal Story I clearly remember my younger sister (by three years) struggling with the concept of budgeting while she was in high school and working in her first job. She called me at college to share her frustration about not having any money in her account. She said to me, "How can I be overdrawn? I still have checks left!"

—Viki Sox Fecas

Strategies for Using Checking Accounts Effectively

◆ Whenever you write a check or make an ATM withdrawal, immediately subtract its amount from your *balance*—i.e., amount of money remaining in your account to determine your new balance.
◆ Keep a running balance in your checkbook; it will ensure that you know exactly how much money you have in your account at all times. This will reduce the risk that you'll

write a check that "bounces," i.e., a check that you don't have enough money in the bank to cover. If you do bounce a check, you'll probably have to pay a charge to the bank and possibly to the business that attempted to cash your bounced check.

◆ Double check your checkbook balance with each monthly statement you receive from the bank. Be sure to include the service charges your bank makes to your account that appear on your monthly statement. This practice will make it easier to track errors—on either your part or the bank's part. (Banks can and do make mistakes occasionally.)

Advantages of a Checking Account

There are several advantages of a checking account:

◆ you can carry checks instead of cash;

◆ you have access to cash at almost any time through an ATM machine;

◆ it allows you to keep a very visible track record of income and expenses in your checkbook; and

◆ a properly managed checking account can serve as a good credit reference for future loans and purchases.

Credit Card (e.g., MasterCard, Visa, or Discover)

A credit card is basically money loaned to you by the credit-card company that issues you the card, which you pay back to the company on a monthly basis. You can pay the whole bill or a portion of the bill each month—as long as some minimum payment is made. However, for any remaining (unpaid) portion of your bill, you are charged a very high interest rate, which is usually about 18 percent.

Strategies for Selecting a Credit Card

If you decide to use a credit card, pay attention to its *annual percentage rate (APR)*. This is the interest rate you pay for previously unpaid monthly balances, and it can vary depending on the credit-card company. Credit-card companies also vary in terms of their annual service fee. You will likely find companies that charge higher interest rates tend to charge lower annual fees, and vice-versa. As a general rule, if you expect to pay the full balance every month, you're probably better off choosing a credit card that does not charge you an annual service fee. On the other hand, if you think you'll need more time to make the full monthly payments, you may be better off with a credit-card company that offers a low interest rate.

Another feature that differentiates one credit-card company from another is whether or not you're allowed a "grace period"—i.e., a certain period of time after you receive your monthly statement during which you can pay back the company without paying added interest fees. Some companies may allow you a grace period of a full month, while others may provide none and begin charging interest immediately after you fail to pay on the bill's due date.

Credit cards may also differ in terms of the credit limit (a.k.a., a "credit line" or "line of credit"), which refers to the maximum amount of money the company will make available to you. If you are a new customer, most credit-card companies will set a credit limit beyond which you will not be granted any additional credit.

Advantages of a Credit Card

If a credit card is used responsibly, it has some key advantages as a money-management tool. Its features can provide the following advantages:

- It helps you track your spending habits because the credit-company sends you a monthly statement that includes an itemized list of all your card-related purchases, which provides you with a "paper trail" of *what* you purchased that month and *when* you purchased it.

- It allows access to cash whenever and wherever you need it, because any bank or ATM machine that displays your credit card's symbol will give you cash up to a certain limit, usually for a small transaction fee. Keep in mind that some credit card companies charge a higher interest rate for cash advances than purchases.

- It enables you to establish a personal *credit history*. If you use a credit card responsibly, you can establish a good credit history that can be used later in life for big-ticket purchases such as a car or home. In effect, responsible use of a credit card shows others from whom you wish to seek credit (borrow money) that you're financially responsible.

> **Remember:** Do not buy into the belief that the *only* way you can establish a good credit history is by using a credit card. It's not your only option; you can establish a good credit history through responsible use of a checking account and by paying your bills on time.

Strategies for Using Credit Cards Responsibly

While there may be advantages to using a credit card, you only reap those advantages if you use your card strategically. If not, the advantages of a credit card will be quickly and greatly outweighed by its disadvantages. Listed below are some key strategies for using a credit card in a way that maximizes its advantages and minimizes its disadvantages.

- **Use a credit card only as a convenience for making purchases and tracking the purchases you make; do not use it as a tool for obtaining a long-term loan.**

A credit card's main money-management advantage is that it allows you to make purchases with plastic instead of cash. The credit card allows you the convenience of not carrying around cash and enables you to receive a monthly statement of your purchases from the credit-card company, which makes it easier for you to track and analyze your spending habits.

The "credit" provided by a credit card should be seen simply as a short-term loan that must be paid back at the end of every month.

> **Remember:** Do not use credit cards for long-term credit or long-term loans because their interest rates are outrageously high. Paying such a high rate of interest for a loan represents a very ineffective (and irresponsible) money-management strategy.

- **Limit yourself to one card.**

More credit cards mean more accounts to keep track of and more opportunities to accumulate debt. You don't need additional credit cards from department stores or gas stations, or any other profit-making business because they duplicate what your personal credit card already does (plus they charge extremely high interest rates for late payments).

- **Pay off your balance each month in full and on time.**

If you pay the full amount of your bill each month, this means that you're using your credit card effectively to obtain an interest-free, short-term (one-month) loan. You're just paying *principal*—the total amount of money borrowed and nothing more. However, if your payment is late and you need to pay interest, you pay more for the items you purchased than their actual ticket price. For instance, if you have an unpaid balance of $500 on your monthly credit bill for merchandise purchased the previous month, and you are charged the typical 18% credit-card interest rate for late payment, you end-up paying $590: $500 (merchandise) + $90 (18% interest to the credit-card company).

In fact, credit-card companies make their money or profit from the interest they collect from cardholders who do not pay back their credit on time. Just as procrastinating doing your work is a poor time-management habit, procrastinating paying your credit-card bills is a poor money-management habit that can cost you dearly in the long run because of the high interest rate you pay.

Avoid paying these huge interest rates and prevent credit-card companies from becoming rich at your expense by paying your total balance on time. If you cannot pay the total amount owed, pay off as much of it as you possibly can rather than making the minimum monthly payment. If you keep making only the minimum payment each month and continue using your credit card, you'll begin to pile up huge amounts of debt.

> **Remember:** If you keep charging on your credit card while you have an unpaid balance or debt, you no longer have a grace period to pay back your charges; instead, interest is charged immediately on all your purchases.

Pause for Reflection

1. Do you have a credit card?

2. If yes, do you pay off your entire balance each month?

3. a. If you don't pay off your entire balance each month, what would you say is your average unpaid balance per month?

   b. What changes would you have to make in your money-management habits to be able to pay off your entire balance each month?

Charge Card (e.g., American Express)

A charge card works very similar to a credit card in that you are given a short-term loan for one month; the only difference is that you must pay your bill in full at the end of each month, and you cannot carry over any debt from one month to the next. Its major disadvantage relative to a credit card is that it has less flexibility—no matter what your expenses may be for a particular month, you must still pay up or lose your ability to acquire credit for the next month. For people who habitually fail to pay their monthly credit-card bill on time, this makes a charge card a smarter money-management tool than a credit card because the cardholder cannot continue to accumulate debt.

Debit Card

A debit card looks almost identical to a credit card (e.g., it has a MasterCard or Visa logo), but it works differently. When you use a debit card, money is immediately taken out or subtracted from your checking account. Thus, you're only using money that's already in your account (rather than borrowing money), and you don't receive a bill at the end of the month. If you attempt to purchase something with a debit card that costs more than the amount of money you have in your account, your card will not allow you to do so. Just like a bounced check, a debit card will not permit you to pay out any money that is not in your account. Like a check or ATM withdrawal, a purchase made with a debit card should immediately be subtracted from your balance.

A major advantage of the debit card is that it provides you with the convenience of "plastic," just like a credit card, but it prevents you from spending beyond your means and accumulating debt. For this reason, financial advisors often recommend using a debit card instead of a credit card (Knox, 2004; Tyson, 2003).

BOX 10.1 *Snapshot* SUMMARY

Financial Literacy: Understanding the Vocabulary of Money Management

As you read each of the financial terms in the following list, place a mark by any one whose meaning you did not previously know.

Account: a formal business arrangement in which a bank provides financial services to a customer (e.g., checking account or savings account).

Balance: amount of money in an account, or the amount of unpaid debt.

Budget: a plan for coordinating income and expenses such that sufficient money is available to cover or pay for expenses.

Credit: money obtained with the understanding that it will be paid back, either with or without interest.

Credit Line (a.k.a., *Credit Limit*): maximum amount of money (credit) made available to a borrower.

Debt: amount of money owed.

Default: failure to meet a financial obligation (e.g., a student who fails to repay a college loan "defaults" on that loan).

Deferred Student Payment Plans: a plan that allows student borrowers to temporarily defer or postpone loan payments for some acceptable reason (e.g., to pursue an internship or volunteer work after college).

Grant: money received that does not have to be repaid.

Insurance Premium: amount paid in regular installments to an insurance company in order to remain insured.

Interest: amount of money paid to a customer for deposited money (as in a bank account) or money paid by a customer for borrowed money (e.g., interest on a loan); interest is usually calculated as a percentage of the total amount of money deposited or borrowed.

Interest-Bearing Account: a bank account that earns interest if the customer keeps a sufficiently large sum of money in the bank.

Loan Consolidation: consolidating (combining) separate student loans into one new, larger loan in order to make the process of tracking, budgeting, and repayment easier. (Loan consolidation typically requires the borrower to pay slightly more interest.)

Loan Premium: amount of money loaned without interest.

Merit-Based Scholarship: money awarded on the basis of performance or achievement that does not have to be repaid.

Need-Based Scholarship: money awarded on the basis of financial need that does not have to be repaid.

Principal: the total amount of money borrowed or deposited, not counting interest.

Yield: revenue or profit produced by an investment above and beyond the original amount invested (e.g., higher lifetime income and other monetary benefits acquired from a college education that exceeds the amount of money invested in or spent on a college education).

Financial Tools for Saving Money

If you're taking in more money than you're spending, you are saving money, and you can invest the money you've saved in an account that will allow you to earn interest on your savings. This account can help you build up a *cash reserve* that can be used for future needs or used immediately for emergencies. Two major financial tools available to you for earning interest on savings are:

1. savings accounts and
2. money-market accounts.

Savings Account

A savings account can be opened at virtually any bank and will earn you interest on the money placed in your account. Usually, no minimum amount of money needs to be deposited to open a savings account, and you don't need to maintain a minimum amount of money in the account.

Money-Market Account

This account is just like a checking account; however, it allows you to write only a limited number of checks, and you're not charged for the checks you use.

If you plan on writing no more than three checks per month, and can continually maintain a minimum balance in your account, you're better off investing your savings in a money-market account than in a savings account because a money-market account will typically pay a higher rate of interest.

Developing Personal Money-Saving Strategies and Habits

The ultimate goal of money management is to save money and avoid debt. Here are some specific strategies for accomplishing this goal.

Prepare a personal budget.

A budget is simply a plan for coordinating income and expenses to ensure that your cash flow leaves you with sufficient money to cover your expenses. A budget helps you maintain awareness of your financial state or condition, and enables you to be your own accountant by keeping track of your money.

Just like managing and budgeting our time, the key first step in managing and budgeting our money involves prioritizing. In the case of money management, prioritizing first involves identifying our most important expenses—necessities that are indispensable and that we must have to survive—as opposed to incidentals that are dispensable because we can really live without them.

Some people can easily confuse essentials and incidentals. For instance, if a piece of merchandise happens to be on sale, what this means is that it may be a great bargain for consumers; however, it doesn't mean that we have to consume (purchase) it before somebody else does.

Remember: Remaining consciously aware of the distinction between life's *essentials* that must be purchased, and *incidentals* that may or may not be purchased, is an important first step toward preparing an effective budget that enables you to save money and escape debt.

· — · CLASSIC QUOTE · — ·

A penny saved is a penny earned.

—Ben Franklin, eighteenth-century inventor, politician, and co-signer of the *Declaration of Independence*

STUDENT PERSPECTIVE

"I need to pay attention to my balance more closely and actually allot certain amounts for certain things."

—First-year student

STUDENT PERSPECTIVE

"I shouldn't buy random stuff (like hair dye) and other stuff when I don't need it."

—First-year student

We need to be aware of whether we're spending money on *impulse* or out of *habit* rather than out of actual need or after thoughtful reflection.

The fact is that humans spend money for a host of psychological reasons (conscious or subconscious) that are totally unrelated to actual need. For example, they spend to build up their self-esteem or self-image, to combat personal boredom, or to seek stimulation and an emotional "high" (Furnham & Argyle, 1998). Furthermore, people can become obsessed with spending money, shop compulsively, and become addicted to purchasing products. In fact, just as Alcoholics Anonymous (AA) exists as a support group for alcoholics, Debtors Anonymous (DA) exists as a support group for "shopaholics," and it includes a similar 12-step recovery program.

Make all your bills visible and pay them off as soon as possible.

When your bills are visible, they become memorable and you're less likely to forget to pay them, or forget to pay them on time. To increase the visibility of your bill payments, keep a financial calendar on which you record key fiscal deadlines for the academic year (e.g., due dates for tuition payments, residential bills, and financial-aid applications). Also, try to get in the habit of paying a bill as soon as you open it and have it in your hands, rather than setting it aside and running the risk of forgetting to pay it or losing it.

Live within your means.

This strategy is simple: Don't purchase what you can't afford. If you are spending more money than you're taking in, it means you're living *beyond* your means. To begin living *within* your means, you have two options:

1. Decrease your expenses (e.g., reduce your spending), or
2. Increase your income.

Since the vast majority of college students are already working while attending college (Orszag & Whitmore, 2001) and working so many hours that it's interfering with their academic performance or progress (King, 2005), the best option for most college students who find themselves in debt is to reduce their spending and begin living within their means.

 Pause for Reflection

Are you currently working for money while attending college?

If you're not working, are you sacrificing anything that you want or need because you lack money?

If you are working:

a. How many hours per week do you currently work?

b. Do you think that working is interfering in any way with your academic performance or progress?

c. Would it be possible for you to reduce the number of weekly hours you now work and still be able to make ends meet?

Economize

We can be frugal or thrifty without compromising the quality of our purchases by being intelligent consumers who use critical thinking skills when purchasing products. For example, we can pay less to see the exact same movie in the late afternoon than at night. Also, why pay more for brand-name products that are exactly the same as products with a different name? For instance, why pay 33 percent more for Advil or Tylenol when exactly the same amount of pain-relieving ingredient (ibuprofen or acetaminophen) is contained in generic brands? Often, when you pay extra for brand-name products, what you're paying for is the extra advertising that companies pay to the media and to celebrities to promote their products.

 Remember: Advertising creates product familiarity, not product quality. The more money manufacturers pay for advertising and creating a "well-known" or "brand-name" product, the more money you pay for the product—not necessarily because you're acquiring a product of higher quality, but most often because you're covering its high cost of advertising.

Don't let peer pressure determine your spending habits.

Downsize

Cut down or cut out spending for products that you don't need. Don't engage in conspicuous consumption just to "keep up with the Joneses" (your neighbors or friends), and don't allow peer pressure to determine your spending habits. Let your spending habits reflect your ability to think critically rather than your tendency to conform socially.

Live with others rather than living alone.

Although you lose privacy when you live with others, you save money. There are also social benefits of living with others if you enjoy being with them.

Give gifts of time rather than money.

Spending money on gifts for family, friends, and romantic partners is not the only way to show that you care. The point of gift giving is not to show others you aren't cheap or to show off your lavish spending skills. Instead, show off your social sensitivity by doing something special or making something meaningful for them. Gifts of time and kindness can often be more personal and more special than store-bought gifts.

Personal Story When my wife (Mary) and I were first dating, Mary was aware that I was trying to gain weight because I was on the thin side. (All right, I was skinny.) One day when I came home from school, I found this hand-delivered package in front of my apartment door. I opened it up and there was a homemade loaf of whole-wheat bread made from scratch by Mary. That gift didn't cost her much money, but the fact that she took the time to do it and remembered to do something that was important to me (gaining weight), it really touched me, and it's a gift that I've never forgotten. In fact, since I eventually married Mary and we're still happily married, I guess you could say that inexpensive loaf of bread was the "gift that kept on giving."

—Joe Cuseo

Develop your own set of money-saving strategies and habits.

You can save money by starting to do little things that can eventually become regular money-saving habits and add up to big savings over time. Consider the following list of habit-forming tips for saving money that were suggested by students in a first-year seminar class:

◆ Don't carry a lot of extra money in your wallet. (It's just like food; if it's easy to get to, you'll be more likely to eat it up.)

◆ Shop with a list—get in, get what you need, and get out.

◆ Put all your extra change in a jar.

◆ Put extra cash in a piggy bank that requires you to smash the piggy to get at it.

◆ Seal your savings in an envelope.

◆ Immediately get extra money into the bank (and out of your hands).

◆ Bring (don't buy) your lunch.

◆ Take full advantage of your meal plan—you've already paid for it, so don't pay twice for your meals by buying food elsewhere.

◆ Use e-mail instead of the telephone.

◆ Hide your credit card or put it in the freezer, so that you don't use it on impulse.

◆ Use cash (instead of credit cards) because you can give yourself a set amount of it and can clearly see how much of it you have at the start of a week and how much is left at any point during the week.

Pause for Reflection

Do you use any of the strategies on the above list?

Have you developed any effective strategies that do not appear on the list?

When making purchases, always think in terms of their long-term total cost.

It's convenient and tempting for consumers to think in the short term ("I see it; I like it; I want it; and I want it now.") However, long-term thinking is one of the essential keys to successful money management and financial planning. Those small (monthly) installment plans that businesses offer to get us to buy expensive products may make the cost of products appear immediately attractive and affordable in the short run. However, if you factor in the interest rates you pay on monthly installment plans, plus the length of time (number of months) you're making installment payments, you get a much more accurate picture of the product's total cost over the long run. This longer-range perspective can quickly alert you to the reality that the product's total cost is actually quite expensive and perhaps "out of your league."

Also, a product's sticker price represents its immediate or short-term cost. However, its long-term price sometimes involves additional "hidden costs" that don't relate directly to the product's initial price, but which must be paid for the product's long-term use. For example, the sticker price we pay for clothes does not include the hidden, long-term costs that may be involved if those clothes require dry cleaning. By just taking a moment to check the inside label, we can save ourselves this hidden, long-term cost by purchasing clothes that are machine washable. Or, to use an example of a big ticket purchase, the extra money spent to buy a new car instead of a used car does includes not only paying a higher sticker price, but also paying the hidden costs of licensing and insuring the new car (as well as any interest fees, if the new car was purchased on an installment plan). When you include these hidden and long-term costs in a new car's total cost, buying a good used car instead of a new car is a very effective money-savings strategy.

Remember: Avoid buying costly items impulsively. Instead, take time to reflect on the purchase you intend to make and do a cost analysis of its hidden or long-term costs, then integrate these invisible costs with the product's sticker price to generate an accurate synthesis and clearer picture of the product's total cost.

·—· **CLASSIC QUOTE** ·—·

If you would be wealthy, think of saving as well as getting.

—Ben Franklin

Long-Range Financial Planning: Financing Your College Education

As we previously mentioned, an effective money-management plan should be time sensitive and include the following financial-planning timeframes:

◆ short-range financial plan—e.g., weekly income and expenses

◆ mid-range financial plan—e.g., monthly income and expenses

◆ long-range financial plan—e.g., projected or anticipated income and expenses for the entire college experience, and

◆ extended long-range financial plan that extends into the future—e.g., expected income and debt after graduation, including a plan for repayment of any college loans.

Thus far, our discussion has focused primarily on short- and mid-range financial planning strategies that will keep you out of debt on a monthly or yearly basis. We turn now to issues involving long-term financial planning for your entire college experience and for life after college. While there is no one "correct" strategy for financing a college education that works best for all students, there are some important research findings about the effectiveness of different financing strategies that college students have used, which you should be aware of when doing long-range financial planning for college and beyond.

Research shows that obtaining a student loan and working no more than 15 hours per week is an effective long-range strategy for students to finance their college education and meet their personal expenses. Students who use this strategy are more likely to graduate from college, graduate in a shorter period of time, and graduate with higher grades than students who work part-time for more than 15 hours per week while going to college full-time, or work full-time and go to college part-time (King, 2002; Pascarella & Terenzini, 2005).

Studies also show that borrowing money in the form of a student loan and working part-time for 15 or fewer hours per week is the most effective financial strategy for students at *all income levels*, and it is *especially effective for students with low incomes*. Unfortunately, less than 6 percent of all first-year students use this strategy. Instead, almost 50 percent of first-year students choose a strategy that research shows to be least associated with college success: borrowing nothing and trying to work more than 15 hours per week. Students who use this strategy increase their risk of lowering their grades significantly and withdrawing from college altogether (King, 2005), probably because they have difficulty finding enough time to handle the amount of academic work required by college on top of the work outside of college for more than 15 hours per week.

Other students decide to finance their college education by working full-time and going to college part-time. These students believe it will be less expensive in the long run to attend college on a part-time basis because it will allow them to avoid any debt from student loans. However, studies show that when students go to college part-time so that they can work full-time, it sharply reduces the likelihood that they will complete a college degree (Orszag, Orszag, & Whitmore, 2001).

Even students who manage to eventually graduate from college, but take longer to do so because they have worked more than 15 hours per week for extra income, will eventually lose money in the long run. The longer they take to graduate means the longer they must wait to "cash in" on their college degree and enter higher-paying, full-time positions that require a college diploma. The pay per hour for most part-time jobs that students hold while working in college is less than half what they will earn from working in a full-time position as a college graduate (King, 2005).

Furthermore, studies show that two out of three college students have at least one credit card, and nearly one-half of students with credit cards carry an average balance of more than $1,500 per month (Wahlstrom & Williams, 1997). Debt level this high is likely to push many students into working more than 15 hours a week to pay off their high level of debt. ("I owe, I owe, so off to work I go.") The result is that these students take longer to graduate and earn a college graduate's salary, because they tend to enroll in fewer courses per term to give themselves extra work time to earn enough money to pay off their credit-card debt.

Instead of paying almost 20 percent interest to credit-card companies for their monthly debt, these students would be much better off obtaining a student loan at a much lower interest rate, which they don't begin to pay back until six months after graduation—when they will be making more money in full-time positions as college graduates. Despite the clear advantages of student loans compared to credit card loans, only about 25 percent of college students who use credit cards take out a student loan.

"My school sends me portions of my diploma as I make partial payments on my student loans."

Compared to other loans, student loans have a much lower interest rate, and they don't need to be repaid until after students are awarded their college diploma—which is awarded in its entirety after graduation, not in parts until the entire loan is repaid!

Keep in mind that not all debt is bad. Debt can be good if it represents an investment in something that will *appreciate* with the passage of time, i.e., it will gain in value and eventually turn into profit for the investor. Purchasing a college education on credit is a good investment because it will appreciate over time—in the form of higher salaries for the remainder of the investor's life. In contrast, purchasing a new car is a bad long-term investment because it immediately begins to depreciate or lose monetary value once it is purchased. The instant you drive that new car out of the dealer's lot, you immediately become the proud owner of a used car that's worth much less than what you just paid for it.

Pause for Reflection

In addition to college, what might be other good, long-term investments for you to make now or in the near future?

You may have heard the expression that "time is money." One way to interpret this expression is that when we spend more money, we must spend more time making money to pay for our spending habits. If you're going to college, spending more time to earn money to cover your spending habits often means spending less time studying, learning, completing classes, and earning good grades. You can avoid this vicious cycle by looking at your schoolwork as academic work that "pays" you back in terms of completed courses and higher grades. By putting in more academic time to complete more courses and earn better grades, you are "paid" back by increasing the likelihood you will graduate, graduate sooner, and start earning a full-time salary as a college graduate that will pay you about twice as much money per hour than you earn doing part-time work without a college degree (plus benefits such as medical insurance, dental insurance, and paid vacation time). Furthermore, the time you put into earning higher grades while in college should pay off immediately in your first full-time position after college because research shows that among students graduating in the same field, those with higher grades are more likely to earn higher starting salaries (Pascarella & Terenzini, 2005). Thus, our bottom-line recommendation is: **Work for better grades now; work for better pay later.**

You may need to defer or delay satisfying all your immediate material desires and postpone consumer gratification by making high-priced purchases later. Ultimately, financing a college education may require that you give serious thought to your current lifestyle choices and make firm decisions about what you can live with and live without. For example, a new set of wheels or a more private and spacious apartment may have to wait until you graduate.

Finally, be sure you take full advantage of your Financial Aid Office during your time in college. This is the campus resource that has been designed specifically to help you finance your college education. If you are in any way concerned about whether you are currently using the most effective strategy for financing your education, make an appointment of see a professional in your financial aid office. Also, periodically check with this office to see if you qualify for additional sources of income through different avenues, such as:

◆ part-time employment on campus,
◆ low-interest loans,
◆ grants, or
◆ scholarships.

Lastly, keep a watchful eye out for notices posted near your Financial Aid Office about financial-aid reminders, application deadlines and updates, as well as information about campus workshops designed to help you finance your education and manage your money.

Postponing immediate or impulsive satisfaction of material desires is a key element of effective college financing and long-term financial success.

 Pause for Reflection

Do you need to work part time to meet your college expenses?

If yes, do you have to work more than 15 hours per week to make ends meet?

If yes, is there anything you can do to change that?

●●● Summary and Conclusion

Mastering the skills of managing time and money are critical for success in college and in life beyond college. If we can gain better control over these practical aspects of our life, we can gain greater control over the quality of our life. On the other hand, if we ignore either one of them, we run the risk of increasing our stress level and decreasing our performance level. For instance, research indicates that procrastinators often feel miserable about their habit (Tice & Baumeister, 1997) and the work they produce is of poorer quality (Steel, Brothen, & Wambach, 2001; Wesley, 1994). Poor time management with respect to financial matters actually costs people money; for example, reports from H & R Block indicates that procrastinating on filing tax returns costs Americans an average of $400 a year, due to errors resulting from last-minute rushing to meet the deadline (Kasper, 2004).

There are two key features of both money and time management that cause each of these habits to be candidates for potential problems:

1. They are habits that people can fall into and practice so routinely that they do them without conscious self-awareness, and
2. The negative consequences of bad time- and money-management habits build up gradually and are not fully felt until a later point in time. Many years of research shows that the further away an event in time is, the less likely humans are to think about it and factor it into their day-to-day choices and decisions (Lewin, 1935; Ainslie, 1975; Elster & Lowenstein, 1992).

Just as problems of time and money management may have common causes, they may also have common solutions. The recurring themes of effective time and money management indicate that we should use the following higher-level thinking skills and related practices.

1. We should engage in reflective *analysis* of how we spend our time and money. This will allow us to become more consciously aware of our time-spending and money-spending habits, and enable us to know where all our time and money actually go.
2. We should engage in *synthesis* that integrates or "connects" our current decisions with their short-range, mid-range, and long-range consequences. This will allow us to see how our present actions affect the total, long-term picture (e.g., how current choices and decisions affect what happens at the end of the term, at the end of college, and life after college).
3. We should *evaluate* our priorities and create a plan that ensures we put our time and money into what we value the most (e.g., success in college and life).
4. We should *apply* our plan by putting into practice effective time- and money-management strategies on a day-to-day basis. Studies show that when people repeatedly practice effective life-management strategies, these strategies gradually become part of their regular routine and develop into natural habits. For example, when procrastinators repeatedly practice effective time-management strategies with respect to tasks that they procrastinate on, their procrastination habits begin to fade away and are replaced by more effective time-management habits (Ainslie, 1992; Baumeister, et al., 1994). The same results have been found for effective money-management habits (Health & Soll, 1996; Walker, 1996). Thus, when we become aware of what effective actions we should take and perform these actions consistently, they tend to turn into productive lifelong habits.

These four themes appear to be the keys to effectively managing time and money. They may also be the keys to effectively managing life.

●●● Learning More through Independent Research

Web-Based Resources for Further Information on Managing Time and Money

For additional information relating to the ideas discussed in this chapter, we recommend the following Web sites:

Time Management
www.counseling.uchicago.edu/resources/virtualpamphlets/time_management.shtml
www.time-management-guide.com/procrastination.html

Money Management
www.youngmoney.com/money_management
www.students.gov

Name _____ Date _____

Financial Self-Awareness: Monitoring Money and Tracking Cash Flow

DIRECTIONS:

Step 1.
Use the worksheet that follows these directions to estimate what you expect your income and expenses are per month, and enter them in column 2.

Step 2.
Track your actual income and expenses for a month and enter them in column 3. (To help you do this accurately, keep a file of your cash receipts, bills paid, and checking or credit records for the month.)

Step 3.
After one month of tracking your cash flow, answer the following questions:

1. Did you enter any sources of income or expenses that were not listed on the worksheet? (If yes, what were they?)

2. Were your estimates generally accurate?

3. What specific items or areas had the largest discrepancies between what you estimated they would be and what they actually were?

4. Comparing your bottom-line total for income and expenses, are you satisfied with how your monthly cash flow seems to be going?

5. What changes could you make to create more positive cash flow—i.e., to increase your income or savings and reduce your expenses or debt?

6. How likely is it that you would actually make the changes you mentioned in your response to question #5?

	Estimate	Actual
Income Source:		
Parents/Family		
Work/Job		
Grants/Scholarships		
Loans		
Savings		
Others:		
TOTAL INCOME		
Essentials (Fixed Expenses)		
Living Expenses: Food/Groceries		
Rent/Room & Board		
Utilities (gas/electric)		
Clothing		
Laundry/Dry Cleaning		
Phone		
Computer		
Household Items (dishes, etc.)		
Medical Insurance Expenses		
Debt Payments (loans/credit cards)		
Others:		
School Expenses: Tuition		
Books		
Supplies (print cartridges, etc.)		
Special Fees (lab fees, etc.)		
Others:		
Transportation: Public Transportation (bus fees, etc.)		
Car Insurance		
Car Maintenance		
Fuel (gas)		
Car Payments		
Others:		
Incidentals (*Variable* Expenses)		
Entertainment: Movies/Concerts		
DVDs/CDs		
Restaurants (eating out)		
Personal Appearance/Accessories: Haircuts/Hairstyling		
Cosmetics/Manicures		
Fashionable Clothes		
Jewelry		
Others:		
Hobbies		
Travel (trips home, vacations)		
Gifts		
Others:		
TOTAL EXPENSES		

Procrastination: The Vicious Cycle

Delilah has a major paper due at the end of the term. It's now past midterm and she still hasn't started to work on her paper. She tells herself, "I should have started sooner."

However, Delilah continues to postpone starting her work on the paper and is now beginning to feel anxious and guilty about it. To relieve her growing anxiety and guilt, she starts doing other tasks instead, such as cleaning her room and returning e-mails to people who have written her. This makes Delilah feel a little better because these tasks keep her busy, take her mind off the term paper, and give her the feeling that at least she's getting something accomplished. Time continues to pass, and the deadline for the paper is dangerously close. Delilah now finds herself in a position of having lots of work to do and very little time to do it.

Based on the procrastination research and counseling experiences of Jane Burka and Lenora Yuen, as reported in, *Procrastination: Why You Do It, What to Do About It.*

Reflection and Discussion Questions

1. What do you predict Delilah will do at this point?

2. Why did you make this prediction?

3. What grade do you think Delilah will receive on her paper?

4. What do you think Delilah will do on the next term paper she's assigned?

5. Other than starting sooner, what recommendations would you have for Delilah (and other procrastinators like her) to break this "cycle of procrastination" and prevent it from happening over and over again?

Interpersonal Relationships

Communicating and Relating Effectively to Others

Learning Goals

The primary goal of this chapter is to equip you with a set of social skills and strategies that may be used to enhance the quality of your interpersonal relationships and, ultimately, the quality of your life.

Outline

Activate Your Thinking

There was once a popular song that included the following lyrics: "People who need people are the luckiest people in the world." Would you agree or disagree with these lyrics?

Why?

••• The Importance of Interpersonal Relationships for Success, Health, and Happiness

Our interpersonal relationships can be a source of social support that contributes strongly to our personal success, or they may be a source of social conflict that distracts us from focusing on and achieving our personal goals. For new college students who may find themselves surrounded by multiple social opportunities, one of the key adjustments they must make is striking a healthy balance between too much and too little socializing, as well as finding and forming interpersonal relationships that support rather than sabotage their educational success.

For students living on campus, they face the additional social challenge of sharing private living space for an extended period of time with roommates whom they may never have met before—a social experience they'll probably never encounter again—unless they decide to join the military or are forced to go to prison (Gardner, 1987). Living with roommates can be a powerful learning opportunity and an intimate social experience that can result in roommates remaining "friends for life" (or "enemies 'til death," depending on the quality of their relationship).

Interpersonal intelligence—the ability to relate effectively to others—is considered one major form of human intelligence (Gardner, 1993) and *emotional intelligence*—which includes emotional self-awareness and empathy (sensitivity to the emotions of others)—has been found to be more important for personal and professional success than intellectual ability (IQ) (Goleman, 1995). Research also shows that the ability to effectively communicate with and motivate others is a key characteristic of successful leadership (Avolio, 2004), and the ability of college graduates to communicate and relate well to others is a high-ranking factor in employers' hiring decisions (Felstead, Gallie, & Green, 2002; National Association of Colleges & Employers, 2003).

Most importantly, the development of a strong social support system is one of the major keys to achieving personal health and happiness. Studies show that people who have stronger social support networks are more likely to report being "happy" (Myers, 1993) and have a longer life expectancy (Giles, et al., 2005). In today's world, the importance of a solid social-support network may be particularly critical for health and happiness because advances in communication technology have made it possible for human beings to minimize the amount of direct contact they have with others, which can increase their risk of interpersonal isolation, loneliness, and social avoidance (Putman, 2000).

◆ *Pause for Reflection*

Who are the people in your life that you tend to turn to for social support when you are experiencing stress or need personal encouragement?

••• Developing Effective Interpersonal Skills

Our ability to effectively communicate and converse with others can help us minimize interpersonal conflict, as well as help us receive and provide social support by forming meaningful friendships and/or intimate relationships. Being able to communicate effectively also serves to increase our self-esteem by helping us feel better understood and more accepted by others.

Listed below are our top recommendations for strengthening your interpersonal communication and conversation skills. Some of these strategies may appear to be very simple and obvious, but they are also very powerful. Unfortunately, because they are simple or obvious, we often overlook them or fail to use them consistently. Thus, don't be fooled by the seeming simplicity of the following suggestions and don't underestimate their social impact.

Communication and Conversation Skills

Be a good listener.

Studies show that during a typical day, listening is our most frequent communication activity, followed in order by reading, speaking, and writing (Newton, 1990; Purdy & Borisoff, 1996). One study found that college students spend an average of 52.5 percent of their time each day listening (Barker & Watson, 2000). Listening has been identified as one of the top skills that employees seek when hiring and promoting employees (Maes, et al., 1997; Winsor, et al., 1997).

Listening closely can be challenging, but it is an important interpersonal skill that lets speakers know they are worthy of your complete and undivided attention.

Human relations experts frequently recommend that we should talk less, listen more, and listen more effectively (Nichols & Stevens, 1957; Nichols, 1995). However, being a good listener is easier said than done, because listening closely and sensitively is a very challenging mental task. Studies show that our listening comprehension for spoken messages is less than 50 percent (Nichols & Stevens, 1957; Wolvin & Coakley, 1993). This is not surprising when you consider that we have only one chance to understand words that are spoken to us. If we miss something in a spoken word, we cannot replay a message delivered to us in person like we can re-read words in print. Furthermore, studies show that we can understand spoken language at a rate almost four times faster than the average person speaks (Adler & Towne, 2001); this leaves our mind plenty of spare time to drift off to something else (e.g., think about what we intend to say next). Since we're not actively "doing something" while listening, we can easily fall prey to passive listening, whereby we give the impression that we're totally focused on the speaker's words but part of our mind is actually somewhere else. As listeners, we need to remain active and conscious of this tendency to drift and fight it by devoting our full attention to others when they're speaking. By listening closely to others who speak to us, we send them the message that they're worthy of our complete and undivided attention.

Be aware of nonverbal messages you send while listening.

Whether or not we're truly listening is often communicated nonverbally and silently through body language. It has been said that 90 percent of communication is nonverbal, because human body language often communicates stronger and truer messages than spoken language (Mehrabian, 1972). In fact, one way that researchers studying lying recommend for detecting whether people are not telling the truth is to see if their body language fails to match their spoken language. For example, if they say they are excited or enthusiastic about something, but their nonverbal communication indicates otherwise (e.g., their eyebrows don't raise and they sit motionless), we may have reason to doubt their sincerity (Eckman & Friesen, 1969).

In the case of listening, our body language may be the best way to communicate interest in the speaker's words and interest in the person who is doing the speaking. Similarly, if we're speaking, awareness of our listeners' body language can also send us important clues about whether we are holding or losing their interest.

A good mnemonic device (memory-improvement method) for remembering the nonverbal signals we should send others while listening is the acronym, SOFTEN, standing for:

S = Smile—periodically, but not continually as if your smile is permanently (and artificially) painted on your face.

Sit Still—don't fidget and squirm as if the speaker is making you feel uncomfortable or putting you on the spot.

O = Open posture—not a "closed posture" with arms crossed or hands folded together (like Superman or a Supreme Court judge who's about to pass judgment).

F = Forward leaning—as opposed to leaning back as if you're psychoanalyzing or evaluating.

Face the speaker directly—with both shoulders lining up directly with the speaker, rather than turning away one shoulder as if to give the speaker the "cold shoulder."

T = Touch—a light touch on the arm or hand can be a good way to communicate warmth (but no rubbing, stroking, or touching in ways that could qualify as sexual harassment).

E = Eye contact—periodically, rather than little or no eye contact because this suggests you'd like the conversation to end (much like a student who avoids eye contact with a teacher so as not to be called on in class); but don't make continuous or excessive eye contact because this could be interpreted as staring or glaring.

N = Nod your head—slowly and every once in a while; not repeatedly and rapidly (because this sends the message that you want the speaker to hurry up and finish so you can start talking).

Sending positive nonverbal signals when listening can encourage others to become more self-confident and enthusiastic speakers. This not only benefits those who speak to us, it also benefits us as listeners, because listening to speakers who are more self-confident and enthusiastic makes the challenging task of listening less difficult and more enjoyable.

An interesting exercise you can try in order to gain greater awareness of your nonverbal communication habits is to choose a couple of people whom you trust and know you well, and ask them to imitate your body language. This is an exercise that can often be very revealing (and sometimes hilarious).

Be open to different topics of conversation.

Don't be a closed-minded or selective listener who listens to people like you're listening to the radio, changing stations to select or "tune into" conversational topics that only reflect your favorite interests or personal points of view, while "tuning out" everything else.

Remember: People learn best from others whose interests and viewpoints do not necessarily match their own. Ignoring or blocking out information and ideas about topics that don't immediately interest you or support your particular perspective is not only a poor social skill, it's also a poor learning strategy.

If people express viewpoints that you do not agree with, you don't have to nod in agreement; however, you still owe them the courtesy of listening to what they have to say (rather than shaking your head, frowning, or interrupting them). This isn't just a matter of social etiquette; it's a matter of social ethics. After others finish expressing their point of view, you should then feel free to express your own. Your *informed* opinions are worth expressing, as long as you do *not* express them in an *opinionated* way—i.e., stating them so strongly that it sounds like your viewpoints are the only rational or acceptable ones, while all others are foolish (Gibb, 1961). Expressing opinions in this opinionated fashion is likely to put an immediate end to a potentially useful discussion and possibly a future relationship.

Pause for Reflection

On what topics do you hold strong opinions?

When you express these opinions, how do others typically react to you?

Communicate your ideas precisely and concisely.

When speaking, our goal should be to get directly to the point, stick to it, make it clear, and then get "off stage" to make room for others to speak. We want to avoid being a "stage hog" who rambles on and on, dominates the conversation, and gobbles up more than our fair share of conversation time.

Speaking becomes more concise and precise when the speaker avoids including unnecessary details and empty fillers such as "like," "kinda like," "I mean," "I'm all," "you know," and "you know what I mean." Expressions such as these just fill up and waste conversation time, adding nothing substantial or meaningful to the speaker's message. They may also result in the listener losing patience, interest, and respect for the speaker (Daniels & Horowitz, 1997).

Take time to think about what you're going to say before you actually say it.

Sometimes, short silences in conversation can feel uncomfortable, so we may be tempted to rush in and break the silence by saying just about anything. Although this may be well intended, it can result in speaking before (and without) thinking.

Reflection should precede action, and that includes verbal action (speaking). If our mouth moves faster than our brain, we can wind up putting our foot in our mouth, which results in saying something brainless. Or, worse yet, we may say something we shouldn't have said, or say something in a manner that we didn't intend to phrase it. Often, it may be better to hold back our words and think them through before blurting them out.

Silent spots in the conversation should not always be viewed as a "communication breakdown." Instead, they may indicate that the people involved in the conversation are thinking before speaking, reflecting on what each other has to say, and are feeling comfortable enough with their relationship to allow these meaningful pauses to take place.

Human Relations Skills (a.k.a., "People Skills")

Communicating and conversing well with others is one key element of managing our interpersonal relationships. Another key element involves how well we relate to and treat people in general. There are several strategies you can use to improve this broader set of human relations or "people skills."

Remember the names of people you meet.

Remembering people's names communicates to others that you know them as individuals. It makes the person feel that he or she is more than an anonymous face in a crowd, but is a special and unique individual with a distinctive identity.

Despite the fact that people commonly claim they don't have a good memory for names, there is absolutely no evidence that the ability to remember names is an inherited trait that we're born with and have no control over; instead, it's a skill that can be developed through personal effort and employment of effective learning and memory strategies.

Strategies for Remembering Names

◆ When you first meet people, make it a point to consciously pay attention to the name of each person you meet. Really make a conscious effort to listen for the person's name, rather than focusing on what impression you're making on them, what impression they're making on you, or what you're going to say next.

◆ One way to reinforce your memory for a new name is to say it or rehearse it within a minute or two after you first hear it. For instance, if your friend Gertrude has just introduced you to Geraldine, you might say: "Geraldine, how long have you known Gertrude?" When we use a person's name soon after we've heard it, this quick rehearsal serves to intercept memory loss at the point in time when forgetting is most likely to occur—immediately after we acquire new information (Underwood, 1983).

◆ You can strengthen your memory of an individual's name by associating it with other information you've learned about the person or other information you already know. For instance, you can associate the person's name with: (a) your first impression of the individual's personality, (b) a physical characteristic of the person, (c) the topic of conversation you had with the person, (d) the place where you met the person, or (e) a familiar word that rhymes with the person's name. By making a mental connection between the person's name and some other piece of information you know, you help your brain actually form a neurological connection, which is the biological foundation of human memory.

◆ One strategy that people use to ensure that we don't forget something is to write it down. We can use this same strategy for learning names by keeping a name journal that includes the names of new people we meet plus some information about them (e.g., what they do and what their interests are). You could make it a goal to meet one new person every day and make it a point to remember that person's name by recording it in your journal.

Remember: Developing the habit of remembering names is not only a social skill that can improve your interpersonal interactions and bring you friends, it's also a powerful professional tool that can promote your career success in whatever field you may pursue.

In business, remembering people's names helps to recruit and retain customers; in politics it can win votes; and in education it can promote the teacher's connection and rapport with students.

Refer to people by name when you greet and interact with them.

When you greet a person, be sure to use the person's name in your greeting. Saying, "Hi, Waldo" will mean a lot more to Waldo than simply saying "Hi" or, worse yet, saying "Hi, there"—which sounds like you're just acknowledging something "out there" that could be either a human being or an inanimate object. Continuing to use people's names after you've learned them serves to further strengthen your memory of their names, and it continues to send a message to them that you haven't forgotten their unique identity.

Show interest in others by remembering information about them.

Ask people questions about their personal interests, plans, and experiences. Pay attention to what seems most important to others, what they care about or what concerns them, and introduce these topics when you have conversations with them. For one person that topic may be politics, for another it may be sports, while for another it may be relationships.

When you see people again, ask them about something they brought up in your last conversation. Try to get beyond the standard, generic questions that are routinely asked after people say "hello" (e.g., "What's goin' on?"). Instead, ask about something *specific* that you discussed with them last time you conversed (e.g., "How was that math test you were worried about last week?"). This sends a message to the person that you know his or her personal interests and concerns, and that they are also of interest and concern to you.

Remembering information about someone is an interpersonal skill that will make that person feel important.

When you remember specific information about people, it suggests to them that they are important to you. Our memory often reflects our priorities—we're most likely to remember what's most important to us. So, when you remember people's names and something about them, it suggests to them that they are a high priority to you. Furthermore, you will find that others start showing more interest in you when you show interest in them.

Another surprising, almost contradictory thing can happen when you show more interest in others: You become a person that others consider to be a great conversationalist.

Personal Story One of my most successful teaching strategies is something I do on the first day of class. I ask my students to complete a "student information sheet" that includes their name and some information relating to their past experiences, future plans, and personal interests. I answer the same questions I ask my students by writing my answers on the board while they write theirs on a sheet of paper. (This allows them to get to know me while I get to know them.) After I've collected all their information sheets, I call out the names of individual students, asking them to raise their hand when their name is called, so I can associate their name and face. To help me remember their names, as I call each name, I very rapidly jot down a quick word or abbreviated phrase next to the student's name for later review (e.g., something about a distinctive physical feature or where the student's seated).

I save the students' information sheets, and I refer back to them throughout the term. For example, I record the student's name and strongest interest on a post-it note, and stick the note onto my class notes near topics I'll be covering during the term that relates to the student's interest. When I get to that topic in class (which could be months later), I immediately see the student's names posted by it. When I begin to discuss the topic, I mention the name of the student who had expressed interest in it on the first day of class (e.g., "Gina, we're about to study your favorite topic."). Often what happens is that students really perk up when I mention their name in association with their preferred topic; plus, they're often amazed by my apparent ability to remember their personal interests from the first day of class so much later in the term. Students rarely ask how I managed to remember their personal interests, so they are not aware of my post-it note strategy. Instead, they just think I've got extraordinary social memory and social sensitivity (which is just fine with me).

—Joe Cuseo

Be a positive person.

Simply stated, studies show that others will like a person more when that person is in a good mood (Byrne, 1997). People prefer being around others who are upbeat and enthusiastic. As the old adage goes, "Enthusiasm is contagious," meaning that others can "catch" your good mood and, by so doing, their own mood improves. Also, if you have a good sense of humor, don't be afraid to share it to improve the mood of others. Laughter relaxes both the body and mind, and it generates an increase in the brain's production of endorphins—brain chemicals that produce feelings of euphoria (positive well-being). Thus, helping others to laugh helps them to improve both their mood and their health (McGhee, 1999).

In contrast, when we're consistently "down" or inconsistently moody, we tend to bring others down with us. If this happens too frequently, we may find others becoming less interested in spending time with us.

Be a complimentary person.

Look for the positive in others and praise it when you see it. When you provide others with a sincere compliment, it increases their self-esteem and increases their interest in you. Simply stated, people like to be around others who make them feel good about themselves.

Remember that compliments can be given to people about many things other than their looks. You can also compliment others on their character or actions—which often require more personal effort and are more authentic than mere appearance—which is more obvious and superficial. Even if you have just met someone and enjoyed your initial interaction together, you can compliment that person by simply saying, "I enjoyed this time with you. Let's do it again."

Be a reliable and dependable person.

Good human relations skills also include remembering and following through on our social commitments, such as keeping our appointments by showing up if we say we will and when we say we will. If we don't show up when people expect us to, or show up consistently late, we're basically breaking a social promise and showing disrespect for other people's time. Our forgetfulness or tardiness may make others feel that spending time with them isn't important to us and that they aren't important to us.

Being reliable and dependable also includes academic behavior, such as not missing appointments with instructors or advisors. Missing class, coming to class late, leaving class early, or getting ready to leave class early (e.g., prematurely packing up your books and getting ready to leave), sends a message to your instructors that you don't care very much about what they are saying or that you don't value the time you spend with them. Sending such messages to your instructors may not only affect the quality of your relationships with them, it may also affect the grades you receive from them.

Pause for Reflection
How often do you miss appointments? (Circle one)

Never   Rarely   Sometimes   Often

Why?

How often are you late for appointments? (Circle one)

Never   Rarely   Sometimes   Often

Why?

If you often miss or forget appointments, you may want to acquire an appointment scheduling book and carry it with you each day to remember personal appointments you've made and to record appointments you make during the day.

Be a sharing person.

Studies show that when people disclose or share their feelings with others, it helps them feel understood and feel better about themselves (Reis & Shaver, 1988). When people are uncertain about how to act around others, or whether others will accept them, they may act in a guarded manner that insulates or hides their true feelings and true self so they can protect themselves from possible rejection. This can result in behavior that is distant or cool. (As an old Simon and Garfunkel song goes, "I am a rock, I am an island; and a rock feels no pain, and an island never cries.")

How often have you witnessed this rapid, ritualistic interchange between two individuals?

> Person A: "Hi, how's it goin'?"
> Person B: "Fine, how ya' doin'?"

No real personal information is shared by either person, and chances are that neither one expects nor wants to hear about how the other person is truly feeling (Goffman, 1967). Such social rituals are understandable and acceptable when people first interact with each other. However, if these individuals continue to interact and want to move their relationship forward, they should move beyond these ritualistic routines and move toward mutual sharing of more personal, meaningful information.

As you become more comfortable with others, engage in some self-disclosure—sharing or disclosing a little more of yourself. Naturally, you want to do this gradually and in small doses, rather than by suddenly blowing them away with "hot blasts" of intimacy and private details about your personal life. Selectively sharing some things about yourself serves to show others that you trust them well enough to share a part of yourself.

You can start this sharing process by noticing the things that other people have shared with you and follow up by sharing something about yourself that relates to the same topic or experience they shared with you. Relating a similar experience of your own demonstrates empathy—your ability to understand the feelings of others. It also lets others know that you have something in common, which, in turn, encourages them to share more of themselves with you (Adler & Towne, 2001). Friendships gradually build up through this progressive process of give-

STUDENT PERSPECTIVE

Please take this advice.

Take out those wings that you hide

And use them to fly where no one's gone before.

And soon you will find

The air that you breathe is much fresher

Without the suffocating mask you always wear.

—A poem by Lizze Frazer, college sophomore

STUDENT PERSPECTIVE

"How do you strengthen your trust in a person?"

—Question asked by a first-year student

and-take or sharing of more personal information, which is referred to by human relations specialists as the *intimacy spiral* (Cusinato & L'Abate, 1994).

Be a caring person.

Show authentic concern for other people's feelings. For example, instead of asking the routine question, "How are you?" or, "How's it goin'?" ask the person, "How are you feeling?" Showing concern for others not only helps them feel more comfortable about sharing information with you, it also helps to create more opportunities for you to learn from and about the people you meet.

Be ready and willing to help others who come to you with personal problems.

A good friend and a good person is someone who is willing to help others in need. Your friends and other people you know are likely to come to you occasionally for advice or assistance about personal issues.

Listed below are some strategies that may prepare and enable you to better help others who seek your support.

Strategies

◆ Be a good listener and lend an empathetic ear. By providing a sounding board and letting others bounce their thoughts and feelings off of you, a solution may bounce right back to them simply by giving them a chance to get their personal feelings out in the open and the opportunity to think out loud, which can sometimes lead them to discover an effective solution on their own. Thus, their problem may be solved with your doing little more than listening in a concerned and compassionate way.

◆ Ask questions that will help the person clarify the problem and identify options for solving it. For example, ask questions such as, "Could it be that . . . ?" "Do you think that . . .?" "What if you decided to . . .?" An effective helper assists others in understanding and discovering solutions to their own problems. Often we can provide better help by knowing what questions to ask than by knowing what answers to give. Good questions help others to help themselves by clarifying their problem and by generating possible solutions. In contrast, questions you want to avoid are "trapping questions," such as: "What are you going to do now? What if somebody finds out?" "Will you get in trouble?" Pelting others with prying questions like these are likely to elevate their anxiety about the problem and cause them to feel worse off than better off after seeking your help.

◆ If you have experienced a similar problem and overcame it, share your personal experience. Sharing a similar experience of your own may help others feel that their problem isn't unusual and may help them feel more optimistic about solving it. However, avoid using the common expression, "I know how you feel." Although this statement may be well intended, it's presumptuous to say that you know how someone else feels because it's impossible to get into that person's head and know what he or she is truly feeling or experiencing at the moment.

◆ Be sure not to dismiss or minimize the person's feelings. Avoid saying things like, "Oh, don't worry about it, everything will be alright" or, "You'll get over it." Comments like these make it sound like the person's feelings are unjustified or exaggerated (e.g., "you're making a mountain out of a mole hill"); they may also send the message that you're discounting or doubting the person's feelings.

◆ Try to avoid directly telling or dictating to others what they should do. An effective helper is someone who helps others to clearly see their options and allows them to make their own decision, without making it for them. When people make their own choice, they "own" that decision and any action they take on it serves to bolster their sense of self-control and self-esteem. They also become more independent thinkers who develop self-confidence in their ability to solve their own problems, rather than being dependent on others to solve their problems for them.

◆ If supportive listening and questioning are not enough to help solve the person's problem, the next step would be to work with the person to identify possible solutions. Brainstorming can serve as an effective method for generating possible solutions to personal problems. (For a detailed description of the brainstorming method, see Chapter 6, p. 194.)

◆ If the person cannot make a decision about what to do and seeks your advice about what choice to make, give your advice as a concerned friend, not as an expert authority. For instance, before beginning to give your advice, introduce it by saying, "This is just a suggestion . . ." or, "I wonder if this might . . . ." Offer your recommendations as reasonable possibilities rather than as sure-fired solutions. The last thing you want to do is give the impression that you're performing psychoanalysis on the person by saying things like, "What your problem is . . ." or, "What you need to do is . . . ." Statements such as these can make the person feel like a patient who is helplessly dependent on your expert diagnosis and treatment.

◆ If the problem is too serious or intense for you to help with, encourage the person to seek professional help (e.g., from a personal counselor on campus). You can take your encouragement one step further by actually helping the person take the specific steps needed to get professional assistance by:

a. helping the person identify what questions to ask the professional;

b. helping the person find contact information for the professional (e.g., phone number);

c. helping the person "connect" with the professional while you're together (e.g., having the person phone the professional while you're present or walking with the person to the professional's office); and

d. following up later by asking if the professional assistance proved helpful, and complimenting the person for being open and willing to seek help.

◆ Last and most importantly, if someone comes to you for help or assistance with a personal problem, any information that person shares with you should remain confidential. This respects the person's privacy and reinforces the person's trust and respect for you.

Pause for Reflection

Do you often find people coming to you for advice?

If yes, why do you think they do?

If no, why do you think they don't?

Interact with people as persons, not as objects.

Martin Buber, a highly regarded philosopher and theologian, argues that there are "I-thou" and "I-it" relationships (Buber, 1923). "I-it" relationships are those in which human beings interact with other human beings as if they exist solely for the purpose of getting what they want or need from them. In contrast, "I-thou" relationships are authentic interactions between two human beings that are not qualified or compromised by their particular roles or status; they are interactions in which each person involved is treated as a bona fide human being with human feelings.

We should strive for "I-thou" interactions in all situations, even those interactions in which others are performing their functions, roles, or duties (for example, when interacting with office assistants, cafeteria workers, bus drivers, or groundskeepers). We shouldn't forget that these are *persons* performing these functions, so the same interpersonal skills should be applied to functional interactions as any other human interaction. Although these are functional exchanges whereby the persons are performing functions they're expected or paid to do as a service to us, taking the time to sincerely say "thank you" or "I appreciate it" can go a long way to make them feel appreciated and improve the quality of our interpersonal interaction with them (as well as the quality of service we receive from them).

When communicating online, choose your words carefully, and deliver them sensitively.

When communicating with others online, use the same human relations skills as you would when communicating in person.

The terms "e-mail etiquette" and "netiquette" have crept into our current vocabulary because people sometimes forget to apply principles of social etiquette and interpersonal sensitivity when they communicate electronically. In fact, it may even be more important for us to use effective verbal communication skills when we're communicating online because we don't have nonverbal communication channels available to us to support and clarify our written words. Thus, when communicating electronically, we may need to be especially careful about choosing our words thoughtfully and delivering them sensitively.

Strategies for Meeting People and Forming Friendships

An important element of the college experience is meeting new people, learning from them, and forming new friendships. There are specific strategies you can use to improve the quantity and quality of new people you meet and new friendships you form.

Place yourself in situations and locations where you will come in regular contact with others.

Studies show that friendships form when people regularly cross paths or find themselves in the same place at the same time (Latané, et al., 2005). You can apply this principle by spending as much time on campus as possible, and spending time in places where others are likely to be present (e.g., by eating your meals in the student cafeteria, and studying in the college library). If you have the opportunity to live on campus, do so, because studies show that it helps students make social connections and increases their satisfaction with the college experience (Pascarella & Terenzini, 2005; Tinto, 1993). If you are a commuter student, try to make your college experience as similar as possible to that of a residential student; for example, try to

BOX 11.1 *Snapshot SUMMARY*

Avoiding the Three "Egos": The Types of Person You Don't Want to Be and Don't Want to Be Around

Good friends and good people are those who get outside themselves and get interested in others. The following types of people are more into themselves than other people and, consequently, they're not much fun to be around.

Egotist—an egotistical person is basically someone who is conceited—a braggart who boasts, shows off in front of others (sometimes to cover up feelings of personal inadequacy or low self-esteem), and spends lots of conversation time talking about his or her outstanding features or personal accomplishments.

Egoist—an egoistic person is basically selfish and unwilling to share things with others or do things for others.

Egocentric—an egocentric person views the world as if he or she is always at the center of it (including every conversation), and shows little interest in or empathy for others. The words "me" and "I" appear with relentless frequency when an egocentric person speaks, and you may get the feeling that this person is not talking *with* you but *at* you.

An egocentric person wants to be at the "center" of (and the subject of) every conversation.

spend more than just class time on campus by spending study time on campus and social time by attending campus social or cultural events.

Put yourself in social situations where you're likely to meet people who have similar interests, goals, and values as you.

Research supports the old proverb, "Birds of a feather flock together." People tend to form friendships with others who share similar interests, values, or goals (AhYun, 2002). When people have things in common, they are more likely to form friendships because they are more likely to spend time together doing things relating to their common interests, and they're more likely to get along with each other because they positively reinforce or validate each other's personal interests and values (Festinger, 1954).

One straightforward way to find others with whom you have something in common is by participating in clubs and organizations on campus that reflect your personal interests and values. If you cannot find one, start one of your own. By joining or forming organizations and clubs comprised of people that you have something in common with, you can begin to actively create your own social life and make it happen *for* you, instead of passively waiting and hoping it will happen *to* you.

Also, regularly check your college newspaper, posted flyers on campus, and the Student Information Desk in your Student Activities Center to keep track of social events that are more likely to attract others who share your interests, values, or goals.

Joining a fraternity or sorority.

On some campuses, Greek life (fraternities and sororities) can provide an option for forming friendships by allowing you to share common living quarters (fraternity or sorority house) and common social activities that take place regularly throughout the academic year. However, a fraternity or sorority may not be a good fit for you if you prefer socializing within a smaller circle of friends rather than a larger group of "brothers" or "sisters."

Also, fraternities and sororities can vary in terms of their commitment to education and to the community. Some may de-emphasize academics in favor of social activities, use socially insensitive or dangerous "hazing" (induction) practices, or encourage excessive use of alcohol. For these reasons, some colleges and universities have eliminated fraternities or do not allow students to join them until their sophomore year. One major study showed that joining fraternities during the first year had a strong, negative impact on the academic development of first-year male students. However, joining fraternities after the first year of college did not interfere with male students' academic development. The study also showed that joining a sorority did not interfere with the academic performance of females at any time in their college experience (Pascarella, Flowers, & Whitt, 1999).

Attending parties.

Parties represent a common and convenient way for college students to meet new people. You'll probably have no trouble finding parties on or off campus; attending them is perfectly fine, as long as you don't do it too frequently or intensely. Unfortunately, for some new students, when they leave home for college and escape the direct control of parents, they act like they've just

THE MIND IS A WONDERFUL THING TO WASTE!

Attending parties is one effective way to meet new people, as long as it's done in moderation, not as an obsession that displaces or interferes with your primary purpose for being in college—to get an education.

been released from a minimal security prison (Gardner, 1987). It's as if they've just been cut loose from a restraining noose and are ready to bust loose—like wild (party) animals.

Try to limit your attendance at parties to Fridays and Saturdays, and skip them on nights before class. (Or, if large parties aren't your "scene," don't feel pressured to do them at all.)

 Pause for Reflection
Have you been to college parties on or off campus?

If yes, what were they like?

If no, why haven't you attended one?

Meeting others through *Facebook*.

Created in 2004 by a college sophomore, *Facebook* is an Internet database that's the college equivalent of "MySpace." Through it, you can network with any other college student who has an ".edu" e-mail address. Through the *Facebook* database, you can also join different groups on campus and check for announcements of parties or other social events.

Facebook represents another venue through which you may be able to meet new people and form new friendships. However, remember that *Facebook*, just like Myspace, is public domain and is available to anyone who has Internet access. So, be careful about people you respond to, and be careful about what you post on your site or "wall." For example, recent reports indicate that both schools and employers are checking students' *Facebook* and *Myspace* entries and using that information to help them decide whether to accept or reject applicants (Palank, 2006).

••• Overcoming Shyness

Shyness is a very common human feeling; studies show that over 80 percent of the American population report being shy at some time in their life, and almost one-half report that they are currently "shy" (Zimbardo, 1990). Anytime we approach and attempt to interact with someone new or attempt to form a new friendship, it involves some risk and possible fear of being evaluated negatively or rejected. For people who are shy, this risk may cause them to experience greater apprehension or anxiety than for individuals who aren't shy. Shyness may be considered to be a social fear, and, like any fear, it needs to be faced before it can be overcome. As the old proverb goes, "Nothing ventured, nothing gained."

Personal Story My daughter Sara, like myself (or maybe not), was a fairly shy child. She had a hard time meeting people mainly because she did not join groups very easily.
Sara would come home and say "Daddy I have no one to play with, would you help me find someone?" Although there were children on our street and in school, who would have loved to play with Sara, she would not approach them and acted very shy when they approached her. She did not feel comfortable with being assertive in this area. As a dad who feels he can fix any problem for his children, I decided to set up a process for her to deal

with her shyness. Each week I would set a goal for her to meet two new people. Whenever Sara did this, I would reward her. This task was tough at first, and I went with her for several trial runs until she got the pattern down. She eventually overcame her shyness, and during her entire 2nd- and 3rd-grade years, she made many friends. As a grown woman who is now a 2nd grade teacher, Sara is thought of as a great communicator who is more assertive than her father (or maybe not). Many of her friends (she has too many—especially boys) might say she not only perfected communication, she took it to new heights. Sara loves to talk and she has an answer for everything (which is a trait she gets from her mother).

—*Aaron Thompson*

If you are one of the many people who experience shyness, or if you're in a position to help someone who is struggling with shyness, listed below are some specific, research-based strategies that may be used to overcome shyness (Carducci, 1999; Jones, et al., 1986; Zimbardo, 1990).

Strategies

Increase your awareness of specific situations in which your shyness tends to be most intense.

Studies show that shyness is not a general personality trait that people take with them to all situations. Instead, shyness tends to occur in specific social situations and in the presence of particular people. Research shows that shyness is most likely to be experienced by people when they are in the presence of strangers, members of the opposite sex, and authority figures—people in positions of power or influence (e.g., professors and employers) (Zimbardo, 1977, 1990). Also, shyness is more likely to occur in the following types of social situations:

a. new situations that have never been experienced before (e.g., living with a new room-mate in college);

b. large social groups where the person is the focus of attention;

c. situations in which the person is being evaluated by others (e.g., delivering a speech in class); and

d. situations requiring assertiveness (e.g., standing up for your rights or saying "no" to another person's request) (Carducci, 1999; Zimbardo, 1990).

An important first step toward overcoming shyness is becoming aware of the particular social circumstances or situations in which we experience shyness.

 Pause for Reflection

In what specific social situations, or when interacting with what particular types of people, do you tend to feel most shy?

Become aware of and consciously block-out negative thoughts that can lower your self-confidence or self-esteem in social situations.

Shyness is often related to the person having low self-confidence or self-esteem in certain social situations (Zimbardo, 1977, 1990), which, in turn, triggers a series of negative or pessimistic thoughts (e.g., "I'm not attractive to others," "I'm not an interesting person," or "I know I'll be rejected"). This type of negative thinking can often lead the shy person to engage in behavior that makes the negative thinking come true. For example, if someone doesn't quickly approach you or speak to you and you're shy, you may immediately begin to think that the other person is disinterested in you or feels superior to you. (Of course, this is just your perception or interpretation of the person's behavior; it could be just as likely that the other person didn't notice you yet, or may feel shy about approaching you.) However, if you're very shy, these thoughts about rejection can cause you to behave in such a way that you withdraw from the other person, such as moving farther away or not making eye contact. Your "withdrawing" behavior, in turn, may lead the other person to conclude that you're "standoffish" and unapproachable or "stuck up" and disinterested.

This sequence of thought, action, and reaction illustrates what sociologists call the *self-fulfilling prophecy*—we behave in ways that fulfill our self-beliefs, i.e., we act in ways that make our beliefs come true (Rosenthal & Jacobson, 1968; Insel & Jacobson, 1975). The key to breaking the vicious cycle of the self-fulfilling prophecy is to consciously block out negative thoughts that originally trigger or start the cycle going in the first place.

Carefully observe others who behave in a relaxed and confident manner in social situations where you feel shy.

We can learn to overcome fear by observing how others effectively handle situations in which we are fearful. In fact, a technique used by psychotherapists that has proven to be effective for helping patients overcome a variety of phobias (intense fears) is called "social modeling," which involves the patient observing another person (a model)—either live or on film—who behaves fearlessly and confidently in the situation that the patient fears (Rosenthal & Steffek, 1991). You can apply the same strategy to help reduce shyness in situations where you experience social anxiety by thinking of people you know, or people you've observed, who could serve as models for guiding your actions in situations where you are shy.

Visualize yourself in the situations that trigger shyness for you and practice relaxing in those situations.

Studies show that visualizing a fear situation and practicing relaxation in that situation is an effective strategy for reducing fear (Marshall, Boutilier, & Minnes, 1974). You can practice feeling relaxed in social situations where you feel anxious or shy by using specific self-relaxation techniques. (See pp. 431–433 for a description of relaxation techniques.)

Practice the skills of effective interpersonal communication (e.g., smiling, good eye contact, open posture) so that others may feel more comfortable and confident approaching you.

You can practice skills for effective communication skills and for behaving in a non-shy manner by asking a friend to role play social situations in which you usually feel shy. After the role-play, ask your friend for feedback about both your verbal and nonverbal behavior.

Taking smaller classes is one strategy for overcoming shyness.

STUDENT PERSPECTIVE

"Introduce yourself to other people in class; study in groups; ask your friends to introduce you to others; attend floor parties; and participate in campus workshops on assertiveness training."

—Tips given by first-year students for overcoming shyness and meeting new people

Take as many small classes as you can.

You are more likely to overcome your shyness if you put yourself in situations that will reduce the intensity of your feelings of shyness. Since many people tend to feel more shy in larger groups, try to put yourself in social situations that involve smaller groups. In one major research study conducted at a large university, graduating seniors were asked for specific strategies they would recommend to first-year students, especially shy first-year students, in order to develop their self-confidence. The most frequent recommendation given by seniors was for first-year students to take some smaller classes in which they were expected to speak up (Light, 1992).

In large classes, it's easy to remain shy because you can hide; in fact, it's possible for you to go through the entire term without anyone asking you a question, knowing your name, or even knowing whether you're in class or not.

Pause for Reflection

What are the approximate sizes of the smallest and largest classes you're enrolled in this semester?

Do you notice any difference in how you interact with others, or how others interact with you, in your largest and smallest classes?

Gain a wide base of knowledge in different subject areas.

Increasing your knowledge also increases your self-esteem, your self-confidence, and your ability to converse with others about a variety of different topics. One value of a college education, particularly its liberal arts component, is that it will enable you to expand your knowledge in multiple fields and subject areas. This breadth of knowledge will give you something to say and good questions to ask about a wide variety of topics that may come up in conversations. Take your liberal arts education seriously—not only will it benefit you intellectually, it will benefit you *socially* as well.

You can also strengthen your knowledge base and conversational skills by keeping up with current events. Keeping up with the news will build up your knowledge of newsworthy topics to talk about with others, and will reduce your fear about not knowing what to say, appearing "stupid," or being "left out" of conversations.

Although conversations about the news may appear to be just small talk, they often serve as icebreakers or warm-up exercises that can eventually lead to more personal topics of conversation and to more intimate friendships or relationships.

••• Dating and Romantic Relationships

Overcoming shyness and developing conversational skills can often contribute to the development of romantic relationships. Often these intimate relationships begin through the process of dating. Research shows that college students take different approaches to dating, ranging from not dating at all to dating with the intent of exploring or cementing long-term relationships. Listed below is a summary of the major forms or purposes of college dating adapted from research reviewed by Gordon Seirup (2000).

Approaches to Dating

Postponing Dating Students who adopt this approach feel that the demands of college work and college life are too time-consuming to take on the additional social and emotional burden of dating while in college.

Hooking Up Students who prefer this approach believe that formal dating is unnecessary; they feel that their social and sexual needs are better met more casually by associating with friends and acquaintances. Instead of going out on a one-on-one date, students opting for this approach prefer to first meet and connect with romantic partners in larger group settings, such as college parties.

Casual Dating Students taking this approach do go out on dates, but primarily for the purpose of enjoying themselves and not getting "tied down" to any particular person. Thus, casual daters prefer to go out on a series of successive dates with different partners, and they may date different individuals at the same time. Their primary goal is to meet new people and discover what characteristics they find attractive in others.

Exclusive Dating Students adopting this approach prefer to date only one person for an extended period of time. Although marriage is not the goal, exclusive dating takes casual dating one step further. This form of dating may serve to help the partners develop a clearer idea of what characteristics they may seek in an ideal spouse or long-term mate.

Courtship This form of dating is intended to continue a relationship with the partner until it culminates in marriage or a formal, long-term commitment. Studies suggest that healthy, non-abusive relationships started in college can lead to more egalitarian (equal) marriages later in life (Ganong, et al., 1996).

These approaches to dating do not always occur separately; they may be blended or combined. Also, romantic relationships may evolve or grow into different stages across time. Described below are the characteristics of two major stages that often take place in the evolution or maturation of romantic love.

Romantic Love

Research reveals that romantic love involves two key stages.

1. Passionate Love (Infatuation)

Passionate love represents the very first stage of romantic love, and it often has the following characteristics:

◆ Heavy emphasis is placed on physical elements of the relationship. For example, lots of attention is focused on the partner's physical appearance or attractiveness, and the partners experience a high level of physical arousal and passion (i.e., "erotic love").

◆ Impulsive: Partners quickly or suddenly "fall" into love or are "swept off their feet" (e.g., "love at first sight").

◆ Obsessive: Partners can't stop thinking about each other.

♦ An intense emotional experience characterized by a "rush" of chemical changes in the body (similar to a drug-induced state), which includes:

    a. Release of the hormone adrenalin that triggers faster heart rate and breathing, and

    b. Increased production of brain chemicals that produce feelings of excitement, euphoria, joy, and general well being (Bartels & Siki, 2000).

The intensity of this emotional and chemical experience decreases with the passage of time, typically leveling off within a year after the couple has been together. The decrease in emotional intensity after partners have been together for a period of time is similar to the buildup of tolerance to a drug after use of that drug (Peele & Brodsky, 1991).

♦ Idealistic: The lover's partner and the relationship is perceived as "perfect." For example, the partners may say things like "We're perfect for each other," "Nobody else has a relationship like ours," "We'll be together forever." This is the stage where love can be blind, and the partner's most obvious flaws or weaknesses may not be seen or even acknowledged. This "love is blind" process is similar to the psychological defense mechanism of *denial*, whereby the lover pushes out of conscious awareness any of the partner's personal weaknesses, or any problems that may threaten the security of the relationship, and does not "see" them.

♦ Attachment and Dependency: The lover feels insecure without the partner and cannot bear being separated from him or her (e.g., "I can't live without him"). This type of attachment and dependence follows the principle: "I love you because I am loved" and "I love you because I need you." Thus, it may be difficult to determine whether the person is in love with the partner or is in love with the feeling of being in love and being loved (Fromm, 1970).

♦ Possessiveness and Jealousy: The lover feels that he or she has exclusive rights to the partner and can become very suspicious of the partner or others who interact with the partner in an affectionate manner. This suspiciousness can sometimes border on the illogical or irrational; for example, there can be "insane jealousy" whereby the lover suspects infidelity in the partner when none exists.

♦ "Love sickness" is often experienced if there is a breakup of the relationship. For example, an intense depression or "love withdrawal" may follow the breakup, which can be similar to withdrawal from a pleasure-producing drug.

2. Mature Love

At this more advanced stage of the relationship, the partners gradually "fall out" of first-stage (puppy) love, and gradually grow into a more mature stage of love that has the following characteristics:

♦ The partners become less selfish and self-centered (egocentric), and become more selfless and other-centered (altruistic). Love moves beyond being just a noun—an emotion or feeling within the person (e.g., "I am in love") and becomes an action verb—how the person acts toward and treats the partner (e.g., "S/he loves me"). More emphasis is placed on caring for the partner, rather than being cared for. Mature love follows two principles:

    1. "I am loved because I love" not, "I am in love because I'm loved" and

    2. "I need you because I love you" not, "I love you because I need you." (Fromme, 1980)

♦ There is less of an emotional high experienced at this stage than during early stages of the relationship; for example, the mad rush of hormones and mass production of euphoria-producing brain chemicals is replaced by feelings of emotional serenity (mellowness) and emotional evenness, (rather than "ups and downs"). The love "rush" is replaced by a less intense, but more consistently pleasant emotional state characterized by slightly elevated levels of different brain chemicals (endorphins). This pleasant emotional state does not tend to decrease with time, and it may actually grow stronger as the partners' relationship continues and matures (Bartels & Zeki, 2000).

◆ Physical passion decreases. The "flames of the flesh" do not burn so intensely as in first-stage love, but a romantic afterglow continues. This afterglow is characterized by more emotional intimacy or closeness between the partners, plus greater self-disclosure, trust and emotional honesty, which can often enhance the physical quality of the relationship (Viorst, 1998).

At this more advanced stage of love, interest is focused broadly on the partner as a whole person, rather than narrowly on the partner's physical qualities. Partners genuinely like one another as persons and consider each other to be their "best" or "closest" friend. Partners have a realistic, rather than an idealistic view of each other: Their respective strengths and weaknesses are recognized and accepted.

There is a complementary blend of independence and interdependence in the relationship—sometimes referred to as the paradox (contradiction) of love—whereby both partners maintain their independence and individuality yet both feel more complete and fulfilled when together. Both partners have their individual identity and do not expect the other to give them a personal identity and a sense of self-worth; however, together, their respective identities become more complete.

◆ The partners have mutual trust and confidence in each other's commitment, rather than suspicion, paranoia, or petty jealousy. For example, each partner may have interests and close friends outside the relationship without the other becoming jealous (Hatfield and Walster, 1985).

◆ The partners have mutual concern for each other's growth and fulfillment. For example, they are happy about each other's personal success and accomplishments, rather than being envious or competitive.

There appear to be five characteristics of successful, long-lasting, romantic relationships (Fromm, 1970; Fromme, 1980):

1. **Compatibility:** partners share similar interests, attitudes, and values.

2. **Caring:** partners do not take each other for granted. Instead, they continue to care for each other, appreciate all the good things they do for each other, and do not forget to communicate this appreciation for each other.

3. **Commitment:** partners dedicate time to the relationship—i.e., they take time and make time to work at the relationship to keep it alive and strong.

4. **Compromise:** partners are willing to negotiate or give in on minor disagreements and accept each other's minor imperfections.

5. **Constructive Disagreement:** partners "fight fairly" and do not express disagreement or handle conflict in an aggressive way, but in an assertive and mutually respectful manner.

Brain image © Sebastian Kaulitzki, 2007. Under license from Shutterstock, Inc.

Happy Valentine's Day
I Love You with All My Brain!

Despite expressions like, "I love you with all my heart," romantic love takes place in the human brain and is accompanied by major changes in the production of brain chemicals.

Pause for Reflection

Rate your degree of agreement or disagreement with the following statements:

"All you need is love."

strongly agree   agree   not sure   disagree   strongly disagree

Reason for rating:

"Love makes the world go 'round."

strongly agree   agree   not sure   disagree   strongly disagree

Reason for rating:

"Love is just a four-letter word."

strongly agree   agree   not sure   disagree   strongly disagree

Reason for rating:

"Love stinks."

strongly agree   agree   not sure   disagree   strongly disagree

Reason for rating:

© JupiterImages Corporation.

Although interpersonal conflicts are inevitable, there are strategies for managing them effectively.

●●● Interpersonal Conflicts

Occasional disagreement and conflict between people is an inevitable aspect of social life. Research shows that even the most happily married couples do not experience continual marital bliss, but have occasional disagreements and conflicts (Gottman, 1994). Thus, conflict is something we cannot expect to completely escape or eliminate; we can only hope to contain it, manage it, and prevent it from reaching unmanageable levels. Listed below are tips for handling interpersonal conflict in an effective and humane fashion.

Minimizing and Resolving Interpersonal Conflicts

Pick the right time and place to resolve conflicts.

Don't discuss sensitive issues when you're fatigued, in a fit of anger, or in a hurry (Daniels & Horowitz, 1997). Also, don't discuss them in a public arena, but discuss them privately and solely with the person(s) involved. As the expression goes, "Don't air your dirty laundry in public." Addressing a conflict in public is akin to a public stoning or having the person wear a dunce cap for everyone to see. All this will do is embarrass or humiliate the person with whom you're in conflict, and is likely to cause the person to resist or resent you.

Decompress yourself emotionally before expressing yourself orally.

When you have a conflict with someone, your ultimate objective should be to solve the problem, not unload your anger and get everything off your chest. Impulsively "dumping" on the other person may give you an immediate sense of relief, but it's not likely to produce permanent improvement in the other person's attitude or behavior toward you. Instead of unloading, take some time to cool off and reflect rationally before reacting emotionally. For example, count to 10 and give your emotions time to settle down before you begin to say anything. Pausing for reflection also communicates to the other person that you're giving careful thought and attention to the matter rather than lashing out randomly.

If the conflict is very intense and you're really enraged or outraged, it may be a good idea to write out your thoughts ahead of time. This strategy will give you time to organize and clarify your ideas by first talking silently to yourself (on paper), before talking out loud to the other person (in person).

Give the person a chance to respond.

Just because you're angry doesn't mean that the person you're angry with must lose or forfeit the right to free speech and self-defense. Giving the other person a chance to speak and be heard will increase the likelihood that you'll receive a cooperative response to your request. It will also prevent you from storming in, jumping the gun, and "pulling the trigger" too quickly before being sure you've got all the facts straight.

After listening to the other person's response, you might also check your understanding by summarizing it in your own words (e.g., "What I hear you saying is . . ."). This is an important first step in the conflict-resolution process because conflicts often revolve around a simple misunderstanding, failure to communicate, or a communication breakdown of some sort. Sometimes, just taking the time to really hear where the other person is coming from before launching into a full-scale complaint or criticism can, in itself, reduce or resolve the conflict.

After listening to the person's response, if you disagree with it, still acknowledge the person's perspectives and feelings; do not completely dismiss or discount them.

For instance, don't say: "That's ridiculous" or, "You're not making any sense." Instead, say, "I see how you might feel that way, but . . ." or, "I feel badly that you are under pressure, but. . . ."

If things begin to get nasty, call for a time out or cease fire, and table (postpone) the discussion to allow both of you time to cool off.

When emotion and adrenalin run high, logic and reason often run low. This can result in someone saying something out of anger, which, in turn, stimulates an angry response from the other person; then the anger of both combatants continues to escalate and turns into an intense volley of verbal punches and counterpunches. For example, the conversation may go something like this:

> Person A: "You're out of control."
> Person B: "No, I'm not out of control, you're just overreacting."
> Person A: "*I'm* overreacting, you're the one who's yelling!"
> Person B: "I'm not yelling, *you're* the one who's raising your voice!" . . . etc.

Blow-by-blow exchanges such as these are likely to turn up the emotional heat so high that it's probably best for both fighters to back off, retreat to their respective corners, cool down, and try again later when neither one of them is ready to throw a knockout punch.

Make your point assertively, not passively or aggressively.

When you are *passive*, you don't stand up for your personal rights; you allow others to take advantage of you by allowing them to push you around. You say nothing when you really should say something. You say "yes" when you really want to say "no." When you handle conflict passively, you tend to feel angry, anxious, or resentful about doing nothing and keeping it all inside.

When you are *aggressive*, you stand up for your rights, but you do so in a way that violates the rights of the other person in the conflict by threatening, dominating, humiliating, or bullying that person. You use intense, emotionally loaded words that attack the person (e.g., "You spoiled brat" or, "You're a sociopath!"). You manage to get what you want but at the other person's expense. Later, you tend to feel guilty about overreacting or coming on too strong (e.g., "I knew I shouldn't have said that.") When you are *passive-aggressive*, you get back or get even with the other person by withholding or taking away something (e.g., not speaking to the other person or withdrawing all attention or affection).

In contrast, when you are *assertive*, you strike a healthy middle ground between being aggressive and passive. You handle conflict in a way that protects or restores your rights without taking away or stepping on the rights of others. You approach conflict in an even-tempered way—rather than in an angry or agitated manner; you speak in a normal volume—rather than yelling or screaming; and you communicate at a normal distance—rather than getting up close and "into the face" of the other person involved in the conflict.

Focus on the specific behavior causing the conflict, not the person's general character.

Avoid labeling the person as "selfish," "mean," "inconsiderate," etc. For instance, if you're upset because your roommate doesn't do his share of cleaning, stay away from aggressive labels such as: "You slacker!" or "You lazy bum!" Attacking others with negative labels such as these may just give them the feeling they're under attack. This is likely to put them on the defensive and provoke a counterattack on one of your own characteristics that they're not exactly thrilled about. Before you know it, you may find yourself in a full-scale war of words and mutual character assassinations rather than a small-scale skirmish about the specific behavior of one person.

Rather than focusing on the person's general character, focus on the specific behaviors that are causing the problem (e.g., failing to do the dishes; leaving dirty laundry around the room). This will enable the other person to know exactly what actions need to be taken to take care of the problem. Furthermore, it's much easier for others to change a specific behavior than it is to change their entire character—which would require a complete change in personality (or a frontal lobotomy).

◆ **Use "I" messages to focus on how the other person's behavior or action affects you.**

Using "I" messages that focus on our personal perceptions and feelings sends a message that is less accusatory and less threatening (Narciso & Burkett, 1975). In contrast, "you" messages are more likely to make the other person on the defensive and put them on the offensive—ready to retaliate rather than cooperate (Gibb, 1991). For instance, suppose you've received a grade that is lower than what you think you earned in a course, and you decide to question your instructor about it. This conversation should not begin by saying to the instructor, "*You* gave me the wrong grade" or "*You* made a mistake." These messages may put your professor immediately on the defensive and ready to defend the grade you already received. Your professor will be less threatened and more likely to hear your complaint if you initiate the conversation with an "I statement," such as: "I don't believe I received the correct grade . . ." or, "I think an error may have been made in my final grade."

"I" messages are less aggressive because you're targeting an issue, not a person (Jakubowski & Lange, 1978). Saying, "I feel angry when . . ." rather than, "You make me angry when . . ." sends the message that you're taking responsibility for the way you feel, rather than guilt-tripping the individual for making you feel that way (perhaps without the person even knowing that's how you felt).

Lastly, when using "I" messages, try to describe *precisely what you are feeling*. For instance, saying, "I feel neglected when you don't write or call" more precisely identifies what you're feeling than to say, "I wish you would be more considerate." Describing what you feel in precise terms serves to increase the persuasive power of your message and reduces the risk that the other person will misunderstand or discount it.

Pause for Reflection

Your classmate is not contributing to a group project that you're both supposed to be working on as a team; you're getting frustrated and angry because you're doing virtually all of the work. What might be an "I message" that you could use to communicate your concern in a non-threatening way that could successfully resolve this conflict.

Avoid criticizing in terms of absolute or blanket statements.

Compare the following three pairs of statements:

a. "You're no help at all" versus, "You don't help me enough."
b. "You never try to understand how I feel" versus, "You don't try hard enough to understand how I feel."
c. "I always have to clean up" versus, "I'm doing more than my fair share of the cleaning."

The first statement in each of the above pairs represents an absolute or blanket statement that covers all times, situations, and circumstances—without any room for possible exceptions. Such extreme, blanket criticisms are likely to put the criticized person on the defensive because they state that the person is totally lacking or deficient with respect to some positive behavior. The second statement in each pair states the criticism in terms of degree or amount, which is less likely to threaten the person's self-esteem, and which is probably closer to the truth.

Focus on solving the problem, not winning the argument.

Try not to approach conflict with the attitude that you're going to "get even" or "prove that you're right." Winning the argument but not actually persuading the person to change the behavior that's causing the conflict is like winning a battle but losing the war. Instead, go into the discussion with the attitude that it's a problem to be solved, and that both parties can "win"— i.e., both of you can end-up with a better relationship in the long run if the problem is solved.

End your discussion of the conflict on a warm, constructive note.

Finish the session by making sure that the other person knows there are "no hard feelings" and that you're optimistic the conflict can be resolved and your relationship improved.

If the conflict is resolved because of some change made by the other person, express your appreciation for the individual's effort.

Even if your complaint was legitimate and your request was justified, the person's effort to accommodate your request should not be taken for granted. At the very least, you should not react to the changed behavior with rubbing-it-in comments like, "That's more like it" or, "It's about time!"

Expressing appreciation to the other person for making a change in response to your request not only is a socially sensitive thing to do; it's also a self-serving thing to do, because by recognizing or reinforcing the other person's changed behavior, you increase the likelihood that the positive change in behavior will be maintained and continue.

If you have expressed your concern and given the person ample time to make the change you requested, but nothing changes, then you have the right to take your complaint to a higher level of authority.

For example, if your roommate repeatedly ignores your reasonable and repeated requests to change some behavior that is violating your rights, you can take it a step higher and talk about it with the resident assistant on your floor. If nothing happens at that level, you may have to take the issue one step higher by bringing it to the attention of your resident director. Similarly, if your instructor repeatedly ignores your request to re-evaluate your grade, your next step would be to take it to the chairperson of the professor's department; if nothing happens at that level, then the next step would be to take it to the academic dean at your college or university.

BOX 11.2 *Snapshot* SUMMARY

"Dirty Fighting" Techniques: Ineffective Ways of Handling Interpersonal Conflict

The behaviors demonstrated by the following types of "fighters" represent ineffective ways to resolve conflict, because they tend to cut off all lines of communication and provoke anger in the other person involved in the conflict.

Crisis Ticklers: complain indirectly by hinting at the problem, but not honestly confronting it. For example, if the conflict involves a smoking roommate, the crisis tickler may say to the roommate, "Whew, it's really stuffy in here" (without mentioning that it's due to the smoke-filled air in the room).

Withholders: deal with conflict indirectly by socially withholding or "taking away" something from the other person, such as attention or affection (e.g., walking out of the room, not talking to the person, or totally ignoring the person). This represents a passive-aggressive approach to dealing with conflict because it attempts to hurt or punish the other person by *not* doing something.

Irritators: express resentment indirectly by doing irritating things that are intentionally designed to "bug" the other person (e.g., playing the stereo loudly when the other person is sleeping).

Blamers: are more concerned about finding fault in the other person than in solving the problem and resolving the conflict.

Gunnysackers: over time they gradually collect little things about the other person that annoy them, just like someone would collect things in a gunnysack (burlap bag). Their sack of anger keeps filling up until it reaches a boiling point—at which point it explodes and they unload all of their anger (and all of their complaints) on the other person at one time—bombarding and burying the person in an aggressive avalanche.

Adapted from, *Creative Aggression: The Art of Assertive Living*, by George Bach and Herb Goldberg.

Pause for Reflection

Do you consider yourself to be a leader?

If yes, why?

If no, why not?

••• Developing Leadership Skills

Effective leadership may be defined as the ability to influence people in a positive way (e.g., motivating your peers to do their best), or the ability to produce positive change in an organization or institution, such as improving the quality of a school, business, or a political organization (Kouzes & Posner, 1988; Veechio, 1997).

In college, you have a tremendous opportunity to influence others because you are among peers who are making a life-changing transition into a new social environment. When people find themselves in social situations they're unfamiliar with and that involve less structure and more freedom than they're accustomed to, they often look to others for cues and direction about how to act. Research suggests that peers provide a powerful source of support and direction for students in college (Feldman & Newcomb, 1969; Astin, 1993). This may be particularly true for new college students who are in the process of making a transition to a new social environment. These students are likely to look for support and direction from others whom they see as being most similar to them, such as other new students like you. You may be in a position right now to step forward and exert positive influence on the people around you; you can become a leader as a first-year student. If you accept this challenge, you can create a "win-win-win" scenario for three different parties:

1. Your *peers* win by benefiting from the positive leadership you provide,
2. Your *school* benefits by having a more successful student body, and
3. *You* benefit by developing leadership skills that will contribute to your college success and strengthen your career success after college.

Thus, by developing leadership skills while you're in college, you not only help others succeed, but you help yourself succeed—both in college and beyond.

Truths and Myths about Effective Leadership

Contrary to a common misconception, leadership is not a single personality trait that happens automatically or naturally (e.g., a "natural born" leader). Rather than being a generic trait, leadership is a specific behavior that is reflected in what you *do* or how you *act*. Furthermore, leadership is not some indefinable, magnetic "charisma" that individuals possess and deploy across all situations. Leaders most often demonstrate their leadership behavior in specific types of situations, which is known as *situational leadership* (Fiedler, 1993). Rather than being born with leadership skill as a genetic gift, leadership is often an acquired habit that a person develops with experience and uses in certain social situations or contexts.

Another misconception about leadership is that effective leaders are extroverted, bold, and aggressive (or ruthless). While these traits may have characterized some famous or notorious political leaders, many effective leaders are not aggressive, dominant, or power hungry; instead, they often display their leadership in subtle, sensitive, and caring ways. Leaders don't always roar; instead, they may be "quiet leaders" who possess a quiet strength and encourage others with a soft voice. Other leaders may be effective without doing much talking at all; they lead by example—by being role models who model positive behaviors, skills, and achievements for others to imitate and emulate. Thus, the bottom line on leadership is that it comes in different styles (Locke, 1991), which means that many people have the potential to demonstrate leadership in different ways and in different situations.

While there are different styles of leadership, one characteristic that all effective leaders often have in common is *self-knowledge* (Bennis, 1989). An important first step you can take toward becoming an effective leader is to develop self-awareness of your own leadership strengths or skills, as well as the situations in which your leadership style may be best applied (Zaccaro, Foti, & Kenny, 1991). Self-awareness is also important for enabling effective leaders to know when they may be spreading themselves too thin by taking on too many different leadership roles or responsibilities. Effective leaders shoot for quality, not quantity, by limiting themselves to those leadership roles and situations that best match their leadership interests and talents.

Leadership Situations and Roles for College Students

The ways in which you can demonstrate leadership in college are almost limitless. However, most of them may be grouped into three general roles.

1. **Academic Leadership.** You can demonstrate leadership in the classroom by modeling intellectual curiosity and academic motivation—for example, by being highly attentive and participating in class, and by contributing insightful questions or comments during class discussions. Specific academic leadership roles you can assume on campus include:

    a. leading study groups and group projects,
    b. being a peer tutor in your college's academic-support center, or
    c. serving as a peer-teaching assistant for a college course.

    You can provide academic leadership in any of these roles without necessarily being intellectually gifted or brilliant, but simply by being knowledgeable, reliable, and available as a resource to peers who seek your support.

2. **Social/Emotional Leadership.** You can demonstrate leadership by modeling responsible social behavior, making others feel welcome, drawing out people who may be shy and including them in conversations and activities, and by being a caring person who is willing to

Becoming a resident assistant is one way to demonstrate a social or emotional leadership role.

listen and provide emotional support for others. Specific social or emotional leadership roles you may be able to assume on campus include:

  a. student leader for new-student orientation,
  b. resident assistant in campus housing,
  c. peer mentor,
  d. peer counselor,
  e. peer minister, or
  f. peer mediator.

3. Organizational Leadership. You can also demonstrate leadership by organizing and motivating groups of people to work for worthy social and political causes. This type of leadership may involve such activities as initiating clubs and directing student organizations, effectively delegating tasks and responsibilities, maintaining group cohesiveness and cooperation, and keeping groups on track and making progress toward a common goal. Specific leadership roles you can assume for these purposes include:

  a. student government,
  b. college committees and task forces, and
  c. volunteer work in the local community.

Strategies for Developing Leadership Skills

Since we have defined leadership as the ability to produce positive change in an organization or institution, or to influence people in a positive way, developing leadership skills begins with knowing the organization or institution to which you belong and the people with whom you interact. Here are some key strategies for gaining knowledge in both of these areas.

Learn about your organization or institution.

Learn how your college is organized and how "the system" works, so you can work the system and make it work for you and your leadership cause. For example, become familiar with your college's table of organization or organizational chart, which shows the chain of command or decision-making authority from top to bottom. Also, be familiar with the student organizations and leadership opportunities that exist at your college by reviewing your *Student Handbook*. (We encourage you to complete exercise #2 at the end of the chapter.)

Learn how to effectively communicate with and relate to others.

Effective leadership boils down to effective use of interpersonal communication and human relations skills such as those discussed in this chapter (for example, learning people's names and interests (Hogan, et al., 1994), and being a good listener (Johnson & Bechler, 1998). Although being a dynamic and eloquent speaker can be helpful in certain leadership roles, leaders are often effective not because of their spectacular oratory skills, but because of their outstanding listening and conversational skills. Rather than taking over and controlling conversations with monologues, effective leaders exert their positive influence by allowing participants equal opportunity to engage in dialogue, and by encouraging equal exchange of ideas from all those involved in the conversation or discussion.

Effective leaders may not always lead or dominate the discussion; but when they do speak, they use effective oral communication strategies that allow them to express their ideas clearly, coherently, and persuasively; and they communicate in ways that allow them to mediate and resolve conflicts successfully.

> **· —· CLASSIC QUOTE ·— ·**
>
> *To lead, one must follow.*
>
> —Lao Tzu, ancient Chinese philosopher and founder of Taoism—a philosophy that emphasizes thought before action

In short, effective leadership involves communicating and relating effectively to others. Thus, the interpersonal communication and human relations skills discussed in this chapter should not only improve your social life, they should also develop your leadership potential.

●●● Summary and Conclusion

Communicating and relating effectively with others is an important life skill and one of the most important forms of human intelligence. We should give equal attention to the development of our interpersonal skills as we do our academic and intellectual skills, because research clearly shows that the quality of our relationships plays a pivotal role in promoting our success, health, and happiness.

The quality of our interpersonal relationships rests heavily on our ability to communicate effectively with others, both as recipients and deliverers of information. We need to give full attention to others by listening actively and empathically, and we need to hold the attention of others by communicating clearly and concisely. When relating to others, we need to get outside ourselves and become interested in others by learning and remembering their names and personal information about them. We need to make others feel special by recognizing their unique identity and special interests. We need to be positive when interacting with others by maintaining a good mood, by looking for the positive qualities in others and by being ready to praise or compliment those qualities when we see them. We need to be sharing persons who gradually disclose ourselves to others, and we need to be caring persons who are ready and willing to help others who seek our help. We need to be reliable and dependable, to come through and follow through on our interpersonal commitments, and to do what we say we're going to do. We need to interact with others in a humane and sensitive manner, whether that interaction takes place online, in person, or in the context of interpersonal conflict.

In short, we need to relate to others in a way that acknowledges their humanity and individuality, and preserves or promotes their self-esteem. We should strive to bring out the best in others by being helpful friends, positive role models, and effective leaders.

●●● Learning More through Independent Research

Web-Based Resources for Further Information on Interpersonal Relationships

For additional information relating to the ideas discussed in this chapter, we recommend the following Web sites:

> www.Humanresources.about.com/od/interpersonalcommunication1/
>
> www.articles911.com/Communication/Interpersonal_Communication/
>
> http://hodu.com/ECS-Menu1.shtml

CHAPTER 11

Exercise #1. Identifying Ways of Handling Interpersonal Conflict

Think of a social situation or relationship that is currently causing you the most conflict in your life. Describe how this conflict might be approached in each of the following ways:

1. Passively:

2. Aggressively:

3. Passive-Aggressively:

4. Assertively:

(See pp. 377–378 for descriptions of each of these four approaches.)

Consider practicing the assertive approach by role-playing it with a friend or classmate, and then applying it to the actual situation or relationship in your life where you're currently experiencing conflict.

Exercise #2. Identifying Leadership Opportunities on Your Campus

Consult your *Student Handbook* and list the student organizations and leadership opportunities that exist at your college or university.

_____

_____

_____

_____

_____

1. Which of the above student organizations or leadership positions at your college would best match or capitalize on your particular talents, skills, or interests?

2. In what specific situation(s) or position(s) do you see yourself being a leader?

3. Can you think of any behaviors you tend to display that might allow you to serve as a role model that influences other students in a positive way?

4. In what areas or aspects of college life on your campus do you think student leadership is most needed?

Stuck at Stage One: Meeting Lots of People but Making Few Friends

Since starting college, Sydney has met dozens of new people. He attended all the new-student orientation activities that began before classes started, and he has been attending parties almost every weekend throughout his first term in college. Although he continues to have lots of social contact with his peers and continues to meet new people, it's near Christmas break at the end of his first term and he still hasn't developed a close friendship with anybody at his college. Sydney is disappointed about this because none of his high school or hometown friends are attending his college, so he was really hoping to make new friends on campus.

Reflection and Discussion Questions

1. Would you say that Sydney should be concerned about not having developed any friendships at this point in his college experience, or is he expecting too much too soon?

2. What factors or reasons do you think may be contributing to the fact that Sydney's relationships have not progressed to closer levels of friendship?

3. What could Sydney do to increase his chances of forming closer friendships with the people he's already met or will meet on campus?

4. Who would you recommend to Sydney as a useful source of help or advice for moving beyond meeting new people to forming new friendships?

Health and Wellness

The Physical Dimension

Learning Goals

The goal of this chapter is to help you acquire specific strategies for promoting physical wellness *early* in your college experience, so that you can:

a. put these strategies immediately into practice to promote success during your first year, and

b. build on them to maximize wellness during your later years in college and beyond.

Outline

What Is Wellness?
Why Is Wellness Relevant to College Students?
The Body: The Physical Dimension of Wellness
Nutrition
    Nutrition-Management Strategies
Exercise and Fitness
    Benefits of Exercise for the Mind
    Benefits of Exercise for the Body
    Developing a Fitness Plan
    Guidelines and Strategies for Effective Exercise
Rest and Sleep
    The Value and Purpose of Sleep
    Strategies for Improving Sleep Quality

Alcohol, Drugs, and Risky Behavior
    Alcohol Use among College Students
    Illegal Drugs
    Strategies for Minimizing or Eliminating the
        Negative Effects of Alcohol, Drugs, and Risky
        Behavior
Summary and Conclusion
Learning More through Independent Research
Exercises:
    Nutritional Self-Assessment and
        Self-Improvement
    Wellness Self-Assessment and Self-Improvement
Case Study: Drinking to Death: College Partying
    Gone Wild

Activate Your Thinking

What would you say are the three most important things that humans can do to preserve their health and promote their physical well-being?

1. _____

2. _____

3. _____

•●• What Is Wellness?

Wellness may be described as a state of good health, peak performance, and positive well-being that is produced when different dimensions of the "self" work well together.

While experts disagree on the exact number and nature of the different dimensions of wellness (President's Council on Physical Fitness and Sports, 2001), we feel that wellness is best explained, understood, and developed in terms of three key dimensions of the self (Figure 12.1):

1. Physical,
2. Mental, and
3. Spiritual.

Figure 12.1 Three Key Dimensions of Wellness

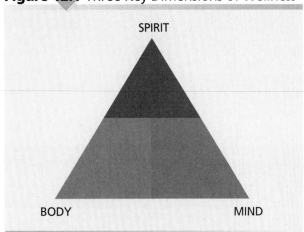

We will discuss the physical dimension of wellness in this chapter. The mental and spiritual dimensions of wellness will be discussed in Chapter 13. If we preserve and promote these three key dimensions of our self, we're more likely to maintain our health, maximize our performance, and attain happiness.

Wellness is not something done in reaction to illness, like trying to get well again after getting sick; it's something that's done proactively to prevent illness from ever occurring in the first place (Corbin, Pangrazi, & Franks, 2000). It involves putting into practice two classic proverbs: "Prevention is the best medicine" and "An ounce of prevention is worth a pound of cure."

Wellness is not a dichotomy that involves only two categories: being either sick or being healthy; instead, it represents a continuum or spectrum that ranges from abnormal (illness) to normal (illness free) to optimal (peak level of health and performance).

As depicted in Figure 12.2, there are three potential interception points for preventing illness, maintaining health, and promoting peak performance, which range from the reactive (after illness) to proactive (before illness):

Figure 12.2 Potential Points for Preventing Illness, Preserving Health, and Promoting Peak Performance

Proactive | Reactive

1. Feeling great and attaining peak levels of performance
2. Not sick, but could be feeling better and performing at higher levels
3. Sick, unable to perform, and trying to regain health

Wellness goes beyond merely maintaining physical health to attaining quality of life—that includes personal satisfaction, happiness, vitality (energy and vigor), and longevity (a longer lifespan).

Why Is Wellness Relevant to College Students?

•—• **CLASSIC QUOTE** •—•

❝ *Wellness is a multidimensional state of being describing the existence of positive health in an individual as exemplified by quality of life and a sense of well-being.* ❞

—Charles Corbin, and Robert Pangrazi, President's Council on Physical Fitness and Sports

When students move directly from high school to college, and move from living at home to living on campus, they are making a major move toward taking sole responsibility for their personal wellness. Mom and Dad are no longer around to monitor their health habits or to remind them about what and when to eat, what hours to keep, and when to go to sleep.

In addition to receiving less guidance and supervision, new college students are making a major life transition; stress tends to increase during times of change or transition. Bad health habits, such as poor nutritional habits, can lead to further stress and moodiness (Khoshaba & Maddi, 1999–2004). In contrast, good health habits are one way to both cope with college stress and maximize college performance.

In the introduction to this book, we noted research that pointed to the advantages of the college experience and college degree. Among the advantages experienced by college graduates are that they experience better physical health, live longer, and experience higher levels of both *psychological well-being* (mental health) and *personal happiness* (life satisfaction). This suggests that students are learning something about wellness and how to promote it by the time they graduate from college. We want you to begin learning about wellness now, so that you can experience its benefits immediately and continue to experience them throughout your college years.

◆ *Pause for Reflection*

If there was one thing about your physical health that you are concerned about or you would like to know more about, what would it be?

The Body: The Physical Dimension of Wellness

A healthy lifestyle for peak performance includes four key elements:

1. Supplying our body with effective fuel (nutrition),
2. Converting the fuel we consume into bodily energy (exercise),
3. Giving our body adequate rest so it can recover from the energy it has expended, and
4. Avoiding risky substances and risky behaviors that can threaten our health and safety.

These four components of the physical dimension of wellness will be discussed in this section.

Nutrition

•—• **CLASSIC QUOTE** •—•

❝ *May the sun bring you new energy by day; may the moon restore you by night. May the rain wash away your worries; may the breeze blow strength into your being. May you walk gently through the world and know its beauty all the days of your life.* ❞

—Apache Indian blessing

Our body needs *nutrients* to replenish its natural biochemicals and repair its tissues. The food we put into our body supplies it with energy in a manner similar to the way gas we pump into a car supplies it with fuel. Consequently, highly nutritious food provides us with high-quality fuel that can power our body and mind to function at maximum capacity and efficiency. Unfortunately, people often pay more attention to the quality of fuel they put into their car than to the quality of food they put into their body. Humans frequently eat without any intentional planning about what they eat. They pick up food on the run or at places where they can get food fast without leaving their cars, or at places where they can get in and out as fast as possible. Even when people slow down and take their time to eat, they often do it while their attention is divided or consumed by something else (e.g., conversation, reading, or watching TV).

We should be eating in a more thoughtful and nutritionally conscious way, rather than just eating out of convenience, habit, or in pursuit of what's most pleasant to our taste buds. Instead of only eating for pleasure, we should also "eat to win," i.e., eat the types of food that will best equip us to defeat disease and promote maximum physical and mental performance.

Studies show that the least nutritious and most unhealthy foods are the ones that receive the greatest amount of media advertising (Caroli, et al., 2004; Hill, 2002). We have been called a "fast food nation" where we've developed the habit of consuming food that can be accessed quickly, conveniently, cheaply, and in large ("super sized") portions (Schlosser, 2001).

Unfortunately, the "fast food" we're consuming in such large quantities also tends to be junk food—i.e., food with the least nutrients, the most calories, and the highest health risks. The availability and convenience of high-calorie, low-cost food is contributing to the fact that Americans are now heavier than at any other time in history. Currently, approximately 65 percent of Americans 20 years and older are either overweight (20 percent over the ideal body weight for their height and age) or obese (30 percent over their ideal weight) (American Obesity Association, 2002). The percentage of Americans who are overweight or obese has risen from 26 percent in 1976 to almost 65 percent in 2003 (Hill, et al., 2003). The most revealing research finding or the "proof in the pudding" is that when people move to America from other countries and begin to adopt American eating habits, they typically put on pounds (Sundquist & Winkleby, 2000).

National surveys of first-year college students indicate that less than 40 percent report that they frequently maintain a healthy diet (Sax, et al., 2004). The phrase "freshman 15" is commonly used to describe the 15-pound weight gain that some students experience during their first year of college (Brody, 2003; Levitsky, et al., 2003). For some first-year students, this weight gain may just be a temporary experience associated with the initial transition to the college eating lifestyle (e.g., all-you-can-eat dining halls, late night pizzas, and junk-food snacks). However, for other students it may signal the start of a longer-lasting pattern of gaining and carrying excess weight. The disadvantage of being overweight isn't merely an issue of appearance, it's a health issue because excess weight increases susceptibility to our leading life-threatening diseases, such as diabetes, heart disease, and certain forms of cancer.

Pause for Reflection

Have your eating habits changed since you've begun college?

If yes, in what way(s) have they changed?

Eating Disorders

While some students may be experiencing the "freshman 15," others may experience eating disorders relating to weight loss and weight control. The disorders described below are more common among females (National Institute of Mental Health, 2001). Studies show that approximately one of every three college females indicate that they worry about their weight, body image, or eating habits (Douglas, et al., 1997; Haberman & Luffey, 1998). This is likely due to the fact that in Western cultures, there is more emphasis or pressure on females than males to maintain lighter body weight and body size. This is an unfortunate cultural standard because it conflicts with the biological reality that the female body is genetically constituted or wired up to contain more fat cells and to store fat more easily than the male body. Since fat is an energy reserve, it's likely that women have been naturally equipped with more ability to store fat because they are the childbearing sex, and this extra fat provides them with an extra energy reserve during pregnancy and delivery.

Below is a short summary of the major eating disorders experienced by college students. People experiencing these disorders often are in denial about their problem, and they typically experience emotional issues along with their eating disorders (e.g., depression and anxiety), which are likely to require professional treatment (American Psychiatric Association Work Group on Eating Disorders, 2000). The earlier these disorders are identified and treated, the better the prognosis or probability of cure. The Counseling Center or Student Health Center is the key campus resource to begin the process of seeking help and treatment for any of the following eating disorders.

Anorexia Nervosa

The self-esteem of people experiencing this disorder is excessively tied to their body weight or shape. They see themselves as overweight and have an intense fear of gaining weight, even though they're dangerously thin. Anorexics deny they're severely underweight and remain obsessed about avoiding eating, eating infrequently, and eating in extremely small portions. Anorexics may also use other methods to lose weight, such as compulsive exercise, diet pills, laxatives, diuretics, or enemas.

Bulimia Nervosa

This eating disorder is characterized by repeated episodes of "binge eating"—eating excessive amounts of food within a limited period of time. Bulimics tend to lose all sense of self-control during their binges, and then they try to compensate for overeating by engaging in extreme behaviors designed to "purge" their guilt and prevent weight gain; for example, they may purge by self-induced vomiting, consuming excessive amounts of laxatives or diuretics, using enemas, or fasting. This binge-purge pattern typically takes place at least twice a week and continues for three or more months.

Unlike anorexia, bulimia is harder to detect because the bulimic's binges and purges take place privately or secretly, and their body weight looks about normal for their age and height. However, similar to anorexics, bulimics fear gaining weight, aren't happy with their body, and have an intense desire to lose weight.

Binge-Eating Disorder

Like bulimia, this eating disorder involves repeated, out-of-control binge eating; however, purging does not occur after binge episodes. To be diagnosed as suffering from binge-eating disorder, the person would have to display at least three of the following symptoms, twice a week, for several months:

a. eating much more rapidly than normal;

b. eating until becoming uncomfortably full;

c. eating large amounts of food when not being physically hungry;

d. eating alone due to feeling embarrassed about others seeing how much he or she eats; and

e. feeling guilty, disgusted, or depressed after overeating.

Since those who suffer from eating disorders typically do not recognize or admit their illness, friends and family members play a key role in helping these individuals receive the help they need before the disorders progress to a life-threatening level. If someone you know is experiencing an eating disorder, consult with a professional at the Health Center or Counseling Center about strategies for approaching and encouraging this person to seek help.

Sources: American Psychiatric Association (1994). National Institute of Mental Health (2006).

Nutrition-Management Strategies

Below is a series of specific nutrition-management strategies, which may be used to increase our body's ability to stay well and perform well.

Develop a nutrition management plan that ensures variety and balance.

Take a look at Figure 12.3, which lists the basic food groups and the portions of each group that are recommended by the American Dietetic Association. The "Food Guide Pyramid" divides food into six basic groups. Since different foods vary in terms of the nature of nutrients they provide (carbohydrates, protein, and fat), no one food group can supply all the nutrients that your body needs. Therefore, your diet should be "balanced" and include all of these food groups, but in different proportions or percentages. To find the daily amount of food you should consume from each of these groups that best meets your personal needs (e.g., your age and gender), go to MyPyramid.gov.

The food pyramid can be used to develop a general plan to ensure you consume each of these food groups every day, resulting in a balanced diet that will minimize your risk of experiencing any nutritional deficits or deficiencies. If this guide to nutrition is followed, there is no need to take vitamins or dietary supplements.

Figure 12.3 Food Guide Pyramid

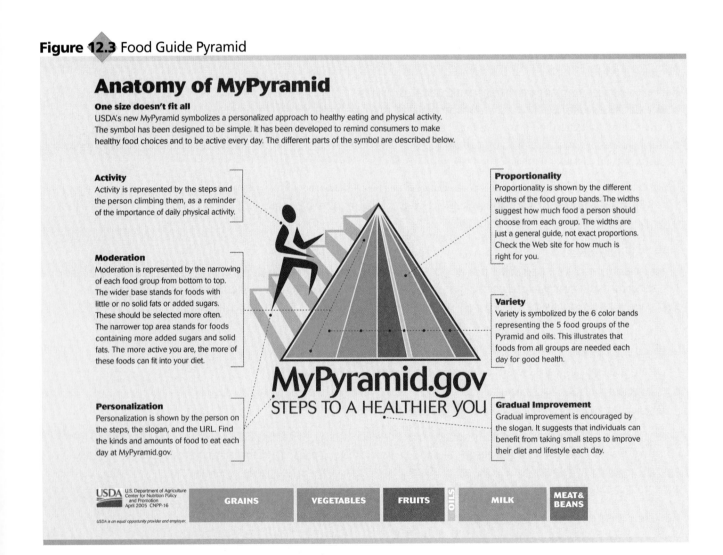

Planning what we eat is essential to ensure we eat what is best for our health and wellness. If we don't plan ahead of time and purchase the food we should eat, we are more likely to eat food that can be accessed conveniently and doesn't require advanced preparation. Unfortunately, foods that can be acquired and consumed most conveniently are fast food and packaged food, which are the least healthy foods. If we are serious about eating in a way that is best for our health and performance, we need to do some advanced nutritional planning.

Personal Story

Growing up in poverty wasn't fun but it was somewhat nutritious for me. What we ate had to be reasonable in price and bought in bulk. Every morning my mother fixed rice or oatmeal for breakfast along with wonderful buttermilk biscuits (probably not nutritious). Every night she fixed pinto beans and cornbread for dinner. We also had fresh vegetables from the garden and apples, hickory nuts, and walnuts from surrounding trees. Meat was not readily available and was only eaten when we killed a chicken or hog that we had raised. My mother believed that these items "stuck to your ribs" and provided a balanced diet. When I left home and went to college, I realized that those items that I complained about while living at home were exactly the food I missed eating. As a college student, I soon determined that my eating habits were not nearly as healthy as they were at home. Cheese sandwiches did not constitute a balanced diet. With the innovation of modern day food sites on many college campuses, students need to take the time to develop good eating habits in college so that they continue to eat the balanced meals they left behind at home.

—Aaron Thompson

Minimize consumption of the following foods because their nutritional value is low (or zero) and they increase the risk of heart disease and cancer.

◆ Reduce intake of fried and fatty foods such as pizza, hamburgers, french fries, donuts, butter, and margarine. These foods not only contain lots of calories, they can increase the risk of heart disease because they contain *saturated fats* and *trans fats*—"bad" fats that tend to stick to blood vessel walls and increase our risk for cardiovascular disease. These fats also increase the risk of certain forms of cancer, such as breast and bowel cancer.

While saturated fats don't have to be completely eliminated from our diet, their intake should be limited. They should comprise less than 1/10th of the total number of calories we consume (National Research Council, 1989). Even if we exercise and are physically active, we still have to be conscious of the food we put into our body. Well-conditioned athletes still can be at risk for heart disease and cancer if they consume foods containing high amounts of saturated fat.

◆ Reduce consumption of processed foods. Processed foods are natural foods that have been altered so they can be preserved, packaged, jarred, canned, or bottled, and then sold to the public in large or bulk quantities. Processed foods contain additives that supplement natural food in order to preserve its shelf life, make it look more pleasing to the eye, or make it more pleasing to the taste buds. These additives typically have no nutritional value and may have unknown or possibly unhealthy effects on the body. For example, processed foods frequently contain added sugar and salt, which tend to promote weight gain and elevate blood pressure, respectively.

Salt and sugar are often added to processed foods just to increase their taste appeal (and sales appeal). Why do many humans find sweeter and saltier processed foods tastier than natural foods? One theory is that processed foods have not been around as long as unprocessed "natural" foods, which have been around for millions of years and were the only foods available to and consumed by our ancient ancestors. Therefore, taste buds of modern man may find "newer" processed foods to be more stimulating because they are more novel and different from the same "old" natural foods that have been eaten for millions of years (Eaton & Konner, 1985; Simopoulos & Pavlou, 1997). Ironically, humans may have developed or evolved a taste preference for the very foods that are the least nutritious, least healthy, and highest in calories. Thus, unfortunately, the foods that are most likely to stimulate our taste buds are also most likely to inflate our fat cells.

◆ Reduce consumption of high-fat dairy products (e.g., cheese, butter, margarine, cream, and whole milk). High-fat dairy products are high in saturated fat and sodium, both of which increase the risk of heart disease. The calcium contained in dairy products is good for us, but we're better off getting that calcium from low-fat dairy products, such as low-fat milk, yogurt, and cottage cheese.

Fruit is a nutritious snack that can also satisfy your craving for something sweet.

◆ Minimize consumption of animal meats, particularly red meat such as hamburger and steak. Many people believe they need to consume a substantial amount of red meat because it contains needed protein. It's true that animal meats provide large amounts of protein, but protein only constitutes 15 percent of our daily calories, and the fact is that Americans consume about twice as much protein as their bodies need (National Research Council, 1989).

Animal meats often contain a large amount of saturated fat, which poses a major risk for heart disease. Thus, it's probably best to reduce the amount of protein we get from animal meats and increase the amount we get from other sources that are low in saturated fat, such as plant sources (e.g., beans and peas), nuts (e.g., peanuts and almonds), and low-fat dairy products (e.g., low-fat milk and yogurt).

Also, if and when you do consume animal meat, you can reduce its health risk by eating lean meats that have less fat, and by removing any fatty skin from the meat (e.g., removing the skin from chicken or turkey). Lastly, it's healthiest not to fry meat because the oils used in the frying process increase the concentration of saturated fat in the meat. Instead of frying, it's better to roast, grill, bake, or broil the meat you eat.

Strategies for Weight Control

◆ Decrease or eliminate junk-food snacks. Replace sugary and salty snacks with healthier munchies, such as fruits, nuts, seeds, and raw vegetables. Many of these healthier snacks are as sweet, crispy, or crunchy as junk food snacks. For instance, natural fruits can provide sweetness with more nutrients and fewer calories than processed sweets (e.g., candy bars and blended coffee drinks). Unfortunately, advertisers have spent millions of dollars to convince consumers that processed sweets are "indescribably delicious." From a consumer standpoint, nutritious snacks represent a better investment of your money because you get a bigger "bang for your buck"—i.e., more key nutrients (and less empty calories) for your snacking dollar.

Pause for Reflection

What type of junk food (if any) do you eat?

Do you think you need to reduce the amount of junk food you're currently eating?

◆ Decrease the tendency to pack most of your calories into one or two large meals per day. Most nutritionists recommend that we should eat large meals less often and small meals more often. There is no research evidence that the American habit of eating three times a day is the best nutritional practice. In fact, six smaller meals or healthy snacks per day may be a more effective way to fuel the body than consuming three, full-sized meals (Khoshaba & Maddi, 1999–2004). When foraging for food, it's unlikely that our ancient ancestors ate three full meals three times a day; instead, they probably ate more frequently and in smaller portions, which provided them with a steady stream of energy throughout the day.

◆ Reduce the total number of calories consumed during your evening meal. The meal you eat closest to bedtime should be your lightest meal with the fewest calories, because you're soon going to be lying down and not expending much physical energy for 7 to 8 hours. Remember that calories are measures of the amount of energy contained in food. One calorie may be described as one unit or degree of energy. If we consume that unit of energy, and don't use it, we don't lose it; instead, we save it and store it as fat. In other words, much like money, if you don't spend your income (caloric intake), you tend to save it in your body's bank of fat cells. Eating lots of calories in the evening, then lying down and sleeping soon thereafter, means those evening calories don't get burned as physical energy; instead, they get stored as body fat.

◆ Reduce the tendency to rush out at the beginning of the day and skip or skimp on breakfast. As its name implies, a good breakfast provides energy that enables you to "break fast" at the start of the day and sustain your energy throughout the day. (It also reduces your desire for unhealthy snacks later in the day.) Your first meal of the day should be the meal where you can consume your most calories because you need energy for the next 16 or so hours that you'll be awake and moving. Unfortunately, Americans tend to do it backwards by skipping or skimping at breakfast and piling on calories at dinner—a time of day when they don't need many calories because they'll soon be lying down and falling asleep.

Make a conscious attempt to increase consumption of natural foods that have been available to humans throughout history.

The following foods aren't processed foods but are *natural* foods that have been available throughout human history. As a general rule, the food that was good for our ancient ancestors and the survival of our species is also good for us now. In fact, these are the foods that provide us with the best protection against our two leading killers: heart disease and cancer.

◆ Feast on fresh fruit. Fruit has multiple nutritional benefits, including high amounts of vitamins (especially A and C) and minerals. Many fruits also contain high amounts of *fiber*, which helps purify the bloodstream, lower the type of cholesterol that can cause heart disease, and rid the body of toxins found in the intestine. Other fruits, such as berries, are rich in *antioxidants*—substances that lower the risk of cancer by attacking oxidants (toxins) in the body that can damage genetic DNA and weaken the immune system. (Blueberries are thought to contain the most antioxidants, followed by blackberries, raspberries, and strawberries.) Keep in mind that fresh fruit is superior to canned fruit—which has been processed and artificially preserved. Also, if weight control is an issue, fresh fruit is superior to dried fruit—which contains more calories.

◆ Go wild on fresh (or frozen) vegetables. Fresh or frozen vegetables are superior to canned and processed vegetables. The natural oils in certain vegetables (e.g., olive, corn, avocado, and soy) are rich sources of unsaturated fat. *Unsaturated* fats, also known as "essential fatty acids," are considered to be "good" fats because they don't congregate or coagulate in our bloodstream but remain as liquid in our system; therefore, they don't degenerate into fat on the walls of blood vessels (Erasmus, 1993). Unsaturated fats also help wash away or flush out bad fats from our bloodstream. In addition to containing unsaturated fats, many vegetables (e.g., raw carrots and green beans) contain fiber that reduces the risk of heart disease and certain forms of cancer.

Pause for Reflection

Do you eat fresh fruit and vegetables on a daily basis?

If yes, why?

If no, why not?

◆ Go for grains. Whole-wheat bread, whole-wheat pasta, whole-grain cereals, oatmeal, and bran are examples of healthy grains. Note that the word "whole" should appear in the product's name (e.g., whole-wheat bread and whole-grain cereal). This is the key to determining that the grain is natural and not processed; for example, whole-wheat bread is made from a natural grain, but wheat or white bread has been processed. Thus, make sure it says "whole-wheat" if you are looking for an unbleached non-processed grain bread.

    Natural grains contain *complex carbohydrates* that the body uses to produce energy in a steady, ongoing fashion. Complex carbohydrates are called "complex" because their molecular structure is harder for the body to digest and break down into blood sugar. Since their more complex molecular structure slows down the digestion process, allowing them to be absorbed into the bloodstream more slowly, thereby delivering energy to the body more gradually and evenly over an extended period of time (similar to a coated pill or time-released capsule). Thus, grains are an excellent source of food for producing steady, long-term energy (e.g., athletic activities that require endurance and stamina). Grains are also high in fiber, which helps fight heart disease and certain forms of cancer. Lastly, many complex carbohydrates also contain an amino acid that helps produce serotonin—a brain chemical associated with relaxation and feelings of emotional serenity or "mellowness" (DesMaisons, 1998).

◆ Feed freely on fish. Fish are high in protein and low in saturated fat; and the natural oil in fish is high in unsaturated fat, which flushes out and washes away cholesterol-forming fats from the bloodstream (Khoshaba & Maddi, 1999–2004). Thus, a diet high in unsaturated fats (and low in saturated fats) reduces risk for non-genetic forms of cardiovascular disease such as high blood pressure, heart attacks, and strokes. This explains why fish-eating Eskimos have a significantly lower rate of cardiovascular disease than non-Eskimos (Feskens & Kromhout, 1993). However, be cautious about eating too much fish that may contain high levels of mercury such as shark, swordfish, red snapper, and orange roughy. Eating a variety of fish will help minimize this risk (American Heart Association, 2006).

◆ Consume lots of legumes. The word "legumes" derives from the Latin root "legumend," meaning "to gather." They include plants and seeds, such as beans (black, red, and navy), lentils, brussels sprouts, peas, and peanuts. Such foods are great sources of fiber, protein, iron, and B vitamins; plus, they are naturally cholesterol-free and low in saturated fat. In fact, the natural oil contained in these foods contains unsaturated fats—"good fats" that can reduce buildup of bad cholesterol in the bloodstream.

It's interesting to note in developing countries that are poorer economically than the U.S., people rely mainly on legumes, grains, fruits, and vegetables. Despite their poorer economy and poorer medical care, people living in underdeveloped countries have significantly lower rates of heart disease and diet-related cancers than do people living (and eating) in the United States (U.S. Department of Health & Human Services, 2000).

◆ Drink more water. Most people don't get the recommended amount of water (seven, 8-ounce glasses per day). We need to hydrate our bodies. The body uses water much like a car uses motor oil and transmission fluid to drive nutrients (fuel) to their proper destinations, and to drive waste products out of the system. Water also improves our nervous system's ability to conduct electrochemical signals, which may benefit the brain's ability to process information more easily and more rapidly. Don't only drink water when you are very thirsty; drink it regularly and try to consume 50 to 60 ounces a day. Besides all of its internal benefits, water has the cosmetic benefit of improving the appearance of your skin.

◆ If you're a woman, make a conscious effort to consume more calcium. Females should take in at least 1,200 mg of calcium per day (Gershoff & Whitney, 1996) in order to reduce their risk of *osteoporosis*—thinning of bones and loss of bone mass or density, which increases the risk of fractures and curvature of the upper spine. Although osteoporosis can happen in men as well as women, it occurs much more often among females. It's estimated that one of three women over the age of 40 will develop osteoporosis (Bohme & Budden, 2001). Because societal pressures make women more weight-conscious than men, females may try to avoid high-calcium dairy products because they are high in calories. However, women can get lots of calcium without lots of calories by consuming low-fat, low-calorie, dairy products, such as cottage cheese and low-fat yogurt. Also, sizable amounts of calcium are contained in other low-calorie foods, such as certain fish (e.g., salmon), vegetables (e.g., broccoli), and fruit (e.g., oranges) (Gershoff & Whitney, 1996). Calcium dietary supplements can also help a woman get the optimum level of calcium each day.

STUDENT PERSPECTIVE

"I always drink lots of water and I try to eat as much fruit and veggies as I can with each meal."

—First-year student

Develop more self-awareness of what you eat.

The first step toward effective nutrition management is becoming aware of our current eating habits. Decisions about what to eat are often made without much thought, or even awareness. We can increase awareness of our eating habits by simply taking a little time to read the labels on the food products before we put them into your shopping cart and into your body. Consider keeping a nutritional log or journal of what you eat in a typical week to track its nutrients and caloric content.

Also, become aware of your family history. Have members of your immediate and extended family shown tendencies toward heart disease? Diabetes? Cancer? If so, adopt a diet that will reduce your risk for experiencing the types of illnesses that you may have the genetic potential to develop.

Pause for Reflection

Are you aware of any disease or illness that tends to run in your family?

If yes, is there anything you can do with respect to your diet that may decrease your risk of experiencing this disease or illness?

●●● Exercise and Fitness

Wellness depends not only on fueling our body, but also on moving it. The benefits of physical exercise for improving the longevity and quality of human life are simply extraordinary. The power of exercise is not surprising because physical activity was something that our early ancestors did consistently on a daily basis in order to stay alive. They had no motorized vehicles to move them from point A to point B, and no one sold or served them food. Exercise was part of their daily survival routine of roaming and rummaging for fruit, nuts, and vegetables to eat; or running after and tracking down animals for meat to eat. Just as eating natural (unprocessed) food is better for our health because it's long been part of human history and has contributed to the survival of the human species, so too is exercise a "natural" health-promoting activity (Booth & Vyas, 2001). In fact, if done regularly, exercise may be the most effective "medicine" available to humans for preventing disease and preserving lifelong health.

Personal Story I kept in shape as a young person by playing sports such as basketball and baseball. Every chance that made itself available to my schedule I would play these sports for hours at a time. I enjoyed it so much that I did not realize I was actually exercising. My body fat was practically non-existent, energy was ever-flowing, and my skills in basketball always growing. As a middle-aged person, I now realize the activities I did for fun as a young person I can no longer do because age has caught up with me. At this point in my life, I attempt to remain active in order to keep my body fat in a reasonable double-digit category. This takes good scheduling, forethought, and strong will.

—*Aaron Thompson*

Benefits of Exercise for the Mind and Body

In addition to the multiple benefits of exercise for the body, it also has numerous benefits for the mind. Listed below is a summary of the powerful benefits of physical exercise for our mental health and mental performance. For people who believe that exercise isn't all that good for you and still cling to this belief after reading the following list, it may be safe to conclude that they are either in denial or "on another planet."

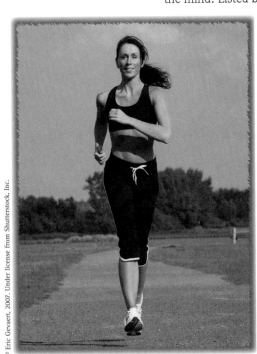

Physical exercise provides benefits for the body and the mind.

Exercise increases mental energy and improves mental performance.

Have you ever noticed how red your face gets when you engage in strenuous physical activity? This rosy complexion is due to the fact that physical activity causes enormous amounts of blood to be pumped into our head region, resulting in more oxygen reaching our brain. The human brain requires more oxygen than any other organ in the human body; it consumes almost 25 percent of the oxygen taken in by our lungs (Drubach, 2000). Since our brain cells cannot store oxygen, they need to receive a continuous supply of it through the flow of oxygen-carrying blood. Exercise increases the heart's ability to pump blood throughout the body and into the brain, and since the brain consumes more oxygen than any other part of the body, it's easy to see why it is the bodily organ that benefits the most from exercise.

Exercise also increases mental alertness by stimulating the body's adrenal glands to produce more adrenalin—an energy-promoting hormone that travels to the brain after it has been released into the bloodstream. Furthermore, exercise increases production of a brain chemical called norepinephrine, which helps form physical connections between brain cells (Howard, 2000). As we mentioned in Chapter 4, the formation of connections between brain cells is the physical foundation of learning and memory.

Exercise elevates mood.

Exercise increases the release of endorphins—natural morphine-like chemicals found in the brain that produce a natural high; and exercise also increases serotonin—a mellowing brain chemical that reduces feelings of tension (anxiety) and depression. Exercise is often prescribed by psychotherapists for patients experiencing mild forms of anxiety or depression (Johnsgard, 2004). In fact, studies show that people who exercise regularly tend to report feeling "happier" (Myers, 1993).

Exercise strengthens self-esteem.

Exercise can improve our self-esteem by giving us a sense of personal achievement or accomplishment, and improving our physical self-image (e.g., improved weight control, body tone, and skin tone).

Exercise deepens and enriches the quality of sleep.

Research on how exercise affects sleep indicates that, if done at least three hours before bedtime, exercise helps us fall asleep, stay asleep, and sleep more deeply (Singh, et al., 1997). In fact, exercise is a common component of treatment programs for people experiencing insomnia (Dement & Vaughan, 2000).

Benefits of Exercise for the Body

Exercise promotes cardiovascular health.

Exercise makes for a healthy heart. The heart is a muscle, and like any other muscle in the body, its size and strength is increased by exercise. A bigger and stronger heart can pump more blood per beat, which reduces the risk of heart disease and stroke (loss of oxygen to the brain) by increasing circulation of oxygen-carrying blood throughout the body and by increasing the body's ability to dissolve blood clots (Khoshaba & Maddi, 1999–2004).

Exercise further reduces the risk of cardiovascular disease by reducing the level of triglycerides (clot-forming fats) in the blood and by increasing levels of the body's "good cholesterol"—High-Density Lipoprotein (HDL), which removes "bad cholesterol"—Low-Density Lipoprotein (LDL) from sticking to and clogging up blood vessels.

Exercise stimulates the immune system.

There are several reasons why exercise improves the functioning of our immune system and enables us to better fight off infectious diseases (e.g., colds and the flu):

◆ Exercise reduces stress, which normally weakens the immune system.
◆ Exercise increases breathing rate and blood flow throughout the body; this helps flush out germs from our system by increasing the circulation of antibodies that are carried through the bloodstream.
◆ Exercise increases body temperature, which helps kill germs in a way that's similar to the way a low-grade fever kills germs when we're sick (May, 2004).

Exercise strengthens muscles and bones.

Exercise reduces muscle tension, which helps prevent muscle strain and pain (e.g., strengthening abdominal muscles can reduce the risk of developing lower back pain). Exercise also maintains bone density and reduces the risk of osteoporosis (brittle bones that bend and break easily). It's noteworthy that bone density before age 20 affects a person's bone density for the remainder of life; thus, regular exercise early in life pays long-term dividends by preventing bone deterioration throughout life.

 Pause for Reflection

Have your exercise habits changed (for better or worse) since you've begun college?

If yes, why do you think this change has taken place?

Exercising effectively promotes weight loss and weight management.

To lose weight, a change must take place in the body's energy balance, such that the number of calories the body expends in physical energy starts to exceed the number of calories it consumes in food. Thus, weight can be lost in only two ways: (1) by consuming a smaller number of calories, and/or (2) by burning a larger number of calories.

The increasing national trend toward weight gain is due not only to Americans consuming more calories; it's also due to their reduced levels of physical activity (American Obesity Association, 2002). Much of this reduction in physical activity is due to the emergence of modern technological conveniences that have made it easier for humans to go about their daily business without exerting themselves in the slightest. For example, almost all TVs now come with remote controls so we don't have to move to change channels, change volume, or turn it on and off. Children now have video games galore that are played "virtually," so kids can have fun playing without actually getting up, running around, or jumping up and down. Consequently, we're playing double jeopardy with our health by eating more and moving less.

Losing weight and maintaining weight loss are best achieved by a combination of diet and exercise. Research suggests that people who have successfully dieted to attain the weight they desire are better able to *maintain* their desired weight by continuing to exercise regularly, without having to continue dieting. In fact, exercise is superior to dieting in one major respect: It raises the body's rate of metabolism—i.e., the rate at which consumed calories are burned as energy rather than stored as fat. In contrast, low-calorie dieting lowers the body's rate of metabolism (Leibel, Rosenbaum, & Hirsch, 1995) and slows down the rate at which calories are burned.

After 2 to 3 weeks of low-calorie dieting without exercising, the body saves more of the calories it does get by storing them as fat. This happens because long-term low-calorie dieting makes the body "think" it's starving, so it tries to compensate and increase its chances of survival by saving more calories as fat so they can be used for future energy (Bennet & Gurin, 1983).

In contrast, exercise actually speeds up basal metabolism—our body's rate of metabolism when we're resting. Thus, in addition to burning fat directly while exercising, our rate of metabolism continues to remain higher after exercise is finished and we move on to do other things. In fact, exercise increases basal metabolism up to 48 hours after exercise is completed. This is a significant weight-control advantage of exercise because our basal metabolism accounts for 2/3 of our total energy expenditure. For example, in one study, overweight women were put on a restricted diet and their metabolic rates started to slow down, as you might expect because it was the body's natural way to store more calories to compensate for the fewer calories their body was taking in on their diet. However, when the dieters combined exercise with their diet, their metabolic rates rose almost to their pre-diet levels, and the women continued to lose weight (Wadden, et al., 1990). Furthermore, contrary to popular belief, exercise does not necessarily increase appetite and cause people to eat more. In fact, it may actually lower appetite among people who are overweight (Gershoff & Whitney, 1996).

Since dieting ultimately slows down basal metabolism and increases fat storage, exercise is the key to effective, long-term weight management (Leibel, et al., 1995).

Developing a Fitness Plan

A comprehensive fitness plan includes a balanced blend of exercises that increase *stamina*, *strength*, and *flexibility*. The following forms of exercise can be used to attain each of these three key fitness goals.

Aerobic Exercise

"Aerobic" literally means "with air" and refers to physical exercise that requires increased consumption of oxygen, causing our lungs and heart to pump faster to take oxygen in and transport it throughout the body (Bailey, 1991; Cooper, 1982). Aerobic exercise is the best type of exercise for promoting stamina (endurance) and cardiovascular health.

Swimming requires continuous movement and is considered an aerobic exercise.

The following activities qualify as aerobic exercise: vigorous walking (a.k.a., "power walking"), jogging, long-distance running, bicycling, swimming, aerobic dancing, skating, cross-country skiing, and sports that require continuous movement (e.g., basketball, handball, racquetball, tennis). To produce maximum benefits, aerobic exercise should be done *continuously* (e.g., 20–30 minutes at a time) and *consistently* (e.g., at least three times per week).

Different forms of aerobic exercise can vary in terms of the amount of *impact* or pressure that they exert on the body's joints, ranging from *high* impact (e.g., running or jogging), to *moderate* impact (walking), to *low* impact (swimming). Low-impact activities put less stress on joints, ligaments, and tendons; therefore, they pose less risk of injury. However, moderate- and high-impact exercise is more effective for stimulating bone growth and provides better protection against osteoporosis.

Anaerobic Exercise

In contrast to "aerobic," the term "anaerobic" literally means "without oxygen" and refers to physical activities that do not require a large increase in oxygen consumption; therefore, they do not force our lungs and heart to work as fast or continuously as aerobic exercise. The major benefits of anaerobic exercise are building body strength and tone (firmness).

Anaerobic exercises such as sit-ups do not require a large increase in oxygen consumption, and mainly serve to strengthen and tone the body.

Strength-building exercises include activities such as lifting weights (e.g., free weights), using strength building machines (e.g., nautilus training), push-ups, and sit-ups (Khoshaba &

Maddi, 1999–2004). These exercises also help maintain bodily posture and tone, increase bone density, and reduce the risk of bone degeneration. Although strength-building exercises do not burn as many calories as aerobic exercises, they do increase the body's muscle-to-fat ratio, which makes the body leaner and slowly raises its metabolism, thereby increasing the rate at which the body burns calories.

There are two major myths about strength-building exercises that need to be dispelled:

Myth #1: Extra muscle mass acquired through strength-building exercises will later turn into fat when the person stops training. This is false because muscle and fat are two entirely different types of body tissue, and one doesn't change or get transformed into the other.

Myth #2: Strength-building exercise requires consumption of large amounts of protein (e.g., eating more meat). This is not true because muscles do not use protein for energy; they use calories for energy, just like the rest of the body.

Flexibility Exercises

Any physical activity that effectively stretches muscles, and extends the range or degree of motion of the body's limbs and joints, will increase the body's flexibility and agility. A body that becomes more flexible and agile becomes less susceptible to muscle stiffness or soreness, and is at lower risk for injury to its muscles and joints. Exercises that promote flexibility and agility include yoga, tai chi, gymnastics, and Pilates. Many of these exercises also have other physical benefits, such as improving posture, balance, and bodily strength.

Phil Date, 2007. Under license from Shutterstock, Inc.

Flexibility exercises stretch your muscles, and increase your range of motion.

Pause for Reflection

What exercises or physical activities do you currently engage in that help you maintain or develop the following key components of physical fitness?

1. Endurance (Stamina)_____

2. Strength _____

3. Flexibility_____

Guidelines and Strategies for Effective Exercise

Specific exercises vary in terms of what they do to and for the body. Nevertheless, there are some general guidelines and strategies, such as those discussed below, that can be applied to virtually any type of exercise routine or personal fitness program.

Warm up before beginning exercising, and cool down after exercising.

Start with a 10-minute warm up of low-intensity movements that are similar to the ones you'll be using in the actual exercise. This increases circulation of blood to the muscles that will be exercised, which will reduce muscle soreness and muscle pulls.

End your exercise routine with a 10-minute cool down, during which you stretch the muscles that were used while exercising. Stretch the muscle until it burns a little bit, and release it;

this will stretch the muscle and reduce its tightness or tension. Cooling down after exercise improves circulation to the exercised muscles and enables them to return more gradually to a tension-free state, which will minimize the risk of muscle cramps, pulls, or tears.

Seek total fitness by cross training.

A balanced, comprehensive fitness program is one that involves *cross training*, which combines different exercises to achieve total fitness; for example, it includes aerobic exercises that promote endurance and weight control as well as anaerobic exercises that build strength, tone, and flexibility. A total fitness plan also includes exercising a variety of muscle groups on a rotational basis (e.g., upper-body muscles one day, lower-body muscles the next). This strategy will give your muscle tissue extra time to rest and fully repair itself before its next physical performance.

Exercising with regularity and consistency is as important as exercising with intensity.

Doing exercise regularly, and allowing strength and stamina to increase gradually, is the key to attaining fitness and avoiding injury. One test you can perform to be sure that you're training your body rather than straining it or overextending yourself is to see if you can talk while you're exercising; if you can't do it without having to catch your breath, then you may be over-doing it. As your body begins to adapt or adjust to an exercise and you find that you can do it and talk simultaneously, you can then gradually increase its intensity, frequency, or duration.

Personal Story I had a habit of exercising too intensely—to the point where I over-fatigued my muscles and left my body feeling sore for days after I worked out. Like many people, I exercise while listening to music to make the exercise routine a little more stimulating. I've since discovered that listening to music through headphones while exercising may be used as a strategy for helping me determine whether I'm exercising too intensely. I've found that if I can't sing along with the music without having to stop and catch my breath, I know I'm not overdoing it. This strategy has helped me manage my exercise-intensity level and reduce my day-after-exercise soreness. (Plus, I've gained more confidence as a singer. My singing sounds much better to me when I hear it while my ears are covered with headphones!)

—Joe Cuseo

Take advantage of the exercise and fitness resources on your campus.

You paid for use of the campus gym or recreation center with your college tuition, so take advantage of this and other exercise resources on campus. Also, your college is likely to offer physical education courses that you can take for credit toward your college degree. Typically, these courses are offered for one unit of credit so they can be easily added to your course schedule. There may also be exercise-related groups or clubs on campus that you can join. If there are, consider joining them; they can provide you with a motivating support group that may make exercise less monotonous and more socially stimulating.

Take advantage of natural opportunities for physical activity that present themselves during the day.

Exercise can take place at places other than a gym or fitness center, and at times other than those that are officially designated as workout times. Opportunities for exercise often occur naturally as we go about our daily activities. For example, if you can walk or ride your bike to class, do that instead of driving a car or riding a bus. If you can climb some stairs instead of taking an elevator, take the route that's more physically challenging and requires more bodily activity.

Use exercise as a strategy for improving your academic performance.

Here are two simple strategies that can be used to combine physical activity with academic activity in a way that may improve your mental performance:

1. Take study breaks that involve physical activity (e.g., a short jog or brisk walk). Study breaks that include physical activity not only refresh the mind by giving it a break from studying, they also stimulate the mind by increasing blood flow to your brain; this will help you retain what you've already studied and regain concentration for what you're about to study.

2. Before exams, take a brisk walk. This will increase mental alertness by increasing oxygen flow to the brain, and it will also decrease tension by increasing the brain's production of emotionally "mellowing" brain chemicals (e.g., serotonin and endorphins).

Wellness is built on a balanced foundation of nutrition, exercise, and rest.

••• Rest and Sleep

Sleep experts agree that humans in today's information-loaded, multitasking world are not getting the quantity and quality of sleep they need to perform at peak levels (Mitler, Dinges, & Dement, 1994).

College students, in particular, tend to have very ineffective sleep habits. Heavier academic workloads, more opportunities to socialize, and tendencies toward procrastination often result in last-minute, late-night, or all-night study binges, often leaving college students with irregular sleep schedules and occasional sleep loss.

How much sleep do we need or should we get? The answer to this question lies in our genes and varies from person to person. On the average, adults need 7 to 8 hours of sleep each day and teenagers need slightly more—about 9 hours (Roffwarg, Muzio, & Dement, 1966). Research shows that college students get an average of less than 7 hours of sleep each night (Hicks in Zimbardo, et al., 2006), which means that they're not getting the amount of sleep needed for optimal academic performance.

Attempting to train our body to sleep less is likely to be an exercise in futility, because what we're actually trying to do is force our body to do something that it's not naturally (genetically) inclined to do; eventually, we pay the price for the sleep we've lost with lower energy and poorer performance. When our body is deprived of the sleep it needs, it accumulates "sleep debt," which, like financial debt, must be eventually "paid back" by getting extra sleep at a later time (Dement & Vaughan, 1999). If our sleep debt isn't paid back, negative consequences are likely to occur in terms of our health, mood, and performance (Van Dongen, et al., 2003). For example, studies have shown that the effects of sleep loss on driving are similar to the effects of alcohol (Arndt, et al., 2001; Fletcher et al., 2003), and students who get less sleep than their body requires earn lower grades than students who get sufficient sleep (Spinweber in Zimbardo, et al., 2006).

 Pause for Reflection

What amount of sleep per night do you think you need to perform at your highest level?

How many nights per week do you typically get this amount of sleep?

If you're not getting this optimal amount of sleep each night, what is preventing you from doing so?

The Value and Purpose of Sleep

Resting and reenergizing the body is the most obvious purpose of sleep (Dement & Vaughan, 1999). However, there are other benefits of sleep that are less well known but equally important for our physical and mental health (Dement & Vaughan, 2000; Horne, 1988). Some of the lesser known but equally important benefits of sleep are described below.

Sleep restores and preserves the power of our immune system.

Studies show that when humans and other animals lose sleep, their production of disease-fighting antibodies is reduced and they become more susceptible to illness, such as common colds and the flu (Blakeslee, 1993).

Sleep helps us cope with daily stress.

In addition to its physical benefits for the body, sleep also has *psychological* benefits for the mind, particularly dream sleep. Sleep research shows that the percentage of time we spend in dream sleep increases when we are experiencing stress (Greenberg, Pillard, & Pearlman, 1972). Apparently, dream sleep is our brain's way of coping with stress in our daily lives. It's thought that the biochemical changes that take place in our brain during dream sleep serve to restore imbalances in brain chemistry that are caused by stress. Support for this theory comes from studies showing that loss of dream sleep results in loss of emotional stability (Voelker, 2004); and if the dream sleep loss is extreme, we begin to lose our grip on reality. For example, if humans are deprived of dream sleep for more than 2 to 3 days, they become delirious and begin to hallucinate. Less extreme amounts of dream-sleep loss can create or aggravate emotional problems, such as anxiety and depression. You've probably noticed how infants can become very irritable and cranky when they're tired. The truth is that people of any age become more tense and irritable when they've lost needed sleep. Getting quality sleep, especially dream sleep, is essential for maintaining a good mood and a positive frame of mind. Indeed, research reveals that people who sleep well are more likely to report that they feel "happy" (Myers, 1993).

Sleep helps the brain form and store memories.

When we're asleep, our brain does not receive the external stimulation it normally gets while we're awake, so at night, it has a chance to turn inward and focus on information that it received earlier in the day. Thus, the brain gets an opportunity to replay, rehearse, and retain previously received information at night without being interrupted by external stimulation (sights, sounds, etc.) or being pressured to take in new information (Hobson, 1988). Brain imaging research indicates that when we enter dream sleep, parts of our brain involved with thinking and memory become active (Ogawa, Nittono, & Hori, 2002). Perhaps this is why the brain-wave pattern we experience while dreaming is very similar to the pattern experienced when we're wide awake and actively learning (Figure 12.4). This suggests that the brain is actively learning and remembering information during dream sleep.

Figure 12.4 Brain Waves Experienced While Dreaming and Learning

Brain-Wave Pattern Associated
with the *Dream* Stage of *Sleep*

Brain-Wave Pattern Associated with
an *Awake* State of *Active Learning*

The importance of dream sleep for learning and memory is suggested by the fact that the
brain-wave pattern we experience while dreaming is not very different from the pattern we
experience while we're awake and actively learning.

Further evidence supporting the importance of dream sleep for human memory is provided by studies showing that loss of dream sleep at night results in poorer memory for information learned earlier in the day (Peigneux, et al., 2001). For instance, adolescents who get minimal sleep have a more difficult time retaining new information learned in school (Horne, 1988).

Sleep promotes creative problem solving.

Research evidence and numerous reports of individuals suggest that humans discover solutions to workday problems and experience creative ideas during sleep, particularly dream sleep (Wagner, et al., 2004). Research on highly creative people indicates that one of their distinguishing characteristics is their openness to a wide variety of experiences, including imaginative and fantasized experiences that occur during unusual states of consciousness, such as dream sleep (Ayers, Beaton, & Hunt, 1999). Musicians, artists, authors, and inventors sometimes rely on their dreams as a source of creative ideas and alternative solutions (Feldman, 1994).

These creative breakthroughs are best explained by the fact that during sleep humans enter into a more relaxed, subconscious state. Furthermore, during dream sleep, the front-right half of the brain is more active than when humans are wide awake and fully conscious. The front-right half of the human brain is responsible for visual imagination, and greater activity in this section of the brain during dream sleep may enable the dreamer to "see" things from a different, more *visually imaginative* perspective (Joseph, 1988). In contrast, when we're awake and fully conscious, the part of our brain that is more dominant is the left half, which tends to think in words rather than visual images, and specializes in logical thinking rather than imaginative thinking.

Personal Story In high school, my most difficult subject was geometry. During my junior year, I took a final exam in this subject that counted for almost 50% of my course grade. Naturally, I was very nervous both before and during the exam. I took the exam in the afternoon and when I went to bed that evening, I woke up in a cold sweat at about 4:00 a.m. I just had a dream in which I "saw" the correct solution to one of the major problems I had struggled with on the test. I immediately got out of bed to check my test notes and, amazingly, I did solve the problem correctly in my dream but didn't solve it correctly on the exam.

At the time, I couldn't understand how I could possibly solve a complex problem correctly while I was deeply asleep, yet fail to solve it correctly when I was fully awake! I know now that it was probably because I was more relaxed while sleeping, and because I was thinking about the problem from a more visual and imaginative perspective than when I was wide awake and worried.

—Joe Cuseo

BOX
12.2 *Snapshot* SUMMARY

Tips for Remembering Your Dreams

Generally, we all have a difficult time recalling our dreams because dreams take place during a very deep stage of sleep, during which our level of conscious awareness is low. This is unfortunate because dreams can sometimes provide us with self-insights, creative ideas, and unique problem-solving perspectives or solutions. The good news is that we may be able to improve our dream memory by engaging in certain practices, such as the following:

■ Just before going to sleep, tell yourself that you're going to remember your dreams and think about what you'd like to dream about. Since we tend to dream about what's on our mind, if we think about what we'd like to dream about before falling sleep, we'll be more likely to have a dream about it.

■ Try to go to bed when you're moderately tired, rather than completely exhausted. If you're extremely tired, you tend to sleep more deeply, and the more deeply you sleep, the less conscious you are of your dreams and, therefore, the less likely you are to recall them.

■ Avoid alcohol and virtually all other types of depressant or sedative drugs before bedtime because they tend to suppress the amount of time we spend dreaming, and they also block memory for the dreams we do have.

■ Have pencil and paper or a tape recorder at your bedside. When you attempt to recall a dream, write it down or tape-record it immediately after you wake up. Even if it is vague, you will probably be able to slowly fill in some of the details when you start writing or talking about it. Dreams fade from memory very quickly, so it's crucial to make a record of them as soon as possible after you've experienced them.

■ Use an alarm clock, not a clock radio, to wake you up. You're more likely to remember your last dream if you wake up suddenly or abruptly from sleep. A clock radio allows you to wake up too gradually, and your dream may fade from your memory or become distorted by the music or news you hear on the radio—which can get mixed into your dream and "contaminate" it.

■ When you wake up, the first thing you should ask yourself is: "Have I been dreaming?" You should immediately think about the past (i.e., what happened during the night); try to avoid the natural tendency to think about the present or future (e.g., what day of the week it is, or what you have to do that day).

■ Keep a note pad with you during the day in case you encounter people or events that may trigger your memory of a dream you had the previous night. Sometimes, an event or incident that takes place during the next day can serve as a *memory cue* that reminds us of a dream we had the night before, enabling us to retrieve a dream that may have been forgotten. For example, if we dreamed about a particular person and happened to see that person the next day, the person's face may serve as a retrieval cue that triggers our recall of a dream we had the previous night that included this person.

■ Keep a dream journal. By keeping track of your dreams, you may discover some interesting patterns across time that relate to different experiences or stages in your life.

Sources: Cartwright, R. D. (1978) *A primer on sleep and dreaming*. Faraday, A. (1974). *The dream game*. Holland, M., and Tarlow, G. (1980). *Using psychology*.

Strategies for Improving Sleep Quality

Since sleep has powerful benefits for both the body and mind, if we can improve the quality of our sleep, we may be able to improve our physical and mental well-being. Listed below is a series of specific strategies for improving sleep quality that should also serve to improve personal health and performance.

Increase awareness of your sleep habits by keeping a sleep log or sleep journal.

In this journal, make special note of nights when you slept well or poorly and note what you did before going to bed on those nights. Tracking your sleep experiences in a journal may enable you to find patterns that reveal relationships between certain things you do (or don't do) during the day on nights that you sleep well. If you detect such a pattern, you may have detected a potential routine that you can follow regularly to ensure that you get consistently high-quality sleep.

Attempt to get into a regular sleep schedule by going to sleep and getting up at about the same time each day.

An irregular sleep schedule can disrupt the quality of sleep. This is what happens to people when they experience "jet lag." Traveling to a new time zone often requires travelers to change their sleep schedule to accommodate a different time zone, which can disrupt the quality of their sleep (Rader & Hicks, 1987). Our body likes to work on a "biological rhythm" of set cycles; if you can get your body into a regular sleep schedule or cycle, you're more likely to establish a biological rhythm that makes it easier for you to fall asleep, stay asleep, and awake naturally from sleep according to your own "internal" alarm clock.

Preserving a somewhat stable sleep schedule is particularly important around midterms and finals when students often disrupt their normal sleep patterns to cram in last-minute studying, which means they stay up later, get up earlier, or don't go to sleep at all. To be most physically and mentally alert for upcoming exams, sleep research shows that you should get yourself on a regular sleep schedule of going to bed and getting up at about the same time at least one week in advance of exams (Dement, 1999).

Pause for Reflection
Do you have or need an alarm clock to wake up in the morning?

Why?

Sleep in the same place each night.

We are creatures of habit, and if our brain gets in the habit of associating the same environmental cues (e.g., sights, smells, sounds) with falling asleep, we're more likely to fall asleep when we place ourselves in that same environment. By repeatedly sleeping in the same environment (e.g., the same room, the same side of the bed, the same sound of a humming fan), these stimuli or sensations become repeatedly paired and associated with sleep; therefore, whenever we place ourselves in that environment, our body is more likely to respond automatically by falling asleep (Hauri & Linde, 1996).

Make sure the temperature of your sleep room is not too hot (no higher than 70 degrees).

Warm temperatures often make us feel sleepy, but they usually don't help us stay asleep or sleep well. This is why people have trouble sleeping on hot summer evenings. High-quality, uninterrupted sleep is more likely to take place at cooler, more comfortable room temperatures (Coates, 1977).

Attempt to get into a relaxing bedtime ritual each night.

Taking a hot bath or shower, consuming hot milk, or listening to relaxing music are bedtime rituals that can get you into a worry-free state and help you fall asleep sooner. Also, making a list of things you intend to do the next day before going to bed may help you fall asleep by helping you worry less about all the things you have to do. Since you've made a list of what those things are, you've assured yourself that you won't forget to do them.

Light studying or reviewing previously studied material may also be a good thing to do before going to bed, because sleep can help you better retain what you've experienced just before going to sleep. Many years of studies show that the best thing you can do after attempting to learn something is to "sleep on it," probably because your brain can then focus on processing it without interference from outside distractions (Jenkins & Dallenbach, 1924).

Avoid intense mental activity just before going to sleep.

Light mental work may serve as a relaxing pre-sleep ritual, but cramming intensely for a difficult exam or doing intensive writing before bedtime is likely to generate a state of mental arousal, which will interfere with your ability to "wind down" and fall asleep.

Avoid intense physical exercise before going to sleep.

Physical exercise generates an increase in muscle tension and mental energy (oxygen flow to the brain), which energizes you and keeps you from falling asleep. If you're going to exercise in the evening, it should be done at least three hours before going to sleep (Hauri & Linde, 1996).

Doing intense work right before going to sleep is likely to interfere with your ability to fall asleep.

Avoid consuming sleep-interfering foods, beverages, or drugs in late afternoon or evening.

In particular, avoid the following substances near bedtime:

a. caffeine—because it's a stimulant, it's likely to stimulate your nervous system and keep you awake

b. nicotine—also because it's a stimulant

c. alcohol—because it interferes with and reduces the quality of dream sleep

d. gas-producing foods—for example, peanuts, beans, fruits, raw vegetables, or high-fat snacks, because your stomach has to work hard to digest them, and this internal energy (and noise) can interrupt or disrupt your sleep. In fact, eating anything near bedtime is not a good idea because the internal activity your body engages in to digest the food is likely to reduce the depth and quality of your sleep.

Modify your environment.

If you are consistently awakened by noise (e.g., a snoring roommate or barking dog), sleep with earplugs or a steady background sound (e.g., a humming fan). If you find that your sleep is frequently disturbed by light or brightness, consider wearing eyeshades to bed.

When planning your daily work schedule, be aware of your natural biological rhythms—your peak periods and down times.

Studies show that humans vary in terms of when they naturally prefer to fall asleep and wake up; some are early birds who prefer to go to sleep early and wake up early, and others are night owls who prefer to stay up late at night and get up late in the morning (Natale & Ciogna, 1996). (Teenagers more often fall into the category of "night owls.") As a result of these differences in sleeping preferences, individuals will vary with respect to the times of day when they experience their highest and lowest levels of physical energy. Naturally, early birds are more likely to be "morning" people whose peak energy period occurs before noon; and night owls are likely to be more productive in the late afternoon and evening. Also, many people experience a post-lunch dip in energy in the early afternoon (Monk, 2005).

Be aware of your most productive hours of the day and schedule your highest priority work and most challenging tasks at times when you tend to work at peak effectiveness. For example, schedule your out-of-class work so that you're tackling academic tasks that require intense thinking (e.g., technical writing or complex problem-solving) at times of the day when you tend to be most productive, and schedule lighter work (e.g., light reading or routine tasks) at times when your energy level tends to be lower. Also, keep your natural peak and down times in mind when you schedule your courses. Attempt to arrange your class schedule in such a way that you experience your most challenging courses at times of the day when your body and mind are most ready to accept that challenge.

You may also want to schedule physical activity just before the time of day when you tend to experience your lowest levels of energy. The energizing aftereffects of exercise should carry into the time period when you normally feel most sluggish and should boost your energy and level of performance during that period. For example, if your mental energy tends to be low in the late afternoon, exercising in the mid-afternoon may be a good way to combat your usual late-afternoon sluggishness and enable you to use that time more productively.

 Pause for Reflection

Does your energy level tend to vary at different times during the day?

If yes, do you tend to do anything in particular during your periods of highest and lowest energy?

Do you think you could make more productive use of your time during either of these periods?

●●● Alcohol, Drugs, and Risky Behavior

In addition to putting healthy nutrients into our body, exercising, and resting our body, another key aspect of physical wellness is keeping risky substances out of our body and keeping away from risky behaviors that can jeopardize our health and impair our performance.

Alcohol Use among College Students

In the United States alcohol is "legal" for people 21 years of age and older. However, whether you're of legal age or not, it's likely that alcohol has already been available to you and will continue to be available to you in college. Since alcohol is a substance seen frequently at college parties and social gatherings, it's likely that you will be confronted with decisions about alcohol, which is likely to involve two choices:

1. To drink or not to drink; and
2. To drink responsibly or irresponsibly.

Irresponsible drinking of alcohol is the number one drug problem on college campuses.

Obviously, the best way to avoid irresponsible drinking is not to drink at all. This is the safest option, particularly if there is a history of alcohol abuse in your family. If you choose to drink, make sure that it's *your* choice and not a choice that others are making for you, due to social pressure or peer conformity. Although there are many reasons why students drink or do any drug, research shows that the most common reason why first-year students consume alcohol is to fit in socially (Meilman & Presley, 2005). Research shows that first-year college students drink more than they did in high school (Astin, 2005); however, college students tend to overestimate the number of their peers who drink and the amount they drink. This overestimation can lead students to believe that if they don't drink, they're not doing what's expected or "normal" (DeJong & Linkenback, 1999). Student beliefs that college partying and college drinking go hand in hand may also be strongly influenced by media portrayals of college students as wild party animals. For example, magazines rank the "top party schools," videos or DVDs depict college students who've "gone wild," and movies have been made whose entire plot or premise revolves around the drunken escapades of college students (e.g., "Animal House," "Back to School," "Spring Break I," "Spring Break II").

Unfortunately, irresponsible drinking is the number one drug problem on college campuses. Although alcohol is a "legal" substance (if you're 21 years of age or older), and it is a liquid or beverage that people drink rather than inject, smoke, or snort, the fact still remains that alcohol is a mind-altering drug when it's consumed in a large enough quantity (dose). Just as THC is the mind-altering ingredient in marijuana, ethyl alcohol is the mind-altering ingredient of beer, wine, and hard liquor (Figure 12.5).

Figure 12.5 Ethyl Alcohol: The Mind-Altering Ingredient Contained in Alcohol

$$\begin{array}{ccc} H & H & \\ | & | & \\ H-C-C-O-H \\ | & | & \\ H & H & \end{array}$$

Also, like any other drug, alcohol abuse is a form of drug abuse. Approximately 7 to 8 percent of people who drink develop alcohol addiction or dependency (alcoholism) (Julien, 2004). However, among college students, the most frequent form of alcohol abuse is *binge drinking*—consuming large amounts of alcohol in a short amount of time, resulting in a state of intoxication or inebriation (a.k.a., a drunken state).

Binge drinking is a form of alcohol abuse because it has direct, negative effects on the drinker's:

a. behavior—for example, class absence (Engs, 1977; Engs & Hanson, 1986). Research indicates that repeatedly getting drunk can reduce the size and effectiveness of the part of the brain involved with memory formation (Brown, et al., 2000), which suggests that the more often we get drunk, the dumber we get (Weschsler & Wuethrich, 2002).

b. body—for example, it results in acute alcohol withdrawal syndrome (better known as a "hangover"), and

c. mind—for example, memory loss (in extreme form, known as "blackouts").

Furthermore, binge drinking can have indirect negative effects on an individual's health and safety by reducing the drinker's inhibitions about engaging in risk-taking behavior, which increases the risk of personal accidents, injuries, and illnesses. Arguably, no other drug reduces a person's inhibitions as dramatically as alcohol. After consuming significant amounts of alcohol, humans can become much less cautious about doing things they normally wouldn't do. This chemically induced sense of courage (sometimes referred to as "liquid courage") can override the process of logical thinking and decision-making, thereby increasing the drinker's willingness to engage in irrationally risky behavior. Essentially, when some people drink, they begin to think they're invincible, immortal, and infertile. They become more willing to partake in behaviors that increase their risk of physical accidents—for example, reckless driving that increases their risk of serious injury or death, and reckless sex (unprotected sex) that increases their risk of "social" accidents—for example, accidental pregnancy or sexually transmitted infection.

It's noteworthy that the legal age for consuming alcohol was once lowered to age 18, but it was eventually raised back to 21 because the number of drunk-driving accidents and deaths among teenage drinkers increased dramatically when the legal age was reduced to 18 (MADD, 2006). Traffic accidents still account for more deaths of people between the ages of 15 and 24 than any other single cause (U.S. National Center for Health Statistics, 2003).

Also, drinking increases the risk of aggressive behavior, such as: fighting, damaging property, sexual assault (e.g., date rape), and sexual harassment (Abbey, 2002; Bushman & Cooper, 1990). See Box 12.3 for a summary of sexually aggressive behaviors, all of which are more likely to occur when a person is under the influence of alcohol.

Since alcohol is a depressant drug that depresses or slows down the human nervous system, it increases aggressive and sexual behavior by slowing down signals normally sent from the front part of the upper brain (the "human brain"), which is responsible for rational thinking and normally inhibits or controls the lower, middle part of the brain (the "animal brain"), which is responsible for basic animal drives, such as sex and aggression (Figure 12.6). When the upper brain's messages are slowed down by alcohol, the animal brain is freed from the signals that normally restrain or inhibit it, allowing its basic drives to be released or expressed; thus, the less inhibited drinker is more likely to engage in aggressive or sexual behavior.

Figure 12.6 How Alcohol Works in the Brain to Reduce Personal Inhibitions

Alcohol slows down or suppresses signals sent from our upper "human" brain that normally control or inhibit the lower "animal" brain.

Alcohol

"Human Brain"

●●●●●● = controlling (inhibiting) signals

↓ = slows down (suppresses) signals

"Animal Brain"

Brain image © David Huntley, 2007. Under license from Shutterstock, Inc.

BOX 12.3 *Snapshot* SUMMARY

Threats to Sexual Wellness: Aggressive Sexual Behavior

Sexual Assault, a.k.a., Sexual Violence

Rape is a form of sexual assault, which is defined legally as nonconsensual (unwanted) sexual penetration that is obtained through physical force, by threat of bodily harm, or when the victim is incapable of giving consent due to alcohol or drug intoxication (Fenske, Miller, & Trivedi, 1996). Rape occurs in two major forms:

1. Stranger Rape—when a total stranger forces sexual intercourse on the victim.
2. Acquaintance Rape or Date Rape—when the victim knows, or is dating, the person who forces unwanted sexual intercourse. It's estimated that about 85 percent of reported rapes are committed by an acquaintance (Dobkin & Sippy, 1995). Alcohol is frequently associated with acquaintance rapes because it lowers the rapist's inhibitions and reduces the victim's ability to judge whether she is in a potentially dangerous situation. (Most acquaintance rape is committed by men against women; however, it also occurs in homosexual relationships.) Since the victim is familiar with the offender, s/he may feel at fault or conclude that what happened is not sexual assault.

Recommendations for women to reduce the risk of rape and sexual assault:

▪ Don't drink to excess or associate with others who drink to excess.
▪ Go to parties with at least one other friend so you can keep an eye out for each other.
▪ Clearly and firmly communicate your sexual intentions and limits (e.g., If you say "no," make absolutely sure that he knows that you mean what you say and you say what you mean).
▪ Distinguish lust from love. If you just met someone who makes sexual advances toward you, that person lusts you but doesn't love you.
▪ Take a self-defense class.
▪ Carry mace or pepper spray.

Recommendations for men:

▪ Don't assume a woman wants to have sex just because she's:
   a. very friendly,
   b. dressed in a certain way, or
   c. drinking alcohol.

(continued)

- If a woman says "no," don't assume that she really means "yes."
- Don't interpret sexual rejection as personal rejection.

Sexual Harassment

Sexual harassment may be defined as unwelcome sexual advances or requests for sexual favors in exchange for a grade, job, or promotion. Harassment can take the following forms:

a. Verbal—e.g., sexual comments about your body or clothes; sexual jokes or teasing,

b. Nonverbal—e.g., staring or glaring at your body or obscene gestures, or

c. Physical—e.g., contact by touching, pinching, or rubbing up against your body.

Recommendations for Dealing with Sexual Harassment:

- Make your objections clear and firm. Tell the harasser directly that you are offended by the unwanted behavior and that you consider it sexual harassment.
- Keep a written record of any harassment. Record the date, place, and specific details about the harassing behavior.
- Become aware of the sexual harassment policy at your school. (Your school's policy is likely to be found in the *Student Handbook* or may be available from the Office of Human Resources on campus.)
- If you're unsure about whether you are experiencing sexual harassment, or what to do about it, seek help from the Counseling Center on campus.

Abusive Relationships

An abusive relationship may be defined as one in which one partner abuses the other—physically, verbally, or emotionally. Abusive individuals often are dependent on their partners for their sense of self-worth. They commonly have low self-esteem and fear their partner will abandon them, so they attempt to prevent this abandonment by over-controlling their partner. Frequently, abusers feel powerless or weak in other areas of their life and overcompensate by attempting to gain power, personal strength, and exerting power over their partner.

Potential Signs of Abuse:

a. Abuser tries to dominate or control all aspects of the partner's life,

b. Abuser frequently yells, shouts, intimidates, or makes physical threats,

c. Abuser constantly puts down the partner and damages the partner's self-esteem,

d. Abuser displays intense and irrational jealousy,

e. Abuser demands affection or sex when the partner is not interested,

f. The abused partner behaves differently and is more inhibited when the abuser is around, or

g. The abused partner fears the abuser.

Strategies for Avoiding or Escaping Abusive Relationships

- Avoid isolation by continuing to maintain social ties with others outside of the relationship.
- To help you see your relationship more clearly, ask friends for feedback on how they see it. (Love can sometimes be "blind"; it's possible to be in denial about an abusive relationship and not see what is really going on.)
- Speak with a professional counselor on campus to help you see your relationships more objectively and help you cope or escape from any relationship that you sense is becoming abusive.

References: ETR Associates (2000). *Acquaintance rape.* Santa Cruz, CA.
ETR Associates (2001). *Sexual harassment.* Santa Cruz, CA.
http://sexualviolence.uchicago.edu/daterape.shtml
http://webpages.marshall.edu/~pressman1/rape.html
http://www.uhs.berkeley.edu/home/healthtopics/sexual assault/saalcohol.shtml

During the prohibition era (1920–1933) laws were passed in America that made alcohol illegal for anyone to consume at any age.

1. Why do you think prohibition laws were passed in the first place?

2. Why do you think that alcohol still continued to be produced illegally during the prohibition era ("bootleg liquor"), which eventually led to the abolition or elimination of prohibition laws?

Illegal Drugs

In addition to alcohol, there are other substances likely to be encountered on college campuses that are illegal for anyone to use at any age. Among the most commonly used illegal drugs by college students are the following:

- *Marijuana* (a.k.a., "weed" or "pot")—primarily a depressant or sedative drug that slows down the nervous system and produces a "mellow" feeling of relaxation.
- *Ecstasy* (a.k.a., "X")—a stimulant typically taken in pill form that speeds up the nervous system and reduces social inhibitions.
- *Cocaine* (a.k.a., "coke" or "crack")—a stimulant that's typically snorted or smoked, and produces a strong "rush" of euphoria.
- *Amphetamines* (a.k.a., "speed" or "meth")—a strong stimulant that increases energy and general arousal, which is usually taken in pill form, but may also be smoked or injected.
- *Hallucinogens* (a.k.a., "psychedelics")—drugs that alter or distort perception, which are typically swallowed—e.g., LSD (a.k.a., "acid") and hallucinogenic mushrooms (a.k.a., "shrooms").
- *Narcotics* (e.g., heroin and prescription pain pills)—depressant or sedative drugs that slow down the nervous system and produce feelings of relaxation; heroin is injected or smoked, and it typically produces an intense "rush" of euphoria.

All of these drugs are potentially habit forming. If they are injected (shot directly into a vein) or smoked (inhaled through the lungs), they can be particularly risky because these routes allow the drug to reach the brain faster and with greater impact. Thus, a "higher" peak effect is experienced and is experienced more rapidly, which is followed by a sharp drop or "crash" after the drug produces its peak effect (Figure 12.7). This roller-coaster effect produces a greater desire or craving to use the drug again, which increases the risk of dependency or addiction.

Listed below are common signs that use of any drug (including alcohol) is moving in the direction of drug dependency or addiction:

- Increasing frequency of use
- Increasing the amount (dose) used
- Difficulty cutting back (e.g., unable to use less frequently or in smaller amounts)
- Difficulty controlling or limiting the amount taken after starting
- Using the drug alone

Figure 12.7 Drugs Smoked Produce a Higher and More Rapid Peak Effect

When a drug is smoked (or injected), it reaches the brain faster and produces a higher peak effect, followed by a sharper drop or "crash," which increases the risk of addiction.

- Hiding or hoarding the drug
- Lying about drug use
- Reacting angrily or defensively when questioned about drug use
- Being in denial about abusing the drug (e.g., "I don't have a problem.")
- Rationalizing drug abuse (e.g., "Everyone's doing it; it's no big deal.")
- When continuing to use the drug means more to the user than the personal and interpersonal problems caused by its use.

Addiction is a potential problem and major motive for repeated use of any drug. However, there are multiple motives or reasons for using drugs besides addiction. A summary of the major motives for drug use is provided in Box 12.4. Being aware of what motivates humans to use drugs can help promote self-awareness of motives for personal use, and it can also promote awareness of healthier ways to experience the same psychological effects produced by drugs.

BOX 12.4 Snapshot SUMMARY

Drug Use among College Students: Common Causes and Major Motives

1. **Social Pressure:** using drugs to fit in or be cool (for example, smoking marijuana because it's available at parties and everyone else is doing it).
2. **Recreational ("Party") Use:** taking a drug for fun or pleasure (e.g., drinking alcohol at parties to loosen inhibitions and have a good time.).
3. **Experimental Use:** using a drug out of curiosity—to test out its effects (e.g., trying LSD to see what it's like to have a psychedelic or hallucinogenic experience).
4. **Therapeutic Use:** taking a prescription or over-the-counter drug as treatment for a mental or emotional disorder (e.g., taking Prozac for depression or Ritalin to treat attention deficit disorder).
5. **Performance Enhancement:** taking a drug to improve physical or mental performance (e.g., taking steroids to improve athletic performance or stimulants to stay awake all night and cram for an exam).
6. **Escapism:** using a drug to escape or eliminate a personal problem or an unpleasant emotional state (e.g., taking amphetamines to escape depression or boredom).
7. **Addiction:** habitual use of a drug that's motivated by physical or psychological dependence (e.g., continuing to use nicotine or cocaine because stopping will result in withdrawal symptoms—such as anxiety or depression).

What drugs (if any) have you seen being used on your campus?

How would the type and frequency of drug use on your campus compare to what you saw in high school?

Which of the motives for drug use listed in Box 12.4 would you say are the most common reasons for drug use on your campus?

ALTERED
STATE
UNIVERSITY

Don't blow it on drugs!

There are other, safer ways to "blow your mind" besides mind-altering substances.

Strategies for Minimizing or Eliminating the Negative Effects of Alcohol, Drugs, and Risky Behavior

Alcohol

Don't let yourself be pressured into drinking.

 Remember: College students tend to overestimate the number of their peers who drink, so don't feel you're uncool, unusual, or abnormal if you prefer not to drink.

If you decide to drink, maintain awareness of how much you're drinking on any occasion, and continually monitor your physical and mental state.

Don't continue to drink after you've reached a state of moderate relaxation or a mild loss of inhibition. Drinking to the point where you're drunk, or bordering on intoxication, doesn't promote your physical health or your social life. You're not exactly the life of the party if you're slurring your speech, vomiting in the restroom, nodding out, or about to fall sound asleep.

The key to drinking responsibly and in moderation is to have a plan in mind for managing your drinking. Such a plan can include strategies such as:

a. drinking slowly,

b. eating while drinking,

c. alternating between drinking alcoholic and non-alcoholic beverages, and

d. tapering off your drinking after the first hour of a party or social gathering (Vogler & Bartyz, 1992).

Lastly, don't forget that alcohol is costly, both in terms of money and calories. Thus, reducing or eliminating your drinking is a good money-management and weight-management strategy.

If you're a woman who drinks, or who frequents places where other people drink, remain aware of the possibility of date-rape drugs being dropped into your drink.

Drugs such as Gamma-hydroxybutyric acid (a.k.a., "GHB" or "G") and Rohypnol (a.k.a., "roofies" or "roaches" induce sleep and memory loss, and they are particularly powerful when taken with alcohol. To guard against this risk, don't let others give you drinks and hold onto your drink at all times (e.g., don't leave it, go to the restroom, and then come back to drink it again).

Drugs

If you find yourself in a situation where an illegal drug is available to you, our bottom-line recommendation is this: Don't check it out. If you're in doubt, keep it out—don't put anything you're unsure about into your body.

We acknowledge that the college years are a time for exploring and experimenting with different ideas, experiences, feelings, and states of consciousness. However, doing illegal drugs just isn't worth the risk. Even if you're aware of how an illegal drug affects people in general, you don't know how it's going to affect you in particular because each individual has a unique genetic make-up. Unlike legal drugs that have to pass through rigorous testing by the FDA (Federal Drug Administration) before they are approved for public consumption, you can't be sure how an illegal drug has been produced and packaged from one time to the next; and you don't know if, or what, it may have been "cut" (mixed) with during the production process. Thus, you're not just taking a criminal risk by using a drug that's illegal; you're also taking a physical risk by consuming a drug that may have unpredictable effects on your body and mind.

If you haven't smoked cigarettes, don't even think about starting.

The active ingredient in cigarettes, *nicotine*, is one of the most highly addictive drugs known to man (Jarvik, 1995). There are people who've been able to beat alcohol addiction and heroin addiction, but have not been able to kick their nicotine habit (Stolerman & Jarvis, 1995). In addition to its high potential for addiction, the health disadvantages of cigarette smoking are numerous and serious, which include increased susceptibility to our two leading killers: heart disease and cancer (Freund, Belanger, D'Agostino, & Kannel, 1993).

Women who smoke and use oral contraceptive pills develop a higher risk of heart diseases and stroke (Halperin, 2002). Cigarette smoking also sharply increases a woman's risk of experiencing prenatal problems during pregnancy and giving birth to newborns with health problems. These risks are not eliminated if an expectant mother stops smoking at the start of pregnancy;

instead, smoking needs to be stopped at least one full year prior to pregnancy before its health risks to the fetus are significantly reduced (Fingerhut, Kleinman, & Kendrick, 1990).

It's noteworthy that some women use cigarette smoking as a weight-control strategy because it elevates metabolism and burns calories. However, cigarette smoking produces only about a 7 percent increase in the rate of metabolism; in contrast, physical exercise increases the rate of metabolism by an average of 15 percent (Audrain, et al., 1995). You can do the math: Exercising burns calories at about twice the rate of smoking, which makes exercise a much more effective way of burning calories and managing weight than nicotine.

Pause for Reflection

Do you smoke cigarettes?

If yes, when and why did you start smoking?

Have your smoking habits changed since you've begun college?

If yes, why?

THE FAR SIDE® BY GARY LARSON

The real reason dinosaurs became extinct

Cigarette smoking sharply increases susceptibility to our two leading killers: heart disease and cancer.

Minimize Your Risk of Contracting Sexually Transmitted Infections (STIs)

STIs represent a group of contagious infections that are spread through sexual contact. More than 25 different types of STIs have been identified, and virtually all of them are easily treated if detected early. (See Box 12.5 for a summary of the major types of STIs.) However, if STIs are ignored, some of them can progress to the point where they cause internal infections and possible infertility (Cates, Herndon, Schulz, & Darroch, 2004).

Experiencing pain during or after urination, or have unusual discharge from the penis or vaginal areas, may be early signs of an STI. However, sometimes the symptoms can be subtle; so if you have any doubt, play it safe and check it out immediately by visiting the Health Center on your campus. Any advice or treatment you receive there will remain completely confidential.

If you're a male and sexually active, you can reduce your risk and your partner's risk of contracting a STI by using a latex condom (Holmes, Levine, & Weaver, 2004) (polyurethane could be an alternative if there is an allergic reaction to latex). If you're a sexually active female, insist that your partner use a latex condom. You can reduce your risk of catching a sexually transmitted infection by having sex with fewer partners.

Naturally, the easiest and most foolproof way to eliminate risk for STI (and unwanted pregnancy) is by not engaging in sexual intercourse. While having sexual feelings is normal and healthy, it doesn't mean you have to act on these feelings by expressing and satisfying them through sexual intercourse. You can choose abstinence, which doesn't mean that you cannot express physical affection or that you've decided never to have sex; it just means that you're choosing not to have sexual intercourse at this point in your life.

If you decide to have sex and happen to contract an STI, immediately inform anyone you've had sex with, so that he or she may receive early treatment before the disease progresses. This isn't just a nice or polite thing to do; it's the right (ethical) thing to do.

Sexually Transmitted Infections (STIs)

STIs represent a group of contagious infections that are spread through sexual contact. The more sexual partners you have, the greater the risk of contracting an STI. Latex condoms provide the best protection.

More than 25 different types of STIs have been identified, but the following bacteria and viruses account for the majority of infections. These infections are typically very treatable, but if they are ignored, they can lead to internal infections and possible infertility.

STIs Caused by Bacteria

Gonorrhea

A common STI with few symptoms but serious consequences if it is left untreated. Men typically experience creamy, yellow-colored, pus-like discharge from the penis, and burning when urinating. Women experience few early symptoms, but the disease can lead to later pelvic infections and possible infertility. The best way to detect gonorrhea, or any other STI that produces early symptoms that are not visible, is to have a laboratory test done by a doctor or healthcare provider. Gonorrhea can be treated and completely cured with antibiotics.

Chlamydia

This is the number-one bacterial STI; it's estimated to infect more than 10 percent of college students. Symptoms include a clear, mucous-like discharge and a burning sensation when urinating. Men may experience pain in the testes, and women may experience pain in the abdomen. However, women typically experience few or no early symptoms.

Genital Herpes

Typically produces painful blisters on the genitals or in the anus, which may itch and burn, especially during and following urination. Symptoms may disappear and come back, but are never cured. Later attacks tend to be less severe than the first attack. The frequency and intensity of outbreaks can be reduced with prescription medication (e.g., acyclovir capsules).

Syphilis

Men first experience ulcers (open sores) on the penis. Women may first develop ulcers in the vagina, but they can be overlooked, allowing the disease to progress. Syphilis is totally curable with antibiotics.

STIs Caused by Viruses

Human Papilloma Virus (HPV)

Overall, this is the most common STI among young, sexually active people. HPV is a virus that may cause warts in the genital area, but it typically does not produce noticeable symptoms in its early stages. Sometimes, the disease may also cause lesions (abnormal tissue changes) that are not visible, but when they appear, they look like small hard, cauliflower-like spots. Men can experience warts on the penis. HPV is treatable with laser or chemical treatment, which basically burn off the lesions. If untreated, HPV can lead to cancer of the cervix in women.

Human Immunodeficiency Virus (HIV)

Early symptoms include fever, night sweats, swollen lymph nodes, diarrhea, chronic fatigue, and weight loss. About one-half of people with HIV experience these flu-like symptoms, but one-half show no symptoms at all. Thus, the disease may go undetected until the person is given a blood test for some other reason. Most cases of HIV are transmitted through sexual contact; however, the disease may also be contracted through the sharing of intravenous needles. The most serious form of HIV is *Acquired Immune Deficiency Syndrome (AIDS)*, which is a life-threatening condition, because the person's immune system becomes severely impaired and leaves the infected person vulnerable to cancer and diseases of the nervous system.

(continued)

Hepatitis B or *Hepatitis C*
About one-half of the people with hepatitis experience flu-like symptoms, and one-half show no symptoms at all. Thus, the disease may go undetected until the person is given a blood test for some other reason.

Pubic Lice (a.k.a., "Crabs")
Caused by tiny lice that are called "crabs" (because they look like sea crabs), which breed in pubic hair around the genitals. These creatures are not dangerous but can cause intense itching.

••• Summary and Conclusion

The physical dimension of wellness includes strategic decisions about how we eat, exercise, sleep, and protect our body from unhealthy substances and unnecessary risks.

The research studies and scholarly wisdom reviewed in this chapter suggest that physical wellness is most effectively promoted if we adopt the following strategies with respect to our body.

1. Pay more attention to nutrition. In particular, we should increase consumption of natural fruits, vegetables, legumes, whole grains, fish, and water and decrease our consumption of processed, fatty, and fried foods. Although the expression, "you are what you eat," may be a bit exaggerated, it does contain a kernel of truth; the food we consume does influence our health, our emotions, and our performance.

2. Be more physically active. To counteract the sedentary lifestyle created by life in modern society and to attain total fitness, we should engage in a balanced blend of exercises that build stamina, strength, and flexibility.

3. Be careful not to cheat on sleep. Humans currently do not get enough sleep to perform at their highest levels. College students, in particular, need to get more sleep and develop more regular or consistent sleep habits.

4. Drink alcohol responsibly or not at all. We need to avoid excessive consumption of alcohol or use of other mind-altering substances that can threaten our physical health, impair our mental judgment, and increase our tendency to engage in dangerous, risk-taking behavior.

5. Minimize risk of contracting sexually transmitted infections. We have basically three options for doing so: using latex condoms during sex, limiting our number of sexual partners, or choosing not to be sexually active.

••• Learning More through Independent Research

Web-Based Resources for Further Information on Health and Wellness

For additional information relating to the ideas discussed in this chapter, we recommend the following Web sites:

Nutrition: www.eatright.org (American Dietetic Association)

Fitness: www.fitness.gov/home_resources.htm (The President's Council on Physical Fitness and Sports)

Sleep: www.sleepfoundation.org (National Sleep Foundation)

Alcohol and Drugs: www.nida.nih.gov (National Institute on Drug Abuse)

CHAPTER 12

Exercise #1. Nutritional Self-Assessment and Self-Improvement

Go online to www.mypyramid.gov

In the boxes on the right side of the screen, fill in your age, gender, and daily level of physical activity.

Click "select" to get a nutritional guide that is customized to your age, gender, and exercise habits.

For each of the five food groups, record the amount that is recommended for you to consume on a daily basis, and next to it, your estimate of the amount you now consume.

Basic Food Type	Amount Recommended	Amount Consumed
1. Grains		
2. Vegetables		
3. Fruits		
4. Milk Products		
5. Meat and Beans		

For any food group you're consuming less than the recommended amounts, click on that group to find foods you could consume to meet the recommended daily amount. Record below any items that you would be willing to consume in greater amounts to meet the daily recommendation.

_____

_____

_____

_____

_____

How likely is it that you will add these food items to your regular diet?

Very likely _____
Possibly   _____
Unlikely   _____

If you did not answer "very likely," what would inhibit or prevent you from adding these food items to your regular diet?

Exercise #2. Wellness Self-Assessment and Self-Improvement

STEP 1.

For each of the aspects of wellness listed below, rate yourself in terms of how close you think you are to doing what you should be doing (1 = furthest from the ideal; 5 = closest to the ideal).

	Nowhere Close to What I Should Be Doing		Not Bad, but Should Be Better		Right Where I Should Be
	1	2	3	4	5
Nutrition	1	2	3	4	5
Exercise	1	2	3	4	5
Sleep	1	2	3	4	5
Alcohol and Drugs	1	2	3	4	5

STEP 2.

For each of the above areas where there's the widest gap between where you are now and where you should be, what would be the most important thing you could do to reduce this gap?

▼ CASE STUDY

Drinking to Death: College Partying Gone Wild

At least 50 college students nationwide die each year as a result of drinking incidents on or near campus. During a one-month period in the fall of 1997, three college students died as a result of binge drinking at college parties. One involved an 18-year-old, first-year student at a private university who collapsed after drinking a mixture of beer and rum, fell into a coma at his fraternity house, and died three days later. He had a blood-alcohol level of over .40, which is about equal to gulping down 20 shots of liquor in one hour.

The second incident involved a student from a public university in the South who died of alcohol poisoning (overdose). The third student died at another public university in the Northeast where, after an evening of partying and heavy drinking, he accidentally fell off a building in the middle of the night and fell through the roof of a greenhouse. Some colleges in the Northeast now have student volunteers roaming the campus on cold, winter nights to make sure that no students freeze to death after passing out from an intense bout of binge-drinking.

Strategies that are being considered to stop or reduce the problem of dangerous binge drinking include:

a. A state governor announcing that he is going to launch a series of radio ads designed to discourage underage drinking,

b. A senator who has filed bills to toughen penalties for those who violate underage drinking laws, such as producing and using fake identification cards, and

c. A group of city council members who are going to look into stiffening penalties for liquor stores that deliver directly to fraternity houses.

Sources: *Los Angeles Times*, October 4, 1997; *Los Angeles Times*, April 10, 2000.

Reflection and Discussion Questions

1. How would you rank the potential effectiveness of the three strategies for stopping or reducing the problem of binge drinking mentioned in the last paragraph (1 representing the most effective strategy and 3 representing the least effective)?

    _____

    _____

    _____

2. Comparing your highest ranked and lowest ranked choices, what reasons(s) do you have for:

    a. ranking the first one as most effective, and

    b. ranking the last one as least effective?

3. What other strategies do you think would be effective for stopping or reducing dangerous binge drinking among college students?

Health and Wellness

Mental and Spiritual Dimensions

13

Activate Your Thinking

What would you say are the three most important things humans can do to attain mental health and happiness?

_____

_____

_____

SPIRIT

BODY   MIND

In addition to the body, two other key dimensions of wellness are mind and spirit. Our mental state can strongly influence our physical health and personal performance. In particular, two elements of the mind play a major role in wellness:

1. Emotions and
2. Thoughts.

••• Emotions and Wellness

Research indicates that positive emotions, such as optimism and excitement, serve to promote learning by increasing the brain's ability to take in, store, and retrieve information (Rosenfield, 1988). For example, in one study involving nearly 4,000 first-year college students, it was found that students' level of optimism or hope for success during their first term on campus was a more accurate predictor of their first-year grades than were their SAT scores or high school grade-point average (Snyder, et al., 1991).

In contrast, negative emotions such as anxiety and fear can interfere with the brain's ability to (a) store memories (Jacobs & Nadel, 1985), (b) retrieve stored memories (O'Keefe & Nadel, 1985), and (c) engage in higher-level thinking (Caine & Caine, 1991).

As mentioned in Chapter 3, one type of intelligence is *intrapersonal* intelligence—the ability to be aware of our own feelings or emotions (Gardner, 1983). More recently, the term *emotional intelligence* has been coined to describe our ability to identify and monitor our emotions, and to be aware of how our emotions influence our thoughts and actions (Salovey & Mayer, 1990; Goleman, 1995). The connection between emotional intelligence and successful performance is demonstrated by research showing that people who are able to control their emotions and use them in a positive way tend to persist longer at challenging tasks (Simunek, et al., 2000) and are more likely to experience professional success (Goleman, 1995; Saarni, 1999). Succeeding in college is a challenging task that can test your emotional control and your ability to persist to graduation. Studies show that college students report higher levels of stress after beginning college than they did prior to college (Bartlett, 2002; Sax, 2003). However, if students control this stress and keep it at manageable levels, it can be a positive experience that stimulates learning and personal development.

Students who score higher on tests of emotional intelligence and emotional management have been found to achieve higher grade-point averages at the end of their first year of college (Schutte, et al., 1998). Additional research shows that new college students who take first-year seminars or college success courses, which include information on emotional control and emotional-skill development, are more likely to be successful during their first year of college (Schutte, Malouff, et al., 2002).

•—• CLASSIC QUOTE •—•

Future shock [is] the shattering stress and disorientation that we induce in individuals by subjecting them to too much change in too short a time.

—Alvin Toffler, American science-fiction author

••• Stress and Anxiety

Students entering college today are reporting higher levels of stress (Astin, Parrot, Korn, & Sax, 1997; Sax, et al., 1999) and lower levels of mental health (Kadison & DiGeronimo, 2004) than they have in years past. This increased level of stress may reflect the fact that we're now living in an era of rapid technological change and information overload. In fact, psychiatric terms such as "internet addiction" and "information fatigue syndrome" are now being used to refer to emotional disorders relating to psychological dependency on the Internet and excessive stress relating to information overload (Waddington, 1996; Young, 1996).

What exactly is *stress*? The etymology of the word "stress" derives from a Latin root that means, "to draw tight." Thus, stress isn't necessarily bad. For example, a tightened guitar string provides better sound than a string that's too lax or loose; a tightened bow delivers a more powerful arrow shot; and a tightened muscle provides more strength or speed. Such productive stress is sometimes referred to as *eustress*—which is derived from the root "eu" meaning "good" (as in the words euphoria—good mood, and eulogy—good words).

The biology of stress derives from the "fight or flight" reaction that is wired into our body for survival purposes. This automatic reaction prepares us to handle danger or threat by flooding our body with chemicals (e.g., adrenalin) in the same way that our ancient ancestors had to engage in fight or flight (escape) when confronted by life-threatening predators.

COUNSELING OFFICE
Hours: 24–7

Anxiety Disorders
Drug Addiction
Internet Addiction
Information Fatigue Syndrome

Today's technological revolution and information explosion may be making life particularly stressful.

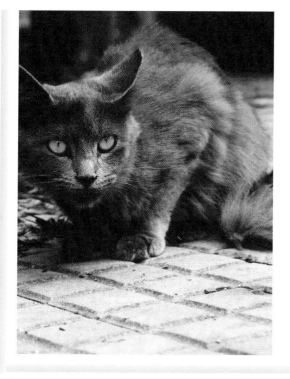

© JupiterImages Corporation.

The "fight-or-flight" reaction occurs when we're under stress because it's a throwback to the time when ancient humans needed to fight with or flee from potential predators. However, unlike other animals, stress doesn't cause our hair to rise up and appear more intimidating to foes (but we still can get "goose bumps" when we're nervous, and we still refer to scary events as "hair raising" experiences).

If stress occurs for a short period of time and in a manageable amount, it can benefit us by improving:

a.   our physical performance (e.g., strength and speed),

b.   our mental performance (e.g., attention and memory), and

c.   our mood (e.g., hope and optimism).

⟁ Pause for Reflection

Can you think of a situation in which you performed at a higher level because you were somewhat nervous or experienced a moderate amount of stress?

Research indicates that college students' stress levels tend to rise when they are experiencing a wave of exams, such as finals.

However, if stress is extreme or excessive, and continues for a prolonged period of time, it moves from being productive to being destructive. Using our guitar-string analogy, if a guitar string is too tight, it's likely to snap or break, which would not be productive. Such unproductive stress is often referred to as *distress*—from the root "dis" meaning "bad" (as in the words discomfort and disease). Extreme stress produces intense anxiety or anxiety disorders (e.g., panic attacks), and if a high level of stress persists for a prolonged period of time, it can trigger psychosomatic illness— from "psyche" ("mind") causing illness in the "soma" ("body"). For instance, prolonged distress can trigger high blood pressure, which may account for why high blood pressure is also referred to as "hypertension." Also, prolonged stress can suppress our immune system, leaving us more vulnerable to flu, colds, and other infectious diseases. Studies show that college students' immune systems produce fewer antibodies at very stressful times during the academic term, such as during periods of intense testing (e.g., midterms and finals) (Jemott & Magloire, 1985; Kielcolt-Glaser & Glaser, 1986).

Excess stress can also interfere with mental performance because the feelings and thoughts that accompany anxiety begin to preoccupy our mind and take up space in our working memory, leaving less of it available for concentrating on the information we're trying to learn and retain. Studies show that students who experience higher levels of academic stress or performance anxiety are more likely to use ineffective "surface" approaches to learning that rely merely on memorization (Ramsden & Entwistle, 1981), rather than using more effective "deep" learning strategies that seek meaning and understanding. (For more detailed information about "surface" versus "deep" learning, see Chapter 4.) Also, high levels of test anxiety are more likely to result in careless concentration errors on exams (e.g., overlooking key words in test questions), and can interfere with memory for information that's been studied (Jacobs and Nadel, 1985; O'Keefe & Nadel, 1985; Tobias, 1985).

Although there is considerable research pointing to the negative effects of excess stress, we still need to keep in mind that stress can work either for or against us; we can be either energized or sabotaged by stress depending on its level of intensity and the length of time it continues. We cannot expect to stop or eliminate stress altogether, nor should we want to; we can only hope to contain it and maintain it at a level where it's more productive than destructive. In fact, many years of research indicate that personal performance is best when it takes place under conditions of *moderate stress*, which creates a sense of challenge, rather than too much stress, which creates performance anxiety, or too little stress, which results in lack of intensity or indifference (Sapolsky, 2004; Yerkes & Dodson, 1908) (Figure 13.1).

Figure 13.1 Relationship Between Arousal and Performance

Moderate challenge that produces moderate stress often results in maximum (peak) performance.

Source: Williams, Landers, & Boutcher (1993)

Good | Maximum Performance

Performance

Poor | Poor Performance   Poor Performance

Low (Underaroused) | Moderate (Optimally aroused) | High (Overaroused)

Emotional Arousal

Box 13.1 provides a short summary of the key signs or symptoms of extreme stress that may indicate that stress has reached a level of distress or high anxiety. If these symptoms continue to occur for two or more weeks, action should be taken to reduce it.

BOX 13.1 *Snapshot* SUMMARY

High Anxiety: Signs of Distress

- Jitteriness or shaking—especially the hands
- Accelerated heart rate or heart palpitations—intense, irregular heartbeat
- Muscle tension—tightness in the chest, upper shoulders, or a tight feeling ("lump") in the throat (the expressions "uptight" and "choking" stem from these symptoms of upper-body tension)
- Body aches—due to increased muscle tension (e.g., "tension headaches" in the back of the head; lower backache), or chest pain—which can become so extreme that the person may feel that a heart attack is taking place
- Sweating—e.g., sweaty (clammy) palms
- Cold, pale hands or feet (the expressions "white knuckles" and "cold feet" derive from these symptoms)
- Dry mouth—due to production of less saliva (the expression, "cotton mouth" stems from this loss of saliva)
- Stomach discomfort or indigestion—due to increased secretion of stomach acid (the expression "feeling butterflies in my stomach" relates to this symptom)
- Elimination problems—e.g., constipation or diarrhea
- Feeling faint or dizzy—due to constriction of blood vessels that decreases oxygen flow to the brain
- Weakness and fatigue—due to being in a sustained (chronic) state of arousal and muscle tension
- Menstrual changes—such as missing periods or experiencing irregular menstrual periods
- Difficulty sleeping—such as insomnia, or interrupted (fitful) sleep
- Increased susceptibility to colds, flu, and other infections—due to suppression of the body's immune system

Pause for Reflection

How would you rate your level of anxiety in the following situations?

1.	*Taking tests or exams*	high moderate low
2.	*Interacting in social situations*	high moderate low
3.	*Making decisions about the future*	high moderate low

Researched-Based Techniques for Stress Management

If we perceive our level of stress reaching a point where it's beginning to interfere with the quality of our performance or the quality of our life, we need to take steps to reduce it. Listed below are three key stress-management methods whose positive effects have been documented by psychological and biological research (Benson & Klipper, 1990; Everly, 1989; Lehrer & Woolfolk, 1993).

1. Deep (Diaphragmatic) Breathing

The type of breathing associated with excessive stress is hyperventilation—fast, shallow, and irregular breathing that occurs through the mouth. Breathing associated with relaxation is just the opposite—slow, deep, and regular breathing that originates from the stomach.

Usually, breathing is something we do automatically or involuntarily; however, with some concentration and effort we can control our breathing by controlling our diaphragm—the body's muscle that enables us to expand and contract our lungs. By voluntarily controlling our diaphragm muscle, we can slow down our breathing rate, which, in turn, can bring down our stress level.

It's important to realize that our rate of breathing sets the pace for the rate at which other systems in our body operate. For example, when our breathing slows down, our heart rate slows down, our blood pressure goes down, and our muscle tension is reduced. Thus, by slowing down our breathing, we can produce a "wave" or "ripple effect" of relaxation across other systems of our body that slows them down as well. Deep breathing's ability to trigger relaxation throughout the body makes it one of the most powerful stress-management techniques available to us.

You can practice diaphragmatic breathing by breathing with your mouth closed (but your lips not pressed tightly together), keeping your chest still, and allowing your stomach to rise and fall at a slow, steady pace. To help you produce this type of breathing, imagine a candle in front of you that you're blowing on and trying to make it flicker without blowing it out. To be sure you're breathing deeply and consistently through your stomach, put one hand on your chest and be sure your chest remains still while you breathe; and place your other hand on your stomach to be sure that it rises and falls as you breathe in and out.

By practicing diaphragmatic breathing consistently, it can soon become very natural to you, and you'll be able to quickly shift into deep breathing anytime you feel yourself becoming anxious or tense (e.g., before a big exam or speech).

2. Progressive Muscle Relaxation

This stress-management method is similar to stretching exercises that are used for relaxing and loosening muscles before and after physical exercise. To achieve total body (head-to-toe) muscle relaxation, progressively tense and release the five sets of muscles listed below. Hold the tension in the muscle area for about 5 seconds and release it slowly.

a. Wrinkle your forehead muscles, and then release them.
b. Shrug your shoulders up as if to touch your ears, and then drop them.
c. Make a fist with both hands, and then open them.
d. Tighten your stomach muscles, and then release them.
e. Tighten your toes by curling them under your feet, and then raise them as high as possible.

To help tense your muscles, imagine you're using them to push or lift a heavy object. When relaxing your muscles, take a deep breath and think or say the word "relax." By breathing deeply and thinking or hearing the word "relax" each time you relax your muscles, this word becomes associated with your muscles becoming relaxed. Thus, if you find yourself in a stressful situation, you can take a deep breath, think or say the word "relax," and then your muscles may immediately release tension because that's what they've been trained or conditioned to do.

3. Mental Imagery

We can use our imagination to create sensory experiences that promote relaxation. For example, you can create your own relaxing "mental movie" or "imaginary DVD" by visually placing yourself in a setting that is calm, comfortable, and soothing. You can visualize ocean waves, floating clouds, floating in a warm sauna, or any sensory experience that tends to relax you. The more senses you use in your imagined situation, the more real it will seem to be and the more powerful its relaxing effects will be (Fezler, 1989). Try to use all your senses—try to "see" it, "hear" it, "smell" it, "touch" it, and "feel" it. You can also use musical imagination to create your own "mental CD" of calming background music that helps you relax.

Lastly, when using your imagination, close your eyes and move your eyeballs upward—as if you're looking at the sky or ceiling. Research indicates that this upward eye movement tends to trigger "alpha waves"—brainwaves that are associated with a state of mental relaxation (Liebertz, 2005a).

© JupiterImages Corporation.

Mental imagery is a stress management technique you can practice anywhere.

> *Personal Story* My wife, Mary, is a kindergarten teacher. Whenever her young students start misbehaving and the situation becomes stressful (e.g., during lunchtime when the kids are running wildly, arguing vociferously, and screaming at maximum volume), Mary "plays" relaxing songs in her head. She reports that her musical imagination always works to soothe her nerves, enabling her to remain calm and even-tempered when she must confront children who need to be scolded or disciplined.
>
> *—Joe Cuseo*

Stress-Reduction Strategies and Practices

In addition to formal stress-management techniques, such as diaphragmatic breathing, progressive muscle relaxation, and mental imagery, there are other simpler strategies or practices that can be used to reduce stress.

Reduce or avoid intake of alcohol and caffeine.

The substances we put into our body physically can affect us emotionally. Because alcohol is a sedative or "downer" drug that slows down the nervous system, people often turn to it as a strategy to cope with stress and promote relaxation (Carpenter & Hasin, 1998). However, if too much alcohol is consumed, it has just the opposite effect because it stimulates release of cortisol—a hormone that activates and elevates the body's stress response.

Since stress can cause fatigue, people may also be tempted to use caffeine to regain energy. However, caffeine is a stimulant drug that not only stimulates alertness, it also stimulates the part of our involuntary nervous system that's associated with stress and arousal. Thus, caffeine is likely to increase feelings of nervous tension (hence, the expression, "coffee nerves"). If you tend to get somewhat nervous or anxious in situations that test your mental performance, such as exams or speeches, the last substance you want to put into your system just before performance time is something that's going to further stimulate your tension.

While we're on the subject of alcohol and caffeine, this may be the time to point out that it's a myth that giving caffeine (e.g., a cup of coffee) to someone who is drunk will help sober them. Caffeine does not reduce the body's blood-alcohol level, so it will not make the drunken person feel any less intoxicated. Since caffeine stimulates the nervous system, it will make a drunken person feel less sleepy, but not any less drunk nor any more capable of operating heavy machinery—such as driving a car.

Decrease your intake of simple sugars (e.g., chocolates, candies, sugary sodas), and increase your intake of foods that are high in complex carbohydrates.

Foods high in complex carbohydrates (e.g., brown rice, potatoes, pasta, legumes, whole grain bread, and cereals) elevate a brain chemical called serotonin, which increases feelings of calmness and serenity. Although it may be tempting to put something sweet in your mouth when you're stressed and tired, simple sugars will only deliver a short-term shot of nervous energy.

If you tend to eat when you're stressed, chew on something other than high-sugar, high-calorie foods (e.g., chew sugarless gum or suck on a mint), or explore other ways to relieve tension, rather than relying on oral stimulation.

Journaling

Dealing with stressful feelings by writing about them in a personal journal can provide a safe and regular outlet for releasing steam and coping with stress. Also, writing about our emotions enables us to deal with them more consciously and rationally, reducing the risk that we'll suppress or repress them into our subconscious.

Take time for humor and laughter.

Research on the power of humor for reducing tension is clear and convincing. For example, one research study involved college students who were unexpectedly given an assignment to deliver an impromptu (off the top of their head) speech. This sudden assignment resulted in the students' heart rate elevating to an average of 110 beats per minute during their speech. However, students who watched humorous episodes of sitcoms before delivering their impromptu speeches displayed a lower average heart rate of 80–85 beats per minute, indicating that humor served to lower their level of anxiety (O'Brien, cited in Howard, 2000). Research also shows that if our immune system is suppressed or weakened by stress, humor strengthens it by blocking the body's production of the stress hormone, cortisol, which is responsible for suppressing our immune system when we are stressed (Berk in Leibertz, 2005b).

••• Depression

Along with stress and anxiety, depression is another emotional problem that commonly afflicts humans. Excess stress can turn into anxiety—a heightened state of tension, arousal, and nervous energy; or, it can lead to depression—an emotional state characterized by a loss of optimism, hope, and energy. As its name implies, when people are depressed, their mood is pushed "down" or "lowered." In contrast to anxiety, which typically involves worry or tension about something that is currently happening or is about to happen (e.g., experiencing test anxiety before an upcoming exam), depression more often relates to something that has already happened. In particular, depression is frequently related to a *loss* of some sort, such as a lost *relationship* (e.g., departed friend, broken romance, death of a family member) or a lost *opportunity* (e.g., losing a job, failing a course, or failing to be accepted into a major) (Bowlby, 1980; Price, Choi, & Vinokur, 2002). It is natural and normal to feel dejected after losses such as these.

Remember: If dejection reaches a point where we can't concentrate and complete our day-to-day tasks, and this continues for an extended period of time, we may be experiencing what psychologists call *clinical depression,* i.e., depression so serious that it requires professional treatment.

Box 13.2 provides a summary of key symptoms or signs that may indicate the presence of depression. If these symptoms continue to occur for two or more weeks, action should be taken to relieve them.

BOX 13.2 *Snapshot* **SUMMARY**   **Key Signs of Depression**

- Feeling "low," "down," dejected, sad, or blue
- Pessimistic feelings about the future—e.g., expecting failure, feeling helpless or hopeless
- Decreased sense of humor
- Difficulty finding pleasure, joy, or "fun" in anything
- Lack of concentration
- Loss of motivation or interest in things that previously were found to be exciting or stimulating
- Stooped posture (e.g., hung head, drawn face)
- Slower and softer speech rate
- Decreased animation and slower bodily movements
- Loss of energy
- Changes in sleeping patterns (e.g., sleeping more or less than usual)
- Changes in eating patterns (e.g., eating more or less than usual)
- Social withdrawal
- Neglect of physical appearance
- Consistently low self-esteem—for example, thinking: "I'm a loser."
- Strong feelings of worthlessness or guilt—for example, thinking: "I'm a failure."
- Suicidal thoughts—e.g., thoughts like: "I can't take it anymore," "People would be better off without me," or, "I don't deserve to live."

Pause for Reflection

Have you, or a member of your family, ever experienced depression?

What do you think was the primary cause or factor that triggered the depression?

Strategies for Coping with Depression

Depression can range widely in intensity from mild to moderate to severe. Moderate and severe forms of depression frequently require professional counseling or psychotherapy, and their cause often has genetic roots that involve inherited imbalances in brain chemistry.

The following strategies are offered primarily for milder cases of depression that are more amenable to self-help and self-control. Nevertheless, these strategies may also be used in combination with professional help or psychiatric medication to further reduce the intensity and frequency of depression.

Focus on the present and the future, not the past.

Consciously fight the tendency to dwell on past losses or failures because they can no longer be changed or controlled. Instead, focus on things you still can control, which are occurring now and will occur in the future.

When you're feeling "down," deliberately make an effort to bring yourself "up" by engaging in positive or upbeat behavior.

If our behavior is upbeat, our mind (mood) often follows suit. "Put on a happy face" may actually be an effective depression-reduction strategy because smiling produces certain changes in our facial muscles, which, in turn, trigger changes in brain chemistry that improves mood (Leibertz, 2005); in contrast, frowning activates a different set of facial muscles that reduce production of mood-elevating brain chemicals (Myers, 1993).

Continue to engage in activities that are fun and enjoyable for you (e.g., socialize with friends; partake in your usual recreational activities).

Don't fall into the downward spiral of ceasing to do the things you find rewarding because you're too down to do them, which brings you down even further because you're taking away the very things that normally bring you up. Interestingly, the root of the word "recreation" means to "re-create" or "create again," which suggests that recreation can revive, restore, and renew us—physically and emotionally.

Intentionally seek out humor and laughter.

In addition to reducing anxiety, laughter can also lighten and brighten a dark mood. Furthermore, humor improves memory (Nielson, in Liebertz, 2005), which is an important advantage for people experiencing depression, because depression interferes with concentration and memory. Research supporting the benefits of humor for the body and mind is so well established that humor has become a legitimate academic field of study, known as gelontology—the study of laughter (from the Greek word, "gelos" for "laughter" and "ology" meaning "study of").

Continue to accomplish things.

Continuing to stay busy and getting things done when we feel down can help boost our mood by increasing our self-esteem. Getting something done that also involves doing something nice for someone less fortunate than ourselves can be particularly effective for elevating mood because it helps us realize that our issues are often much less serious and more manageable than the problems faced by others.

Make a conscious effort to focus on your personal strengths and accomplishments.

Another way to beat back the blues is by keeping track of the good developments in your life. One way to do this is by keeping a "positive events journal" in which you note the good experiences in your life, including things you're grateful for, as well as your accomplishments and achievements. Positive journal entries such as these will leave you with an uplift-

One strategy for coping with depression is to write down the positive events in your life in a journal.

ing visible record that you can review anytime you're feeling down. Furthermore, a positive events journal can provide you with a starting point for developing a formal resume, portfolio, and "personal strengths sheet" that you can provide for your personal references or the individuals who write your letters of recommendation. (More information on letters of recommendation, resumes, and portfolios is provided in Chapter 9.)

If you are unable to overcome depression on your own, be open to seeking help from others.

College students today are more likely to seek professional help if they're feeling depressed (Kadison & DiGeronimo, 2004). This is good news because it suggests that seeking help is no longer being viewed as a source of embarrassment, or sign of personal weakness. Instead, seeking help indicates that people have the courage to share their feelings with others and the motivation to improve their quality of life.

In some cases, you may be able to help yourself overcome emotional problems through personal effort and the use of effective coping strategies. This is particularly true if you are experiencing depression or anxiety in milder forms and for limited periods of time. However, overcoming more serious and long-lasting episodes of clinical depression or anxiety is not as simple as people make it out to be when they say things like, "just deal with it," "get over it," or "snap out of it."

In mild cases of anxiety and depression, it's true that a person may be able to "deal with" or "get over" it, but in more serious cases, depression and anxiety may be strongly related to genetic factors that are beyond the person's control. Furthermore, the genes that can cause emotional problems often have a delayed effect, and their influence doesn't kick in until the late teens and early 20s. Thus, individuals who may have experienced no emotional problems during childhood may begin to experience them for the first time while they're in college. These cases of depression and anxiety often cannot be solved by willpower alone because they're often triggered by imbalances in brain chemicals caused by the individual's genetic make-up.

Certainly, we wouldn't tell a diabetic: "Come on, snap out of it. Get your insulin up!" This would be ridiculous because we know that this illness is caused by a chemical imbalance (shortage of insulin) in the body. Similarly, emotional disorders can be caused by a chemical imbalance (shortage of serotonin) in the brain—which is also part of the body. Just as it's obvious that we should not expect people suffering from diabetes to be able to exert self-control over a problem caused by their blood chemistry, we shouldn't expect people suffering from serious cases of emotional illness to be able to exert self-control over a problem caused by their brain chemistry.

In cases where professional assistance is needed for depression, anxiety, or any other emotional problem, an effective (and convenient) place to start is the Counseling Office on campus. Psychologists in this office can provide professional counseling and they can also make referrals to psychiatrists (MDs) in case medication is needed. Medications for emotional disorders are designed to compensate or correct chemical imbalances in the brain. Thus, taking medication for emotional disorders may be viewed as a way of helping the brain produce chemicals that it should be producing, but is not producing on its own because of its genetic make-up. When humans experience intense physical pain, we understand and accept their need to take pain-killing drugs (e.g., Advil or prescription pain-killers) to provide relief for their symptoms. Similarly, we should understand that humans experiencing intense emotional pain (e.g., depression or anxiety) may need to take psychiatric medication to provide relief for their symptoms.

If you thought you were experiencing a serious episode of anxiety or depression, would you feel comfortable seeking help from a professional?

If yes, why? If no, why not?

●●● Thinking and Wellness

In addition to emotions, another key element of the human mind that can affect overall wellness is our thoughts, or the way we think. Two key elements of thinking that can affect both our mental and physical well-being are:

1. The amount of higher-level thinking we do, and
2. The amount of positive thinking we do.

Higher-Level Thinking and Health

Research shows that people who spend more time engaged in higher-level thinking tend to experience better mental and physical health. Simply put: Those who use their mind don't lose their mind—that is, they're less likely to lose their memory or experience dementia (e.g., Alzheimer's disease) during their later years (Wilson, Mendes, & Barnes, 2002). While there is a tendency to divide the "mind" (mental) and "body" (physical) into separate categories, thinking is not merely a mental activity; it's also a physical activity that exercises the brain, much like physical activity exercises muscles in other parts of the body. Higher-level thinking requires physical energy and stimulates biological activity among brain cells, invigorating them and making them less susceptible to deterioration. Studies show that use of higher-level thinking skills increases both the number and strength of connections between brain cells ("Optimizing Those Brain Cells," 2002).

Furthermore, thinking is a naturally stimulating activity that represents a very inexpensive form of self-entertainment. It doesn't cost anything to do it; you don't need to purchase heavy machinery or high-tech equipment; you can do it anywhere at any time, when you're alone or with others; you can do it while you're standing in line, sitting in the bathroom, or lying in bed; and you can do it with your eyes open or closed.

Contrary to common belief, problem solving and other forms of higher-level thinking will not "fry" your brain but will stimulate and exercise it, reducing the likelihood that you'll experience Alzheimer's disease and other causes of memory loss in later life.

Optimistic versus Pessimistic Thinking

Just as engaging in higher-level thinking can promote wellness, so too can engaging in *optimistic* (positive) thinking rather than pessimistic (negative) thinking. The differences between pessimism and optimism are artfully captured by the following familiar metaphors:

◆ An optimist sees a half-filled glass as half full; a pessimist sees it as half empty.
◆ An optimist sees a doughnut; a pessimist sees its hole.
◆ An optimist sees a cloud's silver lining; a pessimist sees a cloud.

Less metaphorically, pessimistic students view exams as sources of threat and potential failure; optimistic students view them as challenges and as opportunities to demonstrate their learning.

Research indicates that pessimistic thinking is associated with poorer personal performance (Peterson, 1990; Peterson & Barrett, 1987) and lower life expectancy (Peterson, 1998). The good news is that research also shows that individuals can learn to perceive situations less pessimistically, and when they learn to think more optimistically (e.g., thinking they have more influence or control over the outcome of events), they improve their academic performance (Wilson & Linville, 1982, 1985) and their personal performance in other areas of life (Perry, et al., 1993).

How Thinking Influences Emotions and Actions

Research indicates that the part of the human brain involved in higher-level thinking (the brain's upper area—known as the cortex) has many connections to the part of the brain responsible for emotions (the limbic system—located in the middle of the brain) (Goleman, 1995; Zull, 1998). Thus, the brain is wired in such a way that thinking can directly influence emotions or feelings.

Since thoughts can precede and influence emotions, by changing the way we think, we may be able to change the emotions we experience, and change them in a way that improves our performance and wellness. Thinking can affect how we feel and perform by affecting:

a. perceptions of current experiences,
b. reactions to previous experiences, and
c. expectations of future experiences.

How you think affects your perceptions of current experiences.

Stress involves a rush of adrenalin throughout the body, but how this rush is perceived or interpreted determines whether it is experienced as excitement or tension. For instance, the rush of adrenalin experienced during a horror movie or a scary ride may be interpreted as thrilling fun or spine-chilling fear. Similarly, if you experience a rush of adrenalin during a test, you could interpret it to mean that you're "psyched up" for the challenge or "psyched out" by the pressure.

How you think affects your reactions to previous experiences.

The thoughts that follow an experience can affect how you react to it and what action you take with respect to it. For instance, what you think about a poor performance (e.g., a poor test grade) can affect your emotional reaction to that grade and what you do about it. You can react to the poor grade by scolding yourself and knocking yourself further down with self-putdowns ("I'm a loser"), or by building yourself back up with positive pep talk ("I'm going to learn from these mistakes and rebound stronger on the next one").

If a poor past performance is not seen as a personal failure but as an opportunity to learn and correct your mistakes, it enables you to convert setbacks into comebacks. Here are some notable people who turned early setbacks into very successful comebacks:

◆ Louis Pasteur, famous bacteriologist, who failed his admission test to the University of Paris;
◆ Albert Einstein, Nobel Prize-winning physicist, who failed math in elementary school;
◆ Thomas Edison, prolific inventor, who was once expelled from school as "uneducable";
◆ Johnny Unitas, Hall-of-Fame football player, who was cut twice from professional football teams early in his career.

In response to their early setbacks, these successful people didn't get bitter; they got better. Getting mad or sad about setbacks is likely to cause stress and depression; in contrast, thinking about how to better your performance is more likely to result in actually doing something to improve your future performances, which, in turn, will elevate self-esteem and contribute positively to your overall wellness.

How you think affects your expectations of future experiences.

Just as afterthoughts can affect your reaction to something after it has happened, your forethoughts can affect what you *expect* to happen. Your expectations of things to come can either be positive or negative. For example, before a test you could think: "I'm poised, confident, and ready to do it!" or, you could think: "I know I'm going to fail this test; I just know it."

Our expectations can lead to what sociologists and psychologists call a "self-fulfilling prophecy," which refers to how negative thoughts or beliefs can lead to behaviors that make our beliefs turn out to be true. For instance, if you expect you're going to be rejected by people, you may unconsciously develop patterns of rejecting others first; for example, by looking away, walking away, and staying away from others. Naturally, all of these behaviors will increase the probability that you will, in fact, be rejected and thereby confirm your pessimistic belief.

On the other hand, positive expectations can lead to a positive self-fulfilling prophecy. For instance, if you expect your social interactions to go well, you're more likely to display confidence and enthusiasm when interacting with others, which will increase the likelihood that others will approach and accept you, thereby making your positive expectation come true.

Pause for Reflection

Would you consider yourself to be generally an optimistic or a pessimistic person?

In what specific situations do you tend to think:

a. *optimistically?*

b. *pessimistically?*

Catastrophic Thinking

Sometimes, situations or experiences can be made worse by overreacting to them and exaggerating their significance. In other words, you can make "a mountain out of a molehill" by blowing something way out of proportion and magnifying its negative aspects. This is what psychologists call "catastrophic" thinking, which is another form of negative thinking that should be avoided if you want to promote wellness. Here are some classic examples of catastrophic thinking:

◆   You're having difficulty with the first item on a test and you begin to think that you're going to flunk the entire exam.

◆   You have one misunderstanding with your new roommate and you become absolutely convinced that the entire year will be one long battle.

◆   You haven't been able to get to sleep for ten minutes and you convince yourself that you'll be lying awake for hours and be totally wiped out the next day.

Researchers have identified three recurrent themes or common elements that seem to characterize all forms of catastrophic and pessimistic thinking (Beck, 1976; Seligman, 1991):

1. **Personalizing:** assuming that you are the cause of a negative event, i.e., you believe it's entirely your fault or that you're totally responsible (e.g., "I made this happen." "The relationship failed because I'm just not lovable." "I failed that test because I'm not very bright.");

2. **Pervasiveness:** assuming that the consequences of a negative event are going to pervade or penetrate every aspect of your life (e.g., thinking that a bad romantic experience is going to ruin you—socially, emotionally, and academically);

3. **Permanence:** thinking that a negative experience is never going to improve or change for the better (e.g., "Things will never be the same." "I'll never get over this.")

Strategies for Replacing Negative Thinking with Positive Thinking

Information typically passes first through emotional areas of the brain, before being passed on to centers of the brain involved in thinking and reasoning (LeDoux, 1998). Thus, our brain tends to react to an event emotionally before it does rationally. In fact, emotions can be triggered so quickly that they can determine our reaction to a situation before rational thinking gets a chance to regulate or control them. Also, if the emotion being experienced is very intense, it can completely preempt or "short-circuit" rational thinking.

In order to prevent a flood of emotions from overtaking or hijacking your train of thought, you need to make a very conscious effort to think and reason rationally in response to them, so that you can decrease their negative impact on your performance and your health. For instance, if you find yourself beginning to feel overwhelmed by stress, you may need to think or say, "Before I get carried away, let me think this through," or, "I need to stop and think before doing anything." An entire field of psychotherapy, known as *rational-emotive therapy* or *cognitive therapy,* uses this approach to help people develop specific thinking strategies to cope with, control, and cure emotional problems, such as anxiety and depression (Ellis, 1975, 2001).

Described below is a series of specific strategies for thinking positively that may be used to help manage emotions, maintain mental health, and attain overall wellness.

Develop self-awareness of your thinking patterns or habits.

Becoming more aware of the nature of your thoughts is the first step to controlling them. Thinking often takes the form of "self-talk"—that is, when we think, we're talking to ourselves silently (or sometimes out loud). Therefore, negative thinking often involves negative self-talk (e.g., "I'm a loser." "What's happening to me is just horrible." "There's absolutely nothing I can do."). One way we can become more aware of our self-talk is to write down the words we use in a "thought journal," making special note of pessimistic or catastrophic thought patterns that should be changed.

Block negative thoughts.

You can block or put a stop to negative thoughts the instant you start having them by practicing what psychologists call "internal screaming" (e.g., using commanding thoughts like: "Cool it!" "Get out!" "Get lost!" or "Go to hell!"). Also, negative thoughts may be blocked by intentionally changing the subject of thought, i.e., switching our "mental channel" to a different program.

Substitute positive thoughts for negative thoughts.

In addition to blocking or ignoring negative thoughts, you can also attack and replace them with positive alternative thoughts. Let's say you happen to see some students turning in their tests before you finished and you start having a catastrophic thought like, "They all must be smarter than I am!" You can stop that thought and substitute the following thought: "They're getting up and getting out because they're giving up." Or, "They're rushing out without taking the time to carefully review it before turning it in." The key to this thought-substitution strategy is to develop a set of specific, positive statements and practice them so well that you think of them automatically and immediately to replace negative thoughts. For example, you can develop your own special "positive self-talk" vocabulary for dealing with personal setbacks or disappointments that could include expressions such as: "Nobody's perfect." "Tomorrow's another day." "It's over with and it can't be changed anyway." "I gave it my best shot." "I've seen worse." "This isn't the end of the world." "Later, I'll look back at this and laugh." By rehearsing and repeatedly using these optimistic expressions, you can develop a habit of thinking good thoughts that routinely take the place of negative thoughts.

Use critical thinking skills to question the logic or truth behind your negative thoughts.

When you're having pessimistic or catastrophic thoughts, ask yourself questions such as:

- What actual evidence do I have for thinking this way?
- What other interpretations or explanations for this event might be possible and plausible?
- Are there any real advantages to my thinking this way?
- If I think in a more positive way, what consequences are likely to follow?

For example, let's say you're feeling nervous, and you say to yourself: "Geez, my heart's beating so hard, it feels like it's going to jump right out of my chest!" If you start thinking critically about this thought, you would immediately become aware that it's outrageously irrational. You can then use your critical thinking skills to challenge it and defeat it by coming to a much more rational and productive conclusion, such as: "Wait a second, although hearts are made of muscle, they don't have the leaping ability of frogs, so it's highly unlikely that my heart is going to leap out of my body and leave me heartless. Therefore, I'm not going to focus on my heart or my anxiety, but on the situation in front of me and what I can do about it!"

Put your personal issues into a larger framework or global perspective.

For example, when things begin to get you down, you might ask yourself: "Is what I'm experiencing really that bad compared to other people in the world who are suffering from starvation, chronic pain, or dying from incurable diseases?" Viewed from this broader perspective, many of the things that worry or depress us become almost petty in comparison.

"Restructure" or "reframe" negative thoughts.

Cognitive "restructuring" or "reframing" is a thinking strategy whereby you change your perception or interpretation of a potentially negative experience by mentally converting or transforming it into something more positive (Beck, 1976). For instance, if you can't find a parking space near campus, rather than reacting to it with frustration and anger because you'll need to park far away, you can reframe your reaction to this event by viewing it as an opportunity to get some needed exercise. Similarly, if you're stuck in a long line waiting to take care of some bureaucratic business, instead of seething or doing a slow burn by perceiving the situation as a total waste of your time, you could reframe it as an opportunity that allows you some time to slow down and do some introspective or imaginative thinking.

Make productive use of your mind's capacity for fantasy and visual imagery.

Fantasy is not merely an escape from reality or an impractical waste of time, it can also be used as an effective thought-control and wellness-promoting strategy. For example, whenever you're nervous about doing something difficult or dealing with something stressful, you can use your imagination to visualize how you'll overcome your fear and experience success. You can use fantasy to create your own imaginary "hero" or personal success story; for instance, if you're shy, you can help reduce your shyness by mentally visualizing yourself meeting people, interacting with others confidently, and making new friends.

Pause for Reflection

Have you ever used your imagination to visualize yourself being successful or doing something successfully?

If yes, what was the situation you imagined yourself in, and what did you visualize yourself doing successfully in that situation?

●●● The Spiritual Dimension of Wellness

In addition to the body and mind, there is a third dimension to wellness: the *spirit*. Spirituality is the most difficult dimension of wellness to define precisely; it is an abstract concept that can have different meanings to different people. The National Wellness Institute defines spirituality as,

> *"Seeking meaning and purpose in human existence. It includes the development of a deep appreciation of the depth and expanse of life and natural forces that exist in the universe" (National Wellness Institute, 2005).*

We will use this definition as a starting point or foundation for building a broader definition of spiritual wellness that includes diverse spiritual perspectives and viewpoints.

Elements of Spirituality

We think that there are three key components of a comprehensive definition of spirituality that embraces multiple spiritual perspectives:

1. An inward search for the meaning and purpose of life,
2. An outward search for connection between the self and the larger world or universe, and
3. A transcendent search for the mystical or supernatural—for something or someone that transcends the natural world.

What follows is a closer look at each of these components of spirituality, accompanied by an explanation of why each of them plays an important role in promoting total wellness and personal happiness.

Spirituality involves a search for the meaning and purpose of life.

A spiritual focus shifts our attention away from the exterior and material world toward our inner or interior life (Astin, 2004). You may have the drive to succeed in life, and use every possible success strategy and resource at your disposal, but you're not likely to feel you have succeeded until you answer larger questions about what it means to be successful, and what is your mission, purpose, or direction in life. This aspect of spirituality is an important component of our quest for personal identity (Tisdell, 2003).

The need to focus less on the exterior or material world and more on an interior search for meaning is highlighted by research showing that Americans have grown progressively wealthier during the course of the last half-century, but they have not grown progressively happier (Kassin, 2006) (Figure 13.2).

Figure 13.2 Relationship Between Material Wealth and Personal Happiness

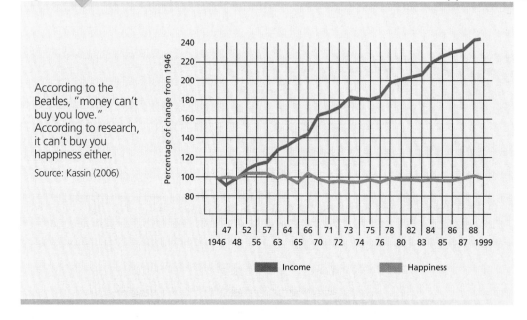

According to the Beatles, "money can't buy you love." According to research, it can't buy you happiness either.

Source: Kassin (2006)

Being rich, famous, or powerful doesn't ensure happiness. While it is true that you need money to meet your basic material needs (e.g., food, shelter, and clothing), it doesn't necessarily meet your "higher" spiritual needs for personal meaning and self-fulfillment. In fact, research indicates that people who have a stronger spiritual focus report being happier (Myers, 1993).

A spiritual focus can contribute to happiness by helping humans cope with "existential anxiety"—the feeling that life has no meaning or purpose and will simply terminate with death (Frankl, 1946; Tillich, 1952). Spirituality can also help people attain and maintain inner calm when the outer world is rife with unrest and uncertainty. Perhaps this aspect of spirituality accounts for the finding that even though alcohol consumption and abuse is increasing among college students in general, students who identify themselves as "spiritual" drink far less than their peers (Higher Education Institute, 2004).

"I've got the bowl, the bone, the big yard. I know I *should* be happy."

© The New Yorker Collection 1992 Mike Twohy from cartoonbank.com. All Rights Reserved.

Success and happiness are not synonymous.

Personal Story When my son was three years old and in preschool, his teacher talked about the Christian belief that Christ died on the cross and then rose from the dead on Easter morning. My son heard his teacher tell this story in the morning, held it in his head all day, and as soon as his mother (my wife) came to pick him up in the afternoon, he ran to her as fast as he could, and with a face full of tears, he blurted out: "Mommy, we're all gonna die!"

That was my three-year-old son's first awareness of his own mortality; also, it may have been his first spiritual thought, and his first encounter with existential anxiety. Whatever it was, he certainly felt a strong need to make sense of death and find a way to cope with it before he could feel happy again.

—*Joe Cuseo*

Spirituality involves a search for connection between the self and the larger world or universe.

In addition to an inward search for meaning, spirituality may also involve an outward search to understand and connect with the world around us. This search may include looking for a connection between the self and the larger social world that is *humanity*, or a connection between the self and the larger physical world that embraces *nature and the universe*.

Finding a personal connection between ourselves and something larger than ourself may reduce feelings of being disconnected, isolated, or alienated. It may promote wellness by allowing us to experience a common bond with the rest of humanity and a feeling of unity with the physical world that surrounds us.

Spirituality involves a search for the mystical or supernatural—for something or someone that transcends the natural world.

Spiritual questions launch humans on a quest for the mystical or mysterious, for what has not yet been or may never be fully understood. This involves a search for what might *transcend* human existence and the existence of the universe or a search for the *supernatural*—for something or someone that is above and beyond the natural world, and which may account for the origin of the universe and human existence.

For some people, this aspect of the spiritual quest has led them to become *theists* who believe in God or a Supreme Being. For other people, this search has led them to a *religion*—an organized system of beliefs that they share with others, which often includes a set of worship practices and rituals directed toward a Supreme Being, as well as a set of moral guidelines for living an ethical life (Argyle & Beit-Hallahmi, 1975).

While spirituality and religion are related, they are not synonymous. Religion represents one specific way to address or answer broad spiritual questions; thus, religion may be understood as a particular route or avenue (among other routes and avenues) through which to experience spirituality (Dalton, et al., 2006).

Another important distinction between spirituality and religion is that spirituality represents an individual experience that is inner, personal, and private; in contrast, religion represents a more outward, external, and public expression of one's inner spirituality (Palmer, 1999; Plante & Sherman, 2001; Spilka, et al., 2003).

 Pause for Reflection

Would you characterize yourself as someone who is:

a. *spiritual?   Yes   No   Why?*

b. *religious?   Yes   No   Why?*

What experiences in your life do you think have influenced or led you to answer the above questions in the way that you did?

Strategies for Developing and Promoting the Spiritual Dimension of Wellness

While you're in college, use your learning experiences to actively explore, examine, develop, or refine your personal philosophy about life's meaning and purpose.

Surveys show that fewer students are entering college with the idea that the college experience will help them "develop a meaningful philosophy of life." At the same time, more students are entering college with the idea that its purpose is to help them get a job and make more money (Astin, et al., 2002). While it is true that college will help its graduates find gainful employment and meet their material needs, it's also true that college plays a key role in helping students explore spiritual questions relating to life's purpose and meaning. Liberal arts courses, in particular, are designed to answer these larger questions. Take these courses seriously, and, if your major permits, take more of them as electives—above and beyond the bare minimum number needed to complete your general-education requirements.

Remain open to exploring and further examining questions relating to how humans conceive of and believe in a higher power or Supreme Being.

You can do so by taking courses in theology or religious studies, and by participating in co-curricular activities and organizations that focus on this element of spiritual development.

Practice meditation.

Meditation is a practice that was originated by the Buddhist religion. Briefly stated, meditation involves an intense focusing or narrowing of concentration on a single sound, sight, or thought while simultaneously ignoring everything else, such as distracting, stress-producing thoughts and feelings.

Meditation has proven to be an effective stress-management technique (Davidson, et al., 2003), and recent research suggests that it can produce long-lasting positive changes in brain activity. Studies of Buddhist monks who are well practiced in meditation show that they have significantly greater activity in areas of their brain that are associated with learning and happiness (Lutz, et al., 2004).

Meditation has proven to be an effective stress-management technique, which may also have long-lasting positive effects on brain activity.

Build time into your schedule for spiritual matters.

 STUDENT PERSPECTIVE

"I love to go to the public library to reduce stress. I turn my cell phone off and get away from everyone."

—First-year student

Plan for periodic quiet time in a quiet place where you can engage in silent reflection.

You need to take time now and then to slow down, step away from the rat race, get off the fast track to success, think less about "getting ahead" and think more about where you're headed. The things that are ultimately most important for your overall health and happiness often take a back seat to things that are "more urgent." As we mentioned in Chapter 10, many years of research shows that the further away an event is in time, the less likely humans are to think about it and factor it into their day-to-day choices and decisions (Lewin, 1935; Loewenstein & Elster, 1992). This is unfortunate because our long-term life plans should be our first priority, not what we're doing today, tomorrow, next month, next year, or even five years from now. You could say that spiritual thinking about our larger purpose in life and our eventual mortality is the first and foremost step toward effective long-range planning.

The importance of spending some time in our "spiritual room" is especially true for human life in today's high-tech, multitasking world. We are now fully wired with wireless tools (and toys) for electronic communication and stimulation; we're becoming more preoccupied with immediate consumption of information and with the delivery and reception of instant communication. Thus, more of our attention is being consumed by the virtual world that currently engulfs us, which may distract us from the "inner" (personal) world within us and the "outer" (natural) world that surrounds us.

Just as we've taken time to develop our technological intelligence, so too should we take time to develop our "spiritual intelligence" (Gardner, 1999). Spiritual questions are powerful, intellectually stimulating questions that require us to use higher-level thinking skills to ponder "higher" issues relating to the meaning and purpose of life, how to place individual life in the context of something larger or beyond the self, and how to make long-range decisions about what life path is most meaningful for us to follow (Zohar & Marshall, 2000).

It's revealing that in Western cultures, creativity focuses on the production of tangible products that are displayed in public. In Eastern cultures, creativity is viewed as a personal process involving a spiritual quest for inner meaning or purpose (Lubart, 1999).

CLASSIC QUOTES

Attention should be focused internally to experience a quiet body and a calm mind.

—Buddha, 563–483 BC; founder of the Buddhist religion

Everyone is a house with four rooms: a physical, a mental, an emotional, and a spiritual. Most of us tend to live in one room most of the time but unless we go into every room every day, even if only to keep it aired, we are not complete.

—Native American proverb

CLASSIC QUOTE

Always being in touch means never being able to get away. The Wireless Man sits amid nature's grandeur and says, "It's beautiful. But it's not moving." He's addicted to the perpetual flux of the information networks. He's a speed freak, an info junkie. He wants to slow down, but can't.

—David Brooks, "Time to Do Everything Except Think," *Newsweek*, April 30, 2001

••• **Summary and Conclusion**

This chapter builds on the ideas presented in the previous chapter on physical wellness and highlights the fact that in addition to physical health, wellness also embraces mental and spiritual dimensions of the self. Thus, being "well" depends on how well you attend to three key elements of human existence:

STUDENT PERSPECTIVE

"How will I know if I am going the 'right way'?"
"How am I going to leave my mark when I finally pass away?"

—Questions raised by two college students during focus group interviews on the topic of spirituality (Higher Education Research Institute, 2004)

1. The body (discussed in Chapter 12)—what we put into and keep out of it (nutrition and substances), what we do with it (exercise), and how well we rest it (sleep);

2. The mind—how we manage our emotions (stress) and thoughts (positive or negative thinking);

3. The spirit—exploring the meaning and purpose of life, and coming to grips with the connection between ourselves as individuals and the larger world around and beyond us.

The research studies and scholarly wisdom reviewed in this chapter suggest that our wellness is most effectively promoted when we address the three key elements of our mind and spirit.

1. We need to maintain awareness of our emotions and monitor our stress, keeping it at a moderate level in order to achieve optimal performance. We should also develop our own set of self-help strategies for coping with the two most troublesome human emotions: anxiety and depression; and we should be willing to seek help from others when we cannot cope with these emotions on our own.

2. We need to be mentally active and use higher-level thinking skills to exercise our brain, just as we should physically exercise other parts of our body. By exercising our brain, we promote its long-term health and reduce its susceptibility to memory loss later in life. In addition to engaging in higher-level thinking, we need to engage in positive thinking to prevent pessimistic thoughts from having a negative effect on our emotional health and personal performance.

3. Last, but certainly not least, we need to attend to our spiritual needs by taking the time to turn inward and reflect on larger issues relating to the meaning and purpose of life. The need for spiritual reflection is particularly important in today's multitasking, technology-driven world, which keeps us constantly "plugged into" the outer world of information and communication, leaving less time and opportunity to "tune into" the inner world of self-reflection.

••• Learning More through Independent Research

Web-Based Resources for Further Information on Health and Wellness

For additional information relating to the ideas discussed in this chapter, we recommend the following Web sites:

Thinking and wellness: www.habitsmart.com

Emotional Health: www.nimh.nih.gov/publicat/index.cfm (National Institute of Mental Health)

Spirituality: www.collegevalues.org

Exercise #1. College Stress: Identifying Potential Sources and Possible Solutions

STEP 1.

Read through the following 30 college stressors and rate them in terms of how stressful each one is for you on a scale from 1 to 5 (with 1 being the lowest level of stress and 5 being the highest).

STEP 2.

Review your ratings and identify three of your top (highest-rated) stressors, and identify: (a) a coping strategy you may use on your own to deal with that source of stress, and (b) a campus resource you could use to obtain help with that source of stress.

Potential Stressors	Stress Rating (1= lowest; 5 = highest)				
Tests and exams	1	2	3	4	5
Assignments	1	2	3	4	5
Class workload	1	2	3	4	5
Pace of courses	1	2	3	4	5
Performing up to expectations	1	2	3	4	5
Handling personal freedom	1	2	3	4	5
Time pressure (e.g., not enough time)	1	2	3	4	5
Organizational pressure (e.g., losing things)	1	2	3	4	5
Living independently	1	2	3	4	5
The future	1	2	3	4	5
Decisions about a major or career	1	2	3	4	5
Moral and ethical decisions	1	2	3	4	5
Finding meaning in life	1	2	3	4	5
Emotional issues	1	2	3	4	5
Physical health	1	2	3	4	5
Social life	1	2	3	4	5
Intimate relationships	1	2	3	4	5
Sexuality	1	2	3	4	5
Family responsibilities	1	2	3	4	5
Family conflicts	1	2	3	4	5
Peer pressure	1	2	3	4	5
Family pressure	1	2	3	4	5
Loneliness or isolation	1	2	3	4	5
Roommate conflicts	1	2	3	4	5
Conflict with professors	1	2	3	4	5
Campus policies or procedures	1	2	3	4	5
Transportation	1	2	3	4	5
Technology	1	2	3	4	5
Safety	1	2	3	4	5

Exercise #2. Converting Setbacks into Comebacks: Transforming Pessimism into Optimism

In Hamlet, Shakespeare wrote: "There is nothing good or bad, but thinking makes it so." His point was that our experiences have the potential to be positive or negative, depending on how we interpret them and react to them.

Listed below is a series of statements representing negative interpretations and reactions to situations, events, or experiences. For each of these statements:

a. Note whether you have either experienced or observed this type of thinking, and note the situation(s) in which it took place.

b. Replace the negative statement with a statement that would represent a more positive interpretation or reaction. (For help in constructing these positive statements, see our discussion of thought-substitution strategies on page 441.)

1. "I'm just not good at this."

2. "There's nothing I can do about it."

3. "Things will never be the same."

4. "Nothing is going to change."

5. "This always happens to me."

6. "This is unbearable."

7. "Everybody is going to think I'm a loser."

8. "I'm trapped, and there's no way out."

▼ **CASE STUDY**

Blue and Lonesome

Lola and Leo were high school sweethearts. After high school graduation, each of them went to different colleges that were about a three-hour drive apart. Midway through their first term in college, Leo calls Lola to tell her that he is breaking up with her because their "long-distance relationship isn't working out" and he wants to meet and date other women.

Following the breakup, Lola begins to feel depressed. She's eating less, socializing less, and she's having trouble sleeping and concentrating on her schoolwork. Three weeks have now passed since Leo broke up with her, and she's beginning to think that she will never be the same and that she will never develop a relationship with anyone like she had with Leo.

Reflection and Discussion Questions

1. How realistic do you think this case is? Why?

2. What additional information would you need to accurately determine how serious Lola's emotional condition is?

3. What do you anticipate will be the most likely outcomes of this case (i.e., what do you expect will happen to Lola)?

4. What do you think needs to take place in order for Lola to recover from this social setback and move on with her life?

Epilogue:
Thriving in College and Beyond

A Matter of Principles and Character

••• Revisiting the Principles of College Success

In the first chapter of this text, we mentioned that research on human learning and student development pointed to four powerful principles of college success:

1. *active involvement,*
2. *utilizing resources,*
3. *interpersonal interaction* and *collaboration,* and
4. *self-reflection.*

These principles form the four major *bases* or cornerstones of college success, which provided the *foundation* for the specific strategies recommended in this book. We will conclude this text by recapping how these four bases contribute to college success and demonstrating how they can also promote development of character—a lifelong quality that is essential for personal success beyond college.

Active Involvement

This principle rests on a solid foundation of research, which indicates that success in college depends on students becoming *active agents* in the learning process who are willing to invest a significant amount of *time, effort,* and *energy* in the college experience.

The importance of this principle emerged at the very start of this book when we noted that the positive impact of college is magnified when students become actively involved in planning their course work and participating in campus life. We saw this principle in action again in the chapters on learning and memory, where it was shown that deep, long-lasting learning involves active *construction* (building) of knowledge and *transformation* of information into a form that has personal meaning to the learner.

In short, the principle of active involvement suggests that students maximize their learning and development when they get "into" the college experience and do it with passion and enthusiasm. Actively involved students do not hold back or do college half-heartedly; they do it whole-heartedly—by putting their whole "heart and soul" into it.

Social Interaction/Collaboration

A large body of research indicates that learning is significantly strengthened when it takes place in a *social* context that involves human *interaction* and interpersonal *collaboration* (Cuseo, 1996; 2002). You can embrace this interactive and collaborative spirit by seeking input and support from others, and by being open to the ideas of others. As we pointed out in Chapter 8 (Diversity), interaction and collaboration with individuals from diverse cultural backgrounds is one particular form of interpersonal interaction that has especially powerful effects on promoting deep learning, higher-level thinking, and social development.

You can also capture the spirit of collaboration by building *success-supporting social networks,* surrounding yourself with other success-seeking and high-achieving students. In addition, be on the lookout for more experienced students, college alumni, and career professionals, all of whom can serve as potential mentors or supportive role models.

Last, and perhaps most important, studies show that people who have strong social support networks are happier (Myers, 1993), healthier (Maddi, 2002), and live longer (Giles, et al., 2005).

Utilizing Resources

Success results from a combination of what students do for themselves and how effectively they capitalize on the multiple resources that their college provides them. Studies show that students who utilize campus resources report higher levels of satisfaction with the college experience and get more out of their college experience (Pascaralla & Terenzini, 1991, 2005). Typically, successful students are *resourceful* students who seek out and take full advantage of their resources to help them develop academically, emotionally, physically, and spiritually.

Self-Reflection

Self-awareness is an essential pre-requisite for success. As we noted in Chapter 2, "know thyself" is among the most frequently cited goals of higher education and one of the cardinal characteristics of a highly educated person. Effective learning not only requires action, it also requires *reflection*. Humans do not learn deeply by engaging in mindless repetition and memorization, but by thoughtful *reflection* and *connection* of what they're learning to what they already know.

Effective learning also involves periodically pausing to reflect on whether you truly *understand* or *comprehend* what you're attempting to learn and whether you are using effective learning strategies. Reflection ensures that you "watch yourself" while you learn, which enables you to maintain self-awareness of your learning habits and allows you to "know yourself" as a learner.

Deepening your self-awareness also puts you in a better position to select and pursue a career path that's true to yourself—a path that is truly compatible with your personal interests, values, and talents. Furthermore, maintaining awareness of your developing skills and personal qualities will put you in a better position to successfully present your strengths to future employers.

Last and perhaps most important, taking time for internal reflection is particularly important in today's high-tech world that bombards us with multiple modes of communication, massive loads of information, and endless amounts of external stimulation. We need to make a conscious effort to call "time out" and turn off all this sensory stimulation from the outside world, and "tune into" the inner world of personal reflection if we hope to find meaning and direction in our life.

In sum, success in college and beyond is more likely to be achieved by students who are:

1. Actively involved,
2. Interactive and collaborative,
3. Resourceful, and
4. Reflective.

These four principles represent more than just college-specific tips or strategies; they are *life-long-learning* skills and *life-success* principles that can be applied to all aspects of life throughout life. In Chapter 1, we represented these principles visually as four bases in a diamond of *college* success. These principles may also be represented as four bases in a diamond of *personal* success:

The Diamond of Personal Success: Four Core Principles

Interpersonal *Interaction/Collaboration*

Self-*Reflection*   PERSONAL SUCCESS   Utilizing *Resources*

Active
Involvement

□ = Supporting Bases of Personal Success
▼ = Primary ("Home") Base of Personal Success

◆ *Pause for Reflection*

Thus far in your college experience, which of the four principles of success do you think you have most consistently put into practice?

Which of the four personal-success principles do you think you need to devote more attention to than you have thus far in your college experience?

●●● **Personal Character**

While success in college and beyond cannot happen without both awareness and use of effective learning and living principles, it takes something more. Ultimately, success emerges from the inside out. Effective actions and good deeds emerge from positive attributes found within us; when they are combined, they form our personal *character*.

Success stems from something larger than the application of principles and strategies. We become successful human beings when our effective actions become a natural extension of who we are and how we live. At first, practicing strategies for doing well in college and leading a productive life may require deliberate concentration and conscious effort because these behaviors may be new to you. However, if these effortful actions occur frequently enough, they become transformed into regular and natural habits.

When we engage in good habits in this regular fashion, they become personal virtues. A *virtue* may be defined as a characteristic or trait that is valued as good or admirable, and a person who possesses a collection of important virtues is said to be a person of *character* (Peterson & Seligman, 2004).

Research suggests that the following five virtues are especially important for success in college and in life after college:

1. Wisdom,
2. Initiative,
3. Motivation,

4. Integrity, and

5. Civic Responsibility.

We'll turn now to a discussion of each of these key virtues and highlight their relevance for success in college and beyond.

Wisdom

When we use knowledge to guide our actions to do what is good or excellent, we are demonstrating *wisdom* (Staudinger & Baltes, 1994). The four research-based principles of success that provide the foundation of this book (i.e., involvement, collaboration, resourcefulness, and reflection) are grounded in a large body of knowledge on educational and personal success. If you use these four knowledge-based principles to inform and guide your behaviors, you are acting wisely or exhibiting wisdom.

Initiative

When you take charge of your life by attempting to gain control over the outcomes and events in your life, you are demonstrating *initiative*. In contrast, lack of initiative stems from feeling powerless and allowing things to happen to us passively, without making an effort to change them.

People with personal initiative have what psychologists call an *internal locus of control*—they believe that the source (locus) of control over events and outcomes in their life resides primarily within them, i.e., control is "internal" rather than being determined by "external" factors beyond their control—such as luck, chance, or fate (Rotter, 1966).

Research indicates that individuals with a strong internal locus of control display the following characteristics:

a. Greater independence and self-direction (Van Overwalle, Mervielde, & De Schuyer, 1995),

b. More accurate self-assessment (Hashaw, Hammond, & Rogers, 1990; Lefcourt, 1982),

c. Higher levels of learning and academic performance (Wilhite, 1990), and

d. Better physical health (Maddi, 2002; Seligman, 1991).

An internal locus of control also contributes to the development of another positive trait, which psychologists call *self-efficacy*—the belief that we have the capacity or power to produce positive outcomes in our life (Bandura, 1994). A strong sense of self-efficacy increases our motivation by increasing our willingness to initiate action, to put forth effort, and to persist or persevere in the face of setbacks and adversity (Bandura, 1997; 1986). Students with a strong sense of *academic* self-efficacy have been found to

a. Put forth great effort in their studies,

b. Use active-learning strategies,

c. Capitalize on campus resources, and

d. Persist in the face of obstacles (Multon, Brown, & Lent, 1991; Zimmerman, 1995).

Individuals with initiative do not have a false sense of entitlement; they don't feel they are "entitled to" or are "owed" anything without taking the personal initiative to attain it. For example, studies show that college graduates who successfully convert their college degree into successful career entry are individuals who take the initiative to become actively involved in the job-hunting process and use multiple job-search strategies (Brown & Krane, 2000). They

·—· **CLASSIC QUOTE** ·—·

Mere knowledge is not power; it is only possibility. Action is power; and its highest manifestation is when it is directed by knowledge.

—Francis Bacon (1561-1626), English philosopher, lawyer, and champion of modern science

·—· **CLASSIC QUOTE** ·—·

What lies behind us and what lies in front of us are small matters compared to what lies within us.

—Ralph Waldo Emerson, 19th-century philosopher, author, and abolitionist

·—· **CLASSIC QUOTE** ·—·

Man who stand on hill with mouth open will wait long time for roast duck to drop in.

—Confucius, famous Chinese philosopher who emphasized sincerity and social justice do not take a passive approach that assumes a good position will be handed to them or will just fall into their lap, nor do they feel that they are owed a good job simply because they have a college degree.

Pause for Reflection

In what area(s) of your life do you feel that you have been able to exert the most control and are producing the most positive results?

What area(s) of your life do you wish you had more control over and were producing better results?

Motivation

The word motivation derives from the Latin "movere," which means "to move." Success comes to those who truly want it and who exert effort to move in the direction of success. Having an arsenal of effective strategies at your disposal, such as those provided in this text, provides only the potential for success. Realizing this potential requires personal motivation to put these strategies into actual practice. As the old saying goes, "You can lead a horse to water, but you can't make him drink." In other words, if there's no will, there's no way.

Motivation consists of different elements or components that may be referred to as the "three Ds" of motivation:

a. drive,
b. dedication, and
c. determination.

Drive

Drive is the force within us that provides us with the energy needed to overcome inertia and initiate action. People who possess drive make a forceful effort to convert their goals and dreams into concrete actions and behaviors.

They are not "dreamers" who simply dream; they are "doers" who take action on their dreams and strive to transform the ideal into the real. People with drive will hustle—they go all out, all the time; they give 100%, 100% of the time; they are willing to go "beyond the call of duty" and go "the extra mile" to achieve their dreams.

Dedication

Dedication includes such positive qualities as commitment, devotion, and diligence. These motivational qualities enable us to keep going, steadily sustaining our effort and our endurance over an extended period of time. Dedicated people are willing to "grind it out," to take all the small steps and to diligently do all the little things that need to be done, which gradually build up and add up to a big accomplishment.

People with dedication put in the day-to-day perspiration needed to attain their future aspirations. They are truly committed to their goals and are willing to undergo needed short-term strain and pain for long-term gain. They possess the self-control and self-restraint to resist giving in to impulses for immediate gratification or the temptation to do what they "feel like" doing at the moment or in the short run.

They have the dedication and self-discipline to sacrifice their short-term needs or desires and get done what must be done in order to get them where they want to be in the long run.

Studies show that individuals with commitment—who become deeply involved and dedicated to what they do—are more likely to be healthy and happy (Maddi, 2002).

Determination

People who are determined show a relentless tenacity in pursuit of their goals. They have the fortitude to persist in the face of frustration and they have the resilience to bounce back after setbacks. When the going gets tough, they keep going. If they encounter something on the road to their goal that's hard to do, they work harder to do it; they don't give up or give in, they dig deeper and give more.

In fact, people who are determined often seek out *challenges*. Rather than remaining stagnant and simply doing what's safe, secure, or easy, they "stay hungry" and display an ongoing commitment to personal growth and development; they keep striving and driving to be the best they can possibly be in all aspects of their life.

Research indicates that people who seek challenges and continual self-development throughout life are more likely to be happy (Myers, 1993) and healthy (Maddi, 2002).

Integrity

In addition to pursuing performance excellence, people of character also pursue ethical excellence. They not only do what is smart; they also do what is *good* or *right*. People with integrity possess a strong set of personal values, which serves to guide them in the right moral direction.

The term *value* derives from the Latin root "valere," meaning to be of "worth" or to be "strong" (as in the words, "valuable" and "valor"). This is a particularly important virtue for college students to possess because the freedom of college brings with it new freedom to make personal choices and decisions about what life path to pursue and what people to associate with, which often serve as a test of their true priorities and values.

Individuals with integrity are "inner-directed"—their actions reflect their inner conscience; when they are unsure about what choice or decision to make, they look inward and let their own conscience guide their action. They are not "outer-directed" people whose personal standards of conduct are determined by looking outward to see what others are doing (Riesman, Glazer, & Denney, 2001). For example, college students with integrity do not cheat and rationalize their cheating as being acceptable because "other people are doing it." They don't look to others to determine their own values and they don't conform to the norm if the norm is wrong.

Unlike a chameleon, which changes its color to fit the environment it happens to be in, the behavior of people with integrity is not determined by their social environment—by the reactions or approval of others around them. Instead, their sense of self-respect, self-worth, and self-satisfaction come from within—from the internal feeling of pride that comes from knowing they did what was right and what they should have done.

People with integrity display *honesty*. They admit when they're wrong or when they haven't done what they should have done. They feel remorse or guilt when they haven't lived up to their own ethical standards, and they use this guilt productively to motivate them to do what's right in the future. When they are wrong, they don't play the role of victim and look for something or someone else to blame; they're willing to accept the blame or "take the heat" when they're wrong and to take responsibility for making it right.

People with integrity also possess *authenticity*—they are genuine or "real"—how they appear to be is who they really are. It's noteworthy that the word "integrity" comes from the same word root as "integrate." This captures the idea that people with integrity have an integrated or unified sense of self. Their "outer" self—how they appear to others, is in harmony with their inner self—who they really are.

How you see yourself is your *self-concept* or *personal identity* which derives from the Latin "identitas" for "being the same" (as in the words "identical" and "identify"). In contrast, your *personality* is how others see you. Personality originates from the Latin "persona," which was a mask worn by actors in ancient Greek and Roman plays who portrayed fictional characters. People of integrity don't wear masks or play roles. Their public persona or outer personality is consistent with their private self or inner identity.

Said in another way, people with integrity have "got it together"; they are individuals whose inner character and outer personality come together to form an integrated and unified human being.

People with integrity also integrate their professed or stated values and their actual behavior. Their convictions and actions are aligned or in sync; they are models of consistency rather than hypocrisy. They say what they mean and they mean what they say. They don't give lip service to their values by just stating or announcing them; they embody them and live by them.

People with integrity not only "talk the talk," they also "walk the talk" by practicing what they preach and remaining truthful to their values. Their actions and commitments are consistent with their ideals and convictions.

 Pause for Reflection

Since beginning college, have you observed any instances or examples of personal integrity that you thought were admirable?

What were the situations and what was done in these situations to demonstrate integrity?

Civic Responsibility

People of character are good *citizens*. They model what it means to live in a civilized community by displaying *civility*—they are respectful of and sensitive to the rights of others. In exercising their own rights and freedoms, they do not step on (or stomp on) the rights and freedoms of others.

Civically responsible people treat their fellow citizens in a humane and compassionate manner, and they are also willing to confront others who violate the rights of their fellow citizens. People with civic character are model citizens whose actions visibly demonstrate to others that they actively oppose any attempts to disrespect or dehumanize fellow members of their community.

Civic character is also demonstrated through *civic engagement*. Civically minded and civically responsible people are actively engaged in their community, trying to make it the best it can be by partaking in the democratic process and participating in its governance.

Civically responsible people show civic concern by stepping beyond their individual interests to actively promote the welfare of others in their community. They show kindness and commitment to their community by selflessly volunteering their time and energy to help fellow citizens, particularly those who are in need.

When people give to others and contribute to the good of the larger group of which they are a part, they experience a sense of self-satisfaction and personal reward. Studies show that individuals who go beyond themselves to focus on the needs of others are more likely to report feeling "happy" (Myers, 1993). Furthermore, when we contribute to the lives of others, we're more likely to feel that we're doing something meaningful with our own life.

Five Virtues Possessed by People with Character: A Visual Summary

••• Conclusion and Farewell

It is our hope that the ideas presented in this book will enable you to get off to a good start in college, as well as contribute to your success throughout your college years and beyond. We recommend that you save this book, use its recommended strategies beyond the first year of college, and continue to use them until they become natural, lifelong habits. It often takes time for effective habits to take hold and take effect. If you remain patient and continue to use effective strategies consistently, their positive effects will begin to accumulate and their power will increase with the passage of time.

Remember: College success isn't a short sprint; it's a long-distance run that takes years to complete. What matters most is not how fast you start but when and if you cross the finish line. That finish line is your college graduation ceremony—where a crowd of cheering family, friends, faculty, and fellow students will be waiting to celebrate your accomplishment.

Finally, don't forget that graduation is also known as *commencement*, which means to start or begin. College graduation doesn't represent the end of your education; instead, it is the beginning of a life of ongoing learning and development. The skills you acquire by the time you graduate will continue to be used to further promote your growth and development throughout the remaining years of your life. It could be said that your growth after college is likely to follow a pattern similar to that of the Chinese bamboo tree. The first four years of this tree's growth takes place underground, after which it emerges from the ground and grows as high as 80 feet (Covey, Merrill, & Merrill, 1996). Similarly, your four academic years in college will provide the underlying roots for lifelong growth. We hope that you will continue to grow until you achieve and exceed your highest dreams.

All the best,

Joe Cuseo
Viki Sox Fecas
Aaron Thompson

P.S.: We would love to receive any feedback you can provide us about this book. We'd like to learn about your general reaction to the text and if you successfully applied any of the strategies we've recommended. We would also be interested in your ideas about what we should continue to include in future editions of this text and what we should change to improve it. You can be assured that any feedback you provide us will be taken seriously. Please send us any ideas you may have for us to this e-address (website):

www.kendallhunt.com/cuseo

We'll be sure to read your comments and write back to you.

References

Abbey, A. (2002). Alcohol-related sexual assault: A common problem among college students. *Journal of Studies on Alcohol, 14*, 118–128.

AC Neilsen Research Services (2000). *Employer satisfaction with graduate skills*. Department of Education, Training and Youth Affairs. Canberra: AGPS. Retrieved October, 25, 2006, from http:www.dest.gov.au/ty/publications/employability_skills/final_report.pdf

Academic Integrity at Princeton (2003). *Examples of plagiarism*. Retrieved October 21, 2006, from http://www.princeton.du/pr/pub/integrity/pages/plagiarism.html

Ackerman, S. (1992). *Discovering the brain*. Washington, D.C.: National Academy Press.

Acredolo, C., & O'Connor, J. (1991). On the difficulty of detecting cognitive uncertainty. *Human Development, 34*, 204–223.

Adler, R. B., & Towne, M. (2001). *Looking out, looking in: Interpersonal communication* (10th ed.). Orlando, FL: Harcourt Brace.

Ahlum-Heather, M. E., & DiVesta, F. J. (1986). The effect of a conscious controlled verbalization of a cognitive strategy on transfer in problem solving. *Memory and Cognition, 14*(3), 281–285.

AhYun, K. (2002). Similarity and attraction. In M. Allen, R. W. Preiss, B. M. Gayle, & N. A. Burrell (Eds.), *Interpersonal communication research* (pp. 145–167). Mahwah, NJ: Erlbaum.

Ainslie, G. (1975). Specious reward: A behavioral theory of impulsiveness and impulse control. *Psychological Bulletin, 82*, 463–496.

Ainslie, G. (1992). *Picoeconomics: The strategic interaction of successive motivational states within the person*. New York: Cambridge University Press.

Alkon, D. L. (1992). *Memory's voice: Deciphering the brain-mind code*. New York: HarperCollins.

Allport. G. W. (1954). *The nature of prejudice*. Cambridge, MA: Addison-Wesley.

Amabile, T., Hadley, C. N., & Kramer, S. J. (2002). Creativity under the gun. *Harvard Business Review, 80*(8), 52–61.

Ambron, J. (1991). History of WAC and its role in community colleges. In L. C. Stanley & J. Ambron (Eds.), *Writing across the curriculum in community colleges* (pp. 3–8). New Direction for Community Colleges, no. 73. San Francisco: Jossey-Bass.

American College Testing (2003). *National college dropout and graduation rates, 2002*. Retrieved June 4, 2004, from http://www.act.org/news

American Heart Association (2006). *Fish, levels of mercury and omega-3 fatty acids*. Retrieved Jan. 13, 2007, from http://americanheart.org/presenter.jthml?identifier=3013797

American Obesity Association (2002). *Obesity in the U.S.* Retrieved April 26, 2006, from http://www.obesity.org/subs/fastfacts/obesity_US.shtml

American Psychiatric Association (1994). Diagnostic and Statistical Manual for Mental Disorders (4th ed.) (DSM-IV). Washington, DC: American Psychiatric Press.

American Psychiatric Association Work Group on Eating Disorders (2000). Practice guidelines for the treatment of patients with eating disorders. *American Journal of Psychiatry, 157,* 1–39.

Amir, Y. (1969). Contact hypothesis in ethnic relations. *Psychological Bulletin, 71*, 319– 342.

Amir, Y. (1976). The role of intergroup contact in change of prejudice and ethnic relations. In P. A. Katz (Ed.), *Towards the elimination of racism* (pp. 245–308). New York: Pergamon Press.

Andersen, P. A. (1985). Nonverbal immediacy in interpersonal communication. In A. W. Siegmean & S. Feldstein (Eds.), *Multichannel integrations of nonverbal behavior* (pp. 1–36). Hillsdale, NJ: Lawrence Erlbaum.

Anderson, P. V. (1985). What survey research tells us about writing at work. In L. Odell & D. Goswami (Eds.), *Writing in nonacademic settings* (pp. 3–85). New York: Guilford Press.

Anderson, J. R. (2000). *Cognitive psychology and its implications.* Worth Publishers.

Anderson, C. J. (2003). The psychology of doing nothing: Forms of decision avoidance result from reason and emotion. *Psychological Bulletin, 129,* 139–167.

Anderson, J. R., & Bower, G. H. (1974). Interference in memory for multiple contexts. *Memory and Cognition, 2,* 509–514.

Anderson, M. & Fienberg, S. E. (2000). Race and ethnicity and the controversy over the U.S. census. *Current Sociology, 48*(3), 87–110.

Anderson, L. W., & Krathwohl, D. R. (Eds.)(2001). *A taxonomy for learning, teaching, and assessing: A revision of Bloom's taxonomy of educational objectives.* New York: Addison Wesley Longman.

Applebee, A. N. (1981). *Writing in the secondary school.* Urbana, Ill.: National Council of Teachers of English.

Applebee, A. N. (1984). Writing and reasoning. *Review of Educational Research, 54*(4), 577–596.

Applebee, A. N., Langer, J. A., Jenkins, L. B., Mullis, I. V. S., & Foertsch, M. A. (1990). *Learning to write in our nation's schools: instruction and achievement in 1988 at grades 4, 8, and 12.* Princeton, NJ: The National Assessment of Educational Progress.

Argyle, M., & Beit-Hallahmi, B. (1975). *The social psychology of religion.* London: Routledge.

Arnedt, J. T., Wilde, G. J. S., Munt, P. W., & MacLean, A. W. (2001). How do prolonged wakefulness and alcohol compare in the decrements they produce on a simulated driving task? *Accident Analysis and Prevention, 33,* 337–344.

Aronson, E., Wilson, T. D., & Akert, R. M. (2005). *Social psychology* (5th ed.). Upper Saddle River, NJ: Pearson/Prentice Hall.

Association of American Colleges & Universities (2002). *Greater expectations: A new vision for learning as a nation goes to college.* Washington, D.C.: Author.

Astin, A. W. (1993). *What matters in college?* San Francisco: Jossey-Bass.

Astin, A. W. (2004). Why spirituality deserves a central place in higher education. *Spirituality in Higher Education Newsletter, 1*(2), pp. 1–12.

Astin, A. W., Oseguera, L., Sax, L. J., & Korn, W. S. (2002). *The American freshman: Thirty-five year trends.* Los Angeles, CA: Higher Education Research Institute, Graduate School of Education & Information Studies. University of California, Los Angeles.

Astin, A. W., Parrot, S. A., Korn, W. S., & Sax, L. J. (1997). *The American freshman: Thirty year trends, 1966–1996.* Higher Education Research Institute, University of California, Los Angeles.

Astin, A. W., Vogelgesang, L. J., Ikeda, E. K., & Yee, J. A. (2000). *How service-learning affects students.* Higher Education Research Institute, University of California, Los Angeles.

Atkinson, R. C. (1975). Mnemotechnics in second-language learning. *American Psychologist, 30,* 821–828.

Audrain, J. E., Klesges, R. C., & Flesges, L. M. (1995). Relationship between obesity and the metabolic effects of smoking in women. *Health Psychology, 14,* 116–123.

Avolio, B. J. (2005). *Leadership development in balance: Made/born.* Mahwah, NJ: Lawrence Erlbaum Associates.

Ayers, L., Beaton, S., & Hunt, H. (1999). The significance of transpersonal experiences, emotional conflict, and cognitive abilities in creativity. *Empirical Studies of the Arts, 17*(1), 73–82.

Baer, J. M. (1993). *Creativity and divergent thinking.* Hillsdale, NJ: Erlbaum.

Bahrick, H. P., & Phelps, E. (1987). Retention of Spanish vocabulary over 8 years. *Journal of Experimental Psychology, Learning, Memory, & Cognition, 13,* 344–349.

Bailey, C. (1991). *The new fit or fat.* Boston: Houghton Mifflin.

Bandura, A. (1994). Self-efficacy. In V. S. Ramachaudran (Ed.), *Encyclopedia of human behavior, Volume 4* (pp. 71–81). New York: Academic Press.

Bandura, A. (1986). *Social foundations of thought and action: A social cognitive theory.* Englewood Cliffs, NJ: Prentice-Hall.

Bandura, A. (1997). *Self-efficacy: The exercise of control.* New York: Freeman & Co.

Barefoot, B. O. (Ed.) (1993). *Exploring the evidence: Reporting outcomes of freshman seminars.* Monograph Series No. 11. National Resource Center for The Freshman Year Experience. Columbia, SC: University of South Carolina.

Barefoot, B. O., Warnock, C. L., Dickinson, M. P., Richardson, S. E., & Roberts, M. R. (Eds.) (1998). *Exploring the evidence, Volume II: Reporting outcomes of first-year seminars.* (Monograph No. 29). Columbia, SC: National Resource Center for The First-Year Experience and Students in Transition, University of South Carolina.

Barker, L., Edwards, R., Gaines, C., Gladney, K., & Holley, F. (1980). An investigation of proportional time spent in various communication activities by college students. *Journal of Applied Communication Research, 8,* 101–110.

Barker, L., & Watson, K. W. (2000). *Listen up: How to improve relationships, reduce stress, and be more productive by using the power of listening.* New York: St. Martin's Press.

Baron, R. A., Byrne, D., & Brauscombe, N. R. (2006). *Social psychology* (11th ed.). Boston: Pearson.

Bartels, A., & Zeki, S. (2000). The neural basis of romantic love. *European Journal of Neuroscience, 12,* 172–193.

Basadur, M., Runco, M. A., & Vega, L. A. (2000). Understanding how creative thinking skills, attitudes, and behaviors work together. *Journal of Creative Behavior, 34*(2), 77– 100.

Bassham, G., Irwin, W., Nardone, H., Wallace, J. M. (2005). *Critical thinking* (2nd ed.). New York: McGraw-Hill.

Bates, G. A. (1994). *The next step: College.* Bloomington, IN: Phi Delta Kappa.

Baumeister, R. F., Heatherton, T. F., & Tice, D. M. (1994). *Losing control: How and why people fail at self-regulation.* San Diego, CA: Academic Press.

Baxter Magolda, M. (1992). *Knowing and reasoning in college: Gender-related patterns in students' intellectual development.* San Francisco: Jossey-Bass.

Bean, J. C. (2003). *Engaging ideas.* San Francisco: Jossey-Bass.

Beck, A. T. (1976). *Cognitive therapy and the emotional disorders.* Boston: International Universities Press.

Beck, B. L., Koons, S. R., & Milgram, D. L. (2000). Correlates and consequences of behavioral procrastination: The effects of academic procrastination, self-consciousness, self-esteem and self-handicapping. *Journal of Social Behavior and Personality, 15,* 3–13.

Belenky, M. F., Clinchy, B., Goldberger, N. R., & Tarule, J. M. (1986). *Women's ways of knowing: The development of self, voice, and mind.* New York: Basic Books.

Bellah, R. N., Madsen, R., Sullivan, W. M., Swidler, A., & Tipton, S. M. (1985). *Habits of the heart: Individualism and commitment in American life.* Berkeley: University of California Press.

Benjamin, L. T., Jr., Cavell, T. A., & Shallenberger, W. R., III (1984). Staying with initial answers on objective tests: Is it a myth? *Teaching of Psychology, 11,* 133–141.

Benjamin, M., McKeachie, W. J., Lin, Y.-G., & Holinger. D. (1981). Test anxiety: Deficits in information processing. *Journal of Educational Psychology, 73,* 816–824.

Bennet, W., & Gurin, J. (1983). *The dieter's dilemma.* New York: Basic Books.

Bennis, W. (1989). *On becoming a leader.* Reading, MA: Addison-Wesley.

Benson, H., & Klipper, M. Z. (1990). *The relaxation response.* New York: Avon.

Biggs, J. B. (1987). *Student approaches to learning and studying.* Hawthorn, Victoria: Australian Council for Educational Research.

Biglan, A. (1973). The characteristics of subject matter in different academic areas. *Journal of Applied Psychology, 57,* 195–203.

Bishop, S. (1986). Education for political freedom. *Liberal Education, 72*(4), 322–325.

Bjork, R. (1994). Memory and metamemory considerations in the training of human beings. In J. Metcalfe & A. P. Shimamura (Eds.), *Metacognition: Knowing about knowing* (pp. 185–206). Cambridge, MA: MIT Press.

Blair, I. V. (2002). The malleability of automatic stereotypes and prejudice. *Personality & Social Psychology Review, 6*(3), 242–261.

Blakeslee, S. (1993, Aug. 3). Mystery of sleep yields as studies reveal immune tie. *The New York Times,* pp. C1, C6.

Bohme, K., & Budden, F. (2001). *The silent thief: Osteoporosis, exercises and strategies for prevention and treatment.* Buffalo, NY: Firefly.

Boice, R. (1994). *How writers journey to comfort and fluency: A psychological adventure.* Westport, CT: Praeger.

Bolles, R. N. (1998). *The new quick job-hunting map.* Toronto, Canada: Ten Speed Press.

Booth, F. W., & Vyas, D. R. (2001). Genes, environment, and exercise. *Advances in Experimental Medicine and Biology, 502,* 13–20.

Boudreau, C., & Kromrey, J. (1994). A longitudinal study of the retention and academic performance of participants in a freshman orientation course. *Journal of College Student Development, 35,* 444–449.

Bowen, H. R. (1977). *Investment in learning: The individual and social value of American higher education.* San Francisco: Jossey-Bass.

Bowen, H. R. (1997). *Investment in learning: The individual and social value of American higher education* (2nd ed.). Baltimore: The Johns Hopkins Press.

Bower, L. H. (1972). Mental imagery and associative learning. In L. W. Gregg (Ed.), *Cognition in learning and memory*. New York: Wiley.

Bower, G. H. (1973). "How to . . . uh . . . remember!" *Psychology Today* (October), 63–70.

Bower, G. H., Clark, M. C., Lesgold, A. M., & Winzenz, D. (1969). Hierarchical retrieval schemes in recall of categorized word lists. *Journal of Verbal Learning and Verbal Behavior, 8,* 323–343.

Bowlby, J. (1980). *Attachment and loss: Volume 3. Loss, sadness, and depression*. New York: Basic Books.

Boyer, E. L. (1987). *College: The undergraduate experience in America*. New York: Harper & Row.

Boyer, E. L. & Kaplan, M. (1977). *Educating for survival*. New Rochelle, NY: Change Magazine Press.

Bradshaw, D. (1995). Learning theory: Harnessing the strength of a neglected resource. In D.C.A. Bradshaw (Ed.), *Bringing learning to life: The learning revolution, the economy and the individual* (pp. 79–92). London, UK: The Falmer Press.

Bransford, J. D., Brown, A. L., & Cocking, R. R. (1999). *How people learn: Brain, mind, experience and school*. Washington, D.C.: National Academy Press.

Breivik, P. S. (1998). *Student learning in the information age*. American Council on Education, Oryx Press Series on Higher Education. Phoenix: The Oryx Press.

Bridgeman, B. (2003). *Psychology and evolution: The Origins of mind*. Thousand Oaks, CA: Sage.

Britton, J. and others (1975). *The development of writing abilities*. London: Macmillan.

Brody, J. E. (2003, August 18). Skipping a college course: Weight gain 101. *The New York Times*, p. D7.

Brown, R. D. (1988). Self-quiz on testing and grading issues. *Teaching at UNL, 10*(2), pp. 1–3. The Teaching and Learning Center, University of Nebraska-Lincoln.

Brown, D. (2003). *Career information, career counseling, and career development* (8th ed.). Boston: Allyn & Bacon.

Brown, T. D., Dane, F. C., & Durham, M. D. (1998). Perception of race and ethnicity. *Journal of Social Behavior & Personality, 13*(2), 295–306.

Brown, S. D., & Krane, N. E. R. (2000). Four (or five) sessions and a cloud of dust: Old assumptions and new observations about career counseling. In S. D. Brown & R. W. Lent (Eds.), *Handbook of counseling psychology* (3rd ed.)(pp. 740–766). New York: Wiley.

Brown, R. W., & McNeil, D. (1966). The "tip of the tongue" phenomenon. *Journal of Verbal Learning and Verbal Behavior, 5,* 325–327.

Brown, S. A., Tapert, S. F., Granholm, E., & Delis, D. C. (2000). Neurocognitive functioning of adolescents: Effects of protracted alcohol use. *Alcoholism: Clinical & Experimental Research, 24*(2), 164–171.

Bruffee, K. A. (1993). *Collaborative learning: Higher education, interdependence, and the authority of knowledge*. Baltimore: Johns Hopkins University Press.

Bryan, W. A., Mann, G. T., Nelson, R. B., & North, R. A. (1981). The co-curricular transcript—what do employers think? A national survey. *National Association of Student Personnel Administrators Journal, 9*(1), 20–34.

Buber, M. (1923). *I and thou* (Translation, 1970). New York: Touchstone.

Burka, J. B., & Yuen, L. M. (1983). *Procrastination: Why you do it, what to do about it*. Reading, MA: Addison-Wesley.

Bushman, B. J., & Cooper, H. M. (1990). Effects of alcohol on human aggression: An integrative research review. *Psychological Bulletin, 107*(3), 341–354.

Business Council of Australia and Australian Chamber of Commerce & Industry (2002). *Employability skills for the future*. Canberra, Australia: AGPS. Retrieved October, 25, 2006 from http:www.dest.gov.au/ty/publications/employability_skills/final_report.pdf

Business/Higher Education Round Table (1991). *Aiming higher: The concerns and attitudes of leading business executives and university heads to education priorities in Australia in the 1990s* (Commissioned Report no. 1). Melbourne, Australia.

Business/Higher Education Round Table (1992). *Educating for excellence part 2: Achieving excellence in university professional education* (Commissioned Report no. 2). Melbourne, Australia.

Buzan, T. (1991). *Use your perfect memory* (3rd ed.). New York: Penguin Books.

Caine, R. N., & Caine, G. (1991). *Teaching and the human brain*. Alexandria, VA: Association for Supervision and Curriculum Development.

Campbell, T. A., & Campbell, D. E. (1997, December). Faculty/student mentor program: Effects on academic performance and retention. *Research in Higher Education, 38,* 727–742.

Caplan, P. J., & Caplan, J. B. (1994). *Thinking critically about research on sex and gender*. New York: HarperCollins College Publishers.

Carducci, B. J. (1999). *Shyness: A bold new approach.* New York: HarperCollins.

Carney, R. N., & Levin, J. R. (2001). Remembering the names of unfamiliar animals: Keywords as keys to their Kingdom. *Applied Cognitive Psychology, 15*(2), 133–143.

Caroli, M., Argentieri, L., Cardone, M., & Masi, A. (2004). Role of television in childhood obesity prevention. *International Journal of Obesity Related Metabolic Disorders, 28* (Supplement 3), S104–108.

Carpenter, K. M., & Hasin, D. S. (1998). A prospective evaluation of the relationship between reasons for drinking and DSM-IV alcohol-use disorders. *Addictive Behaviors, 23*(1), 41–46.

Carroll, J. B. (1964). *Language and thought.* Englewood Cliffs, NJ: Prentice-Hall.

Carter, R. (1998). *Mapping the mind.* Berkeley and Los Angeles: University of California Press.

Cates, J. R., Herndon, N. L., Schulz, S. L., & Darroch, J. E. (2004). *Our voices, our lives, our futures: Youth and sexually transmitted diseases.* Chapel Hill, NC: University of North Carolina at Chapel Hill School of Journalism and Mass Communication.

Cheney, L. V. (1989). *50 hours: A core curriculum for college students.* Washington D.C.: National Endowment for the Humanities.

Chi, M., de Leeuw, N., Chiu, M. H., & LaVancher, C. (1994). Eliciting self-explanations improves understanding. *Cognitive Science, 18*, 439–477.

Chickering, A. W., & Schlossberg, N. K. (1998). Moving on: Seniors as people in transition. In J. N. Gardner, G. Van der Veer, & Associates, *The senior year experience* (pp. 37–50). San Francisco: Jossey-Bass.

Chronicle of Higher Education (2003, August 30). Almanac 2003–04. *The Chronicle of Higher Education, 49*(1). Washington, D.C.: Author.

Claxton, C. S., & Murrell, P. H. (1988). *Learning styles: Implications for improving practice.* ASHE-ERIC Educational Report No. 4. Washington D.C.: Association for the Study of Higher Education.

Coates, T. J. (1977). *How to sleep better: A drug-free program for overcoming insomnia.* Englewood Cliffs, NJ: Prentice-Hall.

Collins, A. M., & Loftus, E. F. (1975). A spreading activation theory of semantic processing. *Psychological Review, 82*, 407–428.

Colombo, G., Cullen, R., & Lisle, B. (1995). *Rereading America: Cultural contexts for critical thinking and writing.* Boston: Bedford Books of St. Martin's Press.

Conaway, M. A. (1982). Listening: Learning tool and retention agent. In A. S. Algier & K. W. Algier (Eds.), *Improving reading and study skills* (pp. 51–63). San Francisco: Jossey-Bass.

Connolly, P. (1989). Writing and the ecology of learning. In P. Connolly & T. Vilardi (Eds.), *Writing to learn mathematics and science* (pp. 1–14). New York: Teachers College Press, Columbia University.

Cook, S. W. (1984). Cooperative interaction in multiethnic contexts. In N. Miller & M. B. Brewer (Eds.), *Groups in contact: The psychology of desegregation.* New York: Academic Press.

Cook, L. (1991). Learning style awareness and academic achievement among community college students. *Community/Junior College Quarterly of Research and Practice, 15*, 419–425.

Cooper, K. (1982). *The aerobics program for total well-being.* New York: Bantam.

Corbin, C. B., Pangrazi, R. P., & Franks, B. D. (2000). Definitions: Health, fitness, and physical activity. *President's Council on Physical Fitness and Sports Research Digest, 3*(9), pp. 1–8.

Covey, S. R. (1990). *Seven habits of highly effective people* (2nd ed). New York: Fireside.

Covey, S. R., Merrill, A. R., & Merrill, R. R. (1996). *First things first: To live, to love, to learn, to leave a legacy.* New York: Fireside.

Cowan, N. (2001). The magical number 4 in short-term memory: A reconsideration of mental storage capacity. *Behavioral and Brain Sciences, 24*, 87–114.

Coward, A. (1990). *Pattern thinking.* New York: Praeger Publishers.

Craik, F. I. M., & Lockhart, R. S. (1972). Levels of processing: A framework for memory research. *Journal of Verbal Learning and Verbal Behavior, 11*, 671–684.

Craik, F. I. M., & Tulving, E. (1975). Depth of processing and the retention of words in episodic memory. *Journal of Experimental Psychology: General, 104*, 268–294.

Crawford, H. J., & Strapp, C. H. (1994). Effects of vocal and instrumental music on visuospatial and verbal performance as moderated by studying preference and personality. *Personality and Individual Differences, 16*(2), 237–245.

Cronon, W. (1998). "Only connect": The Goals of a Liberal Education. *The American Scholar* (Autumn), 73–80.

Crosby, O. (2002). Informational interviewing: Get the scoop on careers. *Occupational Outlook Quarterly* (Summer), 32–37.

Cross, K. P. (1982). Thirty years passed: Trends in general education. In B. L. Johnson (Ed.), *General education in two-year colleges* (pp. 11–20). San Francisco: Jossey-Bass.

Cross, K. P. (1993). Reaction to "Enhancing the productivity of learning" by D. B. Johnstone. *AAHE Bulletin, 46*(4), p. 7.

Csikszentmihalyi, M. (1996). *Creativity: Flow and the psychology of discovery and invention.* New York: HarperCollins.

Cummings, M. C. (2002). *Democracy under pressure* (9th ed.). Belmont, CA: Wadsworth.

Cuseo, J. B. (1991). *The freshman orientation seminar: A research-based rationale for its value, delivery, and content.* Columbia, SC: National Resource Center for The Freshman Year Experience, University of South Carolina.

Cuseo, J. B. (1996). *Cooperative learning: A pedagogy for addressing contemporary challenges and critical issues in higher education.* Stillwater, OK: New Forums Press.

Cuseo, J. B. (2002). *Igniting student involvement, peer interaction, and teamwork: A taxonomy of specific cooperative learning structures and collaborative learning strategies.* Stillwater, OK: New Forums Press.

Cuseo, J. B. (2003). Comprehensive academic support for students during the first year of college. In G. L. Kramer & Associates, *Student academic services: An integrated approach* (pp. 271–310). San Francisco: Jossey-Bass.

Cuseo, J. (2005). "Decided," "undecided," and "in transition": Implications for academic advisement, career counseling, and student retention. In R. S. Feldman (Ed.), *Improving the first year of college: Research and practice* (pp. 27–50). Mahwah, NJ: Lawrence Erlbaum Associates.

Cusinato, M., & L'Abate, L. (1994). A spiral model of intimacy. In S. M. Johnson & L. S. Greenberg (Eds.), *The heart of the matter: Emotion in marital therapy.* New York: Brunner/Mazel.

Czaja, R., Blair, J., Bickart, B., & Eastman, E. (1994). Respondent strategies for recall of crime victimization incidents. *Journal of Official Statistics, 10*(3), 257–276.

Dalton, J. C., Eberhardt, D., Bracken, J., & Echols, K. (2006). Inward journeys: Forms and patterns of college student spirituality. *Journal of College & Character, 7*(8), 1–21. Retrieved December 17, 2006, from http://www.collegevalues.org/pdfs/Dalton.pdf

Daly, W. T. (1992). The academy, the economy, and the liberal arts. *Academe* (July/August), 10–12.

Daniels, D., & Horowitz, L. J. (1997). *Being and caring: A psychology for living.* Prospect Heights, IL: Waveland Press.

Davidson, R. J., Kabat-Zinn, J., Schumacher, J., Rosenkranz, M. D., Santorelli, S. F., Urbanowski, F., Harrington, A., & Bonus, K. F. (2003). Alteration in brain and immune function produced by mindfulness meditation. *Psychosomatic Medicine, 65*(4), 564–570.

DeJong, W., & Linkenback, J. (1999). Telling it like it is: Using social norms marketing campaigns to reduce student drinking. *AAHE Bulletin, 52*(4), pp. 11–13, 16.

Dement, W. C. (1974). *Some must watch while some must sleep.* San Francisco: W. H. Freeman.

Dement, W. C., & Vaughan, C. (1999). *The promise of sleep.* New York: Delacorte Press.

Dement, W. C., & Vaughan, C. (2000). *The promise of sleep: A pioneer in sleep medicine explores the vital connection between health, happiness, and a good night's sleep.* New York: Dell.

DesMaisons, K. (1998). *Potatoes not Prozac.* London: Simon & Schuster.

Donald, J. G. (2002). *Learning to think: Disciplinary perspectives.* San Francisco: Jossey-Bass.

Dorfman, J., Shames, J., & Kihlstrom, J. F. (1996). Intuition, incubation, and insight. In G. Underwood (Ed.), *Implicit cognition.* New York: Oxford University Press.

Douglas, K. A., Collins, J. L., Warren, C., Kahn, L., Gold, R., Clayton, S., Ross, J. G., & Kolbe, L. J. (1997). Results from the 1995 national college health risk behavior survey. *Journal of American College Health, 46*, 55–66.

Drubach, D. (2000). *The brain explained.* Englewood Cliffs, NJ: Prentice-Hall.

Druckman, D., & Bjork, R. A. (Eds.)(1991). *In the mind's eye: Enhancing human performance.* Washington, D.C.: National Academy Press.

Dryden, G. & Vos, J. (1999). *The learning revolution: To change the way the world learns.* Torrance, CA & Auckland, New Zealand: The Learning Web.

Dudenhyer, J. P., Jr. (1976). An experiment in grading papers. *College Composition and Communication, 27*(4), 406–407.

Dunn, R., Dunn, K., & Price, G. (1990). *Learning style inventory.* Lawrence, KS: Price Systems.

Dunn, R., Griggs, S., Olson, J., Beasley, M., & Gorman, B. (1995). A meta-analytic validation of the Dunn and Dunn learning-styles model. *Journal of Educational Research, 88*, 353–362.

Dupuy, G. M., & Vance, R. M. (1996, Oct. 26). *Launching your career: A transition module for seniors.* Paper presented at the Second National Conference on Students in Transition, San Antonio, Texas.

Eaton, S. B., & Konner, M. (1985). Paleolithic nutrition: A consideration of its nature and current implications. *New England Journal of Medicine, 312,* 283.

Eble, K. E. (1966). *A perfect education.* New York: Macmillan.

Eckman, P., & Friesen, W. V. (1969). Nonverbal leakage and clues to deception. *Psychiatry, 32,* 88–106.

Education Commission of the States (1995). *Making quality count in undergraduate education.* Denver, CO: ECS Distribution Center.

Education Commission of the States (1996). *Bridging the gap between neuroscience and education.* Denver, CO: Author.

Einstein, G. O., Morris, J., & Smith, S. (1985). Note-taking, individual differences, and memory for lecture information. *Journal of Educational Psychology, 77*(5), 522–532.

Elbow, P. (1973). *Writing without teachers.* New York: Oxford University Press.

Elder, L., & Paul, R. (2002). *The miniature guide to taking charge of the human mind.* Dillon Beach, CA: The Foundation for Critical Thinking.

Ellin, A. (1993). "Post-parchment depression." *Boston Phoenix,* September.

Ellis, A. (1975). *A new guide to rational living.* Englewood Cliffs, NJ: Prentice Hall.

Ellis, A. (1995). Changing rational-emotive therapy (RET) to rational emotive behavior therapy (REBT). *Journal of Rational-Emotive & Cognitive Behavior Therapy, 13*(2), 85–89.

Ellis, A. (2000). *How to control your anxiety before it controls you.* New York: Citadel Press/Kensington Publishing.

Ellis, A. (2001). *Overcoming destructive beliefs, feelings, and behaviors: New directions for rational-emotive behavior therapy.* Amherst, NY: Prometheus Books.

Ellis, A., & Knaus, W. J. (1977). *Overcoming procrastination.* New York: Signet Books.

Engs, R. C. (1977). Drinking patterns and drinking problems of college students. *Journal of Studies on Alcohol, 38,* 2144–2156.

Engs, R., & Hanson, D. (1986). Age-specific alcohol prohibition and college students' drinking problems. *Psychological Reports, 59,* 979–984.

Entwistle, N. J., & Marton, F. (1984). Changing conceptions of learning and research. In F. Marton et al. (Eds.), *The experience of learning.* Edinburgh: Scottish Academic Press.

Entwistle N. J., & Ramsden, P. (1983). *Understanding student learning.* London: Croom Helm.

Erasmus, U. (1993). *Fats that heal, fats that kill.* Burnaby, British Columbia: Alive Books.

Erickson, B. L., Peters, C. B., & Strommer, D. W. (2006). *Teaching first-year college students.* San Francisco: Jossey-Bass.

Erickson, B. L., & Strommer, D. W. (1991). *Teaching college freshmen.* San Francisco: Jossey-Bass.

Ericsson, K. A., & Charness, N. (1994). Expert performance. *American Psychologist, 49*(8), 725–747.

Everly, G. S. (1989). *A clinical guide to the treatment of the human stress response.* New York: Plenum Press.

Ewell, P. T. (1997). Organizing for learning. *AAHE Bulletin, 50*(4), pp. 3–6.

Family Care Foundation (2005). *If the world were a village of 100 people.* Retrieved December 19, 2006, from http:www.familycare.org.news/if_the_world.htm

Feagin, J. R., & McKinney, K. D. (2003). *The many costs of racism.* Lanham, MD: Rowman & Littlefield.

Feldman, D. H. (1994). Creativity: dreams, insights, and transformation. In D. H. Feldman, M. Csikszentmihalyi, & H. Gardner (Eds.), *Changing creativity* (pp. 85–102). Westport, CT: Praeger.

Feldman, K. A., & Newcomb, T. M. (1997). *The impact of college on students.* New Brunswick, NJ: Transaction Publishers (originally published in 1969 by Jossey-Bass).

Feldman, K. A., & Paulsen, M. B. (Eds.) (1994). *Teaching and learning in the college classroom.* Needham Heights, MA: Ginn Press.

Felstead, A., Gallie, D., & Green, F. (2002). *Work skills in Britain 1986–2001.* Retrieved December 22, 2006, from http://www.kent.ac.uk/economics/staff/gfg/WorkSkills1986–2001.pdf

Ferris, K. R. (1982). Educational predictors of professional pay and performance. *Accounting, Organization, and Society, 7*(3), 225–230.

Feskens, E. J., & Kromhout, D. (1993). Epidemiologic studies on Eskimos and fish intake. *Annals of the New York Academy of Science, 683,* 9–15.

Festinger, L. (1954). A theory of social comparison processes. *Human Relations, 7,* 117–140.

Fidler, P., & Godwin, M. (1994). Retaining African-American students through the freshman seminar. *Journal of Developmental Education, 17,* 34–41.

Fiedler, F. E. (1993). The leadership situation and the black box in contingency theories. In M. M. Chemers & R. Ayman (Eds.), *Leadership theory and research* (pp. 2–28). New York: Academic Press.

Fingerhut, L. A., Kleinman, J. C., & Kendrick, J. S. (1990). Smoking before, during, and after pregnancy. *American Journal of Public Health, 80*(5), 541–544.

Fisher, J. L., Harris, J. L., & Harris, M. B. (1973). Effect of note-taking and review on recall. *Journal of Educational Psychology, 65*(3), 321–325.

Fixman, C. S. (1990). The foreign language needs of U.S.-based corporations. *Annals of the American Academy of Political and Social Science, 511*, 25–46.

Flavell, J. H. (1985). *Cognitive development* (2nd ed.). Englewood Cliffs, NJ: Prentice-Hall.

Fletcher, A., Lamond, N., van den Heuvel, C. J., & Dawson, D. (2003). Prediction of performance during sleep deprivation and alcohol intoxication using a quantitative model of work-related fatigue. *SleepResearch Online, 5*, 67–75.

Flett, G. L., Blankstein, K. R., Hewitt, P. L., & Koledin, S. (1992). Components of perfectionism and procrastination in college students. *Social Behavior & Personality, 20*, 85–94.

Ford, P. L. (Ed.) (1903). *The works of Thomas Jefferson.* New York: Knickerbocker Press.

Frankl, V. E. (1946). *Man's search for meaning.* London: Hodder & Stoughton.

Freund, K. M., Belanger, A. J., D'Agostino, R. B., & Kannel, W. B. (1993). The health risks of smoking. The Framingham study: 34 years of follow-up. *Annals of Epidemiology, 3*(4), 417–424.

Fromm, E. (1970). *The art of loving.* New York: Bantam.

Fromme, A. (1980). *The ability to love.* Chatsworth, CA: Wilshire Book Company.

Frost, S. H. (1991). *Academic advising for student success: A system of shared responsibility.* ASHE-ERIC Higher Education Report, No. 3. The George Washington School of Education and Human Development, Washington, D.C.

Furnham, A., & Argyle, M. (1998). *The psychology of money.* New York: Routledge.

Gamson, Z. F. (1984). *Liberating education.* San Francisco: Jossey-Bass.

Ganong, L. H., Coleman, M., Thompson, A., & Goodwin-Watkins, C. (1996). African American and European American college students' expectations for self and future partners. *Journal of Family Issues, 17*(6), 758–775.

Gardiner, L. F. (2005). Transforming the environment for learning: A crisis of quality. *To Improve the Academy, 23*, 3–23.

Gardner, J. N. (1987, January). *The freshman year experience movement: Present status and future directions.* Address delivered at The Freshman Year Experience Conference—West, Irvine, CA.

Gardner, H. (1983). *Frames of mind: The theory of multiple intelligences.* New York: Basic Books.

Gardner, H. (1993). *Multiple intelligences: The theory of multiple intelligences* (2nd ed.). New York: Basic Books.

Gardner, H. (1999). *Intelligence reframed: Multiple intelligences for the 21st century.* New York: Basic Books.

Gardner, P. D. (1991, March). *Learning the ropes: Socialization and assimilation into the workplace.* Paper presented at the Second National Conference on The Senior Year Experience, San Antonio, TX.

Garfield, C. A. (1984). *Peak performance: Mental training techniques of the world's greatest athletes.* Los Angeles: Tarcher.

Gemmil, G. (1989). The dynamics of scapegoating in small groups. *Small Group Behavior, 20*, 406–418.

Gere, A. R. (1987). *Writing groups: history, theory, and implications.* Carbondale, IL: Southern Illinois University Press.

Gershoff, S., & Whitney, C. (1996). *The Tufts University guide to total nutrition.* New York: HarperPerennial

Gibb, J. R. (1961). Defensive communication. *The Journal of Communication* (September) *11*, p. 3.

Gibb, H. R. (1991). *Trust: A new vision of human relationships for business, education, family, and personal living* (2nd ed.). North Hollywood, CA: Newcastle.

Giles, R. M., Johnson, M. R., Knight, K. E., Zammett, S., & Weinman, J. (1982). Recall of lecture information: A question of what, when, and where. *Medical Education, 16*(5), 264–268.

Giles, L. C., Glonek, F. V., Luszcz, M. A., & Andrews, G. R. (2005). Effect of social networks on 10-year survival in very old Australians: The Australia longitudinal study of aging. *Journal of Epidemiology and Community Health, 59*, 574–579.

Glass, J., & Garrett, M. (1995). Student participation in a college orientation course: retention, and grade point average. *Community College Journal of Research and Practice, 19,* 117–132.

Glassman, J. K. (2000, June 9). The technology revolution: Road to freedom or road to serfdom? *Heritage Lectures*, No. 668. Washington, DC: The Heritage Foundation.

Glenberg, A. M., Bradley, M. M., Kraus, T. A., & Renzaglia, G. J. (1983). Studies of the long-term recency effect: Support for a contextually guided retrieval hypothesis. *Journal of Experimental Psychology: Learning, Memory, and Cognition, 9*, 231–255.

Glenberg, A. M., Schroeder, J. L., & Robertson, D. A. (1998). Averting the gaze disengages the environment and facilitates remembering. *Memory & Cognition, 26*(4), 651–658.

Goffman, E. (1956). *The presentation of self in everyday life.* Edinburgh, UK: University of Edinburgh, Social Sciences Research Centre.

Goffman, E. (Ed.) (1967). *Interaction ritual: Essays in face-to-face behavior.* Chicago: Aldine.

Goleman, D. (1992, Oct. 27). Voters assailed by unfair persuasion. *The New York Times*, pp. C1–C3.

Goleman, D. (1995). *Emotional intelligence: Why it can matter more than IQ.* New York: Bantam Books.

Gordon, W. C. (1989). *Learning and memory.* Belmont: Wadsworth.

Gordon, V. N., & Steele, G. E. (2003). Undecided first-year students: A 25-year longitudinal study. *Journal of The First-Year Experience, 15*(1), 19–38.

Gottman, J. (1994). *Why marriages succeed and fail.* New York: Fireside.

Graf, P. (1982). The memorial consequence of generation and transformation. *Journal of Verbal Learning and Verbal Behavior, 21*, 539–548.

Green, M. G. (Ed.) (1989). *Minorities on campus: A handbook for enhancing diversity.* Washington, D.C.: American Council on Education.

Greenberg, R., Pillard, R., & Pearlman, C. (1972). The effect of dream (Stage REM) deprivation on adaptation to stress. *Psychosomatic Medicine, 34*, 257–262.

Griffin, C. W. (1982). *Teaching writing in all disciplines.* New York: Directions for Teaching and Learning, No. 12. San Francisco: Jossey-Bass.

Grunder, P., & Hellmich, D. (1996). Academic persistence and achievement of remedial students in a community college's success program. *Community College Review, 24*, 21–33.

Guilford, J. P. (1967). *The nature of human intelligence.* New York: McGraw-Hill.

Gullette, M. M. (1989). Leading discussion in a lecture course. *Change, 24*(2), pp. 32–39.

Haas, R. (1994). *Eat smart, think smart.* New York: HarperCollins.

Haberman, S., & Luffey, D. (1998). Weighing in college students' diet and exercise behaviors. *Journal of American College Health, 46*, 189–191.

Hall, E. T., & Hall, M. R. (1986). *Hidden differences: How to communicate with the Germans.* Hamburg, West Germany: Gruner & Jahr.

Hall, R. M., & Sandler, B. R. (1982). *The classroom climate: A chilly one for women.* Association of American Colleges' Project on the Status of Women. Washington, DC: Association of American Colleges.

Hall, R. M., & Sandler, B. R. (1984). *Out of the classroom: A chilly campus climate for women.* Association of American Colleges' Project on the Status of Women. Washington, DC: Association of American Colleges.

Halperin, A. C. (2002). *State of the union: Smoking on US college campuses.* Washington, DC: A report from the American Legacy Foundation. Retrieved August 13, 2006, from http:www.ttac.org/college/facts/references/html

Hamilton, D. L., & Sherman, S. J. (1989). Illusory correlations: Implications for streotype theory and research. In D. Bar-Tal, C. F. Graumann, A. W. Kruglanski, & W. Stroebe (Eds.), *Stereotyping and prejudice: Changing conceptions* (pp. 59–82). New York: Springer-Verlag.

Harriott, J., & Ferrari, J. R. (1996). Prevalence of procrastination among samples of adults. *Psychological Reports, 78*, 611–616.

Hart, L. A. (1983). *Human brain and human learning.* White Plains, NY: Longman.

Hartley, J. (1998). *Learning and studying: a research perspective.* London: Routledge.

Hartley, J., & Marshall, S. (1974). On notes and note taking. *Universities Quarterly, 28*, 225–235.

Harvey, L., Moon, S., Geall, V., & Bower, R. (1997). *Graduates' work: Organisational change and students' attributes.* Birmingham: Centre for Research into Quality, University of Central England.

Hashaw, R. M., Hammond, C. J., & Rogers, P. H. (1990). Academic locus of control and the collegiate experience. *Research & Teaching in Developmental Education, 7*(1), 45–54.

Hatfield, E., & Walster, G. W. (1985). *A new look at love.* Lanham, MD: University Press of America.

Hauri, P., & Linde, S. (1996). *No more sleepless nights.* New York: John Wiley & Sons.

"Haven't filed yet? Tackle those taxes." (2003, April 11). *USA Today*, p. 3b.

Health, C., & Soll, J. (1996). Mental budgeting and consumer decisions. *Journal of Consumer Research, 23*, 40–52.

Heath, H. (1977). *Maturity and competence: A transcultural view.* New York: Halsted Press.

Helkowski, C. & Shehan, M. (2004). Too sure, too soon: When choosing should wait. *About Campus*, (May/June), 19–24.

Herman, R. E. (2000). Liberal arts: The key to the future. *USA Today Magazine* (November), *129*, p. 34

Hersh, R. (1994). What our publics want, but think they don't get, from a liberal arts education: Ted Marchese interviews Richard Hersh. *AAHE Bulletin* (November), pp. 8–10.

Hersh, R. (1997). Intentions and perceptions: A national survey of public attitudes toward liberal arts education. *Change, 29*(2), pp. 16–23.

Higbee, K. L. (2001). *Your memory: How it works and how to improve it.* New York: Marlowe & Company.

Higher Education Council (1992). *The quality of higher education: Discussion papers.* (National Board of Employment, Education, & Training), Cantaberra, Australian Capital Territory: Australian Government Publishing Service.

Higher Education Institute (2004). *The spiritual life of college students: A national study of college students' search for meaning and purpose.* Los Angeles, CA: Higher Education Research Institute, Graduate School of Education & Information Studies. University of California, Los Angeles.

Hildenbrand, M., & Gore, P. A., Jr. (2005). Career development in the first-year seminar: Best practice versus actual practice. In P. A. Gore (Ed.), *Facilitating the career development of students in transition* (Monograph No. 43) (pp. 45–60). Columbia, SC: University of South Carolina, National Resource Center for The First-Year Experience and Students in Transition.

Hill, A. J. (2002). Developmental issues in attitudes toward food and diet. *Proceedings of the Nutrition Society, 61*(2), 259–268.

Hill, J. O., Wyat, H. R., Reed, G. W., & Peters, J. C. (2003). Obesity and environment: Where do we go from here? *Science, 299*, 853–855.

Hillocks, G. (1986). What works in teaching composition: A meta-analysis of experimental treatment studies. *American Journal of Education, 93*(1), 133–170.

Hobson, J. A. (1988). *The dreaming brain.* New York: Basic Books.

Hobson, E. H. (2004). *Getting students to read: Fourteen tips.* IDEA Paper #40. Manhattan, KS: The IDEA Center.

Hogan, R., Curphy, G. J., & Hogan, J. (1994). What we know about leadership: Effectiveness and personality. *American Psychologist, 49*, 493–504.

Holmes, K. K., Levine, R., & Weaver, M. (2004). Effectiveness of condoms in preventing sexually transmitted infections. *Bulletin of the World Health Organization, 82*, 254–464.

Horn, C. E. (1995). *Enhancing the connection between higher education and the workplace.* Denver, CO: The State Higher Education Executive Offices and The Education Commission of the States.

Horne, J. (1988). *Why we sleep: The functions of sleep in humans and other mammals.* New York: Oxford University Press.

Howard, A. (1986). College experiences and managerial performance. *Journal of Applied Psychology, 71*, 530–552.

Howard, P. J. (2000). *The owner's manual for the brain: Everyday applications of mind-brain research* (2nd ed.). Atlanta, GA: Bard Press.

Howe, M. J. (1970). Note-taking strategy, review, and long-term retention of verbal information. *Journal of Educational Psychology, 63*, 285.

Hugenberg, K., & Bodenhausen, G. V. (2003). Facing prejudice: Implicit prejudice and the perception of facial threat. *Psychological Science, 14*, 640–643.

Hunter, M. A., & Linder, C. W. (2005). First-year seminars. In M. L. Upcraft, J. N. Gardner, B. O. Barefoot, & Associates, *Challenging and supporting the first-year student: A handbook for improving the first year of college* (pp. 275–291). San Francisco: Jossey-Bass.

Indiana University (2004). *Selling your liberal arts degree to employers.* Bloomington, IN: Indiana University, Arts & Sciences Placement Office. Retrieved July 7, 2004, from http://www.indiana.edu/~career/fulltime/selling_liberal_arts.html

Insel, P. M., & Jacobson, L. (1975). *What do you expect? An inquiry into self-fulfilling prophecies.* Menlo Park: CA: Cummings Publishing.

Institute for Research on Higher Education (1995). Connecting schools and employers: Work-related education and training. *Change, 27*(3), pp. 39–46.

Institute of International Education (2001). *Open doors.* Retrieved July 7, 2005, from www.opendoorsweb.org/2001%20Files/layout_htm

Jablonski, N. G., & Chaplin, G. (2002). Skin deep. *Scientific American* (October), 75–81.

Jacobs, W. J., & Nadel, L. (1985). Stress-induced recovery of fears and phobias. *Psychological Review, 92*(4), 512–531.

Jakubowski, P., & Lange, A. J. (1978). *The assertive option: Your rights and responsibilities.* Champaign, IL: Research Press.

Janis, I. L. (1982). *Groupthink: Psychological studies of policy decisions and fiascoes.* (2nd ed.). Boston: Houghton Mifflin.

Jarvik, M. E. (1995). The scientific case that nicotine is addictive: Comment. *Psychopharmacology, 117*(1), 18–20.

Jemott, J. B., & Magloire, K. (1988). Academic stress, social support, and secretory immunoglobin. *Journal of Personality and Social Psychology, 55*, 803–810.

Jenkins, J. G., & Dallenbach, K. M. (1924). Oblivescence during sleep and waking. *American Journal of Psychology, 35*, 605–612.

Jensen, E. (1998). *Teaching with the brain in mind.* Alexandria, VA: Association for Supervision and Curriculum Development.

Johnsgard, K. W. (2004). *Conquering depression and anxiety through exercise.* New York: Prometheus.

Johnson, D. W., Johnson, R. T., & Smith, K. A. (1991). *Cooperative learning: Increasing college faculty instructional productivity.* ASHE-ERIC Higher Education Report No. 4. Washington, D.C.: Association for the Study of Higher Education.

Johnson, D., Johnson, R., & Smith, K. (1998). Cooperative learning returns to college: What evidence is there that it works? *Change, 30*, 26–35.

Joint Science Academies Statement (2005). *Global response to climate change.* Retrieved August 29, 2005, from http://nationalacademies.org/onpi/06072005.pdf

Jones, W. T. (1990). Perspectives on ethnicity. In L. V. Moore (Ed.), *Evolving theoretical perspectives on students* (pp. 59–72). San Francisco: Jossey-Bass.

Jones, W. H., Cheek, J. M., & Biggs, S. R. (1986). *Shyness: Perspectives on research and treatment.* New York: Plenum.

Jones, L., & Petruzzi, D. C. (1995). Test anxiety: A review of theory and current treatment. *Journal of College Student Psychotherapy, 10*(1), 3–15.

Joseph, R. (1988). The right cerebral hemisphere: emotion, music, visual-spatial skills, body-image, dreams, and awareness. *Journal of Clinical Psychology, 44*(5), 630–673.

Judd, C. M., Ryan, C. S., & Parke, B. (1991). Accuracy in the judgment of in-group and out-group variability. *Journal of Personality and Social Psychology, 61*, 366–379.

Julien, R. M. (2004). *A primer of drug action.* New York: Worth.

Kachgal, M. M., Hansen, L. S., & Nutter, K. J. (2001). Academic procrastination prevention/intervention: Strategies and recommendations. *Journal of Developmental Education, 25*, 14–24.

Kadison, R. D., & DiGeronimo, T. F. (2004). *College of the overwhelmed: The campus mental health crisis and what to do about it.* San Francisco: Jossey-Bass.

Kagan, S., & Kagan, M. (1998). *Multiple intelligences: The complete MI book.* San Clemente, CA: Kagan Cooperative Learning.

Karelis, C. H. (1986). A note on democracy and liberal education. *Liberal Education, 72*(4), 319–322.

Kasper, G. (2004, March). *Tax procrastination: Survey finds 29% have yet to begin taxes.* Retrieved June 6, 2006, from http://www.preweb.com/releases/2004/3/prweb114250.htm

Kassin, S. (2006). *Psychology in modules.* Upper Saddle Back River, NJ: Pearson.

Katz, J., & Henry, M. (1993). *Turning professors into teachers: A new approach to faculty development and student learning.* Phoenix: American Council on Education and Oryx Press.

Kaufman, J. C., & Baer, J. (2002). Could Steven Spielberg manage the Yankees?: Creative thinking in different domains. *Korean Journal of Thinking & Problem Solving, 12*(2), 5–14.

Kearns, D. (1989). Getting schools back on track. *Newsweek* (November), pp. 8–9.

Kember, D., Jamieson, Q. W., Pomfret, M., & Wong, E. T. T. (1995). Learning approaches, study time and academic performance. *Higher Education, 29*, 329–343.

Khoshaba, D. M., & Maddi, S. R. (1999–2004). *HardiTraining: Managing stressful change.* Newport Beach, CA: The Hardiness Institute.

Kielcolt-Glaser, J. K., & Glaser, R. (1986). Psychological influences on immunity. *Psychosomatics, 27*, 621–625.

Kiecolt, J. K., Glaser, R., Strain, E., Stout, J., Tarr, K., Holliday, J., & Speicher, C. (1986). Modulation of cellular immunity in medical students. *Journal of Behavioral Medicine, 9*, 5–21.

Kiewra, K. A. (1985). Students' note-taking behaviors and the efficacy of providing the instructor's notes for review. *Contemporary Educational Psychology, 10*, 378–386.

Kierwa, K. A. (2000). Fish giver or fishing teacher? The lure of strategy instruction. *Teaching at UNL, 22*(3), pp. 1–3. Lincoln, NE: University of Nebraska-Lincoln.

Kiewra, K. A., & Fletcher, H. J. (1984). The relationship between notetaking variables and achievement measures. *Human Learning, 3*, 273–280.

Kiewra, K. A., Hart, K., Scoular, J., Stephen, M., Sterup, G., & Tyler, B. (2000). Fish giver or fishing teacher? The lure of strategy instruction. *Teaching at UNL, 22*(3), Lincoln NE: Teaching & Learning Center, University of Nebraska.

Kincaid, J. P., & Wickens, D. D. (1970). Temporal gradient of release from proactive inhibition. *Journal of Experimental Psychology, 86*, 313–316.

King, A. (1990). Enhancing peer interaction and learning in the classroom through reciprocal questioning. *American Educational Research Journal, 27*(4), 664–687.

King, A. (1995). Guided peer questioning: A cooperative learning approach to critical thinking. *Cooperative Learning and College Teaching, 5*(2), pp. 15–19.

King, J. E. (2002). *Crucial choices: How students' financial decisions affect their academic success.* Washington, DC: American Council on Education.

King, J. E. (2005). Academic success and financial decisions: Helping students make crucial choices. In R. S. Feldman (Ed.), *Improving the first year of college: Research and practice* (pp. 3–26). Mahwah, NJ: Lawrence Erlbaum Associates.

King, P. M., & Kitchener, K. S. (1994). *Developing reflective judgment: Understanding and promoting intellectual growth and critical thinking in adolescents and adults.* San Francisco: Jossey–Bass.

Kintsch, W. (1968). Recognition and free recall of organized lists. *Journal of Experimental Psychology, 78*, 481–487.

Kintsch, W. (1970). *Learning, memory, and conceptual processes.* Hoboken, NJ: John Wiley & Sons.

Kintsch, W. (1982). *Memory and cognition.* Melbourne, FL: Krieger.

Kintsch, W. (1994). Text comprehension, memory, and learning. *American Psychologist, 49*, 294–303.

Kitchener, K., Wood, P., & Jensen, L. (2000, August). *Curricular, co-curricular, and institutional influence on real-world problem-solving.* Paper presented at the annual meeting of the American Psychological Association, Boston.

Klein, S. P., & Hart, F. M. (1968). Chance and systematic factors affecting essay grades. *Journal of Educational Measurement, 5*, 197–206.

Knapp, J. R., & Karabenick, S. A. (1988). Incidence of formal and informal academic help-seeking in higher education. *Journal of College Student Development, 29*(3), 223–227.

Knoll, A. H. (2003). *Life on a young planet: The first three billion years of evolution on earth.* Princeton, NJ: Princeton University Press.

Knouse, S., Tanner, J., & Harris, E. (1999). The relation of college internships, college performance, and subsequent job opportunity. *Journal of Employment Counseling, 36*, 35–43.

Knox, S. (2004). *Financial basics: A money management guide for students.* Columbus, OH: Ohio State University Press.

Kolb, D. A. (1976). Management and learning process. *California Management Review, 18*(3), 21–31.

Kolb, D. A. (1985). *Learning styles inventory.* Boston: McBer.

Kouzes, J. M., & Posner, B. Z. (1988). *The leadership challenge: How to get extraordinary things done in organizations.* San Francisco: Jossey-Bass.

Kowalewski, D., Holstein, E., & Schneider, V. (1989). The validity of selected correlates of unexcused absences in a four-year private college. *Educational and Psychological Measurement, 49*, 985–991.

Kruger, J., Wirtz, D., & Miller, D. (2005). Counterfactual thinking and the first instinct fallacy. *Journal of Personality and Social Psychology, 88*, 725–735.

Kuh, G. D. (1993). In their own words: What students learn outside the classroom. *American Educational Research Journal, 30*, 277–304.

Kuh, G. D. (1995). The other curriculum: Out-of-class experiences associated with student learning and personal development. *Journal of Higher Education, 66*(2), 123–153.

Kuh, G. D. (2002, February 17). *Student engagement in the first year of college.* Plenary address presented at the Annual Conference of The First-Year Experience, Kissimmee, Florida.

Kuh, G. D., Douglas, K. B., Lund, J. P., & Ramin-Gyurnek, J. (1994). *Student learning outside the classroom: Transcending artificial boundaries.* ASHE-ERIC Higher Education Report, No. 8. Washington, D.C.: George Washington University, School of Education and Human Development.

Kuhn, L. (1988). What should we tell students about answer changing? *Research Serving Teaching, 1*(8). Cape Girardeau, MO: Center for Teaching and Learning, Southeast Missouri State University.

Kulik, J. A., & Kulik, C.-L. C. (1979). College teaching. In P. L. Peterson & H. J. Walberg (Eds.), *Research on teaching: Concepts, findings, and implications.* Berkeley, CA: McCutcheon.

Kurfiss, J. G. (1988). *Critical thinking: theory, research, practice, and possibilities.* ASHE-ERIC, Report No. 2. Washington, DC: Association for the Study of Higher Education.

La Berge, D. (1995). *Attentional processing.* Cambridge, MA: Harvard University Press.

Ladas, H. S. (1980). Note-taking on lectures: An information-processing approach. *Educational Psychologist, 15*(1), 44–53.

Lakein, A. (1973). *How to get control of your time and your life.* New York: New American Library.

Lay, C. H., & Silverman, S. (1996). Trait procrastination, time management, and dilatory behavior. *Personality & Individual Differences, 21*, 61–67.

Langer, J. A., & Applebee, A. N. (1987). *How writing shapes thinking.* NCTE Research Report No. 22. Urbana, IL: National Council of Teachers of English.

Latané, B., Liu, J. H., Nowak, A., Bonevento, N., & Zheng, L. (1995). Distance matters: Physical space and social impact. *Personality and Social Psychology Bulletin, 21*, 795–805.

Laur-Ernst, U. (1990). German vocational education survey. In B. G. Scheckley, L. Lamdin, & M. T. Keeton (Eds.), *The skills employers seek and employees need: Employability in a high performance economy* (pp. 109–113). Chicago: Council for Adult and Experiential Education.

Leahy, R. (1990). What the College Writing Center is—and isn't. *College Teaching, 38*(2), 43–48.

LeDoux, J. E. (1996). *The emotional brain: The mysterious underpinnings of emotional life.* New York: Touchstone.

Lefcourt, H. M. (1982). *Locus of control: Current trends in theory and research.* Hillsdale, NJ: Erlbaum.

Lehrer, P. M., & Woolfolk, R. L. (1993). *Principles and practice of stress management,* Vol. 2. New York: Guilford Press.

Leibel, R. L., Rosenbaum, M., & Hirsch, J. (1995). Changes in energy expenditure resulting from altered body weight. *New England Journal of Medicine, 332*, 621–628.

Leuwerke, W. C., Robbins, S. B., Sawyer, R., & Hovland, M. (2004). Predicting engineering major status from mathematics achievement and interest congruence. *Journal of Career Assessment, 12*, 135–149.

Levin, D. T. (2000). Race as a visual feature: Using visual search and perceptual discrimination tasks to understand face categories and the cross-race recognition deficit. *Journal of Experimental Psychology: General, 129*(4), 559–574.

Levine, A. (1989). *Shaping higher education's future—demographic realities and opportunities, 1990–2000.* San Francisco: Jossey-Bass.

Levine, L. W. (1996). *The opening of the American mind: Canons, culture, and history.* Boston: Beacon Press.

Levine, A., & Cureton, J. S. (1998). *When hopes and fears collide.* San Francisco: Jossey-Bass.

Levitsky, D. A., Nussbaum, M., Halbmaier, C. A., Mrdjenovic, G. (2003, July). *The freshman 15: A model for the study of techniques to curb the 'epidemic' of obesity.* Annual meeting of the Society of the Study of Ingestive Behavior, University of Groningen, Haren, The Netherlands.

Levitz, R., & Noel, L. (1989). Connecting student to the institution: Keys to retention and success. In M. L. Upcraft, J. N. Gardner, & Associates, *The freshman year experience* (pp. 65–81). San Francisco: Jossey-Bass.

Lewin, K. (1935). *A dynamic theory of personality.* New York: McGraw Hill.

Liebertz, C. (2005a). Want clear thinking? Relax. *Scientific American Mind, 16*(3), pp. 88–89.

Liebertz, C. (2005b). A healthy laugh. *Scientific American Mind, 16*(3), pp. 90–91.

Light, R. L. (1990). *The Harvard assessment seminars.* Cambridge, MA: Harvard University Press.

Light, R. L. (1992). *The Harvard assessment seminars, second report.* Cambridge, MA: Harvard University Press.

Light, R. J. (2001). *Making the most of college: Students speak their minds.* Cambridge, MA: Harvard University Press.

Linn, R. L., & Gronlund, N. E. (1995). *Measurement and assessment in teaching* (7th ed.). Englewood Cliffs, NJ: Prentice-Hall.

Linville, P. W., Fischer, G. W., & Salovey, P. (1989). Perceived distributions of the characteristics of in-group and out-group members: Empirical evidence and a computer simulation. *Journal of Personality and Social Psychology, 57*, 165–188.

Lock, R. D. (2000). *Taking charge of your career direction* (4th ed.). Belmont, CA: Wadsworth/Thomson Learning.

Locke, E. (1977). An empirical study of lecture note-taking among college students. *Journal of Educational Research, 77*, 93–99.

Locke, E. A. (1991). *The essentials of leadership.* New York: Lexington Books.

Loftus, E. F. (1979). The malleability of human memory. *American Scientist, 67*(3), 312–320.

Loftus, E. F. (1980). *Memory: Surprising new insights into how we remember and how we forget.* Reading, MA: Addison-Wesley.

Lopez, G. E., Gurin, P., & Nagda, B. A. (1998). Education and understanding structural causes for group inequalities. *Journal of Political Psychology, 19*(2), 305–329.

Lorayne, H., & Lucas, J. (1974). *The memory book.* New York: Stein & Day.

Love, P., & Love, A. G. (1995). *Enhancing student learning: Intellectual, social, and emotional integration.* ASHE-ERIC Higher Education Report No. 4. Washington, D.C.: The George Washington University. Graduate School of Education and Human Development.

Elster, J., & Lowenstein, G. (Eds.) (1992). *Choice over time.* New York: Russell Sage Foundation.

Lubart, T. I. (1999). Creativity across cultures. In R. J. Sternberg (Ed.*),* *Handbook of creativity* (pp. 339–350). New York: Cambridge University Press.

Luotto, J. A., Stoll, E. L., & Hoglund-Ketttmann, N. (2001). *Communication skills for collaborative learning* (2nd ed.): Dubuque, IA: Kendall/Hunt.

Lutz, A., Greischar, N. B., Rawlings, M. R., & Davidson, R. J. (2004). Long-term meditators self-induce high-amplitude gamma synchrony during mental practice. *Proceedings of the National Academy of Science, 101*, 16369–16373.

MacGregor, J. (1991). What differences do learning communities make? *Washington Center News, 6*(1), pp. 4–9

Mackes (2003). Employers describe perfect job candidate. *NACEWeb Press Releases.* Retrieved July 13, 2004, from http://www.naceweb.org/press

MADD (2006). *Why 21?* Retrieved Dec. 16, 2006, from http://www/madd.org/stats/4846

Maddi, S. R. (2002). The story of hardiness: Twenty years of theorizing, research, and practice. *Consulting Psychology Journal: Practice and Research, 54*(3), 175–185.

Maes, J. D., Weldy, T. G., & Icenogle, M. L. (1997). A managerial perspective: Oral communication competency is most important for business students in the workplace. *The Journal of Business Communication, 34*(1), 67–80.

Magolda, M. B. B. (1992). *Knowing and reasoning in college.* San Francisco: Jossey-Bass.

Maier, N. R. F. (1970). *Problem solving and creativity in individuals and groups.* Belmont, CA: Brooks/Cole.

Mandler, G. (1967). Organization and memory. In K. W. Spence & J. T. Spence (Eds.), *The psychology of learning and motivation: Advances in research and theory* (Volume 1) (pp. 328–372). New York: Academic Press.

Marchese, T. J. (1990). A new conversation about undergraduate teaching: An interview with Professor Richard J. Light, convener of the Harvard Assessment Seminars. *AAHE Bulletin, 42*(9), 3–8.

Marshall, W. L., Boutilier, J., & Minnes, P. M. (1974). The modification of phobic behavior by covert reinforcement. *Behavior Therapy, 5*, 469–480.

Martin, P. Y., & Benton, D. (1999). The influence of a glucose drink on a demanding working memory task. *Physiology & Behavior, 67*(1), 69–74.

Marton, F., & Saljo, R. (1984). Approaches to learning. In F. Marton et al. (Eds.), *The experience of learning.* Edinburgh: Scottish Academic Press.

Marton, F., Housell, D. J., & Entwistle, N. J. (1997) (Eds.). *The experience of learning* (2nd ed.). Edinburg: Scottish Academic Press.

Marzano, R. J., Pickering, D. J., & Pollock, J. (2001). *Classroom instruction that works: Research-based strategies for increasing student achievement.* Alexandria, VA: Association for Supervision and Curriculum Development.

Massey, D. (2003). *The source of the river: The social origins of freshmen at America's selective colleges and universities.* Princeton, NJ: Princeton University Press.

May, M., Galper, L., & Carr, J. (2004). *Am I hungry? What to do when diets don't work.* Phoenix, AZ: Nourish Publishing.

McArthur, L. Z., & Friedman, S. A. (1980). Illusory correlation in impression formation: Variations in the shared distinctiveness effect as a function of the distinctive person's age, race, and sex. *Journal of Personality and Social Psychology, 39*, 615–624.

McGhee, P. (1999). *Health, healing and the American system.* Dubuque: Kendall/Hunt.

McGuiness, D., & Pribram, K. (1980). The neurophysiology of attention: Emotional and motivational controls. In M. D. Wittrock (Ed.), *The brain and psychology* (pp. 95–139). New York: Academic Press.

Mehrabian, A. (1972). *Nonverbal communication.* Chicago: Adline-Atherton.

Meilman, P. W., & Presley, C. A. (2005). The first-year experience and alcohol use. In M. L. Upcraft, J. N. Gardner, & B. O. Barefoot, & Associates, *Challenging and supporting the first-year student: A handbook for improving the first year of college* (pp. 445–468). San Francisco: Jossey-Bass.

Meyers, C. (1986). *Teaching students to think critically: A guide for faculty in all disciplines.* San Francisco: Jossey-Bass.

Middleton, F., & Strick, P. (1994). Anatomical evidence for cerebellar and basal ganglia involvement in higher brain function. *Science, 226*, 51584: 458–461.

Millard, B. (2004, November 7). *A purpose-based approach to navigating college transitions.* Preconference workshop presented at the Eleventh National Conference on Students in Transition, Nashville, Tennessee.

Miller, G. (1988). *The meaning of general education.* New York: Teachers College Press.

Miller, M. A. (2003). The meaning of the baccalaureate. *About Campus* (Sept./October), pp. 2–8.

Millman, J., Bishop, C., & Ebel, R. (1965). An analysis of test-wiseness. *Educational and Psychological Measurement, 25*, 707–727.

Milner, A. D., & Goodale, M. A. (1998). *The visual brain in action.* (Oxford Psychology Series, No. 27). Oxford: Oxford University Press.

Milton, O. (1982). *Will that be on the final?* Springfield, Ill.: Charles C. Thomas.

Minninger, J. (1984). *Total recall: How to boost your memory power.* Emmaus, PA: Rodale.

Mitler, M. M., Dinges, D. F., & Dement, W. C. (1994). Sleep medicine, public policy, and public health. In M. H. Kryger, T. Roth, & W. C. Dement (Eds.), *Principles and practice of sleep medicine* (2nd ed.). Philadelphia: Saunders.

Molnar, S. (1991). *Human variation: race, type, and ethnic groups* (3rd ed.). Englewood Cliffs, NJ: Prentice-Hall.

Monk, T. H. (2005). The post-lunch dip in performance. *Clinical Sports Medicine, 24*(2), 15–23.

Motley, M. T. (1997). *Overcoming your fear of public speaking: A proven method.* Boston, MA: Houghton Mifflin.

Multon, K. D., Brown, S. D., & Lent, R. W. (1991). Relation of self-efficacy beliefs to academic outcomes: A meta-analytic investigation. *Journal of Counseling Psychology, 38*(1), 30–38.

Murname, K., & Shiffrin, R. M. (1991). Interference and the representation of events in memory. *Journal of Experimental Psychology: Learning, Memory, & Cognition, 17*, 855–874.

Murray, D. M. (1984). *Write to learn* (2nd ed.). New York: Holt, Rinehart, & Winston.

Murray, D. M. (1993). *Write to learn* (4th ed.). Fort Worth: Harcourt Brace.

Myers, I. B. (1976). *Introduction to type.* Gainesville, FL: Center for the Application of Psychological Type.

Myers, D. G. (1993). *The pursuit of happiness: Who is happy—and why?* New York: Morrow.

Myers, D. G., & McCaulley, N. H. (1985). *Manual: A guide to the development and use of the Myers-Briggs Type Indicator.* Palo Alto, CA: Consulting Psychologists Press.

Nadel L., & Willner, J. (1980). Context and conditioning. A place for space. *Journal of Comparative and Physiological Psychology, 8*, 218–228.

Nagda, B. R., Gurin, P., & Lopez, G. E. (2003). Transformative pedagogy for democracy and social justice. *Race, Ethnicity, & Education, 6*(2), 165–191.

Nagda, B. R., Gurin, P., & Johnson, S. M. (2005). Living, doing and thinking diversity: How does pre-college diversity experience affect first-year students' engagement with college diversity? In R. S. Feldman (Ed.), *Improving the first year of college: Research and practice* (pp. 73–110). Mahwah, NJ: Lawrence Erlbaum Associates.

Naisbitt, J. (1982). *Megatrends: Ten new directions transforming our lives.* New York: Warner Books.

Narciso, J., & Burkett, D. (1975). *Disclose yourself: Discover the "me" in relationships.* Englewood Cliffs, NJ: Prentice-Hall.

Natale, V., & Ciogna, P. (1996). Circadian regulation of subjective alertness in morning and evening types. *EDRA: Environmental Design Research Association, 20*(4), 491–497.

National Association of Colleges and Employers (NACE) (2003). *Job Outlook 2003 survey.* Bethlehem, PA: Author.

National Forum on Information Literacy (2005). *Forum overview.* Retrieved Oct. 17, 2005, from http://www.infolit.org

National Institute of Mental Health (2001). *Eating disorders: Facts about eating disorders and the search for solutions*. Retrieved August 7, 2006, from http://www.nimh.nih.gov/publicat/eatingdisorders.cfm

National Institute of Mental Health (2006). *The numbers count: Mental disorders in America*. Retrieved December 16, 2006, from http:www.nimh.nih.gov.pulicat/numbers.cfm

National Research Council (1989). *Diet and health: Implications for reducing chronic disease risk*. Committee on Diet and Health, Washington, DC: National Academy Press.

National Resources Defense Council (2005). *Global warming: A summary of recent findings on the changing global climate*. Retrieved Nov. 11, 2005, from http://www.nrdc.org/global/Warming/fgwscience.asp

National Wellness Institute (2005). *The six dimensional wellness model*. Retrieved August 11, 2006, from http://www.nationalwellness.org/SitePrint.ph?id=391&tiername=Free%20Resource%20

Neer, M. R. (1987). The development of an instrument to measure classroom apprehension. *Communication Education, 36*, 154–166.

Newell, A., & Rosenbloom, P. S. (1981). Mechanisms of skill acquisition of the law of practice. In J. R. Anderson (Ed.), *Cognitive skills and their acquisition*. Hillsdale, NJ: Erlbaum.

Newton, T. (1990, September). *Improving students' listening skills*. IDEA Paper No. 23. Manhattan, KS: Center for Faculty Evaluation and Development.

Nicholas, R. W. (1991). Cultures in the curriculum. *Liberal Education, 77*(3), 16–21.

Nichols, M. P. (1995). *The lost art of listening*. New York: Guilford Press.

Nichols, R. G., & Stevens, L. A. (1957). *Are you listening?* New York: McGraw-Hill.

Niles, S. G., & Harris-Bowlsbey, J. (2002). *Career development interventions in the 21st century*. Upper Saddle River, NJ: Pearson Education.

Noel, L. (1985). Increasing student retention: New challenges and potential. In L. Noel & Associates (Eds.), *Increasing student retention* (pp. 1–27). San Francisco: Jossey-Bass.

Norman, D. A. (1982). *Learning and memory*. San Francisco: W. H. Freeman.

Nummela, R. M., & Rosengren, T. M. (1986). What's happening in students' brains may redefine teaching. *Educational Leadership, 43*(8), 49–53.

Nystrand, M. (1986). *The structure of written communication: Studies in reciprocity between writers and readers*. Orlando, FL: Academic Press.

Office of Research (1994). *What employers expect of college graduates: International knowledge and second language skills*. Washington, D.C.: Office of Educational Research and Improvement (OERI), U.S. Department of Education.

Ogawa, K., Nittono, H., & Hori, T. (2002). Brain potentials associated with the onset and offset of rapid eye movement (REM) during REM sleep. *Psychiatry & Clinical Neurosciences, 56*, 259–260.

O'Keefe, J., & Nadel, L. (1978). *The hippocampus as a cognitive map*. Oxford: Clarendon Press.

Oller, D. K. (1981). Infant vocalizations: Exploration and reflectivity. In R. E. Stark (Ed.), *Language behavior in infancy and early childhood* (pp. 85–104). New York: Elsevier/North-Holland.

Onwuegbuzie, A. J. (2000). Academic procrastinators and perfectionistic tendencies among graduate students. *Journal of Social Behavior and Personality, 15*, 103–109.

Orszag, J. M., Orszag, P. R., & Whitmore, D. M. (2001). *Learning and earning: Working in college*. Retrieved July 19, 2006 from http://www.brockport.edu/career01/upromise.htm

Ottinger, C. (1990). College graduates in the labor market: Today and the future. *Research Briefs, 1*(5), pp. 1–2. Washington, D.C.: American Council on Education, Division of Policy Analysis & Research,

Pace, C. R. (1990a). Measuring the quality of student effort. *Current Issues in Higher Education, 2*(1), (Monograph). Washington, D.C.: American Association for Higher Education.

Pace, C. R. (1990b). *The undergraduates*. Los Angeles: Center for the Study of Evaluation, University of California, Los Angeles.

Paivio, A. (1990). *Mental representations: A dual coding approach*. New York: Oxford University Press.

Palank, J. (2006, July 17, 2006). *Face it: 'Book' no secret to employers*. Retrieved August 21, 2006, from http:www.washtimes.com/business/20060717-12942-1800r.htm

Palmer, P. J. (1999). *The active life: A spirituality of work, creativity and caring*. San Francisco: Jossey-Bass.

Paolini, S., Hewstone, M., Cairns, E., & Voci, A. (2004). Effects of direct and indirect cross-group friendships on judgments of Catholics and Protestants in Northern Ireland: The mediating role of an anxiety-reduction mechanism. *Personality and Social Psychology Bulletin, 30*, 770–786.

Papalia, D. E., & Olds, S. W. (1990). *A child's world: Infancy through adolescence* (5th ed.). New York: McGraw-Hill.

Pascarella, E. T. (2001). Cognitive growth in college: Surprising and reassuring findings from The National Study of Student Learning. *Change* (November/December), pp. 21– 27.

Pascarella, E., Flowers, L., & Whitt, E. (1999). *Cognitive effects of Greek affiliation in college: Additional evidence.* Unpublished manuscript, University of Iowa, Iowa City.

Pascarella, E., Palmer, B., Moye, M., & Pierson, C. (2001). Do diversity experiences influence the development of critical thinking? *Journal of College Student Development, 42,* 257–291.

Pascarella, E. & Terenzini, P. (1991). *How college affects students: Findings and insights from twenty years of research.* San Francisco: Jossey-Bass.

Pascarella, E. T., & Terenzini, P. T. (2005). *How college affects students: A third decade of research* (volume 2). San Francisco: Jossey-Bass.

Paul, R. (1995). *Critical thinking: How to prepare students for a rapidly changing world.* Dillon Beach, CA: The Foundation for Critical Thinking.

Paul, R. W., & Elder, L. (2002). *Critical thinking: Tools for taking charge of your professional and personal life.* Upper Saddle River, NJ: Pearson Education.

Paul, R., & Elder, L. (2004). *The nature and functions of critical and creative thinking.* Dillon Beach, CA: The Foundation for Critical Thinking.

Peele, S., & Brodsky, A. (1991). *Love and addiction.* New York: Signet Books.

Peigneux, P. P., Laureys, S., Delbeuck, X. & Maquet, P. (2001, Dec. 21). Sleeping brain, learning brain: The role of sleep for memory systems. *Neuroreport, 12*(18), pp. A111–124.

Perry, W. G. (1970, 1999). *Forms of intellectual and ethical development during the college years: A scheme.* New York: Holt, Rinehart & Winston.

Perry, R., Hechter, F., Menec, V., & Weinberg, L. (1993). Enhancing achievement motivation and performance in college students: An attributional retraining perspective. *Research in Higher Education, 34,* 687–723.

Peterson, C. (1990). Explanatory style in the classroom and in the playing field. In S. Graham & V. S. Folkes (Eds.), *Attribution theory: Applications to achievement, mental health, and interpersonal conflict.* Hillsdale, NJ: Erlbaum.

Peterson, C., & Barrett, L. (1987). Explanatory style and academic performance among university freshmen. *Journal of Personality and Social Psychology, 53,* 603–607.

Peterson, C., & Seligman, M. E. P. (2004). *Character strengths and virtues—a handbook and classification.* New York: Oxford University Press.

Peterson, C., Seligman, M. E. P., Yurko, K. H., Martin, L. R., & Friedman, H. S. (1998). Catastrophizing and untimely death. *Psychological Science, 9,* 49–52.

Piaget, J. (1978). *Success and understanding.* Cambridge, MA: Harvard University Press.

Piaget, J. (1985). *The equilibration of cognitive structures: The central problem of intellectual development.* Chicago, IL: University of Chicago Press.

Pinker, S. (1994). *The language instinct.* New York: HarperCollins.

Pintrich, P. R. (Ed.) (1995). *Understanding self-regulated learning.* New Directions for Teaching and Learning, no. 63. San Francisco: Jossey-Bass.

Plante, T. G., & Sherman, A. S. (Eds.) (2001). *Faith and health: Psychological perspectives.* New York: Guilford.

Policy Center on the First Year of College (2003). *Second national survey of first-year academic practices, 2002.* Retrieved August 10, 2005, from http://www.brevard.edu/fyc/survey2002/findings.htm

Pope, L. (1990). *Looking beyond the ivy league.* New York: Penguin Press.

Pope, R. L., Miklitsch, T. A., & Weigand, M. J. (2005). First-year students: Embracing their diversity, enhancing our practice. In R. S. Feldman (Ed.*), Improving the first year of college: Research and practice* (pp. 51–72). Mahwah, NJ: Lawrence Erlbaum Associates.

Postsecondary Education Opportunity (2000). Private economic benefit/cost ratios of a college investment for men and women, 1967–1999. *The Environmental Scanning Research Letter of Opportunity for Postsecondary Education,* Number 101 (November), pp. 1–6.

Postsecondary Education Opportunity (2001). *Enrollment rates for females 18 to 34 years, 1950–2000.* Number 113 (November). Washington, DC: Center for the Study of Opportunity in Higher Education.

Potts, J. T. (1987). Predicting procrastination on academic tasks with self-report personality measures. (Doctoral dissertation, Hofstra University). *Dissertation Abstracts International, 48,* 1543.

President's Council on Physical Fitness and Sports (2001). Toward a uniform definition of wellness: A commentary. *Research Digest,* Series 3, No. 15, pp. 1–8.

Pribram, K. H. (1991). *Brain and perception: Holonomy and structure in figural processing.* Hillsdale, NJ: Erlbaum.

Price, R. H., Choi, J. N., & Vinokur, A. D. (2002). Links in the chain of adversity following job loss: How financial strain and loss of personal control lead to depression, impaired functioning, and poor health. *Journal of Occupational Health Psychology, 7*(4), 302–312.

Purdue University Online Writing Lab (1995–2004). *Writing a research paper*. Retrieved August 18, 2005, from http://owl.english.purdue.edu/workshops/hypertext/ResearchW/notes.html

Purdy, M., & Borisoff, D. (Eds.) (1996). *Listening in everyday life: A personal and professional approach.* Lanham, MD: University Press of America.

Putman, R. D. (2000). *Bowling alone: The collapse and revival of American community.* New York: Simon & Schuster.

QHE (Quality in Higher Education) (1993). *Update (6).* The newsletter of the quality in higher education project, University of Central England, Birmingham.

QHE (Quality in Higher Education) (1994). *Update (7).* The newsletter of the quality in higher education project, University of Central England, Birmingham.

Rader, P. E., & Hicks, R. A. (1987, April). *Jet lag desynchronization and self-assessment of business-related performance.* Paper presented at the Western Psychological Association, Long Beach, CA.

Ramsden, P. (2003). *Learning to teach in higher education* (2nd ed.). London and New York: RoutledgeFalmer.

Ramsden, P., & Entwistle, N. J. (1981). Effects of academic departments on students' approaches to studying. *British Journal of Educational Psychology, 51*, 368–383.

Ratcliff, J. L. (1997). What is a curriculum and what should it be? In J. G. Gaff, J. L Ratcliff, and Associates, *Handbook of the undergraduate curriculum: A comprehensive guide to purposes, structures, practices, and change* (pp. 5–29). San Francisco: Jossey-Bass.

Redelmeier, D. A., & Tibshirani, R. J. (1997). Association between cellular-telephone calls and motor vehicle collisions. *New England Journal of Medicine, 336*(7), 453–458.

Reed, S. K. (1996). *Cognition: Theory and applications* (3rd ed.). Pacific Grove, CA: Brooks/Cole.

Reis, H. T., & Shaver, P. (1988). Intimacy as an interpersonal process. In S. W. Durck (Ed.), *Handbook of personal relationships* (pp. 367–389). New York: Wiley.

Rennels, M. R., & Chaudhari, R. B. (1988). *Eye-contact and grade distribution. Perceptual and Motor Skills, 67* (October), 627–632.

Rennie, D., & Brewer, L. (1987). A grounded theory of thesis blocking. *Teaching of Psychology, 14*(1), 10–16.

Resnick, L. B. (1986). *Education and learning to think.* Special Report. Pittsburgh: University of Pittsburgh, Commission on Behavioral and Social Sciences Education.

Rhoads, J. (2005). *The transition to college: Top ten issues identified by students.* Retrieved June 30, 2006, from http://advising.wichita.edu/lasac/pubs/aah/trans.htm

Richmond, V. P., & McCloskey, J. C. (1997). *Communication apprehension: Avoidance and effectiveness* (5th ed.). Boston, MA: Allyn & Bacon.

Riesman, D., Glazer, N., & Denney, R. (2001). *The lonely crowd: A study of the changing American character* (revised ed.). New Haven, CT: Yale University Press.

Ring, T. (1997, October). Issuers face a visit to the dean's office. *Credit Card Management, 10*, 34–39.

Riquelme, H. (2002). Can people creative in imagery interpret ambiguous figures faster than people less creative in imagery? *Journal of Creative Behavior, 36*(2), 105–116.

Roediger, H. L., III, & McDermott, K. B. (2000). Tricks of memory. *Current Directions in Psychological Science, 9*, 123–127.

Roffwarg, H. P., Muzio, J. N., & Dement, W. C. (1966). Ontogenetic development of the human sleep-dream cycle. *Science, 152*, 604–619.

Roos, L. L., Wise, S. L., Yoes, M. E., & Rocklin, T. R. (1996). Conducting self-adapted testing using MicroCAT. *Educational and Psychological Measurement, 56*, 821–827.

Rose, S. P. R. (1993). *The making of memory.* New York: Anchor Books.

Rosenfield, I. (1988). *The invention of memory: A new view of the brain.* New York: Basic Books.

Rosenthal, R., & Jacobson, L. (1968). *Pygmalion in the classroom.* New York: Holt, Rinehart & Winston.

Rosenthal, T. L., & Steffek, B. D. (1991). Modeling methods. In F. H. Kanfer & A. P. Goldstein (Eds.), *Helping people change.* Elmsford, NY: Pergamon.

Rothblum, E. D., Solomon, L. J., & Murakami, J. (1986). Affective, cognitive, and behavioral differences between high and low procrastinators. *Journal of Counseling Psychology, 33*(4), 387–394.

Rotter, J. (1966). Generalized expectancies for internal versus external controls of reinforcement. *Psychological Monographs: General and Applied, 80*(609), 1–28.

Ruggiero, V. R. (2004). *Beyond feelings: A guide to critical thinking*. New York: McGraw-Hill.

Rudman, L. A., & Fairchild, K. (2004). Reactions to counter-stereotypic behavior: The role of backlash in cultural stereotype maintenance. *Journal of Personality and Social Psychology, 87*, 157–176.

Rumberger, R. W., & Levin, H. M. (1987). *Computers in small business*. Washington D.C.: Institute for Enterprise Advancement.

Runco, M. A. (2004). Creativity. *Annual Review of Psychology, 55*, 657–687.

Saarni, C. (1999). *The development of emotional competence*. New York: Guilford.

Sadker, M., & Sadker, D. (1994). *Failing at fairness: How America's schools cheat girls*. New York: Charles Scribner's Sons.

Salovey, P., & Mayer, J. D. (1990). Emotional intelligence. *Imagination, Cognition, and Personality, 9*, 185–211.

Sapolsky, R. (2004). *Why zebras don't get ulcers*. New York: W. H. Freeman.

Savitz, F. (1985). Effects of easy examination questions placed at the beginning of science multiple-choice examinations. *Journal of Instructional Psychology, 12*(1), 6–10.

Sax, L. J. (2003). Our incoming students: What are they like? *About Campus* (July–August), pp. 15–20.

Sax, L. J., Astin, A. W., Korn, W. S., & Mahoney, K. M. (1999). *The American freshman: National norms for fall 1999*. Los Angeles, CA: Higher Education Research Institute, UCLA Graduate School of Education & Information, Studies.

Sax, L. J., Lindholm, J. A., Astin, A. W., Korn, W. S., & Mahoney, K. M. (2004). *The American freshman: National norms for fall, 2004*. Los Angeles: Higher Education Research Institute, UCLA.

Schab, F. R. (1990). Odors and the remembrance of things past. *Journal of Experimental Psychology: Learning, Memory, and Cognition, 16*(4), 648–655.

Schacter, D. L. (1992). Understanding implicit memory. *American Psychologist, 47*(4), 559–569.

Scheckley, B. G., & Keeton, M. T. (1997). *A review of the research on learning: Implications for the instruction of adult learners*. College Park, MD: Institute for Research on Adults in Higher Education, University of Maryland.

Schlosser, E. (2001). *Fast food nation: The dark side of the all-American meal*. Boston: Houghton Mifflin.

Schmeck, R. (1981). Improving learning by improving thinking. *Educational Leadership, 38*, 384–385.

Schneider, W., & Chein, J. M. (2003). Controlled and automatic processing: Behavior, theory, and biological mechanisms. *Cognitive Science, 27*, 525–559.

Schutte, N. S., Malouff, J. M., and others (1998). Development and validation of emotional intelligence. *Personality and Individual Differences, 26*, 167–177.

Schutte, N. S., & Malouff, J. M. (2002). Incorporating emotional skills content in a college transition course enhances student retention. *Journal of The First-Year Experience, 14*(1), pp. 7–21.

Secretary's Commission on Achieving Necessary Skills (SCANS) (1992). *Learning a living: A blueprint for high performance. SCANS Report for America 2000*. Washington, D.C.: U.S. Department of Labor.

Sedlacek, W. (1987). Black students on white campuses: 20 years of research. *Journal of College Student Personnel, 28*, 484–495.

Segall, M. H., Campbell, D. T., & Herskovits, M. J. (1966). The influence of culture on visual perception. Indianapolis: Bobbs-Merrill.

Seligman, M. E. P. (1991). *Learned optimism*. New York: Knopf.

Senge, P. (1990). *The fifth dimension*. New York: Currency/Doubleday.

Shanley, M., & Witten, C. (1990). University 101 freshman seminar course: A longitudinal study of persistence, retention, and graduation rates. *NASPA Journal, 27*, 344–352.

Shatz, M. A., & Best, J. B. (1987). Students' reasons for changing answers on objective tests. *Teaching of Psychology, 14*(4), 241–242.

Shelgon, R. (2003). *No direction home: The life and music of Bob Dylan*. New York: William Morrow.

Sherif, M., Harvey, D. J., White, B. J., Hood, W. R., & Sherif, C. W. (1961). *The Robbers' cave experiment*. Norman, OK: Institute of Group Relations.

Sidle, M., & McReynolds, J. (1999). The freshman year experience: Student retention and srudent success. *NASPA Journal, 36*, 288–300.

Simopoulos, A. P., & Pavlou, K. N. (Eds.) (1997). Genetic variation and dietary response. *World Review of Nutrition and Dietics*. Bosel, Switzerland: S Karger.

Simunek, M., Schutte, N. S., Hollander, S., & McKenley, J. (2000). *The relationship between ability to understand and regulate emotions, mood, and self-esteem*. Paper presented at the Conference of the American Psychological Society, Miami, FL.

Singh, N. A., Clements, K. M., & Fiatarone, M. A. (1997). A randomized controlled trial of the effect of exercise on sleep. *Sleep, 20*, 95–101.

Slavin, R. E. (1995). *Cooperative learning* (2nd ed.). Boston: Allyn & Bacon.

Smith, B. L. (1983–84). An interview with Elaine Maimon. *1983–84 Current Issues in Higher Education.* Washington, D.C.: American Association for Higher Education.

Smith, R. L. (1994). The world of business. In W. C. Hartel, S. W. Schwartz, S. D. Blume, & J. N. Gardner (Eds.), *Ready for the real world* (pp. 123–135). Belmont, CA: Wadsworth Publishing.

Smith, D. (1997). How diversity influences learning. *Liberal Education, 83*(2), 42–48.

Smith, D. D. (2005). Experiential learning, service learning, and career development. In P.A. Gore (Ed.), *Facilitating the career development of students in transition* (Monograph No. 43) (pp. 205–222). Columbia, SC: University of South Carolina, National Resource Center for The First-Year Experience and Students in Transition.

Smith, A. P., Clark, R., & Gallagher, J. (1999). Breakfast cereal and caffeinated coffee: Effects on working memory, attention, mood, and cardiovascular function. *Physiology & Behavior, 67*(1), 9–17.

Smith, S. M., Glenberg, A., & Bjork, R. A. (1978). Environmental context and human memory. *Memory & Cognition, 6*, 342–353.

Smith, T., Snyder, C. R., & Handelsman, M. M. (1982). On the self-serving function of an academic wooden leg: Test anxiety as a self-handicapping strategy. *Journal of Personality & Social Psychology, 42*, 314–321.

Smith, J. B., Walter, T. L., & Hoey, G. (1992). Support programs and student self-efficacy: Do first-year students know when they need help? *Journal of The Freshman Year Experience, 4*(2), 41–67.

Snyder, C. R., Harris, C., Anderson, J. R., Holleran, S. A., Irving, L. M., Sigmon, S. T., Yoshinobu, L., Gibb, J., Langelle, C., & Harney, P. (1991). The will and the ways: Development and validation of an individual-differences measure of hope. *Journal of Personality and Social Psychology, 60*, 570–585.

Soloman, L. J., & Rothblum, E. D. (1984). Academic procrastination: Frequency and cognitive-behavioral correlates. *Journal of Counseling Psychology, 31*, 503–509.

Spear, K. (1988). *Sharing writing: Peer response groups in English classes.* Portsmouth, NH: Boynton/Cook.

Spilka, B., Hood, R. W., Hunsberger, B., & Gorsuch, R. (2003). *The psychology of religion: An empirical approach* (3rd ed.). New York: Guilford Press.

Sprenger, M. (1999). *Learning and memory: The brain in action.* Alexandria, VA: Association for Supervision and Curriculum Development.

Squire, L. (1986). Mechanism of memory. *Science, 232*, 1612–1619.

Stangor, C., Sechrist, G. B., & Jost, T. J. (2001). Changing racial beliefs by providing consensus information. *Personality and Social Psychology Bulletin, 27*, 486–496.

Stark, J. S., Lowther, R. J., Bentley, M. P., Ryan, G. G., Martens, M. L., Genthon, P. A., & Shaw, K. M. (1990). *Planning introductory college courses: Influences on faculty.* Ann Arbor: University of Michigan: National Center for Research to Improve Postsecondary Teaching and Learning. (ERIC Document Reproduction Services No. 330 277 370)

Starke, M. C., Harth, M., & Sirianni, F. (2001). Retention, bonding, and academic achievement: Success of a first-year seminar. *Journal of The First-Year Experience & Students in Transition, 13*(2), 7–35.

Staudinger, U. M., & Baltes, P. B. (1994). Psychology of wisdom. In R. J. Sternberg (Ed.), *Encyclopedia of intelligence, Volume 1* (pp. 143–152). New York: Macmillan.

Steel, P. (2003). *The nature of procrastination: A meta-analytic and theoretical review of self-regulatory failure.* Retrieved June 28, 2006, from www.haskayne.ucalgary.ca/research/workingpapers

Steel, P., Brothen, T., & Wambach, C. (2001). Procrastination and personality, performance, and mood. *Personality & Individual Differences*, 30, 95–106.

Stein, B. S. (1978). Depth of processing reexamined: The effects of the precision of encoding and testing appropriateness. *Journal of Verbal Learning and Verbal Behavior, 17*, 165–174.

Sternberg, R. J. (2001). What is the common thread of creativity? *American Psychologist, 56*(4), 360–362.

Stolerman, I. P., & Jarvis, M. J. (1995). The scientific case that nicotine is addictive. *Psychopharmacology, 117*(1), 2–10.

Strage, A. A. (2000). Service-learning: Enhancing student learning outcomes in a college-level course. *Michigan Journal of Community Service Learning, 7*, 5–13.

Strommer, D. W. (1993). Not quite good enough: Drifting about in higher education. *AAHE Bulletin, 45*(10), pp. 14–15.

Suinn, R. M. (1985). Imagery rehearsal applications to performance enhancement. *Behavior Therapist, 8*, 155–159.

Sullivan, R. E. (1993, March 18). Greatly reduced expectations. *Rolling Stone*, pp. 2–4.

Sundquist, J., & Winkleby, M. (2000, June). Country of birth, acculturation status and abdominal obesity in a national sample of Mexican-American women and men. *International Journal of Epidemiology, 29,* 470–477.

Susswein, R. (1995). College students and credit cards: A privilege earned? *Credit World, 83,* 21–23.

Svinicki, M. D., & Dixon, N. M. (1987). The Kolb model modified for classroom activities. *College Teaching, 35*(4), 141–146.

Tafjel, H. (1982). *Social identity and intergroup behavior.* Cambridge, England: Cambridge University Press.

Taylor, S. E., Peplau, L. A., & Sears, D. O. (2006). *Social psychology* (12th ed.). Upper Saddle River, NJ: Pearson/Prentice-Hall.

Tchudi, S. N. (1986). *Teaching writing in the content areas: College level.* New York: National Educational Association.

Teigen, K. H. (1994). Yerkes-Dodson—A law for all seasons. *Theory & Psychology, 4,* 525–547.

Terenzini, P. T., & Pascarella, E. T. (2004, July). *How college affects students: A third decade of research.* Plenary address to the Academic Affairs Summer Conference of the American Association of State Colleges and Universities. Albuquerque, New Mexico.

Thayer, R. E. (1996). *The origin of everyday moods: Managing energy, tension, and stress.* New York: Oxford University Press.

The Board of Trustees of the University of Illinois (2005). *Career Preparation.* College of Liberal Arts & Sciences, University of Illinois at Urbana Champaign. Retrieved December 16, 2006, from http://www.las.uiuc.edu/students/career/businesscareers.html

The Conference Board of Canada (2000). *Employability skills 2000+.* Ottawa: The Conference Board of Canada.

The Echo Boomers (2004, Oct. 3). Retrieved Oct. 22, 2004, from http://www.cbsnews.com/stories/2004/10/01/60minutes/printable646890.shtml

The Pennsylvania State University (2005). *How to avoid plagiarism.* Retrieved Oct. 15, 2005, from http://tlt.its.psu/suggestions/cyberplag/cyberplagexamples.html

Thomson, R. (1998). University of Vermont. In B. O. Barefoot, C. L. Warnock, M. P. Dickinson, S. E. Richardson, & M. R. Roberts (Eds.) (1998). *Exploring the evidence, Volume II: Reporting outcomes of first-year seminars* (Monograph No. 29) (pp. 77–78). Columbia, SC: University of South Carolina, National Resource Center for The First-Year Experience and Students in Transition.

Thompson, R. F. (1981). Peer grading: some promising advantages for composition research and the classroom. *Research in the Teaching of English, 15*(2), 172–174.

Thornburg, D. D. (1994). *Education in the communication age.* San Carlos, CA: Starsong.

Tice, D. M., & Baumeister, R. F. (1997). Longitudinal study of procrastination, performance, stress, and health: The costs and benefits of dawdling. *Psychological Science, 8,* 454–458.

Tierney, W. G. (Ed.) (1998). *The responsive university: Restructuring for high performance.* Baltimore: Johns Hopkins Press.

Tillich, P. (1952). *The courage to be.* Newhaven: Yale University Press.

Tinto, V. (1993). *Leaving college: Rethinking the causes and cures of student attrition* (2nd ed.). Chicago: University of Chicago Press.

Tinto, V. (1997). Classrooms as communities: Exploring the educational character of student persistence. *The Journal of Higher Education, 68,* 599–623.

Tinto, V. (2000). Linking learning and leaving: Exploring the role of the college classroom in student departure. In J. M. Braxton (Ed.), *Reworking the student departure puzzle* (pp. 81–94). Nashville: Vanderbilt University Press.

Tisdell, E. J. (2003). *Exploring spirituality and culture in adult and higher education.* San Francisco: Jossey-Bass.

Tobias, S. (1985). Test anxiety: Interference, defective skills, and cognitive capacity. *Educational Psychologist, 20*(3), 135–142.

Tobolowsky, B. F. (2005). *The 2003 national survey on first-year seminars: Continuing innovations in the collegiate curriculum* (Monograph No. 41). Columbia, SC: University of South Carolina, National Resource Center for The First-Year Experience and Students in Transition.

Torrance, E. P. (1963). *Education and the creative potential.* Minneapolis: The University of Minnesota Press.

Torres, V. (2003). Student diversity and academic services: Balancing the needs of all students. In G. L. Kramer & Associates, *Student academic services: An integrated approach* (pp. 333–352). San Francisco: Jossey-Bass.

Tulving, E. (1983). *Elements of episodic memory.* Oxford: Clarendon Press/Oxford University Press.

Tulving, E. (1985). Memory and consciousness. *Canadian Psychology, 26,* 1–12.

Tyson, E. (2003). *Personal finance for dummies.* Indianapolis: IDG Books.

Ulus, I. H., & Wurtman, R. J. (1977). Trans-synaptic induction of adrenomedullary tyrosine hydroxylase activity by choline: Evidence that choline administration can increase cholinergic transmission. *Proceeding of the National Academy of Science, 74*(2), 798–800.

Underwood, B. J. (1983). *Attributes of memory.* Glenview, IL: Scott, Foresman, & Company.

United States Bureau of Labor Statistics (2005). *Number of jobs, labor market experience, and earnings growth: Results from a longitudinal survey.* Washington, D.C.: Author. Retrieved September 24, 2005, from http://www.bls.gov/news.release/nlsoy.toc.htm

U.S. Census Bureau (2000). *Racial and ethnic classifications in census 2000 and beyond.* Retrieved December 19, 2006, from http://census.gov/population/www/socdemo/race/racefactcb.html

U.S. Census Bureau (2003). *Current population survey, March 2002.* Washington, DC: Government Printing Office.

U.S. Census Bureau (2004). *The face of our population.* Retrieved December 12, 2006, from http://factfinder.census.gov/jsp/saff/SAFFInfojsp?_pageId=tp9_race_ethnicity

U.S. Department of Education, National Center for Education Statistics (2002). *Profile of undergraduate students in U. S. postsecondary institutions: 1999–2000.* Washington, DC: Government Printing Office.

U.S. Department of Health & Human Services (2000). *Healthy people 2010: Understanding and improving health.* Washington, DC: Government Printing Office.

U.S. National Center for Health Statistics (2003). *National vital statistics report,* Volume 51, No. 5.

Van Dongen, H. P. A., Maislin, G., Mullington, J. M., & Dinges, D. F. (2003). The cumulative cost of additional wakefulness: Dose-response effects on neurobehavioral functions and sleep physiology from chronic sleep restriction and total sleep deprivation. *Sleep, 26,* 117–126.

Van Overwalle, F. I., Mervielde, I., & De Schuyer, J. (1995). Structural modeling of the relationships between attributional dimensions, emotions, and performance of college freshmen. *Cognition and Emotion, 9*(1), 59–85.

Veechio, R. (1997). *Leadership.* Notre Dame, IN: University of Notre Dame Press.

Viorst, J. (1998). *Necessary losses.* New York: Fireside.

Voelker, R. (2004). Stress, sleep loss, and substance abuse create potent recipe for college depression. *Journal of the American Medical Association, 291,* 2177–2179.

Vogler, R. E. & Bartz, W. R. (1992). *Teenagers and alcohol: When saying no isn't enough.* Philadelphia: The Charles Press.

Vogt, P. (1994). Students, professors point out each other's irritating behaviors. *Recruitment and Retention in Higher Education, 8*(7), p. 1.

Vygotsky, L. S. (1978). Internalization of higher cognitive functions. In M. Cole, V. John-Steiner, S. Scribner, & E. Souberman (Eds. & Trans.), *Mind in society: The development of higher psychological processes* (pp. 52–57). Cambridge: Harvard University Press.

Wadden, T. A., Thomas, A., Foster, G. D., Letizia, K. A., & Mullen, J. L. (1990). Long-term effects of dieting on resting metabolic rate in obese outpatients. *Journal of the American Medical Association, 264,* 707–711.

Waddington, P. (1996). *Dying for information: An investigation into the effects of information overload in the USA and worldwide.* London: Reuters Limited.

Wade, C. & Tavris, C. (1990). Thinking critically and creatively. *Skeptical Inquirer, 14,* 372–377.

Wagner, U., Gais, S., Haider, H., Verleger, R., & Born, J. (2004). Sleep inspires insight. *Nature, 427,* 352–355.

Wagner, M. J., & Tilney, G. (1983). The effect of "superlearning" techniques on the vocabulary acquisition and alpha brainwave production of language learners. *TESOL Quarterly, 7*(1), 5–17.

Wahlstrom, C., & Williams, B. K. (1997, Spring). Dealing with students' naïveté about money. *The Keystone* (Newsletter of the Wadsworth College Success Series), pp. 4–5.

Walker, C. M. (1996). Financial management, coping, and debt in households under financial strain. *Journal of Economic Psychology, 17,* 789–807.

Walsh, K. (2005). *Suggestions from more experienced classmates.* Retrieved June 12, 2006, from http://www.uni.edu/walsh/introtips.html

Walter, T. W., Knudsbig, G. M., & Smith, D. E. P. (2003). *Critical thinking: Building the basics* (2nd ed.). Belmont, CA: Wadsworth.

Walter, T. L., & Smith, J. (April, 1990). *Self-assessment and academic support: Do students know they need help?* Paper presented at the annual Freshman Year Experience Conference, Austin, Texas.

Watkins, D. A. (1983). Depth of processing and the quality of learning outcomes. *Instructional Science, 12*, 49–58.

Webber, R. A. (1991). *Breaking your time barriers: Becoming a strategic time manager.* Englewood Cliffs, NJ: Prentic-Hall.

Weschsler, H., & Wuethrich, B. (2002). *Dying to drink: Confronting binge drinking on college campuses.* Emmaus, PA: Rodale.

Weinstein, C. E. (1982). A metacurriculum for remediating learning-strategies deficits in academically underprepared students. In L. Noel & R. Levitz (Eds.), *How to succeed with academically underprepared students.* Iowa City, Iowa: American College Testing Service, National Center for Advancing Educational Practice.

Weinstein, C. F. (1994). Students at risk for academic failure. In K. W. Prichard & R. M. Sawyer (Eds.), *Handbook of college teaching: Theory and applications* (pp. 375–385). Westport, CT: Greenwood Press.

Weinstein, C. F., & Meyer, D. K. (1991). Cognitive learning strategies. In R. J. Menges & M .D. Svinicki (Eds.), *College teaching: From theory to practice* (pp. 15–26). New Directions for Teaching and Learning, no. 45. San Francisco: Jossey-Bass.

Weinstein, C. E., & Underwood, V. L. (1985). Learning strategies: The how of learning. In J. W. Segal, S. F. Chapman, & R. Glaser (Eds.), *Thinking and learning skills* (pp. 241–258). Hillsdale, NJ: Erlbaum.

Wesley, J. C. (1994). Effects of ability, high school achievement, and procrastinatory behavior on college performance. *Educational & Psychological Measurement, 54*, 404–408.

Wheelright, J. (2005). Human, study thyself. *Discover* (March), pp. 39–45.

Whitman, N. A. (1988). *Peer teaching: To teach is to learn twice.* ASHE-ERIC Higher Education Report No. 4. Washington, D.C.: Association for the Study of Higher Education.

Wilder, D. A. (1984). Inter-group contact: The typical member and the exception to the rule. *Journal of Experimental Psychology, 20*, 177–194

Wilhite, S. (1990). Self-efficacy, locus of control, self-assessment of memory ability, and student activities as predictors of college course achievement. *Journal of Educational Psychology, 82*(4), 696–700.

Williams, J. M., Landers, & Boutcher, S. H. (1993). Arousal-performance relationships. *Sport Psychology: Personal Growth to Peak Performance, 3*, 170–184.

Willingham, W. W. (1985). *Success in college: The role of personal qualities and academic ability.* New York: College Entrance Examination Board.

Wilson, T. D., & Linville, P. W. (1982). Improving the academic performance of college freshmen: Attribution therapy revisited. *Journal of Personality and Social Psychology, 42*, 811–819.

Wilson, T. D., & Linville, P. W. (1985). Improving the academic performance of college freshmen using attributional techniques. *Journal of Personality and Social Psychology, 49*, 287–293.

Wilson, R., Mendes, C., Barnes, L., and others (2002). Participation in cognitively stimulating activities and risk of incident Alzheimer's disease. *Journal of the American Medical Association, 287*(6), 742–748.

Winsor, J. L., Curtis, D. B., & Stephens, R. D. (1997). National preferences in business and communication education: A survey update. *JACA, 3*(September), 170–179.

Wolvin, A. D., & Coakley, (1993). *Perspectives on listening.* Norwood, NJ: Ablex Publishing.

Wright, D. J. (Ed.) (1987). *Responding to the needs of today's minority students.* New Directions for Student Services, No. 38. San Francisco: Jossey-Bass.

Wyckoff, S. C. (1999). The academic advising process in higher education: History, research, and improvement. *Recruitment & Retention in Higher Education, 13*(1), pp. 1–3.

Yerkes, R. M., & Dodson, J. D. (1908). The relationship of strength and stimulus to rapidity of habit formation. *Journal of Neurological Psychology, 184*, 59–82.

Young, K. S. (1996, Aug. 10). *Pathological Internet use: The emergence of a new clinical disorder.* Paper presented at the annual meeting of the American Psychological Association, Toronto, Canada.

Zaccaro, S. J., Foti, R. J., & Kenny, D. A. (1991). Self-monitoring and trait-based variance in leadership: An investigation of leader flexibility across multiple group situations. *Journal of Applied Psychology, 76*, 308–315.

Zajonc, R. B. (2001). Mere exposure: A gateway to the subliminal. *Current Directions in Psychological Science, 10*, 224–228.

Zeidner, M. (1995). Adaptive coping with test situations: A review of the literature. *Educational Psychologist, 30*(3), 123–133.

Zimbardo, P. G. (1977, 1990). *Shyness: What it is, what to do about it.* Reading, MA: Addison-Wesley.

Zimbardo, P. G., Johnson, R. L., & Weber, A. L. (2006). *Psychology: Core concepts* (5th ed.). Boston: Allyn & Bacon.

Zimmerman, B. J. (1995). *Self-efficacy and educational development.* In A. Bandura (Ed.), Self-efficacy in changing societies. New York: Cambridge University Press.

Zinsser, W. (1988). *Writing to learn.* New York: HarperCollins.

Zohar, D., & Marshall, I. (2000). *SQ: Connecting with your spiritual intelligence.* New York: Bloomsbury.

Zull, J. E. (1998). The brain, the body, learning, and teaching. *The National Teaching & Learning Forum, 7*(3), pp. 1–5.

Glossary

Ability (Aptitude): the capacity to do something well or to have the potential to do it well.

Academic Advisor: a professional who advises college students on course selection, helps students understand college procedures, and helps guide their academic progress toward completion of a college degree.

Academic Dismissal: denying a student to continue college enrollment because of a cumulative GPA that continues to remain below a minimum level (e.g., below 2.0).

Academic Probation: a period of time (usually one term) during which students with a GPA that is too low (e.g., less than 2.0) are given a chance to improve their grades; if the students' GPA does not meet or exceed the college's minimum requirement after this probationary period, they may be academically dismissed from the college.

Academic Support Center: place on campus where students can obtain individual assistance from professionals and trained peers to support and strengthen their academic performance.

Administrators: college personnel whose primary responsibility is the governance of the college or a unit within the college, such as an academic department or student support service.

Career: the sum total of vocational experiences throughout an individual's work life.

Career Advancement: working up the career ladder to higher levels of decision-making responsibility and socioeconomic status.

Career Development Center: key campus resource for learning about the nature of different careers and for strategies on how to locate career-related work experiences.

Career Development Courses: college courses that typically include self-assessment of career interests, information about different careers, and strategies for career preparation.

Career Entry: gaining entry into a career and beginning a career path.

Citation: an acknowledgment of the source of any piece of information included in a written paper or oral report that doesn't represent one's own work or thoughts.

Co-curricular Experience: learning and development that occurs outside the classroom.

Communication Skills: skills necessary for accurate comprehension and articulate expression of ideas, which include reading, writing, speaking, listening, and multimedia skills.

Commuter Students: college students who do not live on campus.

Concentration: a cluster of approximately three courses in the same subject area.

Concept: a larger system or network of related ideas.

Concept (Idea) Map: a visual diagram that represents or maps out main categories of ideas and their relationships in a visual-spatial format.

Cooperative Education (Co-op) Programs: programs in which students gain work experience relating to their college major, either by stopping their course work temporarily to work full-time at the co-op position, or by continuing to take classes while working part-time at the co-op position.

Core Courses: courses required of all students, regardless of their particular major.

Cover (Application) Letter: letter written by an applicant who is applying for an employment position or admission to a school.

Cramming: packing study time into one study session immediately before an exam.

Creative Thinking: a form of higher-level thinking skill that involves producing a new and different idea, method, strategy, or work product.

Critical Thinking: a form of higher-level thinking that involves making well-informed evaluations or judgments.

Culture: a distinctive way or style of living that characterize a group of people who share the same social system, heritage, and traditions.

Cum Laude: graduating "with honors" (e.g., achieving a cumulative GPA of 3.3).

Cumulative GPA: a student's grade-point average for all academic terms combined.

Curriculum: the total set of courses offered by a college or university.

Dean's List: achieving an outstanding GPA for a particular term (e.g., 3.5 or higher).

Diversity: interacting with and learning from peers of varied backgrounds and lifestyles.

Diversity Appreciation: becoming interested in and valuing the experiences of different groups of people and willingness to learn more about them.

Diversity (Multicultural) Courses: courses designed to promote diversity awareness and appreciation of multiple cultures.

Documentation: information sources that serve as references to support or reinforce conclusions in a written paper or oral presentation.

Electives: courses that students are not required to take but that they elect or choose to take.

Experiential Learning: out-of-class experiences that promote learning and development.

Faculty: a collection of instructors on campus whose primary role is to teach courses that comprise the college curriculum.

Free Electives: courses that students may elect to enroll in, which count toward your college degree but are not required for either general education or an academic major.

Freshman Fifteen: a phrase commonly used to describe the 15-pound weight gain that some students experience during their first year of college.

Graduate Assistant (GA): a graduate student who receives financial assistance to pursue graduate studies by working in a university office or college professor.

Grade Points: the amount of points earned for a course, which is calculated by multiplying the course grade multiplied by the number of credits carried by the course.

Grade Point Average (GPA): translation of students' letter grades into a numeric system, whereby the total number of grade points earned in all courses is divided by total number of course units.

Graduate School: university-related education pursued after completing a four-year, bachelor's degree.

Grant: money received that does not have to be repaid.

Greek Life: a term that refers to both fraternities (usually all male) and sororities (usually all female).

Hazing: a rite of induction to a social or other organization, most commonly associated with fraternities.

Higher-Level Thinking: thinking at a higher or more complex level than merely acquiring factual knowledge or memorizing information.

Holistic (or Whole Person) Development: development of the total self, which includes intellectual, social, emotional, physical, spiritual, ethical, vocational, and personal development.

Human Diversity: the variety of differences that exist among people who comprise humanity (the human species).

Humanity: the common elements of the human experience that are shared by all human beings.

Hypothesis: an informed guess that might be true, but still needs to be tested to confirm or verify its truth.

Illustrate: to provide concrete examples or specific instances.

Independent Study: a project that allows a student to receive academic credit for an in-depth study of a topic of his or her choice by working independently with a faculty member without enrolling in a formal course that meets in a classroom according to a set schedule.

Information Interview: an interview with a professional currently working in a career to obtain inside information on what the career is really like.

Information Literacy: the ability to find, evaluate, and use information.

Intellectual (Cognitive) Development: acquiring knowledge, learning how to learn, and how to think deeply.

Interdisciplinary: courses or programs that are designed to help students integrate knowledge from two or more academic disciplines (fields of study).

Interests: what someone likes or enjoys doing.

International Student: a student attending college in one nation who is a citizen of a different nation.

International Study (Study Abroad) Program: doing coursework at a college or university in another country that counts toward graduation, and which is typically done for one or two academic terms.

Internship: work experience related to a college major for which students receive academic credit, and in some cases, financial compensation.

Interpret: to draw a conclusion about something, and support that conclusion with evidence.

Job Shadowing: a program that allows a student to follow (shadow) and observe a professional during a typical workday.

Justify: to back-up one's arguments and viewpoints with evidence.

Leadership: ability to influence people in a positive way (e.g., motivating your peers to do their best), or the ability to produce positive change in an organization or institution, (e.g., improving the quality of a school, business, or a political organization).

Leadership Courses: courses in which students learn how to advance and eventually assume important leadership positions in a company or organization.

Learning Community: a program offered by some colleges and universities in which the same group of students takes the same block of courses together during the same academic term.

Learning Style: the way in which individuals prefer to perceive information (receive or take it in), and process information (deal with it once it has been taken in).

Liberal Arts: the component of a college education that provides the essential foundation or backbone for the college curriculum, and which is designed to equip students with a versatile set of skills to promote their success in any academic major or career.

Lifelong Learning Skills: skills that include learning how to learn and how to continue learning that can be used throughout the remainder of one's personal and professional life.

Magna Cum Laude: graduating with "high honors" (e.g., achieving a cumulative GPA of 3.5).

Major: the academic field students choose to specialize in while in college.

Mentor: someone who serves as a role model and personal guide to help students reach their educational or occupational goals.

Merit-Based Scholarship: money awarded on the basis of performance or achievement that does not have to be repaid.

Meta-Cognition: thinking about the process of thinking.

Midterm: the midpoint of an academic term.

Minor: a second field of study that is designed to complement and strengthen a major, which usually consists of about half the number of courses required for a college major (e.g., 6–7 courses for a minor).

Mnemonic Devices (Mnemonics): specific memory-improvement methods designed to prevent forgetting, which often involve such memory-improvement principles as: meaning, organization, visualization, or rhythm and rhyme.

MLA Style: a style of citing references in a research report that is endorsed by the Modern Language Association (MLA) and is commonly used by academic fields in the Humanities and Fine Arts (e.g., English and Philosophy).

Multicultural Competence: ability to understand cultural differences and to interact effectively with people from multiple cultural backgrounds.

Multidimensional Thinking: a form of higher-level thinking that involves taking multiple perspectives and considering multiple theories.

Multiple Intelligences: the notion that humans display intelligence or mental skills in many other forms besides their ability to perform on intellectual tests, such as the IQ or SAT.

Need: a key element of life planning that represents something stronger than an interest, and which makes a person's life more satisfying or fulfilling.

Need-Based Scholarship: money awarded to students on the basis of financial need that does not have to be repaid.

Netiquette: applying the principles of social etiquette and interpersonal sensitivity when communicating online.

Online Resources: resources that can be used to search for and locate information including online card catalogues, Internet search engines, and electronic databases.

Oral Communication Skills: ability to speak in a concise, confident, and eloquent fashion.

Oversubscribed (Impacted) Major: a major that has more students interested in it than there are openings for students to be accepted.

Paraphrase: restating or rephrasing information in one's own words.

Part-to-Whole Method: a study strategy that involves dividing study time into smaller parts or units, and then learning these parts in several short, separate study sessions in advance of exams.

Persuasive Speech: an oral presentation intended to persuade or convince the audience to agree with a certain conclusion or position by providing supporting evidence.

Plagiarism: deliberate or unintentional use of someone else's work without acknowledging it, giving the impression that it is one's own work.

Portfolio: a collection of work materials or products that illustrate an individual's skills and talents, or demonstrates that individual's educational and personal development.

Pre-Writing: an early stage in the writing process where the focus is on generating and organizing ideas, rather than expressing or communicating ideas to someone else.

Primary Sources: information obtained from first-hand sources or original documents.

Process-of-Elimination Method: a multiple-choice test-taking strategy that involves "weeding out" or eliminating choices that are clearly wrong and continuing to do so until the choices are narrowed down to one answer that seems to be the best choice available.

Procrastination: the tendency to postpone making a decision or taking action until the very last moment.

Professional School: formal education pursued after a bachelor's degree in school that prepare students for an "applied" profession (e.g., Pharmacy, Medicine, or Law).

Pre-requisite Course: a course that must be completed before students can enroll in a more advanced course.

Proofreading: a final "microscopic" form of editing that focuses on detecting mechanical errors relating to such things as referencing, grammar, punctuation, and spelling.

Recall Test Question: a type of test question that requires students to generate or produce the correct answer on their own, such as a short-answer question or an essay question.

Recitation (Reciting): a study strategy that involves verbally stating information to be remembered without looking at it.

Recognition Test Question: a type of test question that requires students to select or choose a correct answer from answers that are provided to them (e.g., multiple-choice, true-false, and matching questions).

Reconstruction: a process of rebuilding a memory part-by-part or piece-by-piece.

Re-entry Student: a student who matriculated as a traditional (just out of high school) student, but who left college to meet other job or family demands and has returned to complete a degree or obtain job training.

Reference (Referral) Letter: a letter of reference typically written by a faculty member, adviser, or employer, for students who are applying for entry into positions or schools after college, or for students during the college experience when they apply for special academic programs, student leadership positions on campus, or part-time employment.

Reflection: a thoughtful, personal review of what one has already done, is in the process of doing, or is planning to do.

Research Skills: ability to locate, access, retrieve, organize, and evaluate information from a variety of sources, including library and technology-based (computer) systems.

Restricted Electives: courses that students must take, but have the option of choosing them from a restricted set or list of possible courses that have been specified by the college.

Resume: a written summary or outline that effectively organizes and highlights an individual's strongest qualities, personal accomplishments, and skills, as well as personal credentials and awards.

Rough Draft: an early stage in the writing process whereby a first (rough) draft is created that converts the writer's major ideas into sentences, without worrying about the mechanics of writing (e.g., punctuation, grammar, or spelling).

Scholarly: a criterion or standard for critically evaluating the quality of an information source; typically, a source is considered to be "scholarly" if it has been reviewed by a panel or board of impartial experts in the field before being published.

Secondary Sources: publications that rely on or respond to primary sources that have been previously published (e.g., a textbook that draws its information from published research studies or an article that critically reviews a published novel or movie).

Self-Assessment: process of evaluating one's own characteristics, traits, or habits, and their relative strengths and weaknesses.

Self-Monitoring: the process of maintaining awareness of one's own thoughts or actions, and how effective they are.

Semester (Term) GPA: GPA for one semester or academic term.

Senior Seminar (Capstone) Course: course designed to put a "cap" or final touch on the college experience, helping seniors to tie ideas together in their major and/or make a smooth transition from college to life after college.

Service Learning: a form of experiential learning in which students serve or help others, while they simultaneously acquire skills through hands-on experience that can be used to strengthen their resume, and explore fields of work that may relate to their future career interests.

Sexually Transmitted Infections (STIs): a group of contagious infections that are spread through sexual contact.

Shadow Majors: students who have been admitted to their college or university, but have not yet been admitted to their intended major.

Shallow (Surface-Oriented) Learning: an approach to learning in which students spend most of their study time repeating and memorizing information in the exact form that it was presented to them.

Student Development (Co-Curricular) Transcript: an official document issued by the college that validates a student's co-curricular achievements which the student can have sent to prospective employers or schools.

Summa Cum Laude: graduating with "highest honors" (e.g., achieving a cumulative GPA of 3.8).

Syllabus: an academic document that serves as a contract between instructor and student, which outlines course requirements, attendance policies, grading scale, course topic outlines by date, test dates and dates for completing reading and other assignments, as well as information about the instructor (e.g., office location and office hours).

Synthesis: a form of higher-level thinking that involves building up ideas by integrating (connecting) separate pieces of information to form a larger whole or more comprehensive product.

Teaching Assistant (TA): a graduate student who receives financial assistance to pursue graduate studies by teaching undergraduate courses, leading course discussions, and/or helping professors grade papers or conduct labs.

Test Anxiety: a state of emotional tension that can weaken test performance by interfering with memory and thinking.

Test-Wise: the ability to use the characteristics of the test question itself (such as its wording or format) to increase the probability of choosing the correct answer.

Theory: a body of conceptually related concepts and general principles that help to organize, understand, and apply knowledge that has been acquired in a particular field of study.

Thesis Statement: an important sentence in the introduction of a paper that serves as a one-sentence summary of the key point or main argument a writer intends to make, and support with evidence, in the body of the paper.

Transferable Skills: skills that can be transferred or applied across a wide range of subjects, careers, and life situations.

Values: what a person strongly believes in and cares about, or feels is important to do and should be done.

Visual Aids: charts, graphs, diagrams, or concept maps that improve learning and memory by enabling the learner to visualize information as a picture or image and connect separate pieces of information to form a meaningful whole.

Visual Memory: memory that relies on the sense of vision.

Visualization: a memory-improvement strategy that involves creating a mental image or picture of what is to be remembered, or by imagining it being placed at a familiar site or location.

Vocational (Occupational) Development: exploring career options, making career choices wisely, and developing skills needed for career success.

Waive: to give-up a right to access information (e.g., waiving the right to see a letter of recommendation).

Wellness: a state of optimal health, peak performance, and positive well-being that is produced when different dimensions of the "self" (body, spirit and mind) are attended to and effectively integrated.

Work-study Program: a federal program that supplies colleges and universities with funds to provide on-campus employment for students who are in financial need.

Written Communication Skills: ability to write in a clear, creative, or persuasive manner.

Learning the Language of Higher Education

A Dictionary of College Vocabulary

Academic Affairs: unit or division of the college that deals primarily with the college curriculum, course instruction, and campus services that support academic success (e.g., library and learning center).

Academic Calendar: the scheduling system used by a college or university to divide the academic year into shorter terms (e.g., semesters, trimesters, or quarters).

Academic Credits (Units): what students are credited with after completing courses that are counted toward completion of their college degree; course credit is typically counted in terms of how many hours the class meets each week (e.g., a course meets for three hours per week counts for 3 credits).

Academic Standing: where a student stands academically (cumulative GPA) at a given point in their college experience (e.g., after one term or one year).

Academic Transcript: a list of all courses a student has enrolled in, the grades received in those courses, and the student's grade-point average.

Advanced Placement (AP) Tests: tests designed to measure college-level work that are taken while a student is in high school; if the student scores high enough, then college credit is awarded in the subject area tested or the student is granted advanced placement in a college course.

Analysis (Analytical Thinking): a form of higher-level thinking skill, which involves breaking down information and identifying its key parts or underlying elements and detecting what is most important or relevant.

APA Style: a particular style of citing references in a research report or term paper that is endorsed by the American Psychological Association (APA) and is most commonly used in fields that comprise the Behavioral Sciences (e.g., Psychology and Sociology) and Natural Sciences (e.g., Biology and Chemistry).

Associate Degree (A.A./A.S. Degree): two-year college degree that represents completion of general education requirements and prepares students for transfer to a four-year college or university.

Bachelor's (Baccalaureate) Degree: degree awarded by four-year colleges and universities, which represents the completion of general education requirements plus completion of an academic specialization in a particular major.

Breadth Requirements: required general-education courses that span a wide-range of different subject areas.

Certificate: credential received by students at a community college or technical college who have completed a one- or two-year vocational or occupational training program, which allows them entry into a specific occupation or career.

College Catalog (a.k.a., College Bulletin): an official publication of a college or university that identifies its mission, curriculum, academic policies and procedures, as well as the names and educational background of the faculty.

Combined bachelor/graduate degree program: a program offered by some universities that allows students to apply for simultaneous admission to both undergraduate and graduate school in a particular field and to receive both a bachelor's degree and a graduate degree in that field after completing the combined program (e.g., a Bachelor's and Master's degree in physical therapy).

Counseling Services: personal counseling provided by professionals on campus, that is designed to promote self-awareness and self-development in emotional and social aspects of life.

Cross-registration: a collaborative program offered by two colleges or universities that allow students who are enrolled at one institution to register for and take courses at another institution.

Dean: a college or university administrator who is responsible for running a particular unit of the college.

Distance Learning: enrolling in and completing courses online rather than in person.

Doctoral Degree: an advanced degree obtained after completion of the bachelor's (baccalaureate) degree, which typically requires 5 to 6 years of full-time study in graduate school, including completion of a thesis or doctoral dissertation.

Double Major: attaining a bachelor's degree in two majors by meeting the course requirements of both academic fields.

Drop/Add: the process of changing an academic schedule by dropping courses or adding courses to a pre-existing schedule; at most colleges and universities, adding and dropping courses can be done during the first week of the academic term.

Fine Arts: a division of the liberal arts curriculum that focuses largely on artistic performance and appreciation of artistic expression by pursuing such questions as: What is beautiful? How do humans express and appreciate aesthetic (sensory) experiences, imagination, creativity, style, grace, and elegance?

Full-time Student: a student who typically enrolls and completes at least 24 units per academic year.

General-Education Curriculum: collection of courses designed to provide a "general" or "broad" rather than narrow education, and develop skills needed for success in any major or career.

Graduate Record Examination (GRE): a standardized test for admission to graduate schools, which is used in a manner similar to the way that the SAT and ACT tests are used for admission to undergraduate colleges and universities.

Graduate Student: student who has completed a 4-year (Bachelor's) degree and is enrolled in graduate school to obtain an advanced degree (e.g., Master's or Ph.D.).

Health Services: on-campus services provided to help students who are experiencing physical illnesses or injuries, and to educate students on matters relating to health and wellness.

Higher Education: formal education beyond high school.

Honors Program: a special program of courses and other learning experiences designed for college students who have demonstrated exceptionally high levels of academic achievement.

Humanities: division of the liberal arts curriculum that focuses on the human experience, human culture, and questions that arise in a human's life, such as: Why are we here? What is the meaning or purpose of our existence? How should we live? What is the good life? Is there life after death?

Impacted Major: an academic major in which there are more students wishing to enter the program than there are spaces available in the program; thus, students must formally apply and qualify for admission to the major by going through a competitive screening process.

Inter-Term (a.k.a., January Interim or Maymester): a short academic term, typically running 3 to 4 weeks during which students enroll in only one course, which is studied intensively.

Learning Habits: the usual approaches, methods, or techniques a student uses while attempting to learn.

Living-Learning Environment: on-campus student residence that is designed and organized in such a way that student learning experiences are integrated into their living environment (e.g., study groups, tutoring, and student development workshops).

Lower-Division Courses: courses taken by college students during their freshman and sophomore years.

Master's Degree: degree obtained after completion of the bachelor's (baccalaureate) degree, which typically requires 2 to 3 years of full-time study in graduate school.

Matriculation: the process of initially enrolling in or registering for college (The term is derived from the term, 'matricula'—a list or register of persons belonging to a society or community).

Multicultural Center: place on campus that is designed to provide a place for interaction among and between members of diverse cultural groups.

Natural Sciences: a division of the liberal arts curriculum that focuses on observing the physical world and explaining natural phenomena, asking such questions as: What causes physical events in the natural world? How can we predict and control physical events and improve the quality of interaction between humans and the natural environment?

Non-Resident Status: out-of-state students who typically pay higher tuition than in-state students because they are not residents of the state in which their college is located.

Orientation: an educational program designed to help students make a smooth transition to college that is delivered to students before their first academic term.

Part-Time Student: a student who typically enrolls and completes less than 24 units per academic year.

Pass/Fail (Credit/No Credit) Grading: a grading option offered in some courses whereby students do not receive a letter grade (A–F), but only a grade of "pass" (credit) or "fail" (no credit).

Phi Beta Kappa: a national honor society that recognizes outstanding academic achievement of students at 4-year colleges and universities.

Phi Theta Kappa: a national honor society that recognizes outstanding academic achievement of students at 2-year colleges.

Placement Tests: tests administered to new students upon entry to a college or university designed to assess their basic academic skills (e.g., reading, writing, mathematics) in order to place them in courses that are neither too advanced nor too elementary for their particular level of skill development.

Postsecondary Education: formal education beyond secondary (high school) education.

Pre-professional Coursework: undergraduate courses that are required or strongly recommended for gaining entry into professional school (e.g., medical school or law school).

Proficiency Tests: tests given to college students before graduation that are designed to assess whether they can perform certain academic skills (e.g., writing) at a level advanced enough to qualify them for college graduation.

Quarter System: a system for scheduling courses in which the academic year is divided into four quarters (fall, winter, spring, and summer terms), each of which lasts approximately 10–11 weeks.

Registrar's Office: campus office that maintains college transcripts and other official records associated with student coursework and academic performance.

Resident Assistant: undergraduate student (sophomore, junior or senior) whose role is to enforce rules in student residences and help new students adjust successfully to residence hall life.

Resident Director: student development professional who is in charge of residential (dormitory) life and the person to whom resident assistants report.

Resident Status: in-state students who typically pay lower tuition than out-of-state students because they are residents of the state in which their college is located.

Residential Students: students who live on campus or in a housing unit owned and operated by the college.

Semester System: a system for scheduling courses in which the academic year is divided into two terms (fall and spring) that are approximately 15–16 weeks long.

Self-Regulation: adjusting learning strategies in a way that best meets the specific demands of the subject being learned.

Social and Behavioral Sciences: a division of the liberal arts curriculum that focuses on the observation of human behavior, individually and in groups, asking such questions as: What causes humans to behave the way they do? How can we predict, control, or improve human behavior and interpersonal interaction?

Student Activities: co-curricular experiences offered outside the classroom that are designed to promote student learning and student involvement in campus life.

Student-Designed (Interdisciplinary) Major: an academic program offered at some colleges and universities in which a student works with a college representative or committee to develop a major that is not officially offered by the institution.

Student Development Services (Student Affairs): division of the college that provides student support on issues relating to social and emotional adjustment, involvement in campus life outside the classroom, and leadership development.

Student Handbook: an official publication of a college or university that identifies student roles and responsibilities, violations of college rules and policies, and opportunities for student involvement in co-curricular programs, such as student clubs, campus organizations, and student leadership positions.

Summer Session: courses offered during the summer between spring and fall terms that typically run for 4 to 6 weeks.

Transfer Program: two-year college program that provides general education and pre-major coursework to prepare students for successful transfer to a four-year college or university.

Trimester System: a system for scheduling courses in which the academic year is divided into three terms (fall, winter, spring) that are approximately 12–13 weeks long.

Undeclared: students who have not committed to a college major.

Undergraduate: student who is enrolled in a 2-year or 4-year college.

University: an educational institution that offers not only undergraduate degrees, but graduate degrees as well.

Upper-division Courses: courses taken by college students during their junior and senior years.

Vocational/Technical Programs: community college programs of study that train students for a particular occupation or trade and immediate employment after completing a two-year associate degree (e.g., Associate of Applied Science) or a one-year certificate program.

Volunteerism: volunteering personal time to help others.

Withdrawal: dropping a class after the drop/add deadline, which results in a student receiving a "W" for the course and no academic credit.

Writing Center: a campus support service where students can receive assistance at any stage of the writing process, whether it be collecting and organizing ideas, composing a first draft, or proofreading a final draft.

Index

breathing exercises, 432
Brewer, Lawrence, 282–283
broad topics, 216
Buber, Martin, 366
budget
    defined, 339
    preparation of, 340–341
bulimia nervosa, 391
business education, 44–45, 81
Byrd, James, 282–283

C

caffeine
    stress and, 433–434
    test-taking and, 162
calcium, 397
calories, intake of, 395, 400–401
campus resources
    learning strategies and, 140–141
    master list of, 31–35
    utilizing, 2, 8–15
candy, test-taking and, 162
capstone courses, for seniors, 306
cardiovascular health, 399
career preparation, 285–317. see also time
        management
    career, defined, 298
    career compatibility, 298–301
    career development centers, 11, 95, 290,
        312
    career entry and development, 301–312
    case study, 317
    college major selection and, 77–82
    diversity and, 261, 274
    early planning for, 286
    independent research for, 314
    information interviews for, 292, 315–316
    liberal arts education and, 49–51
    personal characteristics and, 289
    personal needs to consider in, 288
    researching career options, 290–297
    self-awareness and, 287–290
    self-projection and, 28–29
caring, in romantic relationships, 375
cash flow
    checking accounts, 335–336
    credit cards, 333, 336–339
catalogs, 218
catastrophic thinking, 440–443
categorization, 149
causal analysis, 183
character. see personal character
charge cards, 338
checking accounts, 335–336
checklists, 226
Chicago Manual of Style, The (University of
        Chicago Press), 223
chlamydia, 420
chronological perspective, 58–60, 184–188

cigarettes, 418–419
circular reasoning, 196
citations, of research sources, 222–223
civic responsibility, 463
classes. see also college majors; note taking
    active involvement in, 2–8
    in career development, 292
    college transcript and, 304–306
    diversity incorporated in, 272
    overcoming shyness in, 372
    visiting, before registering, 95
    working independently outside classroom,
        3–4, 58
classification, 149
classism, 268
clock maps, 232
cocaine, 415
co-curricular activities
    career preparation and, 291–292,
        306–307
    co-curricular transcript, 307
    diversity and, 272
    involvement in, 13–14
    liberal arts education and, 55–59
cognitive dissonance, 204–205
cognitive therapy, 441
collaboration, with peers, 21–24, 276
college, cost of, 333, 344–347. see also
        money management
college catalogs/bulletins, 15, 92
college libraries, 10
college majors, 74–75. see also career
        preparation
    career plan flexibility and, 77–79
    changing, 76
    foundation for effective decisions about,
        90
    graduate school and, 79–80
    self-awareness and, 82–90
    timing of declaration, 75–76
college minors, 91, 96–97
college population, diversity and, 256–257
college success, 1–36, 455
    active involvement and, 2–8, 456
    campus resource utilization, 2, 8–15, 457
    checklist for, 29–30
    "diamond" of, 2, 458
    self-reflection, 2, 24–29, 457
    social interaction and collaboration, 2,
        15–24, 456
college timeline. see also career preparation
    career planning during, 286
    for different degrees, 80
college transcript, 304–306
commencement, 464
commitment, in romantic relationships, 375
communication. see also interpersonal
        relationships; speaking; writing
    diversity and, 261
    for interpersonal relationships, 357–359

language and, 255
    leadership and, 383–384
    liberal arts education and, 47, 49
communication age, 216
community
    diversity and, 277–278
    social-spatial perspective and, 60
comparison, as study strategy, 128–129
compatibility, in romantic relationships, 375
complaints, 380
compliments, 362
comprehension, 181–182. see also higher-
        level thinking
    self-monitoring strategies, 137–138
    writing-to-learn strategy, 227
compromise, in romantic relationships, 375
computation skills, 47
computer-based research terms, 218
concept maps, 150, 151, 232–233
conceptual organization, for writing, 232
conceptual thinking, 184
concern, for others, 364–365
conclusion, of papers, 234
condoms, 419
conflict, 376
    "dirty fighting" techniques, 380
    resolution, 376–381
constructive disagreement, in romantic
        relationships, 375
contemporary element, of chronological
        perspective, 59
contingency plans, time management and,
        325
contraception, 418, 419
contrast, as study strategy, 128–129
convergent thinking, 198
conversation skills, 357–359. see also
        communication
cool down routines, for exercise, 402–403
cooperative education (co-op) programs,
        294–295
core curriculum, 41. see also liberal arts
        education
Council of Biology Editors (CBE) style, 223
counseling centers, 12, 437
coursework, outside classroom, 3–4, 58
courtship, 373
cover letters, 308–310
"crabs," 421
creative thinking, 183, 197–199, 202. see
        also higher-level thinking
    sleep and, 406
    strategies for, 205–207
credibility, 217
credit
    cards, 333, 336–339, 345
    defined, 339
    history, 337
    limit, 336
    line, 339

critical thinking, 183, 192–195, 197–199, 202. *see also* higher-level thinking
   diversity and, 275
   liberal arts education and, 47–48, 49
   positive/negative thoughts and, 442
criticism, 379
cross-cultural differences, 253, 274, 305. *see also* diversity
cross training, 403
culture
   cross-cultural differences, 253, 274, 305
   cultural perspective, 184–188
   diversity and, 253, 271–272
   multicultural differences, 253, 274, 306
   spirituality and, 447
currency, of information, 219
Cuseo, Joe, personal reflections of
   career preparation, 295–296, 302
   collaborating with peers, 22
   diversity, 254
   higher-level thinking, 198, 220, 227
   interpersonal relationships, 361–362
   learning centers, 9
   learning strategies, 107, 134
   learning styles, 86, 89
   liberal arts education, 38, 64, 66–67
   memory, 133, 148, 149, 152
   mental health, 433
   mental health, spirituality, 445
   money management, 342
   physical health, 403, 406
   strategic learning, 107
   writing, 227

D

dairy, 394
databases, 218
date rape, 413, 418
dating, 372–376
deadlines. *see* time management
debit cards, 338–339
debt, 345–346
   credit cards and, 337
   defined, 339
decision-making, about career options, 299
declarative knowledge, 138
dedication, 460–461
deductive reasoning, 191–194, 202
deep (diaphragmatic) breathing, 432
deep learning, 107, 108–110, 136
default, 339
democracy
   diversity and, 278
   higher-level thinking skills and, 208
   liberal arts and, 38–39
denial, 195
dependability, 362–363

depression, 434–435
   coping strategies, 435–438
   exercise for, 399
   signs of, 435
descriptors, 218
determination, 461
devil's advocate role, 204–205
dialectical (dialogic) thinking, 188–189
"diamond" of success, 2, 458
dictionaries, 124
Dictionary of Occupational Titles (DOT), 291
diet. *see* nutrition
dietary fat, 393, 394
"dirty fighting" techniques, 380
disability services, 10
disciplines, defined, 45–46
discrimination, 263–269. *see also* prejudice
distress, 431. *see also* anxiety
distributed practice method
   avoiding procrastination and, 331
   for studying, 129–130
divergent thinking, 198
diversity, 251–283
   career preparation and, 261
   case study, 282–283
   college population and, 256–257
   courses in, 306
   discrimination and, 263–269
   emotion and, 256
   fight-or-flight reaction and, 265
   humanity and, 252
   independent research on, 279–280
   interpersonal interaction and, 272–279
   liberal arts education and, 257–258
   optical illusion example, 260–261
   prejudice and, 262–269
   self-awareness and, 258
   self-awareness exercises, 281–282
   self-reflection and, 269–272
   social development and, 261
   spectrum of, 252–256
   thinking skills and, 258–261
   of workforce, 306
documentation, 217
dogmatism, 195
Dominski, Paul, 49
double standard, 195
downsizing, 342
drafts, of written works, 233–237
dreams
   benefits of, 405–406
   remembering, 407
drive, 460
drugs
   resisting pressure, 418
   smoking of, 416
   types of, 415
   use among college students, 416
dual coding, 133

dualistic thinking, 189, 209
durability
   memory and, 109
   of skills, 46, 50

E

eating disorders, 391
Eble, Kenneth, 62
economizing, 342
ecstasy, 415
editing, of written works, 235–236
education, as college major, 81
educational planning, 73–104. *see also* academic advisement
   awareness of options and, 91–97
   case study, 104
   college major, timing of declaration, 75–76
   college major and career choice, 77–82
   college majors and, 74–75
   independent research of majors, 99
   long-range, 76–77
   long-range graduation plan, 102–103
   planning exercises for, 101–102
   self-awareness and, 82–90
egocentrism, 258, 367
egoists, 367
egotists, 367
elective courses, 92, 93–94, 98
e-mail
   etiquette, 366
   interaction with instructors by, 17
emotion. *see also* health
   appealing to, 197
   brain and, 180
   conflict resolution and, 377
   effect of thoughts on, 439–440
   facial expressions and, 256
   positive mindset for speeches, 245
   social/emotional leadership, 382–383
   wellness and, 428 (see also health)
emotional development, 51, 53, 56
emotional intelligence, 356
emotional learning, 135
employers, skills required by, 49–51. *see also* career preparation
employment opportunities, 298–299. *see also* career preparation
Encyclopedia of Careers and Vocational Guidance (Ferguson Press), 291
endorphins, 399
episodic knowledge, 138–139
"E pluribus Unum," 254
essay questions, strategies for, 168–170
essential fatty acids, 395–396
ethical development, 51, 53, 56, 57
ethnic groups (ethnicity), 253–254
ethnocentrism, 209, 266, 268
ethyl alcohol, 411. *see also* alcohol

I

Idea of a University, The (Newman), 50, 62
imagery, 149–150
"I" messages, 378–379
immune system, 399, 405. *see also* health
income, 333–334
incubation, 205
independent study courses, 292
independent work habits, 58
individualism, 255–256, 270
inductive reasoning, 192, 194–195, 202
infatuation, 373–374
inferential reasoning, 183, 191–192
  deductive, 191–194
  inductive, 192, 194–195
informal writing, 225–226
information age, 216
information integration, for studying, 129
information interviews, 292, 315–316
information literacy, 216
informative speeches, 241
"in-groups," defined, 209
initiative, 459–460
instructors. *see also* faculty
  student-faculty interaction, 16–17
  team-instructor conferences, 22–23
insurance premiums, 339
integrity, 461–462
intellectual development, 51, 52, 56
intelligence
  interpersonal, 356
  multiple intelligences, 84–85
interdisciplinary courses, 70
interest (financial), 339, 345–346
interest rates, 337–338
interests
  career choice and, 289
  self-awareness and, 83–85, 90–97
international courses, 305
international perspective, 61
international students, 257
Internet
  e-mail, 17, 366
  Facebook, MySpace, 369
  on-line communication, 275
internships, 293–295
interpersonal relationships, 355–386. *see also* social interaction
  abusive relationships, 414
  avoiding "egos," 367
  case study, 386
  communication and conversation skills for, 357–359
  dating and romantic relationships, 372–376
  diversity and, 272–279
  exercises, 385–386
  human relations skills for, 359–366
  importance of, 356

independent research on, 384
interpersonal conflicts in, 376–381
interpersonal (social) skills, 56–57
leadership skills and, 381–384
meeting people, 366–369
overcoming shyness, 369–372
rape, 413
interpersonal (social) intelligence, 85, 356
interviews
  informational, 292, 315–316
  for jobs, 312
"in the first place," 154
intrapersonal (self) intelligence, 85, 428
introduction, to papers, 234
invoices, 341
involvement. *see* active involvement
"I-thou"/"I-it" interactions, 366

J

James Byrd Foundation for Racial Healing, 283
Jasper County, Texas, 282–283
Jefferson, Thomas, 39
job opportunities, 298–299. *see also* career preparation
job shadowing programs, 292–293
journals, 225, 270
  career-development, 302
  to cope with depression, 436–437
  of dreams, 407
  sleep and, 408
  for stress reduction, 434
"jumping to a conclusion," 196
junk food, 394

K

Kearns, David, 49
key words, 218
King, John, 282–283
knowledge, 41. *see also* higher-level thinking; liberal arts education
  acquiring, 108
  awareness strategies, 138–139
  factual, 181–182
  socially constructed, 260
Kolb, David, 87–88
Ku Klux Klan, 283

L

language, 255
leadership, 13, 56
  courses in, 305
  developing skills for, 381–384
  diversity and, 276–277
learning. *see also* memory
  diversity and, 259–261
  skills, career preparation and, 301–303

skills for, 48
sleep and, 405–406
learning centers, 9, 86
learning community programs, 23–24
learning styles, 85–90. *see also* strategic learning
  Learning Styles Inventory (LSI), 87–88
  Myers-Briggs Type Indicator (MBTI), 86–87
Learning Styles Inventory (LSI), 87–88
legumes, 396–397
letters of application, 308–310
letters of recommendation, 310–312
liberal arts education, 37–72
  career planning and, 77–82
  career success and, 49–51
  case study, 72
  co-curriculum, 55–57
  college goals and, 66–67
  curriculum, 41–44
  diversity and, 258–259
  generalists vs. specialists, 63–65, 81–82
  history of, 38–39
  liberal arts, defined, 38
  meaning and purpose of, 38–40
  personal freedom responsibility, 39–40
  planning exercises for, 69–72
  skill-building and, 46–48, 65–66
  social benefits of, 372
  spirituality and, 446
  value of, 44–48
  whole-person development and, 51–55
  world perspective and, 57–63
libraries, 10, 22
life goals, 287. *see also* career preparation; self-awareness
lifelong learning skills, 48, 49
life-management skills, 319–353
  importance of, 320
  independent research on, 349
  money management, 332–333
  money management, financial tools for, 335–344
  money management, improving, 333–335
  money management, long-range planning, 344–347
  money management exercises, 351–353
  time management, 320–321
  time management, improving, 321–323
  time management, procrastination and, 327–332
  time management planning, 324–327
lifestyle, money management and, 341
linguistic intelligence, 85
link system, 153–154
listening
  in classes, 4–6
  conflict resolution and, 377
  higher-level thinking and, 203

P

paired-associate recall, 157–158
parallel co-op programs, 294–295
paraphrasing, as learning strategy, 137
participation, in classes, 5–7
parties, 368–369
part-time work, 296–297
part-to-whole method, for studying, 130–131
passionate love, 373–374
passive behavior, 378
"peer reviewed/refereed" publications, 218
peers
    cognitive dissonance and, 204
    collaboration with, 21–24, 126
    diversity among, 272–279. *see also* diversity
    feedback for writing from, 236
    interaction with, 19–20
    speaking and, 239–240
    strategies for making connections with, 24
    study groups, 135–136
"people skills," 359–366
perception. *see also* learning styles
    group, 267
    mental health and, 439
    selective, 195, 262–263
    as stage of learning and memory process, 110–112
Perfect Education, The (Eble), 62
performance, arousal and, 430
permanence, of thoughts, 441
persistence, creative thinking and, 207
personal action, diversity and, 271–272
personal character, 455, 458–459, 463–464
    civic responsibility, 463
    initiative, 459–460
    integrity, 461–462
    motivation, 460–461
    wisdom, 459
personal development, 51, 55, 56, 57
personal finance. *see* money management
personal freedom responsibility, 39–40
personal identity, 287. *see also* self-awareness
personalization, of thoughts, 441
personal life, career options and, 300–301
personal perspective, 184–188
perspective, 65–66
    liberal arts education and, 45–46, 57–63
    multidimensional thinking and, 184–188, 201
persuasive speeches, 241
pervasiveness, of thoughts, 441
pessimistic thinking, 438–439
physical activity. *see* exercise
physical appearance, 271
physical development, 51, 54, 56

physical education and wellness, 43–44, 45
physical health. *see* health
place, perspective and, 184–188
plagiarism, 223
portfolio, 307–308
positive attitude, 362, 438–443
prejudice
    belief systems about group inferiority, 268–269
    diversity and, 262–269
    ethnocentrism and, 266
    familiarity and stranger anxiety, 265–266
    fight-or-flight reaction and, 265
    higher-level thinking and, 209
    majority groups' attitude and, 267
    self-esteem and, 267–269
primary sources, 221
principal, 337, 339
prioritization, time management and, 323
problem solving
    creative thinking for, 205–207
    interpersonal conflict resolution and, 379
    sleep and, 406, 407
procedural knowledge, 138
procrastination. *see also* time management
    defined, 327–328
    myths about, 328–329
    psychological causes of, 329–330
    self-help strategies for, 330–332
productivity, biological rhythm and, 134
professional organizations, 95–96
progressive muscle relaxation, 432
proofreading, 237–238
psychological well-being, 389. *see also* health
pubic lice ("crabs"), 421
purchases, cost of, 343–344

Q

questions
    self-questioning strategies for higher-level thinking, 199–203
    skipping, on tests, 163
"quilt" metaphor, 254

R

racial groups (race), 254–256
racism, 268
rape, 413–414, 418
rational-emotive therapy, 441
reading. *see also* studying
    for career research, 290–291
    comprehension and retention, 7–8
    higher-level thinking and, 204
    with peers, 22
    writing and, 235
    writing-to-learn strategy and, 227

reading comprehension, 122–126
recall test questions, 156–161
recitation, 158–159
recognition test questions, 156
reconstruction, 147
recreation
    to cope with depression, 436
    importance of, 325
red herring, 196
references, for job search, 310–312
references, for research, 220–221
reflection
    conversation skills and, 359
    note-taking and, 121
reframing, of negative thoughts, 442–443
refutation, 190, 201
regionalism, 268
rehearsal, of speeches, 242–243
relearning savings time, 130–131
reliability, 362
religion, 446
religious bigotry, 269
research, 215. *see also* speaking; writing
    of campus resources, 15
    case study, 250
    citing sources, 222–224
    collaboration with peers, 22
    for college course selection, 92–95
    communication skills and, 216
    computer-based terms, 218
    evaluating references, 220–221
    evaluating sources of information for, 217–220
    exercises, 249
    higher-level thinking and, 221
    identifying topic for, 216
    independent research on, 247
    liberal arts education and, 47
    locating sources of information for, 217
    plagiarism, 223
resource utilization, 2, 8–15, 457
rest. *see* sleep
restructuring, of negative thoughts, 442–443
resume, 308–310
retention, of textbook material, 122–126
retrieval, of memories, 113–114, 159–161
review, of completed written assignments, 238
review, studying and, 131
rhetorical deception, 196
rhythm, memory and, 151–152
Rohypnol (roofies, roaches), 418
romantic relationships, 372–376

S

"salad bowl" metaphor, 254
salt, 393–394
saturated fats, 393, 394